W9-DGL-023

THE PLANT OPERATIONS HANDBOOK

A Tactical Guide to Everyday Management

Gerhard J. Plenert
Director, Productivity and Quality Research Group
Brigham Young University
Institute of Business Management

BUSINESS ONE IRWIN
Homewood, Illinois 60430

This publication is designed to provide accurate and authoritative information in regard to the subject matter covered. It is sold with the understanding that neither the author nor the publisher is engaged in rendering legal, accounting, or other professional service. If legal advice or other expert assistance is required, the services of a competent professional person should be sought.

From a Declaration of Principles jointly adopted by a Committee of the American Bar Association and a Committee of Publishers.

Sponsoring editor: Jean Marie Geracie
Project editor: Gladys True
Production manager: Ann Cassady
Designer: Heidi J. Baughman
Compositor: Bi-Comp, Inc.
Typeface: 11/13 Century Schoolbook
Printer: Arcata Graphics/Kingsport

Library of Congress Cataloging-in-Publication Data

Plenert, Gerhard Johannes.
The plant operations handbook : a tactical guide to everyday management / Gerhard J. Plenert.
p. cm.
Includes index.
ISBN 1-55623-707-3
1. Factory management—Handbooks, manuals, etc. 2. Production management—Handbooks, manuals, etc. I. Title.
TS155.P523 1993
658.5—dc20 92–28397

Printed in the United States of America

1 2 3 4 5 6 7 8 9 0 K 9 8 7 6 5 4 3 2

To My Wife, Renee Sangray Plenert,
Whose Patience and Love Make It All Worthwhile

About the Author

The author, Gerhard J. Plenert, PhD, CPIM, has spent 15 years working in management for private industry. His specialties are production/operations management and management information systems. He has traveled throughout the world in this capacity. He recently returned to school to earn his PhD at the Colorado School of Mines. Mr. Plenert spent four years teaching and doing research at California State University, Chico (CSUC). He recently joined Brigham Young University (BYU) in the Institute of Business Management. He was the director of the California Productivity and Quality Center at CSUC and is now the director of the Productivity and Quality Research Group at BYU. His research specialty is in international industrial management with an emphasis on developing countries. Mr. Plenert recently published a book titled *International Management and Production—Survival Techniques for Corporate America,* Tab Professional and Reference Books, 1990.

Mr. Plenert realizes that the subject matter of this book is very fluid and dynamic. He is very interested in your experiences, comments, ideas, and recommendations and would find them helpful in further editions of this book. Please send your comments to him at:

Brigham Young University
Institute of Business Management
660 TNRB
Provo, Utah 84602

Preface

If every factory in the world worked in exactly the same way, this book would have been very easy to write. Unfortunately, my experience is that no two factories work alike. Even when the factories are producing the same product and are right next to each other, they often operate differently because of management style and influence. Therefore, it is difficult to come up with one book and then claim that this is the perfect way to run a factory. That is why I will not make that claim. It reminds me of Newton's law of manufacturing: *"For every expert with a perfect solution there is an equal and opposite expert with a perfect solution."*

This book is a book of simplistic ideas that have proven effective in the past and I hope most of them will fit into your plant in some form or another. However, they are not all intended to fit perfectly—which brings us to the purpose of this book. It is designed to be a starting point, not the final answer. Use it to help you out. Let it be an idea generator for you. But do not treat it as the final solution to all problems.

One weakness of this book is that it doesn't cover all of the current and relevant production and operations management topics. But this is also a strength. It doesn't bog the reader down with unnecessary details and theories, many of which haven't passed the test of time. It simply presents the user with a bag of tricks that works. Once you have the principles of this book working well in your organization you can expand on concepts such as (not discussed in detail in this book):

- Computerization
  - CIM, DSS, ES, AI
- JIT
  - KANBAN
  - global management
- Advanced manufacturing topics
  - OPT (theory of constraints)
  - CAD/CAM
  - bill of energy
  - BAM
  - risk and uncertainty assessment
- Quality
  - TQC

- TQM
- QC
- ILQC
- statistical process control

Process manufacturing

International manufacturing

- logistics

Accounting interface

Construction

- long lead time manufacturing

Short lead time manufacturing

But the key is to get the basics working first. Without the basics, advancing to these other topics is just a waste of time.

Gerhard J. Plenert

Acknowledgments

To give credit where credit is due I would have to go to the earliest days of my work experience when I worked in a variety of small- to medium-sized plants in Oregon. Later I worked for NCR Corporation and Clark Equipment Company in plants all over the world, as far away as Indonesia, Australia, Chile, and Germany, and as close as Ohio and Mexico. I received broad exposure to a variety of developing manufacturing facilities just like those systems described in this book. These experiences gave me the background I needed to write this book.

I also need to recognize Jeffrey Krames and Jean Marie Geracie who were my mentors and helped make this book a reality at Business One Irwin. I need to recognize my academic setting at Brigham Young University, which gave me the resources to make this book a reality. And I need to recognize my family: my wife, Renee Sangray Plenert, and my children, Heidi Lynette Plenert, Dawn Jenelle Plenert, Gregory Johannes Plenert, Gerick Johannes Plenert, Joshua Johannes Plenert, Natasha Ida Plenert, Zackary Johannes Plenert, and Chelsey Jean Plenert, who gave me the time I needed to make this book work. I hope they can all learn to live with me again now that this book is completed.

G. J. P.

Contents

List of Charts

Introduction

Have you ever wondered what your boss does? Are you sure you understand the information needs of your employees? Have you ever wondered if there is a better way to do your job? Don't feel alone. You're one of the millions of managers and future managers throughout the United States that spends most of their time fighting fires and never really has a chance to think. That's what this book is designed to help you do: *Think!* Think about your job function. Think about how to *Help!:* Help you organize better. Help you monitor, plan, and control more effectively. Help you avoid expediting (rush jobs). Help you satisfy the information needs of your boss without causing chaos. Help you support your employees better by not giving them unnecessary frustrations, burdens, or time crunches.

This book is designed to:

1. Describe a function and show how it integrates into the total operation of a factory.
2. Describe the tools available to help that function perform better.
3. Show how the tools should be used, giving examples of their usage.
4. Demonstrate the benefits of each tool.
5. Supply you with sample forms, lists, charts, etc., so that you can implement the tools immediately.

The key features of this book are:

1. Easy to read instructions on "how to"
2. Examples demonstrating each concept discussed
3. Charts, tables, graphs, checklists, and diagrams on nearly every page
4. Control lists and/or sample documents that can be photocopied directly out of the book and used immediately in the operation of the factory.
5. Large margins and spacing between lines so users can write notes and thoughts into the book as they use it.

This book is not a textbook filled with theory. Rather, this book is a map, filled with directions, routes, and alternatives. It's not meant to be read and thrown on a shelf; it's meant to be used and abused, written in, scribbled on, and photocopied. It should be the only job-related book that you have that gets more use than your yellow pages. This book will help you now and later as you move through the various stages of management. Different parts of the book will get more use as you move up through management. This is not a book with heavy thoughts and great theories; rather, it's the hammer that will help you get the job done.

The best way to approach the book is to first read the entire book quickly from cover to cover. Don't attempt to memorize or study anything thoroughly. As you read through it, mark those areas that you feel are important to your job function. After you've gone through the book once, go back and look at those areas that you highlighted and review them thoroughly. Take those ideas that will help you the most and give them a try. You'll be pleasantly surprised. After about six months, do this process again. Go through the whole book, highlight areas of interest, and study those areas thoroughly. You'll be amazed at the number of ideas that didn't seem important the first time that now suddenly seem useful. You should be expanding your base of understanding and doing your job better. If you repeat the process of reviewing the book on a regular basis, before long you'll know the topics discussed in this book well enough to share their operation with others. Soon you'll be helping everyone.

So let's get started. Read on and, remember, by learning how to do your job better, you will make that old boring job you've been working at suddenly come to life and seem exciting.

PART

I INTRODUCTORY TOPICS

Chapter

1 How to Use This Book

How to Use This Book
The Strengths of This Book
Why Is Change Necessary?

How to Use This Book

To get the most out of this book, carefully read the preface, introduction, and Chapters 1 through 6. These chapters will give you an overall picture of the manufacturing environment. Chapter 4 even gives you some idea of where to look for details about a few of these concepts, especially those that are important to your job function.

The second step in using this book is to read quickly through the remainder of the chapters. This will give you a feel for where your job function fits in with the rest of the organization. It will put your job in perspective. As you read through the rest of the book, mark the sections that directly relate to your function.

The third step in the use of this book is to go back and carefully read those areas of the book that you marked. Look at the tools and elements discussed and see how you can improve your function by implementing some of these ideas.

The last step in the use of this book is to repeat this process every six months to one year. As your function changes, so will your information requirements. Reviewing this book will help you reanalyze your position and put it into perspective with the company as a whole.

The Strengths of This Book

The strengths of this book lie in the following areas:

1. Easy to understand explanation of the job function.

2. Easy to understand explanation of the key tools available to that job function; not a lot of theory.

3. Examples of the operation of a particular job function. These examples are focused on demonstrating the benefits that can be achieved by implementing a particular technique.

4. Sample forms, lists, charts, tables, graphs, checklists, diagrams, etc., that you can photocopy and use directly, or modify if necessary, to help you in your job function. The objective is to give you control lists and/or sample documents that can be photocopied directly out of the book and used immediately in the operation of the factory.

5. Large margins and spacing between lines so that you can write notes and thoughts into the book as you use it.

6. Completeness for all levels of management. This book cannot possibly discuss all areas of management and all types of industry. It focuses on the discrete manufacturer that is Economic Order Quantity (EOQ) or Material Requirements Planning (MRP) based. It shows how planning is done at the different levels of management. It demonstrates what types of information need to be transferred between the levels of management. It identifies the control systems that should be in place at each of these levels and describes the feedback mechanisms that need to be in place to assure proper responsiveness. In summary, the book will help your company build an integrated top-to-bottom information loop.[1]

7. This book will help you as you move through the ranks of tactical and operational management. It will help you understand your new function and your new boss. It will help you work better with your peers. It is intended to be a personal road map that you keep with you through all your stages of growth. This book will also help you understand external functions such as management information systems, finance, accounting, and any other function that may be of interest to your function and your needs.

Why Is Change Necessary?

Two basic questions still need to be answered: "Why should we go through all this?" The reason for doing this is in order to change. "Why is change necessary at all?" There are several reasons for change. The first is competition, whether from at home or abroad. We need to improve to stay on top of our competitors. Another reason for change is to take advantage of technological advancements such as automation or computerization. Another reason for change is because our customers' habits change. Customer awareness programs, environmental consciousness, resource scarcity, governmental regulations, and economic swings will affect the way we produce goods.

Now you're ready to change and improve. Read on to get your function in perspective with everyone else's. And don't forget to note those areas that require further study. One of my favorite quotes comes from the book *Breakthrough Thinking* by Nadler and Hibino:

> The definition of insanity is continuing to do the same things and expecting different results.

---

[1] I originally planned to put a glossary of terms in the back of this book, but as I started to write it, it started to look exactly like the *APICS Dictionary,* so I decided that rather than make you pay for a reprint of the *APICS Dictionary,* I would let you buy your own copy (if you don't already have one). To get your copy, write to APICS (American Production and Inventory Control Society), 500 West Annandale Road, Falls Church, Virginia, 22046-4274, USA.

Chapter

2 The Manufacturing Organization

One of the frustrations of manufacturing is that titles and terminology become very confusing. Often the same function will have several different names. For this reason this chapter begins by defining some of the terminology used in this book. The best place to start is by diagramming the job functions that occur in a factory.

The Organizational Structure

Chart 2.1 diagrams the directorship and job functions of the typical plant. The ownership elects the board of directors; the board of directors hires the chief executive officer (CEO); and the CEO is responsible for running the organization. He hires the vice presidents, and so on down the chain. In many small- to medium-sized organizations the same individuals are involved in the ownership, directorship, CEO, and even some of the vice president positions.

The three key vice presidential job functions that make or break an organization are the operations, the financial (funding), and the marketing (sales) functions. These functions interact in order to keep the company in balance. For example, Chart 2.2 shows how this balance works. This balancing act between these three functional areas helps

CHART 2.1 Corporate Job Structure

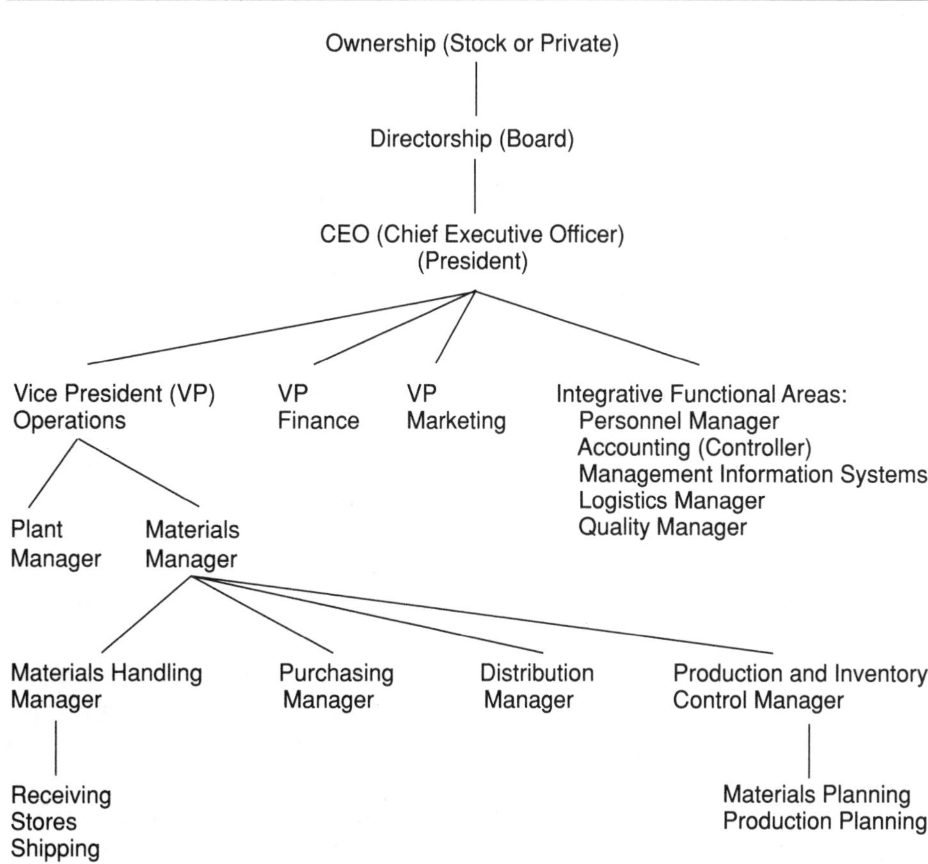

CHART 2.2 Objectives of the Conflicting VP Functions

	Marketing	Finance	Operations
Inventory	High finished goods	None	High raw materials
Funding	High sales expenditures	None	High equipment expenditures
Product types	Flexibility	Minimize cost	Standardization

CHART 2.3 Vice Presidential Functional Areas

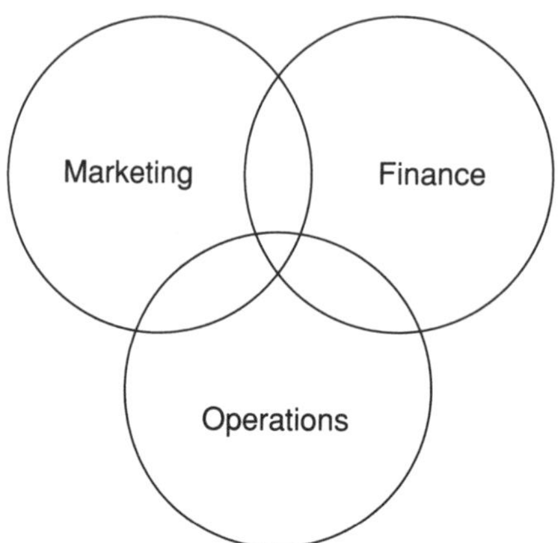

keep the organization from spending too much of its resources in one area. Rather than think of this as a balancing act, however, it more appropriately should be thought of as a consolidation of efforts, where the different functional areas work together sharing resources to achieve a common corporate goal. These overlaps are often diagrammed as shown on Chart 2.3.

The organization may have other vice presidential level positions that are considered support functions. These are included in Chart 2.1 under the "Integrative Functional Areas" section. The personnel manager deals with personnel problems, benefits programs, and union relations. The accounting area keeps records on the financial transactions of the organization. In some organizations accounting may be found under the VP of finance. Management information systems (MIS) is the computer operations department. Often this department is found under the accounting function, even though often more than two-thirds of their work is operations oriented. The logistics manager handles the distribution of sold goods and the receipt of purchased goods. This function may be found under the operations department. The last integrative area, quality management, is responsible for the customers' acceptance of the product and may include the engineering function. Often the quality and engineering functions are found under the operations VP.

For best control, MIS should be independent and not under the control of a specific department. This will allow them to treat all functions in the organization as customers without showing favoritism to any. The same philosophy is true of the quality function. If its independence is maintained, it can validate the quality (customer acceptance) of all areas without being pressured by the operations or marketing area to release products that are below corporate standards.

Chapter 4 will reflect on the organizational structure discussed in this chapter and will discuss the job functions of each of these individuals. The job functions will then be tied into the corporate information flow diagram.

Planning, Operations, and Control Functions

Another way of looking at this organizational structure and its interaction is to think of it in terms of a plant-wide program of planning, operations, and control. The vice presidents of finance, marketing, and operations, and the functional levels above these VPs, do the corporate planning. The managers under these three functions do the implementation and run the operation of these plans for each functional area. Control occurs through the feedback information provided by the integrative functional areas. This information is used by each area to cross-check the performance of the other functional areas.

Within each functional area we will also find planning, operations, and control functions. Each job function plans what they will do, does it, and checks to see if it was done correctly. This book will show how each of these steps occurs at each level of the organization.

Organizational Trade-offs

As we have already seen, manufacturing is a balancing act. The primary challenge is to select the best trade-offs that will help to achieve the goals of the factory. Chapter 6 will discuss what these goals should look like for the factory as a whole. In the operations area there are also trade-offs. Here the balancing act occurs between issues such as (Chart 2.4):

- Cost
  - Labor
  - Materials
  - Plant and equipment
  - Overhead
- Quality
  - Product design and engineering
  - Service
  - Dependability
- Flexibility
  - Turnaround time
  - Product features

CHART 2.4 Operations Trade-offs

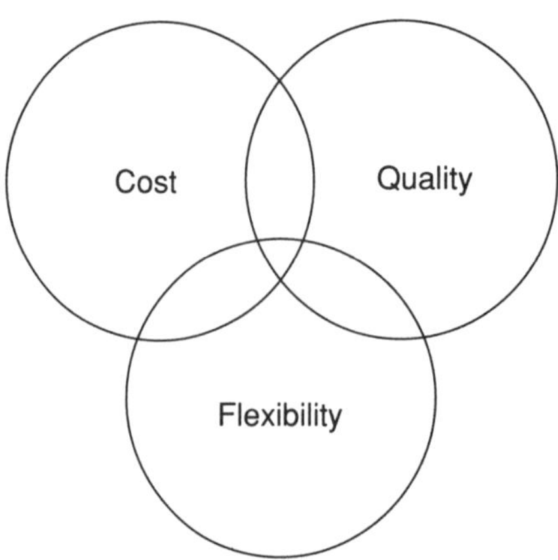

To evaluate these trade-offs, an analysis of the costs and benefits of different options becomes necessary, and in very complicated situations where the number of options becomes very large, a decision tree becomes a useful tool.

Types of Manufacturing

As mentioned earlier, there is no perfect solution for manufacturing problems that will cover all situations. One of the reasons for this is found in the large number of different types of manufacturing. This is again an area where there are many different definitions for each of the manufacturing classifications. We will establish our own set of simplistic definitions for use in this book.

Process Manufacturing

Process manufacturing has production lead times that are very short. Generally, a product is poured into one end of the process and comes pouring out of the other end. Very little labor is involved in the process; it is primarily materials-intensive. There are usually no definable pieces of product in the raw materials or work-in-process stages. Examples of process manufacturing include oil refining, chemical processing, pharmaceuticals, steel and other metal manufacturing, food and beverages, textiles, paper, etc.

Discrete Manufacturing

Discrete manufacturing occurs when you have two or more different pieces and you slam, bang, glue, weld, bolt, or somehow attach them together. It typically has interrupted flow in the manufacturing process and is much more labor-intensive. Within discrete manufacturing there are three categories of manufacturing: departmentalized, job shop, and flow.

Departmentalized Discrete. In this type of discrete manufacturing, a highly repetitive product is made. In each of the production process steps, the product is moved to a specific department that specializes in that particular production process. For example, drilling is done in the drilling department, welding is done in the welding department, and inspection is done in the quality control department. This is probably the most common form of discrete manufacturing in the United States. Labor efficiency is usually emphasized.

Job Shop. This type of manufacturing involves employees who are artists or experts in their fields. The product manufactured is usually one of a kind or very few of a kind. These manufacturers generally build the machines, tools, dies, and jigs for the other types of manufacturing.

Flow Discrete. Flow discrete manufacturing entails a work line that is laid out in the sequence in which the product is to be built. The work line includes all the machines and employees needed to produce the product. The traditional American assembly line is a flow discrete process. The newer KANBAN[1] lines also fall into this category.

With these definitions of the different types of manufacturing, we realize that each operational process will be run differently. Strategic and tactical management tools are very similar across the different types of manufacturing, but operations management tools can differ dramatically. As the different operations tools are discussed in this book (see Chapter 4) you will be given a feel for how each tool is best used.

The Manufacturing Cycle

The manufacturing cycle is composed of a series of inputs being processed, and this process creates a specific output. A diagram of the manufacturing cycle can be seen in Chart 2.5. This cycle involves:

1. A planning mechanism that specifies what we would like to see happen. This includes the planning of the inputs and the planning of the production process.

2. A control mechanism that monitors what is actually happening. As inputs are processed, the outputs are monitored for quantity and quality. These measures become the control information that is used to monitor the actual progress in the plan.

[1] KANBAN is part of a leading edge just-in-time system from Japan that attempts to approach all of the manufacturing functions with a type of assembly-line technique. KANBAN is an advanced topic and, hence, is not part of the focus of this book, but should be considered after most of the rest of the functions outlined in this book are working correctly.

CHART 2.5 Manufacturing Cycle

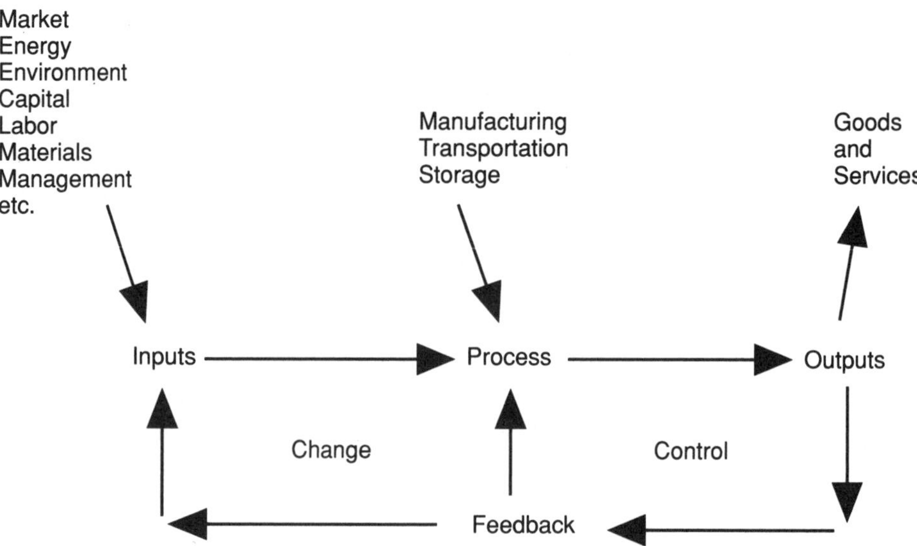

3. A feedback mechanism that reports back what actually happens in units produced, timing, and quality. The data that are generated by the monitoring process feed back to the inputs and the process functions.

4. Last is a change mechanism that integrates back into the planning mechanism. This integration implements the corrective action to both inputs and the process functions on what should be done, when it should be done, and how it should be done. This change mechanism is necessary to bring the inputs and process back in line with the initial plan.

Selection of Operations Management Tools

As we already mentioned, the operations areas differ significantly from one manufacturer to another. Therefore, each may use a different selection of management tools. When looking at the manufacturing cycle, there are several factors which affect the selection of operations management tools. Of prime importance is *time*. How long does the manufacturing cycle take? Another way of stating this same question is to ask: "What is the manufacturing lead time of the products produced at this factory?" What we are trying to identify is the planning horizon. The chapter on routings will discuss in detail how a planning horizon is calculated. For our purposes here, let's estimate how long it takes to build a product from start to finish. If this time is less than one or two days, you have a flow discrete or a process manufacturing facility and you need a different set of tools than if your planning horizon lies between one week to about one year. In the latter case you are probably a departmentalized discrete or a job shop manufacturer. If your lead time goes beyond a year, your manufacturing process starts to look like that of a construction project. Although the strategic and tactical management tools discussed in this book would fit all three time environments, the operations management tools of this book orient themselves primarily around the one-week to one-year planning horizon category.

Another factor in the selection of operations management tools occurs when taking a look at the resource focus of the facility. Determining which resource is the most critical to the process will define the production planning tools that you should use. This topic is discussed in Chapter 6.

Summary

Having looked at a few of the definitional issues of manufacturing planning we can now move forward with a look at the manufacturing data base. This is the subject of Chapter 3.

Chapter

3 The Manufacturing Data Base

Data Base

The term *Data Base* can scare anyone off. Usually it brings forth visions of lots of work and very little meaningful information. Before we get started removing these fears, let's define a few of the terms that get thrown around by data base groupies.

The *data base* is the collection of all data that is stored for future analysis. *Data base* does not equal *computer*. Computers have a data base, but your data base does not have to be on a computer. Your data base may be a file drawer full of one year's worth of purchase invoices. Perhaps you want to keep some portions of your data base on the computer, such as the bookkeeping, or accounts receivable, or inventory. Or perhaps your data base in a particular area is so small that a computer is more hassle than it's worth. Don't feel alone. Toyota runs their entire production planning and control process without a computer for just the same reasons. But computers do offer an enormous time savings and error-reducing benefit in certain areas—*if* used correctly.

Data are the things that are collected and thrown into the data base. For example, time cards, invoices, reject slips, shipping documents, etc., are all data and can be incorporated into the data base in different ways (filed in the file drawer or typed into a computer—or both).

Information is manipulated and analyzed data. For example, if you have a file of all accounts receivable transactions, you could run a report of who is past due and by how much. That report is information. Information is used for decision-making processes. There are different forms of information generating systems. These include:

1. *Electronic Data Processing (EDP):* The process of taking data and sorting and printing it.

2. *Management Information Systems (MIS):* The use of data to create summary reports or exception (problem) reports. These are systems with one correct answer. Most accounting systems fall into this category.

3. *Decision Support Systems (DSS):* DSS systems create information that does not have one correct answer. Answers come in the form of ranges, options, and variances. The results require some intuitive interpretation by a manager before decisions can be made. Most manufacturing operations management falls into this category.

Garbage In—Garbage Out

Garbage in—garbage out (GIGO) suggests that information isn't any better than the data used to build it. Missing data or incorrect data will make the information worthless.

Chart 3.1 diagrams the data collection and information generation process. The input is the data, which become part of a data base; the output is information; and the process is the manipulation of the data base in various ways to create the desired output.

CHART 3.1 Input—Process—Output

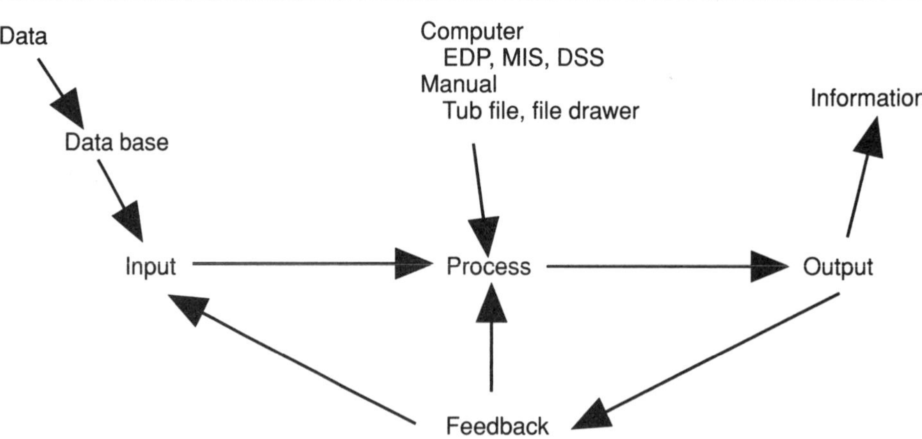

Data Base Construction

Data base construction is a topic worth discussing because we tend to find factories that are at the extremes. Either they collect data on everything, and then don't know what to do with it, or they don't collect any data at all. Both situations can be equally detrimental when it comes to running a factory. There are three keywords that are critical when planning the manufacturing data base. They are integration, simplicity, and focus.

Integration

The full impact of information and data *integration* is discussed in Chapter 4. This chapter describes the total information flow of an organization.

We need to look at how data and information fit into the manufacturing cycle (Chart 2.5). The primary function of data is in the feedback loop. Data are a collection of transactions that have recently occurred. For example, inventory receipts and inventory releases are data. These data are collected to provide information such as the current balance of each inventory item, which provides further information about what inventory items should be purchased and how often each item of inventory is used. From this example we see that inventory data help monitor and control what is happening to each item of inventory. The collection of the data into a data base allows informational reports to be generated. These reports are the feedback mechanism of the system that cause additional planning and change activity. Planning activity is like setting up purchase requests, and change activity is like checking to see why we are using twice as much of an inventory item as our planning system said we should.

Simplicity

Simplicity suggests that if the data element isn't used in the generation of meaningful information, or if it doesn't help fulfill the corporate goals, we shouldn't waste our time collecting it. Chapter 6 discusses the process of selecting what data are appropriate for collection. The following example will go into more detail on this concept.

Focus

Focus suggests that all data collection and information gathering processes should be done with a specific goal and direction in mind. The systems discussed in this book should be focused toward the corporate goal discussed in Chapter 6. Systems should not be implemented at random; rather, they should be selectively placed like building blocks toward the achievement of a planned purpose. An example that will help explain is given here.

For the small- to medium-sized manufacturer, some of the fads of data collection can be destructive rather than helpful. One example is the ABC (activity-based costing) systems, which suggest that data should be collected on as many cost elements as possible so that you understand all aspects of your operation as completely as possible. This concept is supported by many of the big accounting firms. However, for the small- to medium-sized firm, these types of concepts are a grandiose overkill. Even IBM, the king of data collection, has backed off of the ABC system because of the overhead cost and bureaucracy it has caused within their own organization. Activity-based costing is neither simple, nor is it focused.

For inventory control, however, data collection is important. We could shut the entire operation of the factory down if we didn't have the correct level of inventory needed in the production process. But what about filling out time cards to the detail where employees have to record when they take breaks? Does the time spent recording these transactions really help achieve the goal of the organization? Does this show data collection focus? Often this level of detail data collection is imposed on employees who compose less than 10 percent of the value-added cost component. This same facility does not track scrap and pilferage of materials, which makes up 60 percent of the value-added cost component. The message we are giving our employees in a situation like this is that keeping breaks short is more important than worrying about someone stealing tools. This example may seem ridiculous, but so is the data collection system that transmits this set of values to our employees.

Value Added

In the last paragraph, a few terms were used that need further explanation. The most important is the concept of *value added.* Understanding how to manipulate the value-added part of a manufactured product is to

CHART 3.2 Value-Added Breakdown

Labor	5 to 15 percent
Materials	40 to 70 percent
Overhead	15 to 50 percent

understand why the Japanese target certain industries and avoid others. Here is how it works.

In your plant you purchase raw materials (input into the production cycle, Chart 2.5). These raw materials are converted into a finished good that we sell (output into the production cycle, Chart 2.5). The difference between the selling price and the cost of the raw materials (finished goods minus raw materials) is what "value" your plant has "added" to the raw materials product. The Japanese target those industries where the value-added portion is the highest. For example, if we purchase the raw materials for $10, and sell the product for $30, we have added $20 of value to the product we sold. If the actual cost is only $15 to generate this $20 of increased value, we are much better off than if the actual cost to us was $19. The Japanese select those industries that give them the most bang for the buck. We need to learn this lesson as well.

Going on with my explanation of value added, for the small- to medium-sized discrete manufacturer, the value-added components usually break down somewhere in the ranges shown in Chart 3.2. To calculate your own value-added components, see Chart 6.A1 under the "Cost of Production" section. In this example labor was 59.7 percent, materials was 32.8 percent, and overhead was 7.5 percent.

Returning to my comments on focused data collection where we discussed the collection of data about breaks, doesn't it seem backward to focus our importance on a resource component (labor) that is only 5 to 15 percent of the value-added component, and ignore the importance of a data element that is 40 to 70 percent of the value-added component (materials)?

Motivation

One critical method of motivating our employees is through the measurement systems we establish. As ridiculous as the example may seem, if murdering someone during a robbery had a smaller prison penalty than letting them live, wouldn't we suddenly see an upswing in the number of murders? This measurement system says that murder is OK, just like the lack of a measurement system for scrap and pilferage that we discussed earlier says that the company turns a blind eye to the misuse of materials. If, however, we quit measuring breaks and started measuring scrap and pilferage, we may see that employees now spend twice as much time at breaks, but if we also see a 50 percent reduction in wasted materials, wasn't it worth it? Remember that a change to materials costs (in this example) has six times the impact on value-added costs as a change to labor costs (in the example, labor was 10 percent of the value-added component and materials was 60 percent).

Restated simplistically: *Your measurement system is also the motivation system that directs employees and tells them what is important to management.* Don't measure it unless you care about it! Remember, *simplicity* and *focus.*

What Data Do We Collect?

The planning of what data to collect so that they are focused, simple, integrated, and properly motivate employees is not a one-time decision. Chapter 6 will help you establish the data base and information needs plan. You will select the appropriate goals of the organization, select the most critical resources that affect that goal, and lay out a data collection and data base building procedure that will help you in the control, feedback, and change process (see Chart 2.5). Once the data base and information generation tools have been selected, we need to monitor them for a period of time to see if they are giving us the desired effect. We want to make sure we are measuring the right things to the level of completeness we need, and we want to make sure our employees are receiving the correct messages through our measurement process. We may need to modify our data collection and information generation process occasionally to fine-tune it toward this goal. Regularly checking on the data and information systems will keep the data base and the operation of your entire factory on track.

Computerization

If you are inclined to install a computer system, let me give you a few guidelines. These will be called the "Rules of Systems Analysis when Computerizing." They have been listed in Chart 3.3 for easy reference and also summarized in Chart 3.4.

CHART 3.3 Rules of Systems Analysis when Computerizing

1. When analyzing a system, analyze the output first.

1.1. There are three pieces to every system, the input, the process, and the output (see Chart 3.1). The most important of these is the output. The output is the information we hope to obtain from the system. It is the goal of the system. Plan this first.

1.2. The second piece that needs to be analyzed is the input. We need to make sure that we can collect the data that will be needed to achieve the desired output.

1.3. The last piece that needs to be analyzed is the process. This is the computer system. This piece is analyzed last because we need to know where we are going (output) and where we are starting from (input) before we worry about what route to take (process).

2. Buy the system, not the hardware.

2.1. First define the needs of your system. What do you expect out of it in the way of information (reports)?

2.2. Next, investigate the different systems options. APICS and several other organizations publish regular evaluations of the systems software products that are available. They list costs and features. This will help you narrow down which systems will fit your needs best.

2.3. Next, contact selected vendors for demonstrations of their software. Again, narrow down the selection process to two to four choices.

2.4. Test run the systems that you are the most comfortable with using your actual data, not some dummy demonstrated data. Often, at this stage, we find problems such as decimal places are not significant enough or product numbers are not large enough.

2.5. After selecting the software that will fit the best, you can start considering your different hardware options. If you are already tied to a piece of computer hardware, perhaps this step is not needed. But if you have not tied yourself to a piece of hardware, now is the time to try out different pieces to see which gives the best performance on your selected software product.

3. Don't computerize something that doesn't work manually. If the process you want to computerize cannot be performed manually on a small scale, then computerization will simply give you high-speed garbage. Make sure that the data collection process is complete and that all the data exist to give you accurate results.

For example, inventory control systems exist where inventory is issued to a specific work order, and inventory receipts are recorded. But if an employee breaks a part that they are working on, they often run back to the stockroom and get another part. The appropriate paperwork is not filled out because that would embarrass the employee. So what happens is that occasionally the inventory system will claim that there is sufficient inventory, when in fact there isn't. In one example, the company chose to install a computer system because this would "force employees to keep accurate records." *Wrong!* The breakages still weren't recorded and the company now had high-speed GIGO. The problem didn't go away until they took the employee identification requirement off the breakage replacement slips. This is not the only solution, nor is it necessarily the best solution. The point is that sometimes we have to set our priorities correctly, and inventory inaccuracies have been known to shut down production lines.

The computer cannot solve problems in data collection. These problems need to be solved before you install the computer.

4. Don't dump the manual system. Computers break down. Don't let the computer be the "God" of your plant to the point where you can't operate without it. It should help you, not obstruct you. Therefore, keep a manual backup system handy that you can jump

CHART 3.3 *(concluded)*

to if there is a computer failure. Don't run both the computer and the manual system. Keep the old system handy in case you need it.

Don't throw the manual system away simply because you are now computerized.

5. Your point of view is most often wrong. When selecting a system, talk to the users. Find out what the users of the information need. Find out what would be helpful to those individuals that generate the data. Don't assume you know it all.

6. Make sure your system passes the "beer truck test." Assume you have an employee that, while walking home from work one day, gets hit by a beer truck. Will your organization's systems and computer still be able to function? Don't become overly dependent on any one person (including yourself). Cross train your employees on all job functions. This will also help them keep tabs on each other.

Another important aspect to the beer truck test is documentation. Make sure that instructions and procedures are written down and that other employees know how to use them. It can be nearly impossible to figure out what is in someone's head after the beer truck strikes.

7. Make the right thing easier to do than the wrong thing. Employees take the easy way out. If reporting scrap or waste is a burdensome process, you can bet your data will be inaccurate. Make the process of recording data easy, and make inventory error reconciliation a burdensome task. That way employees will try to keep the data correct.

8. Do your homework. Often systems exist to solve a symptom, not a problem. Dig out the real problem. Ask "Why does this exist?" over and over until the root of the problem is found. This process is discussed further in Chapter 6.

9. Install a computer only if it makes life easier. Simplicity is the key. Does the computer help by improving accuracy, timeliness, or by handling large volumes of data? If the computer doesn't help make life easier, for example, if the information needed is small and the time is not an issue, don't use the computer. One example is fixed asset reporting. If you only have a few fixed assets, you only need a depreciation report annually, and you have over a month to do the report, so is it worth spending two months of employee time to develop a customized fixed asset system? Probably not!

10. Don't build a data base and then not use it. As mentioned earlier, don't set up an inventory data base and then use it only for inventory balances. Since you have the data collected you should also use it for usage history analyses and inventory costing.

11. Parallel. When installing a new computerized system, don't just turn the computer on and throw the old manual stuff away. Don't be that trusting. Run both the computer and the manual system simultaneously for about a month to see if the results coming out of both systems are the same. If they're different, find out why and continue paralleling until they are the same.

12. Backups. Computers break down, scratch disks, and commit all sorts of vicious crimes on your data base. Keep at least two copies of everything, preferably three. Take one copy home with you so that it isn't in the same place as the other copies. Computers have been known to be broken or stolen. You can replace the computer fairly easily—but reinputting your data base can take months.

Once a week (at least) copy everything from the computer data base onto a backup disk and place that disk in a safe place. Rotate the backups so that every other week you use a different backup disk. Then, if failure occurs, the most you'll ever have to recover is one week's worth of data. Also, keep the source documents (invoices, job sheets, time cards, etc.) for at least two weeks so that you can reinput them if need be.

13. Keep it simple. Keep it focused. Keep it integrated. These are points stressed throughout this chapter.

CHART 3.4 Summary of Rules of Systems Analysis when Computerizing

1. When analyzing a system, analyze the output first.
   - **1.1.** Plan the output first.
   - **1.2.** Plan the input next.
   - **1.3.** Plan the process last.
2. Buy the system, not the hardware.
   - **2.1.** Define the needs of your system.
   - **2.2.** Investigate the different systems options.
   - **2.3.** Contact the vendors for demonstrations.
   - **2.4.** Test run the systems.
   - **2.5.** Consider your different hardware options.
3. Don't computerize something that doesn't work manually.
4. Don't dump the manual system.
5. Your point of view is most often wrong.
6. Make sure your system passes the "beer truck test."
7. Make the right thing easier to do.
8. Do your homework.
9. Install a computer only if it makes life easier.
10. Don't build a data base and then not use it.
11. Parallel.
12. Backup.
13. Keep it simple, focused, and integrated.

Summary

Now that you have a better feel for what a data base is, we are ready to go to Chapter 4. This chapter integrates the manufacturing cycle of Chart 2.5 with the job functions of Chart 2.1 and the information integration needs of Chart 3.1. Everything ties together, and if we have a good understanding of how these ties work, we will be better able to plan out the operation of our factory.

Chapter

4 What Is POM?

Three Levels of Management

The three levels of management are strategic, tactical, and operational (Chart 4.1). Strategic management sets the goals and directions of the organization (five or more years in the planning horizon). Tactical management turns these goals into a plan of action (one- to three-year planning horizon). Operational management implements the plans (one-hour to one-year planning horizon). Referring back to Chart 2.1, strategic management covers the ownership, directorship, and CEO. Tactical management covers the CEO, VPs, and the plant and materials managers. Operations management covers the plant and materials managers and on down the management chain. POM is the abbreviation for "production and operations management," another name for operations management. This book is broken up into the three segments of management. Strategic management is covered in Chapter 6; tactical is covered in Chapter 7; and operations management is covered in Chapters 8 on.

For most management functions, the use of mathematical models or tools is only 20 percent of the job function. However, the understanding and correct use of these tools is what will make the other 80 percent (dealing with people) effective.

As promised earlier, this chapter goes into detail on the integration and flow of information and data through the factory. It will turn this information flow into a diagram and then tie this diagram to the manufacturing cycle of Chart 2.5, to the job functions of Chart 2.1, and to the information integration needs of Chart 3.1.

Information and its required data are often treated as separate modules. For example, we may find an accounting system, an accounts payable system, an accounts receivable system, an order processing system, a forecasting system, etc. Each of these "systems" is treated as a separate entity with some occasional data transfer occurring between

CHART 4.1 Levels of Management

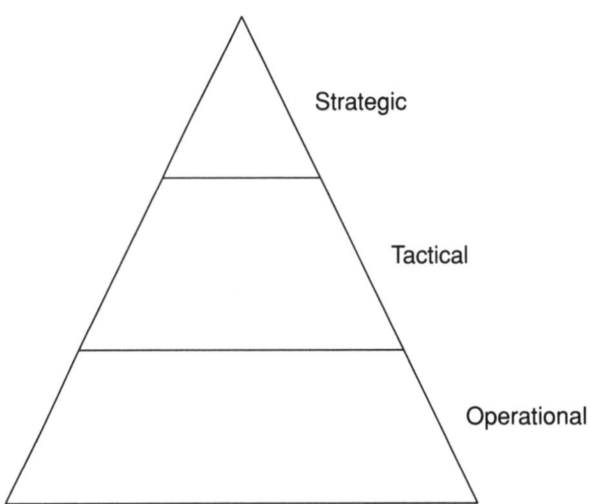

the systems. But the corporate-wide data collection process and information generation process need to be integrated in order to function correctly.

Information Flow

Each of the three levels of management (strategic, tactical, and operational) influences the other. There are specific "systems" used by each of these management levels that integrate with the other levels of management. The remainder of this chapter will look at the information requirements of each of these levels of management. It will analyze what they are, how they are used, and how they integrate into the total flow of information, data, and the feedback mechanism.

Manufacturing Information Flow

The information flow process starts with the *business plan,* which is designed by strategic management. This plan defines the goals and directions of the corporation. Once the business plan (BP) has defined these goals, the rest of the information processing system is built to support this goal. For example, a *forecast* (F) needs to be developed so that these goals are achieved. This forecast is not always a dollar sales forecast, although in the United States it usually is. If the goal is market share, then some market share percentage or some measure of the number of units sold is used. The forecast can be relieved (replaced) by *customer orders* (C/O). The total demand for production on the factory is the combination of the forecast and the customer orders.

The next information processing segment is the *rough-cut capacity plan* (RCC). This plan highlights the total available resources that the organization has at its disposal. A balancing act is now performed between F + C/O (forecast plus customer orders) and the RCC (rough-cut capacity). The forecast plus the customer orders define the demand placed on the plant's resources, and the rough-cut capacity plan defines resource availability. The resources most often selected for these measures are materials, labor hours, and machine hours. Each product that is forecast places a demand on the factory for a specific number of labor hours, machine hours, and units of material. This demand can be multiplied by the number of units anticipated to be produced. The result is measured against the available capacity. Occasionally products may need to be produced and held in storage for sale in another time period. This storage will cover an anticipated increase in demand. A compromise plan will result. This compromise plan is called the *aggregate production schedule* (APS). If we diagram the process to this point, the diagram would look like Chart 4.2.

At this point a vision of the total integration process should begin to unfold. We will continue to move down the information flow diagram by looking at the next step, the *master production schedule* (MPS). The

CHART 4.2 Strategic to Tactical Management

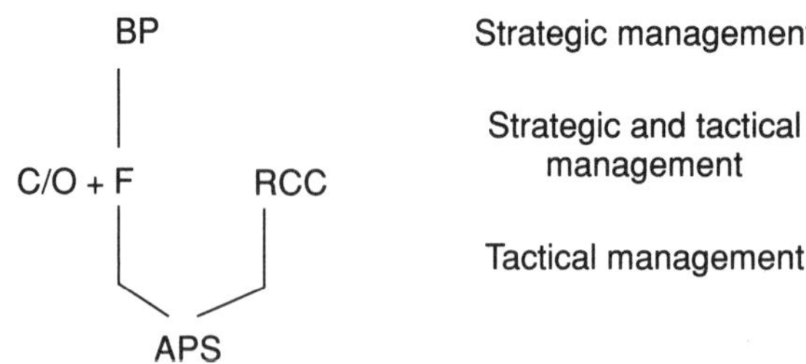

CHART 4.3 Bill of Materials

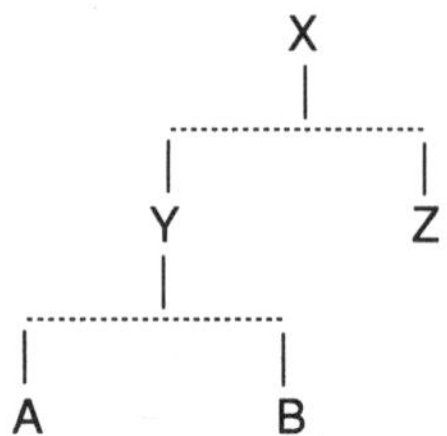

MPS is the detailing of the APS. What happens in the move to the MPS is that we break the rough numbers of the APS out into specific, definable products that have an identity. Products analyzed in the F, C/O, RCC, and APS were discussed as families of products. The step moving from the APS to the MPS takes these families and breaks them into specific products.

The master production schedule is the first of five inputs that go into the production planning (PP) process. The MPS defines the number of end products to be produced. The second input is the *bill of materials* (BofM), which defines the product makeup of every end product. An example of a bill of materials is seen in Chart 4.3. Here product X is made up of product Y and product Z. Product Y, in turn, is made up of products A and B.

The third input into the production planning process is the *routings* (R). The routings define job functions and time. For example, the routing for product Y in the diagram above would specify all the production steps required to combine A with B to create Y. The routing describes what the labor steps are, how much time each labor step takes, and how much machine time each step takes.

Both the routing and the bill of materials information are used when we define the capacity demanded by the forecast in the creation of the aggregate production schedule. These give specific information on machine hours, labor hours, and material usage demands for each product to be created.

The fourth input into the production plan is the *inventory status information* (I). This is simply the count of all the inventory in the factory at any point in time.

The fifth input is the *purchase and production orders* (P/PO) in process. This last input tells the system what is already being produced or what is already being shipped but has not yet arrived. If we were to diagram the information flow diagram at this point it would look like Chart 4.4.

The function of the production plan is to

1. Take the total number of units to be produced, as defined by the MPS.
2. Calculate the number of units of materials required for each product using the BofM.
3. Define how much labor and machine time will be required for each of these production steps using the routing.
4. Use the routing to further define when the materials, labor hours, and machine hours will be needed.
5. Adjust those needs downward by the number of units of inventory we already have on hand.
6. Further adjust the needs downward based on the items that have already been purchased but have not yet arrived or items that are currently in production but are not yet finished.

In this book we will discuss two types of production planning models. The first is called *economic order quantity* (EOQ). This model only plans inventory. It does not consider labor or machinery schedules. It is the most basic form of production planner. EOQ works best in an environment where demand is steady and constant and the parts costs are evenly distributed (there is no part that is exceptionally expensive). This system can be run manually or with a simple computerized inventory control package.

CHART 4.4 Strategic to Operational Management

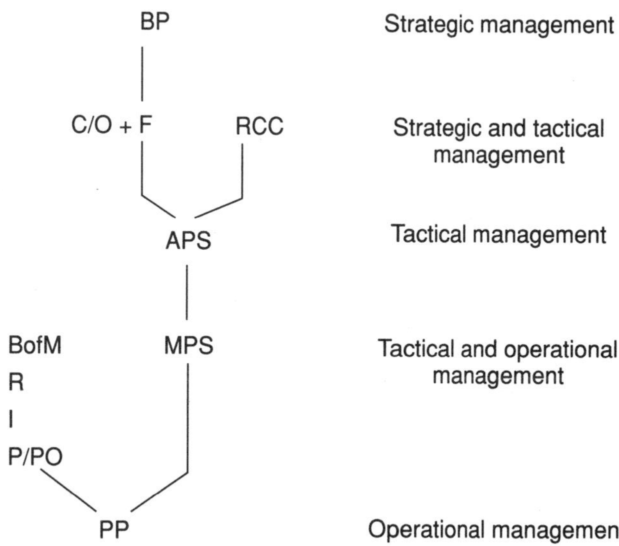

The second type of production planning model discussed in this book is *material requirements planning* (MRP). MRP considers material, labor, and machinery in planning the schedules. It offers advantages for plants with intermittent demand and expensive parts scheduling. However, because of the added control offered by MRP it is much more complex than EOQ and will probably require the use of a computer package with an MRP scheduler. This book will explain MRP so that you can use it manually. Understanding how MRP functions manually is extremely helpful even when using a computer system because this will help you take advantage of the system and know what to expect from the system.

Continuing with our analysis of the information flow diagram, we come to the outputs of the production planning process. Using an EOQ scheduler will give you a purchasing schedule as an output. Using MRP will give you both of the following outputs:

1. A *production schedule* (PROD) is generated that creates shop orders for items that still need to be produced in order to achieve the MPS schedule.
2. A *purchasing schedule* (PURCH) is generated that lists purchases of materials that are needed in order to complete the desired product satisfactorily.

The results of all these calculations are seen in Chapter 16, which is on material requirements planning outputs. At this point, an updated information flow diagram would look like Chart 4.5. The production schedule (PROD) starts work on the factory floor. As items are produced, inventory is used up, and new items of inventory are created.

CHART 4.5 Strategic through Operational Management

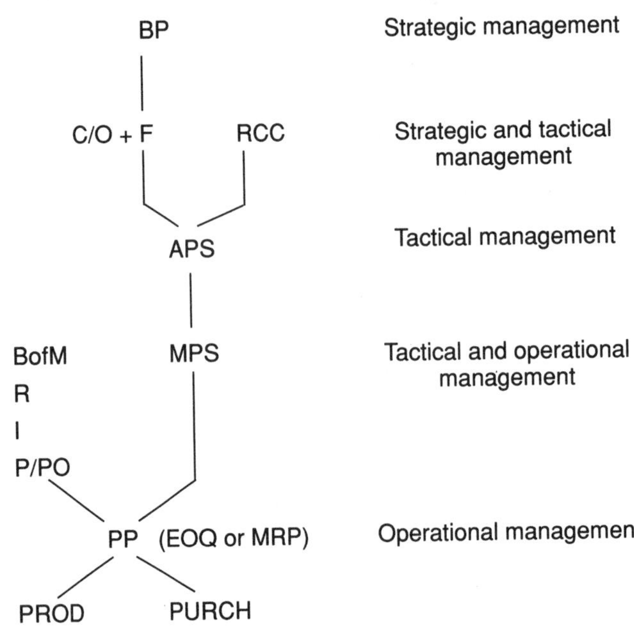

This updates the I and P/PO inputs to the PP. Similarly, the purchasing schedule (PURCH) causes items to be purchased and brought into inventory, updating these same two inputs. As products are completed and sold, adjustments need to be made to the MPS, which will reduce the number of products still needing to be produced.

When using MRP as a production scheduler, two more elements enter into the production flow diagram. The first is *capacity requirements planning* (CRP). This system plans the production schedule generated by the MRP system (PROD) on a department-by-department basis. This is a departmental tool assisting the department in planning its capacity.

Coming out of CRP is a *shop floor control scheduler* (SFC). This is a data collection and shop floor control mechanism that monitors progress on the factory floor. The data it collects feed the information flow diagram and affect future schedules.

The last element that needs to be integrated into this process is the *logistics system* (LOG). Logistics applies when products are purchased and special shipping arrangements must be made. It also applies when products are sold and shipped and when warehousing occurs at either the shipping or receiving ends. The final production information and data flow diagram would look like Chart 4.6.

At this point it is important to reflect on the concept of integration. Each of the elements of this information flow diagram needs to be integrated. They cannot be treated as isolated entities. What is infor-

CHART 4.6 Information Flow Diagram

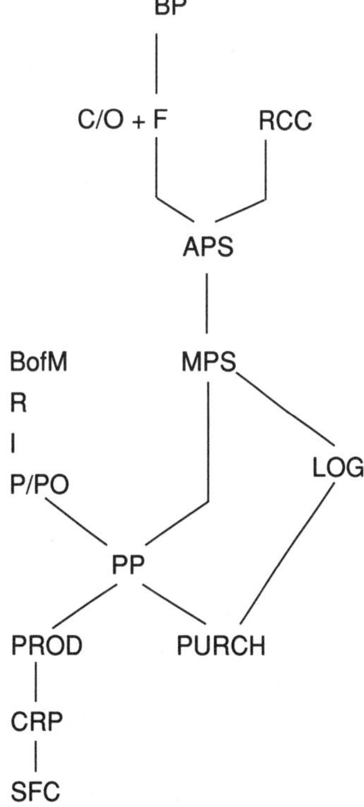

mation to one entity becomes data to the next one up the line. Feedback between the entities is common and important.

The diagramming process used in this chapter has been greatly simplified in order to help us understand how the overall process works. But many monkey wrenches occur in real life that complicate these diagrams significantly, making integration and feedback even more critical. Here are a few examples:

1. What happens to RCC, APS, MPS, and PROD if a machine breaks down and it takes several days for it to be repaired?
2. What happens to R, RCC, APS, MPS, and PROD if a new employee is hired and this new employee has only half the efficiency of the old employee he or she replaced?
3. What happens to I, P/PO, and PROD if an error in production occurs and several hundred units of product need to be scrapped?
4. What happens to R, APS, MPS, and PROD if a new machine is brought in that increases the total output?
5. What happens to BofM, APS, MPS, PROD, and PURCH if engineering improves product design and product X is no longer composed of Y and Z, but is now composed of W and Z?

Accounting Information Flow

The accounting information flow process is an area with which most information processors are familiar. This is primarily because accounting is the first area that is usually automated. It is highly repetitive and lends itself easily to MIS (management information systems, see Chapter 3) concepts, whereas the production information flow incorporates primarily DSS (decision support systems) techniques. Next we need to discuss briefly the accounting information flow because it becomes important when we try to integrate it with the production information flow process.

Using the same top-down approach that was used for the production information flow process, we would start with the *balance sheet* (BS), which indicates the financial status of the corporation at a specific point in time. The BS is composed of three areas: the *assets* (A), the *liabilities* (L), and the *owners equity* (OE). Assets are composed of inventory (I), accounts receivable (AR), cash (C), fixed assets (FA), and other similar assets (OA). Liabilities are composed of accounts payable (AP), payroll (P), and a collection of other liabilities (OL). Equity is composed of current ownership of the corporation (CO), which is adjusted by recent profits or losses (P/L). A diagram of this process would look like Chart 4.7. Information is fed into these financial analysis elements from several sources. For example, accounts receivable and cash information comes from sales. Inventory information comes from I in the production flow diagram. Fixed assets are defined in the rough-cut capacity plan as resources available and are depreciated by their planned usage. Accounts payable and cash reductions come from purchasing. Payroll information comes from the PROD output of the production plan, which is

CHART 4.7 Financial Information Flow

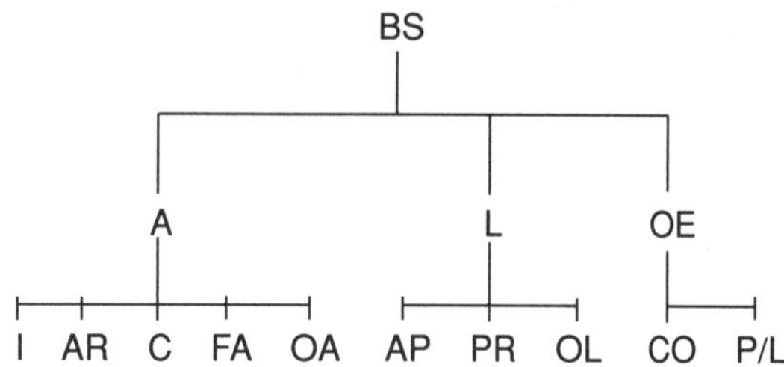

CHART 4.8 Total Flow of Financial Information

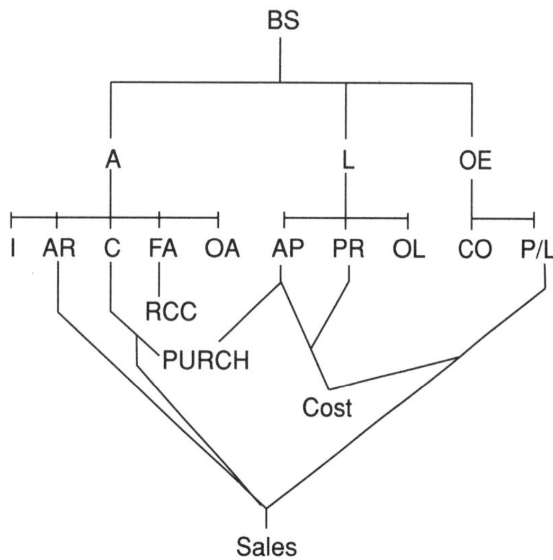

fed through a costing system. Profit and loss information comes from income (sales) reduced by costs. Adding these elements into the diagram would result in Chart 4.8.

Integration of the Manufacturing and Accounting Information Flows

Integration needs to occur between these two information flow systems because of the large number of interfaces that occur. To simplify this integration process we will take only the inputs that go directly into the accounting system. These also have integration points in the production system. These are:

Inventory (I)
Sales
Costs
Purchasing (PURCH)
Fixed assets (FA)
Payroll (PR)
Accounts payable (AP)

CHART 4.9 The Manufacturing and Accounting Integrated Information Flow Diagram

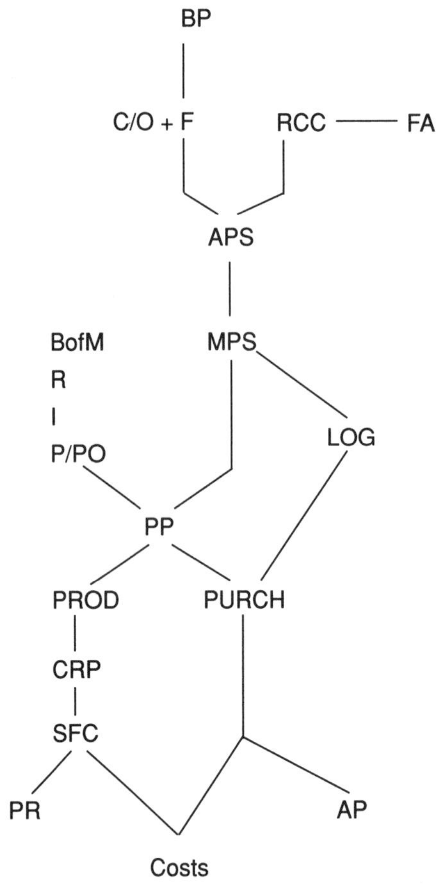

Redrawing the production flow diagram with these added elements of integration would make the chart look like Chart 4.9.

Sales is an input into future forecast projections, and sales gets feedback from the MPS on products that have been shipped. Costs receive input from both the purchasing and the production schedule feedback process, which indicates what was purchased and what labor has been expended. Fixed asset information requires information about what machines exist and how many hours each machine has operated.

From this analysis, it is impossible to see how a corporate-wide system can run as a collection of isolated systems. These systems must be integrated in order to be effective.

Organizational Structure

With the organizational structure diagram in Chart 2.1, we can start placing labels on the information flow diagram of Chart 4.9. Chart 4.10 redisplays Chart 4.9 with some of the appropriate job titles inserted.

CHART 4.10 The Manufacturing and Accounting Integrated Information Flow Diagram

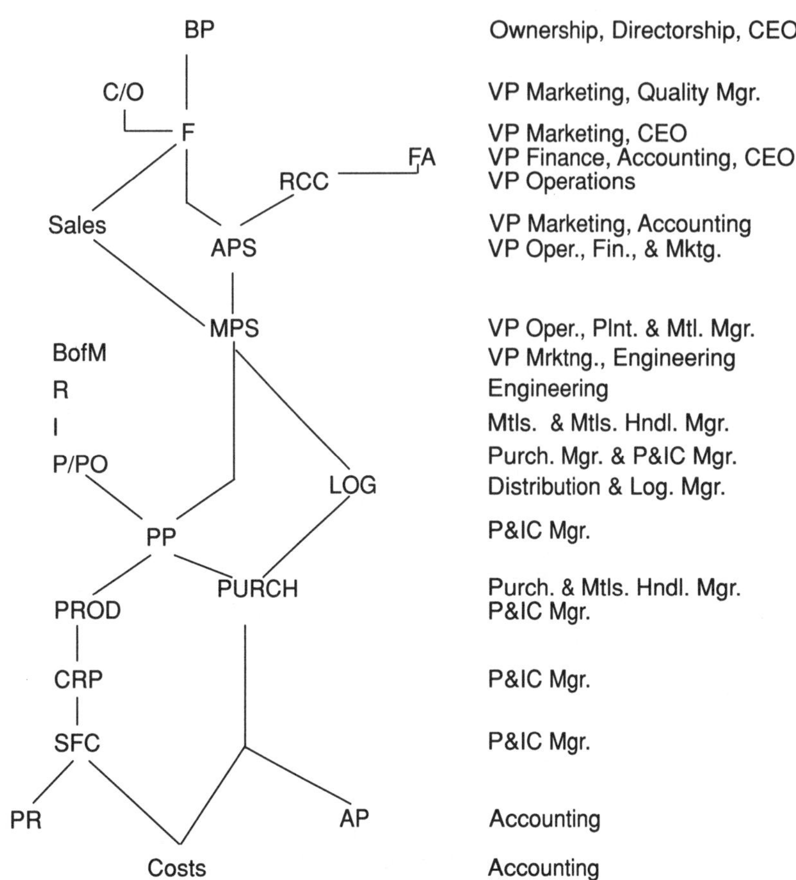

Referring back to the accounting information flow on Chart 4.8, all functions listed here are performed by the integrative functional areas of accounting and management information systems.

The Manufacturing Cycle

The manufacturing cycle of Chart 2.5 also needs to be integrated with the production information flow diagram of Chart 4.9. At each stage of the information flow we find inputs, a process, outputs, and a feedback mechanism that offers control and change. Chart 4.11 attempts to show some of the obvious flows but it is important to realize that these flows are highly integrated and can get very complex.

CHART 4.11 Integration of the Production Information Flow Steps and the Manufacturing Cycle

System	Inputs	Process	Outputs	Feedback (Control & Change)
Business plan (BP)	Guidance and direction of ownership and directorship	Written by CEO and directorship	Goals and objectives of organization	
Forecast (F)	Sales history	Mathematical modeling	Anticipated sales for at least one year	
Customer orders (C/O)	Sales orders	Relieve forecast	Shipment and delivery of goods	Corrections to forecast
Rough-cut capacity analysis (RCC)	Materials, labor, & machinery data & performance history	Mathematically calculate the capacities	Capacity plan	
Aggregate production schedule (APS)	RCC, C/O, F	Mathematical aggregate planning	APS	F or RCC adjustments
Logistics/distribution/warehousing (LOG)	MPS, PURCH	Mathematical modeling	Logistics plan	MPS or PURCH adjustments
Master production schedule (MPS)	APS, C/O, F history	Distribution of APS	MPS	APS & F adjustments
Inventory (I)	PURCH, issues and receipts, quality inspections	Inventory balance updating	I balance, usage, and cost information	PURCH, BofM
Production plan (PP)	I, BofM, P/PO, R, MPS	MRP generation	PURCH and PROD schedules	MPS adjustments
Bill of materials (BofM)	Engineering change information	BofM explosion	Parts requirements list, PP input	Engineering modifications
Routings (R)	Engineering time measurements	Planning horizon calculation	Production lead times, PP input	Engineering modifications
Purchase and production orders (P/PO, PURCH, & PROD)	PP	Order generation	PURCH & PROD	PP adjustments
Capacity requirements planning (CRP)	PP, PROD	Mathematical capacity evaluation	CRP	MPS, PROD
Shop Floor Control (SFC)	CRP	Data collection	Data, data base	Corrective feedback for PP and all its inputs

Integration Needs and the Manufacturing Information Flow Diagram

Computers can exist or not exist at any of the stages diagrammed in Chart 4.9. The use of a computer should always stress the points made in Chapter 3: *integration, simplicity, and focus*. The first of these three points that needs to be considered when looking at computerization is simplicity. Computers can simplify, but they can also complicate. For most organizations, computerizing the inventory system would make data collection and processing easier. Each piece of data is used in a variety of different ways: to update inventory balances, to generate usage history, and for inventory costing. However, computerization of systems like the business plan, rough-cut capacity, or the forecast is often more trouble than it's worth. These systems are used infrequently and the results normally only serve one main purpose. A general rule of thumb would be *if a computer simplifies the process, use it; if it complicates the process, forget it.*

Focus for your data and information system comes from properly planning the information flow process (Chart 4.9). Integration comes from placing all these system pieces together into one coordinated, focused pie. Integration also means consistency. If you're going to establish a computerized inventory system to track inventory balances, don't cost the inventory manually. Be consistent. If you're going to computerize inventory and go through all the trouble of setting it up, take advantage of all the information benefits available to you from that data base you have established.

Summary

Understanding the integration of the total information flow of a corporation is critical if effective systems are to be installed. We need to integrate the total flow of information. We need to stop thinking in terms of independent modules. We need to plan these systems so that they have focus and simplicity. This book will help you do just that!

In these first four chapters we have looked at a factory from a planning and control perspective. The next chapter (Chapter 5) takes a different perspective. It looks at a factory from the point of view of a new product idea. This will give you a slightly different perspective on integration. So let's move forward and broaden our perspective.

Chapter

5 Development of a New Product from Idea to Implementation

New Product Idea Generation

This chapter will look at the planning of a factory from a slightly different perspective. Up to now we have stressed the planning and control aspects (Chart 2.5) and the information flow aspects (Chart 4.9). This book will stress both of these perspectives as we go through the process of organizing your factory. However, it is also important to look at the flow of a factory from the perspective of a new product being developed. This chapter will discuss the product development perspective and tie it back into the information flow perspective discussed in Chapter 4.

When a new product idea is to be developed, the ideas come from several sources. Many of the best ideas come from customers, and we need to lend a listening ear in their direction. Many also come from the nonmarketing personnel of your organization. Employees should be invited to submit ideas and should be rewarded for the good ones. Ideas also come from vendors, especially product improvement ideas.

Break-Even Analysis

The ideas that are generated get filtered through the marketing organization. Marketing is responsible for screening these ideas. If the ideas are compatible with the goals of the organization (see Chapter 6), a financial analysis is performed. To do this analysis, marketing will work with engineering, production, and purchasing to try to estimate the cost of producing the new product. Two cost estimates are needed. The first is a cost to setup. This is a one-time cost (fixed cost) of what it will take to acquire machinery and retooling to prepare the plant for the production process required by the new product. The second cost estimate is the cost of production. This is the cost estimate of what it will take to produce each item in a mass production situation (variable cost).

Marketing needs to make some estimates of the sales potential of the suggested product. Two numbers are needed. The first is an estimate of the selling price. The second is an estimate of the annual sales volume.

With the four estimates (fixed and variable costs, sales volume, and sales price) an analysis can be performed to see if the product shows enough profitability to be worth producing. This process is called a *break-even analysis*. The steps for this process are outlined in Chart 5.1. Chart 5.2 offers some sample data and Chart 5.3 shows how the calculations of Chart 5.1 should be performed. It also offers an interpretation of the information calculated.

Chart 5.4 gives us a graphical look at the data in Charts 5.2 and 5.3. This graphical display is not necessary for you to do if you are performing break-even analyses, but it is helpful so that we can visualize what is happening.

CHART 5.1 Break-Even Analysis

[1]	Estimate the fixed costs of setup (total cost of setup)	———
[2]	Estimate the variable cost of producing the product (cost per unit produced)	———
[3]	Estimate the number of units sold per year	———
[4]	Estimate the sales price of the product (price per unit sold)	———
[5]	Estimate the number of years over which you want to amortize the fixed costs (number of years in which you want to recover the fixed costs of [1])	———
[6]	Calculate the annual fixed cost component ([1]/[5])	———
[7]	Calculate the profit margin of each product sold ([4] − [2])	———
[8]	Calculate the break-even units ([6]/[7])	———
[9]	Calculate total annual sales ([3] × [4])	———
[10]	Calculate total marginal cost of sales ([3] × [2])	———
[11]	Calculate total annual profits ([9] − [6] − [10])	———

CHART 5.2 Sample Break-Even Data

[1]	Estimate the fixed costs of setup (total cost of setup)	$ 5,000
[2]	Estimate the variable cost of producing the product (cost per unit produced)	$ 100
[3]	Estimate the number of units sold per year	10,000
[4]	Estimate the sales price of the product (price per unit sold)	$ 200
[5]	Estimate the number of years over which you want to amortize the fixed costs (number of years in which you want to recover the fixed costs of [1])	5 years

CHART 5.3 Break-Even Analysis

[1]	$ 5,000	
[2]	100	
[3]	10,000	
[4]	200	
[5]	5	
[6]	Calculate the annual fixed cost component ([1]/[5] = 5,000/5) This amount ($1,000) is how much will be costed annually against the profits of the product for the first five years in an attempt to recover the fixed cost outlay.	$ 1,000
[7]	Calculate the profit margin of each product sold ([4] − [2] = 200 − 100) This is how much we earn on each product sold before considering the fixed costs.	$ 100
[8]	Calculate the break-even units ([6]/[7] = 1,000/100) This number is how many units must be sold each year in order to break even (cover all costs with the sales amount). No profits can be made on this product until you have sold at least 10 units. Your profits will begin on the eleventh unit sold.	10 units
[9]	Calculate total annual sales ([3] × [4] = 10,000 × 200) This is the total estimated sales dollar volume.	$2,000,000
[10]	Calculate total marginal cost of sales ([3] × [2] = 10,000 × 100) This is what it will cost to produce the items sold each year. This number does not include the fixed cost coverage.	$1,000,000
[11]	Calculate total annual profits ([9] − [6] − [10] = 2,000,000 − 1,000 − 1,000,000) This should be your total annual profits from producing this product if all the estimates are correct. It is often smart (based on experience) to assume there are a few miscalculations and to divide this number in half.	$ 999,000

CHART 5.4 Annual Break-Even Analysis Graph

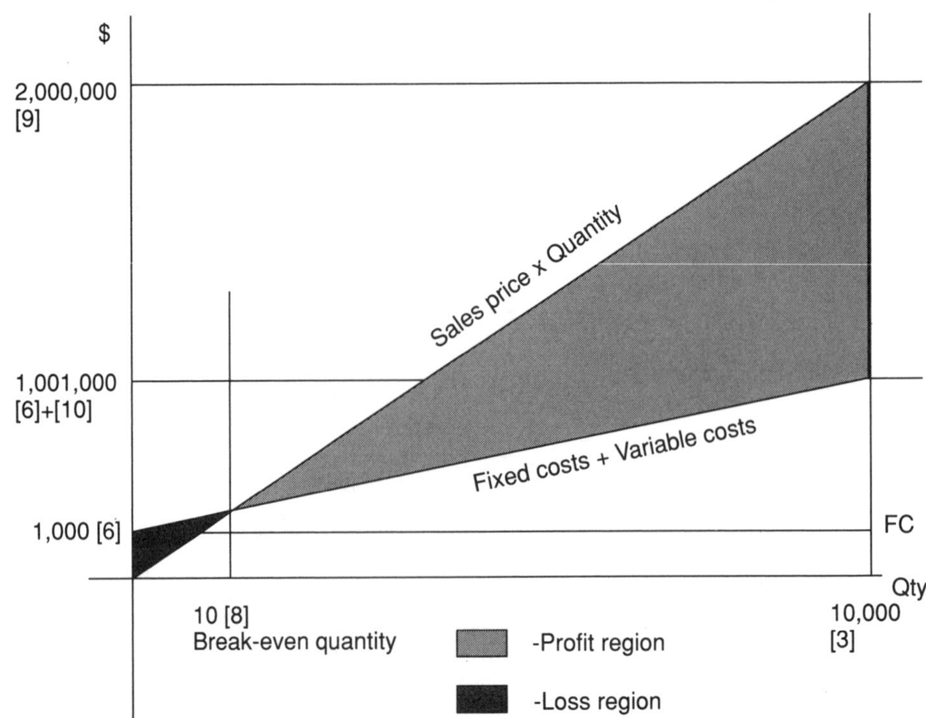

A typical marketing organization will have several product options to consider. The selection of which product options are the most feasible is done by performing a break-even analysis on each of the options. The new product idea showing the best annual profits should be implemented first.

Risk Assessment

Two other considerations are involved in the selection of a product idea. The first is disruption of the status quo. Although a new product idea may be a good one, it is often avoided because it doesn't fit in well with the other products currently under production. Implementing this new product would be disruptive to the organization. Unless the profitability of this product is dramatic, it may not be worth the trouble.

A second consideration (this is optional because it may be too much trouble and too hard to estimate) in the selection of a new product idea is to estimate the probability of success. This process is called *risk assessment*. For example, if the product in Charts 5.2 and 5.3 only has a 60 percent probability of success, then it may not be as desirable as a product with a 75 percent chance of success even though the annual profit estimate is higher. Chart 5.5 is the worksheet for risk assessment and Chart 5.6 demonstrates how to calculate the risk assessment of the product idea in Chart 5.2. Once the risk assessments are made, compare the profitability of each of the new product ideas and see which is

CHART 5.5 Risk Assessment Worksheet (Continuation of Chart 5.1)

[12]	Estimate the probability of success	____
[13]	Calculate the annual profitability of success ([12] × [11])	____
[14]	Calculate the probability of failure (1.0 − [12])	____
[15]	Calculate the cost of failure ([14] × [1])	____
[16]	Calculate the risk assessed annual profits ([13] − [15])	____

CHART 5.6 Risk Assessment Example (Using the Product of Charts 5.2 and 5.3)

[12]	Estimate the probability of success	60 percent
[13]	Calculate the annual profitability of success ([12] × [11] = .60 × 999,000)	$599,400
[14]	Calculate the probability of failure (1.0 − [12] = 1.00 − .60)	40 percent
[15]	Calculate the cost of failure ([14] × [1] = .40 × 5,000)	$ 2,000
[16]	Calculate the risk assessed annual profits ([13] − [15] = 599,400 − 2,000) This value is a more realistic estimate of what you stand to gain (or lose if negative) using the estimated probabilities of success.	$597,400

still the most profitable. Then select the option with the most profitability first.

Engineering

Having selected which products should receive further consideration, marketing now turns to engineering for a prototyping process. Only about 15 percent of the new product ideas get past this point. This is where a model or example of the product is actually made. This process proves the feasibility of the product and its previous cost estimates. It is possible that a break-even analysis may have to be repeated at this point if any of the previous estimates are changed. Only about 5 percent of the new product ideas get past this point.

The chapter on engineering (Chapter 15) goes into detail about the functions of the engineering organizations, but it is helpful at this point to define the different groups.

Product Engineering

These are the individuals that are responsible for designing the features and functions of the new product. They design how the product will work and how it will look.

Manufacturing Engineering

These individuals design how the product will be made. There are two categories of engineers within this category:

1. *Processing Engineering:* These individuals design the jigs and fixtures that will be used to hold the materials, they design the bits that will drill the materials, and they identify the step-by-step materials handling process that is necessary to turn the materials into the desired manufactured product.
2. *Industrial Engineering:* These individuals define the labor and machine steps necessary to convert the materials into the desired new form.

It is the analysis performed by these engineers that determines what it will take in materials, labor, and machine time to make this new product. Then the accountants will add a loaded cost factor to cover overhead. This combination of numbers will then identify the costs associated with the new product to be manufactured.

If all goes well and the new product idea is to be implemented into the production cycle, we then move forward with the production planning process. This is described in this book starting with Chapter 7 where we establish a forecast for the new product (assuming the product isn't part of a family of products that has already been forecast).

One area that is nearly as important as the installation of new products is the elimination of old products. Plants seem to never want to separate themselves from products that have died. They keep inventories of the components and materials that went into these old products, even though these materials are not used anywhere else in the manufacturing process. As much as two-thirds of the inventory items in a factory have been found to be irrelevant. We need to purge our factories of these old components because they are just taking up space and costing us inventory dollars.

Summary

This chapter discussed the process required in building a new product. Now we should have a feel for how new product ideas are planned and implemented into the production planning system. It is important to remember the words of Oliver Wendel Holmes:

> It's not so important where you stand as in what direction you are moving.

In the next chapter we will be looking at the strategic manufacturing functions. These are the inputs into the operations management systems, which is the subject of this book.

Chapter 6 Strategic Management

Benchmarking

SIC Classifications

The term *manufacturing* covers a broad area. We will start this chapter with a few more definitions to help us understand what manufacturing is. We begin with a classification system called *Standard Industrial Classification (SIC) codes,* which classify every type of business in the United States. Your business, whatever it is, is classified in one of these SIC categories. A selective and summarized list of these SIC codes is given in Chart 6.1. Only those SIC codes that are relevant for discussion in this book are included. One of the major benefits of SIC coding is the opportunity it presents for a comparison process called *benchmarking*. We can go to the local library and get the federal business directory for the last few years and look at how all companies that are in your line of business have performed (on the average).[1] With this information we can look at our own company and see how it stacks up against its competitors.

We can take this benchmarking process further by identifying specifically which companies fall into each SIC category (from another federal directory). We can then look at companies within our region or at companies that are direct competitors. Assuming that these competitors have publicly held ownership we can obtain their annual report and directly compare their financial numbers with ours. From these comparisons we can find our weak points and work on strengthening them. We can also find the weak points of our competitors and we may be able to use some of them to our advantage.

The most basic measure of success for an organization is profitability taken from the profit and loss statement. A few additional measures are also helpful in determining why the profit level isn't what it should be or how it can be improved even more. These measures help give direction from one year to the next. This same type of comparative analysis is also valuable when looking at customers. Is the customer

CHART 6.1 SIC Classification Codes

Four-digit numbers where the first three digits are

010–090 Agriculture and related
100–140 Extraction industries
150–170 Construction
200–390 Manufacturing
400–470 Transportation
500–519 Wholesale distribution

[1] One of the most popular tables of industrial ratios is the *Industrial Norms and Key Business Ratios* put out by Dun and Bradstreet Information Services. This report will give all the average ratios, the average profit and loss statement, and the average balance sheet for one year for each SIC code. It is available in most of the business libraries.

stable, when compared to their competitors? Or we can look at our vendors. Do we feel comfortable in the long term working with this vendor? (See Appendix 6.A for a detailed discussion of the techniques available for measuring corporate performance.)

Plant-wide Operational Measures of Performance

Operations managers at the highest levels of management are concerned with four key measures of performance:

Quality
Cost
Productivity
Efficiency

Quality

The definition of quality differs from country to country. In the United States, quality usually means "meeting engineering standards." If the product is built as specified by the engineering drawings, it passes the test of corporate quality. But other countries, like Japan, and some U.S. companies, primarily the award-winning ones, have modified the definition of quality. They prefer to define it as "producing a product that the customer enjoys, likes, and appreciates so much that the customer wouldn't think of buying from anyone else." The difference in the two definitions is simple. In the first case we ask the engineers what quality is; in the second case we ask the customer what it is. Keep these differences in mind as you formulate your own definition of quality. Is the engineer or the customer more important to the sale of your product?

Quality measures at the corporate level show customer, vendor, and internal performance. Using your definition of quality, which of these measures is the most important? It may be desirable to break these data down into more detail. For example, which customers are dissatisfied? We may find that most of the returns are coming from a very few customers. Talk to them and find out why.

Vendor quality analysis may also need to be broken down into more detail. Perhaps most of your quality problems are happening with one vendor or on one product. Ask "Why?"

Internal quality issues are also important. Breaking this data down may show that a certain department or a certain process is causing all the quality problems. Find out why. Perhaps you are working with a faulty piece of equipment and its scrap rate may justify its replacement. Or perhaps an employee needs additional training. Or perhaps reengineering is needed to make the process easier and less risky. Perhaps the tolerances are tighter than they need to be and you are wasting parts unnecessarily.

Cost

Cost issues are discussed in Appendix 6.A in Charts 6.A1 and 6.A3 under the "Cost of Sales" and "Cost of Production" issues. Costs of production can be broken down by department or product to see if costs for a certain area of production, or for a certain process, are increasing. Again, the key is to ask "Why?"

Productivity

Productivity is a highly confusing term. It means different things to different individuals. For example, if asked "What is the most productive country in the world?" most people would say something like Japan, Germany, or Korea. However, the answer is the United States. If asked "Which country is showing the most productivity growth?" the answer could be one of these other countries. By manipulating the definition of productivity, anyone can be the most productive. Therefore, the only meaningful measure of productivity is when you compare your current situation to your past situation.

The definition of productivity is

$$\text{Productivity} = \frac{\text{Output}}{\text{Input}}$$

The question becomes "What is output and what is input?" Output for you should be net sales. Input can be any basis of measure.

Efficiency

The last of the operational measures that needs to be discussed is efficiency. Normally, efficiency is used to measure the performance of an employee. Very simply stated, efficiency measures, when used this way, are a comparison of an employee's performance with some standard level of performance. These standards are developed during the engineering design process (see Chapter 5). These standards are placed into the routings and are updated on a yearly basis using actual history. An employee is at 100 percent efficiency if his or her performance is equal to the standard. If an employee performs better than the standard (produces more pieces per hour), then the efficiency value will be greater than 100 percent. This is often used for the calculation of bonuses and incentive pay.

This same form of efficiency calculation can be used to monitor the performance of machinery. Using a machine standard from the routings, we can validate the expected number of pieces produced and calculate efficiency. Machine efficiency helps monitor equipment that may be growing old and ineffective.

Efficiency calculations will be discussed again after we have discussed the development of standards. Then we can discuss examples of how efficiency measures work.

Now we have a basis of measurement tools that can be used to monitor the performance of the overall organization. These tools will help us highlight trouble spots in the factory. We will now start to work our way down the production information flow diagram (Chart 4.9) starting at the top with strategic management. We will look at the planning, control, and feedback functions (Chart 2.5) of each of the steps in this information flow process. We will learn how to make each of these work better in your organization. (See Appendix 6.A for a detailed discussion of the techniques available for measuring performance.)

Goal Planning

Financial Goals

What is the purpose of a goal? It is to give purpose and direction for what you are doing. A goal should be:

Simple
Precise
Measurable
Focused
Achievable
Sharable.

The typical business plan of a company reads like a wish list of all good things and is totally worthless. Having lots of goals is as useful as not having any. The goals soon get in each other's way. For example, the set of goals given in Chart 6.2 (taken from an actual company) is very typical of most companies. There are several important points that need to be made about these goals in Chart 6.2:

1. These goals are all financial.
2. These goals are in conflict with each other.
3. These goals are not focused, nor are they simple.
4. Establishing a measurement system that will achieve all these goals simultaneously is impossible.

CHART 6.2 Typical Corporate Goals

Maximize sales
Increase market share
Reduce costs
Maximize profits
Increase return on investment

Nonfinancial Goals

All the previous goals are financial. This is an important point because most of the leading edge, award-winning, and more successful companies have moved away from financial goals to goals such as:

Improved quality
Customer satisfaction
Employee permanence and stability

What happens is that more of the company's profits that would have traditionally gone to the stockholders are now retained in the company. These profits are focused on these new goals. What is interesting is that achieving these nonfinancial goals also results in achieving the financial goals. In Chart 6.3 I have relisted these nonfinancial goals, shown how they are measurable, and shown some ways that they can be strengthened.

The second point that I made is that the set of goals in Chart 6.2 is in conflict with each other. There are several ways I can prove this. The easiest way is by having you look at the output of your own factory (assuming that you are typical). What you'll find is something like

CHART 6.3 Nonfinancial Corporate Goals

Improved Quality
Measured by returns percentage (see Chart 6.A1 under "Quality") and by size of market share growth (see Chart 6.A1 under "Sales Growth").

Quality can be strengthened by talking with your customers. This can be done by surveys, bringing the customer into your plant, sending your engineers out to the customer to work in their plant, etc. Contact and openness with the customer is critical.

Customer Satisfaction
This category is a little broader than the previous goal of improved quality. This includes all the measures and strengthening issues of quality, but also includes issues such as customer courtesy, customer service at the time of the sale, customer service after the sale with respect to follow up and maintenance. This also includes giving the customer what they want in the way of technological advances. The measures for this include returns percentage and size of market share growth but also require a customer evaluation of your performance (some type of survey).

This area, like the area on quality, is strengthened by communication and responsiveness to the customer.

Employee Permanence and Stability
This is an important goal that is used quite often in Japan. The primary reason for the popularity of this goal is because it supports a participative relationship with the employees, rather than the adversarial one (employers see employees as a cost element and employees see employers as cattle drivers) that is typical of U.S. firms.

The primary measure of this goal is employee turnover. To measure turnover, divide the number of employees hired and fired over the last year by the average number of employees on the payroll for the year. If this ratio goes down from one year to the next, then it shows that you are being responsive to your employees' needs.

$$\text{Employee Turnover Ratio} = \frac{\text{Number of Employees Hired + Fired + Quit During the Year}}{\text{Total Average Number of Employees for the Year}}$$

Again the key to strengthening this area is to stay in touch with the employees; communicate with them.

CHART 6.4 Conflicting Financial Goals

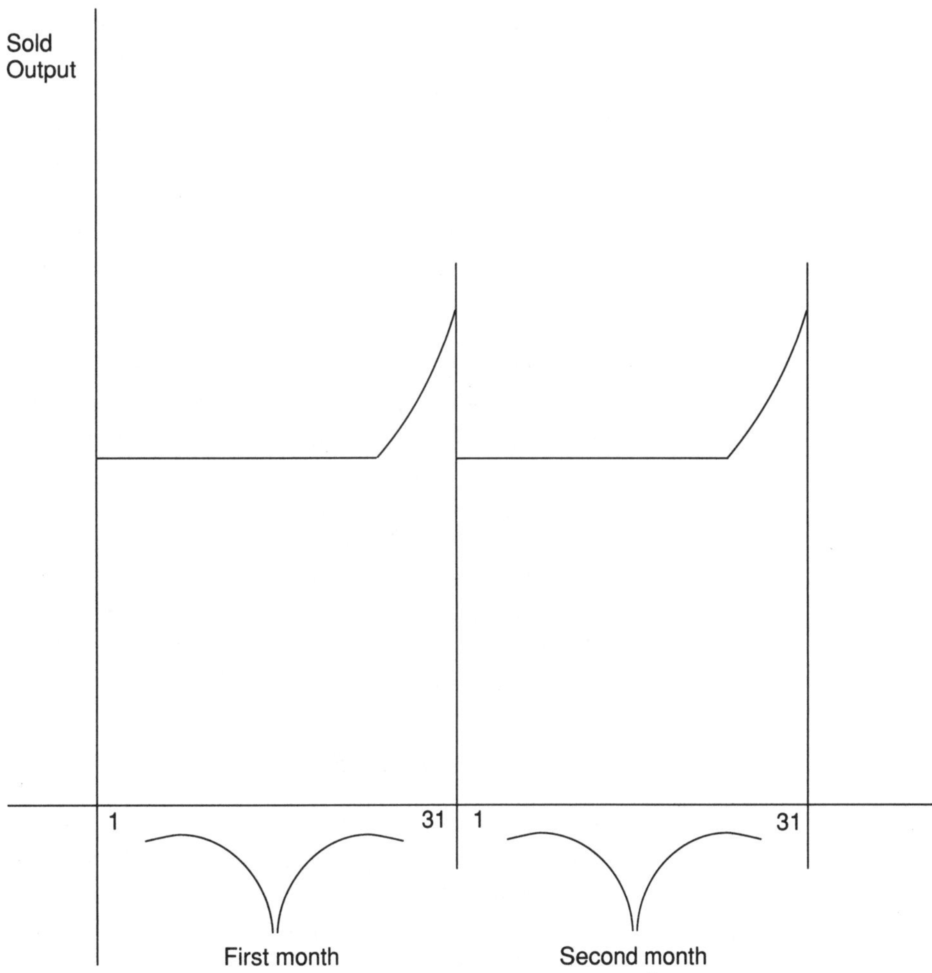

Chart 6.4. About the first 90 percent of the month we have steady output. This is because we are working efficiently toward the goals of increased profits (reduced costs). Then, during the last 10 percent of the month we put on a rush trying to push as much product out the door as possible. We have thrown efficiency, profit, and cost reduction to the wind. We send people scurrying around the plant (these product chasers are called "expediters") in an attempt to get employees to work in smaller batch sizes so that we can get a few extra product units out the door. We are now working toward the goal of increased sales. Obviously, from this example, we see that these goals are in conflict. At one time of the month we are working toward one goal, while at another time of the month we are working toward another goal.

In your basic economics class you learned about the production function. This function taught us that the volume at which we produce to achieve maximum sales is not the same volume at which we produce to achieve maximum profits. So which is your goal—sales, profits, cost reductions, market share, or return on investment? Several are in conflict with each other. You can't have them all as your goal (unless you're happy with not really achieving any of them).

This leads to the first and fourth points that I made about the goals in Chart 6.2. These goals are not focused, nor are they simple. The company of Chart 6.4 shows a lack of focus. They are basically running the plant two different ways. Since these goals are in conflict, which measurement system is appropriate? The one used during the first 90 percent of the month would be efficiency, productivity, and cost of production (see Appendix 6.A). The measurement system used during the last 10 percent of the month would be a sales growth measure. Stressing both will result in the type of chaos shown in Chart 6.4. We need to have *focus* and *simplicity* in our goals. Set your goal, build a measurement system around it, and stick to it.

In my book *International Management and Production: Survival Techniques for Corporate America,* I stress that "as long as we are playing catch up, the best we can ever do is get caught up." We need to stop copying the goals and business plans of other companies; we need to instead step out and make our own marks.

Much of what we need to do in goal setting is break away from tradition. As was stressed in the book *Breakthrough Thinking,* we need to "do the right things before we do things right." We need to select the correct goals before we start setting goals.

Secondary Goals

There is nothing wrong with having secondary goals as long as they strengthen, rather than conflict with, the primary goal. Let me give you an example. If your primary goal is employee permanence and stability, then it would be appropriate to ask what secondary goal would support this primary goal? If we want the employees to have jobs, then we want the plant to be around as long as possible. To do this, we need to make sure we manufacture the product as long as possible. We need to control the market and the production of the product. An appropriate secondary goal would be to control market share. Then the next question is: How do we control market share? This may take a little price cutting or gouging until you control the market. Then you can make the price whatever you want. But a more important way to control market share is by using the definition of quality discussed earlier, which is "to make a product the customer enjoys, likes, and appreciates so much that they wouldn't think of buying from anyone else." I have reviewed this chain of primary and secondary goals in Chart 6.5.

Another type of secondary goal is to break a goal down by departments or management levels. It would be helpful if each department

CHART 6.5 Example of Primary and Secondary Corporate Goals

Primary—Employee permanence and stability
Secondary—Control market share
Second secondary—Quality product

were able to define a subgoal that would demonstrate that organization's efforts toward the primary goal. This subgoal would be measurable within the organization and would be more useful to the specific organization than the primary goal. These subgoals include the development of a measurement system, which will be discussed later in this chapter.

Goal Communication

One of the biggest "sins" of goal making is not to communicate the goal to the individuals that are responsible for achieving the goals. Numerous companies have said "we don't show our employees our business plan because it is confidential," meaning that only strategic management employees are allowed to look at them. The question that should be asked is "How can you expect the employees to hit a target they cannot see?" Employees need to know what the goal is, how it is going to be measured, whether or not you are making progress toward the goal, and they should receive part of the reward of achieving the goal. *A hidden goal is as useful as no goal, for no one will know if you succeeded.*

If you fail to plan, you plan to fail. Once you have selected a goal you need to build a planning, control, and feedback system around that goal.

Resource Matching/Data Measurement

The last section emphasized the importance of developing a focused goal for our organization. What we need to do in this section is to identify which resources have the greatest influence on that goal. Having identified those key resources, we can then move forward with establishing a measurement system that focuses on those resources.

We need to start by defining the resources of a factory. The list of resources that you develop for your organization will differ from someone else's list. Don't waste a lot of time analyzing resources that have very little effect on your operation. What you're looking for are the "biggies." After you have built your list, watch for the biggest of the "biggies," but focus your selection on the corporate goal you established earlier.

With your list of resources you should now assign percentages of importance to each item. The next step is to ABC classify these resources. This means that we list them in order of most influential to least influential. At this point we know what our critical resources are and now we are ready to build a planning, control, and measurement system around these critical resources.

In the development of a planning, control, and measurement system we need to look at each resource and decide what is critical about that resource. This entire book discusses planning, control, and measurement systems.

At this point we have achieved focus in our goals and focus in our resources. This helps us build focus into our measurement system. We also have a general feeling of how effectively our organization is performing. We know some of the key areas for improvement. But before we develop the planning, control, feedback, and measurement systems in detail we need to complete our strategic management process and put our focus into a business plan. (See Appendix 6.B for a detailed discussion of the procedure used for resource matching).

Budgets

There are only a few "dirty" words in manufacturing operations. One of these happens to be *budget.* A budget system is a measurement system, an evaluation system, and a control system, all wrapped up into one bundle. The art of "meeting your budget" is not an art of achievement, rather it is an art of manipulation. Consider a plant in which the manufacturing manager was being chastised for exceeding his budget in labor costs. His solution was to lay several employees off and then pay them to work at home doing the same process. This way the work was classified as a material purchase rather than a labor cost. The plant manager meets budget in labor costs by shifting the cost burden to someone else's budget.

The original function of a budget is for planning. The idea is simple, if we sell $100 of a product, we should expect $50 of materials cost, $10 of labor cost, and $30 of burden, giving us $10 of profit. Using this ratio we can calculate what the labor, materials, and burden costs should be regardless of what amount we choose to sell. These principles are good, but they do not promote improvement. For example, if we can reduce labor cost by $5 by purchasing a component outside, but the result is that we increase materials costs by $3, then we declare that labor is in budget but materials are out of budget, and we chastise the materials purchasing people. However, we increased profits by $2, and that should be the real measure of performance, not meeting a budget.

Use a budget the way it is intended to be used, as a benchmark, not as absolute law. If a deviation from the budget is explainable, don't worry about it. Only worry about those deviations that are not explainable. Then the budget will help you find improvements rather than occupy your time looking for ways to manipulate it. Even worse, each year you try to adjust to an unrealistically distorted budget, you end up distorting it even more. Allow, and even encourage, budget deviations by letting them be justified with simple explanations.

CHART 6.6 Costing System Information Flow Diagram

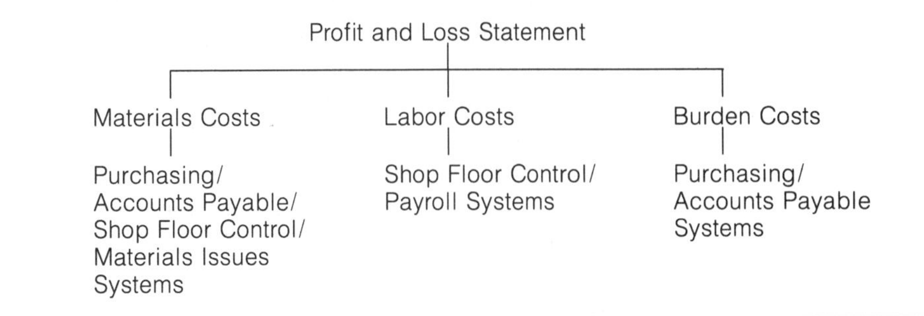

Costing Systems

The costing system is the data collection and information generation system that provides the detail to be used later in the creation of the profit and loss statements. The costing system includes several branches, all of which consolidate into this report. To start with, look at the diagram in Chart 6.6.

Materials cost values come from the purchase cost of a product (purchasing/accounts payable) and are then distributed to an end product based on the amount of usage of the material (shop floor control/ materials issues). Labor costs come from the time cards used by the payroll system and these costs are distributed based on the job sheets of the shop floor control system. Burden costs are a collection of purchase costs for "everything else" and these costs are reported through the accounts payable and purchasing systems.

A summary of these data results in the cost data that are fed into the profit and loss statements. This information then becomes the data and the basis for the creation of the operating budget as we saw in the previous section of this chapter. A quick look back at Charts 4.8 and 4.9 will help you understand how costs fit into both the manufacturing systems information flow and the accounting information flow.

Cost/Benefit Analysis

Part of the process of generating a business plan is to make decisions about the future of a business. For example, should we build a new factory?, should we expand the existing factory?, should we increase our level of automation?, etc. Each of these decisions has an anticipated benefit and a corresponding cost. But we can't do everything. So we have to decide what the costs and benefits of each alternative is and select the most appealing alternative. The result is called a cost/benefit analysis. Let's look at an example. Let's assume we manufacture manual transmissions and we are considering building a new factory to manufacture the transaxle transmissions. The first thing we need to do is come up with the break-even analysis of the new product as discussed in Chapter 5. This break-even analysis would give us the fixed and variable manufacturing costs of this new transaxle product (see Charts 5.2 and 5.4). We can start plugging these numbers into our sample cost/ benefit analysis chart (see Chart 6.7). We are assuming a sales level of \$2,000 for the new transaxles. We assume that all the costs will be proportionately the same as are the costs of operation for the current plant. In other words, we will generate a budget for the new plant based on the same cost-to-sales relationships that we had in the current plant. To calculate the budget, use the following procedure. The new additional category of financing costs was added because this is a new cost associated with the construction of this plant. This cost is in addition to the costs of operation at the existing plant. This is the cost of paying for the financing of the outlays (plant and equipment) that went into the new plant.

1. Marketing forecasts sales for the next three years as \$2,000, \$2,000, and \$2,200, respectively.

2. Engineering has performed a break-even analysis on this new product (see Chapter 5) and has determined the direct costs associated with building the new product. This includes direct labor, direct materials, and usually direct overhead (sometimes overhead will need to be estimated using the procedure in step 3). For a sales level of \$2,000, the costs are direct labor = \$800, net purchases = \$440, and direct overhead = \$100.

3. The \$2,000 in new net sales is divided by this last year's gross sales of \$5,000. (See Chart 6.A2 for the data that these calculations are based on.) This gives us a ratio of .4 = (2,000/5,000). Then we simply multiply each of the other values (in this case, returns and indirect costs of operation) by this ratio to get the estimated costs of operation, assuming that we run the new plant the same way we ran the old plant last year. For example, indirect cost of operation for the new plant is 420 = .4 × 1,050.

CHART 6.7 Cost/Benefit Example

	Year 1	Year 2	Year 3
Sales (benefits)			
Gross sales	2,000	2,000	2,200
Returns	140–	140–	154–
Net sales	**1,860**	**1,860**	**2,046**
Cost of sales			
Direct labor	800	800	880
Materials			
Gross purchases	520	520	572
Returns to vendor	80–	80–	88–
Net purchases	440	440	484
Direct overhead	100	100	110
Total cost of sales	**1,340**	**1,340**	**1,474**
Indirect costs of operation	420	420	462
Financing costs	100	100	50
Net profit/loss (cash flow)	**0**	**0**	**60**
(This is a before-tax cash flow)			

4. Insert the estimate for the new additional cost of financing the new plant.

5. Calculate to obtain our estimated net profit or loss for next year's operation of the new plant.

6. Repeat this procedure for each of the projected years of operation. Note that sales may change, thereby affecting the ratios. Also, financing costs may change.

Note that in Chart 6.7 we break even for the first two years and don't turn a profit until the third year when some of our interest costs start going down and our anticipated sales increase. The advantage of a cost/benefit analysis is that it lets you look at multiple years and allows you to project into the future.

Some costs and benefits may be unquantifiable. For example, selling the transaxle transmission manufactured at the new plant may also generate goodwill that may in the future help to sell more manual transmissions. This may encourage you to go ahead with the new plant even when the cost/benefit analysis shows a loss.

I have not provided a worksheet for the cost/benefit analysis because it needs to be formatted similar to your profit and loss statement (P/L). Since no two companies have the same profit and loss format, it is nearly impossible to come up with some standard format. Take your P/L, photocopy it covering up the numbers, and use the blanked-out photocopied sheet for a cost/benefit analysis worksheet just like in Chart 6.7.

Present Value Analysis

Usually there is more than one option from which to choose. For example, perhaps we could do some retooling at our current transmission plant and even though we won't be able to produce the full $2,000 worth of new transaxles that we could with the new plant, we would still be able to get into the transaxle market on a smaller scale, at less of an upfront cost. We need to establish some form of comparison to see which project will give us the best return. This technique is called *present value analysis* and works this way: Assume we have four different options (A, B, C, and D) and they are represented by the cash flows expressed in Chart 6.8. (These cash flows come from the profit/loss line

CHART 6.8 Present Value of Cash Flow Example

Option	Year 1	Year 2	Year 3	Year 4
A	0	100	200	300
B	100	100	100	100
C	100−	100	200	300
D	300	100	0	0

Assume an interest rate to carry money would be 10 percent. Get the interest rate from your bank—what rate of interest does your bank pay you for the money you put into the bank?

of the cost/benefit analysis that was done for each respective alternative.) The interest rate serves an important purpose. The idea is that if we earn 10 percent interest, how much money would we need to put in the bank today to have (in the case of option A) $100 in year 2, $200 in year 3, and $400 in year 4. What would be the present value (in today's uninflated dollars) of this cash flow? If we can estimate the present value of each of the cash flows in Chart 6.8, then we will have a basis of comparison allowing us to select which of these options will give the best return.

The procedure for calculating the present value of cash flow is that each value is multiplied by the following formula [note that the (1 + Interest Rate) is raised to the power (year − 1)]:

$$\text{Present Value} = \frac{\text{Future Value}}{(1 + [\text{Interest Rate}])^{(\text{Year}-1)}}$$

The procedure for calculating the present value of the option A cash flow stream would be as follows:

(Present Value of Option A for Year 1)

$$= \frac{\$0}{(1+.10)^{(1-1)}} = \frac{\$0}{1.1^0} = \frac{(\$0)}{1} = \$0$$

(Present Value of Option A for Year 2)

$$= \frac{\$100}{(1+.10)^{(2-1)}} = \frac{\$100}{1.1^1} = \frac{(\$100)}{1.1} = \$90.91$$

(Present Value of Option A for Year 3)

$$= \frac{\$200}{(1+.10)^{(3-1)}} = \frac{\$200}{1.1^2} = \frac{(\$200)}{1.21} = \$165.29$$

(Present Value of Option A for Year 4)

$$= \frac{\$300}{(1+.10)^{(4-1)}} = \frac{\$300}{1.1^3} = \frac{(\$300)}{1.331} = \$225.39$$

Summarizing this into a present value chart would result in Chart 6.9. Here we see that each of the numbers has been converted to its present value equivalent. Then, to get the actual present value of each of the cash flows, simply add the numbers of each stream together, as shown on the right-hand side of Chart 6.9.

Looking at option A in Chart 6.9, if we were to go to the bank and deposit $481.59 at a rate of 10 percent interest, we could withdraw $100 in year 2, $200 in year 3, and exactly $300 in year 4.

CHART 6.9 Present Value of Cash Flow Example—Present Values Calculated

Option	Year 1	Year 2	Year 3	Year 4	TOTAL
A	0	90.91	165.29	225.39	481.59
B	100	90.91	82.64	75.13	348.68
C	100−	90.91	165.29	225.39	381.59
D	300	90.91	0	0	390.91

CHART 6.10 Worksheet for Present Value Cash Flow Calculations

Year	Future Cash Flow	Interest Rate (+1)		Interest Factor		Present Value Cash Flow
1	______	------------------------→				______
2	______	/ ______	=	______	=	______
3	______	/ (______)^2	=	______	=	______
4	______	/ (______)^3	=	______	=	______
5	______	/ (______)^4	=	______	=	______
6	______	/ (______)^5	=	______	=	______
7	______	/ (______)^6	=	______	=	______
		Total Present Value Cash Flow	=			______

CHART 6.11 Worksheet for Present Value Cash Flow Calculations—Example
(Example using option C from Chart 6.8 at 10% interest.)

Year	Future Cash Flow	Interest Rate (+1)		Interest Factor		Present Value Cash Flow
1	−100	------------------------→				−100.00
2	100	/ 1.10	=	1.100	=	90.91
3	200	/ (1.10)^2	=	1.210	=	165.29
4	300	/ (1.10)^3	=	1.331	=	225.39
5	0	/ (1.10)^4	=	1.464	=	0
6	0	/ (1.10)^5	=	1.6105	=	0
7	0	/ (1.10)^6	=	1.77156	=	0
		Total Present Value Cash Flow	=			381.59

The present value cash flow calculation of the four options presented in Chart 6.9 resulted in option A giving us the best overall total present value cash flow. This is the option that would be selected.

Chart 6.10 is a worksheet for the calculation of present value cash flows for any one particular option. Chart 6.11 is the application of option C from Chart 6.8 using the worksheet layout in Chart 6.10.

At this point we have an understanding of how cost data, budgets, cost/benefit analyses, and present value information are used to help us evaluate various options for future growth. The details of the data collection and data base construction for cost information are included in the chapter on purchase planning and shop floor data collection. The options selected through this process will become a part of the business plan.

Formulating the Business Plan

Planning systems are the basis of all control and measurement systems. Without the planning system you have no hope of other pieces of the system working. I have often seen a plant manager install a production planning system such as MRP (material requirements planning) without first installing the necessary elements in the information flow diagram (see Chart 4.9). MRP, which is a production planning system, cannot function properly without a good master production schedule (MPS). Without the MPS, the MRP system is just as good as guessing. And MPS cannot work without a good aggregate production planning system (APS) in place. And the APS is worthless without a good business plan, which leads us to the topic of this chapter.

We are now ready to formulate the business plan. Let us review some of the concepts discussed in detail in the last few chapters:

1. Plan one specific, simplistic goal. The goal must be precise, measurable, focused, and achievable.

2. Develop a set of subgoals breaking the main goal down into workable pieces. Each subgoal must support the main goal. Subgoals can identify specific projects or they can be established by department.

3. Communicate the goal to everyone involved in achieving the goal and give them a subgoal that will help them identify their part in achieving the goal.

4. Identify the resources of the plant.

5. Quantify the resources with respect to the goal and determine which resource(s) have the greatest influence in achieving the goal. Focus your planning, control, and measurement system based on these critical resources. This system will run the operations of the factory on an on-going basis.

6. Goals often involve new projects. These can include the building of a new plant, the purchase of new warehouses, or the updating and automating of equipment on the factory floor. These are projects that change the status quo of the plant. Each project can be implemented in several alternative ways. Evaluate each of these alternatives by developing a break-even analysis (if a new product is involved). Then develop a cost/benefit analysis for each alternative using budget information. Next calculate the present value of the cash flow for each alternative. Then select the alternative that offers the best present value cash flow.

Following the above steps should give you a focused plant that knows where it wants to be. The plant has selected a focus in its planning and control system for the internal operation of the factory. It has also selected specific plant improvement projects that will help it achieve its goals.

Next we need to put all these decisions into a business plan that will communicate our strategy to our investors, our directorship, our CEO, and all the vice presidents and managers in the plant. All these levels of management can then coordinate their focus on the goal.

The business plan does not need to be a book. I have seen many that are excessively large. It needs to be simple, precise, focused, and direct. It should leave room for the managers to do what they do best—make decisions. The format and content of the business plan can vary dramatically from company to company. There is no "correct" way to put it together. But it is important to review and update the business plan annually, so that the focus of the company is not shelved and forgotten. Chart 6.12 suggests a format that may be used as a guideline for you in the preparation of your business plan. This is not the best way, nor is it

CHART 6.12 Suggested Format for the Business Plan

Mission Statement: What is the primary goal of the company? In one sentence state what this company hopes to achieve.

Focus of the company with respect to: (Each of these is a subgoal that focuses on the primary goal with respect to the specific group of individuals.)

- Ownership—What does the ownership hope to gain from the primary goal? How can the ownership measure success in achieving this goal? List about five to ten points that demonstrate this position. Repeat this format for each of the points in this section.
- Industry in general
- Customers
- Employees
- Vendors

Indicate measures of success for each.

Long-Term Goals: (Each of these is a long-term goal and subgoals with respect to the primary goal. Some of these may not be relevant and others may be missing based on your primary goal.)

- Growth—Reflecting on the primary goal of the company, what can be anticipated in the way of growth? This can include sales growth, physical growth, employee growth, market share growth, international growth, or any other form of growth that is meaningful with respect to the primary goal.
- Improvements—Again reflecting on the primary goal, what changes in cost reductions, technology improvements, plant layout and design, marketing strategy, engineering, operational efficiency, productivity, etc., do you want?

Indicate measures of success for each.

Resource Focus: (What are the critical resources and how will they be planned, monitored, and controlled?)

- Capital plan
- People plan
- Product plan
- Systems plan
- etc.

Indicate measures of success for each.

Short-Term Goals: (For the next year.)

1. *Review:* Start by reviewing the long-term goals with respect to the next year (What will we do next year to help achieve the long-term goals in general?)
2. *Marketing Plan:* What specifically will marketing do over the next year to help achieve the primary goal of the organization? Some possible areas of improvement and measurement are (others that fit you may not be listed):
   - Change in sales efforts
   - Changes in advertising
   - Target markets
   - Pricing policy
   - International
3. *New Product Development:* Use the same procedure as in point 2 to discuss expansion projects, new target markets, etc.
4. *Operations Plan:* What specific operational changes are anticipated that will help achieve the primary goal? Specifically discuss each of the following areas (more may be needed to fit your organization):
   - Systems changes
   - Production changes
   - Distribution changes
   - Order processing changes
   - Engineering
   - Computers, data collection
   - Accounting, information generation
   - Quality programs
   - Productivity improvements
   - Communications with employees
   - Safety programs
   - Cost reduction programs
     - Redesign
     - Purchasing
     - Process improvements

(continued)

CHART 6.12 *(concluded)*

Training programs
- Employees
- Marketing/sales personnel
- Customers
- Vendors

5. *Financial Plan:* What is your debt and equity structure and how do you plan to change it? If you are planning to finance new projects, how will they be paid for? If you plan to reduce debt, how will you do it? Will there be any changes in ownership or equity investments? etc.

It is *critical* that a measurement of success be given to each of these areas so that the respective manager knows if he or she is helping to support the corporate goal.

Budget Sheets:

1. Prepare a budget sheet for the next year using the budget format demonstrated in this chapter. Use this budget sheet to calculate comparative numbers between last year and next year to project your anticipated level of improvement (see Chart 6.A1).

2. Break down the budget sheet numbers in point 1 by quarter and possibly also by month. That way you will know every three months if you are progressing toward your goal.

3. Assume you achieve the projected budget of point 1 and generate a new balance sheet for the end of the year. See if the appropriate asset ratio shows improvement (Chart 6.A1 under "Asset Strength" and "Equity Strength").

4. Break down the budget sheet from point 1 by department or division so that a measure of goal achievement can be established.

5. Break down the budget sheet from point 1 by product line (also by region of sales) so that a measure of achievement can be established.

All of these breakdowns may not be meaningful for your organization. Do not force numbers just to have numbers. If the numbers are not trustworthy, you'll end up losing the respect of the individuals that use these numbers for measurement purposes, and they won't trust any of the numbers. *It is better to give too little, but accurate, numbers, than to give too many, but meaningless, numbers that will cause all the numbers to be mistrusted.*

---

the only way to assemble a business plan, but it is a starting point from which to begin.

At this point you should have a good feel for what is contained in a business plan. Again, the primary purpose of the business plan is:

- To help you rethink your long-term goals.
- To break your long-term goals into measurable subgoals.
- To communicate your long- and short-term goals with all levels of ownership, directorship, and management.
- To develop a measurement system that will allow you to benchmark progress toward your goal.

Summary

Having established our business plan, we can now hand it to tactical management (see Chart 4.2). Tactical management will start by establishing a forecast (F) that will satisfy the goals established in the business plan. This forecast will be adjusted by customer orders (C/O). Then they will measure the ability of the plant to achieve these goals (rough-cut capacity plan). They will then generate a compromise plan that will be used to schedule the factory (aggregate production schedule).

APPENDIX 6.A: Manufacturing Performance Measures

The most basic measure of success for an organization is profitability taken from the profit and loss statement. A few additional measures are also helpful in determining why the profit level isn't what it should be or how it can be improved even more. These measures help give direction. A few comparative measurement areas that are interesting to look at when we compare ourselves with our competitors are found in Chart 6.A1. Chart 6.A2 sets up sample general ledger data, and Chart 6.A3 analyzes these data based on the measurement tools listed in Chart 6.A1.

Operating costs when compared to sales should be comparable to your competitors' costs. If they are not comparable, compare each of the components of the cost to total cost to see where you differ from your competitors. You may find that labor costs are much higher than they should be. Now you need to start asking a repetitive chain of "whys." It may work like this:

Why is labor cost higher?

Because we use too much overtime.

Why do we use too much overtime?

Because our schedules don't fit evenly with the load of a shift.

Why are our schedules unbalanced with the workload of a shift?

. . . and on and on until you get to the root of the problem. Don't spend a lot of time solving a symptom (any answer that is not the root of the problem). Spend your time solving the problem. This technique of asking repetitive "whys" is a technique that should be used throughout the book.

The questions of asset strength are often misinterpreted. To an accountant, having more assets is good because you can cover your debts better. But to operations management this usually means inflating your level of inventory, which is bad. Carrying too much inventory is like buying two cars and letting one sit in the garage forever. You have to pay car payments, pay insurance, and tie up valuable assets like cash, and you get no benefit out of it. Inventory should be minimized. So if your level of inventory is comparatively low (to your competitors), which drives your asset-to-debt ratio lower than your competitors, that's OK. What you'll find is that your cost of sales numbers should also be lower, especially in the inventory cost area (unless you hide interest costs into overhead—then overhead should be lower). If your inventory-to-asset percentage is comparable to your competitors, but your asset-to-debt ratio is low, you have too much debt. One excellent solution is to reduce both your inventory and the corresponding debt.

Chart 6.A2 is a sample of the type of accounting data you may be dealing with in your company. This is the same type of information that can be obtained from the SIC tables in the federal directories. (See the footnote on page 44 of this chapter.) I will use Chart 6.A2 data to show

CHART 6.A1 Areas for Benchmarking Comparisons (Your accountant may be helpful in identifying these numbers for you.)

Sales Growth:

Percentage of increase in sales comparing this year to last year should go up.

$$\text{(Sales Increase Ratio)} = \frac{\text{(Total Sales This Year Minus This Year's Returns)}}{\text{(Total Sales Last Year Minus Last Year's Returns)}}$$

Size of market share growth over the years should increase.

$$\text{(Size of Market Share)} = \frac{\text{(Your Net Sales)}}{\text{(Total Sales of the Market)}}$$

$$\text{(Size of Market Share Growth)} = \frac{\text{(Size of Market Share This Year)}}{\text{(Size of Market Share Last Year)}}$$

Cost of Sales:

*Operating costs (labor, materials, and direct overhead) as a percentage of sales.

$$\text{(Operating Costs of Sales Ratio)} = \frac{\text{(Operating Costs [Cost of Sales for Items Sold])}}{\text{(Total Sales Minus Returns)}}$$

Cost of Production:

What percentage of product cost is labor, materials, overhead? Compare this with your competitors and note any significant differences.

$$\text{(Labor Cost of Production)} = \frac{\text{(Total Direct Labor Cost)}}{\text{(Total Direct Labor, Materials, Direct Overhead)}}$$

$$\text{(Total Materials Cost of Production)} = \frac{\text{(Total Materials Cost)}}{\text{(Total Direct Labor, Materials, Direct Overhead)}}$$

$$\text{(Total Direct Overhead Cost of Production)} = \frac{\text{(Total Direct Overhead Cost)}}{\text{(Total Direct Labor, Materials, Direct Overhead)}}$$

Indirect Cost Ratios:

What is the relationship between indirect and direct costs? The lower these values, the better.

$$\text{(Indirect Cost Ratio)} = \frac{\text{(Total Indirect Costs)}}{\text{(Total Costs)}}$$

$$\text{(Indirect/Direct Coverage)} = \frac{\text{(Total Indirect Costs)}}{\text{(Total Direct Costs)}}$$

Asset strength:

*How well do your assets cover your debts?

$$\text{(Asset Ratio)} = \frac{\text{(Total Assets)}}{\text{(Total Debts)}}$$

$$\text{(Current Ratio)} = \frac{\text{(Total Current Assets)}}{\text{(Total Current Debts)}}$$

*What percentage of your assets are tied up in inventory?

$$\text{(Inventory Asset Ratio)} = \frac{\text{(Total Inventory)}}{\text{(Total Current Assets)}}$$

Equity strength:

What percentage of the total assets is owned? Your number should be higher than your competitors' and higher this year than last year.

$$\text{(Equity Strength)} = \frac{\text{(Total Equity)}}{\text{(Total Assets)}}$$

Quality:

Percentage of returns to total sales should go down.

$$\text{(Returns Percentage)} = \frac{\text{(Total Sales Dollar Value of Returns)}}{\text{(Total Gross Sales Dollars)}}$$

Percentage of scrap or reject parts both internal and from the vendor should decrease.

$$\text{(Scrap-Reject Purchase Ratio)} = \frac{\text{(Total Cost of Scrap-Reject Parts Purchased)}}{\text{(Total Cost of All Parts Purchased)}}$$

$$\text{(Scrap-Reject Production Ratio)} = \frac{\text{(Total Cost of Scrap-Reject Parts Produced)}}{\text{(Total Cost of All Parts Produced)}}$$

* See the discussion of these numbers in Chart 6.A3 for an important explanation of their usage.

CHART 6.A2 Sample Accounting Data Taken from Financial Statements

Sample Accounting Data Taken from a Balance Sheet

(This information covers a specific point in time.)

Assets			
Current assets			
Cash	100		
Accounts receivable	300		
Inventory	500		
Other current assets	50		
Total current assets		950	
Long-term assets			
Plant and equipment	1,500		
Other long-term assets	150		
Total long-term assets		1,650	
Total assets			2,600
Liabilities			
Current liabilities			
Accounts payable	250		
Current notes payable	175		
Other current liabilities	25		
Total current liabilities		450	
Long-term liabilities			
Long-term notes	1,000		
Other long-term liabilities	200		
Total long-term liabilities		1,200	
Total liabilities			1,650
Owners' equity			
Initial ownership investment	550		
Increases/decreases in ownership	400		
Total owners' equity			950
Total liabilities plus owners' equity			2,600

Sample Accounting Data Taken From a Profit and Loss Statement

(This statement covers a period of time, usually one fiscal year. The balance sheet should correspond to the end of this period.)

	Current Year		Previous Year	
Sales				
Gross sales	5,000		4,850	
Returns	350–		375–	
Net sales		4,650		4,475
Cost of sales				
Direct labor	2,000		2,100	
Materials				
Gross purchases	1,300		1,350	
Returns to vendor	200–		225–	
Net purchases	1,100		1,125	
Direct overhead	250		325	
Total cost of sales		3,350		3,550
Indirect costs of operation		1,050		900
Net Profit/Loss		250		25

Some Important Data Checks

(Total assets) = (Total liabilities) + (Total owners' equity)
(Net profit/loss) = (Net sales) − (Total cost of sales) − (Indirect costs of operation)
(This year's net profit/loss) = (This year's increases/decreases in ownership) − (Last year's increases/decreases in ownership)
(If any of these do not balance, you have big problems; check with your accountant.)

CHART 6.A3 Examples of Benchmarking Comparisons Using the Data from Chart 6.A2

Sales Growth

$$\text{(Sales Increase Ratio)} = \frac{\text{(Total Sales This Year Minus This Year's Returns)}}{\text{(Total Sales Last Year Minus Last Year's Returns)}} = \frac{4{,}650}{4{,}475} = 1.039$$

This ratio shows a 3.9 percent (.039) increase in sales over last year. When this number is compared with your industry as a whole, it is desirable for it to be greater than the industry average.

Fixes: Poor numbers in this area mean one of two things. (1) Your product isn't selling because of poor marketing or because of poor competitive value (lack of technological content). (2) The quality of the product isn't what it should be, causing a high number of returns or fewer sales. The quality question also suggests that consideration be given to on-time delivery or simply satisfying customer "cosmetic" needs such as service or a friendly attitude. The other measures listed should help you define the problem more clearly.

$$\text{(Size of Market Share)} = \frac{\text{(Your Net Sales)}}{\text{(Total Sales of the Market)}} = \frac{4{,}650}{200{,}000} = .02325$$

The total sales of the market come from the federal tables. Make sure you include all relevant markets. It may include several SIC categories. For the calculations here, I assumed a market size of 200,000 ($200,000 worth of total sales in all relevant SIC categories). The size of market share ratio calculated a value of .02325. This means that you control 2.325 percent of the market.

Fixes: The only way to improve market share is to think a little like the Japanese who are masters at dominating market share. Their philosophy is to make the product so appealing that the customer wouldn't think of going anywhere else to buy the product. Often this is more of a cosmetic appeal than actual product content. Sometimes this means price cutting.

$$\text{(Size of Market Share Growth)} = \frac{\text{(Size of Market Share This Year)}}{\text{(Size of Market Share Last Year)}} = \frac{.02325}{.02355} = .987$$

For purposes of this example I will assume that the market size last year was 190,000. The size of market share ratio would calculate a value of .02355 (4,475/190,000). Comparing the current year's size of market share ratio with last year's size of market share ratio gives us a size of market share growth ratio of .987. A value greater than 1.0 is desirable. The larger the value, the more market share you are controlling. A value less than 1.0 means that you have lost market share.

Fixes: If you are losing market share, you have one of two choices: (1) Try to recover the market share by improving product appeal (see the fixes for the size of market share calculation). (2) Write that market off and look for a new market area. The cost of market share recovery may be too great and a new, similar product may be easier to work with.

Cost of Sales

$$\text{(Operating Costs of Sales Ratio)} = \frac{\text{(Operating Costs [Cost of Sales for Items Sold])}}{\text{(Total Sales Minus Returns)}} = \frac{3{,}350}{4{,}650} = .72$$

The number for (Operating Costs [Cost of Sales for Items Sold]) needs to be handled carefully. If your product has a short lead time (produced in a few days or less), the numbers can be taken directly from the profit and loss statement, as they have been in this example. However, if the manufacturing lead time for the product is long (several weeks or more), we will need to look at only those costs related specifically to the items that were sold during that period. We are trying to identify what it cost to build the items that were sold during the period. We do not want to include costs for items that will be sold during the next period. These costs will need to be included in the operating costs number for next year.

This is another good benchmarking number where you should compare your numbers with the SIC average. If your ratio (in this case .72 or 72 percent) is lower than the average, then you are more profitable than the average. By comparing this number with last year's ratio, which in this case would be .793 or 79.3 percent (3,550/4,475), you would also have shown a profitability improvement in the production process.

Fixes: If your operating costs of sales ratio is high compared to the industry average, you need to analyze your cost of production ratio to see where your problems are. If the costs of sales are increasing this year compared with last year, check the cost of production ratios for last year to see what area is causing the increase.

Cost of Production

$$\text{(Labor Cost of Production)} = \frac{\text{(Total Direct Labor Cost)}}{\text{(Total Direct Labor, Materials, Direct Overhead)}} = \frac{2{,}000}{3{,}350} = .597$$

$$\text{(Total Materials Cost of Production)} = \frac{\text{(Total Materials Cost)}}{\text{(Total Dir Lbr, Mtls, Dir Ovrhd)}} = \frac{1{,}100}{3{,}350} = .328$$

$$\text{(Total Direct Overhead Cost of Production)} = \frac{\text{(Total Direct Overhead Cost)}}{\text{(Total Dir Lbr, Mtls, Dir Ovrhd)}} = \frac{250}{3{,}350} = .075$$

CHART 6.A3 *(continued)*

If your ratios are lower than your competitors', then you are more efficient. However, the sum of the three ratios should add up to 100 percent (59.7% + 32.8% + 7.5%). This means that if one value goes down, another will have to go up to keep the balance. What you want is to see the ratios go down in your highest cost area. In this example, a 1 percent reduction of labor cost (from 59.7% to 59.1%) would require an 8 percent reduction of overhead (from 7.5% to 6.9%). In other words, you get more bang for the effort if you work on cost reductions for your highest cost area first.

If your ratios this year are lower than they were last year, check which area is being reduced and follow the philosophy in the paragraph above. For the sample data, last year's numbers were: labor = .592 = 2,100/3,550; materials = .317 = 1,125/3,550; overhead = .091 = 325/3,550. Labor costs went up, material costs went up, and overhead went down. These results would be considered bad since the two highest cost components increased.

If the cost of sales ratio was high, these ratios help to identify which resource is causing this high cost. If the cost of sales ratio was acceptable these ratios show how your operation stacks up against competitors.

Fixes: If your labor cost ratio is higher this year than last year, or if it is higher than your competitors, it suggests that you are spending more on overtime, you have higher wages, or that you are doing more labor processes. If the materials cost ratio is high, you are either spending more on materials with your vendor, you are wasting more materials through scrap or pilferage, or you are using more subcontractor support. If your overhead cost ratio is high, you need to analyze the components of overhead to see where you may be wasteful. If this overhead ratio is high, but the indirect cost ratio is low, it may be that you are classifying your costs differently (including things in direct overhead that your competitor is including in indirect costs).

Indirect Cost Ratios

$$(\text{Indirect Cost Ratio}) = \frac{(\text{Total Indirect Costs})}{(\text{Total Costs})} = \frac{1{,}050}{3{,}350 + 1{,}050} = .239$$

$$(\text{Indirect/Direct Coverage}) = \frac{(\text{Total Indirect Costs})}{(\text{Total Direct Costs})} = \frac{1{,}050}{3{,}350} = .313$$

The indirect cost ratio tells you what portion of your total operating costs are nonproductive (.239 for this year). The indirect/direct coverage ratio compares your nonoperating costs with your operating costs (.313 for this year). Both ratios tell you basically the same thing. A low ratio in either case indicates a lean administration, which is good. When comparing the two years, the indirect cost ratio for the previous year was .202 = 900/(900 + 3,550), which shows that your indirect costs have increased this year over last year. The indirect/direct coverage ratio for the previous year was .254 = 900/3,550. Again, you are showing a significant increase in overhead costs over last year.

Fixes: If you have a lower ratio in these two categories than your competitors, you're doing good. However, if your ratio is higher, or if it has increased over last year, this indicates that you have too many administrative costs. You need to analyze what your administrative costs are and look for any outstanding large numbers. Any decrease in indirect cost goes directly to profits.

Asset Strength

$$(\text{Asset Ratio}) = \frac{(\text{Total Assets})}{(\text{Total Debts})} = \frac{2{,}600}{1{,}650} = 1.58$$

This ratio shows how well your total assets cover your total debts. In other words, do you have enough to pay your bills? The larger the number you have here (when compared to the federal tables), the more the banks love it. A large number suggests that you have a lot of ownership invested in the company and that the owners' personal risk is high.

Fixes: Poor numbers here can only be improved by getting more investment capital. It is also possible that you have more debts than you need. Perhaps you have a long-term loan to cover inventory and you really don't need that much inventory.

$$(\text{Current Ratio}) = \frac{(\text{Total Current Assets})}{(\text{Total Current Debts})} = \frac{950}{450} = 2.11$$

This ratio is very important to banks, but is often misinterpreted when it comes to operations. Banks consider a large number good because it suggests that you have a lot of liquid assets and you will have no problem paying your current debts. However, one of the reasons for having a large number here is because you have an excessively large inventory that is financed by long-term debts. The inventory increases the current assets, but the long-term debts do not show up in the total current debts number. Therefore, the number can be badly misstated. Operationally, it is better to have a low number here, and have low inventory (see the inventory asset ratio), than to have a high number with high inventories. The asset ratio is more meaningful because it includes both inventory and long term debts.

Fixes: Use this ratio in conjunction with the other asset strength ratios to identify any problems clearly.

$$(\text{Inventory Asset Ratio}) = \frac{(\text{Total Inventory})}{(\text{Total Current Assets})} = \frac{500}{950} = .526$$

(continued)

CHART 6.A3 *(concluded)*

When compared to your competitors, or when compared to last year's numbers, the lower the number you have here, the better. This indicates that you have better control over your inventory.

Fixes: High inventory numbers suggest the need for an inventory reduction program and possibly a program to improve production scheduling so that you won't need as much inventory. I have encountered plants that have as much as two-thirds of their inventory obsolete either because they are no longer using the part in production or because it is a maintenance part for a machine that is no longer used. Inventory reductions reduce debt, which reduces interest expenditures, which goes directly to profits.

Equity strength

$$\text{(Equity Strength)} = \frac{\text{(Total Equity)}}{\text{(Total Assets)}} = \frac{950}{2{,}600} = .365$$

This ratio is similar to the asset ratio. It shows how much ownership there is in the company. Larger ownership generally implies a more stable company.

Fixes: Stability can only be improved by increased equity or decreased debts.

Quality

$$\text{(Returns Percentage)} = \frac{\text{(Total Sales Dollar Value of Returns)}}{\text{(Total Gross Sales Dollars)}} = \frac{350}{5{,}000} = .07$$

This is an important measure of how your customers perceive your quality. In this case the value is .07 or 7 percent returns. There is an important secondary cost of quality associated with a poor number (a high number is a poor number) here: Customers that return products are not likely to buy from you again. They are also more likely to spread the word about bad quality than they are about good quality.

The measurement value is often distorted from the federal tables. Do the best you can. However, comparisons with previous years are extremely helpful to show if you are improving or not. For these data the previous year's value would be .077 = 375/4,850. This shows that you have improved slightly.

Fixes: Find out what the customer wants. Find out what they perceive good quality to be. Higher engineering standards so that there are fewer failures does not necessarily qualify as higher quality from a customer's perspective.

$$\text{(Scrap-Reject Purchase Ratio)} = \frac{\text{(Total Cost of Scrap-Reject Parts Purchased)}}{\text{(Total Cost of All Parts Purchased)}} = \frac{200}{1{,}100} = .182$$

This ratio tells you how your vendors are performing. A low value is good. A decrease over the previous year is even better.

Fixes: You need to work with your vendor if this number is bad. Perhaps there is a misunderstanding on what is desired or needed. Changing vendors is often not the best solution.

$$\text{(Scrap-Reject Production Ratio)} = \frac{\text{(Total Cost of Scrap-Reject Parts Produced)}}{\text{(Total Cost of All Parts Produced)}} = \frac{400}{3{,}350} = .119$$

This ratio tells how your production floor is performing. The value of "Total Cost of Scrap-Reject Parts Produced" is usually not available from the financial statements and has to be obtained from the production floor. I have assumed the number to be 400 for these calculations. Often this number can be camouflaged on the production floor by labeling discarded products as something other than scrap or reject. This number is only as good as the data. A comparison with the previous year's value is extremely valuable.

Fixes: Corrections involve an improvement in the production control, scheduling, and quality evaluation processes, as outlined in this book.

you what each of the terms in Chart 6.A1 means and how each of the benchmarking measurement ratios listed in Chart 6.A1 should be calculated. These calculations are in Chart 6.A3. Also included in Chart 6.A3 is an example of how each of these ratios should be used for comparative purposes. Then, if the calculated numbers are not as good as they should be, suggestions are made for improvements ("fixes"). However, these suggestions are not absolutes. Improving one area may cause problems in another area (remember the balance we talked about in Chapter 2). It is best if you look at all the measures together and try to get a sense of what all the indicators are telling you together, rather than individually.

Chart 6.A4 is a worksheet that will help you calculate the Chart 6.A3 benchmarking values quickly. It is set up to do one year only. Photocopy it so that you can use it for your competitive analysis and for previous years' analyses.

After examining Chart 6.A4, you should feel comfortable analyzing your financial statements from an operational perspective. Even if the data from the federal tables do not seem to be a good fit, you can check your own progress by comparing your financial reports from one year to the next.

This same type of comparative analysis is also valuable when looking at customers. Is the customer stable, when compared to their competitors? Or we can look at our vendors. Do we feel comfortable in the long term working with this vendor?

CHART 6.A4 Benchmarking Worksheet

Information source: ______________________________

Date of information source: ______________________________

Sales growth (All values come from the profit/loss statements.)

Gross sales for current year = __________(a)
Returns for current year = __________(b)
(a) − (b) = __________(c)
Gross sales for previous year = __________(d)
Returns for previous year = __________(e)
(d) − (e) = __________(f)
Sales Increase Ratio = (c)/(f) = __________

Total sales of the market = __________(g)
(This value is taken from the federal tables for this year.)
Size of Market Share = (c)/(g) = __________ (h)

Total sales of the market for last year = __________ (i)
(This value is taken from the federal tables for last year.)
Size of the market share for last year = (f)/(i) = __________ (j)
Size of the Market Share Growth = (h)/(j) = __________

Cost of Sales (All values come from the profit/loss statements.)

Total cost of sales = __________ (k)
(Check that this number includes the costs of items sold this year only—see explanation in Chart 6.A3.)
Operating Cost of Sales Ratio = (k)/(c) = __________

Cost of Production (All values come from the profit/loss statements.)

Total direct labor cost = __________ (l)
Total materials cost = __________ (m)
Total direct overhead cost = __________ (n)
Total direct labor, materials, and direct overhead = (l) + (m) + (n)
= __________ (o)
Labor Cost of Production = (l)/(o) = __________
Total Materials Cost of Production = (m)/(o) = __________
Total Direct Overhead Cost of Production = (n)/(o) = __________

Indirect Cost Ratios (All values come from the profit/loss statements.)

Total indirect costs = __________ (p)
Total costs = (o) + (p) = __________ (q)
Indirect Cost Ratio = (p)/(q) = __________
Indirect/Direct Coverage = (p)/(o) = __________

Asset Strength (All values come from the balance sheet.)

Total current assets = __________ (r)
Total assets = __________ (s)
Total current liabilities = __________ (t)
Total liabilities (debts) = __________ (u)
Total inventory = __________ (v)
Asset Ratio = (s)/(u) = __________
Current Ratio = (r)/(t) = __________
Inventory Asset Ratio = (v)/(r) = __________

Equity Strength

Total equity = (s) − (u) = __________ (w)
Equity Strength = (w)/(s) = __________

Quality

Returns Percentage = (b)/(a) = __________
Total cost of scrap-reject parts purchased = __________ (x)
Total cost of scrap-reject parts produced = __________ (y)
Scrap-Reject Purchase Ratio = (x)/(m) = __________
Scrap-Reject Production Ratio = (y)/(o) = __________

CHART 6.A5 Productivity Calculations

aa) *Direct Labor Hours Productivity*

$$\text{Direct Labor Hours Productivity} = \frac{\text{Net Sales}}{\text{Total Labor Hours}}$$

bb) *Labor Dollars Productivity*

$$\text{Labor Dollars Productivity} = \frac{\text{Net Sales}}{\text{Total Labor Dollars}}$$

cc) *Materials Productivity*

$$\text{Materials Productivity} = \frac{\text{Net Sales}}{\text{Total Materials Cost}}$$

dd) *Total Cost of Sales Productivity*

$$\text{Total Cost of Sales Productivity} = \frac{\text{Net Sales}}{\text{Total Cost of Sales}}$$

ee) *Total Cost of Operation (Direct plus Indirect) Productivity*

$$\text{Total Cost of Operation Productivity} = \frac{\text{Net Sales}}{\text{Total Cost of Operation (Direct + Indirect)}}$$

Plant-wide Operational Measures of Performance

As we discussed earlier in the chapter, operations managers at the highest levels of management are concerned with four key measures of performance:

Quality
Cost
Productivity
Efficiency.

The definition of quality differs from country to country. In the United States, quality usually means "meeting engineering standards."

Cost issues have also been discussed in Charts 6.A1 and 6.A3 under the "Cost of Sales" and "Cost of Production" issues.

The definition of productivity is

$$\text{Productivity} = \frac{\text{Output}}{\text{Input}}$$

The question becomes "What is output and what is input?" Output for you should be net sales. Input can be any basis of measure. For example, all of the calculations listed in Chart 6.A5 are acceptable inputs.

Chart 6.A6 uses the formulas of Chart 6.A5 and the data of Chart 6.A2 to demonstrate the use of these productivity measures. Chart 6.A7 is a worksheet for the calculation of these productivity values.

The last of the operational measures, efficiency, is used to measure the performance of an employee. This will be discussed in detail in Chapter 19.

CHART 6.A6 Productivity Calculations—Examples

aa) *Direct Labor Hours Productivity*

$$\text{Direct Labor Hours Productivity} = \frac{\text{Net Sales}}{\text{Total Labor Hours}} = \frac{4{,}650}{130} = 35.8$$

To perform this measure, we need to know the amount of direct labor hours worked (time actually spent producing the product). Do not include indirect labor hours (cleanup, administrative, maintenance time, etc.) because these hours are considered nonproductive. For purposes of this example, we will assume 130 direct labor hours for the current year and 140 direct labor hours for the previous year.

Productivity for the current year is 35.8 and for the previous year, 32.0 = (4,475/140). This shows an improvement in productivity for the current year. This means that we are getting more output for each direct labor hour expended.

Fixes: If productivity is going down, it is probably an indicator of inefficiencies creeping into the production process. It could be due to new products being introduced or equipment failure. One of the best ways to improve this number is to increase technology with modernized production equipment, thereby making the employees more effective.

bb) *Labor Dollars Productivity*

$$\text{Labor Dollars Productivity} = \frac{\text{Net Sales}}{\text{Total Labor Dollars}} = \frac{4{,}650}{2{,}000} = 2.33$$

Labor dollars productivity for the current year is 2.33 and for the previous year is 2.13 = (4,475/2,100). Again this shows an improvement in productivity for the current year. Generally this measure gives the same result as the direct labor hours productivity ratio. However, it is possible for direct labor hours productivity to go up while labor dollars productivity goes down. This is most likely the result of a significant wage increase.

Fixes: A decrease in labor dollars productivity indicates that you are not getting as much output per labor dollar as you did in the past. You need to start asking why. It could be wage increases or it could be reduced quality causing more returns.

cc) *Materials Productivity*

$$\text{Materials Productivity} = \frac{\text{Net Sales}}{\text{Total Materials Cost}} = \frac{4{,}650}{1{,}100} = 4.23$$

Materials productivity measures the efficient use of material purchases. For the current year the value is 4.23 and for the previous year it was 3.98 = (4,475/1,125). Again, you are showing an increase in productivity for the current year.

Fixes: A decrease in materials productivity generally indicates excessive waste or scrappage. Waste and scrap should be monitored if they are not already. This could also indicate that you are not returning rejected materials to the vendor.

dd) *Total Cost of Sales Productivity*

$$\text{Total Cost of Sales Productivity} = \frac{\text{Net Sales}}{\text{Total Cost of Sales}} = \frac{4{,}650}{3{,}350} = 1.39$$

Total cost of sales productivity indicates productivity of all the direct costs. If this measure is not improving, it generally indicates an increase in waste on the factory floor and this needs to be checked. For the current year the value is 1.39; for the previous year it was 1.26 = (4,475/3,550). Again, you have shown an improvement.

Fixes: If this value is decreasing you are probably showing a lot of waste in the production process.

ee) *Total Cost of Operation (Direct plus Indirect) Productivity*

$$\text{Total Cost of Operation Productivity} = \frac{\text{Net Sales}}{\text{Total Cost of Operation}} = \frac{4{,}650}{3{,}350 + 1{,}050} = 1.06$$

Total cost of operation productivity indicates performance on the dollars spent for running the entire facility. A decrease here indicates overall inefficiency. If this number is decreasing but the total cost of sales productivity number is increasing, this is a direct indicator that administrative costs are becoming disproportionately high and need to be trimmed back. The current value is 1.06. The previous value is 1.01 = (4,475/[3,550 + 900]). This again demonstrates an increase in productivity for this sample data.

Fixes: A decrease here indicates total inefficiency and the other measures of productivity need to be analyzed to determine where the inefficiency lies.

CHART 6.A7 Productivity Calculations—Worksheet

(Many of these values are taken from Chart 6.4A and the letters referenced will be the same as from that sheet.)

Direct Labor Hours Productivity:

Direct labor hours = __________ (z)

Direct labor hours productivity = (c)/(z) = __________

Labor Dollars Productivity:

Labor dollars productivity = (c)/(l) = __________

Materials Productivity:

Materials productivity = (c)/(m) = __________

Total Cost of Sales Productivity:

Total cost of sales productivity = (c)/(o) = __________

Total Cost of Operation (Direct plus Indirect) Productivity:

Total cost of operation productivity = (c)/(q) = __________

Summary

Now we have a basis of measurement tools that can be used to monitor the performance of the overall organization. These tools will help us highlight trouble spots in the factory.

APPENDIX 6.B: Resource Matching

We need to identify which resources have the greatest influence on the goal of the organization (see the main chapter for a discussion of goals). Having identified those key resources, we can then move forward with establishing a measurement system that focuses on those key resources.

We need to start by defining the resources of a factory. Chart 6.B1 lists most (but not all) of these resources by category. The list of resources that you develop for your organization will differ from this list. Chart 6.B1 is only intended as a starting point. Don't waste a lot of time analyzing resources that have very little effect on your operation. What you're looking for are the "biggies." After you have built your list, watch for the biggest of the "biggies," but focus your selection on the corporate goal you established earlier. Let me give you an example.

Cadillac, a recent Baldrige Award winner,[2] made a presentation at a recent awards conference.[3] Chart 6.B2 shows a chart that was pre-

[2] The Baldrige Award is the national award for excellence in manufacturing. It looks for improvement in the areas of productivity and quality. To obtain more information about the Baldrige Award, or other national manufacturing awards, contact the American Productivity and Quality Center (APQC) in Houston, Texas.

[3] The conference was held in Logan, Utah, and was called "Partners in Business." It is an annual conference. This presentation was made during the 1991 conference.

CHART 6.B1 List of Resources

Traditional	External
Materials	Vendors
Labor	Customers
Machinery	Governmental
Burden	Political environment
Financial	Internal
Capital	Maintenance
Debt	Unions
Infrastructure	Level of automation/technology
Energy	Management style
Communications	Resource dependence
Roadways	Design/engineering
Education system	Other
	Plant location
	Economic potential

CHART 6.B2 Cadillac—Old Versus New Priorities

Old goal—Profitability
New goal—Customer satisfaction

	Old	New
Design costs	5%	70%
Material costs	50%	20%
Labor costs	15%	5%
Burden costs	30%	5%

sented, which demonstrates the change of focus that they made as an organization. Down the left side is a list of some of their key resources (summarized). Across the top are their old and new focuses. The old focus demonstrates their priorities under a goal of increased profits. The new focus demonstrates their priorities under a goal of customer satisfaction.

Under Cadillac's old goal of profitability, material costs were the greatest influence on profitability. Under Cadillac's new goal of customer satisfaction, design and engineering expenditures had the greatest influence. Cadillac modified their planning and control system and the corresponding measurement system to stress engineering issues, with materials issues as secondary, rather than materials issues as primary with burden issues as secondary.[4]

How did Cadillac come up with these percentages? The first column (old), is easy to calculate. These numbers come from the profit and loss statement and the ratios are calculated similar to the way the calculations were done in Chart 6.A1 under the section titled "Cost of Production." The second column is a little trickier. It required a survey. They

went out and asked their customers which of these components was the

[4] Burden costs include all the other costs of operation, such as management, administrative, and energy costs.

most important in the way the customer perceived quality. This is an example of the questions asked in the survey. It takes several questions like this to get the customer's feeling for priorities. What is the most important:

- comfortably designed seats?
- expensive upholstery on the seats?
- hand-sewn seat covers?

A series of questions like this will give you a feel for what is important to the customer. From this survey you can then formulate a list similar to the "new" list in Chart 6.B2. If you are surveying people, don't survey them with a resource list that covers more than five or six categories. They'll soon get tired of it. Do an initial survey to find out where the customer's preferences lie. A later survey can be used to determine a more detailed breakdown of the most important and influential category.

If you use an employee-based goal, you do the same type of thing that you did with a customer-based goal. Instead of surveying the customers, however, you survey the employees and ask them what is important to them.

At this point you now have a list of resources and you have percentages of importance attached to them. The next step is to ABC classify these resources. But first we will need to explain what ABC classification analysis is. *ABC classification* (also called the Parieto principle or the 80–20 rule) is one of the most valuable tools of manufacturing. The concept is very simple. It claims that 80 percent (approximately) of the trouble is caused by 20 percent (approximately) of your children. Or, 80 percent of your inventory activity occurs to 20 percent of your products. You'll be amazed at how consistent this principle is as we work our way through this book. In the case of resource prioritization, we are saying that 80 percent of the resource influence on your corporate goal is caused by 20 percent of the resources.

Looking at Chart 6.B3 we can see an example of ABC classification in use, the top usage 20 percent (in this example 2/12 = 17 percent) are considered "A" items (they cover 71.3 percent of the activity). The next 40 percent (in this example 4/12 = 33 percent) of the items cover another 15 percent of the influence and are considered "B" items. The last 40 percent are the "C" items, but they only cover about 5 percent of the activity (in this case 50 percent covers 2.9 percent of the activity). This model suggests that if we focus on the "A" items, we'll get the most bang for our effort.

The Cadillac list is fairly short with only four items. ABC classification requires at least 10 items to prove itself. But you can see in the Cadillac chart that under the "old" goals, a focus on materials and burden would cover 80 percent of the influence, and under the "new" goals, a focus on design and materials would cover 90 percent of the influence. These high influences are what need to be stressed in the planning, control, and measurement system.

Let me give you a more realistic example. Let's assume a goal of profitability. Chart 6.B4 is a list of the important resources of our

CHART 6.B3 ABC Classification Example

Part Number	Sales $	% of Total	Classification
123	5,684	27.5	A
124	1,234	6.0	B
125	90	.4	C
126	9,056	43.8	A
127	234	1.1	C
128	1,001	4.8	B
129	184	.9	C
130	95	.5	C
131	0	.0	C
132	2,234	10.8	B
133	864	4.2	B
134	0	.0	C
Total $	20,676	100.0	

Total A percentage = 71.3%, # of products = 2
Total B percentage = 25.8%, # of products = 4
Total C percentage = 2.9%, # of products = 6

By focusing more control effort on Parts #123 and 126, and very little on the "C" parts, we get better control of our more critical (money making) products.

CHART 6.B4 Sample List of Critical Resources and Their Influence on Profit

	Percentage of Influence
Materials	50%
Labor	8%
Machinery	24%
Direct burden	3%
Debt	5%
Energy	3%
Communications	2%
Maintenance	2%
Design/engineering	2%
Other	1%

sample organization showing the influence that each resource has on total profitability (the percentage ratios are calculated similar to the way the calculations were done in Chart 6.A1 under the section titled "Cost of Production"). The "A" items of Chart 6.B4 are materials and machinery. These two items are 20 percent (2/10) of all the items and they cover 74 percent (50 + 24) of all the activity. The "B" items would be labor (8%), debt (5%), direct burden (3%), and energy (3%), giving a total coverage of 40 percent of the products (4/10) and a coverage of 19 percent (8 + 5 + 3 + 3) of the activity. That leaves communications (2%), maintenance (2%), design/engineering (2%), and other (1%) as our "C" items. The "C" items have 40 percent of the products (4/10) for a 7 percent (2 + 2 + 2 + 1) activity coverage.

ABC classification systems will reappear several times throughout the book. They are a valuable tool for focusing on the most critical elements of any system.

Returning to the discussion of resource focus, Chart 6.B5 is a worksheet that you can use for defining your critical resource. Fill in the evaluation information on the worksheet. Total the evaluations on the bottom. Then calculate percentages in the percentage of usage column. Using these percentages, sequence the products. Then classify the products as outlined in the following procedure, starting with the largest percentage first.

Chart 6.B6 is an example using the worksheet of Chart 6.B5. In Chart 6.B6 we see an example of cost being the goal that we are trying to optimize. The steps are as follows:

1. First make sure all the cost components (taken from cost of sales from the profit and loss statement, see Chart 6.A2) are written in on the worksheet. Be careful to not lump too much into "Other." Break the numbers down as much as possible. You don't want "Other" to be an "A" item.
2. After posting all the values, total them at the bottom.
3. Calculate the percentage of use by dividing each value by the total.
4. Sequence the products by highest to lowest percentage (second part of Chart 6.B6).
5. Classify the highest usage items up to about 80 percent as "A" items. Classify the next highest group of items up to about 95 percent as "B" items. Classify the remainder of the products as "C" items.

In the example of Chart 6.B6 we see an example of the type of judgment call that may occasionally be necessary. Maintenance should be included as an "A" item if we require the cutoff to be at 80 percent. But looking at maintenance's usage of 7.3 percent, it looks more like a "B" item than an "A" item. I would go with the "B" classification for maintenance.

At this point we know that our critical resources are materials and machinery, so now we are ready to build a planning, control, and measurement system around these two critical resources. Note that, in this example, labor is not significant. I would also expect this to be true in your plant.

In the development of a planning, control, and measurement system, we need to look at each resource and decide what is critical about that resource. This entire book discusses planning, control, and measurement systems. But, just to continue working out my example of Chart 6.B6, we have selected materials and machinery as the critical resources. Our planning, control, and measurement system for these resources can include items such as those listed on Chart 6.B7.

CHART 6.B5 List of Resources—Evaluation

	Evaluation Amount	Percentage of Usage
Traditional		
Materials	________	____
Labor	________	____
Machinery	________	____
Burden	________	____
Financial		
Capital	________	____
Debt	________	____
Infrastructure		
Energy	________	____
Communications	________	____
Roadways	________	____
Education system	________	____
External		
Vendors	________	____
Customers	________	____
Governmental	________	____
Political environment	________	____
Internal		
Maintenance	________	____
Unions	________	____
Levels of automation/technology	________	____
Management style	________	____
Resource dependence	________	____
Design/engineering	________	____
Other		
Plant location	________	____
Economic potential	________	____
Other	________	____
____________	________	____
____________	________	____
____________	________	____
____________	________	____
Total Evaluation	________	____*

Resequencing: Sequence the above list by percentage starting with the highest down to the lowest.

Resource Description	Usage %	Accumulative %	Classification
________	____	____	____
________	____	____	____
________	____	____	____
________	____	____	____
________	____	____	____
________	____	____	____
________	____	____	____
________	____	____	____
________	____	____	____
________	____	____	____
________	____	____	____
________	____	____	____
________	____	____	____
________	____	____	____
________	____	____	____
________	____	____	____

*Check to make sure the percentages total to 100.

CHART 6.B6 List of Resources Evaluation—Example

	Evaluation Amount	Percentage of Usage
Traditional		
Materials	45,000	44.7
Labor	6,500	6.5
Machinery	27,900	27.7
Burden	4,800	4.8
Financial		
Capital		
Debt	2,800	2.8
Infrastructure		
Energy	1,750	1.7
Communications	950	.9
Roadways	1,300	1.3
Education system	200	.2
External		
Vendors		
Customers		
Governmental		
Political environment		
Internal		
Maintenance	7,400	7.3
Unions		
Levels of automation/technology		
Management style		
Resource dependence		
Design/engineering		
Other		
Plant location		
Economic potential		
Other	2,100	2.1
Total Evaluation	100,700	100.0*

Resequencing: Sequence the above list by percentage starting with the highest down to the lowest.

Resource Description	Usage %	Accumulative %	Classification
Materials	44.7	44.7	A
Machinery	27.7	72.4	A
Maintenance	7.3	79.7	A or B
Labor	6.5	86.2	B
Burden	4.8	91.0	B
Debt	2.8	93.8	B
Other	2.1	95.9	B
Energy	1.7	97.6	C
Roadways	1.3	98.9	C
Communications	.9	99.8	C
Education system	.2	100.0	C

*Check to make sure the percentages total to 100.

CHART 6.B7 Planning, Control, and Measurement Systems for Materials and Machinery (Many of these topics have not yet been discussed and will be discussed in more detail later in the book.)

This is a list of potential danger areas that need to be checked using the data collection system.

Materials

- Potential Problems
  - Engineering
    - Do the drawings minimize materials usage (cost)?
  - Purchasing
    - Do we take advantage of discounts?
    - Do we overpurchase excessively?
    - Is the vendor selection process valid?
  - Receiving
    - Do materials received match quantities purchased?
    - Are faulty materials inspected and returned promptly?
  - Stores
    - Do we know where the materials are stored?
    - Do we have accurate inventory counts?
    - Do we cycle count?
  - Picking
    - Do we only issue the amount of materials required?
    - Do we track all issues for scrap and breakage?
  - Shipping
    - Are quality problems reported and solved?
    - Are returns taken care of promptly?
- Corrective Systems
  - Bill of materials
  - Material requirements planning
  - Shop floor control

Machinery

- Potential Problems
  - Engineering
    - Is machine usage effective?
    - Is the product designed for minimum machine usage?
  - Machine
    - Is the machine causing too much part breakage?
    - Does the machine need to be replaced?
    - Are we using the best (cheapest) machine for the job?
  - Corrective Systems
    - Routings
    - Material requirements planning
    - Capacity requirements planning
    - Shop floor control

If trade-offs occur, such as if reducing machine time for a part requires more material, the trade-off should favor our highest cost element, which in the example of Chart 6.B6 is materials.

Summary

At this point we have achieved focus in our goals and focus in our resources. This helps us build focus into our measurement system.

Chapter

7 Tactical Management

Why Forecast?

Forecasting really doesn't need to be scary. It can be very simple. It all depends on how you want to approach it. In Chapter 6 we discussed the business plan, which defined for us our sales goals in order to achieve the primary goal of the organization. The forecast looks at history and attempts to predict the future based on what has happened in the past. Immediately you can see one of the basic fallacies of a forecast: "What if the future isn't the same as the past?" What if we are introducing some new products or changing some product lines? What if we anticipate a recession? There are a million reasons why the forecast can be wrong, but the simple fact is that we don't have anything better for predicting the future—and so we use it.

Some people will claim that you need to do the forecast before you do the business plan because you need to see where sales are going before you can build your business plan around it. That's true if your primary goal supports maintaining a steady sales growth at the same rate as in the past. Often this is not the case. Often you may develop a forecast "assuming everything remains the same" and then adjust these numbers to fit the goals of the business plan. Either way, the forecast is a starting point for the planning process.

Features Common to Forecasts

Let's discuss some features common to all forecasts. These concerns are not reasons to eliminate forecasting, rather they are considerations that need to be kept in mind when you do a forecast.

1. *The data are more important than the modeling technique.* No forecast is any better than the quality of the data (Chapter 3). The data make the model a success or a failure. The key word here is *biases*. A bias is data that aren't objective, that have some distorting influence. For example, if you wanted to know what percentage of people in the world liked lawyers, but in your survey you only asked lawyers for their opinion, you'd be biased toward lawyers. Data that are biased will generate distorted results. There's no magic way around it.

2. *Sophisticated models are not needed.* Hundreds of models could be used. However, the simpler models are more than adequate for handling forecasting for the small- to medium-sized discrete manufacturer. In those cases where complex models were used, the simplistic models were better predictors. In the remaining cases, the sophisticated model was better, but not significantly better to justify the torture that you need to go through to use the model.

3. As we have already suggested, *a forecast assumes that past events can predict future events.* This suggests that the underlying causes behind past sales will remain the same in the future. Any anticipated future events will need to be built into the predictions after the forecasting model has done the best it can with the historical data.

4. *Forecasts are rarely correct.* If you want to know exactly what the future holds, go to a palm reader! If you want the best "educated guess" of the future, try forecasting. But realize that it is nothing more than an educated guess. Don't expect perfection. Allow for some deviation (variance) in the answers.

5. *Group forecasting is the most accurate.* When forecasting, forecast at the highest level possible. Don't forecast individual products if you can forecast a family of products. The reason is that each forecast has an error factor associated with it called a *variance.* If you individually forecast 10 products from the same family and then add their forecasts, you'll get a very different total than if you generated one forecast for the entire family. That's because the variances of each of the 10 products added together give one large variance, whereas the variance for the overall family forecast was just the variance of one forecast.

Total sales forecasting may not be as helpful as family or product line forecasting because business plans are usually based on a plan for each product line.

Forecasting for resources, for example, inventory level forecasts, is not as helpful as sales forecasts because the inventory level is dependent on the number and types of products you plan to sell. You should forecast sales, then calculate the levels of the resource requirements through the production planning process.

6. *Forecast accuracy decreases as the time period of the forecast increases.* The further out you go, the less accurate the forecast becomes. The further we get away from the center of the data, the larger the chance for error (variance). A point is reached at which number crunching isn't any more accurate than guessing.

7. *Determine the purpose, level of accuracy, and time horizon for your forecast.* Don't forecast for the fun of it. Will the forecast help you in detailing your business plan? Will it help you establish your aggregate production schedule? If not, don't waste your time. Just take the total sales number from the business plan and divide it by 12 and you have your monthly forecast for the next year. If you are trying to quantitatively forecast more than one (at most two) years, forget it. The accuracy just isn't good enough.

Types of Forecasts

There are two major categories of forecasts. The number-crunching kind is called the *quantitative forecast,* and the "best guess" kind is called the *qualitative forecast.* Qualitative forecasts include things such as customer surveys, sales force compositions (have each salesperson make a prediction and add all these numbers up), executive opinion (best guess), and panels of experts. We won't spend any time on the qualitative forecasts simply because once you have collected the data, the work is done. Simply collect the data, add it up, and you have your forecast. Then proceed to the next section of this chapter.

Qualitative forecasts are important if you are trying to project further out into the future (three years or more), or if you are trying to forecast a new product for which no sufficient history is available.

Quantitative forecasts are important for short-term forecasts (less than two years) when several years worth of history is available to base the projection on (three or more). The two types of quantitative forecasts are *time series* and *associative*. Associative methods are what economists use to predict the future of our economy. They are extremely complex and are an overkill for what we are trying to do here. Time series quantitative forecasting methods use the history of sales to predict the future of sales.

Basic Steps in Forecasting

The basic steps required to generate a forecast are:

1. *Collect data on the history of sales for as many years back as possible.* This history should be in monthly increments, so that we can give a more accurate monthly projection of future sales. If you can't do monthly sales, then at least do quarterly. The worksheets in this chapter (see Appendix 7.F) have been set up for monthly so if you do quarterly forecasts, they will have to be modified accordingly.

   The sales number can be either in dollar sales or in units sold. But if you're using units sold, don't mix apples with oranges. Don't lump unrelated items such as lawn mowers and toasters together. Make sure the families of products are related.

   If you don't have at least two years worth of data on a particular family of products, as a bare minimum, don't bother forecasting. You need at least three or four years worth to put any credibility into the forecast. If the time period for data you have is too short, the variance becomes very large, and your best guess is probably as accurate as a mathematically calculated forecast.

   If you do not have a sufficient amount of data, or if you are trying to predict too far into the future, go back to the discussion of qualitative forecasts in the previous section. Generate a "best guess" forecast using one of the techniques mentioned there and proceed.

2. *Deseasonalize* your data, which means take the seasonality effects out of it. This cleans up the data so that you can run a straight line through it. It's easier to project where a straight line is going rather than where a curving line is going.

3. *Apply the deseasonalized data to several models and calculate the error factor for each model.*

4. *Select the best model.* Use the appropriate tests to do the model selection.

5. *Generate the forecast* using the model that was selected as being the best model.

6. *Put seasonality back into the generated forecast.* With seasonality placed back into the projected numbers, we now have our forecasted prediction.

7. *Monitor the performance of the forecast.* By watching how well

CHART 7.1 The Steps in Forecasting

1. Collect data
   - Monthly increments
   - Forecast by family of product
   - Don't mix apples with oranges
   - At least two years worth of data
2. Deseasonalize
3. Apply the deseasonalized data to several models and calculate the error factor for each model
4. Select the best model
5. Generate the forecast
6. Put seasonality back into the generated forecast
7. Monitor the performance of the forecast

the forecast has predicted the future (comparing forecasted numbers with actual numbers), we can decide when we should generate a new forecast. This will probably occur at least quarterly, when you need to go back to step 1 and start over. And that's the life of a forecaster—constantly trying out different models to find out which is working best and using it to make predictions. Chart 7.1 summarizes the steps of forecasting.

With your forecast you can now determine what the demand will be on our factory. Next we will see how customer orders affect the forecast. Then we continue with the planning process to see how available capacity and demand on capacity (forecast plus customer orders) are balanced to generate an aggregate production schedule. See Appendix 7.F for the details behind calculating a forecast.

Customer Order Processing

Customer order processing serves several functions. One of its primary planning functions is to convert anticipated demand (the forecast) into actual demand. This function also serves as a feedback and control mechanism on the accuracy of the forecast.

A second function of customer order processing occurs when the order is shipped. At that point, the customer order becomes a sale. The sales transaction serves to monitor our performance on the customer orders. It also helps us in forecasting the future sales of new or changing products. This sales transaction feeds into the accounting system as a cash or accounts receivable entry.

A diagram of the functions of customer order processing is shown in Chart 7.2. (This would be a good time to review the diagrams that integrate the total production flow in order to understand how the total integration works—Charts 4.8 and 4.9.)

The method for reporting the customer order may take many forms depending primarily on the number of orders that are taken. If you

CHART 7.2 The Functions of Customer Order Processing

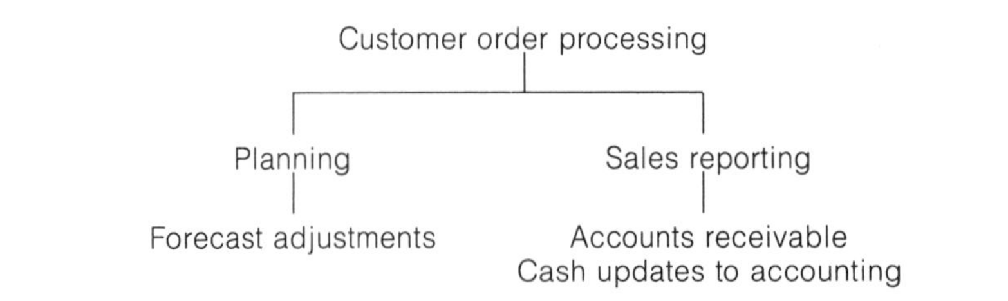

have a high volume of orders, you will want some type of automated system to track the orders and their shipment. If the volume of orders is low—a few per day or less—a simplistic hand-written order form tracking the items listed is enough. The ordering and shipping document may be the same physical piece of paper or a multicarbon form, depending on how often shipments are made. The following functions must be represented:

Order form (what was ordered)

Shipment form (what was shipped)

Invoice (what was billed)

The forecast defines the anticipated demands that are being placed on the organization. These demands are called "adjustable demands" in that they are approximations of when the demand is anticipated and they may be off a month or two in either direction.

There is also a second element that defines the demands on an organization. This is the actual customer orders. Customer orders are considered a "nonadjustable demand" in that they define a demand for a specific point in time. A nonadjustable demand defines a specific point when the customer wants the product to be shipped. To ship it late may mean a dissatisfied customer, and to complete it early would mean that we have to pay inventory and storage costs for the product until we can ship it.

It is important to make a distinction here. The customer order process is distinctly different from the order shipment process. The shipment process is a feedback and control mechanism that demonstrates our plant's performance in terms of the orders. It also reports sales. These functions, however, are discussed in the next section of this chapter. In this section we are primarily concerned with the order itself. Even if a product is shipped immediately, we still need to report the customer order to the planning process.

We generate a report that shows "committed sales" and what part of the forecast is still "available to be promised." This helps the sales force monitor what part of the plant's capacity can still be sold. Total demand (customer orders plus "available to be promised" or the forecast) will now need to be converted into a specific demand on resources. We develop a *bill of resources* for each of these families of products. Then, with this bill of resources, we can calculate the actual demand that is being placed on the factory. The resources that are of greatest concern to most factories are the three M's:

Materials
Machinery
Manpower (labor).

The place to start in the development of a bill of resources is by looking at the *bill of materials* and the *routings* of each of the products in the family. The bill of materials defines the materials requirements for each product. We take the average of each product's requirements and place that value into the bill of resources. Similarly, we use the routing information to define the labor and machinery requirements for each product and average this out for the family.

At this point we can now calculate the demand for each resource as required by each product family. We multiply the demand times the bill of resources to calculate the *total resources demanded by family*. Summarizing by resource gives us the *total resources demanded.*

At this point we have identified the combined demand that our forecast (customer orders plus available to promise quantity) has placed on each of our resource areas. Next we will analyze the available capacity in each of these areas. Then we will build a compromise plan in the form of an *aggregate production schedule,* which balances the demand on resources with the resource capacity availability. See Appendix 7.G for details on customer order processing and Appendix 7.A for details on aggregate production scheduling.

Rough-Cut Capacity Plan

Rough-cut capacity planning (RCC) is the other half of the balancing act that was started with our discussion of forecasting. Forecasting, and the corresponding customer orders, defined the demand on our factory. Rough-cut capacity planning defines the available capacity that we have to satisfy that demand. Chart 7.G11 defines the capacity needs of each family of product. Chart 7.3 relists the resources under evaluation. What we need to do in this chapter is determine the availability of each of these resources. Let's do it by discussing the measurement process for each resource individually.

Materials

The amount of available materials is dependent on your vendor, your cash flow, and the purchasing lead time. If your vendor has a limit on how much he/she could sell to you, that's your capacity. If you have a cash flow limit on the purchase of materials, that cash flow limit has to be divided between all the material resource requirements, which may limit the amount of materials you can actually purchase. If your lead time for the receipt of the product is excessively long, for example, six months or longer, this may place a barrier on how much material you

CHART 7.3 Resources Evaluated

	Unit of Measure
Materials	
Bar stock	Feet
Purchased parts	Dollars
Sheet metal	Square feet
Machinery	
Lathe	Hours
Drill press	Hours
Manpower	
Painting	Hours
Assembly	Hours
Welding	Hours
Grinding	Hours

will have available over the next six months. Note that the unit of measure should be something that is standard for all parts in a particular category.

If lead time, vendor sourcing, and cash flow are not a problem, then perhaps you do not have a materials constraint in one or more areas. Capacity analysis for these particular areas is of no value. It is only important if we have the possibility of running out of capacity in an area.

Machinery

The measurement of machine capacity is fairly easy. Evaluate the following for each category of machine under consideration (in this example, lathes and drill presses):

Number of shifts, a

Number of effective machine usage hours you get out of one shift—for how much of the shift time can the machine effectively be used for production runs? (don't include maintenance, cleanup, or setup), b

Number of machines available on a shift, c

Number of working days in the month, d

Multiply these values together ($a \times b \times c \times d$) to get available capacity. For example, we run two shifts in the lathe department and have four lathes in the department. We have 22 working days in the month under analysis. The shifts are 8 hours long but we have on the average one setup per day lasting about 2 hours. We also have cleanup at the end of the shift lasting about one-half hour. Over the last 6 months we have had 52 hours of production time lost in maintenance so that averages about 0.4 hours per day (52 hours divided by 26 weeks at 5 days per week = 52/(26 × 5) = 0.4 hours). That leaves us a maximum of 5.1 hours of production time per day (8 total hours minus 2 hours of setup, minus one-half hour of cleanup, minus 0.4 hours of maintenance = 8 − 2 − 0.5 − 0.4 = 5.1 hours).

Some reasons for reducing available capacity are not considered acceptable in this calculation process. For example, if we only have one employee working on two machines, each machine may not be utilized to maximum efficiency. This is machine capacity that actually exists but we have simply chosen not to use it.

We need to multiply the daily one-machine capacity of 5.1 hours times the number of shifts (2), times the number of machines (4), times the number of working days in the month (22). This gives us a total capacity of:

$$(5.1) \times (2) \times (4) \times (22) = 897.6 \text{ hours per month}$$

This same process is repeated for the rough-cut capacity calculation of each of the departments under consideration.

Manpower (Labor)

The procedure for calculating productive labor capacity is similar to the procedure used in calculating machine capacity. The employee is not doing productive functions during the entire eight hours on the job. There are breaks, cleanups, meetings, downtime, setups, etc., all affecting the total productive output. For example, in painting we may have the following situation:

8-hour shifts

1-hour lunch

2 breaks at 15 minutes each

0.5-hour cleanup time

0.5-hour startup time

0.5-hour per day average machine shutdown time due to machine breakdown (see the section on machine capacity to see how this is calculated)

1 hour average per day setup time

The effective hours of available capacity on a per-day basis are 8 − 1 − 0.5 − 0.5 − 0.5 − 0.5 − 1 = 4 hours. If we use 22 work days per month, 2 shifts, and 6 employees, we get the following capacity calculation:

4 hours × 22 days × 2 shifts × 6 employees per shift =
1,056 hours of painting labor capacity per month

At this point we know how to get estimates (rough cuts) of the capacity in each area under consideration. For the resources listed in Chart 7.3, let's assume that the rough-cut capacities calculated are those listed in Chart 7.4.

CHART 7.4 Rough-Cut Capacities of Resources Evaluated

	Monthly Capacities
Materials	
Bar stock	No limit
Purchased parts	16,000 dollars
Sheet metal	No limit
Machinery	
Lathe	2,000 hours
Drill press	5,000 hours
Manpower	
Painting	250 hours
Assembly	900 hours
Welding	1,500 hours
Grinding	600 hours

Aggregate Production Scheduling

Aggregate production scheduling starts by comparing the available capacities with the demands on capacity. We look for areas where the available capacity is exceeded. If no area is exceeded, then we can build everything. However, if there are some areas that are over their capacity, then we need to either cut back the production during these periods or expand the capacity. If we cut back the production, we look to see if the production can be shifted to an earlier period where the capacity has not been exceeded. If this occurs, then we need to calculate the cost of carrying inventory from the previous period until the period of demand. This cost may turn out to be excessive. However, if this is not possible, we may have to reduce the amount of anticipated sales.

Capacity expansions can occur in several different ways. For example, outside vendors can be used, or extra shifts, or overtime, or simply hire more people and machinery. The end result of the aggregate planning process is that we now have a production load for that factory that both satisfies the forecast and meets capacity limitations. For a detailed discussion on the development of an aggregate production schedule, see Appendix 7.A.

Plant Layouts

We will now discuss plant layouts, even though a number of the smaller details relative to plant layouts won't be discussed until the chapter on shop floor control. The layout of the production process within the plant can make a significant difference in determining what areas of the plant are bottlenecks. Capacity shifts can be made by simply reorganizing the facility.

In Chapter 2 we discussed three types of discrete manufacturing. These will now be tied into a discussion of plant layouts. The first type of plant layout is the "functional" layout. In this layout we have a plant that is broken up into functional areas (departments) as in Chart 7.5. The objective of this arrangement is usually to take advantage of labor specialization. By keeping similar laborers and machines grouped together, we can maximize the efficiency of that particular function.

Departmentalized discrete manufacturing uses functional layouts. Job shops will often use functional layouts even though they may also use project layouts (the third layout type). Occasionally, a plant may need to be laid out functionally because of the limitations of the existing facility in items like foundations, venting, or energy. The optimal technique for laying out the functional plant is so that there is some type of flow from raw materials, through the production stages, through assembly, and ending in finished goods and shipping. The shorter the distances that materials have to be moved, the better.

The major advantage of the functional layout is flexibility. Product modifications are easy to implement. It simply modifies the routing of the product. The product is produced in batch quantities so that we can take advantage of the efficiencies gained by this type of production.

In the functional layout we brought the product to the machine. In the product layout, the second type of plant layout, we bring the machine to the product. The assembly line is a familiar example of the product layout (see Chart 7.6). In Chapter 2, the flow discrete manufacturer uses a product plant layout. Other production processes, that are not necessarily assembly, follow the product layout strategy in an attempt to copy some of the Japanese planning philosophies. Certain processes within a plant can be performed as a series of steps, similar to an assembly line. These product layout processes are called *group technology manufacturing cells* or *U-lines*. The big advantage of the product layout strategy is the lack of work-in-process inventory. The idea is

CHART 7.5 Functional Layout

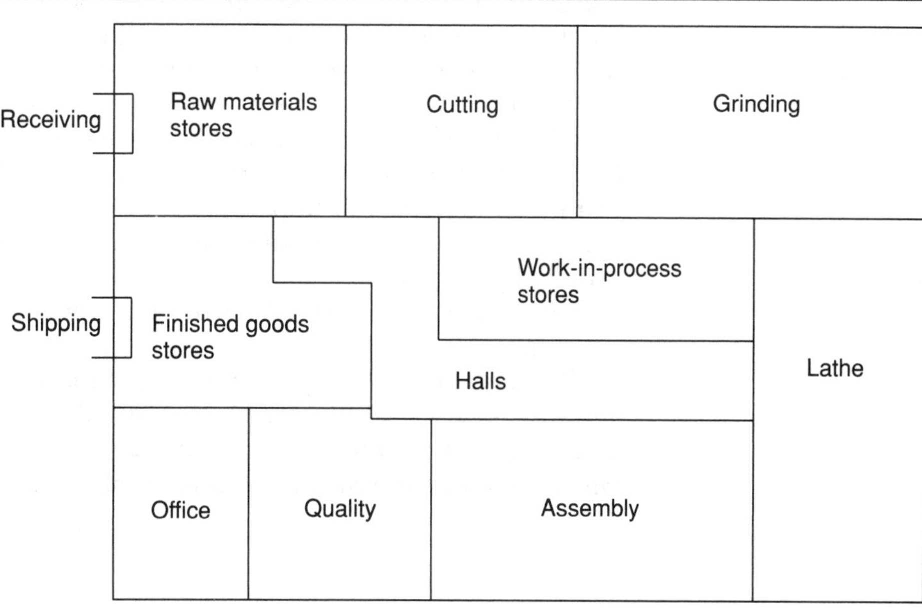

CHART 7.6 Product Layout

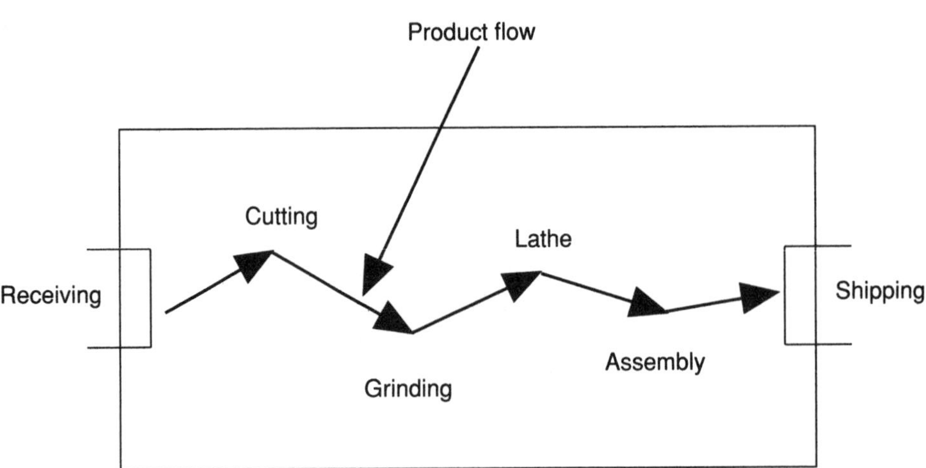

that you work on a product, and when you are done you hand it to the next person in the process. You have very little inventory on the line, but you may have employees or machines that are not being utilized efficiently. The chapter on shop floor control has a section on assembly line balancing that will help you minimize this waste.

Product layouts give us inventory movement efficiencies. Less inventory means less debt, which means fewer interest payments, which means the product can be produced cheaper. However, by achieving this level of inventory efficiency, we lose labor and machinery efficiency. We also lose flexibility because once a production line has been set up and all the machines are moved into place, modifications are difficult.

3. The third plant layout is called the project layout. In the project layout we have a product that is hard to move around the plant. For example, a mobile home or an airplane is built using a project layout. Materials, machinery, and labor are all brought to the place of manufacture. Some job shops follow this type of project layout strategy, in which the product specifies the plant layout.

The type of plant layout you use will probably vary between the functional and product layouts. This decision should be based on a trade-off between product variability (features, options, and functions) and inventory cost minimization. However, even in the functional layout, some parts of the product can be manufactured using the product layout if that part is extremely repetitive. By using the proper blend of factory layouts, capacities can be increased without major capital outlays.

We have now planned the aggregate production schedule. We are now ready to take this schedule and turn it into a detailed plan of production by product types within each family. This will be called a *master production schedule* and is discussed soon.

Distribution Requirements: Planning/Logistics/Warehousing

Distribution requirement planning is a system that incorporates not only the sales and shipping functions of an organization, but also the purchasing and receiving functions. It plans the trafficking and storage of goods that are coming out of or going into the plant. For a detailed discussion of distribution requirements, see Appendix 7.C.

Master Production Schedule

The master production schedule takes the aggregate production schedule and adds details. In the aggregate production schedule we have defined the production load by month for each family of parts. In the master production schedule we break these families down so that we know exactly what product we should be building and how many of each should be built.

The tool that helps us define the master production schedule is the *planning bill of materials* (which is totally different from the bill of materials that you'll be reading about). The planning bill of materials looks at the breakdown of the family of parts over the last year. We look at the total sales for each of these products and for their families over the last year. From the breakdown of the sales we are able to draw up a planning bill of materials for each family of parts based on gross sales as a percentage of total sales.

Using the planning bill of materials based on last year's sales we can now allocate the newly planned aggregate production schedule based on these same percentages. In this manner we can see the breakdown of the family into its individual components. We now have a master production schedule for each of the specific part numbers that we produce in our plant.

It may be helpful to calculate an *available to promise report* at this point. This report would reflect actual customer orders and show what products are still "available to be promised" to the customer. This report may be helpful if your orders are small, for example, just a few bikes at a time. For most of us, however, the available to promise calculations done at the forecast level are adequate.

At this point in our planning process, all customer orders have been planned through the forecast/aggregate production schedule/master production schedule process. All customer orders, the forecast, and the aggregate production schedule will be satisfied by the master production schedule. The products will be built and placed into finished goods inventory. Then they will be shipped to the customer from this inventory location. In the case of our example, some customer orders may be built earlier than they are needed because we have shifted some of the demand for production into earlier months. For details about how to develop a master production schedule, see Appendix 7.E.

Summary

With the master production schedule in hand, we are now ready to move forward with the operations management functions. The first of these functions is the production planning function that includes alternatives like inventory planning, economic order quantity (EOQ), and materials requirements planning (MRP). We start this process of looking at the operations management functions by going through a discussion of inventory. Then we move on to a discussion of other production planning areas.

APPENDIX 7.A: Aggregate Production Scheduling

The easiest way to demonstrate aggregate production scheduling is by example. We start by looking back at Chart 7.4, which listed the capacity limits on each of our resources. We also need to reflect back on Chart 7.G15, which listed the demands on capacity by resource, by month. Chart 7.A1 relists the information from Chart 7.4 and indicates where capacity has been exceeded as seen in Chart 7.G15.

Do not feel that the number of areas of capacity evaluation that I have selected is normal. In reality, I am on the high side. You should go through the process of checking all your capacity areas periodically using a process similar to the one I have done in this chapter to make sure you are focusing on the right capacity bottlenecks. As you will see later in this chapter, the only capacity constraints that are significant are the lathe machine time and the assembly labor time. If we solve these two, we've solved all the rest, because these two have the tightest constraints.

The coverages are calculated by dividing the capacity available by the capacity required. For example, for purchased parts, the capacity was 16,000 and the demand was 22,000.

$$\frac{16{,}000}{22{,}000} = 0.72727 = 72.7 \text{ percent}$$

Months 7, 8, and 12 are the only months with a capacity problem. We need to consider our options for handling this capacity problem. Numerous options exist but I will give you a few examples:

1. Cut back the sales in months 7, 8, and 12 to fit within the capacity limits.
2. Use an outside vendor to satisfy the capacity shortages.
3. Add a third shift to handle the needed capacity.
4. Use overtime to handle the capacity increase.
5. Shift the extra work into prior months where the capacity is not fully utilized.
6. Expand capacity with additional machinery and people.

CHART 7.A1 Capacity Comparison (Comparing Charts 7.G15 and 7.4)

	Monthly Capacities	Bottleneck
Materials		
Bar stock	No limit	None
Purchased parts	16,000 dollars	Month 12 is 68% covered over by $6,000
Sheet metal	No limit	None
Machinery		
Lathe	2,000 hours	Month 7 is 87% covered over by 300 hours Month 12 is 61% covered over by 1,300 hours
Drill press	5,000 hours	Month 12 is 78% covered over by 1,400 hours
Manpower		
Painting	250 hours	Month 12 is 71% covered over by 100 hours
Assembly	900 hours	Month 7 is 88% covered over by 125 hours Month 8 is 97% covered over by 25 hours Month 12 is 58% covered over by 650 hours
Welding	1,500 hours	Month 7 is 92% covered over by 133 hours Month 12 is 62% covered over by 917 hours
Grinding	600 hours	Month 7 is 97% covered over by 17 hours Month 12 is 64% covered over by 333 hours

What we need to do at this point is analyze each of the options to see which is the most feasible. The tool that does the overall comparison is called a *Make-buy decision analysis*. For make-buy decisions we need to determine the cost of each alternative and then compare these costs to decide which would be the cheapest. We now review each of the options listed and go through the process necessary to calculate these costs.

Cut Back Sales. To evaluate this option, we need to determine how much profit will be lost by losing the sales under consideration. To make this calculation, we need to determine a profit level for each of the products produced. Subtracting the product cost from the product selling price gives you the profit of the product. Chart 7.A2 lists the profits for each product in our example.

In considering month 12, assembly is the tightest constraint. The capacity for assembly is 900 hours and the demand on capacity is 1,550

CHART 7.A2 Profit Level of Each Product

	Profit Level ($20 Average)
Mountain bikes	
Economy	$10
Heavy duty	$20
Super lightweight	$30
Ten-speed bikes	
Men's	$10
Women's	$10
Tricycles (only one model)	$ 5

hours. This puts us 650 hours over capacity. By looking at the capacity evaluation sheets for all three product lines, we could reduce capacity by each of the methods listed in Chart 7.A3. There is no magic way to come up with these methods. You simply try a number of options and see which one works best. If you have a computer and linear programming software, you could do this process using that package. (Appendix 7.B shows how to formulate this problem as a linear programming model.)

Option 1 of Chart 7.A3 eliminated all the tricycles (the least profit) and just enough ten-speed bicycles (the second least profit) to bring the lathe hours in line with capacity. The loss for this option is $3,300 (1,500 + 1,800). In option 2 we eliminated all the ten-speed bicycles and just enough tricycles to cover the lathe capacity. The loss for this option was slightly less at $3,255. Option 3 dropped all the mountain bikes and just enough tricycles to cover the grinding. The loss for option 3 was $5,500. The least expensive option when analyzing month 12 is option 2.

Performing a similar analysis for month 7 results in reducing the ten-speed bikes by 75 and results in a loss of $750. Again, performing the same analysis for month 8 results in reducing tricycles by 17 and results in a loss of $85. The total loss incurred by dropping sales for months 7, 8, and 12 where demand exceeds capacity is $4,090 ($3,255 + $750 + $85).

Use an Outside Vendor. We would want to use the vendor to expand our capacity in those areas where we have a capacity shortage. Looking back on Chart 7.A1 we see the need for 300 additional hours of lathe in month 7 and 1,300 hours of lathe in month 12. We would call a vendor and ask how much these hours of capacity would cost us. We would do a similar process for the additional needed drill press hours, painting hours, etc. For purposes of our calculations here, let's assume that the total additional capacity would cost us about $50,000. Subtract the vendor costs from what it would have cost us to produce the product internally (estimated to be $40,000) and we get the cost of using outside sourcing at $10,000 (50,000 − 40,000).

CHART 7.A3 Product Mix Reductions to Reduce Month 12 Demand

1. Eliminate tricycles (profit loss of 300 × 5 = $1,500)
   Reduce purchased parts by $4,500 (need $1,500 more)
   Reduce lathe by 600 hours (need 700 more)
   Reduce drill press by 1,500 hours (sufficient)
   Reduce painting by 75 hours (need 25 more)
   Reduce assembly by 450 hours (need 200 more)
   Reduce welding by 600 hours (need 317 more)
   Reduce grinding by 300 hours (need 33 more)
   Eliminate 180 ten-speed bikes (60% of the bikes) (profit loss of 180 × 10 = $1,800)
   Reduce purchase parts by $4,500 (sufficient)
   Reduce lathe by 720 hours (sufficient)
   Reduce painting by 90 hours (sufficient)
   Reduce assembly by 360 hours (sufficient)
   Reduce welding by 540 hours (sufficient)
   Reduce grinding by 180 hours (sufficient)
2. Eliminate ten-speed bicycles (profit loss of 300 × 10 = $3,000)
   Reduce purchased parts by $7,500 (sufficient)
   Reduce lathe by 1,200 hours (need 100 more)
   Reduce drill press by 2,400 hours (sufficient)
   Reduce painting by 150 hours (sufficient)
   Reduce assembly by 600 hours (need 50 more)
   Reduce welding by 900 hours (need 17 more)
   Reduce grinding by 300 hours (need 33 more)
   Eliminate 51 tricycles (17% of the bikes) (profit loss of 51 × 5 = $255)
   Reduce lathe by 102 hours (sufficient)
   Reduce assembly by 77 hours (sufficient)
   Reduce welding by 102 hours (sufficient)
   Reduce grinding by 51 hours (sufficient)
3. Eliminate mountain bikes (profit loss of 250 × 20 = $5,000)
   Reduce purchased parts by $10,000 (sufficient)
   Reduce lathe by 1,500 hours (sufficient)
   Reduce drill press by 2,500 hours (sufficient)
   Reduce painting by 125 hours (sufficient)
   Reduce assembly by 500 hours (need 150 more)
   Reduce welding by 917 hours (sufficient)
   Reduce grinding by 333 hours (sufficient)
   Eliminate 100 tricycles (33% of the bikes) (profit loss of 100 × 5 = $500)
   Reduce assembly by 150 hours (sufficient)

Add a Third Shift. The real problem with adding a third shift is finding the work force that is willing to be hired for two months in the year. If we hired them permanently, then for the remainder of the year (10 months) this third shift would have no work to do so we would need to come up with additional product to work on. The cost for this option is extremely difficult to justify. Even if we did add the full shift, the capacity increase in month 12 would not be sufficient to cover the capacity demanded in welding and grinding. One shift of welding capacity is 750 hours per month (1,500/2 shifts = 750). We need 917 welding hours, which is 167 hours more than we would have available even with the third shift. One shift of grinding capacity is 300 hours (600/2 shifts = 300). We need 333 hours.

Overtime. Overtime at time and one-half may help; however, even if we worked the whole third shift in overtime we wouldn't be able to expand welding or grinding capacity enough to handle month 12. See the calculations for the "Add a Third Shift" option.

Shift the Extra Work into Prior Months. If we do the overload work in earlier months, when we have the excess capacity, then we have inventory storage costs. If we assume that it costs $1 per month to store a bicycle, and $0.30 per month to store a tricycle, we can estimate the cost of storage for those items produced earlier. To do this, look back at Charts 7.A1 and 7.G15. From Chart 7.A1 we see what our shortages are. Chart 7.A4 relists these shortages and indicates in which months these shortages can be covered. All the shortages in Chart 7.A4 can be handled in the previous month except in the lathe and grinding departments. These are the departments that will cause the most inventory shift because of their shortage of capacity. Looking back on Chart 7.A3, option 1, we shifted all the tricycles and 180 ten speeds for month 12. We will shift the tricycles the furthest because they cost the least to store. We can shift the 180 ten speeds and 143 tricycles to month 11 (based on assembly capacity limits).

CHART 7.A4 Demand Coverage by Working Early (Comparing Charts 7.G15 and 7.A1)

Materials
- Purchased parts—month 12 is short by $6,000
  - Month 11 handles this shortage

Machinery
- Lathe—month 7 is short by 300 hours
  - Month 6 handles 100 hours
  - Month 5 handles the rest of the shortage
  - Month 12 is short by 1,300 hours
    - Month 11 handles 1,250 hours
    - Month 10 handles the rest of the shortage
- Drill press—month 12 is short by 1,400 hours
  - Month 11 handles this shortage

Manpower
- Painting—month 12 is short by 100 hours
  - Month 11 handles this shortage
- Assembly—month 7 is short by 125 hours
  - Month 6 handles 25 hours (the other 25 hours capacity went to month 8)
  - Month 5 handles the rest of the shortage
  - Month 8 is short by 25 hours
    - Month 6 handles this shortage
  - Month 12 is short by 650 hours
    - Month 11 handles 575 hours
    - Month 10 handles the rest of the shortage
- Welding—month 7 is short by 133 hours
  - Month 6 handles this shortage
  - Month 12 is short by 917 hours
    - Month 11 handles this shortage
- Grinding—month 7 is short by 17 hours
  - Month 6 handles this shortage
  - Month 12 is short by 333 hours
    - Month 11 handles this shortage

Calculation: 180 ten speeds take 180 × 2 = 360 assembly hours. Month 11 has 900 capacity hours minus 325 currently used hours (see Chart 7.G15) minus 360 ten-speed bike hours equals 215 remaining capacity hours (900 − 325 − 360 = 215). These 215 remaining capacity hours can handle 143 tricycles (215/1.5 = 143), which are also moved to month 11.

From our initial 650 shortage hours in assembly (from Chart 7.A1) minus the 360 used hours for ten-speed bikes minus the 215 hours used for tricycles equals 75 assembly hours short (650 − 360 − 215 = 75). This leaves 50 tricycles to be built in month 10 (75/1.5 = 50). (Note that this is the second month of shift.) But this shift still left lathe hours over capacity by approximately the amount of lathe hours in tricycles, so the remainder of the tricycles were shifted to month 10 as well. This left months 10, 11, and 12 within capacity in all areas.

Doing the same thing for the overage in month 8, we shift 17 tricycles to month 6 (because month 7 is also over capacity) using an additional 25.5 hours of capacity during month 6 but bringing month 8's assembly hours within capacity. We also shift 16 tricycles from month 7 to month 6 using the last remaining 24.5 hours of capacity in month 6 assembly capacity. Based on assembly capacity, another 68 tricycles should have been shifted from month 7 to month 5. However, based on lathe capacity hours, the entire remaining 117 units of tricycles needed shifting. By shifting these units to month 5 (a second month of shift), we ended up with months 6, 7, and 8 being within capacity in all areas. However, month 5 was now over capacity in assembly hours and 34 tricycles had to be shifted back even one more month to month 4 (a third month of shift). At this point all months were within capacity in all categories. (Note that this entire process is formulated as a linear programming model in Appendix 7.B.)

Realistically, what we are doing is playing a little game. We plug in the forecast numbers and determine which areas exceed capacity. Then we shift just enough of our cheapest stored product and see if everything is now within capacity. If something else is out of capacity, shift a little more until everybody is happy. Keep doing this until all the months are within capacity. If you can't get all months within capacity, then your plant simply doesn't have enough capacity and you have to look at one of the other capacity modification options. For our example, Chart 7.A5 is a recalculation of Chart 7.G16 showing all the adjustments described here and showing how all capacities are met.

The cost of carrying inventory is:

Month 12:
- 180 ten speeds × $1 × 1 month = 180.00
- 143 tricycles × $.30 × 1 month = 42.90
- 157 tricycles × $.30 × 2 months = 94.20

Month 8:
- 17 tricycles × $.30 × 2 months = 10.20

Month 7:
- 16 tricycles × $.30 × 1 month = 4.80
- 100 tricycles × $.30 × 2 months = 60.00
- 34 tricycles × $.30 × 3 months = 30.60

Total Cost of Inventory Storage = $422.70

CHART 7.A5 Forecast Adjusted to Satisfy Rough-Cut Capacity

	A B C	D	E	F	G	H	I	J	K	L	M	N	O	P	Q
2										Family—Mountain Bikes					
4		Resource	Forecast Quantity												
5		Quantity	*Month*	1	2	3	4	5	6	7	8	9	10	11	12
6			*Forecast*	100	50	50	100	100	150	200	150	50	50	75	250
7	Materials														
8	Bar stock	36.7		3670	1835	1835	3670	3670	5505	7340	5505	1835	1835	2752.5	9175
9	Purchased parts	40		4000	2000	2000	4000	4000	6000	8000	6000	2000	2000	3000	10000
10	Sheet metal	19		1900	950	950	1900	1900	2850	3800	2850	950	950	1425	4750
11	Machinery														
12	Lathe	6		600	300	300	600	600	900	1200	900	300	300	450	1500
13	Drill press	10		1000	500	500	1000	1000	1500	2000	1500	500	500	750	2500
14	Manpower (labor)														
15	Painting	.5		50	25	25	50	50	75	100	75	25	25	37.5	125
16	Assembly	2		200	100	100	200	200	300	400	300	100	100	150	500
17	Welding	3.6667		366.67	183.335	183.335	366.67	366.67	550.005	733.34	550.005	183.335	183.335	275.0025	916.675
18	Grinding	1.3333		133.33	66.665	66.665	133.33	133.33	199.995	266.66	199.995	66.665	66.665	99.9975	333.325
22										Family—Ten-Speed Bikes					
24		Resource	Forecast Quantity												
25		Quantity	*Month*	1	2	3	4	5	6	7	8	9	10	11	12
26			*Forecast*	200	50	50	100	200	200	200	200	100	50	230	120
27	Materials														
28	Bar stock	22.5		4500	1125	1125	2250	4500	4500	4500	4500	2250	1125	5175	2700
29	Purchased parts	25		5000	1250	1250	2500	5000	5000	5000	5000	2500	1250	5750	3000
30	Sheet metal	20		4000	1000	1000	2000	4000	4000	4000	4000	2000	1000	4600	2400
31	Machinery														
32	Lathe	4		800	200	200	400	800	800	800	800	400	200	920	480
33	Drill press	8		1600	400	400	800	1600	1600	1600	1600	800	400	1840	960
34	Manpower (labor)														
35	Painting	.5		100	25	25	50	100	100	100	100	50	25	115	60
36	Assembly	2		400	100	100	200	400	400	400	400	200	100	460	240
37	Welding	3		600	150	150	300	600	600	600	600	300	150	690	360
38	Grinding	1		200	50	50	100	200	200	200	200	100	50	230	120

Family—Tricycles

	Resource Quantity	Forecast Quantity											
		Month	1	2	3	4	5	6	7	8	9	10	11	12
		Forecast	150	50	75	134	200	133	0	133	50	207	193	0
Materials														
Bar stock	10		1500	500	750	1340	2000	1330	0	1330	500	2070	1930	0
Purchased parts	15		2250	750	1125	2010	3000	1995	0	1995	750	3105	2895	0
Sheet metal	10		1500	500	750	1340	2000	1330	0	1330	500	2070	1930	0
Machinery														
Lathe	2		300	100	150	268	400	266	0	266	100	414	386	0
Drill press	5		750	250	375	670	1000	665	0	665	250	1035	965	0
Manpower (labor)														
Painting	.25		37.5	12.5	18.75	33.5	50	33.25	0	33.25	12.5	51.75	48.25	0
Assembly	1.5		225	75	112.5	201	300	199.5	0	199.5	75	310.5	289.5	0
Welding	2		300	100	150	268	400	266	0	266	100	414	386	0
Grinding	1		150	50	75	134	200	133	0	133	50	207	193	0

Consolidated

	Total Resources	Forecast Quantity											
		Month	1	2	3	4	5	6	7	8	9	10	11	12
Materials														
Bar stock	100127.5		9670	3460	3710	7260	10170	11335	11840	11335	4585	5030	9857.5	11875
Purchased parts	115375		11250	4000	4375	8510	12000	12995	13000	12995	5250	6355	11645	13000
Sheet metal	72425		7400	2450	2700	5240	7900	8180	7800	8180	3450	4020	7955	7150
Machinery														
Lathe	17400		1700	600	650	1268	1800	1966	2000	1966	800	914	1756	1980
Drill press	33475		3350	1150	1275	2470	3600	3765	3600	3765	1550	1935	3555	3460
Manpower (labor)														
Painting	1843.75		187.5	62.5	68.75	133.5	200	208.25	200	208.25	87.5	101.75	200.75	185
Assembly	8037.5		825	275	312.5	601	900	899.5	800	899.5	375	510.5	899.5	740
Welding	12608.38		1266.67	433.335	483.335	934.67	1366.67	1416.005	1333.34	1416.005	583.335	747.335	1351.003	1276.675
Grinding	4791.623		483.33	166.665	191.665	367.33	533.33	532.995	466.66	532.995	216.665	323.665	522.9975	453.325

Expand Capacity with Additional Machinery and People. For this option we need to determine if we have enough room in our plant to add additional equipment and people. If we don't, then we need to consider expanding the size of the facility. However, adding machinery to the existing shifts would have the same effect as adding a third shift or as adding overtime. What do we do with the machinery and employees during the remaining 10 months of the year when we would have had sufficient capacity?

To increase capacity sufficiently, we would need lathes, drill presses, painting booths, assembly lines, welding equipment, etc. In effect, we would need about a 50 percent plant size increase and that would be difficult to justify in our example. In your case, perhaps one or two machines would do the job and it might be a reasonable alternative.

Review of the Options

Once again I want to stress that evaluating capacity in as many areas as I have done is only done periodically, every couple of years. Most of the resource capacity areas do very little to help in developing a balance between demand and capacity. In the example we are working on here, lathe machine hours and assembly labor hours are the only capacity limitations that have any significant effect on the final schedule. Let's look back at the six options we have considered using make-buy decision analysis to see which one suits us the best.

1. Cutting back the sales in months 7, 8, and 12 to fit within the capacity limits would cost $4,090.
2. Using an outside vendor to satisfy the capacity shortages would cost about $10,000.
3. Adding a third shift to handle the needed capacity would not work because sufficient capacity could not be generated.
4. Using overtime to handle the capacity increase would not work because sufficient capacity could not be generated.
5. Shifting the extra work into prior months where the capacity is not fully utilized would cost $422.70 in inventory storage costs.
6. Expanding capacity with additional machinery and people would require a major plant expansion and be ineffective.

Before we select the best aggregate production schedule, I would like to draw your attention to the difference in the approaches taken by each of these examples. If, for example, our forecast and capacity came out to be similar to the one in Chart 7.A6, we could build an aggregate production schedule several different ways. For example, we could follow a strategy called the *Chase* aggregate planning strategy where the aggregate plan chases the forecast. In this case, the forecast is the same as the aggregate production schedule. Options 2, 3, 4, and 6 are all different methods of following the chase strategy. There are plants, like the canning of agricultural products, that must run on a chase strategy.

CHART 7.A6 Forecast and Capacity

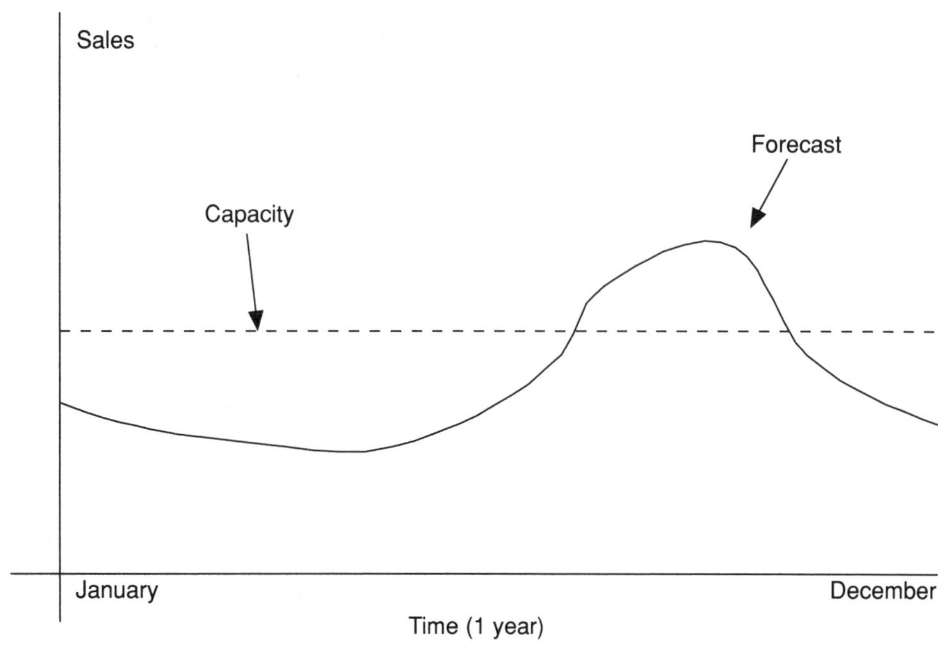

CHART 7.A7 Compromise Strategy

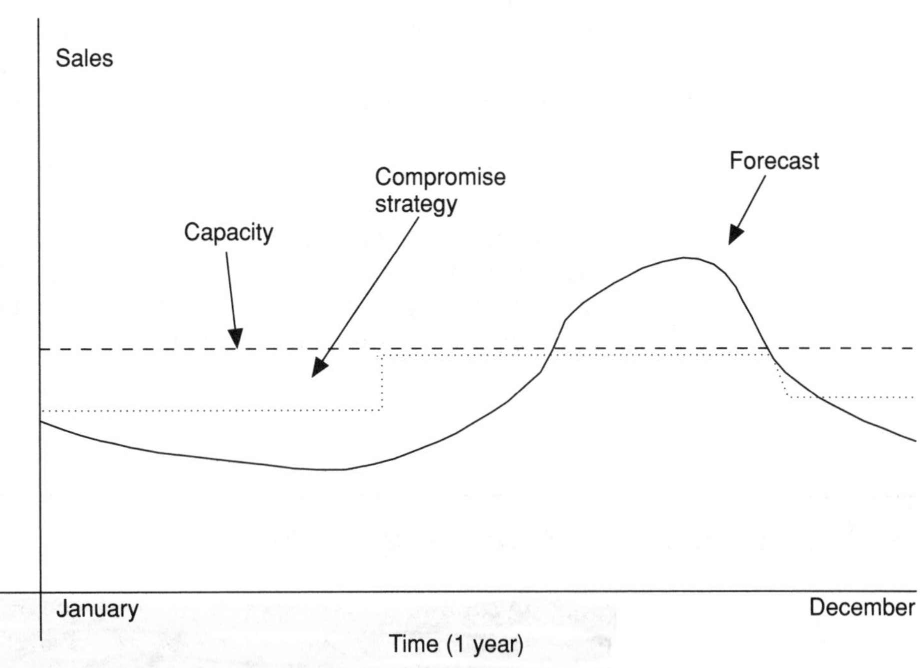

A second method of planning capacity is called the *Levelized* aggregate planning philosophy. In this case we run the plant at the capacity level equal to what the forecast wants. Demand has to match production rather than production matching demand. Option 1 followed a levelized philosophy.

CHART 7.A8 Aggregate Production Schedule

Month	Mountain Bikes	Ten-speed Bikes	Tricycles
1	100	200	150
2	50	50	50
3	50	50	75
4	100	100	134
5	100	200	200
6	150	200	133
7	200	200	0
8	150	200	133
9	50	100	50
10	50	50	207
11	75	230	193
12	250	120	0

A third aggregate planning method is called the *compromise* method. In this technique we try to get the best of all worlds. We modify capacity slightly, but not as much as required by the forecast. We build up some inventory, but not as much as required by a levelized production planning philosophy. There are many different ways that the production load can be adjusted to stay within capacity and still meet the forecast. Chart 7.A7 shows how one of these compromise plans might look. Option 5 in our example is a compromise plan.

We have now considered six different ways of developing an aggregate production schedule. Having used make-buy decision analysis, the most cost advantageous alternative for our example has been demonstrated to be option 5. We build our aggregate production schedule by starting with the forecast and adjusting it based on the changes recommended by option 5, making sure that our customer orders are not adversely affected.

Chart 7.A8 is our newly selected aggregate production schedule. All forecast demands are met and all capacity limitations are met. Customer orders are satisfied even though in some cases the product may be completed earlier than needed.

APPENDIX 7.B: Linear Programming

Linear programming is a mathematical tool that allows us to maximize or minimize some benefit. In the example of this chapter we have two problems; we want to maximize profit and we want to minimize inventory storage time. Numerous linear programming software packages are available, but all of them receive their input similarly. First, let's lay out the profit maximization problem. Looking at Chart 7.A2 we see the profit level for each family of product. We set up an equation that we want to maximize using these profit levels. In this case the objective function would be:

Maximize 20 MB + 10 TS + 5 TR

Where MB = the number of mountain bikes that should be produced each month to maximize profits,

TS = the number of ten-speed bikes that should be produced, and

TR = the number of tricycles that should be produced.

20, 10, and 5 are the average profit earned by the sale of one unit of each item.

The constraints we have are the limits on capacity. From Chart 7.4 we know our capacity limits, and from Chart 7.G11 we know how much capacity each of the families of bikes utilizes. For materials bar stock and sheet metal, there is no limitation, so we do not need to build them into the model. For purchased parts, however, there is a $16,000 limit. Mountain bikes use $40 of purchased parts per bike, ten-speed bikes use $25 per bike, and tricycles use $15 per bike. This information is put into a constraint in the form:

$$40\text{ MB} + 25\text{ TS} + 15\text{ TR} \leq 16{,}000$$

This equation says that for every mountain bike we use $40, $25 per ten speed, and $15 per tricycle, with a cap on spending at $16,000. We work up similar constraints for all the resources that have a limit. The final formulation of the problem would look like:

Objective function:

Maximize 20 MB + 10 TS + 5 TR

Constraints:

$$\begin{array}{rcrcrcr}
40\text{ MB} & + & 25\text{ TS} & + & 15\text{ TR} & \leq & 16{,}000 \\
6\text{ MB} & + & 4\text{ TS} & + & 2\text{ TR} & \leq & 2{,}000 \\
10\text{ MB} & + & 8\text{ TS} & + & 5\text{ TR} & \leq & 5{,}000 \\
0.5\text{ MB} & + & 0.5\text{ TS} & + & 0.25\text{ TR} & \leq & 16{,}000 \\
2\text{ MB} & + & 2\text{ TS} & + & 1.5\text{ TR} & \leq & 2{,}000 \\
3.7\text{ MB} & + & 3\text{ TS} & + & 2\text{ TR} & \leq & 5{,}000 \\
1.3\text{ MB} & + & 1\text{ TS} & + & 1\text{ TR} & \leq & 5{,}000
\end{array}$$

When we plug this information into a linear programming model, we assume that we can utilize all the capacity and that whatever we produce can be sold. The forecast has not come into play at this point. We are just trying to identify the product mix that will maximize our profitability. For this problem, the maximum monthly profit level comes out to be that we should produce 333.33 mountain bikes each month and nothing else. Of course, we probably will not be able to sell that many mountain bikes and we look at the forecast to get a more realistic feel for how we should produce parts. Using the forecast we would then put a priority on mountain bikes, building as many of them as possible. Then we would use the remaining capacity to build ten-speed bikes and tricycles.

The procedure under option 5 (Appendix 7.A), shifting the extra work into prior months, can also be formulated in a linear programming model. In this case we are using the information from the forecast, which specifies monthly demand, and we attempt to minimize the inventory holding cost for products that need to be built early. The objective function would take the form:

Minimize 1 DMB1 + 1 DMB2 + 1 DMB3 + 1 DMB4 + 1 DMB5 + 1 DMB6 + 1 DMB7 + 1 DMB8 + 1 DMB9 + 1 DMB10 + 1 DMB11 + 1 DMB12 + 1 DTS1 + 1 DTS2 + 1 DTS3 + 1 DTS4 + 1 DTS5 + 1 DTS6 + 1 DTS7 + 1 DTS8 + 1 DTS9 + 1 DTS10 + 1 DTS11 + 1 DTS12 + 0.3 DTR1 + 0.3 DTR2 + 0.3 DTR3 + 0.3 DTR4 + 0.3 DTR5 + 0.3 DTR6 + 0.3 DTR7 + 0.3 DTR8 + 0.3 DTR9 + 0.3 DTR10 + 0.3 DTR11 + 0.3 DTR12

Where DMB12 = the quantity of units of production of mountain bikes that had to be shifted from month 12 to month 11. Each of the "D" variables denotes a shift in inventory; the next two letters denote the product family being shifted; and the numbers denote the month.

The numbers 1 and 0.3 denote the cost of carrying that product in inventory for one month as defined in Appendix 7.A under option 5.

Next we need to set up the constraints. The first set of constraints is similar to those in the previous problem. For example, for the first month of the lathe department:

6 MB1 + 4 TS1 + 2 TR1 ≤ 2,000

Where MB1 is the number of mountain bikes produced in month 1, etc.

The 6 is the number of units of lathe time required by each mountain bike.

The 2,000 is the monthly capacity limit of the Lathe Department.

This process needs to be repeated for all months, for all constrained departments. I'm only going to make constraints for the lathe and assembly departments because we know these to be the most tightly constrained, but it wouldn't hurt to do it for all departments just to make sure. The constraints for the lathe and assembly departments would be:

6 MB1 + 4 TS1 + 2 TR1 ≤ 2,000
6 MB2 + 4 TS2 + 2 TR2 ≤ 2,000
. . .
6 MB11 + 4 TS11 + 2 TR11 ≤ 2,000
6 MB12 + 4 TS12 + 2 TR12 ≤ 2,000
2 MB1 + 2 TS1 + 1.5 TR1 ≤ 900
2 MB2 + 2 TS2 + 1.5 TR2 ≤ 900
. . .
2 MB11 + 2 TS11 + 1.5 TR11 ≤ 900
2 MB12 + 2 TS12 + 1.5 TR12 ≤ 900

The next constraints require a little explaining. I will start by showing you the constraint, then we can discuss it. The constraint is:

MB11 + DMB11 − DMB12 = 75

DMB12 is the amount of production shifted from month 12 into month 11. MB11 is the total amount that ends up in month 11. DMB11 is the amount shifted out of month 11 into month 10 and 75 is the forecast for month 11. Rewriting the constraint into the following form is helpful:

MB11 + DMB11 = DMB12 + 75

From this form of the equation, we see that what we kept in month 11 (MB11) plus what is shifted to month 10 (DMB11) has to equal what was shifted into month 11 from month 12 (DMB12) plus the forecast for month 11 (75). We need equations like this for each month. These constraints would look like:

MB1 + DMB1 − DMB2 = 100
MB2 + DMB2 − DMB3 = 50
. . .
MB10 + DMB10 − DMB11 = 50
MB11 + DMB11 − DMB12 = 75
MB12 + DMB12 = 250

A similar set of constraints needs to be set up for the ten-speed bikes and the tricycles. The final formulation of the model is shown in Chart 7.B1. The solution you arrive at with this model depends on which family of variables comes first. Since mountain bikes and ten-speed bikes are both weighted with $1 per month inventory carrying costs, they are equally eligible to be shifted. Therefore, one of two possible solutions is possible, as can be seen in Chart 7.B2. The solution in Chart 7.B2 stressing the ten-speed bikes is almost identical to the solution we arrived at manually (compare with Chart 7.A8).

Linear programming is a powerful tool and can also be used to solve other operations management problems. As we come across some, I will point them out to you.

CHART 7.B1 Inventory Movement Minimization Linear Programming Model

Objective Function

Minimize 1 DMB1 + 1 DMB2 + 1 DMB3 + 1 DMB4 + 1 DMB5 + 1 DMB6 + 1 DMB7 + 1 DMB8 + 1 DMB9 + 1 DMB10 + 1 DMB11 + 1 DMB12 + 1 DTS1 + 1 DTS2 + 1 DTS3 + 1 DTS4 + 1 DTS5 + 1 DTS6 + 1 DTS7 + 1 DTS8 + 1 DTS9 + 1 DTS10 + 1 DTS11 + 1 DTS12 + .3 DTR1 + .3 DTR2 + .3 DTR3 + .3 DTR4 + .3 DTR5 + .3 DTR6 + .3 DTR7 + .3 DTR8 + .3 DTR9 + .3 DTR10 + .3 DTR11 + .3 DTR12

Constraints

6 MB1 + 4 TS1 + 2 TR1 ≤ 2,000
6 MB2 + 4 TS2 + 2 TR2 ≤ 2,000
6 MB3 + 4 TS3 + 2 TR3 ≤ 2,000
6 MB4 + 4 TS4 + 2 TR4 ≤ 2,000
6 MB5 + 4 TS5 + 2 TR5 ≤ 2,000
6 MB6 + 4 TS6 + 2 TR6 ≤ 2,000
6 MB7 + 4 TS7 + 2 TR7 ≤ 2,000
6 MB8 + 4 TS8 + 2 TR8 ≤ 2,000
6 MB9 + 4 TS9 + 2 TR9 ≤ 2,000
6 MB10 + 4 TS10 + 2 TR10 ≤ 2,000
6 MB11 + 4 TS11 + 2 TR11 ≤ 2,000
6 MB12 + 4 TS12 + 2 TR12 ≤ 2,000
2 MB1 + 2 TS1 + 1.5 TR1 ≤ 900
2 MB2 + 2 TS2 + 1.5 TR2 ≤ 900
2 MB3 + 2 TS3 + 1.5 TR3 ≤ 900
2 MB4 + 2 TS4 + 1.5 TR4 ≤ 900
2 MB5 + 2 TS5 + 1.5 TR5 ≤ 900
2 MB6 + 2 TS6 + 1.5 TR6 ≤ 900
2 MB7 + 2 TS7 + 1.5 TR7 ≤ 900
2 MB8 + 2 TS8 + 1.5 TR8 ≤ 900
2 MB9 + 2 TS9 + 1.5 TR9 ≤ 900
2 MB10 + 2 TS10 + 1.5 TR10 ≤ 900
2 MB11 + 2 TS11 + 1.5 TR11 ≤ 900
2 MB12 + 2 TS12 + 1.5 TR12 ≤ 900
MB1 + DMB1 − DMB2 = 100
MB2 + DMB2 − DMB3 = 50
MB3 + DMB3 − DMB4 = 50
MB4 + DMB4 − DMB5 = 100
MB5 + DMB5 − DMB6 = 100
MB6 + DMB6 − DMB7 = 150
MB7 + DMB7 − DMB8 = 200
MB8 + DMB8 − DMB9 = 150
MB9 + DMB9 − DMB10 = 50
MB10 + DMB10 − DMB11 = 50
MB11 + DMB11 − DMB12 = 75
MB12 + DMB12 = 250
TS1 + DTS1 − DTS2 = 200
TS2 + DTS2 − DTS3 = 50
TS3 + DTS3 − DTS4 = 50
TS4 + DTS4 − DTS5 = 100
TS5 + DTS5 − DTS6 = 200
TS6 + DTS6 − DTS7 = 200
TS7 + DTS7 − DTS8 = 200
TS8 + DTS8 − DTS9 = 200
TS9 + DTS9 − DTS10 = 100
TS10 + DTS10 − DTS11 = 50
TS11 + DTS11 − DTS12 = 50
TS12 + DTS12 = 300
TR1 + DTR1 − DTR2 = 150
TR2 + DTR2 − DTR3 = 50
TR3 + DTR3 − DTR4 = 75
TR4 + DTR4 − DTR5 = 100
TR5 + DTR5 − DTR6 = 100
TR6 + DTR6 − DTR7 = 100
TR7 + DTR7 − DTR8 = 150
TR8 + DTR8 − DTR9 = 150
TR9 + DTR9 − DTR10 = 50
TR10 + DTR10 − DTR11 = 50
TR11 + DTR11 − DTR12 = 50
TR12 + DTR12 = 300

CHART 7.B2 Two Solutions to the Inventory Movement Minimization Linear Programming Model

Variables	Stressing Mountain Bikes	Stressing Ten-speed Bikes
MB1	100	100
MB2	50	50
MB3	50	50
MB4	100	100
MB5	110	100
MB6	160	150
MB7	180	200
MB8	150	150
MB9	50	50
MB10	50	50
MB11	191.7	75
MB12	133.3	250
TS1	200	200
TS2	50	50
TS3	50	50
TS4	100	100
TS5	200	200
TS6	200	200
TS7	200	200
TS8	200	200
TS9	100	100
TS10	50	50
TS11	50	225
TS12	300	125
TR1	150	150
TR2	50	50
TR3	75	75
TR4	100	133.3
TR5	186.7	200
TR6	120	133.3
TR7	60	0
TR8	133.3	133.3
TR9	50	50
TR10	50	200
TR11	50	200
TR12	0	0

APPENDIX 7.C: Distribution Requirements: Planning/Logistics/Warehousing

I'm not going to pretend that in one short chapter I can possibly cover the entire field of distribution, logistics, and warehousing. But my focus in this book is on the small- to medium-sized discrete manufacturer. For them, a sophisticated system would be extreme overkill. So what I will present in this chapter are some of the basics. These basics can be expanded to make them as complex as you desire.

Distribution requirements planning (DRP) is a system that incorporates not only the sales and shipping functions of an organization, but also the purchasing and receiving functions. It plans the trafficking and storage of goods that are coming out of or going into the plant. Inventory planning and control will be covered in detail in Chapters 8 and 9 so I will not go into detail about that aspect at this point. However, the added dimension that DRP adds to inventory planning and control is that the same item is stored in a multitude of locations. The inventory control system would need to track where the inventory is located, not just how much. The inventory ledger card talked about in Chapter 9 would need to add a column that indicates location. Some organizations go so far as to make separate cards for each item in each location.

Product Sales and Shipping

As an example, let's walk through what happens when a product is sold. If the sold item is a finished product sitting in finished goods inventory, it can be shipped from inventory. If it needs to be produced, then we follow the procedure of Appendix 7.G—customer order processing. Then when the product has been completed and turned into finished goods inventory, we follow the same procedure as an item shipped from inventory. These are the steps:

1. The customer order (Chart 7.G3) comes in and we generate a picking list (see Chart 7.C1). This picking list is a list of what items need to be picked from inventory in order to satisfy the customer order. Often, the order for a particular part also requires the shipment of an instruction manual and some spare parts. These are not included in the customer order but are included as separate items on the picking list.

2. The picking list goes to the finished goods inventory department and the product is pulled. Shortages are reported for backordering. (See Appendix 7.G on customer order processing to see how backorders are handled.)

3. The product, picking list, and a copy of the customer order used as the shipping order are sent to packaging where they are prepared for shipment. Any special shipping instructions are noted at this time.

4. The product is shipped. If we are using an external carrier, the distribution problem becomes the carrier's problem. If we are using our

CHART 7.C1 Pick List

Customer number ____________ Order date ___/___/___
Shipping instructions ____________ Order number ____________
Customer name/address ____________
Ship to ____________

Product #	Product Description	Order Quantity	Location	Date Shipped	Quantity Shipped

Due date ___/___/___

own trucks, or if we rent a trucking service, we need to plan the routing so that the time spent and miles traveled will be minimized. If we also pick up our own raw materials (backhauls), the shipment scheduling becomes intertwined with the pickup schedule. This scheduling process will be discussed in the next section on "Routing/Transportation Models."

5. The shipping document is filled out with date shipped and carrier information. One copy is sent along with the materials. The other copy is returned to the Order Department so that they know the product was shipped. Then the order and shipping information is forwarded to sales and accounting for sales reporting (Appendix 7.G), carrier reporting (see the end of this appendix), and accounts receivable collections (see Appendix 7.G and Chart 7.G4).

6. A performance report is created detailing the results of the freight/carrier process. This is a process similar to the sales analysis process already discussed near the end of Appendix 7.G (see Charts 7.G18, 7.G19, and 7.G20). In this report we collect data on the timeliness and quality of the shipment process so that it can be improved on if necessary. Freight/carrier analysis is discussed near the end of this chapter.

Routing/Transportation Models

The objective of routing and transportation models is to minimize the travel time (cost) of shipments. Some very complex modeling techniques exist to calculate shipments from multiple plant locations where the same products are produced. These models are beyond what we need for the small- to medium-sized manufacturer with one plant location. However, shipments from a single location to multiple customers with multiple backhauls (pickups from vendors) do occur often. We will cover these types of calculations in detail in the following seven sections:

1. Distribution where each customer shipment requires full load trips
2. Distribution where there are customers and backhauls but each is a full load trip
3. Distribution where multiple customers are serviced during the same trip
4. Distribution with multiple customers and multiple backhauls per trip
5. Mixtures of loads to customers
6. Sectoring
7. Cost or mile optimization

Appendix 7.D shows the linear programming-integer programming (LP-IP) formulations of these problems. See Appendix 7.B for additional clarification about linear programming.

Distribution: Full Load Trips

These problems are best demonstrated with examples. Chart 7.C2 will be used to show the relationship of our plant to five different customers and three different vendors. Chart 7.C3 is a mileage matrix for each of these locations.

For this initial example, we are assuming that we only service customers and that we have no vendor pickups. Each load taken to each customer is a full load and requires a special trip to do. The scheduling of this situation is fairly simple. If there is no capacity problem and you can handle all deliveries, do it. If there is a capacity problem and some of the shipments will need to be made by other carriers, analyze the pricing method of the carrier. If it is a flat-rate carrier, like the post office, have them deliver the farthest shipments. If the carrier rate is by mileage, you deliver the long ones and have the carrier deliver the short trips that are beyond your capacity.

Distribution: Backhauls and Full Load Trips

We will work through a couple of example problems so that you will be able to get a feel for the analysis process. In Chart 7.C4 we have a list of customer deliveries and vendor pickups (backhauls) that need to be made over the next couple of days. The objective is to minimize the total miles driven.

In Example 2.1, I will walk you through the analysis so that you can see how this situation would be solved. Since each trip is a separate full load, we know that there will need to be 14 trips to customers and 10 trips to vendors. Every time we send a truck out, we want that truck to come back loaded with vendor goods, if possible. This should be possible

CHART 7.C2 Routing Map

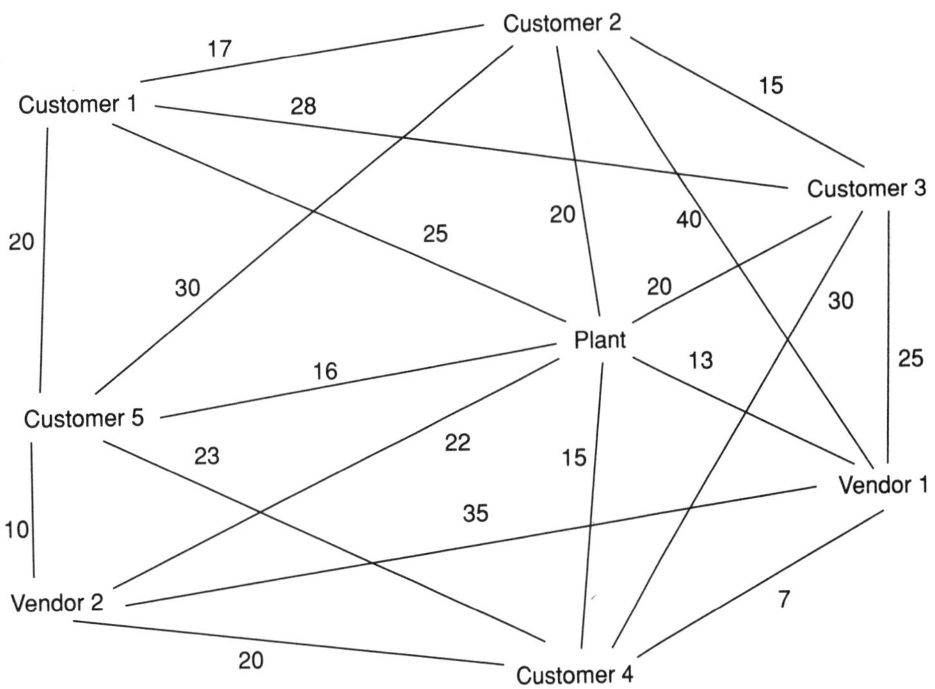

CHART 7.C3 Customer/Vendor Mileage Matrix

	H	C1	C2	C3	C4	C5	V1	V2
Home (H)	0							
Customer 1 (C1)	25	0						
Customer 2 (C2)	20	17	0					
Customer 3 (C3)	20	28	15	0				
Customer 4 (C4)	15	40	35	30	0			
Customer 5 (C5)	16	20	30	36	23	0		
Vendor 1 (V1)	13	38	40	25	7	29	0	
Vendor 2 (V2)	22	30	40	42	20	10	35	0

CHART 7.C4 Trips Required for Example 2

Example 2.1
Customer 1—3 trips
Customer 2—6 trips
Customer 3—1 trip
Customer 4—2 trips
Customer 5—2 trips
Vendor 1 —4 trips
Vendor 2 —6 trips

Example 2.2
Customer 1—2 trips
Customer 2—0 trips
Customer 3—4 trips
Customer 4—1 trip
Customer 5—1 trip
Vendor 1 —4 trips
Vendor 2 —6 trips

10 times. What we want to do is minimize the trip miles out to a customer, over to a vendor, and back to the plant. Vendor 1 is closest to Customer 3 and Customer 4. A trip to Customer 3, then Vendor 1, then back to the plant would be 58 miles. Customer 4, then Vendor 1, would be 35 miles, etc. Following is a list of these options:

Customer 1—Vendor 1 has us going back by the plant
Customer 2—Vendor 1 = 73 miles
Customer 3—Vendor 1 = 58 miles
Customer 4—Vendor 1 = 35 miles
Customer 5—Vendor 1 has us going back by the plant
Customer 1—Vendor 2 = 77 miles
Customer 2—Vendor 2 = 82 miles
Customer 3—Vendor 2 has us going back by the plant
Customer 4—Vendor 2 = 57 miles
Customer 5—Vendor 2 = 48 miles

Next, starting with the shortest, let's start allocating out the trips. The procedure would follow:

Customer 4—Vendor 1—2 trips—Satisfies all of Customer 4 and half of Vendor 1.

Customer 5—Vendor 2—2 trips—Satisfies Customer 5 and one third of Vendor 2.

Customer 4—Vendor 2 is skipped because Customer 4 is already satisfied.

Customer 3—Vendor 1—1 trip—Satisfies Customer 3 but still leaves us one short on Vendor 1.

Customer 2—Vendor 1—1 trip—Satisfies Vendor 1 but still leaves Customer 5 short by five.

Customer 1—Vendor 2—3 trips—Satisfies Customer 1 but still leaves Vendor 2 one short.

Customer 2—Vendor 2—1 trip—Finishes requirements for Vendor 2 and only leaves Customer 2 in need of four additional shipments.

Customer 2—4 trips—Satisfies all the deliveries.

Using the same procedure, we will now solve Example 2.2. In this case we have more vendor pickups than we have customer shipments. The process would be to again look at the shortest combined shipment first:

Customer 4—Vendor 1—1 trip—Satisfies all of Customer 4 and part of Vendor 1.

Customer 5—Vendor 2—1 trip—Satisfies Customer 5 and part of Vendor 2.

Customer 4—Vendor 2 is skipped because Customer 4 is already satisfied.

Customer 3—Vendor 1—3 trips—Satisfies part of Customer 3 and all of Vendor 1.

Customer 2—Vendor 1 is skipped because Vendor 1 is satisfied.

Customer 1—Vendor 2—2 trips—Satisfies Customer 1 but still leaves Vendor 2 three short.

Customer 2—Vendor 2 is skipped because there are no shipments to Customer 2.

Customer 3—Vendor 2 has us going by the plant so we are left with:

Customer 3—1 trip
Vendor 2—3 trips

Distribution: Multiple Customers Serviced in Same Trip

I will again use two examples to demonstrate the scheduling function. The data for these examples are shown in Chart 7.C5. Looking at Example 3.1, the first step is to do the obvious things first, which is to ship the full loads. The percentages represent the percentage of a full load required for this shipment.

Customer 1—Ship the 70% and the 30% load together to the customer.

Customer 2—Ship the 90% load because there isn't any load that is 10% or smaller.

Customer 4—Ship the 80% and the 20% load together.

Customer 5—Ship the 100% load.

Customer 5—Ship the 50% and the 40% load together.

CHART 7.C5 Trips Required for Example 3

Example 3.1
Customer 1—3 loads at 30%, 20%, and 70%
Customer 2—2 loads at 90% and 70%
Customer 3—1 load at 40%
Customer 4—3 loads at 50%, 20%, and 80%
Customer 5—4 loads at 100%, 20%, 40%, and 50%

Example 3.2
Customer 1—3 loads at 30%, 20%, and 70%
Customer 2—2 loads at 90% and 170%
Customer 3—1 load at 60%
Customer 4—3 loads at 50%, 20%, and 30%
Customer 5—4 loads at 100%, 30%, 30%, and 50%

This leaves the following:

Customer 1—20% load
Customer 2—70% load
Customer 3—40% load
Customer 4—50% load
Customer 5—20% load

We attempt to ship the largest load first. Possible load combinations that would ship the 70% load, and their corresponding mileages, are:

C1 and C2 = 90% load at 62 miles
C2 and C5 = 90% load at 66 miles

We ship based on the calculation of the largest percentage, combination, divided by mileage, which in this case is:

C1 and C2 = 90% load at 62 miles
(90%)/(62) = 0.0145

C2 and C5 = 90% load at 66 miles
(90%)/(66) = 0.0136

So based on the larger value we would ship Customer 1 and Customer 2 together.

The next set of combinations is:

C3 + C4 = 90% load at 65 miles
(90%)/(65) = 0.0138

C3 + C5 has us going right by the plant and therefore equals two separate trips

C4 + C5 = 70% load at 54 miles
(70%)/(54) = 0.0130

Since C3 + C4 gives us the most benefit for the trip (largest ratio), we run it together. We end with a separate run to C5. In reality, by this time we will probably have something else to mix with C5's load. The final trip schedule is:

Customer 1—1 trip
Customer 2—1 trip
Customer 4—1 trip
Customer 5—3 trips
Customer 1 then Customer 2—1 trip
Customer 3 then Customer 4—1 trip

We will follow a similar strategy as we work Example 3.2. We start by doing the obvious full loads:

Customer 1—Ship the 30% and the 70% load together.
Customer 2—Ship 100% of the 170% load.
Customer 2—Ship the 90% load.
Customer 4—Ship the 50%, 20%, and 30% loads together.
Customer 5—Ship the 100% load.

Next, we consider the mixed customer loads starting with the largest load first (Customer 2 with 70%):

C1 + C2 = 90% load at 62 miles
(90%)/62 = 0.0145

C2 + C5 = 100% load at 66 miles
(100%)/66 = 0.0152

The largest benefit comes from the Customer 2 (70%) and Customer 5 (30%) combined shipment. Looking at the remaining combinations, we have the following options:

C1 + C3 = 80% at 73 miles
(80%)/73 = 0.011

C3 + C5 requires a trip past the plant and equals two separate trips

C1 + C5 = 100% at 61 miles
(100%)/61 = 0.0164

We ship the Customer 1 (20%) and Customer 5 (30% and 50%) combined load. This leaves us with the 60% Customer 3 load, which gets shipped separately. The final trip schedule is:

Customer 1—1 trip
Customer 2—2 trips
Customer 3—1 trip
Customer 4—1 trip
Customer 5—1 trip
Customer 1 then Customer 5—1 trip
Customer 2 then Customer 5—1 trip

Distribution: Multiple Customers and Multiple Backhauls

Again I will demonstrate this process with two examples. The data can be seen in Chart 7.C6. We start with Example 4.1, looking at the customer analysis we have already done in Example 3.1. I have kept the same customer numbers for both Examples 3.1 and 4.1 so that the customer analysis would not have to be recalculated. Based on the calculations of Example 3.1 we need to make the following trips:

Customer 1—1 trip
Customer 2—1 trip
Customer 4—1 trip
Customer 5—3 trips
Customer 1 then Customer 2—1 trip
Customer 3 then Customer 4—1 trip

Next, we look for vendors with full loads. These are:

Vendor 1—90%
Vendor 2 —70% + 30% or 60% + 40%

The 60% plus 20% combination in Vendor 1 will also be treated as a full load because there is nothing else that can combine with the 60% value. We are left with 50% loads for both vendors. But because the mileage to go to both vendors is equal to the mileage of going to each vendor separately, we will treat these as separate full loads. We are left with the following needed trips for the vendors:

Vendor 1—3 trips
Vendor 2—3 trips

CHART 7.C6 Trips Required for Example 4

Example 4.1
Customer 1—3 loads at 30%, 20%, and 70%
Customer 2—2 loads at 90% and 70%
Customer 3—1 load at 40%
Customer 4—3 loads at 50%, 20%, and 80%
Customer 5—4 loads at 100%, 20%, 40%, and 50%
Vendor 1—4 loads at 90%, 20%, 60%, and 50%
Vendor 2—5 loads at 30%, 40%, 50%, 60%, and 70%

Example 4.2
Customer 1—3 loads at 30%, 20%, and 70%
Customer 2—2 loads at 90% and 70%
Customer 3—1 load at 60%
Customer 4—3 loads at 50%, 20%, and 30%
Customer 5—4 loads at 100%, 30%, 30%, and 50%
Vendor 1—4 loads at 90%, 20%, 60%, and 70%
Vendor 2—5 loads at 30%, 40%, 50%, 80%, and 70%

Next, we analyze which of these has the shortest combined route. The combinations of routes include:

C1 + V1 goes through the plant

C1 + V2 = 77 miles

C2 + V1 = 73 miles (longer than doing each trip separately)

C2 + V2 = 82 miles

C4 + V1 = 35 miles

C4 + V2 = 57 miles

C5 + V1 goes through the plant

C5 + V2 = 48 miles

C1 + C2 + V1 = 95 miles (longer than doing each trip separately)

C1 + C2 + V2 = 89 miles

C3 + C4 + V1 = 70 miles

C3 + C4 + V2 = 92 miles

C1 = 50 miles

C2 = 40 miles

C4 = 30 miles

C5 = 32 miles

V1 = 26 miles

V2 = 44 miles

C1 + C2 = 62 miles

C3 + C4 = 65 miles

We ship the C4 + V1 combination and the three C5 + V2 combinations. This has eliminated all the Vendor 2, Customer 5, and Customer 4 requirements. The next lowest mileage is C4 + V2 but C4 has already been fully shipped. We move on to C3 + C4 + V1 and ship one load. We move on to the next lowest, which is C2 + V1, and ship one of these. At this point we have all the vendor loads shipped and the remaining customer-only loads will be shipped independently. The final shipping loads are:

C5 + V2—3 loads

C4 + V1—1 load

C2 + V1—1 load

C3 + C4 + V1—1 load

C1—1 load

C1 + C2—1 load

Moving forward with our second example (Example 4.2), we again look back at the customer analysis of Example 3.2 where the customer numbers were the same. Based on the calculations of Example 3.2, we would make the following customer shipments:

Customer 1—1 trip
Customer 2—2 trips
Customer 3—1 trip
Customer 4—1 trip
Customer 5—1 trip
Customer 1 then Customer 5—1 trip
Customer 2 then Customer 5—1 trip

Next, we look for vendors with full loads. These are:

Vendor 1—90% or 20% + 70%
Vendor 2—70% + 30% or 50% + 40%

We are left with a 60% load for Vendor 1 and an 80% load for Vendor 2. These loads cannot be combined so they will be treated as full loads. The final list of vendor trips is:

Vendor 1—3 trips
Vendor 2—3 trips

Next, we analyze which of these has the shortest combined route. The combinations of routes include:

C1 + V1 goes through the plant
C1 + V2 = 77 miles
C2 + V1 = 73 miles (longer than doing each trip separately)
C2 + V2 = 82 miles
C3 + V1 = 58 miles
C3 + V2 goes through the plant
C4 + V1 = 35 miles
C4 + V2 = 57 miles
C5 + V1 goes through the plant
C5 + V2 = 48 miles
C1 + C5 + V1 goes through the plant
C1 + C5 + V2 = 77 miles
C2 + C5 + V1 = 99 miles (longer than doing each trip separately)
C2 + C5 + V2 = 82 miles
C1 = 50 miles
C2 = 40 miles
C3 = 40 miles
C4 = 30 miles
C5 = 32 miles
V1 = 26 miles
V2 = 44 miles
C1 + C5 = 61 miles
C2 + C5 = 66 miles

We ship the C4 + V1 combination and the C5 + V2 combination. We move on to C3 + V1 and ship one load. The next lowest mileage is C2 + V1 and we ship one load. We move on to the next lowest, which is C1 + V2 and ship one of these. Then we ship a C1 + C5 + V2. At this point we have all the vendor loads shipped and the customer-only loads remaining will be shipped independently. The final shipping loads are:

C5 + V2—1 load
C4 + V1—1 load
C3 + V1—1 load
C2 + V1—1 load
C1 + V2—1 load
C1 + C5 + V2—1 load
C2—1 load
C2 + C5—1 load

I realize there is a lot of creativity in this process, but like Einstein said, sometimes you have to use a little imagination.

This modeling process can get very complex. For example, we may have combinations of shipments to three or more customers and pickups from three or more vendors. The procedure remains the same, but the number of options can become obnoxious.

Mixed Loads to Customers

Sometimes we have different types of trucks, like a coil truck and a bar stock truck. The bar stock truck cannot haul coils but the coil truck can haul either. The scheduling procedure would be to schedule the most restricted materials first, which in this case would be the coils. Then, once we have the coil shipments planned, we would fill out the coil loads with bar stock and plan the remaining bar stock loads. The procedure is the same as in the process described previously except that we only deal with a limited number of options initially (coils) before we open the scheduling process up to all categories. Then follow the appropriate procedure in the previous sections.

Sectoring

If we have numerous shipments (customers) or many vendors, calculating the mileage between each becomes unreasonable and *sectoring* becomes an important tool. Break your map up into delivery sectors. Everyone within a sector is considered to be at the same delivery point. Deliveries would be scheduled by sector just as if the sector were a customer.

Cost or Mile Optimization

Sometimes cost is more important than mileage, even though they are usually proportionally the same. Sometimes the type of truck required, or tolls, etc., could make a significant difference in which route we would prefer to use. In that case our mileage chart should be made out as a trip cost chart. All other calculations would work the same as if it were mileage with which we were working.

Freight/Carrier Analysis

Freight and carrier analysis is an attempt to stay on top of the quality of shipments to customers. In this process we track shipping costs, breakages, and timing. We want to make sure the customer gets what they want, when they want it, and in good condition. The process starts with the collection of data. As shipments are made from the shipping dock, information about the date of the shipment and the shipper is recorded on the shipping document (see step 5 at the start of this appendix titled "Product Sales and Shipping" and see Chart 7.G4). One copy of this document goes with the materials being shipped; a second goes back to the Order Department to report that the shipment has gone out.

A reporting process needs to be set up so that we can track when the product actually arrived at the customer and if it arrived undamaged. This can be a report filled out by our truckers, if we have our own trucks, or by our carrier, or by the customer. There are many ways to get this information, but the best method for you depends on how many customers you have and on your shipping methods.

The arrival and condition information is collected with the shipment information. Some companies have a Traffic Department, which would handle the data collection and reporting process. Other companies would do this function in the Sales Department as part of the sales reporting process since the completed order information is routed through sales anyway (see Appendix 7.G and Charts 7.G18, 7.G19, and 7.G20). Other companies may do this reporting process in the Accounting Department. Regardless of where the reporting process occurs, the data need to be collected and assimilated into a report. A sample of the input document is found in Chart 7.C7. On this document we record some information found on the order form:

- Customer name and number
- Due date
- Order number
- Shipping costs

Some information is recorded from the shipping document:

- Date shipped
- Carrier
- Load/weight information

CHART 7.C7 Freight/Carrier Data Input Document

Date From __/__/__ to __/__/__

Customer Name	Customer Number	Carrier Name	Carrier Number	Order Number	Date Shipped	Date Due	Date Delivered	Weight	Shipping Costs	Damage Report
					/ /	/ /	/ /			
					/ /	/ /	/ /			
					/ /	/ /	/ /			
					/ /	/ /	/ /			
					/ /	/ /	/ /			
					/ /	/ /	/ /			
					/ /	/ /	/ /			
					/ /	/ /	/ /			
					/ /	/ /	/ /			
					/ /	/ /	/ /			
					/ /	/ /	/ /			
					/ /	/ /	/ /			
					/ /	/ /	/ /			
					/ /	/ /	/ /			
					/ /	/ /	/ /			
					/ /	/ /	/ /			
					/ /	/ /	/ /			
					/ /	/ /	/ /			
					/ /	/ /	/ /			

CHART 7.C8 Freight/Carrier Damage Analysis Report by Carrier

Date __/__/__

Carrier Name	Carrier Number	Damage Costs Month	1	2	3	4	5	6	7	8	9	10	11	12
Damage by month														

Some information comes from the carrier or the customer:

Arrival date

Damage report

This data collection and analysis process can be done very nicely on some type of computerized data base system. It doesn't need to be a large system and it can be the same system you used for sales analysis.

After the data have been collected over a period of time (usually a month), the data are transferred to the analysis reports. Not all of these reports may be appropriate for you. This is just a suggestion of the types of reports that can be generated. Chart 7.C8 is a freight and carrier damage analysis report, which checks on shipment quality. Chart 7.C9

CHART 7.C9 Shipments by Carrier

Date _____/_____/_____

Carrier Name	Carrier Number	Shipments Month	1	2	3	4	5	6	7	8	9	10	11	12
Shipments by month														

CHART 7.C10 Shipments (or Damage Report) to Customer by Carrier

Date _____/_____/_____

Customer Name	Customer Number	Carrier Name	Carrier Number	Shipments Month	1	2	3	4	5	6	7	8	9	10	11	12

is a shipments by carrier report, which shows how much we use a particular carrier. This may be important if we are concerned about favoritism or in negotiating a reduced carrier rate. Chart 7.C10 analyzes the shipments to customers made by different carriers. This is helpful in analyzing customer complaints about shipments. It also helps us recognize preferences. The last report, Chart 7.C11, shows the number of days late (the difference between due date and arrival date) for a particular customer/carrier. This also helps in handling complaints.

With the freight/carrier analysis reports we can gain better control over freight costs, timing, quality, and complaints. This analysis is not necessary on a continuing basis, as is the sales analysis, but it is helpful to do every once in a while to check on potential problem situations.

CHART 7.C11 Days Late to Customer by Carrier

Date ______/______/______

Customer Name	Customer Number	Carrier Name	Carrier Number	Days Late Month	1	2	3	4	5	6	7	8	9	10	11	12

Summary

Distribution planning is a planning tool that you either don't need at all or you can't live without. If you don't need it now, at least remember it for some future time when you may find it valuable. If you do need it, this appendix should provide some of the basics without getting wrapped up into a full-blown extensive system such as the ones larger organizations use. The next step in the information flow will be the development of a master production schedule (MPS). Appendix 7E will discuss this in detail. The MPS will detail out exactly what we have to produce, by product type, rather than by family.

APPENDIX 7.D: Linear-Integer Programming Applied to Distribution and Logistics Planning

This appendix will give you the linear-integer programming formulations for the examples in this chapter. For an additional discussion of linear programming, see Appendix 7.B. Each of the models in this appendix is calculated using a linear-integer programming package where the variables were specified as continuous, binary, or as integers.

A continuous variable will allow any value to be calculated. An integer variable will only allow whole numbers to be calculated. A field specified as a binary number will only allow "0" or "1" to be calculated. Either it is used or it isn't. In the case of the examples we are working, we use *binary* variables to identify whether or not a trip is made. We also use *integer* variables to calculate how many trips are made. We use *continuous* variables to calculate what percentage of any particular trip is wasted. Specifying each variable is important because you can't make a fraction of a trip to a customer—either you go there, or you don't go there.

In Appendix 7.C we walked through a manual procedure for each of the calculations that we are going to do here using linear programming. The manual procedure is not "optimal," which means it isn't guaranteed to be the perfectly best answer. However, it does give a fairly good schedule. As we go through the linear-integer programming solutions, we will occasionally find that slightly better solutions exist. However, we do not want to do the same calculation process by hand that the computer goes through if we are going to do the scheduling manually. It would take us all day to work up a schedule. In most cases the manually calculated answer is adequate. If you want the "optimal" answer, however, use linear-integer programming.

Examples

I will be referring back to previous headings used in Appendix 7.C. I will use the same headings now to identify the same examples recalculated with linear-integer programming.

Distribution: Backhauls and Full Load Trips

The examples for this analysis are found in Chart 7.C4. The linear programming formulation for the first example (Example 2.1) would be:

Objective Function:

Minimize 50 XC1 + 40 XC2 + 40 XC3 + 30 XC4 + 30 XC5
+ 26 XV1 + 44 XV2 + 77 XC1V2 + 73 XC2V1
+ 82 XC2V2 + 58 XC3V1 + 35 XC4V1 + 57 XC4V2
+ 48 XC5V2

Constraints:

XC1V2 + XC1 = 3
XC2V1 + XC2V2 + XC2 = 6
XC3V1 + XC3 = 1
XC4V1 + XC4V2 + XC4 = 2
XC5V2 + XC5 = 2
XC2V1 + XC3V1 + XC4V1 + XV1 = 4
XC1V2 + XC2V2 + XC4V2 + XC5V2 + XV2 = 6

Where the "X" variables represent how many times each trip is made. For example, XC1 is how many trips we made to Customer 1 only. XC1V2 is how many trips we made to Customer 1, then at the same time did a pickup at Vendor 2.

The 50, 40, 40, 30, . . . , values in the objective function are the number of miles each trip takes.

The seven constraints count the number of times we went to each customer or vendor. For example, XC1V2 + XC1 = 3 says that the number of times we did the trip to Customer 1 followed by a pickup at Vendor 2, plus the number of times we just went to Customer 1 and nowhere else has to add up to 3 trips total.

After processing this model through the linear programming processor where each variable was specified as an integer, we come up with the following solution:

XC1 = 0
XC2 = 5
XC3 = 0
XC4 = 0
XC5 = 0
XV1 = 1
XV2 = 0
XC1V2 = 3
XC2V1 = 0
XC2V2 = 1
XC3V1 = 1
XC4V1 = 2
XC4V2 = 0
XC5V2 = 2

This solution tells us that we need to make the trip from Customer 1 to Vendor 2 three times, etc. When we compare this solution to the one we arrived at earlier we see three differences, which are as follows:

Trip	Manual	LP Program
C2	4 (160 miles)	5 (200 miles)
V1	0	1 (26 miles)
C2V1	1 (73 miles)	0
Totals:	(233 miles)	(226 miles)

The computer solution was better than the manual system by 7 miles, which is relatively insignificant when compared to the 763 total miles traveled (using the computer's values). However, if you want optimality, use the computer.

Example 2.2 would have the following formulation:

Objective Function:
Minimize 50 XC1 + 40 XC2 + 40 XC3 + 30 XC4 + 30 XC5
+ 26 XV1 + 44 XV2 + 77 XC1V2 + 73 XC2V1
+ 82 XC2V2 + 58 XC3V1 + 35 XC4V1 + 57 XC4V2
+ 48 XC5V2

Constraints:

XC1V2 + XC1 = 2
XC2V1 + XC2V2 + XC2 = 0
XC3V1 + XC3 = 4
XC4V1 + XC4V2 + XC4 = 1
XC5V2 + XC5 = 1
XC2V1 + XC3V1 + XC4V1 + XV1 = 4
XC1V2 + XC2V2 + XC4V2 + XC5V2 + XV2 = 6

Note that the only difference between this formulation and the previous formulation is in the total number of trips made in the constraints. If you formulate a linear programming model for your situation, this would also be true in your case. You wouldn't need to formulate the model each time. You set it up once, then simply modify the number of trips required and solve the model.

After processing this model through the linear programming processor where each variable was specified as an integer, we come up with the following solution:

XC1 = 0
XC2 = 0
XC3 = 0
XC4 = 0
XC5 = 0
XV1 = 0
XV2 = 2
XC1V2 = 2
XC2V1 = 0
XC2V2 = 0
XC3V1 = 4
XC4V1 = 0
XC4V2 = 1
XC5V2 = 1

When we compare this solution to the one we arrived at earlier using the manual process we see five differences:

Trip	Manual	LP Program
C3	1 (40 miles)	0
V2	3 (132 miles)	2 (88 miles)
C3V1	3 (174 miles)	4 (232 miles)
C4V1	1 (35 miles)	0
C4V2	0	1 (57 miles)
Totals:	(381 miles)	(377 miles)

The computer solution was better than the manual system by 4 miles, which is relatively insignificant when compared to the 579 total miles traveled (using the computer's values).

Distribution: Multiple Customers Serviced in Same Trip

I have again taken the data from the previous examples (Chart 7.C5) and used it to formulate a linear-integer program. Chart 7.D1 is the actual formulation of the problem worked out in detail using a computer package[1] called QS. This formulation, as a linear program, would take about 30 seconds to run. But that would give us fractional results and it is impossible to make half of a trip to a customer. Either you go to the customer or you don't. Therefore, some of these variables are specified as binary and some as integer. Unfortunately, linear-integer programming runs much slower than strict linear programming. I started running this model on an IBM-386PC Turbo processor with one megabyte of memory, and after it had been running 24 hours I came to the conclusion that this is not at all practical and killed the calculation process. You can try running it if you are more patient than I am. But it is unreasonable to wait that long to generate a schedule.

The variables are defined as follows:

C1 = a round-trip to Customer 1 (integer)

C12 = a trip to Customer 1, then to Customer 2, then back (integer)

C1L1S1 = Customer 1, load 1, shipment 1 (binary)

C1B1 = Customer 1, buffer 1 (continuous)

C1S1 = Customer 1, shipment 1 (binary)

The objective function attempts to minimize the total traveled miles. The variables in the objective function are an integer count of how many times each of these trips is made.

The constraints come in two groups. The first group is made up of constraints 1 through 31. Using constraints 1, 2, and 3 as an example, I will explain how these constraints work. These first three constraints are for Customer 1. It is impossible to do all the shipments to Customer 1 in one load, so we set up two shipments (constraints 1 and 2). In constraint 1 we identify each of the loads (0.3, 0.2, and 0.7). By turning on (setting equal to 1) the value of C1L1S2 we are saying that this load (0.3) should be shipped with shipment 1. The C1S1 in this equation turns on (equal to 1) if any one of the loads is shipped in shipment 1. The C1B1 is a buffer that shows how much of each load is wasted. For example, if we ship the 0.2 and the 0.7 loads together, 10% of the truck will be empty and C1B1 will equal 0.1. Constraint 3 counts how many C1 shipments are made by counting C1S1 and C1S2.

Starting with constraint 16 we are dealing with shipments to multiple customers. For example, C12L1S1 says that for a customer 1 (C12L1S1) then customer 2 (C12L1S1) shipment we have 0.3 (see constraint 16) of a load available for shipment and we are calling this Load

---

[1] QS stands for "Quant Systems" and comes as a book with software included. It has several packages in it that would be useful, such as MRP, inventory control, linear and integer programming, forecasting, and shop floor scheduling. It is published by Prentice Hall, Englewood Cliffs, New Jersey. The authors are Yin-Long Chang and Robert S. Sullivan.

CHART 7.D1 QS LP-IP Printout of Routing Example

```
≫ Min 50C1 + 40C2 + 40C3 + 30C4 + 30C5 + 62C12 + 73C13 + 61C15 + 66C25 + 65C34 + 54C45
≫ Subject to
≫ (1) .3C1L1S1 + .2C1L2S1 + .7C1L3S1 - 1C1S1 + 1C1B1 = 0
≫ (2) .3C1L1S2 + .2C1L2S2 + .7C1L3S2 - 1C1S2 + 1C1B2 = 0
≫ (3) 1C1 - 1C1S1 - 1C1S2 = 0
≫ (4) .9C2L1S1 + .7C2L2S1 - 1C2S1 + 1C2B1 = 0
≫ (5) .9C2L1S2 + .7C2L2S2 - 1C2S2 + 1C2B2 = 0
≫ (6) 1C2 - 1C2S1 - 1C2S2 = 0
≫ (7) .4C3L1S1 - 1C3S1 + 1C3B1 = 0
≫ (8) 1C3 - 1C3S1 = 0
≫ (9) .5C4L1S1 + .2C4L2S1 + .8C4L3S1 - 1C4S1 + 1C4B1 = 0
≫ (10) .5C4L1S2 + .2C4L2S2 + .8C4L3S2 - 1C4S2 + 1C4B2 = 0
≫ (11) 1C4 - 1C4S1 - 1C4S2 = 0
≫ (12) 1C5L1S1 + .2C5L2S1 + .4C5L3S1 + .5C5L4S1 - 1C5S1 + 1C5B1 = 0
≫ (13) 1C5L1S2 + .2C5L2S2 + .4C5L3S2 + .5C5L4S2 - 1C5S2 + 1C5B2 = 0
≫ (14) 1C5L1S3 + .2C5L2S3 + .4C5L3S3 + .5C5L4S3 - 1C5S3 + 1C5B3 = 0
≫ (15) 1C5 - 1C5S1 - 1C5S2 - 1C5S3 = 0
≫ (16) .3C12L1S1 + .2C12L2S1 + .7C12L3S1 + .9C12L4S1 + .7C12L5S1 - 1C12S1 + 1C12B1 = 0
≫ (17) 1C12 - 1C12S1 = 0
≫ (18) .3C13L1S1 + .2C13L2S1 + .7C13L3S1 + .4C13L4S1 - 1C13S1 + 1C13B1 = 0
≫ (19) 1C13 - 1C13S1 = 0
≫ (20) .3C15L1S1 + .2C15L2S1 + .7C15L3S1 + 1C15L4S1 + .2C15L5S1 + .4C15L6S1 + .5C15L7S1 - 1C15S1 +
1C15B1 = 0
≫ (21) .3C15L1S2 + .2C15L2S2 + .7C15L3S2 + 1C15L4S2 + .2C15L5S2 + .4C15L6S2 + .5C15L7S2 -
1C15S2 + 1C15B2 = 0
≫ (22) .3C15L1S3 + .2C15L2S3 + .7C15L3S3 + 1C15L4S3 + .2C15L5S3 + .4C15L6S3 + .5C15L7S3 - 1C15S3 +
1C15B3 = 0
≫ (23) 1C15 - 1C15S1 - 1C15S2 - 1C15S3 = 0
≫ (24) .9C25L1S1 - .7C25L2S1 + 1C25L3S1 + .2C25L4S1 + .4C25L5S1 + .5C25L6S1 - 1C25S1 + 1C25B1 = 0
≫ (25) 1C25 - 1C25S1 = 0
≫ (26) .4C34L1S1 + .5C34L2S1 + .2C34L3S1 + .8C34L4S1 - 1C34S1 + 1C34B1 = 0
≫ (27) 1C34 - 1C34S1 = 0
≫ (28) .5C45L1S1 + .2C45L2S1 + .8C45L3S1 + 1C45L4S1 + .2C45L5S1 + .4C45L6S1 + .5C45L7S1 -
1C45S1 + 1C45B1 = 0
≫ (29) .5C45L1S2 + .2C45L2S2 + .8C45L3S2 + 1C45L4S2 + .2C45L5S2 + .4C45L6S2 + .5C45L7S2 - 1C45S2 +
1C45B2 = 0
≫ (30) .5C45L1S3 + .2C45L2S3 + .8C45L3S3 + 1C45L4S3 + .2C45L5S3 + .4C45L6S3 + .5C45L7S3 - 1C45S3 +
1C45B3 = 0
≫ (31) 1C45 - 1C45S1 - 1C45S2 - 1C45S3 = 0
≫ (32) 1C1L1S1 + 1C1L1S2 + 1C12L1S1 + 1C13L1S1 + 1C15L1S1 + 1C15L1S2 + 1C15L1S3 = 1
≫ (33) 1C1L2S1 + 1C1L2S2 + 1C12L2S1 + 1C13L2S1 + 1C15L2S1 + 1C15L2S2 + 1C15L2S3 = 1
≫ (34) 1C1L3S1 + 1C1L3S2 + 1C12L3S1 + 1C13L3S1 + 1C15L3S1 + 1C15L3S2 + 1C15L3S3 = 1
≫ (35) 1C2L1S1 + 1C2L1S2 + 1C12L4S1 + 1C25L1S1 = 1
≫ (36) 1C2L2S1 + 1C2L2S2 + 1C12L5S1 + 1C25L2S1 = 1
≫ (37) 1C3L1S1 + 1C13L4S1 + 1C34L1S1 = 1
≫ (38) 1C4L1S1 + 1C4L1S2 + 1C34L2S1 + 1C45L1S1 + 1C45L1S2 + 1C45L1S3 = 1
≫ (39) 1C4L2S1 + 1C4L2S2 + 1C34L3S1 + 1C45L2S1 + 1C45L2S2 + 1C45L2S3 = 1
≫ (40) 1C4L3S1 + 1C4L3S2 + 1C34L4S1 + 1C45L3S1 + 1C45L3S2 + 1C45L3S3 = 1
≫ (41) 1C5L1S1 + 1C5L1S2 + 1C5L1S3 + 1C15L4S1 + 1C15L4S2 + 1C15L4S3 + 1C25L3S1 + 1C45L4S1 + 1C45L4S2 +
1C45L4S3 = 1
≫ (42) 1C5L2S1 + 1C5L2S2 + 1C5L2S3 + 1C15L5S1 + 1C15L5S2 + 1C15L5S3 + 1C25L4S1 + 1C45L5S1 + 1C45L5S2 +
1C45L5S3 = 1
≫ (43) 1C5L3S1 + 1C5L3S2 + 1C5L3S3 + 1C15L6S1 + 1C15L6S2 + 1C15L6S3 + 1C25L5S1 + 1C45L6S1 + 1C45L6S2 +
1C45L6S3 = 1
≫ (44) 1C5L4S1 + 1C5L4S2 + 1C5L4S3 + 1C15L7S1 + 1C15L7S2 + 1C15L7S3 + 1C25L6S1 + 1C45L7S1 + 1C45L7S2 +
1C45L7S3 = 1
≫ Integer
≫ C1, C2, C3, C4, C5, C12, C13, C15, C25, C34, C45
≫ Binary
≫ C1L1S1, C1L2S1, C1L3S1, C1S1, C1L1S2, C1L2S2, C1L3S2, C1S2, C2L1S1, C2L2S1, C2S1, C2L1S2, C2L2S2, C2S2, C3L1S1,
C3S1, C4L1S1, C4L2S1, C4L3S1, C4S1, C4L1S2, C4L2S2, C4L3S2, C4S2, C5L1S1, C5L2S1, C5L3S1, C5L4S1, C5S1, C5L1S2,
C5L2S2, C5L3S2, C5L4S2, C5S2, C5L1S3, C5L2S3, C5L3S3, C5L4S3, C5S3, C12L1S1, C12L2S1, C12L3S1, C12L4S1, C12L5S1,
C12S1, C13L1S1, C13L2S1, C13L3S1, C13L4S1, C13S1, C15L1S1, C15L2S1, C15L3S1, C15L4S1, C15L5S1, C15L6S1, C15L7S1,
C15S1, C15L1S2, C15L2S2, C15L3S2, C15L4S2, C15L5S2, C15L6S2, C15L7S2, C15S2, C15L1S3, C15L2S3, C15L3S3, C15L4S3,
C15L5S3, C15L6S3, C15L7S3, C15S3, C25L1S1, C25L2S1, C25L3S1, C25L4S1, C25L5S1, C25L6S1, C25S1, C34L1S1, C34L2S1,
C34L3S1, C34L4S1, C34S1, C45L1S1, C45L2S1, C45L3S1, C45L4S1, C45L5S1, C45L6S1, C45L7S1, C45S1, C45L1S2, C45L2S2,
C45L3S2, C45L4S2, C45L5S2, C45L6S2, C45L7S2, C45S2, C45L1S3, C45L2S3, C45L3S3, C45L4S3, C45L5S3, C45L6S3, C45L7S3,
C45S3
```

1 (C12L1S1) of Shipment 1 (C12L1S1). All the loads for Customer 1 and Customer 2 are available for shipment on this combined load.

Constraints 31 through 44 make sure that each load is shipped and that it is shipped only once. In constraint 31, we track every time the 0.3 load for Customer 1 can be shipped, which occurs in C1L1S1, C1L1S2, or in the combined loads of C12L1S1, C13L1S1, C15L1S1, C15L1S2, or C15L1S3. The "=1" says that it can only be shipped (and must be shipped) once in one of these shipments.

Note that some shipments such as C14 do not exist because it would be equivalent to shipping to C1 and then to C4. Also, the number of constraints that exist is dependent on how many possible combination loads can be made.

Now that we know how to achieve the perfect computer solution from Example 3.1, let's look at a more realistic solution. This solution incorporates a little bit of common sense and by doing so makes the model much easier for the poor overworked computer. We use the data in Example 3.1. Displaying these data in matrix format (Chart 7.D2) we see that several loads are full loads and can be immediately eliminated.

The loads that can be eliminated are:

Customer 1—one trip with 0.3 + 0.7

Customer 2—one trip with 0.9

Customer 4—one trip with 0.2 + 0.8

Customer 5—two trips, one with 1.0 and one with 0.4 + 0.5

This leaves us with:

Customer 1—0.2

Customer 2—0.7

Customer 3—0.4

Customer 4—0.5

Customer 5—0.2

Chart 7.D3 shows the computer formulation of this greatly simplified model using the same philosophy and variable identifications as previously. The elapsed computer calculation time is 22 minutes, a lot less time than the previous calculations. The solutions for the number of trips of each type and for which shipments should be made with which loads is shown in Chart 7.D4 (except that the full loads have been eliminated).

CHART 7.D2 Example 3.1 Matrix

	Load 1	Load 2	Load 3	Load 4
Customer 1	0.3	0.2	0.7	
Customer 2	0.9	0.7		
Customer 3	0.4			
Customer 4	0.5	0.2	0.8	
Customer 5	1.0	0.2	0.4	0.5

CHART 7.D3 QS LP-IP Printout of Routing Example 3.1

```
Free format model for ROUTING - CX
>> Min 50C1 + 40C2 + 40C3 + 30C4 + 30C5 + 62C12 + 73C13 + 61C15 + 66C25 + 65C34 + 54C45
   Subject to
>> (1)  -1C1 + .2C1L1S1 + 1C1B1 = 0
>> (2)  -1C2 + .7C2L1S1 + 1C2B1 = 0
>> (3)  -1C3 + .4C3L1S1 + 1C3B1 = 0
>> (4)  -1C4 + .5C4L1S1 + 1C4B1 = 0
>> (5)  -1C5 + .2C5L1S1 + 1C5B1 = 0
>> (6)  -1C12 + .2C12L1S1 + .7C12L2S1 + 1C12B1 = 0
>> (7)  -1C13 + .2C13L1S1 + .4C13L2S1 + 1C13B1 = 0
>> (8)  -1C15 + .2C15L1S1 + .2C15L2S1 + 1C15B1 = 0
>> (9)  -1C25 + .7C25L1S1 + .2C25L2S1 + 1C25B1 = 0
>> (10) -1C34 + .4C34L1S1 + .5C34L2S1 + 1C34B1 = 0
>> (11) -1C45 + .5C45L1S1 + .2C45L2S1 + 1C45B1 = 0
>> (12) 1C1L1S1 + 1C12L1S1 + 1C13L1S1 = 1
>> (13) 1C2L1S1 + 1C12L2S1 + 1C25L1S1 = 1
>> (14) 1C3L1S1 + 1C13L2S1 + 1C34L1S1 = 1
>> (15) 1C4L1S1 + 1C34L2S1 + 1C45L1S1 = 1
>> (16) 1C5L1S1 + 1C15L2S1 + 1C25L2S1  + 1C45L2S1 = 1
>> Bounds
>> C1L1S1 ≤ 1
>> C2L1S1 ≤ 1
>> C3L1S1 ≤ 1
>> C4L1S1 ≤ 1
>> C5L1S1 ≤ 1
>> C12L1S1 ≤ 1
>> C12L2S1 ≤ 1
>> C13L1S1 ≤ 1
>> C13L2S1 ≤ 1
>> C15L1S1 ≤ 1
>> C15L2S1 ≤ 1
>> C25L1S1 ≤ 1
>> C25L2S1 ≤ 1
>> C34L1S1 ≤ 1
>> C34L2S1 ≤ 1
>> C45L1S1 ≤ 1
>> C45L2S1 ≤ 1
>> Integer
>> C1, C2, C3, C4, C5, C12, C13, C15, C25, C34, C45
>> Binary
>> C1L1S1, C2L1S1, C3L1S1, C4L1S1, C5L1S1, C12L1S1, C12L2S1, C13L1S1, C13L2S1, C15L1S1, C15L2S1,
C25L1S1, C25L2S1, C34L1S1, C34L2S1, C45L1S1, C45L2S1
```

CHART 7.D4 Example 3.1 Solution

Variable	Value	Load Variables
These variables tell us how often each type of trip is made and what the load will be for each trip.		
C1	0	
C2	0	
C3	1	C3L1S1 = 1 (0.6)
C4	0	
C5	0	
C12	1	C12L1S1 = 1 (0.2) C12L2S1 = 1 (0.7)
C13	0	
C15	0	
C25	0	
C34	0	
C45	1	C45L1S1 = 1 (0.5) C45L2S1 = 1 (0.2)

The final computer solution would be:

Customer 1—one trip
Customer 2—one trip
Customer 3—one trip
Customer 4—one trip
Customer 5—two trips
Customer 1 then Customer 2—one trip
Customer 4 then Customer 5—one trip

The differences between these results and those achieved manually are:

Trip	Manual	LP Program
C1	1 (50 miles)	1 (50 miles)
C2	1 (40 miles)	1 (40 miles)
C3	0	1 (40 miles)
C4	1 (30 miles)	1 (30 miles)
C5	3 (96 miles)	2 (64 miles)
C12	1 (62 miles)	1 (62 miles)
C34	1 (65 miles)	0
C45	0	1 (54 miles)
Totals:	(343 miles)	(340 miles)

The computer solution is an improvement over the manual system by three miles, which is insignificant.

I have now demonstrated two linear-integer programming methods that can be used for the solution of Example 3.1. For Example 3.2 I will only be using the second method because the first is impractical to use on a regular basis. The matrix for Example 3.2 is shown in Chart 7.D5.

The loads that can be eliminated are:

Customer 1—one trip with 0.3 and 0.7
Customer 2—two trips, one with 1.0 and one with 0.9
Customer 4—one trip with 0.5, 0.2, and 0.3
Customer 5—one trip with 1.0

This leaves us with:

Customer 1—0.2
Customer 2—0.7
Customer 3—0.6
Customer 5—0.3, 0.3, 0.5

CHART 7.D5 Example 3.2 Matrix

	Load 1	Load 2	Load 3	Load 4
Customer 1	0.3	0.2	0.7	
Customer 2	0.9	0.7	1.0	
Customer 3	0.6			
Customer 4	0.5	0.2	0.3	
Customer 5	1.0	0.3	0.3	0.5

Chart 7.D6 shows the computer formulation of this greatly simplified model using the same philosophy and variable identifications as previously. The elapsed computer calculation time is 10.4 minutes. The solutions for this example can be seen in Chart 7.D7.

The final computer solution would be:

Customer 1—one trip

Customer 2—two trips

Customer 3—one trip

CHART 7.D6 QS LP-IP Printout of Routing Example 3.2

```
Free format model for ROUTING – DX
>> Min  50C1 + 40C2 + 40C3 + 30C5 + 62C12 + 73C13 + 61C15 + 66C25
>> Subject to
>> (1)   –1C1 + .2C1L1S1 + 1C1B1 = 0
>> (2)   –1C2 + .7C2L1S1 + 1C2B1 = 0
>> (3)   –1C3 + .6C3L1S1 + 1C3B1 = 0
>> (4)   .3C5L1S1 + .3C5L2S1 + .5C5L3S1 – 1C5S1 + 1C5B1 = 0
>> (5)   .3C5L1S2 + .3C5L2S2 + .5C5L3S2 – 1C5S2 + 1C5B2 = 0
>> (6)   1C5 – 1C5S1 – 1C5S2 = 0
>> (7)   –1C12 + .2C12L1S1 + .7C12L2S1 + 1C12B1 = 0
>> (8)   –1C13 + .2C13L1S1 + .6C13L2S1 + 1C13B1 = 0
>> (9)   –1C15 + .2C15L1S1 + .3C15L2S1 + .3C15L3S1 + .5C15L4S1 + 1C15B1 = 0
>> (10)  –1C25 + .7C25L1S1 + .3C25L2S1 + .3C25L3S1 + 1C25B1 = 0
>> (11)  1C1L1S1 + 1C12L1S1 + 1C13L1S1 + 1C15L1S1 = 1
>> (12)  1C2L1S1 + 1C12L2S1 + 1C25L1S1 = 1
>> (13)  1C3L1S1 + 1C13L2S1 = 1
>> (14)  1C5L1S1 + 1C5L1S2 + 1C15L2S1 + 1C25L2S1 = 1
>> (15)  1C5L2S1 + 1C5L2S2 + 1C15L3S1 + 1C25L3S1 = 1
>> (16)  1C5L3S1 + 1C5L3S2 + 1C15L4S1 = 1
>> Bounds
>> C1L1S1 ≤ 1
>> C2L1S1 ≤ 1
>> C3L1S1 ≤ 1
>> C5L1S1 ≤ 1
>> C5L2S1 ≤ 1
>> C5L3S1 ≤ 1
>> C5S1 ≤ 1
>> C5L1S2 ≤ 1
>> C5L2S2 ≤ 1
>> C5L3S2 ≤ 1
>> C5S2 ≤ 1
>> C12L1S1 ≤ 1
>> C12L2S1 ≤ 1
>> C13L1S1 ≤ 1
>> C13L2S1 ≤ 1
>> C15L1S1 ≤ 1
>> C15L2S1 ≤ 1
>> C15L3S1 ≤ 1
>> C15L4S1 ≤ 1
>> C25L1S1 ≤ 1
>> C25L2S1 ≤ 1
>> C25L3S1 ≤ 1
>> Integer
>> C1, C2, C3, C5, C12, C13, C15, C25
>> Binary
>> C1L1S1, C2L1S1, C3L1S1, C5L1S1, C5L2S1, C5L3S1, C5S1, C5L1S2, C5L2S2, C5L3S2, C5S2, C12L1S1,
C12L2S1, C13L1S1, C13L2S1, C15L1S1, C15L2S1, C15L3S1, C15L4S1, C25L1S1, C25L2S1, C25L3S1
```

CHART 7.D7 Example 3.2 Solution

Variable	Value	Load Variables
These variables tell us how often each type of trip is made and what the load will be for each trip.		
C1	0	
C2	0	
C3	1	C3L1S1 = 1 (0.6)
C5	2	C5L1S1 = 1 (0.3) C5L2S1 = 1 (0.3)
		C5L3S2 = 1 (0.5)
C12	1	C12L1S1 = 1 (0.2) C12L2S1 = 1 (0.7)
C13	0	
C15	0	
C25	0	

Customer 4—one trip

Customer 5—three trips

Customer 1 then Customer 2—one trip

The differences between these results and those achieved manually are:

Trip	Manual	LP Program
C1	1 (50 miles)	1 (50 miles)
C2	2 (80 miles)	2 (80 miles)
C3	1 (40 miles)	1 (40 miles)
C4	1 (30 miles)	1 (30 miles)
C5	1 (32 miles)	3 (96 miles)
C12	0	1 (62 miles)
C15	1 (61 miles)	0
C25	1 (66 miles)	0
Totals:	(359 miles)	(358 miles)

The computer solution was better than the manual system by one mile, which is relatively insignificant.

Distribution: Multiple Customers and Multiple Backhauls

Moving on to the calculation of the examples in Chart 7.C6, I won't even formulate the problem with all the vendor options because neither you nor I have two weeks of available computer time to calculate the solution. The procedure for working out these problems will be similar to the procedure used for the second part of Example 3.1 or for Example 3.2 here. Since I conveniently picked the same customer delivery requirements for Example 4.1 as I had in Example 3.1, I already know the optimal computer-generated product customer delivery mix. It is:

Customer 1—one load of 0.3 + 0.7

Customer 2—one load of 0.9

Customer 3—one load of 0.4

Customer 4—one load of 0.8 + 0.2

Customer 5—one load of 1.0 and a second load of 0.4 + 0.5

Customer 1 then Customer 2—one load of 0.2 + 0.7

Customer 4 then Customer 5—one load of 0.5 + 0.2

Next we need to analyze the vendor pickups. Doing the simple things first we have:

Vendor 1—one load of 0.9 and a second load of 0.6 + 0.2 (0.6 will not schedule with any of the Vendor 2 loads after we have pulled out the full loads)

Vendor 2—one load of 0.3 + 0.7 and a second load of 0.6 + 0.4

That leaves us with:

Vendor 1—0.5

Vendor 2—0.5

Picking up each as a separate load is 26 + 44 = 70 miles and doing them on a combined shipment is also 70 miles, so it doesn't matter which way we do it. We will go with the separate loads giving us three loads for each vendor.

Now that we have the combining of the shipment and pickup loads figured out, we need to analyze which customer shipments should be combined with which vendor pickups. The formulation for the problem is in Chart 7.D8.

The computer-generated solution for the problem is the following:

Customer 1—one trip

Customer 2—one trip

Customer 3 then Vendor 1—one trip

Customer 4 then Vendor 1—one trip

Customer 5 then Vendor 2—two trips

Customer 1 and 2 then Vendor 2—one trip

Customer 4 and 5 then Vendor 1—one trip

Comparing these results with the results we achieved manually we have the following results:

Trip	Manual	LP Program
C1	1 (50 miles)	1 (50 miles)
C2	0	1 (40 miles)
C12	1 (62 miles)	0
C2V1	1 (73 miles)	0
C3V1	0	1 (58 miles)
C4V1	1 (35 miles)	1 (35 miles)
C5V2	3 (144 miles)	2 (96 miles)
C12V1	0	1 (95 miles)
C45V1	0	1 (59 miles)
C34V1	1 (70 miles)	0
Totals:	(434 miles)	(433 miles)

CHART 7.D8 Simplified QS LP-IP Printout

```
Free format model for ROUTING – E
≫ Min  50C1 + 40C2 + 40C3 + 30C4 + 32C5 + 26V1 + 44V2 + 77C1V2 + 73C2V1 + 82C2V2 + 58C3V
≫ 35C4V1 + 57C4V2 + 48C5V2 + 62C12 + 95C12V1 + 89C12V2 + 54C45 + 59C45V1 + 60C45V2
≫ Subject to
≫ (1)  1C1 + 1C1V2 = 1
≫ (2)  1C2 + 1C2V1 + 1C2V2 = 1
≫ (3)  1C3 + 1C3V1 = 1
≫ (4)  1C4 + 1C4V1 + 1C4V2 = 1
≫ (5)  1C5 + 1C5V2 = 2
≫ (6)  1C12 + 1C12V1 + 1C12V2 = 1
≫ (7)  1C45 + 1C45V1 + 1C45V2 = 1
≫ (8)  1V1 + 1C2V1 + 1C3V1 + 1C4V1 + 1C12V1 + 1C45V1 = 3
≫ (9)  1V2 + 1C1V2 + 1C2V2 + 1C4V2 + 1C5V2 + 1C12V2 + 1C45V2 = 3
≫ Integer
≫ C1, C2, C3, C4, C5, V1, V2, C1V2, C2V1, C2V2, C3V1, C4V1, C4V2, C5V2, C12, C12V1, C12V2, C45, C45V1,
C45V2
```

The computer solution was better than the manual system by one mile. The computer time to calculate this solution was two seconds.

Moving on to the second example (Example 4.2), we will follow the same analysis process. The customer shipments that the computer suggested were (see Example 3.2):

Customer 1—one trip

Customer 2—two trips

Customer 3—one trip

Customer 4—one trip

Customer 5—three trips

Customer 1 then Customer 2—one trip

Next we need to analyze the vendor pickups. Doing the simple things first we have:

Vendor 1—one load of 0.9 and a second load of 0.7 + 0.2

Vendor 2—one load of 0.3 + 0.7 and a second load of 0.5 + 0.4

That leaves us with:

Vendor 1—0.6

Vendor 2—0.8

These two loads cannot be combined so we are left with two separate trips giving us three loads for each vendor.

Now that we have the combining of the shipment and pickup loads figured out, we need to analyze which customer shipments should be combined with which vendor pickups. The formulation for the problem is in Chart 7.D9.

The computer-generated solution for the problem is the following:

Customer 1—one trip

Customer 2—two trips

CHART 7.D9 Simplified QS LP-IP Printout

```
Free format model for ROUTING – E
>> Min 50C1 + 40C2 + 40C3 + 30C4 + 32C5 + 26V1 + 44V2 + 77C1V2 + 73C2V1 + 82C2V2 + 58C3V
>> 35C4V1 + 57C4V2 + 48C5V2 + 62C12 + 95C12V1 + 89C12V2 + 54C45 + 59C45V1 + 60C45V2
>> Subject to
>> (1) 1C1 + 1C1V2 = 1
>> (2) 1C2 + 1C2V1 + 1C2V2 = 2
>> (3) 1C3 + 1C3V1 = 1
>> (4) 1C4 + 1C4V1 + 1C4V2 = 1
>> (5) 1C5 + 1C5V2 = 3
>> (6) 1C12 + 1C12V1 + 1C12V2 = 1
>> (7) 1C45 + 1C45V1 + 1C45V2 = 0
>> (8) 1V1 + 1C2V1 + 1C3V1 + 1C4V1 + 1C12V1 + 1C45V1 = 3
>> (9) 1V2 + 1C1V2 + 1C2V2 + 1C4V2 + 1C5V2 + 1C12V2 + 1C45V2 = 3
>> Integer
>> C1, C2, C3, C4, C5, V1, V2, C1V2, C2V1, C2V2, C3V1, C4V1, C4V2, C5V2, C12, C12V1, C12V2, C45, C45V1,
C45V2
```

Vendor 1—one trip

Customer 3 then Vendor 1—one trip

Customer 4 then Vendor 1—one trip

Customer 5 then Vendor 2—three trips

Customers 1 and 2—one trip

Comparing these results with the results we achieved manually we have the following results:

Trip	Manual	LP Program
C1	0	1 (50 miles)
C2	1 (40 miles)	2 (80 miles)
C12	0	1 (62 miles)
C25	1 (66 miles)	0
V1	0	1 (26 miles)
C1V2	1 (77 miles)	0
C2V1	1 (73 miles)	0
C3V1	1 (58 miles)	1 (58 miles)
C4V1	1 (35 miles)	1 (35 miles)
C5V2	1 (48 miles)	3 (144 miles)
C15V2	1 (77 miles)	0
Totals:	(474 miles)	(455 miles)

The computer solution was better than the manual system by 19 miles. The computer time to calculate this solution was two seconds.

We now have examples of each of the linear-integer programming models that are needed in order to solve the routing and scheduling problems in this chapter.

APPENDIX 7.E: Master Production Schedule

As discussed earlier in the chapter, the master production schedule adds detail to the aggregate production schedule. The tool that helps us define the master production schedule is the planning bill of materials (totally different from the bill of materials you'll be reading about). The planning bill of materials looks at the breakdown of the family of parts over the last year. For example, the families we have been working with are shown in Chart 7.E1 (Redrawn from Chart 7.G6). We look at the total sales for each of these products and for their families over the last year. These are displayed in Chart 7.E2. From the breakdown of the sales we are able to draw up a planning bill of materials for each family of parts. Chart 7.E3 shows this planning bill of materials broken down by gross sales and by percentages of total sales.

At this point in this book we have not yet defined what the spare parts list of each of the bicycles looks like. Spare parts can be scheduled individually or as if they were a product of their own. In Chapter 5 we discussed the development of the product. This is where the product structure of the product, and the spare parts, would have been laid out. This becomes the bill of materials. In this book, the definition of what makes up the products, including the spare parts, will be discussed in detail in the chapter on bill of materials. For now, we will treat spare parts like a product and give them the same product number as the

CHART 7.E1 Breakdown of the Product Families

	Model Number
Mountain bikes	
Economy	MB–E
Heavy duty	MB–HD
Super lightweight	MB–SLW
Ten-speed bikes	
Men's	TS–M
Women's	TS–W
Tricycles (only one model)	TRI

CHART 7.E2 Breakdown of Last Year's Sales by Product and Families

	Total Sales
Mountain bikes	1,200
Economy	600
Heavy duty	400
Super lightweight	200
Ten-speed bikes	1,600
Men's	900
Women's	700
Tricycles (only one model)	1,300

CHART 7.E3 Planning Bill of Materials Based on Last Year's Sales

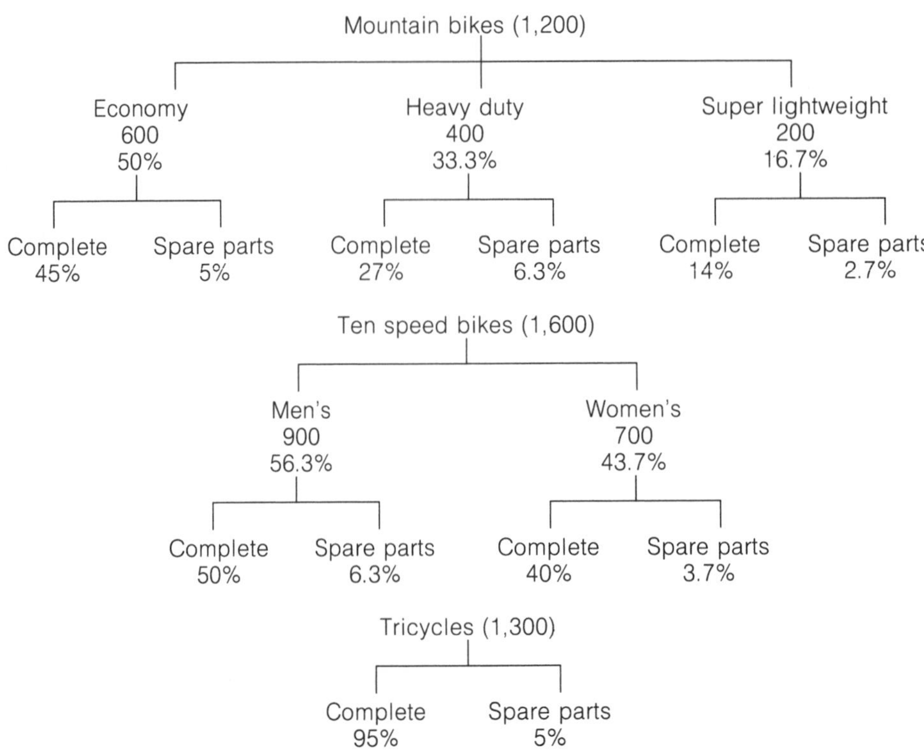

completed product with an extension of "–SP" after the product number.

Using the planning bill of materials based on last year's sales we can now allocate out the newly planned aggregate production schedule. The recently developed aggregate production schedule is displayed in Chart 7.E4. Next to it we can see the breakdown of the family into its individual components. We now have a master production schedule for each of the specific part numbers that we produce in our plant. These values are rounded because it is impossible to make 0.34 bikes. However, the numbers across still add up for each category of product (to avoid capacity conflicts) and the numbers total down for the number of products that should be built of each type.

Chart 7.E5 shows the spreadsheet version of Chart 7.E4 but you still need to do the rounding process yourself, making sure that all the numbers add up as whole numbers by row and by column. Chart 7.E6 shows the formulas for the spreadsheet in Chart 7.E5.

Note that sometimes the spare parts scheduling may be combined. For example, the ten-speed men and ten-speed women spare parts schedules may be combined if there are no differences. In that case we would only have one part number. This difference would be reflected in the planning bill of materials as just one product, for example, TS–SP, rather than the two spare parts we have now (TS–M–SP and TS–W–SP).

CHART 7.E4 Aggregate Production Schedule Converted to Master Production Schedule
(Data from Chart 7.A8)

Mountain Bikes

Month	Family	MB–E	MB–E–SP	MB–HD	MB–HD–SP	MB–SLW	MB–SLW–SP
		45%	5%	27%	6.3%	14%	2.7%
1	100	45	5	27	6	14	3
2	50	23	3	13	3	7	1
3	50	22	2	14	3	7	2
4	100	45	5	27	6	14	3
5	100	45	5	27	6	14	3
6	150	67	8	41	9	21	4
7	200	90	10	54	13	28	5
8	150	68	7	40	10	21	4
9	50	23	2	13	3	7	2
10	50	22	3	14	3	7	1
11	75	34	4	20	5	10	2
12	250	113	12	68	16	35	6
Total	1,325	597	66	358	83	185	36

Ten-speed Bikes

Month	Family	TS–M	TS–M–SP	TS–W	TS–W–SP
		50%	6.3%	40%	3.7%
1	200	100	13	80	7
2	50	25	3	20	2
3	50	25	3	20	2
4	100	50	6	40	4
5	200	100	13	80	7
6	200	100	12	80	8
7	200	100	13	80	7
8	200	100	12	80	8
9	100	50	6	40	4
10	50	25	3	20	2
11	230	115	15	92	8
12	120	60	8	48	4
Total	1,700	850	107	680	63

Tricycles

Month	Family	TRI	TRI–SP
		95%	5%
1	150	143	7
2	50	47	3
3	75	71	4
4	134	127	7
5	200	190	10
6	133	126	7
7	0	0	0
8	133	126	7
9	50	48	2
10	207	197	10
11	193	183	10
12	0	0	0
Total	1,325	1,258	67

CHART 7.E5 Aggregate Production Schedule Converted to Master Production Schedule Using the Spreadsheet

	A	B	C	D	E	F	G	H
1								
2	Mountain Bikes							
3	Month	Family	MB–E	MB–E–SP	MB–HD	MB–HD–SP	MB–SLW	MB–SLW–SP
4			45	5	27	6.3	14	2.7
5	1	100	45	5	27	6.3	14	2.7
6	2	50	22.5	2.5	13.5	3.15	7	1.35
7	3	50	22.5	2.5	13.5	3.15	7	1.35
8	4	100	45	5	27	6.3	14	2.7
9	5	100	45	5	27	6.3	14	2.7
10	6	150	67.5	7.5	40.5	9.45	21	4.05
11	7	200	90	10	54	12.6	28	5.4
12	8	150	67.5	7.5	40.5	9.45	21	4.05
13	9	50	22.5	2.5	13.5	3.15	7	1.35
14	10	50	22.5	2.5	13.5	3.15	7	1.35
15	11	75	33.75	3.75	20.25	4.725	10.5	2.025
16	12	250	112.5	12.5	67.5	15.75	35	6.75
17								
18								
19								
20	Ten-speed Bikes							
21	Month	Family	TS–M	TS–M–SP	TS–W	TS–W–SP		
22			50	6.3	40	3.7		
23	1	200	100	12.6	80	7.4		
24	2	50	25	3.15	20	1.85		
25	3	50	25	3.15	20	1.85		
26	4	100	50	6.3	40	3.7		
27	5	200	100	12.6	80	7.4		
28	6	200	100	12.6	80	7.4		
29	7	200	100	12.6	80	7.4		
30	8	200	100	12.6	80	7.4		
31	9	100	50	6.3	40	3.7		
32	10	50	25	3.15	20	1.85		
33	11	230	115	14.49	92	8.51		
34	12	120	60	7.56	48	4.44		
35								
36								
37								
38	Tricycles							
39	Month	Family	TRI	TRI–SP				
40			95	5				
41	1	150	142.5	7.5				
42	2	50	47.5	2.5				
43	3	75	71.25	3.75				
44	4	134	127.3	6.7				
45	5	200	190	10				
46	6	133	126.35	6.65				
47	7	0	0	0				
48	8	133	126.35	6.65				
49	9	50	47.5	2.5				
50	10	207	196.65	10.35				
51	11	193	183.35	9.65				
52	12	0	0	0				
53								

CHART 7.E6 Aggregate Production Schedule Converted to Master Production Schedule Showing the Spreadsheet Formulas

	A	B	C	D	E	F	G	H
1								
2	Mountain Bikes							
3	Month	Family	MB–E	MB–E–SP	MB–HD	MB–HD–SP	MB–SLW	MB–SLW–SP
4			45	5	27	6.3	14	2.7
5	1	100	C4×B5/100	D4×B5/100	E4×B5/100	F4×B5/100	G4×B5/100	H4×B5/100
6	2	50	C4×B6/100	D4×B6/100	E4×B6/100	F4×B6/100	G4×B6/100	H4×B6/100
7	3	50	C4×B7/100	D4×B7/100	E4×B7/100	F4×B7/100	G4×B7/100	H4×B7/100
8	4	100	C4×B8/100	D4×B8/100	E4×B8/100	F4×B8/100	G4×B8/100	H4×B8/100
9	5	100	C4×B9/100	D4×B9/100	E4×B9/100	F4×B9/100	G4×B9/100	H4×B9/100
10	6	150	C4×B10/100	D4×B10/100	E4×B10/100	F4×B10/100	G4×B10/100	H4×B10/100
11	7	200	C4×B11/100	D4×B11/100	E4×B11/100	F4×B11/100	G4×B11/100	H4×B11/100
12	8	150	C4×B12/100	D4×B12/100	E4×B12/100	F4×B12/100	G4×B12/100	H4×B12/100
13	9	50	C4×B13/100	D4×B13/100	E4×B13/100	F4×B13/100	G4×B13/100	H4×B13/100
14	10	50	C4×B14/100	D4×B14/100	E4×B14/100	F4×B14/100	G4×B14/100	H4×B14/100
15	11	75	C4×B15/100	D4×B15/100	E4×B15/100	F4×B15/100	G4×B15/100	H4×B15/100
16	12	250	C4×B16/100	D4×B16/100	E4×B16/100	F4×B16/100	G4×B16/100	H4×B16/100
17								
18								
19								
20	Ten-Speed Bikes							
21	Month	Family	TS–M	TS–M–SP	TS–W	TS–W–SP		
22			50	6.3	40	3.7		
23	1	200	C22×B23/100	D22×B23/100	E22×B23/100	F22×B23/100		
24	2	50	C22×B24/100	D22×B24/100	E22×B24/100	F22×B24/100		
25	3	50	C22×B25/100	D22×B25/100	E22×B25/100	F22×B25/100		
26	4	100	C22×B26/100	D22×B26/100	E22×B26/100	F22×B26/100		
27	5	200	C22×B27/100	D22×B27/100	E22×B27/100	F22×B27/100		
28	6	200	C22×B28/100	D22×B28/100	E22×B28/100	F22×B28/100		
29	7	200	C22×B29/100	D22×B29/100	E22×B29/100	F22×B29/100		
30	8	200	C22×B30/100	D22×B30/100	E22×B30/100	F22×B30/100		
31	9	100	C22×B31/100	D22×B31/100	E22×B31/100	F22×B31/100		
32	10	50	C22×B32/100	D22×B32/100	E22×B32/100	F22×B32/100		
33	11	230	C22×B33/100	D22×B33/100	E22×B33/100	F22×B33/100		
34	12	120	C22×B34/100	D22×B34/100	E22×B34/100	F22×B34/100		
35								
36								
37								
38	Tricycles							
39	Month	Family	TRI	TRI–SP				
40			95	5				
41	1	150	C40×B41/100	D40×B41/100				
42	2	50	C40×B42/100	D40×B42/100				
43	3	75	C40×B43/100	D40×B43/100				
44	4	134	C40×B44/100	D40×B44/100				
45	5	200	C40×B45/100	D40×B45/100				
46	6	133	C40×B46/100	D40×B46/100				
47	7	0	C40×B47/100	D40×B47/100				
48	8	133	C40×B48/100	D40×B48/100				
49	9	50	C40×B49/100	D40×B49/100				
50	10	207	C40×B50/100	D40×B50/100				
51	11	193	C40×B51/100	D40×B51/100				
52	12	0	C40×B52/100	D40×B52/100				
53								

Master Production Scheduling and Customer Orders

It may be helpful to calculate an available to promise report at this point. This report would reflect actual customer orders and show what products are still "available to be promised" to the customer. The procedure would be identical to the procedure shown in Appendix 7.G (see Chart 7.G8). This report may be helpful if your orders are small, for example, just a few bikes at a time. But for most of us, the available to promise calculations done at the forecast level are adequate.

The calculations and the available to promise report on Chart 7.G8 could also be done by family at the aggregate production level if we are not going to satisfy all the demands of the forecast.

The procedure for calculating the available to promise values at this point (master production level) would be the same as previously (forecast or aggregate production level) except that the available to promise report would be by product number, rather than by product family. In other words, you would have a lot more reports, one for each product number.

At this point in our planning process, all customer orders have been planned out through the forecast/aggregate production schedule/master production scheduling process. All customer orders, the forecast, and the aggregate production schedule will be satisfied by the master production schedule. The products will be built and placed into finished goods inventory. Then they will be shipped to the customer from this inventory location. In the case of our example, some customer orders may be built earlier than they are needed because we have shifted some of the demand for production into earlier months (see Appendix 7.A, Aggregate Production Scheduling).

Relieving the Master Production Schedule

In the planning process, the master production schedule lists the total demands of what needs to be built for each specific product type. As these products are shipped, the master production schedule needs to be "Relieved" of this requirement. In Chart 7.E7 we see an example of how product that is shipped actually reduces the total demand of the master production schedule. It is this relieved master production schedule that will later be used as an input in the development of the production schedule.

CHART 7.E7 Example of Relieving the Master Production Schedule for Tricycles (Data comes from Chart 7.E4)

TRI Month	Demand	Shipped	Remaining
1	143	143	0
2	47	47	0
3	71	71	0
4	127	100	27
5	190	10	180
6	126	33	93
7	0	0	0
8	126	0	126
9	48	0	48
10	197	0	197
11	183	0	183
12	0	0	0
Total	1,258	404	854

APPENDIX 7.F: Forecasting

Let's start by reviewing some of the points made earlier in this chapter.

Features Common to Forecasts

1. The data are more important than the modeling technique.
2. Sophisticated models are not needed.
3. As we have already suggested, a forecast assumes that past events can predict future events.
4. Forecasts are rarely correct.
5. Group forecasting is the most accurate.
6. Forecast accuracy decreases as the time period of the forecast increases.
7. Determine the purpose, level of accuracy, and time horizon for your forecast.

Types of Forecasts

Qualitative forecasts include customer surveys, sales force compositions (have each salesperson make a prediction and add all these numbers up), executive opinion (best guess), or panels of experts.

The two types of quantitative forecasts are time series and associative methods.

Basic Steps in Forecasting

First I will give you the basic steps required to generate a forecast (see Chart 7.F1). Then I will take each of these steps and explain them in detail using examples and giving you worksheets so that you can perform each step on your own. These worksheets can easily be input into a computer spreadsheet package if desired.

Step 1: Collect the Data

Break the actual sales history data into families by month, which is how it should be saved. If you haven't saved it by month, don't arbitrarily break it up. It's better to forecast based on total sales than to use some arbitrary breakdown of the data. If you don't have the data history in this form, start collecting it that way for future forecasts.

The worksheets given here are for a family of products by month. You may need to adjust this worksheet. For example, if your data are quarterly, then record 4 periods per year rather than 12 periods per year (at the bottom of the worksheet you will need to divide by 4 rather than by 12). Record the data into the worksheet in Chart 7.F2, Part A, under the appropriate year in the actual sales column. (See Chart 7.F2, Part B, for an example of how to fill out this worksheet.)

Step 2: Deseasonalize the Data

After you have recorded the data in Chart 7.F2, add each month across to the "Total." Then fill out the "Number of Entries" column, which indicates how many data points you had for each respective month. Follow the example in Chart 7.F2, Part B, to see how the calculations should be done.

Once you have recorded all the Number of Entries, calculate the "Average per Entry" column by dividing the "Total" by the "Number of Entries" for each month. Add down the "Average per Entry" column and put the total on the bottom of the worksheet next to the "Total of the Averages" description. Below the "Total of the Averages" is a "Total of the Averages Divided by Number of Periods" field. Place the "Total of

CHART 7.F1 The Steps in Forecasting

1. Collect data
   - Monthly increments
   - Forecast by family of product
   - Don't mix apples with oranges
   - At least two years' worth of data
2. Deseasonalize
3. Apply the deseasonalized data to several models and calculate the error factor for each model
4. Select the best model
5. Generate the forecast
6. Put seasonality back into the generated forecast
7. Monitor the performance of the forecast

CHART 7.F2 Data Seasonality Factor Worksheet, Part A

Product line ____________ Date __/__/__

Month	Actual Sales								Deseasonalized Sales			
	Year __	Year __	Year __	Year __	Total	# of Entries	Average per Entry	Period Weight	Year __	Year __	Year __	Year __
1	______	______	______	______	____ /	______ =	________ / ZZZ =	______	______	______	______	______
2	______	______	______	______	____ /	______ =	________ / ZZZ =	______	______	______	______	______
3	______	______	______	______	____ /	______ =	________ / ZZZ =	______	______	______	______	______
4	______	______	______	______	____ /	______ =	________ / ZZZ =	______	______	______	______	______
5	______	______	______	______	____ /	______ =	________ / ZZZ =	______	______	______	______	______
6	______	______	______	______	____ /	______ =	________ / ZZZ =	______	______	______	______	______
7	______	______	______	______	____ /	______ =	________ / ZZZ =	______	______	______	______	______
8	______	______	______	______	____ /	______ =	________ / ZZZ =	______	______	______	______	______
9	______	______	______	______	____ /	______ =	________ / ZZZ =	______	______	______	______	______
10	______	______	______	______	____ /	______ =	________ / ZZZ =	______	______	______	______	______
11	______	______	______	______	____ /	______ =	________ / ZZZ =	______	______	______	______	______
12	______	______	______	______	____ /	______ =	________ / ZZZ =	______	______	______	______	______

Total of the averages = ________

Total of the averages divided by the number of periods = ______/12 months = ______ = (ZZZ)

(continued)

CHART 7.F2 *(concluded)* **Sample of Data Seasonality Factor Worksheet, Part B**

Product line Bell bottoms Date 1/ 1/1992

Month	Actual Sales				Total	# of Entries	Average per Entry		Period Weight	Deseasonalized Sales			
	Year 89	Year 90	Year 91	Year __						Year 89	Year 90	Year 91	Year __
1		20	31		51 /	2 =	25.5	/ ZZZ =	.66		30.31	46.97	
2		25	35		60 /	2 =	30	/ ZZZ =	.776		32.20	45.08	
3		28	40		68 /	2 =	34	/ ZZZ =	.88		31.82	45.46	
4	23	30	41		94 /	3 =	31.3	/ ZZZ =	.81	28.36	36.99	50.56	
5	34	42	53		129 /	3 =	43	/ ZZZ =	1.113	30.55	37.74	47.62	
6	37	45	57		139 /	3 =	46.3	/ ZZZ =	1.199	30.86	37.53	47.53	
7	28	37	49		114 /	3 =	38	/ ZZZ =	.98	28.47	37.62	49.82	
8	22	30	45		97 /	3 =	32.3	/ ZZZ =	.837	26.29	35.85	53.78	
9	34	43	58		135 /	3 =	45	/ ZZZ =	1.165	29.19	36.92	49.80	
10	35	43	60		138 /	3 =	46	/ ZZZ =	1.191	29.40	36.12	50.40	
11	37	44	62		143 /	3 =	47.6	/ ZZZ =	1.234	29.99	35.67	50.26	
12	39	50			89 /	2 =	44.5	/ ZZZ =	1.152	33.86	43.41		

Total of the averages = 463.67

Total of the averages divided by the number of periods = 463.67/12 months = 38.639 = (ZZZ)

CHART 7.F3 Actual Sales Data

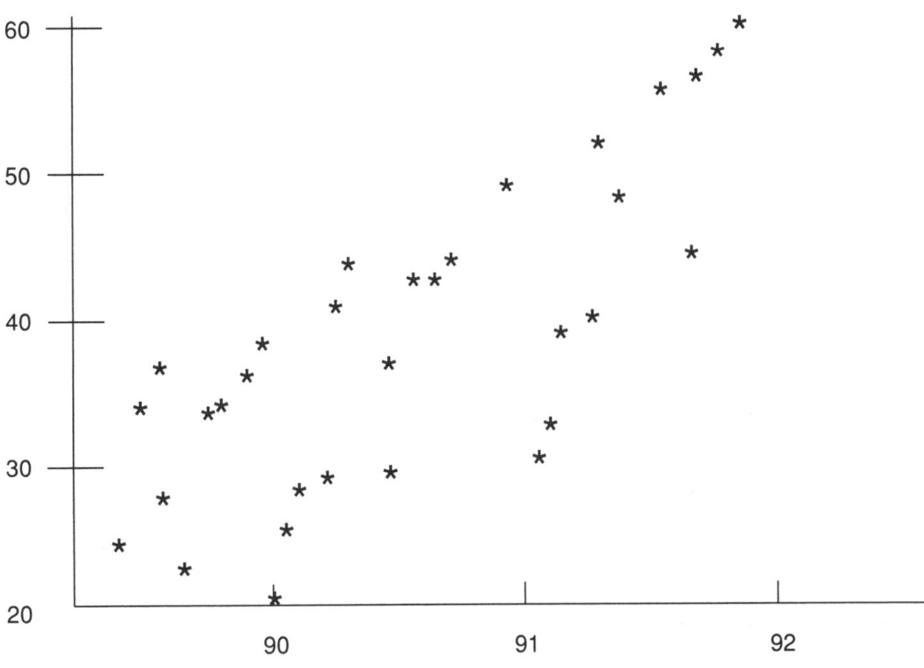

the Averages" amount in this blank and divide by 12 (assuming you are using months). Place the result into the ZZZ blank. Use this ZZZ field to divide all the "Average per Entry" values to come up with the "Period Weight," which is the seasonality factor. What it shows is that in some months you have higher than average sales consistently (values greater than 1.0) and some months you have below average sales consistently (values less than 1.0). This seasonality factor or period weight is what we use to deseasonalize the data.

Chart 7.F3 demonstrates the sporadic nature of the actual sales data. It would be difficult to draw a meaningful projection into the future using these data. Now we will see how deseasonalization can improve the concentration of the data.

To deseasonalize the data continue using the worksheet of Chart 7.F2, Part A. Chart 7.F2, Part B, continues the example of Part A. The "Actual Sales" information and the "Period Weight" information are used from the first part of the worksheet. The "Deseasonalized Sales" information is calculated by dividing each of the "Actual Sales" numbers for a particular period by the "Period Weight" for that period.

I had mentioned earlier that forecasting is also easy to do with a simple computerized spreadsheet package. As I go through the manual forecasting procedures, I will also show you how to do these same worksheets on a spreadsheet. The entire forecasting process will be performed on one spreadsheet. Note that each of the spreadsheet pieces that I show you is a continuation of the previous spreadsheet. Chart 7.F4, Part A, shows how Chart 7.F2, Part B, would look on a spreadsheet. Chart 7.F4, Part B, shows the calculations that are necessary to perform the Chart 7.F2, Part A, calculations. This sample spreadsheet

CHART 7.F4 Deseasonalization Calculations Using a Spreadsheet, Part A

	A	B	C	D	E	F	G	H	I	J	K
1											
2		Deseasonalization Calculations									
3			Actual Sales			# of		Period	Deseasonalized sales		
4	Month	1989	1990	1991	Total	Entries	Average	Weight	1989	1990	1991
5											
6	1		20	31	51	2	25.5	.6599569	0	30.30501	46.97277
7	2		25	35	60	2	30	.7764198	0	32.19907	45.07870
8	3		28	40	68	2	34	.8799425	0	31.82026	45.45752
9	4	23	30	41	94	3	31.3333	.8109274	28.36259	36.99468	50.55940
10	5	34	42	53	129	3	43	1.112868	30.55168	37.74031	47.62468
11	6	37	45	57	139	3	46.33333	1.199137	30.85552	37.52698	47.53417
12	7	28	37	49	114	3	38	.9834651	28.47076	37.62208	49.82383
13	8	22	30	45	97	3	32.33333	.8368081	26.29038	35.85052	53.77577
14	9	34	43	58	135	3	45	1.164630	29.19383	36.92160	49.80123
15	10	35	43	60	138	3	46	1.190510	29.39915	36.11896	50.39855
16	11	37	44	62	143	3	47.66667	1.233645	29.99242	35.66667	50.25758
17	12	39	50		89	2	44.5	1.151689	33.86330	43.41448	0
18					Total of averages		463.6667				
					ZZZ =		38.63889				

CHART 7.F4 *(concluded)* **Part B**

	A	B	C	D	E	F	G	H	I	J	K
1											
2		Deseasonalization Calculations									
3		Actual Sales				# of		Period	Deseasonalized sales		
4	Month	1989	1990	1991	Total	Entries	Average	Weight	1989	1990	1991
5											
6	1		20	31	B6+C6+D6	2	E6/F6	G6/G19	B6/H6	C6/H6	D6/H6
7	2		25	35	B7+C7+D7	2	E7/F7	G7/G19	B7/H7	C7/H7	D7/H7
8	3		28	40	B8+C8+D8	2	E8/F8	G8/G19	B8/H8	C8/H8	D8/H8
9	4	23	30	41	B9+C9+D9	3	E9/F9	G9/G19	B9/H9	C9/H9	D9/H9
10	5	34	42	53	B10+C10+D10	3	E10/F10	G10/G19	B10/H10	C10/H10	D10/H10
11	6	37	45	57	B11+C11+D11	3	E11/F11	G11/G19	B11/H11	C11/H11	D11/H11
12	7	28	37	49	B12+C12+D12	3	E12/F12	G12/G19	B12/H12	C12/H12	D12/H12
13	8	22	30	45	B13+C13+D13	3	E13/F13	G13/G19	B13/H13	C13/H13	D13/H13
14	9	34	43	58	B14+C14+D14	3	E14/F14	G14/G19	B14/H14	C14/H14	D14/H14
15	10	35	43	60	B15+C15+D15	3	E15/F15	G15/G19	B15/H15	C15/H15	D15/H15
16	11	37	44	62	B16+C16+D16	3	E16/F16	G16/G19	B16/H16	C16/H16	D16/H16
17	12	39	50		B17+C17+D17	2	E17/F17	G17/G19	B17/H17	C17/H17	D17/H17
18					Total of averages		SUM(G6:G17)				
19					ZZZ =		G18/12				
20											

uses Supercalc.[2] Any spreadsheet package will work; however, some of the calculations will need to be changed to fit to your particular package.

Chart 7.F5, Part A, shows the deseasonalized data graphically. The data are much more concentrated than on Chart 7.F3. It is much easier to draw a projection line through the data. Chart 7.F5, Part B, overlays the two charts (Chart 7.F3 and Chart 7.F5, Part A). We see from this chart how the seasonal data are pulled in closer to a line of projection around which the deseasonalized data are concentrated. It is not neces-

[2] Supercalc is an easy-to-use spreadsheet package offered by Computer Associates. Their national marketing office can be reached at (516) 227-3300. Supercalc 5 is a registered trademark of Computer Associates International. Any reference to Supercalc refers to this footnote. Material from the Supercalc 5 program is reprinted with the permission of Computer Associates International.

CHART 7.F5 Deseasonalized Sales Data, Part A

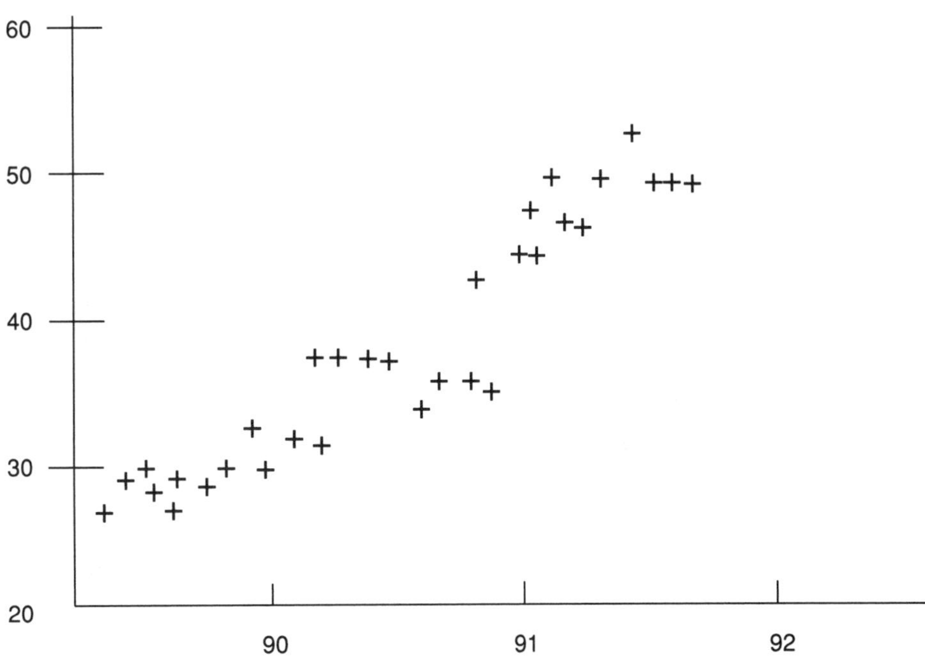

CHART 7.F5 *(concluded)* **Part B**

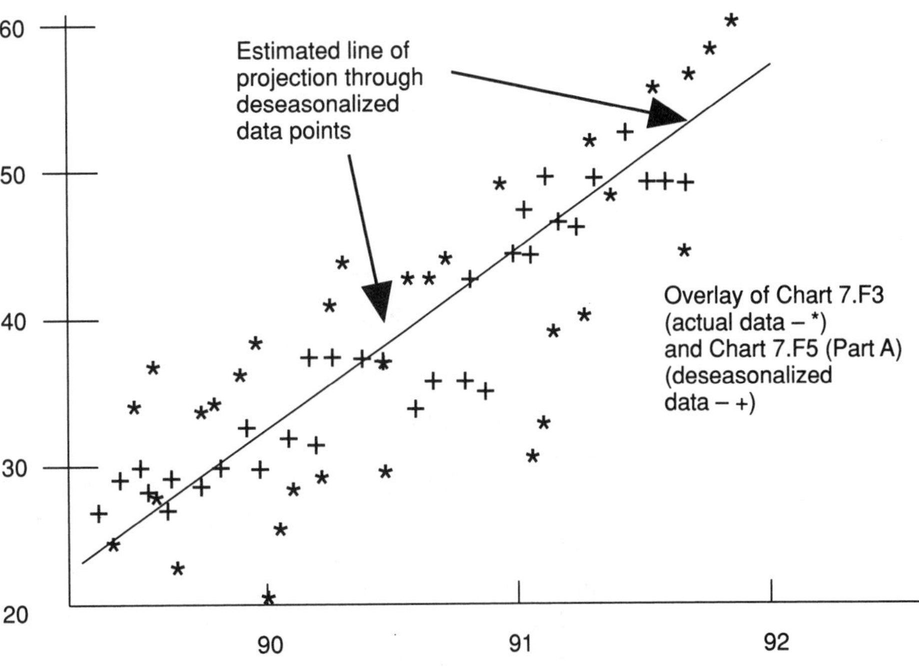

sary to draw these graphs in order to do forecasting. I have displayed these graphs so you can get a better feel for what is happening to the data.

Step 3: Apply Deseasonalized Data to Models

We will be looking at and comparing five specific quantitative time-series forecasting models. The objective is to test each of these models using the historical actual sales data after they have been deseasonalized. We want to find out which model would have done the best job, in the past, of predicting our sales. So we will run our historical, deseasonalized data against each model and calculate the amount of error in the model. The model that causes the least amount of error is the model that would have done the best job in the past (and we assume in the future also). After this step, we will select the best model and make our forecast prediction. The models we are going to use are:

1. Naive forecast
2. Simple moving average (single and double)
   2.1. Two period
   2.2. Three period
3. Weighted moving average (single and double)
   Weights open to the user
4. Exponential smoothing (single and double)
   Alpha factor open to user
5. Simple linear regression

The data I will be using when I give examples of these models are the deseasonalized data from Chart 7.F2, Part B.

Model 1: Naive Forecast. The naive forecast is a very simplistic forecast that says that I will do about the same in sales next month as I did last month (after seasonality has been removed). We input the deseasonalized data of Chart 7.F2, Part A (or the example in Chart 7.F2, Part B) into Chart 7.F6, Parts A and B (or the example of Chart 7.F6, Parts C and D). If one sheet does not have enough space, continue on another sheet (see Chart 7.F6, Parts A and B), but the totals must be for all sheets combined.

After updating the date and deseasonalized actual sales data onto Chart 7.F6, Parts A and B, place the naive forecasts into their appropriate column. Each month's forecast is the previous month's actual value (see the example in Chart 7.F6, Parts C and D). Then calculate the deviations (under the "Absolute Error" column). The absolute error is the difference between the sales value and the forecast value with the minus sign dropped. In other words, if the actual sales are 10 and the forecast is 20, the absolute error is 10. If the actual sales are 20 and the forecast is 10, the absolute error is also 10.

Calculate the error squared by simply squaring the value in the Absolute Error column. I will explain the purpose of these two error columns later when we compare the models to determine which model

CHART 7.F6 Naive Forecast Worksheet, Part A

Product Line ____________
Page _1_ of __ Date __/__/__

Deseasonalized Sales Year/Month	Amount	Naive Forecast	Absolute Error	Error Squared
____/____	______ (a)	(Forecast cannot be calculated in the first month)		
____/____	______ (b)	______ (a)	______	______
____/____	______	______ (b)	______	______
____/____	______	______	______	______
____/____	______	______	______	______
____/____	______	______	______	______
____/____	______	______	______	______
____/____	______	______	______	______
____/____	______	______	______	______
____/____	______	______	______	______
____/____	______	______	______	______
____/____	______	______	______	______
____/____	______	______	______	______
____/____	______	______	______	______
____/____	______	______	______	______
____/____	______	______	______	______
____/____	______	______	______	______
____/____	______	______	______	______
____/____	______ (z)	______	______	______

CHART 7.F6 *(continued)* **Part B**

Product Line ____________
Page __ of __ Date __/__/__

Deseasonalized Sales Year/Month	Amount	Naive Forecast	Absolute Error	Error Squared
(z comes from the previous sheet)				
____/____	______ (a)	______ (z)	______	______
____/____	______ (b)	______ (a)	______	______
____/____	______	______ (b)	______	______
____/____	______	______	______	______
____/____	______	______	______	______
____/____	______	______	______	______
____/____	______	______	______	______
____/____	______	______	______	______
____/____	______	______	______	______
____/____	______	______	______	______
____/____	______	______	______	______
____/____	______	______	______	______
____/____	______	______	______	______
____/____	______	______	______	______
____/____	______	______	______	______
____/____	______	______	______	______
____/____	______	______	______	______
____/____	______	______	______	______
____/____	______ (z)	______	______	______
		Total error factors	______	______
		Divided by n =	______	______ $= n - 1$
Naive forecasts (error values)		MAD =	______	______ = MSE

CHART 7.F6 *(continued)* **Example of Naive Forecast Worksheet, Part C** (Data from Chart 7.F2, Part B)

Product Line Bell Bottoms
Page 1 of 2 Date 1/1/1992

Deseasonalized Sales Year/Month	Amount	Naive Forecast	Absolute Error	Error Squared
89/ 4	28.36 (a)	(Forecast cannot be calculated in the first month)		
89/ 5	30.55 (b)	28.36 (a)	2.1891	4.7921
89/ 6	30.86	30.55 (b)	.3038	.0923
89/ 7	28.47	30.86	2.3848	5.6871
89/ 8	26.29	28.47	2.1804	4.7541
89/ 9	29.19	26.29	2.9034	8.4300
89/10	29.40	29.19	.2053	.0422
89/11	29.99	29.40	.5933	.3520
89/12	33.86	29.99	3.8709	14.9837
90/ 1	30.31	33.86	3.5583	12.6614
90/ 2	32.20	30.31	1.8941	3.5875
90/ 3	31.82	32.20	.3788	.1435
90/ 4	36.99	31.82	5.1744	26.7746
90/ 5	37.74	36.99	.7456	.5560
90/ 6	37.53	37.74	.2133	.0455
90/ 7	37.62	37.53	.0951	.0090
90/ 8	35.85	37.62	1.7716	3.1384
90/ 9	36.92	35.85	1.0711	1.1472
90/10	36.12 (z)	36.92	.8026	.6442

CHART 7.F6 *(concluded)* **Part D** (Data from Chart 7.F2, Part B)

Product Line Bell Bottoms
Page 2 of 2 Date 1/1/1992

Deseasonalized Sales Year/Month	Amount	Naive Forecast	Absolute Error	Error Squared
(z comes from the previous sheet)				
90/11	35.67 (a)	36.12 (z)	.4523	.2046
90/12	43.41 (b)	35.67 (a)	7.7478	60.0286
91/ 1	46.97	43.41 (b)	3.5583	12.6614
91/ 2	45.08	46.97	1.8941	3.5875
91/ 3	45.46	45.08	.3788	.1435
91/ 4	50.56	45.46	5.1019	26.0292
91/ 5	47.62	50.56	2.9347	8.6126
91/ 6	47.53	47.62	.0905	.0082
91/ 7	49.82	47.53	2.2897	5.2425
91/ 8	53.78	49.82	3.9520	15.6179
91/ 9	49.80	53.78	3.9745	15.7970
91/10	50.40	49.80	.5973	.3568
91/11	50.26	50.40	.1410	.0199
/				
/				
/				
/				
/	(z)			
		Total error factors	63.4487	236.1503
		Divided by n =	31	30 = $n - 1$
Naive forecasts (error values)		MAD =	2.0467	7.8717 = MSE

gives the best fit. For now we will simply do the work of coming up with these comparative numbers.

Add the two error columns. Count the number of data points (number of error values) that exist in the column. This value is n. Place the n value where it says "$n =$". Our sample data are for 32 months; however, since we can't calculate a forecast for the first month, we only have 31 error values. Therefore, for the sample data of Chart 7.F6, Parts C and D, n equals 31. Subtract 1 from the n value and place it where it says "$= n - 1$" (for the sample data $n - 1 = 31 - 1 = 30$). Divide the total of the Absolute Error column by n and place the value where it says "MAD =." Divide the total of the "Error Squared" column by "$n - 1$" and place the value where it says "= MSE." These are the error factors we will use for comparison in the next segment (after we have calculated all the error factors for all the models).

The spreadsheet version of Chart 7.F6, Parts C and D, is found in Chart 7.F7, Part A. The calculations necessary to make this spreadsheet work are found in Chart 7.F7, Part B.

Model 2: Simple Moving Average. Simple moving average is a technique that still holds to some of the assumptions of the naive forecast, which is that next month's forecast will be close to that of last month. However, the simple moving average method allows for some fluctuation in demand. The two-period simple moving average takes the previous two months' deseasonalized sales data and averages them using this average as the forecast for next month. A three-period simple moving average uses the last three months' data and averages them for the forecast.

For each of the next three forecasting models (simple moving average, weighted moving average, and exponential smoothing) we will find two versions, a single and a double version. The *single* version is the standard version and is adequate for most businesses. The *double* version is more appropriate for trendy businesses. The worksheets and spreadsheets are set up to do both the single and double versions. Your best option is to calculate both and compare both with all the others when we do our analysis of which model is the best forecaster over all.

Model 2.1: Two-Period Simple Moving Average. Chart 7.F8, Parts A and B, is the input document (worksheet) for two-period simple moving average forecasting. Chart 7.F8, Parts C and D, is the sample of a two-period simple moving average forecast using the deseasonalized sales data generated by Chart 7.F2, Part B.

To fill out the worksheet of Chart 7.F8, Parts A and B, start by inputting the deseasonalized sales information from Chart 7.F2, Part A. Enter the date and amount information down the left-hand side. Go to a second sheet if necessary (see Parts A and B). For more pages, repeatedly use the page on Part B over and over until all the data are posted. The first two sales data points are needed to start the forecasting process. Calculate only the totals on the last sheet covering all sheets in total. See the example on Chart 7.F8, Parts C and D.

Calculate the single forecasts as shown by the formulas. For exam-

CHART 7.F7 Naive Forecast Using a Spreadsheet, Part A

	L	M	N	O	P	Q	R	S
1								
2								
3								
4		Year/	Deseasonalized			Absolute	Error	
5		Month	Sales		Error	Error	Squared	
6		89/4	28.36259					
7		89/5	30.55168		−2.18909	2.189091	4.792119	
8		89/6	30.85552		−.303836	.3038360	.0923163	
9		89/7	28.47076		2.384755	2.384755	5.687058	
10		89/8	26.29038		2.180382	2.180382	4.754067	
11		89/9	29.19383		−2.90345	2.903449	8.430017	
12		89/10	29.39915		−.205327	.2053274	.0421594	
13		89/11	29.99242		−.593270	.5932697	.3519689	
14		89/12	33.86330		−3.87087	3.870872	14.98365	
15		90/1	30.30501		3.558285	3.558285	12.66139	
16		90/2	32.19907		−1.89406	1.894063	3.587475	
17		90/3	31.82026		.3788126	.3788126	.1434990	
18		90/4	36.99468		−5.17442	5.174419	26.77462	
19		90/5	37.74031		−.745629	.7456292	.5559629	
20		90/6	37.52698		.2133317	.2133317	.0455104	
21		90/7	37.62208		−.095098	.0950976	.0090436	
22		90/8	35.85052		1.771561	1.771561	3.138427	
23		90/9	36.92160		−1.07109	1.071089	1.147233	
24		90/10	36.11896		.8026436	.8026436	.6442367	
25		90/11	35.66667		.4522947	.4522947	.2045705	
26		90/12	43.41448		−7.74782	7.747815	60.02864	
27		91/1	46.97277		−3.55828	3.558285	12.66139	
28		91/2	45.07870		1.894063	1.894063	3.587475	
29		91/3	45.45752		−.378813	.3788126	.1434990	
30		91/4	50.55940		−5.10188	5.101881	26.02919	
31		91/5	47.62468		2.934720	2.934720	8.612582	
32		91/6	47.53417		.0905043	.0905043	.0081910	
33		91/7	49.82383		−2.28966	2.289658	5.242533	
34		91/8	53.77577		−3.95194	3.951943	15.61785	
35		91/9	49.80123		3.974539	3.974539	15.79696	
36		91/10	50.39855		−.597316	.5973162	.3567866	
37		91/11	50.25758		.1409750	.1409750	.0198739	
38					Total	63.44872	236.1503	
39					MAD =	2.046733	7.871676	= MSE
40								

CHART 7.F7 *(concluded)* **Part B**

	M	N	O	P	Q	R	S
1							
2							
3							
4	Year/	Deseasonalized			Absolute	Error	
5	Month	Sales		Error	Error	Squared	
6	89/4	I9					
7	89/5	I10		N6-N7	ABS(P7)	Q7×Q7	
8	89/6	I11		N7-N8	ABS(P8)	Q8×Q8	
9	89/7	I12		N9-N9	ABS(P9)	Q9×Q9	
10	89/8	I13		N9-N10	ABS(P10)	Q10×Q10	
11	89/9	I14		N10-N11	ABS(P11)	Q11×Q11	
12	89/10	I15		N11-N12	ABS(P12)	Q12×Q12	
13	89/11	I16		N12-N13	ABS(P13)	Q13×Q13	
14	89/12	I17		N13-N14	ABS(P14)	Q14×Q14	
15	90/1	J6		N14-N15	ABS(P15)	Q15×Q15	
16	90/2	J7		N15-N16	ABS(P16)	Q16×Q16	
17	90/3	J8		N16-N17	ABS(P17)	Q17×Q17	
18	90/4	J9		N17-N18	ABS(P18)	Q18×Q18	
19	90/5	J10		N18-N19	ABS(P19)	Q19×Q19	
20	90/6	J11		N19-N20	ABS(P20)	Q20×Q20	
21	90/7	J12		N20-N21	ABS(P21)	Q21×Q21	
22	90/8	J13		N21-N22	ABS(P22)	Q22×Q22	
23	90/9	J14		N22-N23	ABS(P23)	Q23×Q23	
24	90/10	J15		N23-N24	ABS(P24)	Q24×Q24	
25	90/11	J16		N24-N25	ABS(P25)	Q25×Q25	
26	90/12	J17		N25-N26	ABS(P26)	Q26×Q26	
27	91/1	K6		N26-N27	ABS(P27)	Q27×Q27	
28	91/2	K7		N27-N28	ABS(P28)	Q28×Q28	
29	91/3	K8		N28-N29	ABS(P29)	Q29×Q29	
30	91/4	K9		N29-N30	ABS(P30)	Q30×Q30	
31	91/5	K10		N30-N31	ABS(P31)	Q31×Q31	
32	91/6	K11		N31-N32	ABS(P32)	Q32×Q32	
33	91/7	K12		N32-N33	ABS(P33)	Q33×Q33	
34	91/8	K13		N33-N34	ABS(P34)	Q34×Q34	
35	91/9	K14		N34-N35	ABS(P35)	Q35×Q35	
36	91/10	K15		N35-N36	ABS(P36)	Q36×Q36	
37	91/11	K16		N36-N37	ABS(P37)	Q37×Q37	
38				Total	SUM(Q7:Q37)	SUM(R7:R37)	
39				MAD =	Q38/31	R38/30	= MSE
40							

CHART 7.F8 Two-Period Simple Moving Average Worksheet, Part A

Product line ________ Page 1 of __ Date __/__/__

Deseasonalized Sales Year/Month	Amount		Single Forecast		Absolute Error	Error Squared		Double Forecast	Absolute Error	Error Squared
___/_____	______	(a)								
			(Forecast cannot be calculated for the first two months)							
___/_____	______	(b)						(No forecast exists for the first four months)		
___/_____	______	(c)	(a+b)/2 = ______	(aa)	______	______				
___/_____	______	(d)	(b+c)/2 = ______	(bb)	______	______				
___/_____	______	(e)	(c+d)/2 = ______	(cc)	______	______	(aa+bb)/2 =	______	______	______
___/_____	______	(f)	(d+e)/2 = ______	(dd)	______	______	(bb+cc)/2 =	______	______	______
___/_____	______	(g)	(e+f)/2 = ______	(ee)	______	______	(cc+dd)/2 =	______	______	______
___/_____	______	(h)	(f+g)/2 = ______	(ff)	______	______	(dd+ee)/2 =	______	______	______
___/_____	______	(i)	(g+h)/2 = ______	(gg)	______	______	(ee+ff)/2 =	______	______	______
___/_____	______	(j)	(h+i)/2 = ______	(hh)	______	______	(ff+gg)/2 =	______	______	______
___/_____	______	(k)	(i+j)/2 = ______	(ii)	______	______	(gg+hh)/2 =	______	______	______
___/_____	______	(l)	(j+k)/2 = ______	(jj)	______	______	(hh+ii)/2 =	______	______	______
___/_____	______	(m)	(k+l)/2 = ______	(kk)	______	______	(ii+jj)/2 =	______	______	______
___/_____	______	(n)	(l+m)/2 = ______	(ll)	______	______	(jj+kk)/2 =	______	______	______
___/_____	______	(o)	(m+n)/2 = ______	(mm)	______	______	(kk+ll)/2 =	______	______	______
___/_____	______	(p)	(n+o)/2 = ______	(nn)	______	______	(ll+mm)/2 =	______	______	______
___/_____	______	(q)	(o+p)/2 = ______	(oo)	______	______	(mm+nn)/2 =	______	______	______

CHART 7.F8 *(continued)* **Part B**

Product line __________ Page __ of __ Date __/__/__

Deseasonalized Sales Year/Month	Amount		Single Forecast		Absolute Error	Error Squared		Double Forecast	Absolute Error	Error Squared
			(p and q come from the previous sheet)					(nn and oo come from the previous sheet)		
___/_____	______	(c)	(p+q)/2 = ______	(aa)	______	______	(nn+oo)/2 =	______	______	______
___/_____	______	(d)	(q+c)/2 = ______	(bb)	______	______	(oo+aa)/2 =	______	______	______
___/_____	______	(e)	(c+d)/2 = ______	(cc)	______	______	(aa+bb)/2 =	______	______	______
___/_____	______	(f)	(d+e)/2 = ______	(dd)	______	______	(bb+cc)/2 =	______	______	______
___/_____	______	(g)	(e+f)/2 = ______	(ee)	______	______	(cc+dd)/2 =	______	______	______
___/_____	______	(h)	(f+g)/2 = ______	(ff)	______	______	(dd+ee)/2 =	______	______	______
___/_____	______	(i)	(g+h)/2 = ______	(gg)	______	______	(ee+ff)/2 =	______	______	______
___/_____	______	(j)	(h+i)/2 = ______	(hh)	______	______	(ff+gg)/2 =	______	______	______
___/_____	______	(k)	(i+j)/2 = ______	(ii)	______	______	(gg+hh)/2 =	______	______	______
___/_____	______	(l)	(j+k)/2 = ______	(jj)	______	______	(hh+ii)/2 =	______	______	______
___/_____	______	(m)	(k+l)/2 = ______	(kk)	______	______	(ii+jj)/2 =	______	______	______
___/_____	______	(n)	(l+m)/2 = ______	(ll)	______	______	(jj+kk)/2 =	______	______	______
___/_____	______	(o)	(m+n)/2 = ______	(mm)	______	______	(kk+ll)/2 =	______	______	______
___/_____	______	(p)	(n+o)/2 = ______	(nn)	______	______	(ll+mm)/2 =	______	______	______
___/_____	______	(q)	(o+p)/2 = ______	(oo)	______	______	(mm+nn)/2 =	______	______	______
		Total error factors			______	______			______	______
		Divided by	n =		______	______ = $n-1$		$n-2$ =	______	______ = $n-3$
		Forecast (error values)	MAD =		______	______ = MSE		MAD =	______	______ = MSE

CHART 7.F8 *(continued)* **Example of Two-Period Simple Moving Average Worksheet, Part C**
(Data from Chart 7.F2, Part B)

Product line Bell bottoms Page 1 of 2 Date 1 / 1 /1992

Deseasonalized Sales Year/Month	Amount			Single Forecast		Absolute Error	Error Squared		Double Forecast	Absolute Error	Error Squared
89 / 4	28.36	(a)									
			(Forecast cannot be calculated for the first two months)								
89 / 5	30.55	(b)						(No forecast exists for the first four months)			
89 / 6	30.86	(c)	(a+b)/2 =	29.457	(aa)	1.398	1.955				
89 / 7	28.47	(d)	(b+c)/2 =	30.704	(bb)	2.233	4.986				
89 / 8	26.29	(e)	(c+d)/2 =	29.663	(cc)	3.373	11.376	(aa+bb)/2 =	30.080	3.790	14.364
89 / 9	29.19	(f)	(d+e)/2 =	27.381	(dd)	1.813	3.288	(bb+cc)/2 =	30.183	.990	.979
89 / 10	29.40	(g)	(e+f)/2 =	27.712	(ee)	1.657	2.746	(cc+dd)/2 =	28.522	.877	.770
89 / 11	29.99	(h)	(f+g)/2 =	29.296	(ff)	.696	.484	(dd+ee)/2 =	27.561	2.431	5.910
89 / 12	33.86	(i)	(g+h)/2 =	29.696	(gg)	4.168	17.368	(ee+ff)/2 =	28.519	5.344	28.558
90 / 1	30.31	(j)	(h+i)/2 =	31.928	(hh)	1.623	2.634	(ff+gg)/2 =	29.496	.809	.654
90 / 2	32.20	(k)	(i+j)/2 =	32.084	(ii)	.115	.013	(gg+hh)/2 =	30.812	1.387	1.924
90 / 3	31.82	(l)	(j+k)/2 =	31.252	(jj)	.568	.323	(hh+ii)/2 =	32.006	.186	.035
90 / 4	36.99	(m)	(k+l)/2 =	32.010	(kk)	4.985	24.850	(ii+jj)/2 =	31.668	5.327	28.372
90 / 5	37.74	(n)	(l+m)/2 =	34.407	(ll)	3.333	11.108	(jj+kk)/2 =	31.631	6.109	37.325
90 / 6	37.53	(o)	(m+n)/2 =	37.368	(mm)	.159	.025	(kk+ll)/2 =	33.209	4.318	18.649
90 / 7	37.62	(p)	(n+o)/2 =	37.634	(nn)	.012	.000	(ll+mm)/2 =	35.887	1.735	3.009
90 / 8	35.85	(q)	(o+p)/2 =	37.575	(oo)	1.724	2.972	(mm+nn)/2 =	37.501	1.650	2.723

CHART 7.F8 *(concluded)* **Part D** (Data from Chart 7.F2, Part B)

Product line Bell bottoms Page 2 of 2 Date 1 / 1 /1992

Deseasonalized Sales Year/Month	Amount			Single Forecast		Absolute Error	Error Squared		Double Forecast	Absolute Error	Error Squared	
		(p and q come from the previous sheet)						(nn and oo come from the previous sheet)				
90 / 9	36.92	(c)	(p+q)/2 =	30.736	(aa)	.185	.343	(nn+oo)/2 =	37.604	.682	.466	
90 / 10	36.12	(d)	(q+c)/2 =	36.386	(bb)	.267	.071	(oo+aa)/2 =	37.155	1.036	1.074	
90 / 11	35.67	(e)	(c+d)/2 =	36.520	(cc)	.854	.729	(aa+bb)/2 =	36.561	.895	.800	
90 / 12	43.41	(f)	(d+e)/2 =	35.893	(dd)	7.522	56.575	(bb+cc)/2 =	36.453	6.961	48.460	
91 / 1	46.97	(g)	(e+f)/2 =	39.541	(ee)	7.432	55.237	(cc+dd)/2 =	36.207	10.766	115.912	
91 / 2	45.08	(h)	(f+g)/2 =	45.194	(ff)	.115	.013	(dd+ee)/2 =	37.717	7.362	54.199	
91 / 3	45.46	(i)	(g+h)/2 =	46.026	(gg)	.568	.323	(ee+ff)/2 =	42.367	3.090	9.551	
91 / 4	50.56	(j)	(h+i)/2 =	45.268	(hh)	5.291	27.998	(ff+gg)/2 =	45.610	4.950	24.500	
91 / 5	47.62	(k)	(i+j)/2 =	48.008	(ii)	.384	.147	(gg+hh)/2 =	45.647	1.978	3.912	
91 / 6	47.53	(l)	(j+k)/2 =	49.092	(jj)	1.558	2.427	(hh+ii)/2 =	46.638	.896	.803	
91 / 7	49.82	(m)	(k+l)/2 =	47.579	(kk)	2.244	5.037	(ii+jj)/2 =	48.550	1.274	1.622	
91 / 8	53.78	(n)	(l+m)/2 =	48.679	(ll)	5.097	25.977	(jj+kk)/2 =	48.336	5.440	29.594	
91 / 9	49.80	(o)	(m+n)/2 =	51.800	(mm)	1.999	3.994	(kk+ll)/2 =	48.129	1.672	2.796	
91 / 10	50.40	(p)	(n+o)/2 =	51.789	(nn)	1.390	1.932	(ll+mm)/2 =	50.239	.159	.025	
91 / 11	50.26	(q)	(o+p)/2 =	50.100	(oo)	.158	.025	(mm+nn)/2 =	51.794	1.537	2.361	
		Total error factors				62.920	264.65			83.651	439.35	
		Divided by			$n =$	30	29	$= n - 1$	$n - 2 =$	28	27	$= n - 3$
		Forecast (error values)			MAD =	2.097	9.126	= MSE	MAD =	2.988	16.272	= MSE

ple, (aa) = (a+b)/2. At the top of the second sheet use the last two values of the previous sheet. The first "Absolute Error" column is the difference between the sales amount and the single forecast column with the minus sign dropped. The "Error Squared" column is the square of the "Absolute Error" column.

For the double forecast, the first four entries are not calculated on the first sheet, only on the second sheet and beyond. Do the calculations as shown. For example, the fifth entry is calculated by the formula (aa+bb)/2. The (aa) value is the first single forecast value and the (bb) value is the second.

Having calculated the double forecast, calculate the second "Absolute Error" by subtracting the sales amount from the double forecast and dropping the minus sign. The second "Error Squared" is the square of this second Absolute Error column.

Add up the four error columns from all the worksheets you have used and place the totals on the bottom of the last sheet next to "Total Error Factors." The value of n is the count of the number of single forecast entries you have. In the example of Chart 7.F8, Parts C and D, we have n equal to 30. Calculate $n - 1$, $n - 2$, and $n - 3$ and place these values in their respective positions. Then divide the "Total Error Factors" line by the values in the Divided By line to calculate the "Forecast (Error Values)" line. These are the values that will be used to check out the quality of the two-period simple moving average model when it comes time to select the best model.

Chart 7.F9, (Part A) shows how the spreadsheet calculation of the two-period simple moving average forecast would look. Note that I have not relisted the deseasonalized sales values. They are already in the spreadsheet in column N (See Chart 7.F7, Parts A and B). This will be true of each of the remaining spreadsheet models. Chart 7.F9, Part B, shows the calculations for Chart 7.F9, Part A.

Model 2.2: Three-Period Simple Moving Average. The calculation process for the three-period model is almost identical to the two-period model. The only difference is that three periods are used to generate the forecast rather than two. Chart 7.F10, Parts A and B, is the input document (worksheet) for this model and Chart 7.F10, Parts C, D and E, is the example of how to use this model. Similarly, Chart 7.F10, Part F, shows how these calculations would look on a spreadsheet. Chart 7.F10, Parts G and H, shows the formulas that go with each value of the spreadsheet.

At this point we have validated the performance of five forecasting models (two categories);

Naive forecasting

Simple moving average
- Two-period single moving average
- Two-period double moving average
- Three-period single moving average
- Three-period double moving average

We are now ready to look at a slightly more complicated modeling technique.

CHART 7.F9 Two-Period Simple Moving Average Using a Spreadsheet, Part A

	T	U	V	W	X	Y	Z	AA	AB
1									
2									
3									
4	Forecast		Absolute	Error	Forecast		Absolute	Error	
5	Single	Error	Error	Squared	Double	Error	Error	Squared	
6									
7									
8	29.45713	1.398381	1.398381	1.955471					
9	30.70360	−2.23284	2.232837	4.985563					
10	29.66314	−3.37276	3.372760	11.37551	30.08037	−3.78999	3.789988	14.36401	
11	27.38057	1.813258	1.813258	3.287905	30.18337	−.989541	.9895406	.9791906	
12	27.74210	1.657052	1.657052	2.745821	28.52185	.8773011	.8773011	.7696572	
13	29.29649	.6959334	.6959334	.4843233	27.56134	2.431088	2.431088	5.910191	
14	29.69579	4.167506	4.167506	17.36811	28.51930	5.343999	5.343999	28.55833	
15	31.92786	−1.62285	1.622849	2.633639	29.49614	.8088707	.8088707	.6542719	
16	32.08415	.1149207	.1149207	.0132068	30.81182	1.387249	1.387249	1.924461	
17	31.25204	.5682190	.5682190	.3228728	32.00601	−.185745	.1857453	.0345013	
18	32.00967	4.985013	4.985013	24.85036	31.66810	5.326583	5.326583	28.37249	
19	34.40747	3.332839	3.332839	11.10782	31.63086	6.109455	6.109455	37.32544	
20	37.36750	.1594830	.1594830	.0254348	33.20857	4.318409	4.318409	18.64866	
21	37.63364	−.011568	.0115682	.0001338	35.88748	1.734593	1.734593	3.008812	
22	37.57453	−1.72401	1.724012	2.972217	37.50057	−1.65005	1.650054	2.722679	
23	36.73630	.1853092	.1853092	.0343395	37.60409	−.682481	.6824808	.4657800	
24	36.38606	−.267099	.2670988	.0713418	37.15541	−1.03645	1.036450	1.074229	
25	36.52028	−.853616	.8536165	.7286611	36.56118	−.894511	.8945113	.8001505	
26	35.89281	7.521668	7.521668	56.57549	36.45317	6.961310	6.961310	48.45984	
27	39.54057	7.432193	7.432193	55.23749	36.20655	10.76622	10.76622	115.9115	
28	45.19362	−.114921	.1149207	.0132068	37.71669	7.362010	7.362010	54.19918	
29	46.02574	−.568219	.5682190	.3228728	42.36710	3.090417	3.090417	9.550677	
30	45.26811	5.291287	5.291287	27.99772	45.60968	4.949717	4.949717	24.49970	
31	48.00846	−.383780	.3837797	.1472869	45.64692	1.977754	1.977754	3.911512	
32	49.09204	−1.55786	1.557864	2.426942	46.63828	.8958893	.8958893	.8026176	
33	47.57942	2.244406	2.244406	5.037356	48.55025	1.273583	1.273583	1.622015	
34	48.67900	5.096772	5.096772	25.97708	48.33573	5.440042	5.440042	29.59406	
35	51.79980	−1.99857	1.998567	3.994271	48.12921	1.672021	1.672021	2.795656	
36	51.78850	−1.38995	1.389953	1.931970	50.23940	.1591491	.1591491	.0253284	
37	50.09989	.1576831	.1576831	.0248640	51.79415	−1.53658	1.536577	2.361069	
38		Total	62.91997	264.6493		Total	83.65101	439.3460	
39		MAD =	2.097332	9.125837	= MSE	MAD =	2.987536	16.27207 = MSE	
40									

(*continued*)

CHART 7.F9 *(concluded)* **Part B**

	T	U	V	W	X	Y	Z		
1									
2									
3									
4	Forecast		Absolute	Error	Forecast		Absolute	Error	
5	Single	Error	Error	Squared	Double	Error	Error	Squared	
6									
7									
8	(N6+N7)/2	N8-T8	ABS(U8)	V8×V8					
9	(N7+N8)/2	N9-T9	ABS(U9)	V9×V9					
10	(N8+N9)/2	N10-T10	ABS(U10)	V10×V10	(T8+T9)/2	N10-X10	ABS(Y10)	Z10×Z10	
11	(N9+N10)/2	N11-T11	ABS(U11)	V11×V11	(T9+T10)/2	N11-X11	ABS(Y11)	Z11×Z11	
12	(N10+N11)/2	N12-T12	ABS(U12)	V12×V12	(T10+T11)/2	N12-X12	ABS(Y12)	Z12×Z12	
13	(N11+N12)/2	N13-T13	ABS(U13)	V13×V13	(T11+T12)/2	N13-X13	ABS(Y13)	Z13×Z13	
14	(N12+N13)/2	N14-T14	ABS(U14)	V14×V14	(T12+T13)/2	N14-X14	ABS(Y14)	Z14×Z14	
15	(N13+N14)/2	N15-T15	ABS(U15)	V15×V15	(T13+T14)/2	N15-X15	ABS(Y15)	Z15×Z15	
16	(N14+N15)/2	N16-T16	ABS(U16)	V16×V16	(T14+T15)/2	N16-X16	ABS(Y16)	Z16×Z16	
17	(N15+N16)/2	N17-T17	ABS(U17)	V17×V17	(T15+T16)/2	N17-X17	ABS(Y17)	Z17×Z17	
18	(N16+N17)/2	N18-T18	ABS(U18)	V18×V18	(T16+T17)/2	N18-X18	ABS(Y18)	Z18×Z18	
19	(N17+N18)/2	N19-T19	ABS(U19)	V19×V19	(T17+T18)/2	N19-X19	ABS(Y19)	Z19×Z19	
20	(N18+N19)/2	N20-T20	ABS(U20)	V20×V20	(T18+T19)/2	N20-X20	ABS(Y20)	Z20×Z20	
21	(N19+N20)/2	N21-T21	ABS(U21)	V21×V21	(T19+T20)/2	N21-X21	ABS(Y21)	Z21×Z21	
22	(N20+N21)/2	N22-T22	ABS(U22)	V22×V22	(T20+T21)/2	N22-X22	ABS(Y22)	Z22×Z22	
23	(N21+N22)/2	N23-T23	ABS(U23)	V23×V23	(T21+T22)/2	N23-X23	ABS(Y23)	Z23×Z23	
24	(N22+N23)/2	N24-T24	ABS(U24)	V24×V24	(T22+T23)/2	N24-X24	ABS(Y24)	Z24×Z24	
25	(N23+N24)/2	N25-T25	ABS(U25)	V25×V25	(T23+T24)/2	N25-X25	ABS(Y25)	Z25×Z25	
26	(N24+N25)/2	N26-T26	ABS(U26)	V26×V26	(T24+T25)/2	N26-X26	ABS(Y26)	Z26×Z26	
27	(N25+N26)/2	N27-T27	ABS(U27)	V27×V27	(T25+T26)/2	N27-X27	ABS(Y27)	Z27×Z27	
28	(N26+N27)/2	N28-T28	ABS(U28)	V28×V28	(T26+T27)/2	N28-X28	ABS(Y28)	Z28×Z28	
29	(N27+N28)/2	N29-T29	ABS(U29)	V29×V29	(T27+T28)/2	N29-X29	ABS(Y29)	Z29×Z29	
30	(N28+N29)/2	N30-T30	ABS(U30)	V30×V30	(T28+T29)/2	N30-X30	ABS(Y30)	Z30×Z30	
31	(N29+N30)/2	N31-T31	ABS(U31)	V31×V31	(T29+T30)/2	N31-X31	ABS(Y31)	Z31×Z31	
32	(N30+N31)/2	N32-T32	ABS(U32)	V32×V32	(T30+T31)/2	N32-X32	ABS(Y32)	Z32×Z32	
33	(N31+N32)/2	N33-T33	ABS(U33)	V33×V33	(T31+T32)/2	N33-X33	ABS(Y33)	Z33×Z33	
34	(N32+N33)/2	N34-T34	ABS(U34)	V34×V34	(T32+T33)/2	N34-X34	ABS(Y34)	Z34×Z34	
35	(N33+N34)/2	N35-T35	ABS(U35)	V35×V35	(T33+T34)/2	N35-X35	ABS(Y35)	Z35×Z35	
36	(N34+N35)/2	N36-T36	ABS(U36)	V36×V36	(T34+T35)/2	N36-X36	ABS(Y36)	Z36×Z36	
37	(N35+N36)/2	N37-T37	ABS(U37)	V37×V37	(T35+T36)/2	N37-X37	ABS(Y37)	Z37×Z37	
38		Total	SUM(V8 : V37)	SUM(W8 : W37)		Total	SUM(Z10 : Z37)	SUM(AA10 : AA37)	
39		MAD =	V38/30	W38/29	= MSE	MAD =	Z38/28	AA38/27	= MSE
40									

CHART 7.F10 Three-Period Simple Moving Average Worksheet, Part A

Product line ______ Page 1 of __ Date __/__/__

Deseasonalized Sales Year/Month	Amount			Single Forecast		Absolute Error	Error Squared		Double Forecast	Absolute Error	Error Squared
___/___	______	(a)									
			(Forecast cannot be calculated for the first three months)								
___/___	______	(b)						(No forecast exists for the first six months)			
___/___	______	(c)									
___/___	______	(d)	(a+b+c)/3 =	______	(xa)	______	______				
___/___	______	(e)	(b+c+d)/3 =	______	(xb)	______	______				
___/___	______	(f)	(c+d+e)/3 =	______	(xc)	______	______				
___/___	______	(g)	(d+e+f)/3 =	______	(xd)	______	______	(xa+xb+xc)/3 =	______	______	______
___/___	______	(h)	(e+f+g)/3 =	______	(xe)	______	______	(xb+xc+xd)/3 =	______	______	______
___/___	______	(i)	(f+g+h)/3 =	______	(xf)	______	______	(xc+xd+xe)/3 =	______	______	______
___/___	______	(j)	(g+h+i)/3 =	______	(xg)	______	______	(xd+xe+xf)/3 =	______	______	______
___/___	______	(k)	(h+i+j)/3 =	______	(xh)	______	______	(xe+xf+xg)/3 =	______	______	______
___/___	______	(l)	(i+j+k)/3 =	______	(xi)	______	______	(xf+xg+xh)/3 =	______	______	______
___/___	______	(m)	(j+k+l)/3 =	______	(xj)	______	______	(xg+xh+xi)/3 =	______	______	______
___/___	______	(n)	(k+l+m)/3 =	______	(xk)	______	______	(xh+xi+xj)/3 =	______	______	______
___/___	______	(o)	(l+m+n)/3 =	______	(xl)	______	______	(xi+xj+xk)/3 =	______	______	______
___/___	______	(p)	(m+n+o)/3 =	______	(xm)	______	______	(xj+xk+xl)/3 =	______	______	______
___/___	______	(q)	(n+o+p)/3 =	______	(xn)	______	______	(xk+xl+xm)/3 =	______	______	______

CHART 7.F10 *(continued)* **Part B**

Product line ______ Page __ of __ Date __/__/__

Deseasonalized Sales Year/Month	Amount			Single Forecast		Absolute Error	Error Squared		Double Forecast	Absolute Error	Error Squared	
			(o, p, and q come from the previous sheet)					(xl, xm, and xn come from the previous sheet)				
___/___	______	(d)	(o+p+q)/3 =	______	(xa)	______	______	(xl+xm+xn)/3 =	______	______	______	
___/___	______	(e)	(p+q+d)/3 =	______	(xb)	______	______	(xm+xn+xa)/3 =	______	______	______	
___/___	______	(f)	(q+d+e)/3 =	______	(xc)	______	______	(xn+xa+xb)/3 =	______	______	______	
___/___	______	(g)	(d+e+f)/3 =	______	(xd)	______	______	(xa+xb+xc)/3 =	______	______	______	
___/___	______	(h)	(e+f+g)/3 =	______	(xe)	______	______	(xb+xc+xd)/3 =	______	______	______	
___/___	______	(i)	(f+g+h)/3 =	______	(xf)	______	______	(xc+xd+xe)/3 =	______	______	______	
___/___	______	(j)	(g+h+i)/3 =	______	(xg)	______	______	(xd+xe+xf)/3 =	______	______	______	
___/___	______	(k)	(h+i+j)/3 =	______	(xh)	______	______	(xe+xf+xg)/3 =	______	______	______	
___/___	______	(l)	(i+j+k)/3 =	______	(xi)	______	______	(xf+xg+xh)/3 =	______	______	______	
___/___	______	(m)	(j+k+l)/3 =	______	(xj)	______	______	(xg+xh+xi)/3 =	______	______	______	
___/___	______	(n)	(k+l+m)/3 =	______	(xk)	______	______	(xh+xi+xj)/3 =	______	______	______	
___/___	______	(o)	(l+m+n)/3 =	______	(xl)	______	______	(xi+xj+xk)/3 =	______	______	______	
___/___	______	(p)	(m+n+o)/3 =	______	(xm)	______	______	(xj+xk+xl)/3 =	______	______	______	
___/___	______	(q)	(n+o+p)/3 =	______	(xn)	______	______	(xk+xl+xm)/3 =	______	______	______	
			Total error factors			______	______			______	______	
			Divided by	*n* =		______	______	= *n* − 1	*n* − 3 =	______	______	= *n* − 4
			Forecast (error values)	MAD =		______	______	= MSE	MAD =	______	______	= MSE

(continued)

CHART 7.F10 *(continued)* **Example of Three-Period Simple Moving Average Worksheet, Part C**
(Data from Chart 7.F2, Part B)

Product line Bell bottoms Page 1 of 3 Date 1 / 1 /1992

Deseasonalized Sales Year/Month	Amount			Single Forecast		Absolute Error	Error Squared		Double Forecast	Absolute Error	Error Squared
89 / 4	28.36	(a)		(Forecast cannot be calculated for the first two months)					(No forecast exists for the first four months)		
89 / 5	30.55	(b)									
89 / 6	30.86	(c)									
89 / 7	28.47	(d)	(a+b+c)/3 =	29.923	(xa)	1.453	2.110				
89 / 8	26.29	(e)	(b+c+d)/3 =	29.959	(xb)	3.669	13.461				
89 / 9	29.19	(f)	(c+d+e)/3 =	28.539	(xc)	.665	.429				
89 / 10	29.40	(g)	(d+e+f)/3 =	27.985	(xd)	1.414	2.000	(xa+xb+xc)/3 =	29.474	.075	.006
89 / 11	29.99	(h)	(e+f+g)/3 =	28.294	(xe)	1.698	2.883	(xb+xc+xd)/3 =	28.828	1.165	1.357
89 / 12	33.86	(i)	(f+g+h)/3 =	29.528	(xf)	4.335	18.791	(xc+xd+xe)/3 =	28.273	5.591	31.254
90 / 1	30.31	(j)	(g+h+i)/3 =	31.085	(xg)	.780	.608	(xd+xe+xf)/3 =	28.603	1.702	2.898
90 / 2	32.20	(k)	(h+i+j)/3 =	31.387	(xh)	.812	.660	(xe+xf+xg)/3 =	29.636	2.563	6.570
90 / 3	31.82	(l)	(i+j+k)/3 =	32.122	(xi)	.302	.091	(xf+xg+xh)/3 =	30.667	1.153	1.331
90 / 4	36.99	(m)	(j+k+l)/3 =	31.441	(xj)	5.553	30.838	(xg+xh+xi)/3 =	31.531	5.463	29.847
90 / 5	37.74	(n)	(k+l+m)/3 =	33.671	(xk)	4.069	16.557	(xh+xi+xj)/3 =	31.650	6.090	37.089
90 / 6	37.53	(o)	(l+m+n)/3 =	35.518	(xl)	2.009	4.034	(xi+xj+xk)/3 =	32.412	5.115	26.166
90 / 7	37.62	(p)	(m+n+o)/3 =	37.421	(xm)	.201	.041	(xj+xk+xl)/3 =	33.544	4.078	16.633
90 / 8	35.85	(q)	(n+o+p)/3 =	37.630	(xn)	1.779	3.166	(xk+xl+xm)/3 =	35.537	.314	.098

CHART 7.F10 *(continued)* **Part D** (Data from Chart 7.F2, Part B)

Product line Bell bottoms Page 2 of 3 Date 1 / 1 /1992

Deseasonalized Sales Year/Month	Amount			Single Forecast		Absolute Error	Error Squared		Double Forecast	Absolute Error	Error Squared
			(o, p, and q come from the previous sheet)					(xl, xm, and xn come from the previous sheet)			
90 / 9	36.92	(d)	(o+p+q)/3 =	37.000	(xa)	.078	.006	(xl+xm+xn)/3 =	36.856	.065	.004
90 / 10	36.12	(e)	(p+q+d)/3 =	36.798	(xb)	.679	.461	(xm+xn+xa)/3 =	37.350	1.231	1.516
90 / 11	35.67	(f)	(q+d+e)/3 =	36.297	(xc)	.630	.397	(xn+xa+xb)/3 =	37.143	1.476	2.178
90 / 12	43.41	(g)	(d+e+f)/3 =	36.236	(xd)	7.179	51.534	(xa+xb+xc)/3 =	36.698	6.716	45.107
91 / 1	46.97	(h)	(e+f+g)/3 =	38.400	(xe)	8.573	73.492	(xb+xc+xd)/3 =	36.444	10.529	110.863
91 / 2	45.08	(i)	(f+g+h)/3 =	42.108	(xf)	3.061	9.368	(xc+xd+xe)/3 =	36.978	8.101	65.628
91 / 3	45.46	(j)	(g+h+i)/3 =	45.156	(xg)	.302	.091	(xd+xe+xf)/3 =	38.885	6.573	43.203
91 / 4	50.56	(k)	(h+i+j)/3 =	45.836	(xh)	4.723	22.307	(xe+xf+xg)/3 =	41.858	8.702	75.718
91 / 5	47.62	(l)	(i+j+k)/3 =	47.032	(xi)	.593	.351	(xf+xg+xh)/3 =	44.337	3.288	10.812
91 / 6	47.53	(m)	(j+k+l)/3 =	47.881	(xj)	.346	.120	(xg+xh+xi)/3 =	46.008	1.526	2.330
91 / 7	49.82	(n)	(k+l+m)/3 =	48.573	(xk)	1.251	1.565	(xh+xi+xj)/3 =	46.916	2.908	8.454
91 / 8	53.78	(o)	(l+m+n)/3 =	48.328	(xl)	5.448	29.683	(xi+xj+xk)/3 =	47.828	5.947	35.371
91 / 9	49.80	(p)	(m+n+o)/3 =	50.378	(xm)	.577	.333	(xj+xk+xl)/3 =	48.260	1.541	2.375
91 / 10	50.40	(q)	(n+o+p)/3 =	51.134	(xn)	.735	.540	(xk+xl+xm)/3 =	49.093	1.306	1.705
			Total error factors			______	______			______	______
			Divided by		$n =$	______	______	$= n - 1$	$n - 3 =$	______	______ $= n - 4$
			Forecast (error values)		MAD =	______	______	= MSE	MAD =	______	______ = MSE

CHART 7.F10 *(continued)* **Part E** (Data from Chart 7.F2, Part B)

Product line Bell bottoms — Page 3 of 3 — Date 1 / 1 /1992

Deseasonalized Sales Year/Month	Amount		Single Forecast		Absolute Error	Error Squared		Double Forecast	Absolute Error	Error Squared
		(o, p, and q come from the previous sheet)					(xl, xm, and xn come from the previous sheet)			
91 / 11	50.26	(d) (o+p+q)/3 =	51.325	(xa)	1.068	1.140	(xl+xm+xn)/3 =	49.946	.311	.097
/		(e) (p+q+d)/3 =		(xb)			(xm+xn+xa)/3 =			
/		(f) (q+d+e)/3 =		(xc)			(xn+xa+xb)/3 =			
/		(g) (d+e+f)/3 =		(xd)			(xa+xb+xc)/3 =			
/		(h) (e+f+g)/3 =		(xe)			(xb+xc+xd)/3 =			
/		(i) (f+g+h)/3 =		(xf)			(xc+xd+xe)/3 =			
/		(j) (g+h+i)/3 =		(xg)			(xd+xe+xf)/3 =			
/		(k) (h+i+j)/3 =		(xh)			(xe+xf+xg)/3 =			
/		(l) (i+j+k)/3 =		(xi)			(xf+xg+xh)/3 =			
/		(m) (j+k+l)/3 =		(xj)			(xg+xh+xi)/3 =			
/		(n) (k+l+m)/3 =		(xk)			(xh+xi+xj)/3 =			
/		(o) (l+m+n)/3 =		(xl)			(xi+xj+xk)/3 =			
/		(p) (m+n+o)/3 =		(xm)			(xj+xk+xl)/3 =			
/		(q) (n+o+p)/3 =		(xn)			(xk+xl+xm)/3 =			
		Total error factors			63.972	287.06			93.530	558.61
		Divided by		n =	29	28	= $n-1$ $n-3$ =		26	25 = $n-4$
		Forecast (error values)		MAD =	2.206	10.252	= MSE MAD =		3.597	22.344 = MSE

CHART 7.F10 *(continued)* **Three-Period Simple Moving Average Worksheet, Part F**

	AC	AD	AE	AF	AG	AH	AI	AJ	AK
1									
2									
3									
4	Forecast		Absolute	Error	Forecast		Absolute	Error	
5	Single	Error	Error	Squared	Double	Error	Error	Squared	
6									
7									
8									
9	29.92326	−1.45250	1.452501	2.109759					
10	29.95932	−3.66894	3.668940	13.46112					
11	28.53888	.6549426	.6549426	.4289497					
12	27.98499	1.414166	1.414166	1.999866	29.47382	−.074667	.0746669	.0055751	
13	28.29445	1.697971	1.697971	2.883105	28.82773	1.164694	1.164694	1.356511	
14	29.52847	4.334827	4.334827	18.79073	28.27278	5.590520	5.590520	31.25392	
15	31.08496	−.779947	.7799473	.6083179	28.60264	1.702374	1.702374	2.898078	
16	31.38691	.8121637	.8121637	.6596099	29.63596	2.563114	2.563114	6.569553	
17	32.12246	−.302199	.3021988	.0913241	30.66678	1.153482	1.153482	1.330522	
18	31.44145	5.553232	5.553232	30.83839	31.53144	5.463238	5.463238	29.84697	
19	33.67134	4.068971	4.068971	16.55653	31.65027	6.090037	6.090037	37.08855	
20	35.51842	2.008561	2.008561	4.034317	32.41175	5.115229	5.115229	26.16557	
21	37.42066	.2014196	.2014196	.0405698	33.54374	4.078341	4.078341	16.63287	
22	37.62979	−1.77927	1.779273	3.165811	35.53680	.3137112	.3137112	.0984147	
23	36.99986	−.078252	.0782517	.0061233	36.85629	.0653176	.0653176	.0042664	
24	36.79807	−.679104	.6791041	.4611824	37.35010	−1.23114	1.231139	1.515703	
25	36.29703	−.630361	.6303606	.3973545	37.14257	−1.47590	1.475903	2.178291	
26	36.23574	7.178738	7.178738	51.53427	36.69832	6.716165	6.716165	45.10688	
27	38.40004	8.572730	8.572730	73.49170	36.44361	10.52915	10.52915	110.8631	
28	42.01797	3.060732	3.060732	9.368080	36.97760	8.101101	8.101101	65.62784	
29	45.15532	.3021988	.3021988	.0913241	38.88458	6.572932	6.572932	43.20344	
30	45.83633	4.723068	4.723068	22.30737	41.85778	8.701622	8.701622	75.71822	
31	47.03187	.5928046	.5928046	.3514173	44.33654	3.288138	3.288138	10.81185	
32	47.88053	−.346358	.3463575	.1199635	46.00784	1.526333	1.526333	2.329693	
33	48.57275	1.251081	1.251081	1.565205	46.91624	2.907587	2.907587	8.454060	
34	48.32756	5.448213	5.448213	29.68303	47.82838	5.947389	5.947389	35.37144	
35	50.37793	−.576691	.5766909	.3325723	48.26028	1.540955	1.540955	2.374542	
36	51.13361	−.735062	.7350620	.5403161	49.09274	1.305806	1.305806	1.705129	
37	51.32519	−1.06761	1.067610	1.139792	49.94637	.3112097	.3112097	.0968515	
38		Total	63.97212	287.0581		Total	93.53016	558.6078	
39		MAD =	2.205935	10.25208	= MSE	MAD =	3.597314	22.34431	= MSE
40									

(continued)

CHART 7.F10 *(continued)* **Three-Period Simple Moving Average Using a Spreadsheet, Part G**

	AC	AD	AE	AF	AG
1					
2					
3					
4	Forecast		Absolute	Error	Forecast
5	Single	Error	Error	Squared	Double
6					
7					
8					
9	(N6+N7+N8)/3	N9-AC9	ABS(AD9)	AE9×AE9	
10	(N7+N8+N9)/3	N10-AC10	ABS(AD10)	AE10×AE10	
11	(N8+N9+N10)/3	N11-AC11	ABS(AD11)	AE11×AE11	
12	(N9+N10+N11)/3	N12-AC12	ABS(AD12)	AE12×AE12	(AC9+AC10+AC11)/3
13	(N10+N11+N12)/3	N13-AC13	ABS(AD13)	AE13×AE13	(AC10+AC11+AC12)/3
14	(N11+N12+N13)/3	N14-AC14	ABS(AD14)	AE14×AE14	(AC11+AC12+AC13)/3
15	(N12+N13+N14)/3	N15-AC15	ABS(AD15)	AE15×AE15	(AC12+AC13+AC14)/3
16	(N13+N14+N15)/3	N16-AC16	ABS(AD16)	AE16×AE16	(AC13+AC14+AC15)/3
17	(N14+N15+N16)/3	N17-AC17	ABS(AD17)	AE17×AE17	(AC14+AC15+AC16)/3
18	(N15+N16+N17)/3	N18-AC18	ABS(AD18)	AE18×AE18	(AC15+AC16+AC17)/3
19	(N16+N17+N18)/3	N19-AC19	ABS(AD19)	AE19×AE19	(AC16+AC17+AC18)/3
20	(N17+N18+N19)/3	N20-AC20	ABS(AD20)	AE20×AE20	(AC17+AC18+AC19)/3
21	(N18+N19+N20)/3	N21-AC21	ABS(AD21)	AE21×AE21	(AC18+AC19+AC20)/3
22	(N19+N20+N21)/3	N22-AC22	ABS(AD22)	AE22×AE22	(AC19+AC20+AC21)/3
23	(N20+N21+N22)/3	N23-AC23	ABS(AD23)	AE23×AE23	(AC20+AC21+AC22)/3
24	(N21+N22+N23)/3	N24-AC24	ABS(AD24)	AE24×AE24	(AC21+AC22+AC23)/3
25	(N22+N23+N24)/3	N25-AC25	ABS(AD25)	AE25×AE25	(AC22+AC23+AC24)/3
26	(N23+N24+N25)/3	N26-AC26	ABS(AD26)	AE26×AE26	(AC23+AC24+AC25)/3
27	(N24+N25+N26)/3	N27-AC27	ABS(AD27)	AE27×AE27	(AC24+AC25+AC26)/3
28	(N25+N26+N27)/3	N28-AC28	ABS(AD28)	AE28×AE28	(AC25+AC26+AC27)/3
29	(N26+N27+N28)/3	N29-AC29	ABS(AD29)	AE29×AE29	(AC26+AC27+AC28)/3
30	(N27+N28+N29)/3	N30-AC30	ABS(AD30)	AE30×AE30	(AC27+AC28+AC29)/3
31	(N28+N29+N30)/3	N31-AC31	ABS(AD31)	AE31×AE31	(AC28+AC29+AC30)/3
32	(N29+N30+N31)/3	N32-AC32	ABS(AD32)	AE32×AE32	(AC29+AC30+AC31)/3
33	(N30+N31+N32)/3	N33-AC33	ABS(AD33)	AE33×AE33	(AC30+AC31+AC32)/3
34	(N31+N32+N33)/3	N34-AC34	ABS(AD34)	AE34×AE34	(AC31+AC32+AC33)/3
35	(N32+N33+N34)/3	N35-AC35	ABS(AD35)	AE35×AE35	(AC32+AC33+AC34)/3
36	(N33+N34+N35)/3	N36-AC36	ABS(AD36)	AE36×AE36	(AC33+AC34+AC35)/3
37	(N34+N35+N36)/3	N37-AC37	ABS(AD37)	AE37×AE37	(AC34+AC35+AC36)/3
38		Total	SUM(AE9 : AE37)	SUM(AF9 : AF37)	
39		MAD =	AE38/29	AF38/28	= MSE
40					

CHART 7.F10 *(concluded)* **Part H**

	AH	AI	AJ	AK
1				
2				
3				
4		Absolute	Error	
5	Error	Error	Squared	
6				
7				
8				
9				
10				
11				
12	N12-AG12	ABS(AH12)	AI12×AI12	
13	N13-AG13	ABS(AH13)	AI13×AI13	
14	N14-AG14	ABS(AH14)	AI14×AI14	
15	N15-AG15	ABS(AH15)	AI15×AI15	
16	N16-AG16	ABS(AH16)	AI16×AI16	
17	N17-AG17	ABS(AH17)	AI17×AI17	
18	N18-AG18	ABS(AH18)	AI18×AI18	
19	N19-AG19	ABS(AH19)	AI19×AI19	
20	N20-AG20	ABS(AH20)	AI20×AI20	
21	N21-AG21	ABS(AH21)	AI21×AI21	
22	N22-AG22	ABS(AH22)	AI22×AI22	
23	N23-AG23	ABS(AH23)	AI23×AI23	
24	N24-AG24	ABS(AH24)	AI24×AI24	
25	N25-AG25	ABS(AH25)	AI25×AI25	
26	N26-AG26	ABS(AH26)	AI26×AI26	
27	N27-AG27	ABS(AH27)	AI27×AI27	
28	N28-AG28	ABS(AH28)	AI28×AI28	
29	N29-AG29	ABS(AH29)	AI29×AI29	
30	N30-AG30	ABS(AH30)	AI30×AI30	
31	N31-AG31	ABS(AH31)	AI31×AI31	
32	N32-AG32	ABS(AH32)	AI32×AI32	
33	N33-AG33	ABS(AH33)	AI33×AI33	
34	N34-AG34	ABS(AH34)	AI34×AI34	
35	N35-AG35	ABS(AH35)	AI35×AI35	
36	N36-AG36	ABS(AH36)	AI36×AI36	
37	N37-AG37	ABS(AH37)	AI37×AI37	
38	Total	SUM(AI12:AI37)	SUM(AJ12:AJ37)	
39	MAD =	AI38/26	AJ38/25	= MSE
40				

Model 3: Weighted Moving Average. In this modeling technique, we are attempting to average the last four periods of data. However, we have added one slight twist. We are now able to "weigh" the most current period heavier than older periods. For example, if we use four-period weighted moving average forecasting with weights of 0.4, 0.3, 0.2, and 0.1, then the most recent period would be weighted at 0.4, the period prior to that would be weighted at 0.3, and so on. If we go back to the deseasonalized data of Chart 7.F2, Part B, the forecast for December 1991 would be equal to 0.4 × (50.26) + 0.3 × (50.40) + 0.2 × (49.80) + 0.1 × (53.78) = 50.562. Note that it is very important that the weights add up to 1.0 (which stands for 100%); otherwise the forecast data are worthless.

Chart 7.F11, Parts A and B, is a worksheet for the weighted moving average model. Chart 7.F11, Parts C, D, and E, is an example of how to use Chart 7.F11, Parts A and B, using the same data from Chart 7.F2, Part B, that has been used in the previous examples.

Having assigned the weights (make sure they add up to 1.0), we can now proceed to calculate forecasts for each data point. Since we are dealing with four data points, the first four data points will not have forecasts calculated for them. However, they are needed to calculate the forecast for the fifth period. In this case the calculation would be (see Chart 7.F11, Part C, for April through August 1989):

(First Month times Lowest Weight) plus

(Second Month times Second Lowest Weight) plus

(Third Month times Third Lowest Weight) plus

(Fourth Month times Highest Weight) equals

(Forecast for Fifth Month)

Using the example in Chart 7.F11, Parts C, D, and E, where the weights are 0.4, 0.3, 0.2, and 0.1, the calculation would be:

$$(28.36) \times 0.1 + (30.55) \times 0.2 + (30.86) \times 0.3 + (28.47) \times 0.4 = (29.592)$$

This calculation process repeats itself for each forecast calculation as shown in the formulas on the worksheet.

Once the single forecasts have been calculated, the error factors can be calculated by subtracting the sales amount from the single forecast, dropping the minus sign, and placing the answer in the "Absolute Error" column. The "Error Squared" value is the square of the "Absolute Error" value.

The double forecast is calculated by using the first four data points from the single forecast column. The calculation would be:

(First Month of Single Forecast times Lowest Weight) plus

(Second Month of Single Forecast times Second Lowest Weight) plus

(Third Month of Single Forecast times Third Lowest Weight) plus

(Fourth Month of Single Forecast times Highest Weight) equals

(Forecast for Fifth Month)

CHART 7.F11 Weighted Moving Average Worksheet, Part A

Product line ______ Page 1 of __ Date __/__/__

Deseasonalized Sales Year/Month	Amount		Weights	Single Forecast		Absolute Error	Error Squared		Double Forecast	Absolute Error	Error Squared
___/___	______	(a)	______ (w4) – smallest								
			(Forecast cannot be calculated for the first four months)								
									(No forecast exists for the first eight months)		
___/___	______	(b)	______ (w3)								
___/___	______	(c)	______ (w2)								
___/___	______	(d)	______ (w1) – largest								
___/___	______	(e)	(a×w4+b×w3+c×w2+d×w1) =	______	(ya)	______	______				
___/___	______	(f)	(b×w4+c×w3+d×w2+e×w1) =	______	(yb)	______	______				
___/___	______	(g)	(c×w4+d×w3+e×w2+f×w1) =	______	(yc)	______	______				
___/___	______	(h)	(d×w4+e×w3+f×w2+g×w1) =	______	(yd)	______	______				
___/___	______	(i)	(e×w4+f×w3+g×w2+h×w1) =	______	(ye)	______	______	(ya×w4+yb×w3+yc×w2+yd×w1) =	______	______	______
___/___	______	(j)	(f×w4+g×w3+h×w2+i×w1) =	______	(yf)	______	______	(yb×w4+yc×w3+yd×w2+ye×w1) =	______	______	______
___/___	______	(k)	(g×w4+h×w3+i×w2+j×w1) =	______	(yg)	______	______	(yc×w4+yd×w3+ye×w2+yf×w1) =	______	______	______
___/___	______	(l)	(h×w4+i×w3+j×w2+k×w1) =	______	(yh)	______	______	(yd×w4+ye×w3+yf×w2+yg×w1) =	______	______	______
___/___	______	(m)	(i×w4+j×w3+k×w2+l×w1) =	______	(yi)	______	______	(ye×w4+yf×w3+yg×w2+yh×w1) =	______	______	______
___/___	______	(n)	(j×w4+k×w3+l×w2+m×w1) =	______	(yj)	______	______	(yf×w4+yg×w3+yh×w2+yi×w1) =	______	______	______
___/___	______	(o)	(k×w4+l×w3+m×w2+n×w1) =	______	(yk)	______	______	(yg×w4+yh×w3+yi×w2+yj×w1) =	______	______	______
___/___	______	(p)	(l×w4+m×w3+n×w2+o×w1) =	______	(yl)	______	______	(yh×w4+yi×w3+yj×w2+yk×w1) =	______	______	______
___/___	______	(q)	(m×w4+n×w3+o×w2+p×w1) =	______	(ym)	______	______	(yi×w4+yj×w3+yk×w2+yl×w1) =	______	______	______

(continued)

CHART 7.F11 *(continued)* **Weighted Moving Average Worksheet, Part B**

Product line Bell bottoms   Page 2 of 3   Date 1 / 1 /1992

Deseasonalized Sales Year/Month	Amount		Weights	Single Forecast		Absolute Error	Error Squared		Double Forecast	Absolute Error	Error Squared	
				(n, o, p, and q come from the previous sheet)				(yj, yk, yl, and ym come from the previous sheet)				
____/____	______	(e)	(n×w4+o×w3+p×w2+q×w1) =	______	(ya)	______	______	(yj×w4+yk×w3+yl×w2+ym×w1) =	______	______	______	
____/____	______	(f)	(o×w4+p×w3+q×w2+e×w1) =	______	(yb)	______	______	(yk×w4+yl×w3+ym×w2+ya×w1) =	______	______	______	
____/____	______	(g)	(p×w4+q×w3+e×w2+f×w1) =	______	(yc)	______	______	(yl×w4+ym×w3+ya×w2+yb×w1) =	______	______	______	
____/____	______	(h)	(q×w4+e×w3+f×w2+g×w1) =	______	(yd)	______	______	(ym×w4+ya×w3+yb×w2+yc×w1) =	______	______	______	
____/____	______	(i)	(e×w4+f×w3+g×w2+h×w1) =	______	(ye)	______	______	(ya×w4+yb×w3+yc×w2+yd×w1) =	______	______	______	
____/____	______	(j)	(f×w4+g×w3+h×w2+i×w1) =	______	(yf)	______	______	(yb×w4+yc×w3+yd×w2+ye×w1) =	______	______	______	
____/____	______	(k)	(g×w4+h×w3+i×w2+j×w1) =	______	(yg)	______	______	(yc×w4+yd×w3+ye×w2+yf×w1) =	______	______	______	
____/____	______	(l)	(h×w4+i×w3+j×w2+k×w1) =	______	(yh)	______	______	(yd×w4+ye×w3+yf×w2+yg×w1) =	______	______	______	
____/____	______	(m)	(i×w4+j×w3+k×w2+l×w1) =	______	(yi)	______	______	(ye×w4+yf×w3+yg×w2+yh×w1) =	______	______	______	
____/____	______	(n)	(j×w4+k×w3+l×w2+m×w1) =	______	(yj)	______	______	(yf×w4+yg×w3+yh×w2+yi×w1) =	______	______	______	
____/____	______	(o)	(k×w4+l×w3+m×w2+n×w1) =	______	(yk)	______	______	(yg×w4+yh×w3+yi×w2+yj×w1) =	______	______	______	
____/____	______	(p)	(l×w4+m×w3+n×w2+o×w1) =	______	(yl)	______	______	(yh×w4+yi×w3+yj×w2+yk×w1) =	______	______	______	
____/____	______	(q)	(m×w4+n×w3+o×w2+p×w1) =	______	(ym)	______	______	(yi×w4+yj×w3+yk×w2+yl×w1) =	______	______	______	
			Total error factors			______	______			______	______	
			Divided by	n =		______	______	= $n - 1$	$n - 4$ =	______	______	= $n - 5$
			Forecast (error values)	MAD =		______	______	= MSE	MAD =	______	______	= MSE

CHART 7.F11 *(continued)* **Example of Weighted Moving Average Worksheet, Part C** (Data from Chart 7.F2, Part B)

Product line Bell bottoms Page 1 of 3 Date 1 / 1 /1992

Year/Month	Deseasonalized Sales Amount		Weights	Single Forecast		Absolute Error	Error Squared		Double Forecast	Absolute Error	Error Squared
89 / 4	28.36	(a)	.1 (w4) – smallest	(Forecast cannot be calculated for the first four months)				(No forecast exists for the first eight months)			
89 / 5	30.55	(b)	.2 (w3)								
89 / 6	30.86	(c)	.3 (w2)								
89 / 7	28.47	(d)	.4 (w1) – largest								
89 / 8	26.29	(e)	(a×w4+b×w3+c×w2+d×w1) =	29.592	(ya)	3.301	10.898				
89 / 9	29.19	(f)	(b×w4+c×w3+d×w2+e×w1) =	28.284	(yb)	.910	.828				
89 / 10	29.40	(g)	(c×w4+d×w3+e×w2+f×w1) =	28.344	(yc)	1.055	1.113				
89 / 11	29.99	(h)	(d×w4+e×w3+f×w2+g×w1) =	28.623	(yd)	1.369	1.875				
89 / 12	33.86	(i)	(e×w4+f×w3+g×w2+h×w1) =	29.284	(ye)	4.579	20.965	(ya×w4+yb×w3+yc×w2+yd×w1) =	28.568	5.295	28.036
90 / 1	30.31	(j)	(f×w4+g×w3+h×w2+i×w1) =	31.342	(yf)	1.037	1.076	(yb×w4+yc×w3+yd×w2+ye×w1) =	28.798	1.507	2.271
90 / 2	32.20	(k)	(g×w4+h×w3+i×w2+j×w1) =	31.219	(yg)	.980	.960	(yc×w4+yd×w3+ye×w2+yf×w1) =	29.881	2.318	5.372
90 / 3	31.82	(l)	(h×w4+i×w3+j×w2+k×w1) =	31.743	(yh)	.077	.006	(yd×w4+ye×w3+yf×w2+yg×w1) =	30.610	1.211	1.466
90 / 4	36.99	(m)	(i×w4+j×w3+k×w2+l×w1) =	31.835	(yi)	5.160	26.621	(ye×w4+yf×w3+yg×w2+yh×w1) =	31.260	5.735	32.887
90 / 5	37.74	(n)	(j×w4+k×w3+l×w2+m×w1) =	33.814	(yj)	3.926	15.414	(yf×w4+yg×w3+yh×w2+yi×w1) =	31.635	6.105	37.274
90 / 6	37.53	(o)	(k×w4+l×w3+m×w2+n×w1) =	35.778	(yk)	1.748	3.057	(yg×w4+yh×w3+yi×w2+yj×w1) =	32.547	4.980	24.802
90 / 7	37.62	(p)	(l×w4+m×w3+n×w2+o×w1) =	36.914	(yl)	.708	.502	(yh×w4+yi×w3+yj×w2+yk×w1) =	33.997	3.625	13.141
90 / 8	35.85	(q)	(m×w4+n×w3+o×w2+p×w1) =	37.554	(ym)	1.704	2.903	(yi×w4+yj×w3+yk×w2+yl×w1) =	35.445	.405	.164

(continued)

CHART 7.F11 *(continued)* **Example of Weighted Moving Average Worksheet, Part D** (Data from Chart 7.F2, Part B)

Product line Bell bottoms Page 2 of 3 Date 1 / 1 /1992

Deseasonalized Sales Year/Month	Amount		Weights	Single Forecast		Absolute Error	Error Squared		Double Forecast	Absolute Error	Error Squared
				(n, o, p, and q come from the previous sheet)				(yj, yk, yl, and ym come from the previous sheet)			
90 / 9	36.92	(e)	(n×w4+o×w3+p×w2+q×w1) =	36.906	(ya)	.015	.000	(yj×w4+yk×w3+yl×w2+ym×w1) =	36.633	.288	.083
90 / 10	36.12	(f)	(o×w4+p×w3+q×w2+e×w1) =	36.801	(yb)	.682	.465	(yk×w4+yl×w3+ym×w2+ya×w1) =	36.989	.870	.758
90 / 11	35.67	(g)	(p×w4+q×w3+e×w2+f×w1) =	36.456	(yc)	.790	.624	(yl×w4+ym×w3+ya×w2+yb×w1) =	36.995	1.328	1.763
90 / 12	43.41	(h)	(q×w4+e×w3+f×w2+g×w1) =	36.071	(yd)	7.343	53.916	(ym×w4+ya×w3+yb×w2+yc×w1) =	36.760	6.655	44.289
91 / 1	46.97	(i)	(e×w4+f×w3+g×w2+h×w1) =	38.982	(ye)	7.991	63.856	(ya×w4+yb×w3+yc×w2+yd×w1) =	36.416	10.556	111.437
91 / 2	45.08	(j)	(f×w4+g×w3+h×w2+i×w1) =	42.559	(yf)	2.520	6.351	(yb×w4+yc×w3+yd×w2+ye×w1) =	37.386	7.693	59.184
91 / 3	45.46	(k)	(g×w4+h×w3+i×w2+j×w1) =	44.373	(yg)	1.085	1.176	(yc×w4+yd×w3+ye×w2+yf×w1) =	39.578	5.879	34.569
91 / 4	50.56	(l)	(h×w4+i×w3+j×w2+k×w1) =	45.443	(yh)	5.117	26.181	(yd×w4+ye×w3+yf×w2+yg×w1) =	41.920	8.639	74.634
91 / 5	47.62	(m)	(i×w4+j×w3+k×w2+l×w1) =	47.574	(yi)	.051	.003	(ye×w4+yf×w3+yg×w2+yh×w1) =	43.899	3.726	13.882
91 / 6	47.53	(n)	(j×w4+k×w3+l×w2+m×w1) =	47.817	(yj)	.283	.080	(yf×w4+yg×w3+yh×w2+yi×w1) =	45.793	1.741	3.032
91 / 7	49.82	(o)	(k×w4+l×w3+m×w2+n×w1) =	47.959	(yk)	1.865	3.479	(yg×w4+yh×w3+yi×w2+yj×w1) =	46.925	2.899	8.404
91 / 8	53.78	(p)	(l×w4+m×w3+n×w2+o×w1) =	48.771	(yl)	5.005	25.051	(yh×w4+yi×w3+yj×w2+yk×w1) =	47.588	6.188	38.293
91 / 9	49.80	(q)	(m×w4+n×w3+o×w2+p×w1) =	50.727	(ym)	.926	.857	(yi×w4+yj×w3+yk×w2+yl×w1) =	48.217	1.585	2.511
			Total error factors			____	____			____	____
			Divided by		n =	____	____	= $n - 1$	$n - 4$ =	____	____ = $n - 5$
			Forecast (error values)		MAD =	____	____	= MSE	MAD =	____	____ = MSE

CHART 7.F11 (*concluded*) **Part E** (Data from Chart 7.F2, Part B)

Product line Bell bottoms Page 3 of 3 Date 1 / 1 /1992

Deseasonalized Sales Year/Month	Amount		Weights	Single Forecast		Absolute Error	Error Squared		Double Forecast	Absolute Error	Error Squared
				(n, o, p, and q come from the previous sheet)				(yj, yk, yl, and ym come from the previous sheet)			
91 / 10	50.40	(e)	(n×w4+o×w3+p×w2+q×w1) =	50.771	(ya)	.373	.139	(yj×w4+yk×w3+yl×w2+ym×w1) =	49.295	1.103	1.217
91 / 11	50.26	(f)	(o×w4+p×w3+q×w2+e×w1) =	50.837	(yb)	.580	.336	(yk×w4+yl×w3+ym×w2+ya×w1) =	50.077	.181	.033
/		(g)	(p×w4+q×w3+e×w2+f×w1) =		(yc)			(yl×w4+ym×w3+ya×w2+yb×w1) =			
/		(h)	(q×w4+e×w3+f×w2+g×w1) =		(yd)			(ym×w4+ya×w3+yb×w2+yc×w1) =			
/		(i)	(e×w4+f×w3+g×w2+h×w1) =		(ye)			(ya×w4+yb×w3+yc×w2+yd×w1) =			
/		(j)	(f×w4+g×w3+h×w2+i×w1) =		(yf)			(yb×w4+yc×w3+yd×w2+ye×w1) =			
/		(k)	(g×w4+h×w3+i×w2+j×w1) =		(yg)			(yc×w4+yd×w3+ye×w2+yf×w1) =			
/		(l)	(h×w4+i×w3+j×w2+k×w1) =		(yh)			(yd×w4+ye×w3+yf×w2+yg×w1) =			
/		(m)	(i×w4+j×w3+k×w2+l×w1) =		(yi)			(ye×w4+yf×w3+yg×w2+yh×w1) =			
/		(n)	(j×w4+k×w3+l×w2+m×w1) =		(yj)			(yf×w4+yg×w3+yh×w2+yi×w1) =			
/		(o)	(k×w4+l×w3+m×w2+n×w1) =		(yk)			(yg×w4+yh×w3+yi×w2+yj×w1) =			
/		(p)	(l×w4+m×w3+n×w2+o×w1) =		(yl)			(yh×w4+yi×w3+yj×w2+yk×w1) =			
/		(q)	(m×w4+n×w3+o×w2+p×w1) =		(ym)			(yi×w4+yj×w3+yk×w2+yl×w1) =			
			Total error factors			61.179	268.732			90.514	539.502
			Divided by		n =	28	27	= $n - 1$	$n - 4$ =	24	23 = $n - 5$
			Forecast (error values)		MAD =	2.185	9.953	= MSE	MAD =	3.771	23.457 = MSE

Using the example in Chart 7.F11, Parts C, D, and E, where the weights are 0.4, 0.3, 0.2, and 0.1, the calculation for the first double forecast entry would be:

$$(29.592) \times 0.1 + (28.284) \times 0.2 + (28.344) \times 0.3 + (28.623) \times 0.4 = (28.568)$$

This calculation process repeats itself for each forecast calculation as shown in the formulas on the worksheet.

Once the double forecast has been calculated, the error factors can be calculated by subtracting the sales amount from the double forecast, dropping the minus sign, and placing the answer in the "Absolute Error" column. The "Error Squared" value is the square of the "Absolute Error" value.

Add the totals for the absolute error and error squared columns and place the totals on the last sheet. The value of n is the number of data points in the single forecast column. Calculate n, $n - 1$, $n - 4$, and $n - 5$ and place these values in the appropriate boxes. Divide the "Total Error Factors" by the "Divided by" row to get the MAD and MSE values.

The process of calculating the weighted moving average forecast is very experimental. Any number of weights can be selected. As a forecaster you should try different weights to see which one performs best for your data. For example, for the data of Chart 7.F2, Part B, as demonstrated in Chart 7.F11, Parts C, D, and E, I have tried several weights and have listed the results on Chart 7.F12. The actual process of evaluating these data will be discussed in detail in the section on selecting the best model. Generally what we are looking for is the smallest value possible. In this case, for the data in Chart 7.F12, the best model under the MAD category would be the single forecasting model with the weights of 0.6, 0.3, 0.1, and 0.0. The best model under the MSE category would be the single forecasting model with the weights of 0.9, 0.1, 0.0, and 0.0. The double forecasts did not perform well when compared to the single forecasts.

The spreadsheet version of the calculations performed on Chart 7.F11, Parts C, D, and E, can be seen on Chart 7.F13, Part A. The

CHART 7.F12 Weighted Moving Average Results (Data From Chart 7.F2, Part B)

				Single		Double	
Weights				MAD	MSE	MAD	MSE
0.4	0.3	0.2	0.1	2.185	9.953	3.771	23.457
0.3	0.3	0.2	0.2	2.321	11.100	4.271	27.713
0.5	0.3	0.2	0.0	2.094	9.178	3.360	19.915
0.6	0.2	0.2	0.0	2.070	8.636	3.173	18.597
0.6	0.3	0.1	0.0	2.035	8.715	3.060	17.736
0.6	0.4	0.0	0.0	2.087	8.964	2.965	17.082
0.7	0.3	0.0	0.0	2.058	8.555	2.814	16.262
0.9	0.1	0.0	0.0	2.056	8.250	2.738	15.699
1.0	0.0	0.0	0.0	2.092	8.355	2.832	16.250

CHART 7.F13 Weighted Moving Average Using a Spreadsheet, Part A

	AL	AM	AN	AO	AP	AQ	AR	AS	AT
1									
2									
3	Weights of		.4	.3	.2	.1			
4	Forecast		Absolute	Error	Forecast		Absolute	Error	
5	Single	Error	Error	Squared	Double	Error	Error	Squared	
6									
7									
8									
9									
10	29.59155	−3.30118	3.301176	10.89776					
11	28.28365	.9101768	.9101768	.8284218					
12	28.34435	1.054807	1.054807	1.112617					
13	28.62296	1.369463	1.369463	1.875428					
14	29.28452	4.578777	4.578777	20.96519	28.56837	5.294921	5.294921	28.03619	
15	31.34226	−1.03725	1.037248	1.075884	28.79793	1.507080	1.507080	2.271290	
16	31.21939	.9796806	.9796806	.9597742	29.88129	2.317787	2.317787	5.372139	
17	31.74303	.0772269	.0772269	.0059640	30.60964	1.210626	1.210626	1.465616	
18	31.83516	5.159522	5.159522	26.62067	31.25994	5.734745	5.734745	32.88730	
19	33.81427	3.926043	3.926043	15.41382	31.63508	6.105232	6.105232	37.27385	
20	35.77849	1.748490	1.748490	3.057219	32.54680	4.980178	4.980178	24.80217	
21	36.91385	.7082293	.7082293	.5015888	33.99701	3.625066	3.625066	13.14110	
22	37.55445	−1.70394	1.703939	2.903407	35.44545	.4050612	.4050612	.1640746	
23	36.90626	.0153493	.0153493	.0002356	36.63306	.2885450	.2885450	.0832582	
24	36.80091	−.681948	.6819483	.4650535	36.98946	−.870495	.8704953	.7577620	
25	36.45638	−.789710	.7897101	.6236420	36.99452	−1.32785	1.327849	1.763184	
26	36.07173	7.342754	7.342754	53.91604	36.75952	6.654962	6.654962	44.28852	
27	38.98175	7.991021	7.991021	63.85642	36.41641	10.55636	10.55636	111.4366	
28	42.55868	2.520023	2.520023	6.350515	37.38558	7.693121	7.693121	59.18411	
29	44.37287	1.084642	1.084642	1.176448	39.57798	5.879537	5.879537	34.56896	
30	45.44262	5.116778	5.116778	26.18142	41.92028	8.639121	8.639121	74.63442	
31	47.57403	.0506458	.0506458	.0025650	43.89882	3.725856	3.725856	13.88200	
32	47.81706	−.282891	.2828909	.0800273	45.79284	1.741331	1.741331	3.032235	
33	47.95870	1.865127	1.865127	3.478699	46.92485	2.898984	2.898984	8.404110	
34	48.77066	5.005114	5.005114	25.05117	47.58767	6.188105	6.188105	38.29264	
35	50.72676	−.925526	.9255261	.8565985	48.21669	1.584544	1.584544	2.510780	
36	50.77141	−.372858	.3728584	.1390234	49.29535	1.103202	1.103202	1.217054	
37	50.83733	−.579753	.5797526	.3361131	50.07659	.1809818	.1809818	.0327544	
38		Total	61.17892	268.7317		Total	90.51369	539.5022	
39		MAD =	2.184961	9.953026	= MSE	MAD =	3.771404	23.45662	= MSE
40									

(*continued*)

formulas that were used to do the calculations of worksheet 7.F11, Parts A and B, can be seen on Chart 7.F13, Parts B and C.

Model 4: Exponential Smoothing. The exponential smoothing modeling technique is loved because it is easy to calculate and it uses only one data point to make a forecast prediction. It calculates next month's forecast based on last month's forecast and actual sales. It also allows the same flexibility that we saw in the weighted moving average forecasting model in that it allows you to try several different alpha factors (weights) to see what form of the model is the best predictor. Chart 7.F14, Parts A and B, is the worksheet for this modeling technique. Chart 7.F14, Parts C and D, is the Chart 7.F2, Part B, data applied to the Chart 7.F14, Parts A and B, worksheet.

The calculation process works like this (follow the process on Chart 7.F14, Parts C and D). The first data point (actual sales amount) we have is for 4/89 [28.36 = (a)]. We do not have a forecast for this period.

CHART 7.F13 *(continued)* **Weighted Moving Average Using a Spreadsheet, Part B**

	AL	AM	AN	AO
1				
2				
3	Weights of		.6	.3
4	Forecast		Absolute	Error
5	Single	Error	Error	Squared
6				
7				
8				
9				
10	AQ3×N6+AP3×N7+AO3×N8+AN3×N9	N10-AL10	ABS(AM10)	AN10×AN10
11	AQ3×N7+AP3×N8+AO3×N9+AN3×N10	N11-AL11	ABS(AM11)	AN11×AN11
12	AQ3×N8+AP3×N9+AO3×N10+AN3×N11	N12-AL12	ABS(AM12)	AN12×AN12
13	AQ3×N9+AP3×N10+AO3×N11+AN3×N12	N13-AL13	ABS(AM13)	AN13×AN13
14	AQ3×N10+AP3×N11+AO3×N12+AN3×N13	N14-AL14	ABS(AM14)	AN14×AN14
15	AQ3×N11+AP3×N12+AO3×N13+AN3×N14	N15-AL15	ABS(AM15)	AN15×AN15
16	AQ3×N12+AP3×N13+AO3×N14+AN3×N15	N16-AL16	ABS(AM16)	AN16×AN16
17	AQ3×N13+AP3×N14+AO3×N15+AN3×N16	N17-AL17	ABS(AM17)	AN17×AN17
18	AQ3×N14+AP3×N15+AO3×N16+AN3×N17	N18-AL18	ABS(AM18)	AN18×AN18
19	AQ3×N15+AP3×N16+AO3×N17+AN3×N18	N19-AL19	ABS(AM19)	AN19×AN19
20	AQ3×N16+AP3×N17+AO3×N18+AN3×N19	N20-AL20	ABS(AM20)	AN20×AN20
21	AQ3×N17+AP3×N18+AO3×N19+AN3×N20	N21-AL21	ABS(AM21)	AN21×AN21
22	AQ3×N18+AP3×N19+AO3×N20+AN3×N21	N22-AL22	ABS(AM22)	AN22×AN22
23	AQ3×N19+AP3×N20+AO3×N21+AN3×N22	N23-AL23	ABS(AM23)	AN23×AN23
24	AQ3×N20+AP3×N21+AO3×N22+AN3×N23	N24-AL24	ABS(AM24)	AN24×AN24
25	AQ3×N21+AP3×N22+AO3×N23+AN3×N24	N25-AL25	ABS(AM25)	AN25×AN25
26	AQ3×N22+AP3×N23+AO3×N24+AN3×N25	N26-AL26	ABS(AM26)	AN26×AN26
27	AQ3×N23+AP3×N24+AO3×N25+AN3×N26	N27-AL27	ABS(AM27)	AN27×AN27
28	AQ3×N24+AP3×N25+AO3×N26+AN3×N27	N28-AL28	ABS(AM28)	AN28×AN28
29	AQ3×N25+AP3×N26+AO3×N27+AN3×N28	N29-AL29	ABS(AM29)	AN29×AN29
30	AQ3×N26+AP3×N27+AO3×N28+AN3×N29	N30-AL30	ABS(AM30)	AN30×AN30
31	AQ3×N27+AP3×N28+AO3×N29+AN3×N30	N31-AL31	ABS(AM31)	AN31×AN31
32	AQ3×N28+AP3×N29+AO3×N30+AN3×N31	N32-AL32	ABS(AM32)	AN32×AN32
33	AQ3×N29+AP3×N30+AO3×N31+AN3×N32	N33-AL33	ABS(AM33)	AN33×AN33
34	AQ3×N30+AP3×N31+AO3×N32+AN3×N33	N34-AL34	ABS(AM34)	AN34×AN34
35	AQ3×N31+AP3×N32+AO3×N33+AN3×N34	N35-AL35	ABS(AM35)	AN35×AN35
36	AQ3×N32+AP3×N33+AO3×N34+AN3×N35	N36-AL36	ABS(AM36)	AN36×AN36
37	AQ3×N33+AP3×N34+AO3×N35+AN3×N36	N37-AL37	ABS(AM37)	AN37×AN37
38		Total	SUM(AN10 : AN37)	SUM(AO10 : AO37)
39		MAD =	AN38/28	AO38/27
40				

So we use this sales value as the forecast for the second period, which is 5/89 [forecast equals 28.36 = (zb)]. In this second period we now have both an actual sales amount and a forecast. We use these two values and the alpha value [0.2 in this case = (x)] to calculate the forecast in the third period. The formula as shown on the worksheet is (x) × (b − zb) + zb. The value of (b) is the second period actual sales value of 30.55. The calculation for the forecast in the third period is then (x) × (b − zb) + zb = (0.2) × (30.55 − 28.36) + 28.36 = (0.2) × (2.19) + 28.36 = (0.438) + (28.36) = (28.800), which is the forecast for the third period and equals (zc). Rounding will change your answer slightly from the one calculated here. Similarly, we now use the third-period actual sales amount and the third-period forecast to calculate the fourth-period forecast. The process repeats itself until all actual sales amounts have a corresponding forecast value to compare against.

Calculate the absolute error by subtracting the sales amount from the forecast and dropping any minus signs. The "Error Squared" amount is the square of the "Absolute Error."

CHART 7.F13 (*concluded*) **Part C**

	AP	AQ	AR	AS	AT
1					
2					
3	.1	0			
4	Forecast		Absolute	Error	
5	Double	Error	Error	Squared	
6					
7					
8					
9					
10					
11					
12					
13					
14	AQ3×AL10+AP3×AL11+AO3×AL12+AN3×AL13	N14-AP14	ABS(AQ14)	AR14×AR14	
15	AQ3×AL11+AP3×AL12+AO3×AL13+AN3×AL14	N15-AP15	ABS(AQ15)	AR15×AR15	
16	AQ3×AL12+AP3×AL13+AO3×AL14+AN3×AL15	N16-AP16	ABS(AQ16)	AR16×AR16	
17	AQ3×AL13+AP3×AL14+AO3×AL15+AN3×AL16	N17-AP17	ABS(AQ17)	AR17×AR17	
18	AQ3×AL14+AP3×AL15+AO3×AL16+AN3×AL17	N18-AP18	ABS(AQ18)	AR18×AR18	
19	AQ3×AL15+AP3×AL16+AO3×AL17+AN3×AL18	N19-AP19	ABS(AQ19)	AR19×AR19	
20	AQ3×AL16+AP3×AL17+AO3×AL18+AN3×AL19	N20-AP20	ABS(AQ20)	AR20×AR20	
21	AQ3×AL17+AP3×AL18+AO3×AL19+AN3×AL20	N21-AP21	ABS(AQ21)	AR21×AR21	
22	AQ3×AL18+AP3×AL19+AO3×AL20+AN3×AL21	N22-AP22	ABS(AQ22)	AR22×AR22	
23	AQ3×AL19+AP3×AL20+AO3×AL21+AN3×AL22	N23-AP23	ABS(AQ23)	AR23×AR23	
24	AQ3×AL20+AP3×AL21+AO3×AL22+AN3×AL23	N24-AP24	ABS(AQ24)	AR24×AR24	
25	AQ3×AL21+AP3×AL22+AO3×AL23+AN3×AL24	N25-AP25	ABS(AQ25)	AR25×AR25	
26	AQ3×AL22+AP3×AL23+AO3×AL24+AN3×AL25	N26-AP26	ABS(AQ26)	AR26×AR26	
27	AQ3×AL23+AP3×AL24+AO3×AL25+AN3×AL26	N27-AP27	ABS(AQ27)	AR27×AR27	
28	AQ3×AL24+AP3×AL25+AO3×AL26+AN3×AL27	N28-AP28	ABS(AQ28)	AR28×AR28	
29	AQ3×AL25+AP3×AL26+AO3×AL27+AN3×AL28	N29-AP29	ABS(AQ29)	AR29×AR29	
30	AQ3×AL26+AP3×AL27+AO3×AL28+AN3×AL29	N30-AP30	ABS(AQ30)	AR30×AR30	
31	AQ3×AL27+AP3×AL28+AO3×AL29+AN3×AL30	N31-AP31	ABS(AQ31)	AR31×AR31	
32	AQ3×AL28+AP3×AL29+AO3×AL30+AN3×AL31	N32-AP32	ABS(AQ32)	AR32×AR32	
33	AQ3×AL29+AP3×AL30+AO3×AL31+AN3×AL32	N33-AP33	ABS(AQ33)	AR33×AR33	
34	AQ3×AL30+AP3×AL31+AO3×AL32+AN3×AL33	N34-AP34	ABS(AQ34)	AR34×AR34	
35	AQ3×AL31+AP3×AL32+AO3×AL33+AN3×AL34	N35-AP35	ABS(AQ35)	AR35×AR35	
36	AQ3×AL32+AP3×AL33+AO3×AL34+AN3×AL35	N36-AP36	ABS(AQ36)	AR36×AR36	
37	AQ3×AL33+AP3×AL34+AO3×AL35+AN3×AL36	N37-AP37	ABS(AQ37)	AR37×AR37	
38		Total	SUM(AR14 : AR37)	SUM(AS14 : AS37)	
39	= MSE	MAD =	AR38/24	AS38/23	= MSE
40					

The double forecast is calculated similar to the single forecast, except that we now use the single forecast and the double forecast to calculate each corresponding double forecast. The calculation process works as follows (follow the process on Chart 7.F14, Parts C and D). The first data point (single forecast projection) we have is for 5/89 [28.36 = (zb)]. We do not have a double forecast for this period. So we use this value as the forecast for the third period which is 6/89 [forecast equals 28.36 = (zzc)]. In this third period we now have both a single forecast and a double forecast. We use these two values and the alpha value [0.2 in this case = (x)] to calculate the double forecast in the fourth period. The formula as shown on the work sheet is (x) × (zc − zzc) + zzc. The value of (zc) is the third-period double forecast value of (28.800). The calculation for the double forecast in the fourth period is then (x) × (zc − zzc) + zzc = (0.2) × (28.800 − 28.36) + 28.36 = (0.2) × (0.44) + 28.36 = (0.088) + (28.36) = (28.450), which is the double forecast for the fourth period and equals (zzd). Rounding will change your answer slightly from the one calculated here. Similarly, we now use the fourth-

CHART 7.F14 Exponential Smoothing Worksheet, Part A

Product line ____________ Page 1 of __ Date __/__/__

Deseasonalized Sales Year/Month	Amount		Alpha Factor = ______ (x)	Single Forecast		Absolute Error	Error Squared		Double Forecast		Absolute Error	Error Squared
____/____	______	(a)	For the first month (first sheet) a=zb=zzc									
____/____	______	(b)	a =	______	(zb)	______	______					
____/____	______	(c)	(x)×(b-zb)+zb =	______	(zc)	______	______	zb =	______	(zzc)	______	______
____/____	______	(d)	(x)×(c-zc)+zc =	______	(zd)	______	______	(x)×(zc-zzc)+zzc =	______	(zzd)	______	______
____/____	______	(e)	(x)×(d-zd)+zd =	______	(ze)	______	______	(x)×(zd-zzd)+zzd =	______	(zze)	______	______
____/____	______	(f)	(x)×(e-ze)+ze =	______	(zf)	______	______	(x)×(ze-zze)+zze =	______	(zzf)	______	______
____/____	______	(g)	(x)×(f-zf)+zf =	______	(zg)	______	______	(x)×(zf-zzf)+zzf =	______	(zzg)	______	______
____/____	______	(h)	(x)×(g-zg)+zg =	______	(zh)	______	______	(x)×(zg-zzg)+zzg =	______	(zzh)	______	______
____/____	______	(i)	(x)×(h-zh)+zh =	______	(zi)	______	______	(x)×(zh-zzh)+zzh =	______	(zzi)	______	______
____/____	______	(j)	(x)×(i-zi)+zi =	______	(zj)	______	______	(x)×(zi-zzi)+zzi =	______	(zzj)	______	______
____/____	______	(k)	(x)×(j-zj)+zj =	______	(zk)	______	______	(x)×(zj-zzj)+zzj =	______	(zzk)	______	______
____/____	______	(l)	(x)×(k-zk)+zk =	______	(zl)	______	______	(x)×(zk-zzk)+zzk =	______	(zzl)	______	______
____/____	______	(m)	(x)×(l-zl)+zl =	______	(zm)	______	______	(x)×(zl-zzl)+zzl =	______	(zzm)	______	______
____/____	______	(n)	(x)×(m-zm)+zm =	______	(zn)	______	______	(x)×(zm-zzm)+zzm =	______	(zzn)	______	______
____/____	______	(o)	(x)×(n-zn)+zn =	______	(zo)	______	______	(x)×(zn-zzn)+zzn =	______	(zzo)	______	______
____/____	______	(p)	(x)×(o-zo)+zo =	______	(zp)	______	______	(x)×(zo-zzo)+zzo =	______	(zzp)	______	______
____/____	______	(q)	(x)×(p-zp)+zp =	______	(zq)	______	______	(x)×(zp-zzp)+zzp =	______	(zzq)	______	______

CHART 7.F14 *(continued)* **Part B**

Product line ________ Page __ of __ Date __/__/__

Deseasonalized Sales Year/Month	Amount	Alpha Factor = ____ (x)	Single Forecast	Absolute Error	Error Squared		Double Forecast	Absolute Error	Error Squared	
			(q, zq, and zzq come from the previous sheet)							
___/___	____	(b) (x)×(q-zq)+zq =	____ (zb)	____	____	(x)×(zq-zzq)+zzq =	____ (zzb)	____	____	
___/___	____	(c) (x)×(b-zb)+zb =	____ (zc)	____	____	(x)×(zb-zzb)+zzb =	____ (zzc)	____	____	
___/___	____	(d) (x)×(c-zc)+zc =	____ (zd)	____	____	(x)×(zc-zzc)+zzc =	____ (zzd)	____	____	
___/___	____	(e) (x)×(d-zd)+zd =	____ (ze)	____	____	(x)×(zd-zzd)+zzd =	____ (zze)	____	____	
___/___	____	(f) (x)×(e-ze)+ze =	____ (zf)	____	____	(x)×(ze-zze)+zze =	____ (zzf)	____	____	
___/___	____	(g) (x)×(f-zf)+zf =	____ (zg)	____	____	(x)×(zf-zzf)+zzf =	____ (zzg)	____	____	
___/___	____	(h) (x)×(g-zg)+zg =	____ (zh)	____	____	(x)×(zg-zzg)+zzg =	____ (zzh)	____	____	
___/___	____	(i) (x)×(h-zh)+zh =	____ (zi)	____	____	(x)×(zh-zzh)+zzh =	____ (zzi)	____	____	
___/___	____	(j) (x)×(i-zi)+zi =	____ (zj)	____	____	(x)×(zi-zzi)+zzi =	____ (zzj)	____	____	
___/___	____	(k) (x)×(j-zj)+zj =	____ (zk)	____	____	(x)×(zj-zzj)+zzj =	____ (zzk)	____	____	
___/___	____	(l) (x)×(k-zk)+zk =	____ (zl)	____	____	(x)×(zk-zzk)+zzk =	____ (zzl)	____	____	
___/___	____	(m) (x)×(l-zl)+zl =	____ (zm)	____	____	(x)×(zl-zzl)+zzl =	____ (zzm)	____	____	
___/___	____	(n) (x)×(m-zm)+zm =	____ (zn)	____	____	(x)×(zm-zzm)+zzm =	____ (zzn)	____	____	
___/___	____	(o) (x)×(n-zn)+zn =	____ (zo)	____	____	(x)×(zn-zzn)+zzn =	____ (zzo)	____	____	
___/___	____	(p) (x)×(o-zo)+zo =	____ (zp)	____	____	(x)×(zo-zzo)+zzo =	____ (zzp)	____	____	
___/___	____	(q) (x)×(p-zp)+zp =	____ (zq)	____	____	(x)×(zp-zzp)+zzp =	____ (zzq)	____	____	
		Total error factors		____	____			____	____	
		Divided by	n =	____	____	= $n - 1$	$n - 2$ =	____	____	= $n - 3$
		Forecast (error values)	MAD =	____	____	= MSE	MAD =	____	____	= MSE

(continued)

CHART 7.F14 *(continued)* **Example of Exponential Smoothing Worksheet, Part C** (Data from Chart 7.F2, Part B)

Product line Bell bottoms Page 1 of 2 Date 1 / 1 /1992

Deseasonalized Sales Year/Month	Amount		Alpha Factor = .2 (x)	Single Forecast		Absolute Error	Error Squared		Double Forecast		Absolute Error	Error Squared
89 / 4	28.36	(a)	For the first month (first sheet) a=zb=zzc									
89 / 5	30.55	(b)	(x)×(q-zq)+zq =	28.36	(zb)	2.189	4.792					
89 / 6	30.86	(c)	(x)×(b-zb)+zb =	28.800	(zc)	2.055	4.223	(x)×(zb-zzb)+zzb =	28.36	(zzc)	2.493	6.215
89 / 7	28.47	(d)	(x)×(c-zc)+zc =	29.211	(zd)	.741	.549	(x)×(zc-zzc)+zzc =	28.450	(zzd)	.021	.000
89 / 8	26.29	(e)	(x)×(d-zd)+zd =	29.063	(ze)	2.773	7.689	(x)×(zd-zzd)+zzd =	28.602	(zze)	2.312	5.345
89 / 9	29.19	(f)	(x)×(e-ze)+ze =	28.509	(zf)	.685	.469	(x)×(ze-zze)+zze =	28.695	(zzf)	.499	.249
89 / 10	29.40	(g)	(x)×(f-zf)+zf =	28.646	(zg)	.753	.568	(x)×(zf-zzf)+zzf =	28.657	(zzg)	.742	.550
89 / 11	29.99	(h)	(x)×(g-zg)+zg =	28.796	(zh)	1.196	1.430	(x)×(zg-zzg)+zzg =	28.655	(zzh)	1.337	1.789
89 / 12	33.86	(i)	(x)×(h-zh)+zh =	29.036	(zi)	4.828	23.306	(x)×(zh-zzh)+zzh =	28.683	(zzi)	5.180	26.832
90 / 1	30.31	(j)	(x)×(i-zi)+zi =	30.001	(zj)	.304	.092	(x)×(zi-zzi)+zzi =	28.754	(zzj)	1.551	2.406
90 / 2	32.20	(k)	(x)×(j-zj)+zj =	30.062	(zk)	2.137	4.567	(x)×(zj-zzj)+zzj =	29.003	(zzk)	3.196	10.213
90 / 3	31.82	(l)	(x)×(k-zk)+zk =	30.489	(zl)	1.331	1.771	(x)×(zk-zzk)+zzk =	29.215	(zzl)	2.605	6.787
90 / 4	36.99	(m)	(x)×(l-zl)+zl =	30.756	(zm)	6.239	38.927	(x)×(zl-zzl)+zzl =	29.470	(zzm)	7.525	56.623
90 / 5	37.74	(n)	(x)×(m-zm)+zm =	32.003	(zn)	5.737	32.913	(x)×(zm-zzm)+zzm =	29.727	(zzn)	8.013	64.213
90 / 6	37.53	(o)	(x)×(n-zn)+zn =	33.151	(zo)	4.376	19.151	(x)×(zn-zzn)+zzn =	30.182	(zzo)	7.345	53.945
90 / 7	37.62	(p)	(x)×(o-zo)+zo =	34.026	(zp)	3.596	12.932	(x)×(zo-zzo)+zzo =	30.776	(zzp)	6.846	46.869
90 / 8	35.85	(q)	(x)×(p-zp)+zp =	34.745	(zq)	1.105	1.222	(x)×(zp-zzp)+zzp =	31.426	(zzq)	4.425	19.577

CHART 7.F14 *(concluded)* **Part D** (Data from Chart 7.F2, Part B)

Product line Bell bottoms Page 2 of 2 Date 1 / 1 /1992

Deseasonalized Sales Year/Month	Amount		Alpha Factor = .2 (x)	Single Forecast		Absolute Error	Error Squared		Double Forecast		Absolute Error	Error Squared	
			(q, zq, and zzq come from the previous sheet)										
90 / 9	36.92	(b)	(x)×(q-zq)+zq =	34.966	(zb)	1.955	3.823	(x)×(zq-zzq)+zzq =	32.090	(zzb)	4.832	23.346	
90 / 10	36.12	(c)	(x)×(b-zb)+zb =	35.357	(zc)	.762	.580	(x)×(zb-zzb)+zzb =	32.665	(zzc)	3.454	11.929	
90 / 11	35.67	(d)	(x)×(c-zc)+zc =	35.510	(zd)	.157	.025	(x)×(zc-zzc)+zzc =	33.204	(zzd)	2.463	6.067	
90 / 12	43.41	(e)	(x)×(d-zd)+zd =	35.541	(ze)	7.873	61.991	(x)×(zd-zzd)+zzd =	33.665	(zze)	9.750	95.057	
91 / 1	46.97	(f)	(x)×(e-ze)+ze =	37.116	(zf)	9.857	97.161	(x)×(ze-zze)+zze =	34.040	(zzf)	12.933	167.256	
91 / 2	45.08	(g)	(x)×(f-zf)+zf =	39.087	(zg)	5.992	35.899	(x)×(zf-zzf)+zzf =	34.655	(zzg)	10.424	108.650	
91 / 3	45.46	(h)	(x)×(g-zg)+zg =	40.285	(zh)	5.172	26.750	(x)×(zg-zzg)+zzg =	35.542	(zzh)	9.916	98.326	
91 / 4	50.56	(i)	(x)×(h-zh)+zh =	41.320	(zi)	9.240	85.369	(x)×(zh-zzh)+zzh =	36.490	(zzi)	14.069	197.938	
91 / 5	47.62	(j)	(x)×(i-zi)+zi =	43.168	(zj)	4.457	19.864	(x)×(zi-zzi)+zzi =	37.456	(zzj)	10.168	103.397	
91 / 6	47.53	(k)	(x)×(j-zj)+zj =	44.059	(zk)	3.475	12.076	(x)×(zj-zzj)+zzj =	38.599	(zzk)	8.936	79.845	
91 / 7	49.82	(l)	(x)×(k-zk)+zk =	44.754	(zl)	5.070	25.702	(x)×(zk-zzk)+zzk =	39.691	(zzl)	10.133	102.681	
91 / 8	53.78	(m)	(x)×(l-zl)+zl =	45.768	(zm)	8.008	64.123	(x)×(zl-zzl)+zzl =	40.703	(zzm)	13.072	170.888	
91 / 9	49.80	(n)	(x)×(m-zm)+zm =	47.369	(zn)	2.432	5.913	(x)×(zm-zzm)+zzm =	41.716	(zzn)	8.085	65.366	
91 / 10	50.40	(o)	(x)×(n-zn)+zn =	47.856	(zo)	2.543	6.465	(x)×(zn-zzn)+zzn =	42.847	(zzo)	7.552	57.026	
91 / 11	50.26	(p)	(x)×(o-zo)+zo =	48.364	(zp)	1.893	3.584	(x)×(zo-zzo)+zzo =	43.849	(zzp)	6.409	41.073	
/		(q)	(x)×(p-zp)+zp =		(zq)			(x)×(zp-zzp)+zzp =		(zzq)			
			Total error factors			108.930	603.925				186.284	1630.456	
			Divided by		n =	31	30	= $n-1$	$n-1$ =		30	29	= $n-3$
			Forecast (error values)		MAD =	3.514	20.131	= MSE	MAD =		6.209	56.223	= MSE

period single forecast and the fourth-period double forecast to calculate the fifth-period double forecast. The process repeats itself until all actual sales amounts have a corresponding double forecast value to compare against.

Calculate the double forecast absolute error by subtracting the actual sales amount from the double forecast and dropping any minus signs. The double forecast error squared is the square of the double forecast absolute error.

Add each of the four error columns and place the total into the "Total Error Factors" row of the final data sheet (Chart 7.F14, Part D). The value for n is the count of the number of single forecast data points that were calculated. Calculate n, $n - 1$, and $n - 2$ and place the results into the appropriate "Divided by" slots. Then calculate the "Forecast (Error Values)" by dividing the "Total Error Factors" by the "Divided by" values.

In Chart 7.F14, Parts C and D, we saw one example of an exponential smoothing forecast. The exponential smoothing process works by selecting several alpha factors somewhere between 0.01 and 0.99. It is best to start with factors such as 0.2, 0.4, 0.6, and 0.8. Then, by validating the MAD and MSE values of each of these alpha factors, we can find an interval that needs more breakdown. The example in Chart 7.F14, Parts C and D, shows the calculation procedure for an alpha factor of 0.2. Chart 7.F15 shows these MAD and MSE values plus those for 0.4, 0.6, and 0.8. Then, seeing that the lowest MAD and MSE results were

CHART 7.F15 Exponential Smoothing Results (Data from Chart 7.F2, Part B)

	Single		Double	
Alpha factors	MAD	MSE	MAD	MSE
Step one				
.2	3.514	20.131	6.209	56.223
.4	2.293	10.238	3.764	23.548
.6	2.042	8.230	2.871	15.842
.8	1.996	7.748	2.610	13.767
Step two				
.7	1.994	7.886	2.708	14.406
.9	2.018	7.753	2.618	13.756
Step three				
.69	1.993	7.909	2.720	14.509
.70	1.994	7.886	2.708	14.406
.71	1.994	7.864	2.697	14.311
.72	1.994	7.845	2.685	14.223
.73	1.994	7.827	2.674	14.142
.74	1.995	7.810	2.663	14.069
.75	1.995	7.796	2.652	14.002
.76	1.995	7.783	2.641	13.942
.77	1.996	7.772	2.630	13.889
.78	1.996	7.762	2.622	13.842
.79	1.996	7.754	2.616	13.801
.80	1.996	7.748	2.610	13.767
.81	1.996	7.742	2.604	13.739
.82	1.998	7.738	2.599	13.717

in the single forecast at around 0.8, I proceeded to calculate the forecast for 0.7 and 0.9 (step 2). The lowest single forecast MAD and MSE values seem to vibrate around an alpha value of 0.7 and 0.8. The next step (step 3) is to analyze this region more closely. I have done this by taking alpha values between 0.69 and 0.82 at 0.01-step intervals. These results are shown as "Step Three" on Chart 7.F15. The selection of the best alpha factor is slightly difficult as can be seen from the MAD and MSE values between this range. Using the MAD values, any alpha from about 0.69 to about 0.76 would be "best" (MAD range of about 1.993 to about 1.995). Using only the MSE values the "best" alpha is 0.82 or higher, but less than 0.90 (MSE of about 7.738). Therefore, the selection of the "overall best" alpha value has to be a balance between these two. I would choose an alpha of about 0.81 since that would only raise the MAD from 1.993 (at 0.69) to 1.996 (at 0.81) but reduce the MSE from 7.886 (at 0.69) to 7.742 (at 0.81), which is only slightly above the 7.738 value of 0.82. Therefore the "best" overall exponential smoothing forecast is the single forecast with an alpha factor of 0.81.

Chart 7.F16, Part A, shows the spreadsheet example of how the numbers in Chart 7.F14, Parts C and D, would be calculated. Chart 7.F16, Parts B and C, shows the spreadsheet formulas for the worksheet of Chart 7.F14, Parts A & B.

Model 5: Simple Linear Regression. This model takes the deseasonalized actual sales data and simply draws a straight line through it (refer to Chart 7.F5, Part B). The line that is drawn is the "best fit" through the data. Then, by simply extending the line, we can generate a forecast for any period. The mathematics for this model looks extremely complicated so I won't bore you with it, but the actual calculation of the model is easier than some of the other models that you have already experienced.

Chart 7.F17, Parts A, B, and C, is the worksheet for this model. Chart 7.F17, Parts D, E, and F, applies the deseasonalized data of Chart 7.F2, Part B, to the worksheet of Chart 7.F17, Parts A, B, and C. To calculate this model, place all the deseasonalized sales amounts into their appropriate column as before. This column is called the "Y" column. The "X" column is prenumbered from 1 to the number of data points with which you are dealing. In Chart 7.F17, Parts D, E, and F, we have an example with 32 data points. There is also an "X × X" column where the "X" column is squared. The next column, the "X × Y" column, requires you to multiply the value in the "Y" column times the value in the "X" column.

Before the forecast can be calculated, the third sheet of the worksheet needs to be completed. First we need to determine how many data points we have. In the example of Chart 7.F17, Parts D, E, and F, we have 32 data points ($n = 32$). Then we need to sum the "Y" column and put the value in the "SY" slot. Next we need to sum the "X" column and put the value in the "SX" slot. For the example of Chart 7.F17, Parts D, E, and F, we would sum all the numbers from 1 to 32. Similarly we sum the "X × X" column and put the result in the "SXX" slot. For the example we would sum up all the values in the "X × X" column from 1

CHART 7.F16 Exponential Smoothing Using a Spreadsheet, Part A

	AU	AV	AW	AX	AY	AZ	BA	BB	BC
1									
2									
3	Alpha factor of		.2						
4	Forecast		Absolute	Error	Forecast		Absolute	Error	
5	Single	Error	Error	Squared	Double	Error	Error	Squared	
6									
7	28.36259	2.189091	2.189091	4.792119					
8	28.80041	2.055109	2.055109	4.223472	28.36259	2.492927	2.492927	6.214685	
9	29.21143	−.740668	.7406684	.5485896	28.45015	.0206079	.0206079	.0004247	
10	29.06329	−2.77292	2.772917	7.689068	28.60241	−2.31203	2.312030	5.345481	
11	28.50871	.6851156	.6851156	.4693834	28.69459	.4992421	.4992421	.2492427	
12	28.64573	.7534199	.7534199	.5676416	28.65741	.7417443	.7417443	.5501846	
13	28.79642	1.196006	1.196006	1.430429	28.65508	1.337349	1.337349	1.788502	
14	29.03562	4.827676	4.827676	23.30646	28.68334	5.179952	5.179952	26.83190	
15	30.00115	.3038559	.3038559	.0923284	28.75380	1.551212	1.551212	2.406258	
16	30.06193	2.137148	2.137148	4.567401	29.00327	3.195804	3.195804	10.21316	
17	30.48936	1.330906	1.330906	1.771310	29.21500	2.605260	2.605260	6.787380	
18	30.75554	6.239144	6.239144	38.92692	29.46987	7.524809	7.524809	56.62274	
19	32.00337	5.736944	5.736944	32.91253	29.72701	8.013305	8.013305	64.21305	
20	33.15075	4.376224	4.376224	19.15134	30.18228	7.344701	7.344701	53.94463	
21	34.02600	3.596077	3.596077	12.93177	30.77597	6.846103	6.846103	46.86913	
22	34.74521	1.105301	1.105301	1.221690	31.42598	4.424537	4.424537	19.57653	
23	34.96627	1.955330	1.955330	3.823316	32.08983	4.831780	4.831780	23.34609	
24	35.35734	.7616205	.7616205	.5800658	32.66512	3.453846	3.453846	11.92905	
25	35.50966	.1570017	.1570017	.0246495	33.20356	2.463106	2.463106	6.066893	
26	35.54107	7.873417	7.873417	61.99069	33.66478	9.749701	9.749701	95.05666	
27	37.11575	9.857018	9.857018	97.16081	34.04004	12.93273	12.93273	167.2555	
28	39.08715	5.991551	5.991551	35.89869	34.65518	10.42352	10.42352	108.6498	
29	40.28546	5.172054	5.172054	26.75014	35.54157	9.915942	9.915942	98.32590	
30	41.31987	9.239524	9.239524	85.36880	36.49035	14.06904	14.06904	197.9380	
31	43.16778	4.456899	4.456899	19.86395	37.45626	10.16842	10.16842	103.3968	
32	44.05916	3.475015	3.475015	12.07573	38.59856	8.935612	8.935612	79.84516	
33	44.75416	5.069670	5.069670	25.70155	39.69068	10.13315	10.13315	102.6807	
34	45.76809	8.007678	8.007678	64.12291	40.70338	13.07240	13.07240	170.8876	
35	47.36963	2.431604	2.431604	5.912699	41.71632	8.084915	8.084915	65.36584	
36	47.85595	2.542599	2.542599	6.464812	42.84698	7.551569	7.551569	57.02619	
37	48.36447	1.893105	1.893105	3.583845	43.84878	6.408800	6.408800	41.07272	
38		Total	108.9297	603.9251		Total	186.2841	1630.456	
39		MAD =	3.513861	20.13084	= MSE	MAD =	6.209471	56.22263	= MSE
40									

through 1024. Next we sum the values in the "X × Y" column and put this result in the "SXY" slot.

Now we calculate BT (see Chart 7.F17, Part C) using the formula $(n) \times (\text{SXY}) - (\text{SX}) \times (\text{SY})$. The results of each of these calculations for the sample data can be seen in Chart 7.F17, Parts D, E, and F. We similarly calculate BB using the formula $(n) \times (\text{SXX}) - (\text{SX}) \times (\text{SX})$. The calculation for B is then performed by dividing BT by BB. Next we calculate AT using the formula $(\text{SY}) - (\text{B}) \times (\text{SX})$. The value of A is then calculated by dividing AT by (n). With the values for A and B we now have the equation for the straight line that has been projected through the data points. For the example of Chart 7.F17, Parts D, E, and F, the equation would take the form:

$$\text{Forecast} = \text{A} + (\text{B} \times \text{X})$$

or

$$\text{Forecast} = (24.629) + (.849) \times (\text{X})$$

CHART 7.F16 *(continued)* **Exponential Smoothing Using a Spreadsheet, Part B**

	AU	AV	AW	AX	AY	AZ	BA
1							
2							
3	Alpha factor of		.69				
4	Forecast		Absolute	Error	Forecast		Absolute
5	Single	Error	Error	Squared	Double	Error	Error
6							
7	N6	N7-AU7	ABS(AV7)	AW7×AW7			
8	AW3×(N7-AU7)+AU7	N8-AU8	ABS(AV8)	AW8×AW8	AU7	N8-AY8	ABS(AZ8)
9	AW3×(N8-AU8)+AU8	N9-AU9	ABS(AV9)	AW9×AW9	AW3×(AU8-AY8)+AY8	N9-AY9	ABS(AZ9)
10	AW3×(N9-AU9)+AU9	N10-AU10	ABS(AV10)	AW10×AW1	AW3×(AU9-AY9)+AY9	N10-AY10	ABS(AZ10)
11	AW3×(N10-AU10)+AU10	N11-AU11	ABS(AV11)	AW11×AW1	AW3×(AU10-AY10)+AY10	N11-AY11	ABS(AZ11)
12	AW3×(N11-AU11)+AU11	N12-AU12	ABS(AV12)	AW12×AW1	AW3×(AU11-AY11)+AY11	N12-AY12	ABS(AZ12)
13	AW3×(N12-AU12)+AU12	N13-AU13	ABS(AV13)	AW13×AW1	AW3×(AU12-AY12)+AY12	N13-AY13	ABS(AZ13)
14	AW3×(N13-AU13)+AU13	N14-AU14	ABS(AV14)	AW14×AW1	AW3×(AU13-AY13)+AY13	N14-AY14	ABS(AZ14)
15	AW3×(N14-AU14)+AU14	N15-AU15	ABS(AV15)	AW15×AW1	AW3×(AU14-AY14)+AY14	N15-AY15	ABS(AZ15)
16	AW3×(N15-AU15)+AU15	N16-AU16	ABS(AV16)	AW16×AW1	AW3×(AU15-AY15)+AY15	N16-AY16	ABS(AZ16)
17	AW3×(N16-AU16)+AU16	N17-AU17	ABS(AV17)	AW17×AW1	AW3×(AU16-AY16)+AY16	N17-AY17	ABS(AZ17)
18	AW3×(N17-AU17)+AU17	N18-AU18	ABS(AV18)	AW18×AW1	AW3×(AU17-AY17)+AY17	N18-AY18	ABS(AZ18)
19	AW3×(N18-AU18)+AU18	N19-AU19	ABS(AV19)	AW19×AW1	AW3×(AU18-AY18)+AY18	N19-AY19	ABS(AZ19)
20	AW3×(N19-AU19)+AU19	N20-AU20	ABS(AV20)	AW20×AW2	AW3×(AU19-AY19)+AY19	N20-AY20	ABS(AZ20)
21	AW3×(N20-AU20)+AU20	N21-AU21	ABS(AV21)	AW21×AW2	AW3×(AU20-AY20)+AY20	N21-AY21	ABS(AZ21)
22	AW3×(N21-AU21)+AU21	N22-AU22	ABS(AV22)	AW22×AW2	AW3×(AU21-AY21)+AY21	N22-AY22	ABS(AZ22)
23	AW3×(N22-AU22)+AU22	N23-AU23	ABS(AV23)	AW23×AW2	AW3×(AU22-AY22)+AY22	N23-AY23	ABS(AZ23)
24	AW3×(N23-AU23)+AU23	N24-AU24	ABS(AV24)	AW24×AW2	AW3×(AU23-AY23)+AY23	N24-AY24	ABS(AZ24)
25	AW3×(N24-AU24)+AU24	N25-AU25	ABS(AV25)	AW25×AW2	AW3×(AU24-AY24)+AY24	N25-AY25	ABS(AZ25)
26	AW3×(N25-AU25)+AU25	N26-AU26	ABS(AV26)	AW26×AW2	AW3×(AU25-AY25)+AY25	N26-AY26	ABS(AZ26)
27	AW3×(N26-AU26)+AU26	N27-AU27	ABS(AV27)	AW27×AW2	AW3×(AU26-AY26)+AY26	N27-AY27	ABS(AZ27)
28	AW3×(N27-AU27)+AU27	N28-AU28	ABS(AV28)	AW28×AW2	AW3×(AU27-AY27)+AY27	N28-AY28	ABS(AZ28)
29	AW3×(N28-AU28)+AU28	N29-AU29	ABS(AV29)	AW29×AW2	AW3×(AU28-AY28)+AY28	N29-AY29	ABS(AZ29)
30	AW3×(N29-AU29)+AU29	N30-AU30	ABS(AV30)	AW30×AW3	AW3×(AU29-AY29)+AY29	N30-AY30	ABS(AZ30)
31	AW3×(N30-AU30)+AU30	N31-AU31	ABS(AV31)	AW31×AW3	AW3×(AU30-AY30)+AY30	N31-AY31	ABS(AZ31)
32	AW3×(N31-AU31)+AU31	N32-AU32	ABS(AV32)	AW32×AW3	AW3×(AU31-AY31)+AY31	N32-AY32	ABS(AZ32)
33	AW3×(N32-AU32)+AU32	N33-AU33	ABS(AV33)	AW33×AW3	AW3×(AU32-AY32)+AY32	N33-AY33	ABS(AZ33)
34	AW3×(N33-AU33)+AU33	N34-AU34	ABS(AV34)	AW34×AW3	AW3×(AU33-AY33)+AY33	N34-AY34	ABS(AZ34)
35	AW3×(N34-AU34)+AU34	N35-AU35	ABS(AV35)	AW35×AW3	AW3×(AU34-AY34)+AY34	N35-AY35	ABS(AZ35)
36	AW3×(N35-AU35)+AU35	N36-AU36	ABS(AV36)	AW36×AW3	AW3×(AU35-AY35)+AY35	N36-AY36	ABS(AZ36)
37	AW3×(N36-AU36)+AU36	N37-AU37	ABS(AV37)	AW37×AW3	AW3×(AU36-AY36)+AY36	N37-AY37	ABS(AZ37)
38		Total	SUM(AW7 : AW37)	SUM(AX7 : AX37)		Total	SUM(BA8 : BA37)
39		MAD =	AW38/31	AX38/30 = MSE		MAD =	BA38/30
40							

CHART 7.F16 *(concluded)* **Exponential Smoothing Using a Spreadsheet, Part C**

	BB	BC
1		
2		
3		
4	Error	
5	Squared	
6		
7		
8	BA8×BA8	
9	BA9×BA9	
10	BA10×BA10	
11	BA11×BA11	
12	BA12×BA12	
13	BA13×BA13	
14	BA14×BA14	
15	BA15×BA15	
16	BA16×BA16	
17	BA17×BA17	
18	BA18×BA18	
19	BA19×BA19	
20	BA20×BA20	
21	BA21×BA21	
22	BA22×BA22	
23	BA23×BA23	
24	BA24×BA24	
25	BA25×BA25	
26	BA26×BA26	
27	BA27×BA27	
28	BA28×BA28	
29	BA29×BA29	
30	BA30×BA30	
31	BA31×BA31	
32	BA32×BA32	
33	BA33×BA33	
34	BA34×BA34	
35	BA35×BA35	
36	BA36×BA36	
37	BA37×BA37	
38	SUM(BB8 : BB37)	
39	BB38/29 = MSE	
40		

With this equation we can now go back to the first two data sheets and calculate the forecast for each data point. The formula for each data point already has the value for "X" inserted. For example, the first formula is:

$$\text{Forecast} = A + (B \times 1)$$

or, for the data of Chart 7.F17, Parts D, E, and F,

$$\text{Forecast} = (24.629) + (0.849) \times (1) = 25.478$$

Similarly, the second forecast would be calculated by:

$$\text{Forecast} = A + (B \times 2)$$

or, for the data of Chart 7.F17, Parts D, E, and F,

$$\text{Forecast} = (24.629) + (0.849) \times (2) = 26.327$$

and so on.

Once all the forecasts have been calculated, the "Absolute Error" is calculated by subtracting the "Sales Amount" (Y column) from the "Forecast" and dropping any minus signs. The "Error Squared" column is calculated by squaring the "Absolute Error" column.

Returning to the third page, we now proceed with the remaining calculations. We add up the values of the "Absolute Error" (AE) column and put them in the appropriate blank. We also add up the values of the "Error Squared" (ES) column and place the total in the appropriate slot. We already know the value of *n* and we only need to calculate the value

CHART 7.F17 Simple Linear Regression Worksheet, Part A

Product Line ______ Page 1 of __ Date __/__/__

Deseasonalized Year/Month	Sales Amount (Y)		Period (X)	Period Squared (X×X)	Period Times Amount (X×Y)		Forecast	Absolute Error	Error Squared
___/___	______	(Y01)	1	1	______	A + B × 1 =	______	______	______
___/___	______	(Y02)	2	4	______	A + B × 2 =	______	______	______
___/___	______	(Y03)	3	9	______	A + B × 3 =	______	______	______
___/___	______	(Y04)	4	16	______	A + B × 4 =	______	______	______
___/___	______	(Y05)	5	25	______	A + B × 5 =	______	______	______
___/___	______	(Y06)	6	36	______	A + B × 6 =	______	______	______
___/___	______	(Y07)	7	49	______	A + B × 7 =	______	______	______
___/___	______	(Y08)	8	64	______	A + B × 8 =	______	______	______
___/___	______	(Y09)	9	81	______	A + B × 9 =	______	______	______
___/___	______	(Y10)	10	100	______	A + B × 10 =	______	______	______
___/___	______	(Y11)	11	121	______	A + B × 11 =	______	______	______
___/___	______	(Y12)	12	144	______	A + B × 12 =	______	______	______
___/___	______	(Y13)	13	169	______	A + B × 13 =	______	______	______
___/___	______	(Y14)	14	196	______	A + B × 14 =	______	______	______
___/___	______	(Y15)	15	225	______	A + B × 15 =	______	______	______
___/___	______	(Y16)	16	256	______	A + B × 16 =	______	______	______
___/___	______	(Y17)	17	289	______	A + B × 17 =	______	______	______
___/___	______	(Y18)	18	324	______	A + B × 18 =	______	______	______

CHART 7.F17 *(continued)* **Part B**

Product Line ______ Page 2 of __ Date __/__/__

Deseasonalized Year/Month	Sales Amount (Y)		Period (X)	Period Squared (X×X)	Period Times Amount (X×Y)		Forecast	Absolute Error	Error Squared
___/___	______	(Y19)	19	361	______	A + B × 19 =	______	______	______
___/___	______	(Y20)	20	400	______	A + B × 20 =	______	______	______
___/___	______	(Y21)	21	441	______	A + B × 21 =	______	______	______
___/___	______	(Y22)	22	484	______	A + B × 22 =	______	______	______
___/___	______	(Y23)	23	529	______	A + B × 23 =	______	______	______
___/___	______	(Y24)	24	576	______	A + B × 24 =	______	______	______
___/___	______	(Y25)	25	625	______	A + B × 25 =	______	______	______
___/___	______	(Y26)	26	676	______	A + B × 26 =	______	______	______
___/___	______	(Y27)	27	729	______	A + B × 27 =	______	______	______
___/___	______	(Y28)	28	784	______	A + B × 28 =	______	______	______
___/___	______	(Y29)	29	841	______	A + B × 29 =	______	______	______
___/___	______	(Y30)	30	900	______	A + B × 30 =	______	______	______
___/___	______	(Y31)	31	961	______	A + B × 31 =	______	______	______
___/___	______	(Y32)	32	1024	______	A + B × 32 =	______	______	______
___/___	______	(Y33)	33	1089	______	A + B × 33 =	______	______	______
___/___	______	(Y34)	34	1156	______	A + B × 34 =	______	______	______
___/___	______	(Y35)	35	1225	______	A + B × 35 =	______	______	______
___/___	______	(Y36)	36	1296	______	A + B × 36 =	______	______	______

(continued)

CHART 7.F17 *(continued)* **Simple Linear Regression Worksheet, Part C**

Product Line __________ Date __/__/__

The number of data points in the Y column equals ________ (*n*)
The sum of the Y (Sales Amount) column equals ________ (SY)
The sum of the X (Period) column (use only those X values that have corresponding Y's) equals ________ (SX)
The sum of the X×X (Period Squared) column (use only those X×X values that have corresponding Y's) equals ________ (SXX)
The sum of the X×Y (Period Times Amount) column (use only those X×Y values that have corresponding Y's) equals ________ (SXY)
BT = (*n*) × (SXY) − (SX) × (SY) = ________
BB = (*n*) × (SXX) − (SX) × (SX) = ________
B = BT/BB = ________
AT = (SY) − (B) × (SX) = ________
A = AT/(*n*) = ________
These A and B values are now used to calculate the forecasts and the errors on the previous sheets.
Total of the Absolute Error column = (AE) = ________
Total of the Error Squared column = (ES) = ________
n = 1 = ________
MAD = (AE)/(*n*) = ________
MSE = (ES)/(*n*−1) = ________

CHART 7.F17 *(continued)* **Example of Simple Linear Regression Worksheet, Part D**
(Data from Chart 7.F2, Part B)

Product Line Bell Bottoms Page 1 of 2 Date 1 / 1 /1992

Deseasonalized Sales Year/Month	Amount (Y)		Period (X)	Period Squared (X×X)	Period Times Amount (X×Y)		Forecast	Absolute Error	Error Squared
89 / 4	28.36	(Y01)	1	1	28.363	A + B × 1 =	25.478	2.885	8.321
89 / 5	30.55	(Y02)	2	4	61.103	A + B × 2 =	26.327	4.225	17.847
89 / 6	30.86	(Y03)	3	9	92.567	A + B × 3 =	27.176	3.679	13.538
89 / 7	28.47	(Y04)	4	16	113.883	A + B × 4 =	28.025	.446	.198
89 / 8	26.29	(Y05)	5	25	131.452	A + B × 5 =	28.874	2.584	6.677
89 / 9	29.19	(Y06)	6	36	175.163	A + B × 6 =	29.723	.530	.280
89 / 10	29.40	(Y07)	7	49	205.794	A + B × 7 =	30.573	1.173	1.377
89 / 11	29.99	(Y08)	8	64	239.939	A + B × 8 =	31.422	1.429	2.043
89 / 12	33.86	(Y09)	9	81	304.770	A + B × 9 =	32.271	1.593	2.536
90 / 1	30.31	(Y10)	10	100	303.050	A + B × 10 =	33.120	2.815	7.923
90 / 2	32.20	(Y11)	11	121	354.190	A + B × 11 =	33.969	1.770	3.132
90 / 3	31.82	(Y12)	12	144	381.843	A + B × 12 =	34.818	2.998	8.986
90 / 4	36.99	(Y13)	13	169	480.931	A + B × 13 =	35.667	1.328	1.763
90 / 5	37.74	(Y14)	14	196	528.364	A + B × 14 =	36.516	1.224	1.499
90 / 6	37.53	(Y15)	15	225	562.905	A + B × 15 =	37.365	.162	.026
90 / 7	37.62	(Y16)	16	256	601.953	A + B × 16 =	38.214	.592	.351
90 / 8	35.85	(Y17)	17	289	609.459	A + B × 17 =	39.063	3.213	10.323
90 / 9	36.92	(Y18)	18	324	664.589	A + B × 18 =	39.913	2.991	8.945

CHART 7.F17 *(continued)* **Part E**
(Data from Chart 7.F2, Part B)

Product Line Bell Bottoms Page 2 of 2 Date 1 / 1 /1992

Deseasonalized Sales Year/Month	Amount (Y)		Period (X)	Period Squared (X×X)	Period Times Amount (X×Y)		Forecast	Absolute Error	Error Squared
90 / 10	36.12	(Y19)	19	361	686.260	A + B × 19 =	40.761	4.643	21.554
90 / 11	35.67	(Y20)	20	400	713.333	A + B × 20 =	41.611	5.944	35.332
90 / 12	43.41	(Y21)	21	441	911.704	A + B × 21 =	42.460	.955	.911
91 / 1	46.97	(Y22)	22	484	1033.40	A + B × 22 =	43.309	3.664	13.424
91 / 2	45.08	(Y23)	23	529	1036.81	A + B × 23 =	44.158	.921	.848
91 / 3	45.46	(Y24)	24	576	1090.98	A + B × 24 =	45.007	.450	.203
91 / 4	50.56	(Y25)	25	625	1263.99	A + B × 25 =	45.856	4.703	22.120
91 / 5	47.62	(Y26)	26	676	1238.24	A + B × 26 =	46.705	.919	.845
91 / 6	47.53	(Y27)	27	729	1283.42	A + B × 27 =	47.554	.020	.000
91 / 7	49.82	(Y28)	28	784	1395.07	A + B × 28 =	48.403	1.420	2.018
91 / 8	53.78	(Y29)	29	841	1559.50	A + B × 29 =	49.253	4.523	20.460
91 / 9	49.80	(Y30)	30	900	1494.04	A + B × 30 =	50.102	.300	.090
91 / 10	50.40	(Y31)	31	961	1562.36	A + B × 31 =	50.951	.552	.305
91 / 11	50.26	(Y32)	32	1024	1608.24	A + B × 32 =	51.800	1.542	2.378
/		(Y33)	33	1089		A + B × 33 =			
/		(Y34)	34	1156		A + B × 34 =			
/		(Y35)	35	1225		A + B × 35 =			
/		(Y36)	36	1296		A + B × 36 =			

(continued)

CHART 7.F17 (*continued*) **Example of Simple Linear Regression Worksheet, Part F**
(Data from Chart 7.F2, Part B)

Product Line Bell Bottoms   Date 1 / 1 /1992

The number of data points in the Y column equals 32 (*n*)
The sum of the Y (Sales Amount) column equals 1236.444 (SY)
The sum of the X (Period) column (use only those X values that have corresponding Y's) equals 528 (SX)
The sum of the X×X (Period Squared) column (use only those X×X values that have corresponding Y's) equals 11440 (SXX)
The sum of the X×Y (Period Times Amount) column (use only those X×Y values that have corresponding Y's) equals 22717.65 (SXY)
BT = (*n*) × (SXY) − (SX) × (SY) = (32) × (22717.65) − (528) × (1236.444) = (726964.8) − (652842.43) = (74122.368)
BB = (*n*) × (SXX) − (SX) × (SX) = (32) × (11440) − (528) × (528) = (87296)
B = BT/BB = (74122.368)/(87296) = .849
AT = (SY) − (B) × (SX) = (1236.444) − (.849) × (528) = (1236.444) − (448.321) = (788.123)
A = AT/(*n*) = (788.123)/(32) = (24.629)
These A and B values are now used to calculate the forecasts and the errors on the previous sheets.
Total of the Absolute Error column = (AE) = 66.192
Total of the Error Squared column = (ES) = 216.255
n − 1 = 31
MAD = (AE)/(*n*) = 2.069
MSE = (ES)/(*n*−1) = 6.976

CHART 7.F17 *(continued)* **Simple Linear Regression Using a Spreadsheet, Part G**

	BD	BE	BF	BG	BH	BI	BJ	BK	BL	BM
1										
2	Regression		b =	.8490915						
3	n = 32		a =	24.62888						
4								Absolute	Error	
5	X	X×X	Y	Y×Y	X×Y	Forecast	Error	Error	Squared	
6	1	1	28.36259	804.4364	28.36259	25.47797	2.884618	2.884618	8.321019	
7	2	4	30.55168	933.4051	61.10336	26.32706	4.224617	4.224617	17.84739	
8	3	9	30.85552	952.0628	92.56655	27.17615	3.679362	3.679362	13.53770	
9	4	16	28.47076	810.5842	113.8830	28.02525	.4455149	.445149	.1984835	
10	5	25	26.29038	691.1840	131.4519	28.87434	−2.58396	2.583959	6.676843	
11	6	36	29.19383	852.2795	175.1630	29.72343	−.529601	.5296012	.2804774	
12	7	49	29.39915	864.3103	205.7941	30.57252	−1.17337	1.173365	1.376786	
13	8	64	29.99242	899.5455	239.9394	31.42161	−1.42919	1.429187	2.042576	
14	9	81	33.86330	1146.723	304.7697	32.27070	1.592593	1.592593	2.536353	
15	10	100	30.30501	918.3937	303.0501	33.11979	−2.81478	2.814783	7.923005	
16	11	121	32.19907	1036.780	354.1898	33.96889	−1.76981	1.769812	3.132233	
17	12	144	31.82026	1012.529	381.8431	34.81798	−2.99772	2.997716	8.986300	
18	13	169	36.99468	1368.606	480.9309	35.66707	1.327612	1.327612	1.762554	
19	14	196	37.74031	1424.331	528.3643	36.51616	1.224150	1.224150	1.498543	
20	15	225	37.52698	1408.274	562.9047	37.36525	.1617267	.1617267	.0261555	
21	16	256	37.62208	1415.421	601.9532	38.21434	−.592267	.5922671	.3507803	
22	17	289	35.85052	1285.259	609.4588	39.06343	−3.21292	3.212919	10.32285	
23	18	324	36.92160	1363.205	664.5889	39.91253	−2.99092	2.990921	8.945609	
24	19	361	36.11896	1304.579	686.2603	40.76162	−4.64266	4.642656	21.55426	
25	20	400	35.66667	1272.111	713.3333	41.61071	−5.94404	5.944042	35.33164	
26	21	441	43.41448	1884.817	911.7041	42.45980	.9546813	.9546813	.9114165	
27	22	484	46.97277	2206.441	1033.401	43.30889	3.663875	3.663875	13.42398	
28	23	529	45.07870	2032.090	1036.810	44.15798	.9207202	.9207202	.8477257	
29	24	576	45.45752	2066.386	1090.980	45.00707	.4504413	.4504413	.2028974	
30	25	625	50.55940	2556.253	1263.985	45.85617	4.703231	4.703231	22.12038	
31	26	676	47.62468	2268.110	1238.242	46.70526	.9194190	.9194190	.8453314	
32	27	729	47.53417	2259.498	1283.423	47.55435	−.020177	.0201768	.0004071	
33	28	784	49.82383	2482.414	1395.067	48.40344	1.420389	1.420389	2.017506	
34	29	841	53.77577	2891.834	1559.497	49.25253	4.523241	4.523241	20.45971	
35	30	900	49.80123	2480.163	1494.037	50.10162	−.300389	.3003893	.0902337	
36	31	961	50.39855	2540.014	1562.355	50.95072	−.552165	.5521646	.3048858	
37	32	1024	50.25758	2525.824	1608.242	51.79981	−1.54223	1.542231	2.378477	
38	528	11440	1236.444	49957.86	22717.65	= Sum	Total =	66.19238	216.2545	
39	278784		1528795.	= Squared			MAD =	2.068512	6.975952	= MSE
40										

(continued)

CHART 7.F17 *(continued)* **Simple Linear Regression Using a Spreadsheet, Part H**

	BD	BE	BF	BG	BH	BI
1						
2	Regression			b =(BE3×BH38-BD38×BD38)/(BE3×BE38-BD38)		
3	n = 32		a = (BF38-BG2×BD38)/BE3			
4						
5	X	X×X	Y	Y×Y	X×Y	Forecast
6	1	BD6×BD6	N6	BF6×BF6	BD6×BF6	BG3+BG2×BD6
7	2	BD7×BD7	N7	BF7×BF7	BD7×BF7	BG3+BG2×BD7
8	3	BD8×BD8	N8	BF8×BF8	BD8×BF8	BG3+BG2×BD8
9	4	BD9×BD9	N9	BF9×BF9	BD9×BF9	BG3+BG2×BD9
10	5	BD10×BD10	N10	BF10×BF10	BD10×BF10	BG3+BG2×BD10
11	6	BD11×BD11	N11	BF11×BF11	BD11×BF11	BG3+BG2×BD11
12	7	BD12×BD12	N12	BF12×BF12	BD12×BF12	BG3+BG2×BD12
13	8	BF13×BD13	N13	BF13×BF13	BD13×BF13	BG3+BG2×BD13
14	9	BD14×BD14	N14	BF14×BF14	BD14×BF14	BG3+BG2×BD14
15	10	BD15×BD15	N15	BF15×BF15	BD15×BF15	BG3+BG2×BD15
16	11	BD16×BD16	N16	BF16×BF16	BD16×BF16	BG3+BG2×BD16
17	12	BD17×BD17	N17	BF17×BF17	BD17×BF17	BG3+BG2×BD17
18	13	BD18×BD18	N18	BF18×BF18	BD18×BF18	BG3+BG2×BD18
19	14	BD19×BD19	N19	BF19×BF19	BD19×BF19	BG3+BG2×BD19
20	15	BD20×BD20	N20	BF20×BF20	BD20×BF20	BG3+BG2×BD20
21	16	BD21×BD21	N21	BF21×BF21	BD21×BF21	BG3+BG2×BD21
22	17	BD22×BD22	N22	BF22×BF22	BD22×BF22	BG3+BG2×BD22
23	18	BD23×BD23	N23	BF23×BF23	BD23×BF23	BG3+BG2×BD23
24	19	BD24×BD24	N24	BF24×BF24	BD24×BF24	BG3+BG2×BD24
25	20	BD25×BD25	N25	BF25×BF25	BD25×BF25	BG3+BG2×BD25
26	21	BD26×BD26	N26	BF26×BF26	BD26×BF26	BG3+BG2×BD26
27	22	BD27×BD27	N27	BF27×BF27	BD27×BF27	BG3+BG2×BD27
28	23	BD28×BD28	N28	BF28×BF28	BD28×BF28	BG3+BG2×BD28
29	24	BD29×BD29	N29	BF29×BF29	BD29×BF29	BG3+BG2×BD29
30	25	BD30×BD30	N30	BF30×BF30	BD30×BF30	BG3+BG2×BD30
31	26	BD31×BD31	N31	BF31×BF31	BD31×BF31	BG3+BG2×BD31
32	27	BD32×BD32	N32	BF32×BF32	BD32×BF32	BG3+BG2×BD32
33	28	BF33×BD33	N33	BF33×BF33	BD33×BF33	BG3+BG2×BD33
34	29	BD34×BF34	N34	BF34×BF34	BD34×BF34	BG3+BG2×BD34
35	30	BD35×BD35	N35	BF35×BF35	BD35×BF35	BG3+BG2×BD35
36	31	BD36×BD36	N36	BF36×BF36	BD36×BF36	BG3+BG2×BD36
37	32	BD37×BD37	N37	BF37×BF37	BD37×BF37	BG3+BG2×BD37
38	SUM(BD6 : BD37)	SUM(BE6 : BE37)	SUM(BF6 : BF37)	SUM(BG6 : BG37)	SUM(BH6 : BH37)	= Sum
39	BD38×BD38		BF38×BF38	= Squared		
40						

CHART 7.F17 *(concluded)* **Simple Linear Regression Using a Spreadsheet, Part I**

	BJ	BK	BL	BM
1				
2				
3				
4		Absolute	Error	
5	Error	Error	Squared	
6	BF6-BI6	ABS(BJ6)	BK6×BK6	
7	BF7-BI7	ABS(BJ7)	BK7×BK7	
8	BF8-BI8	ABS(BJ8)	BK8×BK8	
9	BF9-BI9	ABS(BJ9)	BK9×BK9	
10	BF10-BI10	ABS(BJ10)	BK10×BK10	
11	BF11-BI11	ABS(BJ11)	BK11×BK11	
12	BF12-BI12	ABS(BJ12)	BK12×BK12	
13	BF13-BI13	ABS(BJ13)	BK13×BK13	
14	BF14-BI14	ABS(BJ14)	BK14×BK14	
15	BF15-BI15	ABS(BJ15)	BK15×BK15	
16	BF16-BI16	ABS(BJ16)	BK16×BK16	
17	BF17-BI17	ABS(BJ17)	BK17×BK17	
18	BF18-BI18	ABS(BJ18)	BK18×BK18	
19	BF19-BI19	ABS(BJ19)	BK19×BK19	
20	BF20-BI20	ABS(BJ20)	BK20×BK20	
21	BF21-BI21	ABS(BJ21)	BK21×BK21	
22	BF22-BI22	ABS(BJ22)	BK22×BK22	
23	BF23-BI23	ABS(BJ23)	BK23×BK23	
24	BF24-BI24	ABS(BJ24)	BK24×BK24	
25	BF25-BI25	ABS(BJ25)	BK25×BK25	
26	BF26-BI26	ABS(BJ26)	BK26×BK26	
27	BF27-BI27	ABS(BJ27)	BK27×BK27	
28	BF28-BI28	ABS(BJ28)	BK28×BK28	
29	BF29-BI29	ABS(BJ29)	BK29×BK29	
30	BF30-BI30	ABS(BJ30)	BK30×BK30	
31	BF31-BI31	ABS(BJ31)	BK31×BK31	
32	BF32-BI32	ABS(BJ32)	BK32×BK32	
33	BF33-BI33	ABS(BJ33)	BK33×BK33	
34	BF34-BI34	ABS(BJ34)	BK34×BK34	
35	BF35-BI35	ABS(BJ35)	BK35×BK35	
36	BF36-BI36	ABS(BJ36)	BK36×BK36	
37	BF37-BI37	ABS(BJ37)	BK37×BK37	
38	Total =	SUM(BK6 : BK37)	SUM(BL6 : BL37)	
39	MAD =	BK38/32	BL38/31	=MSE
40				

of $n - 1$. We are now ready to calculate MAD, which is AE divided by n. Then we calculate MSE by dividing ES by $n - 1$. In the sample data of Chart 7.F17, Parts D, E, and F, MAD came out to be 2.069 and MSE was calculated at 6.976.

I only supplied enough sheets for 36 data points. If more data points are needed, make sheets similar to the second sheet but continue the numbers starting with 37 for the "X" column, 37 × 37 for the "X × X" column, and "A + B × 37" for the forecast calculation formula.

Chart 7.F17, Part G, demonstrates the regression calculations on a spreadsheet similar to those done in Chart 7.F17, Parts D, E, and F. Chart 7.F17, Parts H and I, shows the calculations that are used for the spreadsheet version of Chart 7.F17, Parts A, B, and C.

Step 4: Select the Best Model

The best model is selected based on the MAD and MSE values, and the model with the lowest values is the one that generates the least errors, making it the best model.

To start this process, we need to review the MAD and MSE values for the models we have tested. Chart 7.F18 is a summary of these values. For a weighted moving average, the best results from Chart 7.F12 are used. For exponential smoothing, the best results from Chart 7.F15 are used.

The information of Chart 7.F18 tells us two things. From the MAD values we learn which forecasting model is the closest "on the average." The winner here appears to be single exponential smoothing with an alpha factor of 0.81. The MSE values tell us which model makes the least "biggies" (big errors) in the forecast prediction process. The MSE winner would be simple linear regression. What you want is for both the MAD and MSE to be at their lowest. No such luck here. But we do need to select a winner in order to decide what forecasting model we should use.

By looking back at the MAD values we see that the three lowest, in order from best to worst, are:

Single exponential smoothing	1.996
Naive	2.047
Single weighted moving average	2.056

Looking back at the MSE values we see that the three lowest, in order from best to worst, are:

Simple linear regression	6.976
Single exponential smoothing	7.742
Naive	7.872

Single exponential smoothing and naive appear on both lists, but single exponential smoothing appears higher on both lists. Therefore, we would select single exponential smoothing with an alpha factor of 0.81 as the overall winner for the best all around forecasting model using the data of Chart 7.F2, Part B.

CHART 7.F18 Review of the Error Factors of Each Model

	Single		Double	
Model	MAD	MSE	MAD	MSE
Naive	2.047	7.872		
Two-period simple moving average	2.097	9.126	2.988	16.272
Three-period simple moving average	2.206	10.252	3.597	22.344
Weighted moving average at 0.9, 0.1, 0.0, 0.0	2.056	8.250	2.738	15.699
Exponential smoothing alpha = 0.81	1.996	7.742	2.604	13.739
Simple linear regression	2.069	6.976		

Step 5: Generate the Forecast

Now we are finally ready to generate a forecast using the model that we selected. Since I don't know which model you will end up selecting during your forecasting process, I will demonstrate the procedure for generating a forecast for the next four months (December 1991 through March 1992) using each of the models shown in Chart 7.F18. I have not supplied the spreadsheet examples for these calculations because they are so easy to do.

Chart 7.F19 shows the forecast using the naive forecasting method. We start with the results of Chart 7.F6, Part D, where the most recent actual sales amount was 50.26 (for November 1991). The forecast for each of the next four months would be this same value.

Two-period simple moving average forecasting would start with the end of Chart 7.F8, Parts C and D, and continue with the forecast predictions. Chart 7.F20, Part A, is a worksheet for generating this forecast. Chart 7.F20, Part B, is an example of how to use the worksheet of Chart 7.F20, Part A, starting with the last two periods of data from Chart 7.F8, Part D. Then we continue the calculation process following the formulas on the worksheet to generate the new forecasts. Notice that when we run out of actual sales values, we start using the forecast

CHART 7.F19 Naive Forecast Projections

Month	Deseasonalized Actual Sales	Deseasonalized Forecasted Sales
11/91	50.26	
12/91		50.26
1/92		50.26
2/92		50.26
3/92		50.26

CHART 7.F20 Two-Period Simple Moving Average Forecast Sheet, Part A

Product Line ________ Page __ of __ Date __/__/__

Deseasonalized Sales Year/Month	Amount		Single Forecast			Double Forecast
(The first two lines of data come from the last two lines of the Chart 7.F8 input sheets)						
____/____	______ (a)		______	(aa)		______
____/____	______ (b)		______	(bb)		______
____/____		(a+b)/2 =	______	(cc)	(aa+bb)/2 =	______
____/____		(b+cc)/2 =	______	(dd)	(bb+cc)/2 =	______
____/____		(cc+dd)/2 =	______	(ee)	=	______
____/____		(dd+ee)/2 =	______	(ff)	=	______
____/____		(ee+ff)/2 =	______	(gg)	=	______
____/____		(ff+gg)/2 =	______	(hh)	=	______
____/____		(gg+hh)/2 =	______	(ii)	=	______
____/____		(hh+ii)/2 =	______	(jj)	=	______
____/____		(ii+jj)/2 =	______	(kk)	=	______
____/____		(jj+kk)/2 =	______	(ll)	=	______
____/____		(kk+ll)/2 =	______	(mm)	=	______
____/____		(ll+mm)/2 =	______	(nn)	=	______

(continued)

CHART 7.F20 (*concluded*) **Example of Two-Period Simple Moving Average Forecast Sheet, Part B,** (Data from Chart 7.F8, Parts C and D)

Product Line Bell bottoms Page 1 of 1 Date 1 / 1 /1992

Deseasonalized Sales Year/Month	Amount		Single Forecast			Double Forecast
(The first two lines of data come from the last two lines of the Chart 7.F8 input sheets)						
91 / 10	50.40 (a)		51.789	(aa)		50.239
91 / 11	50.26 (b)		50.100	(bb)		51.794
91 / 12		(a+b)/2 =	50.33	(cc)	(aa+bb)/2 =	50.949
92 / 1		(b+cc)/2 =	50.295	(dd)	(bb+cc)/2 =	50.215
92 / 2		(cc+dd)/2 =	50.313	(ee)	=	50.313
92 / 3		(dd+ee)/2 =	50.304	(ff)	=	50.304
___/___		(ee+ff)/2 =	______	(gg)	=	______
___/___		(ff+gg)/2 =	______	(hh)	=	______
___/___		(gg+hh)/2 =	______	(ii)	=	______
___/___		(hh+ii)/2 =	______	(jj)	=	______
___/___		(ii+jj)/2 =	______	(kk)	=	______
___/___		(jj+kk)/2 =	______	(ll)	=	______
___/___		(kk+ll)/2 =	______	(mm)	=	______
___/___		(ll+mm)/2 =	______	(nn)	=	______

values in the formula calculations. Also note that the single and double forecasts are the same after the first two predictions.

The three-period simple moving average forecast works similar to the two-period simple moving average forecast. Chart 7.F21, Part A, is the worksheet for this calculation and Chart 7.F21, Part B, is the example of how to use this worksheet when applied to the data of Chart 7.F10, Parts C, D, and E.

For the weighted moving average forecast generation, the worksheet is slightly more complicated. We start with the last eight periods of data. But we cannot start directly with the last eight data entries of Chart 7.F11, Part B. We need to recalculate using the weights that have supplied us with the best MAD and MSE results. In the case of Chart 7.F11, Parts C, D, and E, the weights are 0.4, 0.3, 0.2, and 0.1. The winning weights from Chart 7.F18 are 0.9, 0.1, 0.0, and 0.0.

The worksheet for the weighted moving average model is Chart 7.F22, Part A. Chart 7.F22, Part B, shows how to use this model applying the winning weights. The only information that is transferable from Chart 7.F11, Parts C, D, and E, is the last eight deseasonalized actual sales amounts.

For exponential smoothing the process is slightly trickier. We actually need the fully calculated Chart 7.F14, Parts A and B, worksheet for the winning weight. In the case of Chart 7.F14, Parts C and D, the alpha factor was 0.2. But the winning alpha factor was 0.81. To fill in the worksheet of Chart 7.F23, Part A, which calculates the exponential smoothing forecast, we need the last line from the alpha factor 0.81 calculation process. The information from this line was:

Sales amount = 50.26

Single forecast = 50.399

Double forecast = 50.743

CHART 7.F21 Three-Period Simple Moving Average Forecast Sheet, Part A

Product Line ________ Page __ of __ Date __/__/__

Deseasonalized Sales Year/Month	Amount			Single Forecast			Double Forecast
(The first three lines of data come from the last two lines of the Chart 7.F10 input sheets)							
___/___	______	(a)		______	(aa)		______
___/___	______	(b)		______	(bb)		______
___/___	______	(c)		______	(cc)		______
___/___			(a+b+c)/3 =	______	(dd)	(aa+bb+cc)/3 =	______
___/___			(b+c+dd)/3 =	______	(ee)	(bb+cc+dd)/3 =	______
___/___			(c+dd+ee)/3 =	______	(ff)	(cc+dd+ee)/3 =	______
___/___			(dd+ee+ff)/3 =	______	(gg)	=	______
___/___			(ee+ff+gg)/3 =	______	(hh)	=	______
___/___			(ff+gg+hh)/3 =	______	(ii)	=	______
___/___			(gg+hh+ii)/3 =	______	(jj)	=	______
___/___			(hh+ii+jj)/3 =	______	(kk)	=	______
___/___			(ii+jj+kk)/3 =	______	(ll)	=	______
___/___			(jj+kk+ll)/3 =	______	(mm)	=	______
___/___			(kk+ll+mm)/3 =	______	(nn)	=	______

CHART 7.F21 (*concluded*) **Example of Three-Period Simple Moving Average Forecast Sheet, Part B**
(Data from Chart 7.F10, Parts C and D)

Product Line Bell bottoms Page 1 of 1 Date 1 / 1 /1992

Deseasonalized Sales Year/Month	Amount			Single Forecast			Double Forecast
(The first three lines of data come from the last two lines of the Chart 7.F10 input sheets)							
91 / 9	49.80	(a)		50.378	(aa)		48.260
91 / 10	50.40	(b)		51.134	(bb)		49.093
91 / 11	50.26	(c)		51.325	(cc)		49.946
91 / 12			(a+b+c)/3 =	50.153	(dd)	(aa+bb+cc)/3 =	50.946
92 / 1			(b+c+dd)/3 =	50.271	(ee)	(bb+cc+dd)/3 =	50.871
92 / 2			(c+dd+ee)/3 =	50.228	(ff)	(cc+dd+ee)/3 =	50.583
92 / 3			(dd+ee+ff)/3 =	50.217	(gg)	=	50.217
___/___			(ee+ff+gg)/3 =	______	(hh)	=	______
___/___			(ff+gg+hh)/3 =	______	(ii)	=	______
___/___			(gg+hh+ii)/3 =	______	(jj)	=	______
___/___			(hh+ii+jj)/3 =	______	(kk)	=	______
___/___			(ii+jj+kk)/3 =	______	(ll)	=	______
___/___			(jj+kk+ll)/3 =	______	(mm)	=	______
___/___			(kk+ll+mm)/3 =	______	(nn)	=	______

We start with these values in the example on Chart 7.F23, Part B, and work out the forecasts for the desired number of months. Note that the single forecast is the same value after the second month, and the double forecast converges on the same value as the single forecast after a few months.

Regression is one of the easiest models to calculate. We start with the last "X" value, the "A" value, and the "B" value from Chart 7.F17, Parts A, B, and C. We put this information into Chart 7.F24, Part A, and proceed with the calculation of the forecast as shown. Chart 7.F24, Part B, is an example of the data from Chart 7.F17, Parts D, E, and F, used to generate a forecast.

CHART 7.F22 Weighted Moving Average Forecast Sheet, Part A

Product Line __________ Page __ of __ Date __/__/____

Deseasonalized Sales Year/Month	Amount		Weights		Single Forecast			Double Forecast
(The first eight lines of data come from the last eight lines of the Chart 7.F11 input sheets)								
___/___	______	(a)	______	(w4) – smallest				
___/___	______	(b)	______	(w3)				
___/___	______	(c)	______	(w2)				
___/___	______	(d)	______	(w1) – largest				
___/___	______	(e)		(a×w4+b×w3+c×w2+d×w1) =	______	(ee)		
___/___	______	(f)		(b×w4+c×w3+d×w2+e×w1) =	______	(ff)		
___/___	______	(g)		(c×w4+d×w3+e×w2+f×w1) =	______	(gg)		
___/___	______	(h)		(d×w4+e×w3+f×w2+g×w1) =	______	(hh)		
___/___				(e×w4+f×w3+g×w2+h×w1) =	______	(ii)	(ee×w4+ff×w3+gg×w2+hh×w1) =	______
___/___				(f×w4+g×w3+h×w2+ii×w1) =	______	(jj)	(ff×w4+gg×w3+hh×w2+ii×w1) =	______
___/___				(g×w4+h×w3+ii×w2+jj×w1) =	______	(kk)	(gg×w4+hh×w3+ii×w2+jj×w1) =	______
___/___				(h×w4+ii×w3+jj×w2+kk×w1) =	______	(ll)	(hh×w4+ii×w3+jj×w2+kk×w1) =	______
___/___				(ii×w4+jj×w3+kk×w2+ll×w1) =	______	(mm)	=	______
___/___				(jj×w4+kk×w3+ll×w2+mm×w1) =	______	(nn)	=	______
___/___				(kk×w4+ll×w3+mm×w2+nn×w1) =	______	(oo)	=	______
___/___				(ll×w4+mm×w3+nn×w2+oo×w1) =	______	(pp)	=	______
___/___				(mm×w4+nn×w3+oo×w2+pp×w1) =	______	(qq)	=	______
___/___				(nn×w4+oo×w3+pp×w2+qq×w1) =	______	(rr)	=	______

CHART 7.F22 *(concluded)* **Example of Weighted Moving Average Forecast Sheet, Part B**
(Data from Chart 7.11, Parts C, D, & E)

Product Line Bell Bottoms   Page 1 of 1   Date 1 / 1 /1991

Deseasonalized Sales Year/Month	Amount		Weights		Single Forecast			Double Forecast
(The first eight lines of data come from the last eight lines of the Chart 7.F11 input sheets)								
91 / 4	50.56	(a)	.0	(w4) – smallest				
91 / 5	47.62	(b)	.0	(w3)				
91 / 6	47.53	(c)	.1	(w2)				
91 / 7	49.82	(d)	.9	(w1) – largest				
91 / 8	53.78	(e)		(a×w4+b×w3+c×w2+d×w1) =	49.591	(ee)		
91 / 9	49.80	(f)		(b×w4+c×w3+d×w2+e×w1) =	53.384	(ff)		
91 / 10	50.40	(g)		(c×w4+d×w3+e×w2+f×w1) =	50.198	(gg)		
91 / 11	50.26	(h)		(d×w4+e×w3+f×w2+g×w1) =	50.340	(hh)		
91 / 12				(e×w4+f×w3+g×w2+h×w1) =	50.274	(ii)	(ee×w4+ff×w3+gg×w2+hh×w1) =	50.326
92 / 1				(f×w4+g×w3+h×w2+ii×w1) =	50.273	(jj)	(ff×w4+gg×w3+hh×w2+ii×w1) =	50.281
92 / 2				(g×w4+h×w3+ii×w2+jj×w1) =	50.272	(kk)	(gg×w4+hh×w3+ii×w2+jj×w1) =	50.273
92 / 3				(h×w4+ii×w3+jj×w2+kk×w1) =	50.272	(ll)	(hh×w4+ii×w3+jj×w2+kk×w1) =	50.272
92 / 4				(ii×w4+jj×w3+kk×w2+ll×w1) =	50.272	(mm)	=	50.272
___/___				(jj×w4+kk×w3+ll×w2+mm×w1) =	______	(nn)	=	______
___/___				(kk×w4+ll×w3+mm×w2+nn×w1) =	______	(oo)	=	______
___/___				(ll×w4+mm×w3+nn×w2+oo×w1) =	______	(pp)	=	______
___/___				(mm×w4+nn×w3+oo×w2+pp×w1) =	______	(qq)	=	______
___/___				(nn×w4+oo×w3+pp×w2+qq×w1) =	______	(rr)	=	______

CHART 7.F23 Exponential Smoothing Forecast Sheet, Part A

Product Line __________ Page __ of __ Date __/__/____

Deseasonalized Sales Year/Month	Amount	Alpha Factor = ______ (x)	Single Forecast		Double Forecast	
(The first line of the sales and forecast data comes from the last line of the Chart 7.F14 input sheet for the winning alpha factor)						
___/____	______ (a)		______	(za)	______	(zza)
___/____		(x)×(a−za)+za =	______	(zb)	(x)×(za−zza)+zza = ______	(zzb)
___/____		(zb) =	______		(x)×(zb−zzb)+zzb = ______	(zzc)
___/____		(zb) =	______		(x)×(zb−zzc)+zzc = ______	(zzd)
___/____		(zb) =	______		(x)×(zb−zzd)+zzd = ______	(zze)
___/____		(zb) =	______		(x)×(zb−zze)+zze = ______	(zzf)
___/____		(zb) =	______		(x)×(zb−zzf)+zzf = ______	(zzg)
___/____		(zb) =	______		(x)×(zb−zzg)+zzg = ______	(zzh)
___/____		(zb) =	______		(x)×(zb−zzh)+zzh = ______	(zzi)
___/____		(zb) =	______		(x)×(zb−zzi)+zzi = ______	(zzj)

CHART 7.F23 (*continued*) **Example of Exponential Smoothing Forecast Sheet, Part B**
(Data from Chart 7.F14, Parts C and D, Using an Alpha Factor of .81)

Product Line Bell Bottoms Page 1 of 1 Date 1 / 1 /1992

Deseasonalized Sales Year/Month	Amount	Alpha Factor = .81 (x)	Single Forecast		Double Forecast	
(The first line of the sales and forecast data comes from the last line of the Chart 7.F14 input sheet for the winning alpha factor)						
91 / 11	50.26 (a)		50.399	(za)	50.743	(zza)
91 / 12		(x)×(a−za)+za =	50.286	(zb)	(x)×(za−zza)+zza = 50.464	(zzb)
92 / 1		(zb) =	50.286		(x)×(zb−zzb)+zzb = 50.320	(zzc)
92 / 3		(zb) =	50.286		(x)×(zb−zzc)+zzc = 50.293	(zzd)
92 / 4		(zb) =	50.286		(x)×(zb−zzd)+zzd = 50.288	(zze)
___/____		(zb) =	______		(x)×(zb−zze)+zze = ______	(zzf)
___/____		(zb) =	______		(x)×(zb−zzf)+zzf = ______	(zzg)
___/____		(zb) =	______		(x)×(zb−zzg)+zzg = ______	(zzh)
___/____		(zb) =	______		(x)×(zb−zzh)+zzh = ______	(zzi)
___/____		(zb) =	______		(x)×(zb−zzi)+zzi = ______	(zzj)

At this point we have successfully generated the forecast for each of the five models under consideration. However, you will only need to generate forecasts using one model, the model that has come out the winner in your MAD and MSE analysis. The forecasts from this one winning model are the values that will be applied to the deseasonalization process in the next section.

Step 6: Put Seasonality Back into the Generated Forecast

We have generated a forecast, but the forecast is still not ready for us to apply to our operations. Near the start of this process we removed the seasonality from our data so that we could make a cleaner projection into the future. Now that we have made that projection, we need to restore the effects of seasonality into our data.

For our sample data the winning forecasting method was single exponential smoothing with an alpha factor of 0.81. I will use the data

CHART 7.F24 Simple Linear Regression Forecast Projections, Part A

The last "X" value used was = ________
(from Chart 7.F17, Parts A, B, and C)

The "A" value calculated was = ________
(from Chart 7.F17, Part C)

The "B" value calculated was = ________
(from Chart 7.F17, Part C)

Forecast Predictions (Must Start With The First Month After "X")

Year/Month	"X" value	Forecast
____/____	X+1 = ______ (xa)	A + B × (xa) = ______
____/____	X+2 = ______ (xb)	A + B × (xb) = ______
____/____	X+3 = ______ (xc)	A + B × (xc) = ______
____/____	X+4 = ______ (xd)	A + B × (xd) = ______
____/____	X+5 = ______ (xe)	A + B × (xe) = ______
____/____	X+6 = ______ (xf)	A + B × (xf) = ______
____/____	X+7 = ______ (xg)	A + B × (xg) = ______
____/____	X+8 = ______ (xh)	A + B × (xh) = ______

CHART 7.F24 (*concluded*) **Example of Simple Linear Regression Forecast Projections, Part B** (Data from Chart 7.F17, Parts D, E, and F)

The last "X" value used was = 32
(from Chart 7.F17, Parts A, B, and C)

The "A" value calculated was = 24.629
(from Chart 7.F17, Part C)

The "B" value calculated was = .849
(from Chart 7.F17, Part C)

Forecast Predictions (Must Start With The First Month After "X")

Year/Month	"X" value	Forecast
91 / 12	X+1 = 33 (xa)	A + B × (xa) = 52.646
92 / 1	X+2 = 34 (xb)	A + B × (xb) = 53.495
92 / 2	X+3 = 35 (xc)	A + B × (xc) = 54.344
92 / 3	X+4 = 36 (xd)	A + B × (xd) = 55.193
____/____	X+5 = ______ (xe)	A + B × (xe) = ______
____/____	X+6 = ______ (xf)	A + B × (xf) = ______
____/____	X+7 = ______ (xg)	A + B × (xg) = ______
____/____	X+8 = ______ (xh)	A + B × (xh) = ______

from Chart 7.F23, Part B, to demonstrate how seasonality is reinstalled into the forecasted numbers. The seasonality factors were calculated in Chart 7.F2, Part B, and will now be used to reinstall seasonality into the forecast. Chart 7.F25, Part A, is the worksheet for reinstalling seasonality. Chart 7.F25, Part B, is the example of this process using our winning forecast predictions. To put seasonality back into the forecast, simply multiply the forecast you generated times the period weight. (Note the similarity to Chart 7.F2, Parts A and B, where we initially calculated the seasonality factors.)

Using the numbers from Chart 7.F25, Part B, we are now ready to move forward with the best possible forecast available to us.

CHART 7.F25 Worksheet for Reinstalling Seasonality Back into the Forecast, Part A

Product Line ______ Date __/__/__

Month	Generated Forecast Year __	Generated Forecast Year __	Period Weight	Actual Forecast Year __	Actual Forecast Year __
1					
2					
3					
4					
5					
6					
7					
8					
9					
10					
11					
12					

CHART 7.F25 *(concluded)* **Example of Worksheet for Reinstalling Seasonality Back into the Forecast, Part B**

Product Line Bell Bottoms Date 1/1/92

Month	Generated Forecast Year 91	Generated Forecast Year 92	Period Weight	Actual Forecast Year 91	Actual Forecast Year 92
1		50.286	.66		33.189
2		50.286	.776		39.022
3		50.286	.88		44.252
4					
5					
6					
7					
8					
9					
10					
11					
12	50.286		1.152	57.929	

In summary, our forecast for the next four months is:

December 1991	57.929
January 1992	33.189
February 1992	39.022
March 1992	44.252

Step 7: Monitor the Performance of the Forecast

Forecasting is not a process that we do once and forget about. It is a process that needs to be repeated as often as possible. If you recall the "Features Common to Forecasts" section of this chapter, item 6 stated that forecast accuracy decreases as the time period of the forecast increases. That means that the more periods we forecast out into the future, the greater the chance for error. Therefore, it is important to recalculate the forecast each month with the new "Actual Sales Data," even if we don't reevaluate which model we use each month.

We should reevaluate the model at least quarterly. The reevaluation process is the technique we use to monitor the performance of the forecast. If our "best fit" model is no longer the best predictor, the reevaluation process will change the model we use.

In the "Features Common to Forecasts" section, we also discussed the need to make sure that the generated forecast is in line with the business plan. New product lines will not have a history of sales but they still need to be forecast and put into the production plan. Some adjustment to the calculated forecast may be needed.

Summary

We now have a forecast that tells us what the demand will be on our factory. We should now review how customer orders affect the forecast (Appendix 7.G). Then we continue with the planning process to see how available capacity and demand on capacity (forecast plus customer orders) are balanced out to generate an aggregate production schedule (Appendix 7.A).

APPENDIX 7.G: Customer Order Processing

As discussed earlier, customer order processing serves several functions. One of the primary planning functions it serves is it converts anticipated demand (the forecast) into actual demand. A second function of customer order processing occurs when the order is shipped. A diagram of the functions of customer order processing is shown in Chart 7.G1 (repeat of Chart 7.2). The remainder of this appendix will be broken into three sections; one section on how the order processing paper flow works, one on the planning function, and the last on the sales reporting function.

CHART 7.G1 The Functions of Customer Order Processing

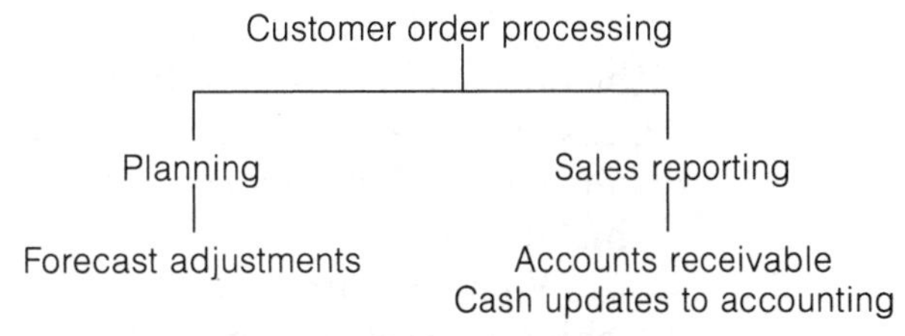

Customer Order Processing

The method for reporting the customer order may take many forms. This depends primarily on the number of orders that are taken. If you have a high volume of orders, you want some type of automated system to track the orders and their shipment. If the volume of orders is low, a few a day or less, a simplistic hand written order form tracking the items listed in Chart 7.G2 is enough. The ordering and shipping document may be one and the same physical piece of paper, or a multicarbon form, depending on how often shipments are made. The following functions must be represented:

Order form (what was ordered)

Shipment form (what was shipped)

Invoice (what was billed)

Chart 7.G3 is an example of what an all-purpose order form would look like. Note that if there are any back orders, they have to be processed as separate orders.

The sample order of Chart 7.G3 is filled out using the following procedure:

1. Order numbers are preassigned to each order so that there are no repeat orders. Back orders look the same except that the order number is prefaced by a "B." This order number is a document tracking number so if a customer has multiple orders you can identify on your statement which order you are billing them for.

2. When the customer phones in an order, fill out the following fields:

Customer number (if one exists)
Order date
Customer name, address, and "ship to" information
Terms (if nonstandard for this customer)
Product #, description, quantity, and price
Due date

3. The order has to be approved by marketing to make sure it is in line with the forecasted work load.

4. The order has to be approved by the credit department to make sure the customer has a good credit history. The credit department will also validate the terms of the agreement.

5. The order processing department makes a file of the outstanding/pending orders in order number and/or customer number sequence. At this point, they may also want to send the customer a confirmation of the order. This can just be a copy of the actual order. Order processing also reports the order, as a firm order, to the production planning system where that department adjusts the forecast (see the next section of this appendix).

6. When the product is shipped, the date shipped information and the shipping cost information is filled in and the order form is sent to the sales department. The sales department reports the completed sales

CHART 7.G2 The Fields of a Customer Order Form

- Order information
  - Order number
  - Date ordered
  - Customer ordering
  - Date wanted
  - Payment terms agreed upon
  - Product wanted
    - Description
    - Quantity
    - Prices agreed upon
  - Shipping instructions
- Shipment information
  - Date shipped
  - Product shipped
    - Description
    - Quantity
    - Back orders
    - Price
    - Shipping costs

CHART 7.G3 Sample Customer Order Form

Customer number ______________________ Order date __/__/__
Terms ______________________ Order number _____
Customer name/address ______________________

Ship to ______________________

Product #	Product Description	Order Quantity	Price	Date Shipped	Quantity Shipped

Due date __/__/__ Shipping cost ________
Order approval (Marketing) ______________ Shipping instructions:

Order approval (Credit) ______________

on the sales report (see the third part of this appendix). Product shipment information is also recorded and used to relieve the Master Production Schedule (see Chart 7.E7).

7. Another copy of the order form is sent to the accounts receivable department. They add the amount of the sales to the accounts receivable report for that particular customer. They also send a copy of the order to the customer and stamp it as an "Invoice." Then the accounts receivable system takes over the billing of the customer and the collection of the debt. The actual invoice may include a charge for the shipping charges as well as the product purchased.

8. If the full amount of the order could not be shipped in step 6, a back order is needed. This can be done in one of two ways.

(a) If we anticipate the shipment to be fairly soon we may hold the order until it has been completed. Then we would proceed with step 6. There may be multiple date and quantity shipped entries for the same product on the same order form.

(b) If we anticipate some delay before the remaining shipment we may want to close out the original order and send it off for billing (steps 6 and 7). We would change the original order quantity on the original order form to reflect the amount actually shipped. We would then create a new order for the remaining balance and use a "B" back order number. The due date of the back order should still be the old due date, not the new anticipated ship date.

A flow chart of this process is given in Chart 7.G4. This will help you follow the order processing procedure on a step-by-step basis.

CHART 7.G4 Order Processing Flow Chart

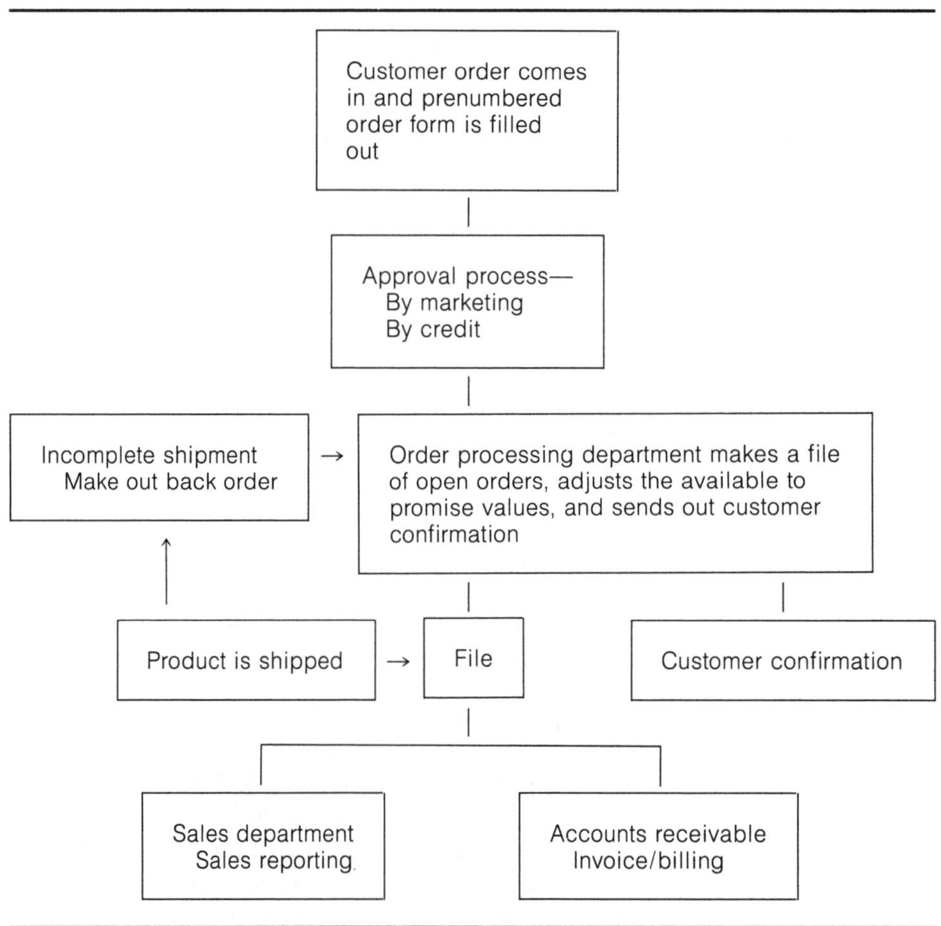

Planning Function

Hopefully, by this point, you now have a forecast for each of your product families. Some of these forecasts may have been developed through the use of quantitative methods such as time series forecasting and some of these forecasts may have been developed using qualitative methods such as a market evaluation. Whatever the origin of the forecast, the VP of Marketing now supplies this forecast to the VP of Operations. Hopefully these forecasts support the goals and objectives of the business plan.

The forecast defines the anticipated demands that are being placed on the organization. These demands are called "adjustable demands" because they are approximations of when the demand is anticipated and they may vary by a month or two in either direction.

There is also a second element that defines the demands on an organization. This is the actual customer orders. Customer orders are considered a "nonadjustable demand" because they define a demand for a specific point in time. A nonadjustable demand defines a specific point when the customer wants the product to be shipped. To ship it late may mean a dissatisfied customer, and to complete it early would mean that we have to pay inventory and storage costs for the product until we can ship it.

It is important to make a distinction here. The customer order process is distinctly different from the order shipment process. The shipment process is a feedback and control mechanism that demonstrates our plant's performance to the orders. It also reports sales. But these functions will be discussed in the next section of this appendix. In this section we are primarily concerned with the order itself. Even if a product is shipped immediately, we still need to report the customer order into the planning process.

At this point I want to return to step 5 of the previous section where the order has been received and approved and is now reported by the ordering department. We need to discuss this reporting process in more

CHART 7.G5 Sample Forecasts

Month	Mountain Bikes	Ten-speed Bikes	Tricycles
1	100	200	150
2	50	50	50
3	50	50	75
4	100	100	100
5	100	200	100
6	150	200	100
7	200	200	150
8	150	200	150
9	50	100	50
10	50	50	50
11	75	50	50
12	250	300	300

detail because it affects the forecast and the entire production planning process of the factory. Let's start by using an example. Chart 7.G5 is the twelve month forecast (anticipated sales) for three product families; mountain bikes, ten-speed bikes, and tricycles. I will use this example throughout the book and build on it as we go along.

Within each of these families of bikes there are several different models. When customers place orders, they order specific models. Chart 7.G6 shows the models of each of these families of bikes and Chart 7.G7 lists some customer orders that we have received.

What we need is a reporting system that shows "committed sales" and what part of the forecast is still "available to be promised." Chart 7.G8 shows how this report would look for each of the families of bikes that we have forecasted in Chart 7.G5. Chart 7.G9 is a blank form that you can use to generate this type of report.

The data of Chart 7.G8 shows the adjustable (available to promise) and the unadjustable (committed) demands that have been placed on the factory. These demands will now need to be converted into a specific demand on resources. We need to develop a "Bill of Resources" for each of these families of products. Then, using the Bill of Resources, we can calculate the actual demand that is being placed on the factory. The resources that are of greatest concern to most factories are the three "M's." They are:

Materials
Machinery
Manpower (labor)

Start in the development of a Bill of Resources by looking at the Bill of Materials and the Routings of each of the products in the family. The

CHART 7.G6 Breakdown of the Families

	Model Number
Mountain bikes	
Economy	MB–E
Heavy duty	MB–HD
Super light weight	MB–SLW
Ten-speed bikes	
Men's	TS–M
Women's	TS–W
Tricycles (only one model)	TRI

CHART 7.G7 Open Customer Orders

Customer Number	Model Number	Quantity	Due Date
21	TS–M	50	March 20
33	TRI	100	June 10
21	MB–E	100	July 1
42	MB–SLW	25	July 10

CHART 7.G8 Forecast/Committed/Available to Promise

Family—Mountain Bikes

Month	Forecast Bikes	Committed Orders	Available to Promise
1	100		100
2	50		50
3	50		50
4	100		100
5	100		100
6	150		150
7	200	125	75
8	150		150
9	50		50
10	50		50
11	75		75
12	250		250

Family—Ten-Speed Bikes

Month	Forecast Bikes	Committed Orders	Available to Promise
1	200		200
2	50		50
3	50	50	0
4	100		100
5	200		200
6	200		200
7	200		200
8	200		200
9	100		100
10	50		50
11	50		50
12	300		300

Family—Tricycles

Month	Forecast Bikes	Committed Orders	Available to Promise
1	150		150
2	50		50
3	75		75
4	100		100
5	100		100
6	100	100	0
7	150		150
8	150		150
9	50		50
10	50		50
11	50		50
12	300		300

Bill of Materials defines the materials requirements for each product. Take the average of each of these requirements and place that value into the Bill of Resources. Similarly, use the Routings to define the labor and machinery requirements for each product and average this out for the family. Chart 7.G10 lists an example of the resource requirements for each of the products in Chart 7.G6.

CHART 7.G9 Available to Promise Report

Product Family—____________

Year/Month	Forecast	Customer Orders	Available to Promise
___/___			
___/___			
___/___			
___/___			
___/___			
___/___			
___/___			
___/___			
___/___			
___/___			
___/___			
___/___			
___/___			
___/___			
___/___			
___/___			

CHART 7.G10 Product Resource Requirements

	Capacity Requirement
Mountain bikes–Economy—Model #MB–E	
Materials	
Bar stock	30 ft.
Purchased parts	$30
Sheet metal	20 sq. ft.
Machinery	
Lathe	6 hours
Drill press	10 hours
Manpower	
Painting	1/2 hour
Assembly	2 hours
Welding	3 hours
Grinding	1 hour
Mountain bikes–Heavy duty—Model #MB–HD	
Materials	
Bar stock	45 ft.
Purchased parts	$40
Sheet metal	22 sq. ft.
Machinery	
Lathe	6 hours
Drill press	10 hours
Manpower	
Painting	1/2 hour
Assembly	2 hours
Welding	4 hours
Grinding	1 hour
Mountain bikes–Super light weight—Model #MB–SLW	
Materials	
Bar stock	35 ft.
Purchased parts	$50
Sheet metal	15 sq. ft.

CHART 7.G10 *(continued)*

	Capacity Requirement
Machinery	
Lathe	6 hours
Drill press	10 hours
Manpower	
Painting	1/2 hour
Assembly	2 hours
Welding	4 hours
Grinding	2 hours
Ten-speed bikes–Men's—Model #TS–M	
Materials	
Bar stock	25 ft.
Purchased parts	$25
Sheet metal	20 sq. ft.
Machinery	
Lathe	4 hours
Drill press	8 hours
Manpower	
Painting	1/2 hour
Assembly	2 hours
Welding	3 hours
Grinding	1 hour
Ten-speed bikes–Women's—Model #TS–W	
Materials	
Bar stock	20 ft.
Purchased parts	$25
Sheet metal	20 sq. ft.
Machinery	
Lathe	4 hours
Drill press	8 hours
Manpower	
Painting	1/2 hour
Assembly	2 hours
Welding	3 hours
Grinding	1 hour
Tricycles–Model #TRI	
Materials	
Bar stock	10 ft.
Purchased parts	$15
Sheet metal	10 sq. ft.
Machinery	
Lathe	2 hours
Drill press	5 hours
Manpower	
Painting	.25 hour
Assembly	1.5 hours
Welding	2 hours
Grinding	1 hour

Chart 7.G11 is the Bill of Resources for each of the family of parts listed in Chart 7.G6. It shows how each of the values is averaged.

At this point I can now calculate the demand for each resource as required by each product family. I combine the demand chart (Chart 7.G8) with the Bill of Resources chart (Chart 7.G11) to calculate the "Total Resources Demanded By Family" worksheet (Chart 7.G12).

CHART 7.G11 Bill of Resources

	Capacity Requirement
Mountain bikes	
Materials	
Bar stock	(30 + 45 + 35)/3 = 36.7 ft.
Purchased parts	(30 + 40 + 50)/3 = $40
Sheet metal	(20 +22 + 15)/3 = 19 sq. ft.
Machinery	
Lathe	(6 + 6 + 6)/3 = 6 hours
Drill press	(10 + 10 + 10)/3 = 10 hours
Manpower	
Painting	(1/2 + 1/2 + 1/2)/3 = 1/2 hour
Assembly	(2 + 2 + 2)/3 = 2 hours
Welding	(3 + 4 + 4)/3 = 3.7 hours
Grinding	(1 + 1 + 2)/3 = 1.3 hours
Ten-speed bikes	
Materials	
Bar stock	(25 + 20)/2 = 22.5 ft.
Purchased parts	(25 + 25)/2 = $25
Sheet metal	(20 + 20)/2 = 20 sq. ft.
Machinery	
Lathe	(4 + 4)/2 = 4 hours
Drill press	(8 + 8)/2 = 8 hours
Manpower	
Painting	(1/2 + 1/2)/2 = 1/2 hour
Assembly	(2 + 2)/2 = 2 hours
Welding	(3 + 3)/2 = 3 hours
Grinding	(1 + 1)/2 = 1 hour
Tricycles–Model #TRI	
Materials	
Bar stock	10 ft.
Purchased parts	$15
Sheet metal	10 sq. ft.
Machinery	
Lathe	2 hours
Drill press	5 hours
Manpower	
Painting	.25 hour
Assembly	1.5 hours
Welding	2 hours
Grinding	1 hour

CHART 7.G12 Total Resources Demanded by Family Worksheet

Family ____________________ Date _/_/_

Resource Description	Quantity	Forecast Month Quantity	1	2	3	4	5	6	7	8	9	10	11	12

CHART 7.G13 Total Resources Demanded-Consolidated

Date __/__/__

Resource Description	Total	Forecast Month	1	2	3	4	5	6	7	8	9	10	11	12

CHART 7.G14 Example of Total Resources Demanded by Family Worksheet (Data from Chart 7.G8 and 7.G11)

Family Mountain bikes Date 1/1/1992

Resource Description	Quantity	Forecast Month / Quantity	1	2	3	4	5	6	7	8	9	10	11	12
			100	50	50	100	100	150	200	150	50	50	75	250
Materials														
Bar stock	36.7		3670	1835	1835	3670	3670	5505	7340	5505	1835	1835	2752.5	9175
Purchased parts	40		4000	2000	2000	4000	4000	6000	8000	6000	2000	2000	3000	100000
Sheet metal	19		1900	950	950	1900	1900	2850	3800	2850	950	950	1425	4750
Machinery														
Lathe	6		600	300	300	600	600	800	1200	900	300	300	450	1500
Drill press	10		1000	500	500	1000	1000	1500	2000	1500	500	500	750	2500
Labor														
Painting	.5		50	25	25	50	50	75	100	75	25	25	37.5	125
Assembly	2		200	100	100	200	200	300	400	300	100	100	150	500
Welding	3.667		366.67	183.34	183.34	366.67	366.67	550	733.34	550	183.34	183.34	275	916.68
Grinding	1.333		133.33	66.67	66.67	133.33	133.33	200	266.66	200	66.67	66.67	100	33.33

CHART 7.G15 Example of Total Resources Demanded-Consolidated (Summary of data from Chart 7.G14)

Date 1/1/1992

Resource Description	Total	Forecast Month	1	2	3	4	5	6	7	8	9	10	11	12
Materials														
Bar stock	100128		9670	3460	3710	6920	9170	11005	13340	11505	4585	3460	4378	18925
Purchased parts	115375		11250	4000	4375	8000	10500	12500	15250	13250	5250	4000	5000	22000
Sheet metal	72425		7400	2450	2700	4900	6900	7850	9300	8350	3450	2450	2925	13750
Machinery														
Lathe	17400		1700	600	650	1200	1600	1900	2300	2000	800	600	750	3300
Drill press	33475		3350	1150	1275	2300	3100	3600	4350	3850	1550	1150	1400	6400
Labor														
Painting	1844		187.5	62.5	68.5	125	175	200	237.5	212.5	87.5	62.5	75	350
Assembly	8038		825	275	312.5	550	750	850	1025	925	375	275	325	1550
Welding	12608		1267	433	483	867	1167	1350	1633	1450	583	433	525	241
Grinding	4792		483	166.7	192	333	433	500	617	550	217	167	200	933

CHART 7.G16 Example of Total Resources Demanded by Family Worksheet and Consolidated Worksheet Using the Spreadsheet

	A B	C	D E	F	G	H	I	J	K	L	M	N	O	P	Q
1															
2	Family—Mountain Bikes														
3															
4		Resource	Forecast Quantity	------------------------											
5		Quantity	Month	1	2	3	4	5	6	7	8	9	10	11	12
6			Forecast	100	50	50	100	100	150	200	150	50	50	75	250
7	Materials														
8	Bar stock	36.7		3670	1835	1835	3670	3670	5505	7340	5505	1835	1835	2752.5	9175
9	Purchased parts	40		4000	2000	2000	4000	4000	6000	8000	6000	2000	2000	3000	10000
10	Sheet metal	19		1900	950	950	1900	1900	2850	3800	2850	950	950	1425	4750
11	Machinery														
12	Lathe	6		600	300	300	600	600	900	1200	900	300	300	450	1500
13	Drill press	10		1000	500	500	1000	1000	1500	2000	1500	500	500	750	2500
14	Manpower (labor)														
15	Painting	.5		50	25	25	50	50	75	100	75	25	25	37.5	125
16	Assembly	2		200	100	100	200	200	300	400	300	100	100	150	500
17	Welding	3.6667		366.67	183.335	183.335	366.67	366.67	550.005	733.34	550.005	183.335	183.335	275.0025	916.675
18	Grinding	1.3333		133.33	66.665	66.665	133.33	133.33	199.995	266.66	199.995	66.665	66.665	99.9975	333.325
19															
20															
21															
22	Family—Ten-speed bikes														
23															
24		Resource	Forecast Quantity	------------------------											
25		Quantity	Month	1	2	3	4	5	6	7	8	9	10	11	12
26			Forecast	200	50	50	100	200	200	200	200	100	50	50	300
27	Materials														
28	Bar stock	22.5		4500	1125	1125	2250	4500	4500	4500	4500	2250	1125	1125	6750
29	Purchased parts	25		5000	1250	1250	2500	5000	5000	5000	5000	2500	1250	1250	7500
30	Sheet metal	20		4000	1000	1000	2000	4000	4000	4000	4000	2000	1000	1000	6000
31	Machinery														
32	Lathe	4		800	200	200	400	800	800	800	800	400	200	200	1200
33	Drill press	8		1600	400	400	800	1600	1600	1600	1600	800	400	400	2400
34	Manpower (labor)														
35	Painting	.5		100	25	25	50	100	100	100	100	50	25	25	150
36	Assembly	2		400	100	100	200	400	400	400	400	200	100	100	600
37	Welding	3		600	150	150	300	600	600	600	600	300	150	150	900
38	Grinding	1		200	50	50	100	200	200	200	200	100	50	50	300
39															
40															
41															

Family—Tricycles

	Resource Quantity	Forecast Quantity Month	1	2	3	4	5	6	7	8	9	10	11	12
		Forecast	150	50	75	100	100	100	150	150	50	50	50	300
Materials														
Bar stock	10		1500	500	750	1000	1000	1000	1500	1500	500	500	500	3000
Purchased parts	15		2250	750	1125	1500	1500	1500	2250	2250	750	750	750	4500
Sheet metal	10		1500	500	750	1000	1000	1000	1500	1500	500	500	500	3000
Machinery														
Lathe	2		300	100	150	200	200	200	300	300	100	100	100	600
Drill press	5		750	250	375	500	500	500	750	750	250	250	250	1500
Manpower (labor)														
Painting	.25		37.5	12.5	18.75	25	25	25	37.5	37.5	12.5	12.5	12.5	75
Assembly	1.5		225	75	112.5	150	150	150	225	225	75	75	75	450
Welding	2		300	100	150	200	200	200	300	300	100	100	100	600
Grinding	1		150	50	75	100	100	100	150	150	50	50	50	300

Consolidated

	Total Resources	Forecast Quantity Month	1	2	3	4	5	6	7	8	9	10	11	12
Materials														
Bar stock	100127.5		9670	3460	3710	6920	9170	11005	13340	11505	4585	3460	4377.5	18925
Purchased parts	115375		11250	4000	4375	8000	10500	12500	15250	13250	5250	4000	5000	22000
Sheet metal	72425		7400	2450	2700	4900	6900	7850	9300	8350	3450	2450	2925	13750
Machinery														
Lathe	17400		1700	600	650	1200	1600	1900	2300	2000	800	600	750	3300
Drill press	33475		3350	1150	1275	2300	3100	3600	4350	3850	1550	1150	1400	6400
Manpower (labor)														
Painting	1843.75		187.5	62.5	68.75	125	175	200	237.5	212.5	87.5	62.5	75	350
Assembly	8037.5		825	275	312.5	550	750	850	1025	925	375	275	325	1550
Welding	12608.38		1266.67	433.335	483.335	866.67	1166.67	1350.005	1633.34	1450.005	583.335	433.335	525.0025	2416.675
Grinding	4791.623		483.33	166.665	191.665	333.33	433.33	499.995	616.66	549.995	216.665	166.665	199.9975	933.325

CHART 7.G17 Examples of the Formulas for Total Resources Demanded by Family Worksheet and Consolidated Worksheet Using the Spreadsheet

	A	B	C	E	F	G	H	I	J
1									
2	Family—Mountain Bikes								
3									
4			Resource	Forecast Quantity	----------	----------	----------		
5			Quantity	Month	1	2	3	4	5
6				Forecast	100	50	50	100	100
7	Materials								
8	Bar stock		36.7		F6×C8	G6×C8	H6×C8	I6×C8	J6×C8
9	Purchased parts		40		F6×C9	G6×C9	H6×C9	I6×C9	J6×C9
10	Sheet metal		19		F6×C10	G6×C10	H6×C10	I6×C10	J6×C10
11	Machinery								
12	Lathe		6		F6×C12	G6×C12	H6×C12	I6×C12	J6×C12
13	Drill press		10		F6×C13	G6×C13	H6×C13	I6×C13	J6×C13
14	Manpower (labor)								
15	Painting		.5		F6×C15	G6×C15	H6×C15	I6×C15	J6×C15
16	Assembly		2		F6×C16	G6×C16	H6×C16	I6×C16	J6×C16
17	Welding		3.6667		F6×C17	G6×C17	H6×C17	I6×C17	J6×C17
18	Grinding		1.3333		F6×C18	G6×C18	H6×C18	I6×C18	J6×C18
19									
20									
21									
22	Family—Ten-Speed Bikes								
23									
24			Resource	Forecast Quantity	----------	----------	----------		
25			Quantity	Month	1	2	3	4	5
26				Forecast	200	50	50	100	200
27	Materials								
28	Bar stock		22.5		F26×C28	G26×C28	H26×C28	I26×C28	J26×C28
29	Purchased parts		25		F26×C29	G26×C29	H26×C29	I26×C29	J26×C29
30	Sheet metal		20		F26×C30	G26×C30	H26×C30	I26×C30	J26×C30
31	Machinery								
32	Lathe		4		F26×C32	G26×C32	H26×C32	I26×C32	J26×C32
33	Drill press		8		F26×C33	G26×C33	H26×C33	I26×C33	J26×C33
34	Manpower (labor)								
35	Painting		.5		F26×C35	G26×C35	H26×C35	I26×C35	J26×C35
36	Assembly		2		F26×C36	G26×C36	H26×C36	I26×C36	J26×C36
37	Welding		3		F26×C37	G26×C37	H26×C37	I26×C37	J26×C37
38	Grinding		1		F26×C38	G26×C38	H26×C38	I26×C38	J26×C38
39									
40									
41									
42	Family—Tricycles								
43									
44			Resource	Forecast Quantity	----------	----------	----------		
45			Quantity	Month	1	2	3	4	5
46				Forecast	150	50	75	100	100
47	Materials								
48	Bar stock		10		F46×C48	G46×C48	H46×C48	I46×C48	J46×C48
49	Purchased parts		15		F46×C49	G46×C49	H46×C49	I46×C49	J46×C49
50	Sheet metal		10		F46×C50	G46×C50	H46×C50	I46×C50	J46×C50
51	Machinery								
52	Lathe		2		F46×C52	G46×C52	H46×C52	I46×C52	J46×C52
53	Drill press		5		F46×C53	G46×C53	H46×C53	I46×C53	J46×C53
54	Manpower (labor)								
55	Painting		.25		F46×C55	G46×C55	H46×C55	I46×C55	J46×C55
56	Assembly		1.5		F46×C56	G46×C56	H46×C56	I46×C56	J46×C56
57	Welding		2		F46×C57	G46×C57	H46×C57	I46×C57	J46×C57
58	Grinding		1		F46×C58	G46×C58	H46×C58	I46×C58	J46×C58
59									
60									
61									
62	Consolidated								
63									
64			Total	Forecast Quantity	----------	----------	----------		
65			Resources	Month	1	2	3	4	5
66	Materials								
67	Bar stock		SUM(F67:Q67)		F8+F28+F48	G8+G28+G48	H8+H28+H48	I8+I28+I48	J8+J28+J48
68	Purchased parts		SUM(F68:Q68)		F9+F29+F49	G9+G29+G49	H9+H29+H49	I9+I29+I49	J9+J29+J49
69	Sheet metal		SUM(F69:Q69)		F10+F30+F50	G10+G30+G50	H10+H30+H50	I10+I30+I50	J10+J30+J50
70	Machinery								
71	Lathe		SUM(F71:Q71)		F12+F32+F52	G12+G32+G52	H12+H32+H52	I12+I32+I52	J12+J32+J52
72	Drill press		SUM(F72:Q72)		F13+F33+F53	G13+G33+G53	H13+H33+H53	I13+I33+I53	J13+J33+J53
73	Manpower (labor)								
74	Painting		SUM(F74:Q74)		F15+F35+F55	G15+G35+G55	H15+H35+H55	I15+I35+I55	J15+J35+J55
75	Assembly		SUM(F75:Q75)		F16+F36+F56	G16+G36+G56	H16+H36+H56	I16+I36+I56	J16+J36+J56
76	Welding		SUM(F76:Q76)		F17+F37+F57	G17+G37+G57	H17+H37+H57	I17+I37+I57	J17+J37+J57
77	Grinding		SUM(F77:Q77)		F18+F38+F58	G18+G38+G58	H18+H38+H58	I18+I38+I58	J18+J38+J58
78									
79									
80									

K	L	M	N	O	P	Q	R
6	7	8	9	10	11	12	
150	200	150	50	50	75	250	
K6×C8	L6×C8	M6×C8	N6×C8	O6×C8	P6×C8	Q6×C8	
K6×C9	L6×C9	M6×C9	N6×C9	O6×C9	P6×C9	Q6×C9	
K6×C10	L6×C10	M6×C10	N6×C10	O6×C10	P6×C10	Q6×C10	
K6×C12	L6×C12	M6×C12	N6×C12	O6×C12	P6×C12	Q6×C12	
K6×C13	L6×C13	M6×C13	N6×C13	O6×C13	P6×C13	Q6×C13	
K6×C15	L6×C15	M6×C15	N6×C15	O6×C15	P6×C15	Q6×C15	
K6×C16	L6×C16	M6×C16	N6×C16	O6×C16	P6×C16	Q6×C16	
K6×C17	L6×C17	M6×C17	N6×C17	O6×C17	P6×C17	Q6×C17	
K6×C18	L6×C18	M6×C18	N6×C18	O6×C18	P6×C18	Q6×C18	
6	7	8	9	10	11	12	
200	200	200	100	50	50	300	
K26×C28	L26×C28	M26×C28	N26×C28	O26×C28	P26×C28	Q26×C28	
K26×C29	L26×C29	M26×C29	N26×C29	O26×C29	P26×C29	Q26×C29	
K26×C30	L26×C30	M26×C30	N26×C30	O26×C30	P26×C30	Q26×C30	
K26×C32	L26×C32	M26×C32	N26×C32	O26×C32	P26×C32	Q26×C32	
K26×C33	L26×C33	M26×C33	N26×C33	O26×C33	P26×C33	Q26×C33	
K26×C35	L26×C35	M26×C35	N26×C35	O26×C35	P26×C35	Q26×C35	
K26×C36	L26×C36	M26×C36	N26×C36	O26×C36	P26×C36	Q26×C36	
K26×C37	L26×C37	M26×C37	N26×C37	O26×C37	P26×C37	Q26×C37	
K26×C38	L26×C38	M26×C38	N26×C38	O26×C38	P26×C38	Q26×C38	
6	7	8	9	10	11	12	
100	150	150	50	50	50	300	
K46×C48	L46×C48	M46×C48	N46×C48	O46×C48	P46×C48	Q46×C48	
K46×C49	L46×C49	M46×C49	N46×C49	O46×C49	P46×C49	Q46×C49	
K46×C50	L46×C50	M46×C50	N46×C50	O46×C50	P46×C50	Q46×C50	
K46×C52	L46×C52	M46×C52	N46×C52	O46×C52	P46×C52	Q46×C52	
K46×C53	L46×C53	M46×C53	N46×C53	O46×C53	P46×C53	Q46×C53	
K46×C55	L46×C55	M46×C55	N46×C55	O46×C55	P46×C55	Q46×C55	
K46×C56	L46×C56	M46×C56	N46×C56	O46×C56	P46×C56	Q46×C56	
K46×C57	L46×C57	M46×C57	N46×C57	O46×C57	P46×C57	Q46×C57	
K46×C58	L46×C58	M46×C58	N46×C58	O46×C58	P46×C58	Q46×C58	
6	7	8	9	10	11	12	
K8+K28+K48	L8+L28+L48	M8+M28+M48	N8+N28+N48	O8+O28+O48	P8+P28+P48	Q8+Q28+Q48	
K9+K29+K49	L9+L29+L49	M9+M29+M49	N9+N29+N49	O9+O29+O49	P9+P29+P49	Q9+Q29+Q49	
K10+K30+K50	L10+L30+L50	M10+M30+M50	N10+N30+N50	O10+O30+O50	P10+P30+P50	Q10+Q30+Q50	
K12+K32+K52	L12+L32+L52	M12+M32+M52	N12+N32+N52	O12+O32+O52	P12+P32+P52	Q12+Q32+Q52	
K13+K33+K53	L13+L33+L53	M13+M33+M53	N13+N33+N53	O13+O33+O53	P13+P33+P53	Q13+Q33+Q53	
K15+K35+K55	L15+L35+L55	M15+M35+M55	N15+N35+N55	O15+O35+O55	P15+P35+P55	Q15+Q35+Q55	
K16+K36+K56	L16+L36+L56	M16+M36+M56	N16+N36+N56	O16+O36+O56	P16+P36+P56	Q16+Q36+Q56	
K17+K37+K57	L17+L37+L57	M17+M37+M57	N17+N37+N57	O17+O37+O57	P17+P37+P57	Q17+Q37+Q57	
K18+K38+K58	L18+L38+L58	M18+M38+M58	N18+N38+N58	O18+O38+O58	P18+P38+P58	Q18+Q38+Q58	

Summarizing Chart 7.G12 by resource gives us the "Total Resources Demanded" worksheet (Chart 7.G13). Chart 7.G14 is an example of how to work Chart 7.G12, and Chart 7.G15 is an example of how to work Chart 7.G13.

For Chart 7.G12 (example Chart 7.G14), we list the resources down the left hand side (from Chart 7.G11) and the forecast amounts across the top (from Chart 7.G8). Then we calculate the amount of each resource that is needed each month by multiplying the forecast amount from the top against the resource amount from the left side. The summarization worksheet (Chart 7.G13—example Chart 7.G15) is calculated by summing up all the family sheets for each resource, for each month. There were three family sheets in the example. I have only shown you the first one (Chart 7.G14). The consolidation example sheet (Chart 7.G15) is the total of all three families.

I have also given you the spreadsheet versions of these worksheets. Chart 7.G16 is the calculation of all the family options in the format of Chart 7.G14. Chart 7.G16 also includes the summarization sheet similar to Chart 7.G15. Chart 7.G17 shows the spreadsheet calculations that will allow you to do the worksheet of Chart 7.G12 and Chart 7.G13.

Note that in this segment I have demonstrated how to calculate demand on resources in the three primary resource areas: materials, machinery, and labor. Most plants in the United States only calculate demand on one of these areas—labor. If this description fits your plant, then the calculation process described here needs to only discuss the demand on the labor resource and is greatly simplified.

At this point we have identified the combined demand that our forecast and customer orders have placed on each of our resource areas. In Chart 7.4 we are able to analyze the available capacity in each of these areas. Then we build a compromise plan in the form of an Aggregate Production Schedule that balances the demand on resources with the resource capacity availability (Appendix 7.A).

Sales Reporting Function

Referring to the segment in this appendix titled "Customer Order Processing," step 6 in the order processing procedure describes the sales department reporting the completed sales on a sales report. This segment will discuss the sales reporting function in more detail.

If we look at Chart 7.G4 we see that when the product is shipped, copies of the order go in two directions. One copy goes to the Accounts Receivable Department, which sends out an invoice and later sends out statements. This accounting process will not be covered in detail here. However, the other copy goes to the Sales Department for sales reporting. This form gets filed by customer number as a completed sale. It is also reported by customer number, product number, and date into the sales system. This process can be done manually or using a small data base computer package. The objective is to generate two reports. One by

CHART 7.G18 Sales Data Collection Form

Date	Customer #	Product #	Quantity	Sales Amount
__/__/____				
__/__/____				
__/__/____				
__/__/____				
__/__/____				
__/__/____				
__/__/____				
__/__/____				
__/__/____				
__/__/____				
__/__/____				
__/__/____				
__/__/____				
__/__/____				
__/__/____				

CHART 7.G19 Sales Analysis Report by Customer

Date __/__/__

Customer Name	Number	Sales Month	1	2	3	4	5	6	7	8	9	10	11	12
Total sales by month														

CHART 7.G20 Sales Analysis Report by Product

Date __/__/__

Product Description	Number	Sales Month	1	2	3	4	5	6	7	8	9	10	11	12
Total sales by month														

customer and one by product, showing the sales performance of the organization.

Chart 7.G18 shows an example of a sales data collection document. Chart 7.G19 shows an example of a customer sales reporting document. Chart 7.G20 shows an example of a product sales reporting document. Chart 7.G21 shows a collection of data that may have been reported on Chart 7.G18. Chart 7.G22 shows the data of Chart 7.G21 reported in the customer sales report. Finally Chart 7.G23 shows the data of Chart 7.G21 reported in a product sales report. There are two versions of the

CHART 7.G21 Example of Sales Data Collection Form

Date	Customer #	Product #	Quantity	Sales Amount
1/1/91	11	MB–HD	100	10,000
1/1/91	12	MB–SLW	50	5,000
2/1/91	11	MB–HD	100	10,000
2/1/91	11	MB–SLW	50	5,000
2/1/91	11	MB–E	100	10,000
3/1/91	12	MB–E	200	20,000
3/1/91	12	TRI	50	3,000
3/1/91	13	TS–M	100	10,000
3/1/91	11	TRI	200	20,000
4/1/91	11	TS–M	50	5,000
5/1/91	12	TS–W	50	5,000
5/1/91	12	TRI	100	6,000
5/1/91	12	MB–HD	100	10,000
6/1/91	13	MB–SLW	50	5,000
6/1/91	13	TRI	100	6,000
7/1/91	14	TS–M	50	5,000
7/1/91	11	TRI	200	12,000
8/1/91	12	MB–HD	50	5,000
8/1/91	12	MB–E	100	10,000
8/1/91	13	MB–E	100	10,000
9/1/91	13	TRI	200	12,000
9/1/91	13	TS–M	50	5,000
10/1/91	13	TS–W	50	5,000
10/1/91	11	MB–HD	100	10,000
10/1/91	12	TRI	100	6,000
11/1/91	11	MB–E	200	10,000
11/1/91	11	MB–HD	50	5,000
12/1/91	12	MB–HD	100	10,000
12/1/91	11	MB–E	50	5,000
12/1/91	12	MB–HD	50	5,000
12/1/91	13	TS–M	100	10,000
12/1/91	14	TRI	100	6,000

CHART 7.G22 Example of Sales Analysis Report by Customer

Date 1/1/1992

Customer Name	Number	Sales Month	1	2	3	4	5	6	7	8	9	10	11	12
Joe	11		10,000	25,000	20,000	5,000			12,000			10,000	15,000	5,000
Sue	12		5,000		23,000		21,000			15,000		6,000		15,000
Jane	13				10,000			11,000		10,000	17,000	5,000		10,000
Fred	14								5,000					6,000
Total sales by month			15,000	25,000	53,000	5,000	21,000	11,000	17,000	25,000	17,000	21,000	15,000	36,000

CHART 7.G23 Example of Sales Analysis Report by Product

Example of Sales Analysis Report by Product (Quantity) Date 1/1/1992

Product Description	Number	Sales Month	1	2	3	4	5	6	7	8	9	10	11	12
Mountain Bike–Economy	MB–E			100	200					200			200	50
Mountain Bike–Heavy	MB–HD		100	100			100			50		100	50	150
Mountain Bike–Light	MB–SLW		50	50				50						
Ten-Speed–Men	TS–M				100	50			50		50			100
Ten-Speed–Women	TS–W						50					50		
Tricycles	TRI				250		100	100	200		200	100		100
Total sales by month			150	250	550	50	250	150	250	250	250	250	250	400

Example of Sales Analysis Report by Product (Dollar) Date 1/1/1992

Product Description	Number	Sales Month	1	2	3	4	5	6	7	8	9	10	11	12
Mountain Bike–Economy	MB–E			10,000	20,000					20,000			10,000	5,000
Mountain Bike–Heavy	MB–HD		10,000	10,000			10,000			5,000		10,000	5,000	15,000
Mountain Bike–Light	MB–SLW		5,000	5,000				5,000						
Ten-Speed–Men	TS–M				10,000	5,000			5,000		5,000			10,000
Ten-Speed–Women	TS–W						5,000					5,000		
Tricycles	TRI				23,000		6,000	6,000	12,000		12,000	6,000		6,000
Total sales by month			15,000	25,000	53,000	5,000	21,000	11,000	17,000	25,000	17,000	21,000	15,000	36,000

product sales report, one by quantity and the other by dollars. Both are helpful in planning future sales projections.

The sales reporting process becomes a basis for analyzing which products are selling best, when the products are selling, and which customers are the strongest customers. The data becomes the basis for future forecasting.

Summary

We have defined the demand that the forecast and the customer orders are making on our plant's resources. The next step is to check on what our plant's available resources actually are. That is the topic of Appendix 7.A. After that we will do a balancing act between the demand for resources and the available resources and create an Aggregate Production Schedule.

PART

II OPERATIONS MANAGEMENT

Chapter

8 Inventory Planning

Inventory Planning as Production Planning

As soon as we pass through the management levels from tactical management to operations management, life starts to get confusing. Not because the process is hard, but rather because there are too many options.

Inventory planning, in some factories is *the* primary and only tool used for planning the production and purchasing functions. As a product is built (or purchased) and put into inventory, its inventory level is tracked. (How many do we have on hand?) Also, when a product is taken out of inventory, its inventory level is tracked. If inventory runs low, more production is scheduled (or purchase orders placed) and more units are built (or purchased) to replenish the shortage. If you plan to follow this type of inventory strategy, you need to follow Chapters 8, 9, and 11 closely. This methodology is simple and is by far the most popular in the United States. Unfortunately, it often requires that we carry more inventory than a more sophisticated system would require.

A second restriction on the use of inventory planning methods for production planning is that demand has to be steady and constant. You can't handle lumpy demand. At this point we are no longer talking about the demand placed on the factory by the forecast. At this point, the demand is placed on the Production Department by the master production schedule (MPS). If the MPS has lumpy demand, a more sophisticated system may be necessary.

If inventory costs are important to you, or if you have lumpy demand, and you want to plan your factory in a way that will minimize inventory costs, you need something more sophisticated. What you need is *demand inventory planning*. This means that you order inventory based on the "demand" for that inventory, rather than on some inventory level that says now is the time to order. For a production strategy of this type, you need all the information in the operations section of this book. The inventory control methods of EOQ are still used for cheap items such as nuts and bolts, and the more expensive items are scheduled with a more sophisticated demand-based production planning tool such as MRP.

Inventory Planning Definitions

As we consider the inventory planning model, we need to start by looking at a few definitions. These definitions are important because we need to agree on what they mean as they are discussed in more detail.

Two-Bin Inventory System. This is a system that is familiar to many people. In this system, when you open the last box of paper, you order more paper. Or when you open the last box of envelopes, you order more envelopes. Out on the factory floor you use this system with nuts, bolts, nails, and washers. When you open the last box, you order more. You use this system for all of the inexpensive materials. You don't want to keep track of how many sheets of paper you have. It would cost you more money to track it than it's worth.

Physical Inventory. Also called periodic review, this is the annual physical inventory that you take to satisfy the tax man. A physical inventory is expensive—not just because you have your work force tied up in counting inventory, but primarily because of the lost production time that occurs while you are taking the physical count. An effective cycle counting system can be used to replace the physical inventory.

ABC Analysis. ABC analysis is a classification system (Chart 8.1). For example, if we want to organize our inventory stores area, we would want the parts that get the most activity to be easily accessible. To do this we look at how much activity (how many requests) we get for each part. The most active 20 percent of the parts will generally have about 80 percent of the activity. We call this top 20 percent the "A" items and place them near the front of the storeroom. The next 40

CHART 8.1 ABC Analysis

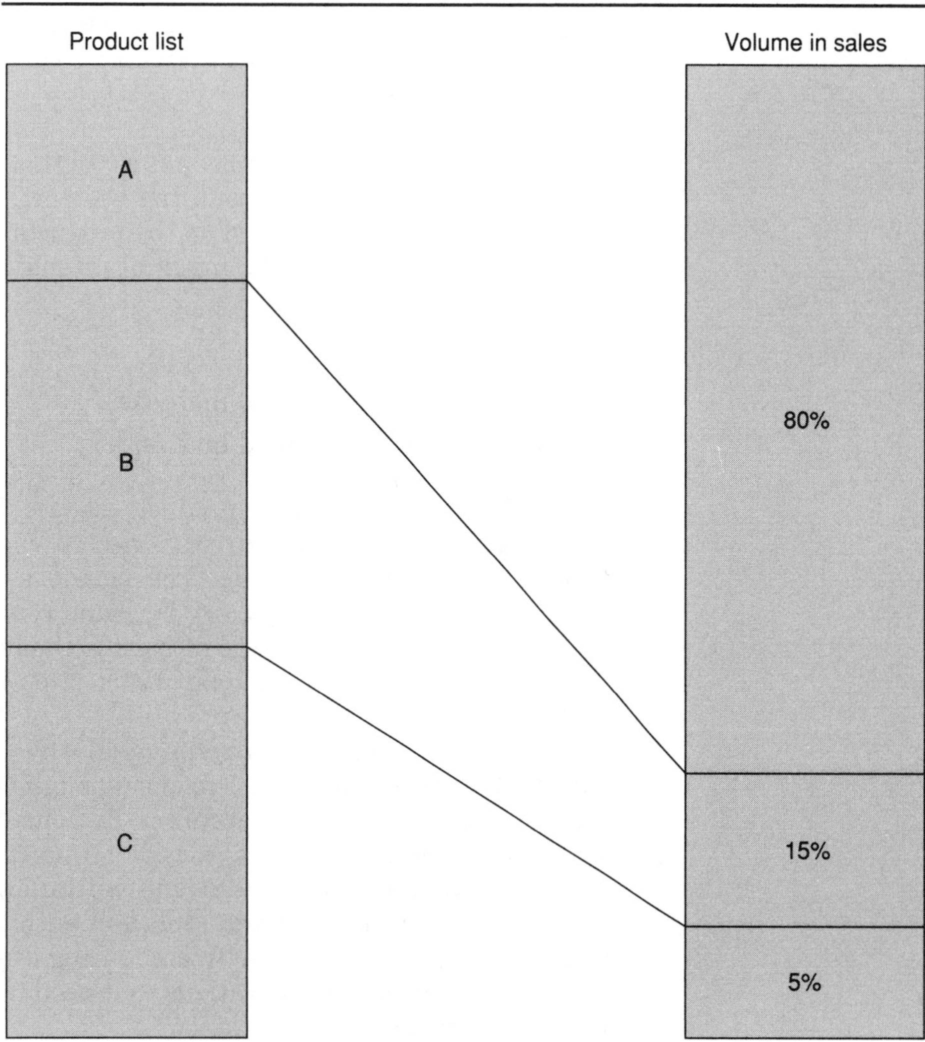

percent of the parts will have about 15 percent of the activity and we call these "B" items. The remaining 40 percent of the parts we label "C" items.

ABC analysis can be used to evaluate which products are the most popular, which products cause the most problems in manufacturing (scrap or rework), which products have the most returns, etc. The ABC classification process works the same way each time. With the ABC classification we can look at those items that are causing the most problems and place an engineering focus or marketing focus on solving those problems.

Perpetual Inventory System. A perpetual inventory system is a system that can tell you the status of your inventory on an ongoing basis. You should be able to go to the system and find the balance of any product in inventory. This does not need to be a computer system. It can be a manual ledger card system. However, the manual system requires that the ledger cards be maintained in one place and controlled by one person. A computer system is easy to set up using a data base and it allows more than one individual to access the data base at any one time. We will discuss how to set up a perpetual inventory system in Chapter 9. Without a perpetual inventory system, cycle counting and most of the inventory planning systems we will be discussing would not be able to function.

Cycle Counting. Cycle counting is a tool that allows us to replace the physical inventory. In cycle counting we start by classifying our products using ABC analysis based on the products' levels of activity. Then we do a spot-check on all the inventory items stressing the "A" items the most. Here is how it works:

All "A" items are counted weekly.

All "B" items are counted monthly.

All "C" items are counted quarterly.

We randomly select which products should be spot-checked (cycle counted) each day, making sure that each item is counted at least once in its appropriate time frame. The person assigned to be the cycle counter will go out on the factory floor and count that particular product. Then the cycle counter will go back to the inventory control system to see if it is correct. If it is wrong, a correction is made and the error is noted.

If the same product is in error regularly, an analysis needs to be made to determine why. If you correct enough of the errors, you should start getting a fairly high accuracy in your cycle counting process. When the percentage correct exceeds 90 percent, it's time to contact your accountant to see if he or she will allow you to eliminate the physical inventory process and replace it with an ongoing cycle counting process. The interaction with accounting is necessary because there are some income tax considerations that need to be satisfied both at the state and national level.

Inventory Balancing Act

Inventory planning is a balancing act. At the strategic level we mentioned the conflict that exists in planning inventories:

- Marketing wants a lot of finished goods.
- Finance wants no inventory because of the financing costs.
- Operations wants plenty of raw materials and work-in-process inventory so that they can avoid production delays.

In inventory planning we attempt to balance these demands so that everyone comes out happy. This is done by looking at the total cost of inventory. We look at all the factors that affect inventory and attempt to minimize the total of all these costs. Chart 8.2 diagrams the inventory cycle. We will start by explaining this diagram.

The Inventory Sawtooth. Chart 8.2 shows the cycle of inventory. It starts at the "M" level (*M*aximum inventory level) and then as time goes on inventory is used up until it reaches the "SS" level (*S*afety *S*tock). At this point a purchase shipment arrives at the plant delivering "Q" (order *Q*uantity) parts and bringing our inventory level back up to M. This cycle repeats itself on the average every "T" days (cycle *T*ime). To minimize the total cost inventory, we need to determine the optimal values for Q, T, SS, and M. Before we can move forward, we need to define a few more terms.

Safety Stock. This is inventory that is kept on hand as a buffer for emergencies. For example, this buffer protects us if an exceptionally large order for parts comes in, or if we damage a few parts, or if a purchase shipment arrives late and we are going to run out of parts. Safety stock is a buffer that we install so that the plant can keep operating even if minor problems in inventory occur.

One of the big risks of safety stock is that it is a permanent fixture.

CHART 8.2 Inventory Sawtooth

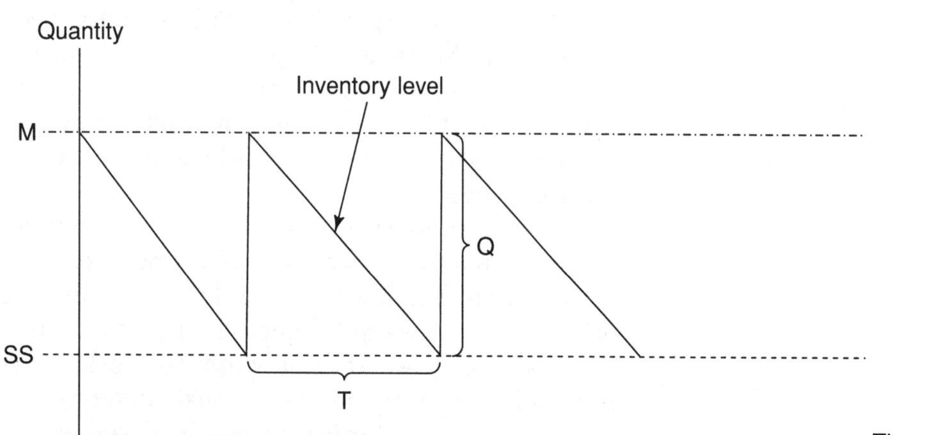

It is a cost that we are always and continually incurring. What often happens is that if a problem occurs, we increase safety stock to protect against it happening again. But then we never bring it back down. A blatant misuse of safety stock occurred in the tool room of a plant. All spare parts had a safety stock so that if the machine broke down they would have the parts on hand to fix it. After a little investigation, we learned that more than 40 percent of the spare parts in stock were for machines that the plant no longer used. However, someone had deemed it safety stock and it had to be maintained because the "system says so."

Cycle Stock. This is inventory that is used up and replaced during each cycle. In Chart 8.2 cycle stock is the inventory between SS and M.

Anticipation Inventory. This is inventory that has been committed for a future sale but has been produced early. It is not part of the safety stock because it has been committed to a sale; neither is it part of the cycle stock that will be used up and replaced this cycle. It is the cumulative difference between the forecast and the aggregate production schedule. For an example using bikes, the anticipation inventory is shown on Chart 8.3. Mountain bikes have no differences. Ten-speed bikes have a difference in month 11 of 180 units, but in month 12 we are short by the same 180 units and the anticipation inventory is used. In tricycles we can see the anticipation inventory was built up and used once during the summer and once during Christmas.

Raw Materials. These are materials that have been purchased but have had no value added (like labor) to them at our plant. An engine is a raw material for an automotive assembly plant.

Work-in-Process. These are materials that have had some value added but are not yet ready for sale.

Finished Goods. These are materials that are completed and ready for sale.

The distinction between raw materials, work-in-process, and finished goods inventory becomes important because they are scheduled differently. For example, raw materials are purchased and therefore use a purchasing model for scheduling. Work-in-process inventory is produced and therefore uses a production model for scheduling. Finished goods are sold and therefore use anticipation inventories in their planning process.

Another important distinction in these inventory types is that when we store inventory, we want to allow "extra" (unplanned) inventory to exist only at the lowest possible cost point, which is raw materials. In other words, if we get a good deal on materials and we purchase more than we need, we do not want to work on them until we need the finished good. Finished goods cost us more in inventory costs, and the entire inventory planning model is based on the fact that you only have the inventory that the model tells you to have and no more.

CHART 8.3 Anticipation Inventory

Mountain Bikes

Month	Forecast	Aggregate Production	Anticipation Inventory
1	100	100	0
2	50	50	0
3	50	50	0
4	100	100	0
5	100	100	0
6	150	150	0
7	200	200	0
8	150	150	0
9	50	50	0
10	50	50	0
11	75	75	0
12	250	250	0

Ten-speed Bikes

Month	Forecast	Aggregate Production	Anticipation Inventory
1	200	200	0
2	50	50	0
3	50	50	0
4	100	100	0
5	200	200	0
6	200	200	0
7	200	200	0
8	200	200	0
9	100	100	0
10	50	50	0
11	50	230	180
12	300	120	0

Tricycles

Month	Forecast	Aggregate Production	Anticipation Inventory
1	150	150	0
2	50	50	0
3	75	75	0
4	100	134	34
5	100	200	134
6	100	133	167
7	150	0	17
8	150	133	0
9	50	50	50
10	50	207	157
11	50	193	300
12	300	0	0

Total Cost of Inventory. Returning to our analysis of the inventory cycle (see Chart 8.2), we remember that the objective of the model is that we are trying to minimize "Total Cost of Inventory." We are now ready to discuss the cost components that make up "Total Cost." There are three basic components. These are:

$$TC = FC + OC + CC$$

where

TC = total cost

FC = fixed costs. These are costs that are considered to be a permanent fixture and do not play a part in the decision of the size of the sawtooth inventory model. Since we are trying to optimize Q, fixed costs do not change with the cost of Q. Only OC and CC have an effect on Q. Fixed costs are made up of:

PC = purchase cost, the cost of all the materials purchased during the year.

QC = quality cost, the costs associated with replacement and scrappage because of poor quality inventory. Even though we bought it cheap, the quality cost may make the product expensive.

SSC = safety stock cost, the cost of storing buffer inventory on a continuous basis.

OFC = other fixed cost, costs that play a role in the total cost of inventory.

OC = ordering cost

CC = carrying cost

The trick to inventory planning is to balance these costs out so that TC is minimized. Chart 8.4 shows how each of the components of TC can be graphed. From this graph we can see that as the order size (Q) increases, the carrying cost (CC) also increases. This is because the sawtooth is larger and the average inventory level is higher (see Chart 8.2).

CHART 8.4 Inventory Total Cost Graph

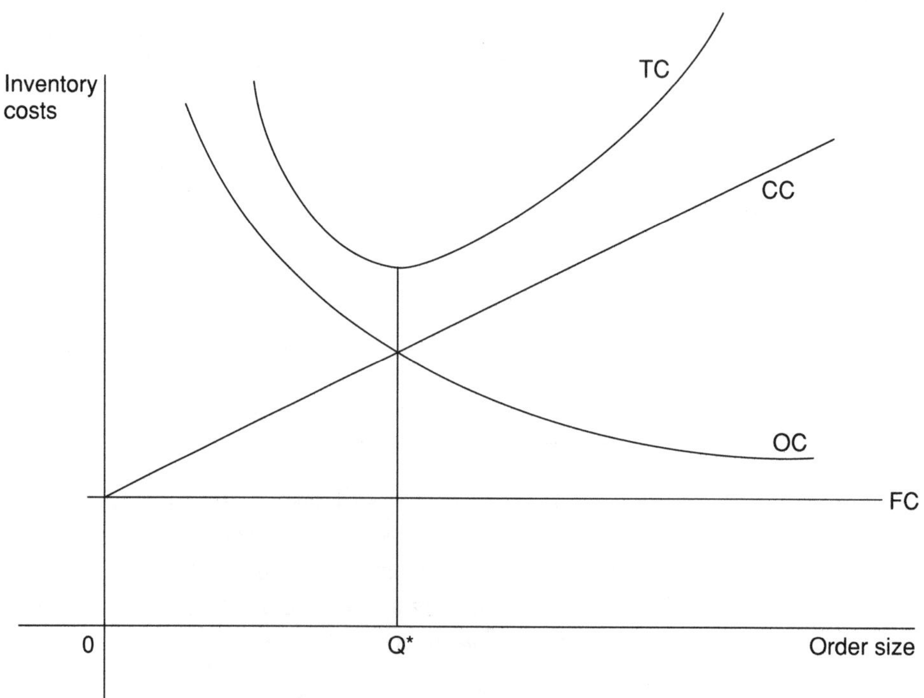

From the graph we also see that as order size (Q) increases, ordering cost (OC) decreases. This is because larger orders means fewer orders. We place purchasing orders fewer times, and we do production setups fewer times as Q gets larger.

The balancing act to find the optimal Q size (Q*) occurs between OC and CC. The FC costs fall out of the evaluation process. Having come this far in the process, we need to make another decision: With what type of production model do we want to work? To answer this question, we need a couple definitions.

Fixed Quantity Ordering System. There are two key elements needed to control this system. One is Q, the other is "ROP." As we use up our inventory, our perpetual inventory system monitors the balance of our inventory. When we hit reorder point ROP we place an order for Q parts. When our inventory level hits safety stock (SS), we receive our

CHART 8.5 Fixed Quantity Ordering System

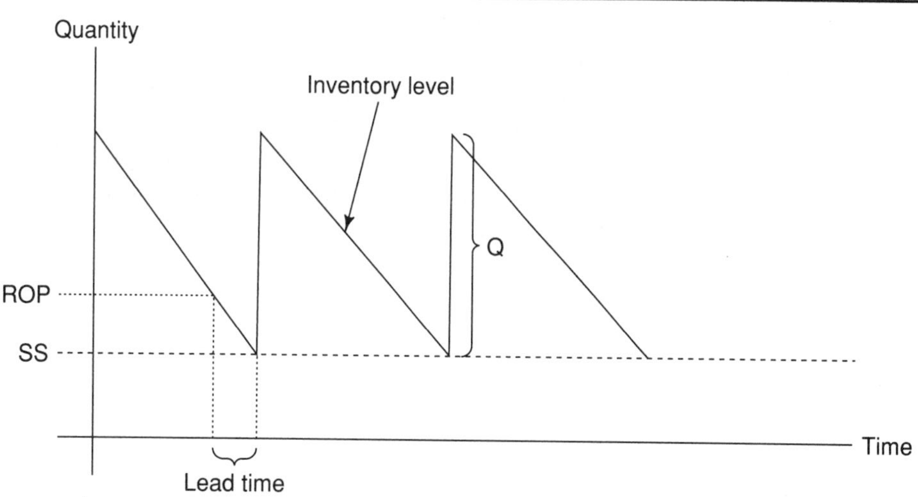

CHART 8.6 Fixed Period Ordering System

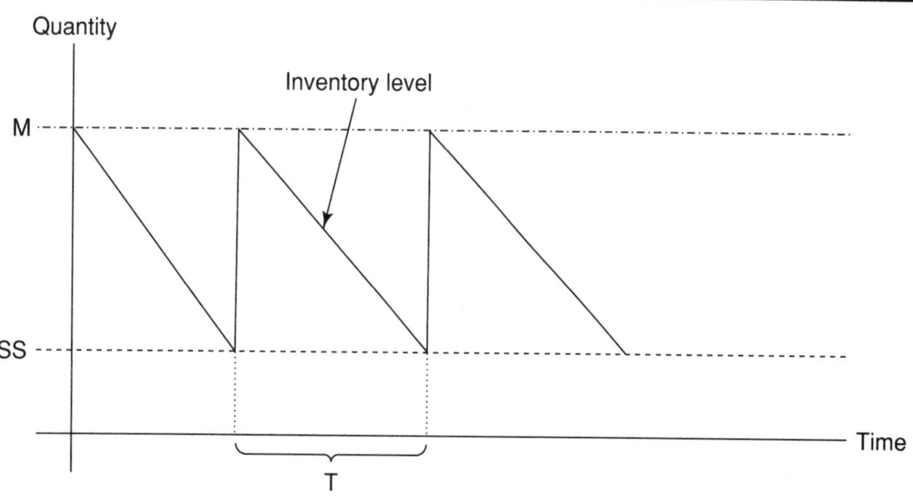

inventory and it is replenished to the maximum level M. This process can be followed in Chart 8.5.

Fixed Period Ordering Systems. If we are hoping to use an inventory planning system but we do not have a perpetual inventory system, then we will not know when our reorder point occurs. In this case we will order inventory based on the time period T between orders. What we do is we mark our calendar every T days and when one of these days occurs we go out and count our inventory level. Then we order enough to get back to the M level of inventory. So the controlling elements in this model are T and M as seen on Chart 8.6.

Summary

Now that we have a basic feeling for how the inventory planning model should function, we can fill in the formulas that calculate each of these values. This calculation process is done in Chapter 11, while Chapter 9 will help you set up a perpetual inventory system so that the reorder point can be monitored. Chapter 10 provides a comparative review of some of the production planning philosophies, thereby setting the stage for the two major production planning philosophies, Economic Order Quantity (Chapter 11) and Material Requirements Planning (Chapter 12).

Chapter

9 Inventory and Stores Control

As mentioned in the previous chapter, the three types of inventory are raw materials (RM), work-in-process (WIP), and finished goods (FG). Each of these requires a slightly different control process. This chapter provides the details of the inventory and stores control steps for each of these types of inventory demonstrating the types of documents that should be used. Then the chapter will review some informational reports that can be generated from this control process. Let's start by taking a close look at raw materials inventory.

Raw Materials

The flow for raw materials (as defined in Chapter 8) is diagrammed in Chart 9.1. Here we see the steps that occur in receiving, inspecting, and accepting raw materials into inventory. I have numbered each of the steps in the flow with an "RM" number for easy identification. In RM2 we discuss the receiving file. This is a file of all the purchase orders that are open and waiting to be received. The file is in vendor and/or purchase order number sequence and, as a shipment arrives at the loading dock, the appropriate purchase order is pulled. In RM3 we match the purchase order against the shipping document to see if they are in agreement. Errors require the intervention of the purchasing agent. Often a standing order will be left by the purchasing agent to accept or reject incorrect shipments from a specific vendor.

In RM6 we transfer the accepted materials to inspection along with the shipping slip and the purchase order. If the order has only been partially shipped, a copy of the purchase order also stays in the receiving file awaiting the remainder of the shipment. Then in RM7 the Quality Control Department verifies the quality of the materials. Errors at this point may also be returned to the vendor.

Assuming all is well, we transfer the accepted materials into the raw materials inventory storage area. Here we do a count of the materials received. This count is reported on the purchasing document and into the perpetual inventory system. The purchasing document and the shipping document are returned to the Purchasing Department to be approved for payment. At this point the accounts payable process takes over and makes the payment to the vendor.

In the inventory storeroom we have a few procedures that we need to discuss in more detail. This process will be discussed in the "Inventory Storeroom" section of this chapter.

Work-in-Process

The flow for work-in-process materials (as defined in Chapter 8) is diagrammed in two charts, 9.2 and 9.4. The reason for this is that work-in-process has an issuing process and a receiving process. The issuing process is diagrammed in Chart 9.2. In Chart 9.2, step WIP1, we note

CHART 9.1 Raw Materials Flow

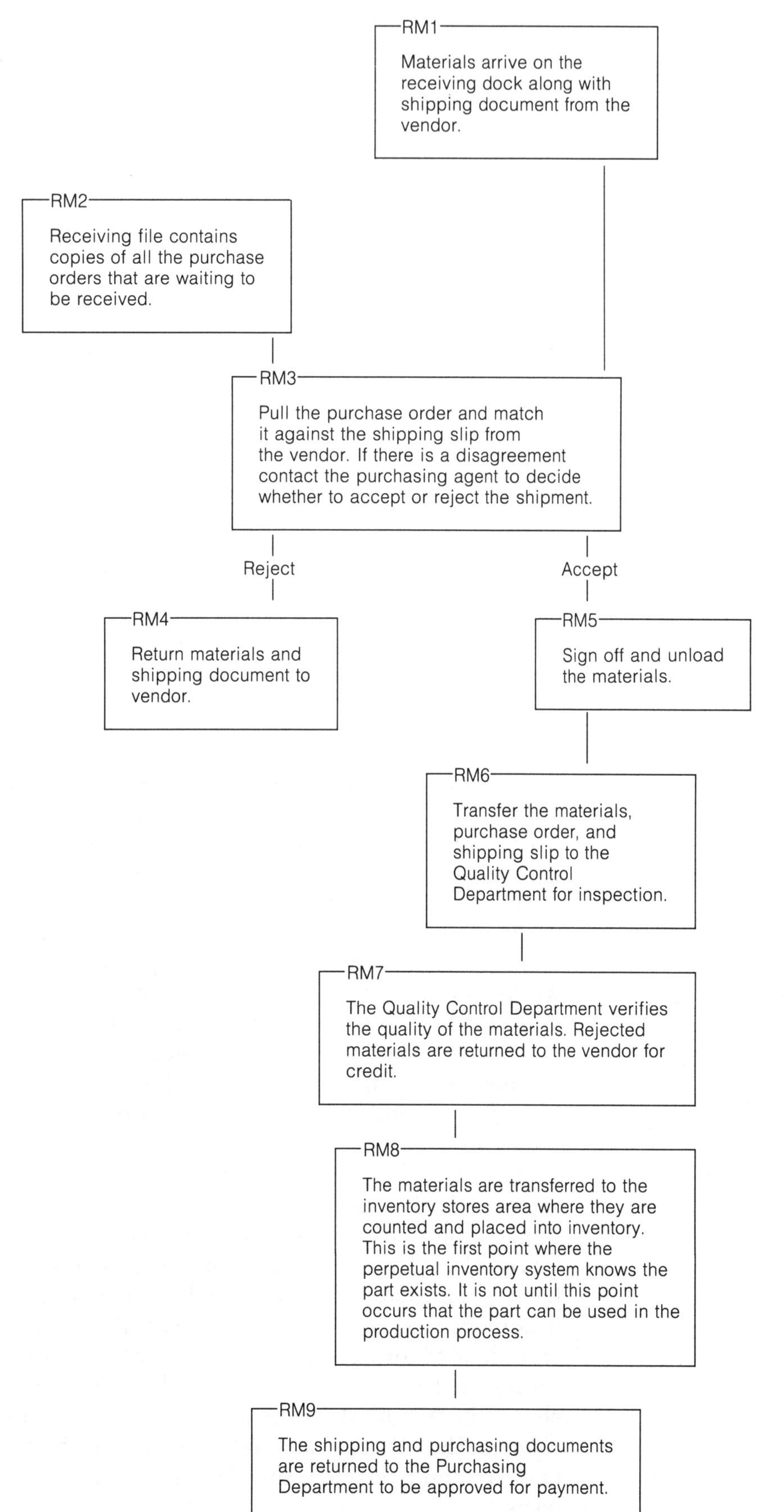

CHART 9.2 Work-in-Process Issues

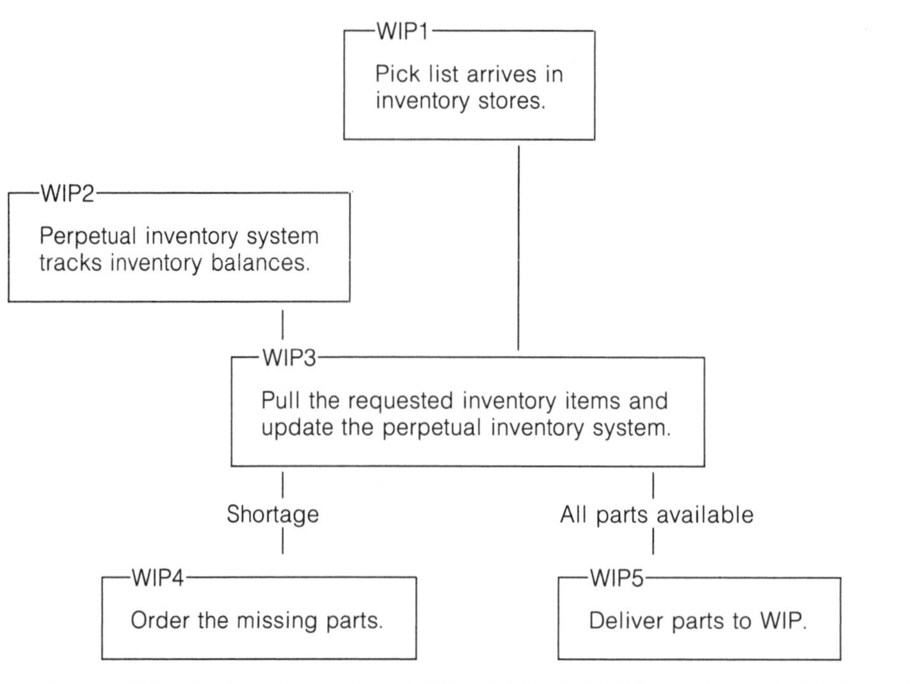

the arrival of the pick list. This pick list is for a set of materials that will be required in the manufacture of a specific batch of products. The definition of what is listed on the pick list occurs in Chapter 13. The discussion of when a pick list is generated occurs in Chapter 19. The purpose of a pick list is to define all of the materials needed for a production process. The inventory storeroom personnel compile all these materials (called the picking process) and deliver them to the work-in-process personnel who will use the materials. Chart 9.3 gives an example of a work-in-process pick list.

Step WIP2 discusses the perpetual inventory tracking system. This system records all issues and receipts into the inventory storage area. This process will be discussed in more detail in the "Inventory Storeroom" section.

Occasionally, issues occur on *nonstandard picks,* which mean that someone on the factory floor lost or broke something and has come to request more materials. These materials need to be reported as picked materials. If they are related to a specific production order, they should be issued as additional picks to that work order using the same picking document that was used previously. If the picks are not related to a specific work order, some nonstandard work order number needs to be established to cover these picks. In this case, the picking document should be filled out in the storeroom and should remain in the storeroom so that these nonstandard picks can be tracked for future reference and analysis (see the section on "Informational and Control Reports").

CHART 9.3 Work-in-Process Pick List

Work order number ______________________ Order date __/__/__
Part number ______________________ Quantity __________
Due date __/__/__ First work center ______________________

Product #	Product Description	Quantity

CHART 9.4 Work-in-Process Receipts

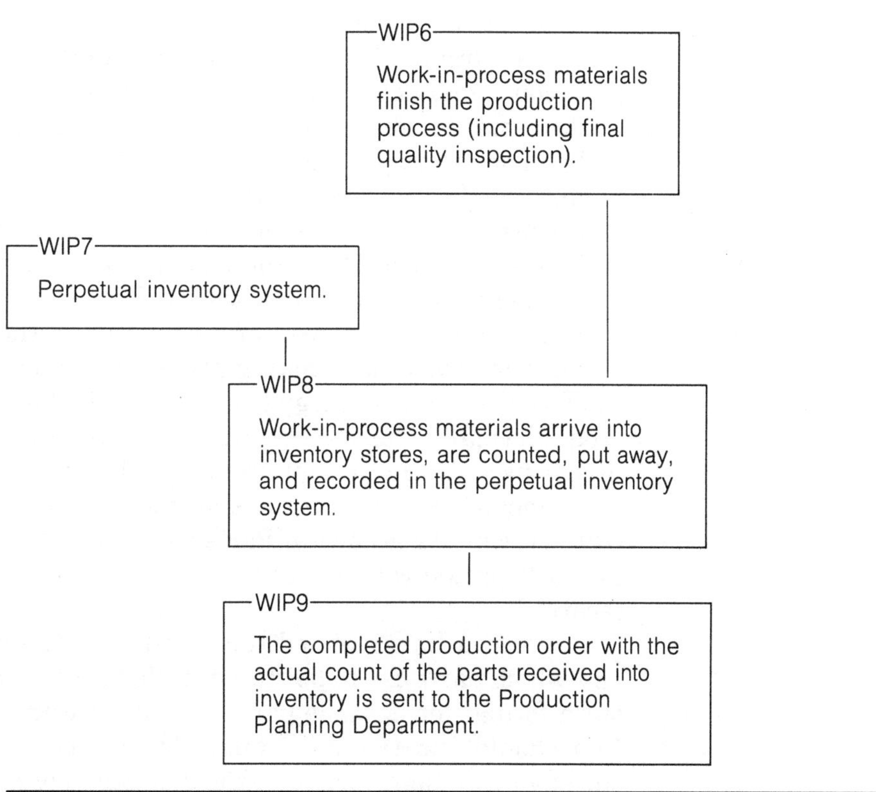

Chart 9.4 diagrams the process of finishing a work-in-process production item and delivering it to the inventory storage area.

Finished Goods

The flow for finished goods inventory (as defined in Chapter 8) is diagrammed in two charts. The reason for this is that, like work-in-process, finished goods also has an issuing process and a receiving process. The issuing process is diagrammed in Chart 9.5 and the receiving process is diagrammed in Chart 9.6.

In Chart 9.5, step FG1, we note the arrival of the pick list. This pick list is for a set of materials that will be shipped to the customer. The inventory stores personnel compile all the listed materials (called the picking process) and deliver them to the shipping area for packaging and shipment. Once again the perpetual inventory system is updated.

Chart 9.6 diagrams the process of completing finished goods and storing them in inventory. The same process is used for customer returns. The returned items are also inspected and delivered to inventory stores.

Inventory Storeroom

Several considerations need to be discussed about the way a storeroom operates. First of all, it is best to consolidate the storeroom function so that you avoid redundancy. You need a raw materials storeroom, a work-in-process storeroom, and a finished goods storeroom, which can all be in one storage area if it is convenient and if this location logically fits into the flow of the manufacturing organization. Normally, the raw materials storage area is near the receiving dock, the finished goods storage area is near the shipping dock, and the work-in-process storage area is near the center of the factory. If it is convenient, try to locate the raw materials and work-in-process items in the same storeroom. This makes the production picking process much easier.

There is also a strategy that needs to be followed within the storage area. Normally the storage area is a locked storeroom with a window that is used for the receipt and issue of parts. Only specific, authorized personnel are allowed in the storeroom area. The reason for this security is inventory accuracy. Parts don't walk away if this type of control exists. This control assures the accurate count of materials issued and received.

Once you have defined the location of the materials storage area, and which parts are to be stored in this area, it is now important to lay out a format for how the parts will be located within the storage area. You should run two ABC analysis reports on the parts that will be stored in your storeroom (see the discussion of ABC analysis in Chapter 8, Chart 8.1). The explanation of how these reports can be generated is

CHART 9.5 Finished Goods Issues

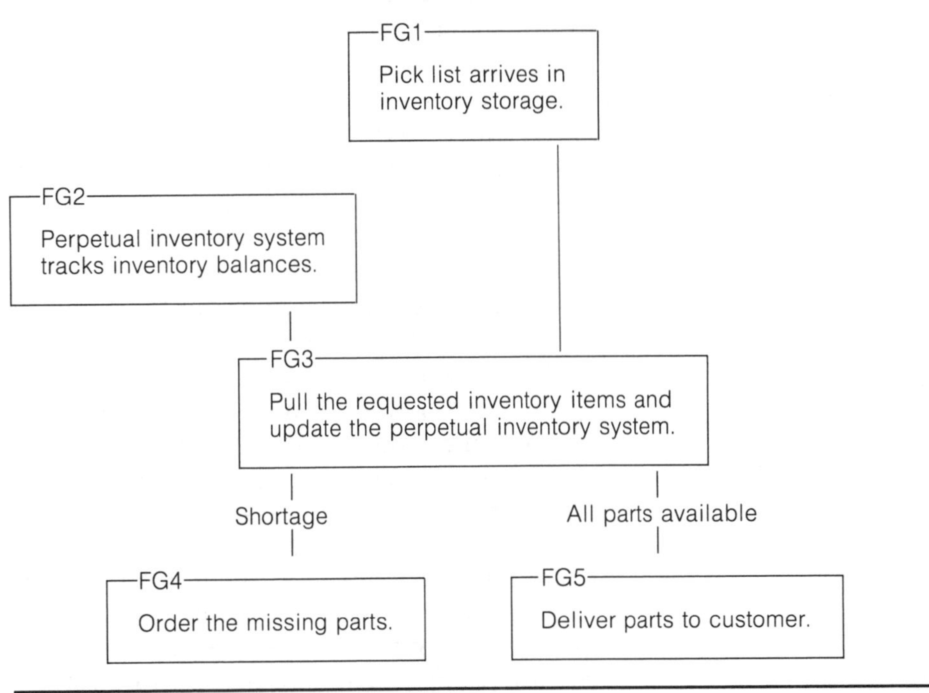

CHART 9.6 Finished Goods Receipts

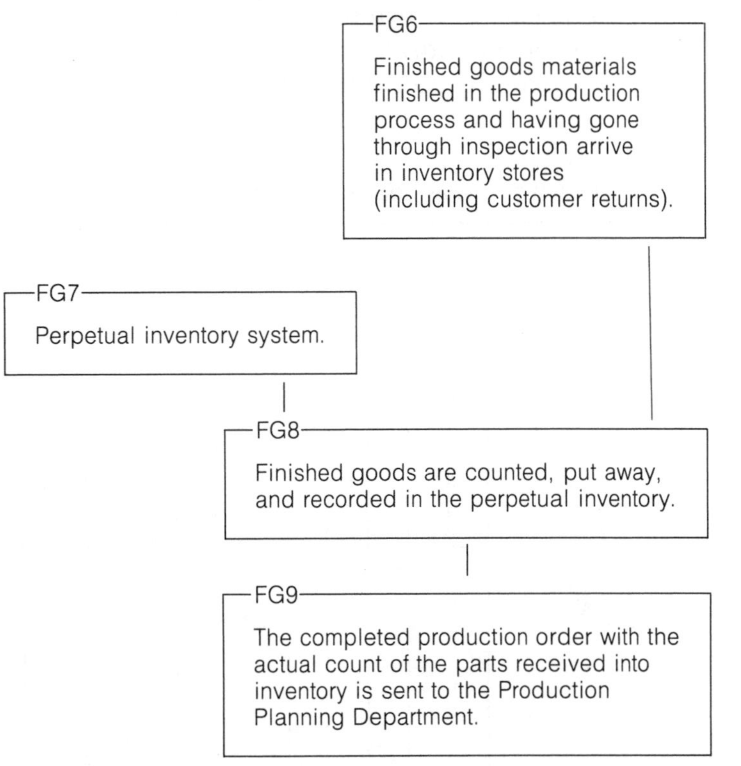

given later in this chapter. These ABC analysis reports should be based on (1) the amount of requests for the part and (2) dollars of inventory maintained on that part.

From this ABC analysis we make two decisions. First of all, some parts are just not worth storing in the storeroom area. For example, if washers have a high number of requests, but the total inventory value of washers is relatively minimal, leave them in an area outside the storeroom where they can be pulled at will. Use a two-bin system for ordering these parts: The last box of washers is kept in the storeroom; when this last box is requested, you place a purchase order for more washers (see the discussion of the two-bin system in Chapter 8).

Those parts that need to be controlled in the storeroom because of their high cost or low usage need to be organized in the storeroom in a way that will make the picking process the easiest. For example, see Chart 9.7 where the "A" items (those items that have a high number of requests) are placed near the front window and the "C" items (those items with very few requests) are placed near the back.

Now that we have organized the parts in our storeroom, we need a system that will track how much inventory is available. This is a perpetual inventory system. A manual perpetual inventory system will be demonstrated, but a computerized system is also easy to set up using a data base package. Numerous inventory control packages are available that will perform the basic functions outlined here.

The key to the perpetual inventory control system is the inventory ledger card. This is a card that is always kept in the storeroom. There is one card for each part that is under the control of the storeroom. Chart 9.8 is an example of an inventory ledger card. Be careful not to keep the same part in multiple areas, thus requiring multiple cards. Duplication can get you into all sorts of confusing situations trying to figure out who has what. If multiple locations for the same part is a requirement of

CHART 9.7 Store Room Layout

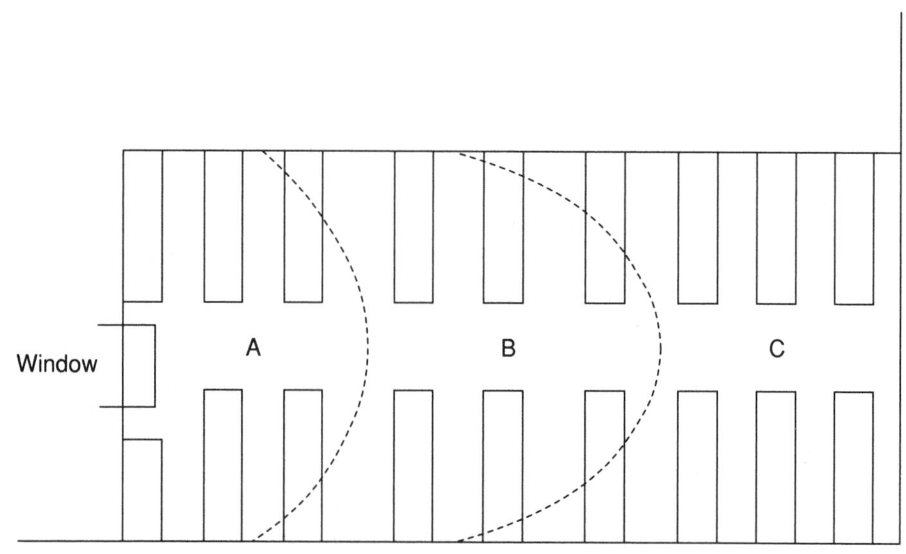

CHART 9.8 Inventory Ledger Card

ABC classification ________ RM WIP FG
Part number ________ Part description ________
Primary vendor ________ EOQ ________
Primary storage location ________ ROP ________
Safety stock ________ Anticipation inventory ________ Total ROP ________

Date	Transaction	Qty. Rcvd.	Qty. Picked	Balance	Trans. By	Order By

CHART 9.9 Inventory Ledger Card Example—Purchased Item

ABC classification ________ RM WIP FG
Part number WHEEL Part description BICYCLE WHEEL
Primary vendor QUICKER WHEEL MFG. EOQ 200
Primary storage location ROW A-45 ROP 125
Safety stock 100 Anticipation inventory ________ Total ROP 225

Date	Transaction	Qty. Rcvd.	Qty. Picked	Balance	Trans. By	Order By
	BALANCE FORWARD			107	GP	
1/1/92	PURCH ORDR #8234	200		307	RS	
1/2/92	PROD ORDR #6235		25	282	GP	
1/2/92	PROD ORDR #6222		10	272	RS	
1/3/92	ISSUE TO REWORK #32		7	265	RS	
1/4/92	PROD ORDR #6224		50	215	RS	RS
1/4/92	ISSUE TO REWORK #33		10	205	RS	

your plant, then you need a computer system where a data base links both inventory storage locations.

The inventory ledger card needs some explanation. We have an example of a filled-out raw materials (purchased items) inventory ledger card in Chart 9.9. Look at both Charts 9.8 and 9.9 as we go through a discussion of how the ledger card should be used. There is one ledger card for each inventory item. These cards are kept in a file in sequence by inventory item number. The card has a part number and description on it. The primary vendor is also indicated. If there are lots of vendors, then this information may not be necessary. The primary location number shows the row and bin number where this part is stored. The "EOQ" (economic order quantity), "ROP" (reorder point), and "Total ROP" indicate when the part should be ordered and how much should be ordered. (The calculations for these numbers and for safety stock are given in Chapter 11.) The "Total ROP" is the sum of ROP and safety stock ("Total ROP" = "ROP" + "Safety Stock"). There is no anticipation inventory for a raw material item. On the top of the card we also indicate the ABC classification of the item. This helps us determine in which area of the inventory storeroom we should store the part. The "RM," "WIP," and "FG" allow us to indicate whether the part is a raw material, work-in-process, or finished goods item. This information will be useful later when we do the inventory reporting. This is also helpful in indicating whether the part requires a purchase requisition (raw material) or a production requisition (work-in-process or finished good). The explanation of how a requisition works follows.

The "Balance Forward" entry in Chart 9.9 shows the balance transferred from the previous card. Cards are pulled at least once a year at physical inventory time and possibly even more often (quarterly or monthly). The balance forward is transferred to the new ledger card. Also, if a card gets filled up, a new card is made up and the inventory balanced is transferred to the new card. The previous card is stapled to the back of the new card.

As activity occurs on the inventory ledger card part, we record the transaction on the card. For example, in Chart 9.9 we see the arrival of a purchase order that added 200 units to our inventory. We also see that two production orders came in taking 25 and 10 units each from inventory. We also see that 7 parts were sent out to be reworked, fixed, corrected, etc. The transactions always need to be recorded exactly as they occur or we will lose the accuracy of the inventory count. The initials of the individual who recorded the transaction are used for identification purposes.

The function of the "EOQ," "ROP," "Total ROP," "Balance," and "Safety Stock" entries is as follows. Each time an issue from stock occurs, we check to see if the balance left in inventory is still large enough to cover safety stock and the reorder point ("Total ROP"). In other words, if the balance is less than "Total ROP," we need to place an order for parts. The amount of parts we order is the EOQ amount. In the example of Chart 9.9, after the 1/3/92 transaction we are left with a balance of 265 units. The next transaction brings this balance down to 215 units. Since this value dropped below 225 units ("ROP" + "Safety Stock" = "Total ROP" = 125 + 100 = 225) which is the "Total ROP," we need to place an order for 200 additional parts (the "EOQ" amount). This order for parts is expected to arrive into inventory when our balance reaches 100 units. The initials of the individual placing the order let us know that the order was placed so that we do not double order or forget to order. With a computer data base system, this process can be done automatically.

The process of "placing an order" needs to be discussed. If you are recording an issue of parts in the example of Chart 9.9 and you notice that the balance is below the "Total ROP," you would record a purchase requisition on the purchase requisition form. These forms are delivered to the Purchasing Department on a daily basis where the actual purchase order is made. When the purchase requisition is filled out, put your initials in the "Ordered By" column of the ledger card. This is your confirmation that an order has already been placed through purchasing. Chart 9.10 is a sample purchase requisition. Chart 9.11 shows how the filled-in requisition would look based on the purchase entry required in the example of Chart 9.9.

Some minor variations are needed for a ledger card for a work-in-process item. Chart 9.12 shows an example of a work-in-process product.

Again there is no anticipation inventory in a work-in-process item. All the inventory receipts come from work orders, which means that we often may not get all the inventory for the full production order into the storage area at once. All the issues are also to production orders. "Total ROP" is again the sum of "ROP" plus "Safety Stock." If the inventory balance falls below the "Total ROP" value, we place a "production requisition" rather than a "purchase requisition" and the production requisition gets transferred to the Production Scheduling Department. A production requisition form can be found in Chart 9.13. Other than these differences, the work-in-process products are processed the same as raw materials items are in the inventory stores area.

CHART 9.10 Purchase Requisition

Date	Part Number	Part Description	Quantity

CHART 9.11 Purchase Requisition Example

Date	Part Number	Part Description	Quantity
1/4/92	WHEEL	BICYCLE WHEEL	200

CHART 9.12 Inventory Ledger Card Example—Work-in-Process Item

ABC classification ________ RM (WIP) FG
Part number SEAT Part description BICYCLE SEAT
Primary vendor ________ EOQ 200
Primary storage location ROW B-23 ROP 125
Safety stock 100 Anticipation inventory ________ Total ROP 225

Date	Transaction	Qty. Rcvd.	Qty. Picked	Balance	Trans. By	Order By
	BALANCE FORWARD			125	GP	
1/1/92	PROD ORDR #10602	200		325	RS	
1/2/92	PROD ORDR #6235		25	300	GP	
1/2/92	PROD ORDR #6222		10	290	RS	
1/3/92	ISSUE TO REWORK #41		7	283	RS	

CHART 9.13 Production Requisition

Date	Part Number	Part Description	Quantity

CHART 9.14 Inventory Ledger Card Example—Finished Goods Item

ABC classification ________ RM WIP (FG)
Part number MB-HD Part description HEAVY-DUTY MTN BIKE
Primary vendor ________ EOQ 50
Primary storage location ROW C-19 ROP 60
Safety stock 40 Anticipation inventory 20 Total ROP 120

Date	Transaction	Qty. Rcvd.	Qty. Picked	Balance	Trans. By	Order By
	BALANCE FORWARD			105	GP	
1/1/92	PROD ORDR #10602	50		155	RS	
1/2/92	PROD ORDR #6235		5	150	GP	
1/2/92	PROD ORDR #6222		10	140	RS	
1/3/92	ISSUE TO REWORK #41		7	133	RS	

There are also some minor variations on how the ledger card would be filled out for a finished goods item. Chart 9.14 shows an example of a finished goods inventory item.

A finished good item may have anticipation inventory. This is inventory that is being stored for a future sale (see Chapter 8). However, the level of anticipation inventory may change each month. Therefore it requires close monitoring. This would also affect the balance of the "Total ROP," which is the sum of the "ROP," the "Safety Stock," and the "Anticipation Inventory" ("Total ROP" = "ROP" + "Safety Stock" + "Anticipation Inventory"). All the inventory receipts come from work orders, which means that we may not get all the inventory for the full production order into the storage area at once. All the issues are to customer orders. If the inventory balance falls below the "Total ROP" value, we place a production requisition, just like we did for a work-in-process item. The same form can be used (see Chart 9.13). Other than these differences, the finished good products are treated the same as the other materials in the inventory stores area.

Critical Issues

All inventory items must be routed through the Inventory Department. If it is a work-in-process item or a raw materials item, it must go through inventory stores before it can be used in production. If it is a finished goods item, it must go through stores before it can go out to the customer. Even if the customer is standing at the door waiting to be handed the part, it still has to be routed through inventory. That is because without this routing, inventory control falls apart. If inventory control is expecting a part to arrive in inventory and it never arrives, the entire ordering and reordering cycle could be thrown off.

Informational and Control Reports

Numerous inventory reports can be written that assist in the analysis and control of one of your most expensive assets—inventory. Examples are now given of each showing how they are used.

Inventory Status

The inventory status report is shown in Chart 9.15. It indicates the current balance and the last month's activity for each part. This report can be run monthly, quarterly, annually, etc. The easiest way would be to run it monthly and then summarize the monthly reports for an annual report. The information from this report is helpful when doing an ABC analyses on the amount of activity or on the inventory costs of the item (see the next report shown in this section; also see the usefulness of this report in the calculation of EOQ values in Chapter 11).

CHART 9.15 Inventory Status Report

Date ____/____/____ Product Type RM WIP FG

Product		Quantities					Number of			Dollar Value				
Name	Number	Balance	Issued	Received	Scrapped	Rework	Issues	Receipts	Unit Price	Balance	Issued	Received	Scrapped	Rework
Totals														

To do the report, pull the ledger cards out of your file one at a time and report the information from the ledger cards on the report. This is also an appropriate time to issue new ledger cards with new "Balance Forward" entries. What this gives you is a monthly report of activity on each part. By issuing new ledger cards at this time, all the new month's activity will be recorded on the new cards. This activity report will then become the basis of many of the other reports.

Three inventory status reports need to be filled out. One for raw materials, one for work-in-process, and one for finished goods. Indicate what type of parts you are working on by circling the appropriate code at the top of the report. (Note the same indication on the top of each ledger card; see Chart 9.8.)

Chart 9.16 is an inventory status report for finished goods items. The "Quantities" and "Numbers of" counts come directly from the ledger cards. For each part, the following information is taken from the ledger card and recorded on the inventory status report. The fields are:

Product name

Product number

Quantity—Balance. This is the balance as of the end of the month. This should be the quantity that is transferred to the top of the next ledger card.

Quantity—Issued. This is the sum of the "Quantity Picked" column of the ledger card for the month. This number should not include issues to rework or scrap. Those numbers go into the "Scrapped" and "Rework" columns.

Quantity—Received. This is the sum of the "Quantity Received" column of the ledger card for the last month.

Quantity—Scrapped. This is the sum of all the issues ("Quantity Picked") to scrap.

Quantity—Rework. This is the sum of all the issues ("Quantity Picked") to rework during the period.

Number of Issues. This is a count of the total number of entries in the "Quantity Picked" column of the inventory ledger card.

Number of Receipts. This is a count of the total number of entries in the "Quantity Received" column of the inventory ledger card.

From the accounting, product costing, or purchasing office we get the information placed in the "Unit Price" column. If the product is a raw material, the information comes from purchasing. If the item is a work-in-process or finished goods item, the costs come from product costing. This unit price value is then multiplied times the "Balance," "Issued," "Received," "Scrapped," and "Rework" columns to get an extended cost value.

Before we are finished with the report, a cross-check should be done. If we take this same report for last month, and look at the "Quantity Balance" for last month, this quantity should cross-check with the value for this month. The check is as follows:

CHART 9.16 Inventory Status Report Example

Date 1 / 1 /1992   Product Type RM WIP FG

Product		Quantities					Number of		Unit	Dollar Value				
Name	Number	Balance	Issued	Received	Scrapped	Rework	Issues	Receipts	Price	Balance	Issued	Received	Scrapped	Rework
Mtn. Bike–Econ	MB–E	100	170	180	10	5	25	30	100.00	10,000	17,000	18,000	1,000	500
Mtn. Bike–HD	MB–HD	50	120	150	10	5	25	30	120.00	6,000	14,400	18,000	1,200	600
Mtn. Bike–SLW	MB–SLW	40	100	90	5	10	20	40	150.00	6,000	15,000	13,500	750	1,500
Ten-speed–M	TS–M	120	200	200	10	10	30	30	75.00	9,000	15,000	15,000	750	750
Ten-speed–W	TS–W	60	180	170	20	5	30	30	75.00	4,500	13,500	12,750	1,500	375
Tricycles	TRI	200	400	410	30	20	100	50	15.00	3,000	6,000	6,150	450	300
Totals							230	210		38,500	80,900	83,400	5,650	4,025

Last Month Quantity Balance
− This Month Quantity Issues
+ This Month Quantity Receipts
− This Month Quantity Scrapped
− This Month Quantity Rework
= This Month Quantity Balance

If this cross-check does not check out for any product, you have an inventory control error that needs to be rectified. Some type of recording error is occurring, or someone is "borrowing" parts. It is important to keep these numbers validated or you may find yourself in need of parts that no longer exist in your inventory.

This calculation process can also be performed on a spreadsheet. The data still need to be collected from the inventory ledger cards and from purchasing or product costing, but the cost calculations can then be done using the spreadsheet. Chart 9.17 shows the data of Chart 9.16 calculated on a spreadsheet. Chart 9.18 shows how the calculations of Chart 9.15 would be performed.

Benefits of the Inventory Status Report

The inventory status report is full of good information. Some of the more important entries are:

Inventory costing. The "Dollar Value Balance" column is a costing of your current inventory assets.

Dollar Value Issued. This column helps you calculate "Cost of Goods Sold."

Dollar Value Received. This column helps you with purchase costing.

Dollar Value Scrapped or Dollar Value Reworked. These columns help you spot potential product wastage problems. Look for excessive numbers in these columns.

The "Number of Issues" and "Number of Receipts" columns help with the ABC analysis for the amount of activity of each product.

Unused Inventories Information. If a product only has balance information, and nothing else, the next question should be—why are we storing this part at all?

Excessive Inventory Analysis. Another valuable piece of information that can be gathered from this report is excessive inventory storage. Compare the "Quantities Balance" column with the "Quantities Issued" column. If the quantities balance is more than half of what you issued, you have too much inventory. If this is a high moving product (lots of activity), then, depending on the amount of activity, your inventory balance should be even lower than the 50 percent estimate. Take a close look at Chapter 11, which discusses the calculation of EOQ and safety stock.

CHART 9.17 Inventory Status Report Using the Spreadsheet

	A	B	C	D	E	F	G	H	I	J	K	L	M	N
1														
2	INVENTORY STATUS REPORT													
3														
4		Quantities					Number of		Unit	Dollar Value				
5		Balance	Issued	Received	Scrapped	Rework	Issues	Receipts	Price	Balance	Issued	Received	Scrapped	Rework
6	MB–E	100	170	180	10	5	25	30	100	10000	17000	18000	1000	500
7	MB–HD	50	120	150	10	5	25	30	120	6000	14400	18000	1200	600
8	MB–SLW	40	100	90	5	10	20	40	150	6000	15000	13500	750	1500
9	TS–M	120	200	200	10	10	30	30	75	9000	15000	15000	750	750
10	TS–W	60	180	170	20	5	30	30	75	4500	13500	12750	1500	375
11	TRI	200	400	410	30	20	100	50	15	3000	6000	6150	450	300
12						TOTALS	230	210		38500	80900	83400	5650	4025
13														

CHART 9.18 Inventory Status Report Using the Spreadsheet and Showing Calculations

	A	B	C	D	E	F	G	H	I	J	K	L	M	N	O
1															
2	INVENTORY STATUS REPORT														
3															
4		Quantities					Number of		Unit	Dollar Value					
5		Balance	Issued	Received	Scrapped	Rework	Issues	Receipts	Price	Balance	Issued	Received	Scrapped	Rework	
6	MB–E	100	170	180	10	5	25	30	100	B6×I6	C6×I6	D6×I6	E6×I6	F6×I6	
7	MB–HD	50	120	150	10	5	25	30	120	B7×I7	C7×I7	D7×I7	E7×I7	F7×I7	
8	MB–SLW	40	100	90	5	10	20	40	150	B8×I8	C8×I8	D8×I8	E8×I8	F8×I8	
9	TS–M	120	200	200	10	10	30	30	75	B9×I9	C9×I9	D9×I9	E9×I9	F9×I9	
10	TS–W	60	180	170	20	5	30	30	75	B10×I10	C10×I10	D10×I10	E10×I10	F10×I10	
11	TRI	200	400	410	30	20	100	50	15	B11×I11	C11×I11	D11×I11	E11×I11	F11×I11	
12						TOTALS	SUM(G6:G11)	SUM(H6:H11)		SUM(J6:J11)	SUM(K6:K11)	SUM(L6:L11)	SUM(M6:M11)	SUM(N6:N11)	
13															

ABC Analysis

Chapter 8 offers a good discussion of the general concept of ABC analysis. In this section we will see how ABC analysis is used to evaluate:

1. the amount of activity each part receives
2. the dollar inventory level of each product

For item 1 we look at the number of times each part had some activity (issues or receipts). This would be the sum of the number of issues and number of receipts columns in the inventory status report (Chart 9.15). For item 2 we would look at the dollar inventory balance of each product (the "Dollar Value Balance" column of the inventory status report). If you have used a spreadsheet to do Chart 9.15, then simply sort on these values to get the ABC listing. If you are doing the process manually, use the inventory status report to look for the largest value of the category on which you are working. Record these from largest to smallest on Chart 9.19.

For example, looking at the example of Chart 9.16, the largest value for dollar value balance is MB–E. The second largest is TS–M, etc. These are listed on Chart 9.20 as an example of an ABC analysis by dollar value balance. Chart 9.21 is an ABC analysis of the data in Chart 9.16 using the amount of activity for classification purposes.

Chart 9.20 lists the products by highest to smallest inventory dollar balance value. Then it calculates a percentage of the dollar value for this product over the total dollar value. For example, MB–E has $10,000 in inventory, which is 10,000/38,500 = 26% of the total inventory dollar value. The "Cumulative %" column is just the sum of the individual percentages. For example, for TS–M, the 26% from MB–E plus the 23% from TS–M equals a total of 49% cumulative. The ABC coding is then identified by taking the first 80% cumulative and classi-

CHART 9.19 ABC Analysis Report

Date ___/___/___ Type RM WIP FG

Product Number	Classification	%	Cumulative %	Code

CHART 9.20 ABC Analysis Report—By Dollar Value Balance

Date 1 / 1 /1992 Type RM WIP (FG)

Product Number	Classification	%	Cumulative %	Code
MB–E	10,000	26	26	A
TS–M	9,000	23	49	A
MB–HD	6,000	16	65	A
MB–SLW	6,000	16	81	A
TS–W	4,500	12	93	B
TRI	3,000	7	100	C

CHART 9.21 ABC Analysis Report—By Activity

Date 1 / 1 /1992 Type RM WIP (FG)

Product Number	Classification	%	Cumulative %	Code
TRI	100 + 50 = 150	34	34	A
MB–SLW	20 + 40 = 60	14	48	A
TS–M	30 + 30 = 60	14	62	A
TS–W	30 + 30 = 60	14	76	A
MB–E	25 + 30 = 55	12	88	B
MB–HD	25 + 30 = 55	12	100	C
	Total = 230 + 210 = 440			

fying it as "A" items. The "B" item cutoff is at 95%, and the rest are "C" items. Since our parts list only has six items, this parts list is too short to demonstrate the ABC classification system (see explanation in Chapter 8). When the parts list gets significantly long, the first cumulative 80% will only use up 20% of the items.

In Chart 9.21 we follow a similar procedure, except we are classifying our parts based on the total activity (the sum of the number of issues plus the number of receipts). The percentage is again the percentage of the total. The cumulative percentage and the coding process work the same as in Chart 9.20.

This ABC classification process can be calculated on the same spreadsheet that we used previously for the inventory status report (Charts 9.17 and 9.18). Chart 9.22 shows the continuation of spreadsheet 9.17, and Chart 9.23 shows the calculations that went into this expansion.

Benefits of the ABC Analysis Report

ABC Analysis can now be used to classify the products for storage location planning purposes and for cycle count planning as discussed in Chapter 8. It can also be run on other categories, such as the scrap and rework columns, to demonstrate which products are causing the most trouble.

CHART 9.22 ABC Analysis Report Using the Spreadsheet

	A	B	C	D	E
14					
15	440	Activity	%	Qume	
16	TRI	150	12.5	12.5	
17	MB–SLW	60	13.63636	26.13636	
18	TS–M	60	13.63636	39.77273	
19	TS–W	60	12.5	52.27273	
20	MB–E	55	34.09091	86.36364	
21	MB–HD	55	13.63636	100	
22					
23			Dollar Balance		
24	MB–E	10000	25.97403	25.97403	
25	TS–M	9000	15.58442	41.55844	
26	MB–HD	6000	23.37662	64.93506	
27	MB–SLW	6000	15.58442	80.51948	
28	TS–W	4500	11.68831	92.20779	
29	TRI	3000	7.792208	100	
30					

CHART 9.23 ABC Analysis Report Using the Spreadsheet and Showing Calculations

	A	B	C	D	E
14					
15	G12 + H12	Activity	%	Qume	
16	TRI	G11 + H11	100 × B21/A15	C16	
17	MB–SLW	G8 + H8	100 × B18/A15	D16 + C17	
18	TS–M	G9 + H9	100 × B19/A15	D17 + C18	
19	TS–W	G10 + H10	100 × B20/A15	D18 + C19	
20	MB–E	G6 + H6	100 × B16/A15	D19 + C20	
21	MB–HD	G7 + H7	100 × B17/A15	D20 + C21	
22					
23			Dollar Balance		
24	MB–E	J6	100 × B24/J12	C24	
25	TS–M	J9	100 × B27/J12	D24 + C25	
26	MB–HD	J7	100 × B25/J12	D25 + C26	
27	MB–SLW	J8	100 × B26/J12	D26 + C27	
28	TS–W	J10	100 × B28/J12	D27 + C28	
29	TRI	J11	100 × B29/J12	D28 + C29	

Summary

Inventory is one of our most critical assets and therefore needs to have a tight control system. The perpetual inventory system and the inventory status reporting system are a "must" in establishing this control. With the inventory control system in place, we are now ready to discuss production planning—what it means and how it works. This is the subject of our next chapter.

Chapter

10 Production Planning—What Does It Mean?

Production Planning Explained

Success lies in the basics. Doing the basics right and not jumping at the magic leads to success. This book is full of the basics. Production planning is one of the most critical of the basics.

In Chapter 4 we were first introduced to the concept of production planning (see Chart 4.10). To examine the portion of this diagram that relates to production planning, we see it redisplayed in Chart 10.1.

The main objective of production planning is to take the gross requirements of the factory (which come from the master production schedule) and convert them into purchase and production orders. For example, we know how many bicycles we want to build (gross requirements). From these gross requirements we want to calculate how many wheels, frames, handlebars, etc., we need to buy (purchase orders). We also need to know when we should start working on assembling these bicycles so that they will be completed on time (production orders).

The production planning process can occur numerous ways, but in this book we will discuss the two most commonly used methods in the United States, the most popular being EOQ (economic order quantity), and the second most popular being MRP (material requirements planning). Each of these methods has advantages and disadvantages, as listed in Chart 10.2.

Because EOQ is very rigid in its assumptions—in particular, EOQ assumes that demand is fixed, constant, and steady—it may require some additional adjustment to the master production schedule so that the demand loads generated by the product requirements are evenly distributed. Otherwise, large lumps of demand may catch the EOQ system unprepared and cause a shortage of parts. This can always be buffered with extra safety stock, but this is a poor solution because it results in higher inventory costs.

As seen on Chart 10.1, the primary input of the production planning process is the master production schedule, which tells us what needs to be completed and when. The other inputs tell us what is needed to perform the manufacturing process. The bill of materials tells us what pieces we need to build or buy and when (see Chapter 13). The routings

CHART 10.1 Production Planning

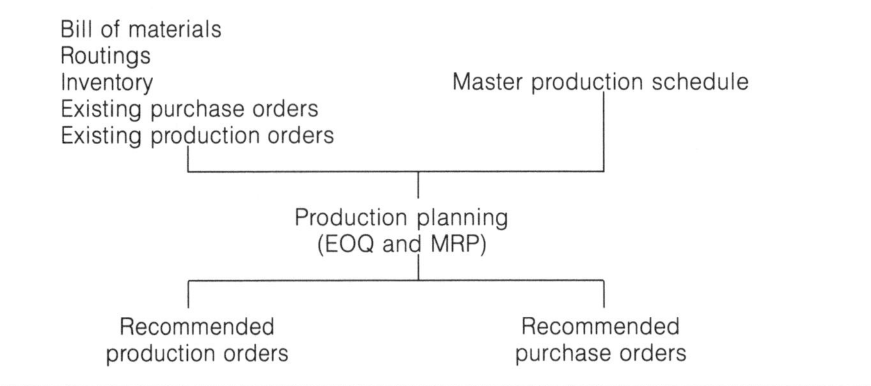

CHART 10.2 EOQ Versus MRP

- EOQ (Economic Order Quantity)
  - Advantages
    - Easy to use
    - Easy to control
    - Can easily be done manually or with minimal automation
  - Disadvantages
    - Only schedules demand that is fixed and constant throughout the year; does not handle demand variability very well
    - Needs to be recalculated about every six months
    - Only schedules materials, not labor
- MRP (Materials Requirements Planning)
  - Advantages
    - Handles demand variability; demand planning
    - Schedules all three of the M's (materials, machinery, and manpower)
    - Offers a significant inventory reduction over EOQ
  - Disadvantages
    - Requires a high level of data accuracy in all areas
    - Requires computer power
    - Much more complicated than EOQ

information tells us how long it takes to purchase or build a product (see Chapter 14). This is referred to as *lead time*. The inventory information tells us what we have in stock so that we don't purchase or build something we already have (see Chapters 8 and 9). The last input, purchase and production orders, is also the output of the production planning system. This input tells us what is already in process. Existing purchase orders tell us what products have been purchased and are in the process of being shipped to us. Existing production orders tell us what items are already being produced.

The two major categories of outputs for production planning are the recommended purchase orders and the recommended production orders. In Chapter 9 we discussed one way in which purchase requisitions (recommended purchase orders) and production requisitions (recommended production orders) are generated. This is the way that an EOQ system would generate these requisitions. (The MRP procedure for generating these requisitions is discussed in Chapters 12 and 16.)

Purchase requisitions are forwarded to the Purchasing Department where the actual purchase order is placed. It then becomes part of the "existing purchase order" input into the production planning process. Production requisitions are forwarded to the production planning office where the production jobs are released onto the production floor (see Chapter 19). These released production orders are now part of the "existing production order" input into the production planning process.

Lead Time

The calculation of lead time is an important consideration in the planning of production and purchase orders. Lead times determine how much earlier we must actually place the purchase order so that the materials will arrive at the factory on time. This is in the case of a purchase order. In the case of a production order, lead time helps us get the materials produced on time. Lead time calculations include the following:

Raw Materials Lead Time. Raw materials are purchased items and their lead time starts when the purchasing agent makes the phone call to place the order for the parts needed. This lead time includes packaging time at the vendor, shipment time, unpacking time, and inspection time. The lead time ends when the materials are in the storeroom and available to be assigned for production. The materials are not usable until then. This process is also explained in Chapter 9.

Work-in-Process Lead Time. Work-in-process items are manufactured items that are not yet completed and ready for sale. Lead time for work-in-process items starts when the production order is released to the factory floor. It includes the time required to pick up the materials from the inventory storeroom, bring them into production, perform the production functions, inspect them, and return the final product to stores.

Finished Goods Lead Time. Finished goods lead time has two different aspects. The first is the time needed to produce the good. This is the only aspect we are interested in when we consider production planning. Production lead time for a finished good is calculated in the same way as work-in-process lead time is calculated. The second aspect of finished goods lead time is the lead time required to pull the part from inventory, package it, and ship it to the customer. This is called *delivery lead time* and is a marketing concern, not a production planning concern.

Summary

A production planning system takes the gross requirements from the master production schedule and converts these requirements into production and purchase orders. The objective of a production planning system is to identify how much product to order and how often and when to place these orders so that production can continue to flow smoothly and so that all customer demands can be met. Chapter 11 discusses the most popular of the production planning methods, EOQ. Chapter 12 discusses the second most popular of these methods, MRP.

Chapter

11 Economic Order Quantity

The EOQ (economic order quantity) process can be a blessing or a curse. EOQ can improve inventory management, but it won't increase quality or productivity. Used correctly, EOQ can generate great inventory savings. However, be careful that you use it correctly, as discussed in this chapter, or else you will end up with it doing you more harm than good.

The EOQ concept is not dead, even though many of the advocates of more sophisticated methods such as MRP (material requirements planning) or JIT (just-in-time) may tell you that it is. In reality, these more sophisticated methods depend on EOQ for many of their basic calculations. For example, MRP uses EOQ for lot sizing (see Chapters 16 and 17). JIT, the Japanese production method, is entirely EOQ based in its assumptions. Having a good understanding of EOQ not only gives you an understanding of the most popular of production control philosophies, it will also help you in the future to understand the more sophisticated methods.

The key to understanding EOQ started back in Chapter 8. Review Chapters 8 and 9 and make sure you understand these concepts before you continue with this chapter. Make sure you feel comfortable with Charts 8.2 and 8.4.

Total Cost Equation

We learned in previous chapters that the objective of inventory planning, and specifically EOQ planning, is to try to minimize the total cost of inventory. The total cost equation as given in Chapter 8 is:

$$TC = FC + OC + CC$$

where

TC = total cost

FC = fixed costs

OC = ordering costs

CC = carrying costs

In EOQ we are trying to determine the optimal order size. This means that we are trying to determine the optimal "Q" at which "TC" will be minimized.

Referring to Chart 8.2, we see the chart redrawn in Chart 11.1. In Chart 11.1 we see two different inventory cycles. The one cycle has large orders (Q_B), the second has small orders (Q_S). The larger orders cause fewer orders to be placed, thereby reducing ordering costs (OC). Unfortunately, the larger orders also force us to carry more inventory, thereby increasing carrying costs (CC). The small orders do just the opposite. They increase ordering costs (OC) because of the large number of orders, but they decrease carrying costs (CC) because of the reduced inventory levels. We need to find the optimal "Q" that will minimize "TC." Looking at Chart 8.4, redrawn as Chart 11.2, we see how the TC equation looks graphically.

CHART 11.1 Sawtooth Size

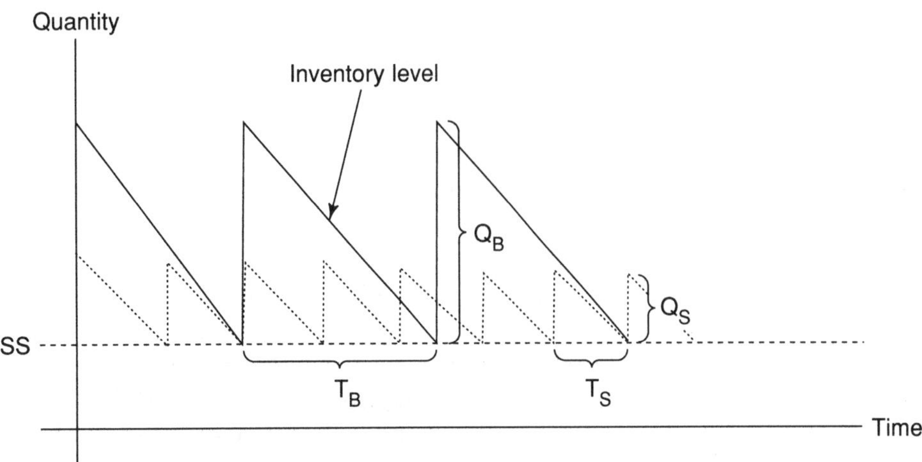

CHART 11.2 Inventory Total Cost Graph

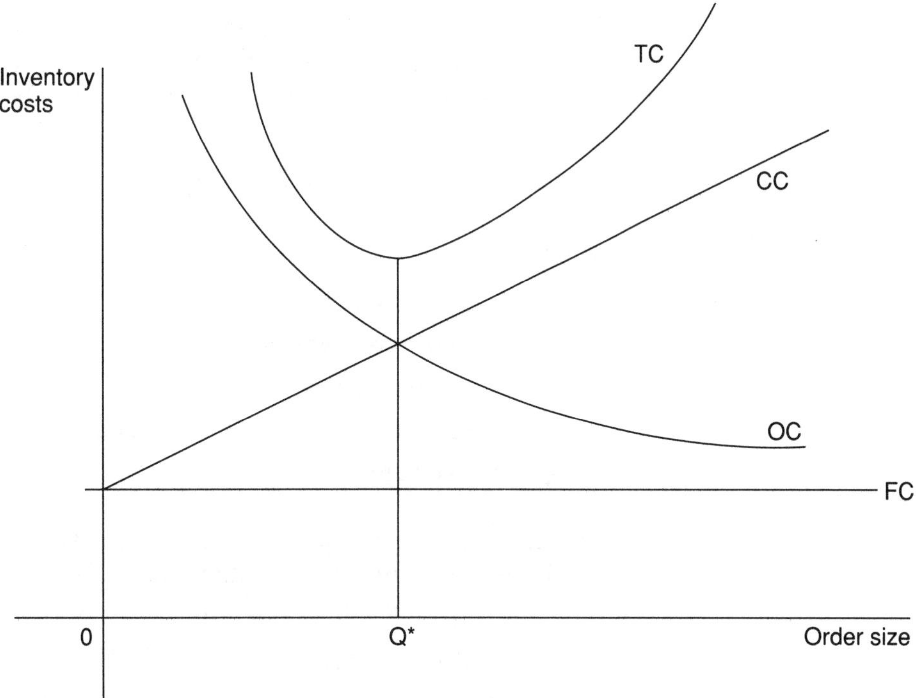

From Chart 11.2 and the total cost equation, we get a feel for the types of things that have an important effect on determining the optimal "Q" size. Let's start again with the total cost equation for the cost of inventory over one year's time:

$$TC = FC + OC + CC$$

Ordering cost (OC) is composed of two factors:

A = the cost of placing an order
B = the number of orders placed

The number of orders placed is calculated by dividing the total demand for the year (D) by the size of each order (Q). So at this point we have:

$$OC = A \times B = A \times \frac{D}{Q}$$

where

D = annual demand
Q = order size

Carrying cost (CC) is composed of the cost of carrying one item in inventory for one year (I) times the average inventory level for the year (X). Each of these terms needs further breakdown. The cost of carrying inventory (I) is composed of the cost of the original item (V) times the percentage rate that it costs us to carry the item in inventory (R). This percentage rate is composed of items such as interest rate or opportunity costs (see below for a more detailed explanation).

The average inventory level (X) is composed of safety stock (SS) plus half the height of the sawtooth (one half of Q). However, we come into a definitional conflict at this point. The cost of carrying safety stock is a permanent, fixed cost. It does not vary with the size of the order and therefore belongs as part of the "FC" term of the "TC" equation. The equation's carrying costs at this point have become:

$$CC = I \times X = (V \times R) \times \left(\frac{Q}{2}\right)$$

where

I = cost of carrying one item in inventory for one year
X = average inventory level
V = price of an item
R = rate paid for the money used for inventory
Q/2 = average sawtooth height

The only other component of the total cost equation (TC) that needs to be discussed is the "FC" component. This component includes all items that are not affected by a change in order size. This includes:

The cost of carrying safety stock (SSC)
The cost of purchasing the inventory (PC)
The cost of quality corrections or improvements (QC)

Then, at this point, the total cost equation would take the form:

$$TC = (SSC + PC + QC) + \left(A \times \frac{D}{Q}\right) + \left(V \times R \times \frac{Q}{2}\right)$$

From Chart 11.2 we see that fixed cost has no effect on the determination of "Q." We further see that the optimal "Q" size occurs at the point where "OC" equals "CC."[1] If we set these two equal to each other, we will arrive at a formula for the optimal "Q" size:

$$OC = A \times \frac{D}{Q} = V \times R \times \frac{Q}{2} = CC$$

Multiplying through by "2 × Q" gives us:

$$2 \times A \times D = V \times R \times Q^2$$

Dividing through by "V × R" and taking the square root of both sides gives us an equation for "Q":

$$Q = \sqrt{\frac{2 \times A \times D}{V \times R}}$$

Now that we know the formula for the optimal order size "Q," we need to make sure we understand how to calculate all the variables that go into this equation. We will eliminate the easy ones first.

Demand (D) is the total number of units of the product that we are analyzing that will be demanded in one year.

Product price (V) is the purchase price if we are dealing with a purchased item, or the manufacturing cost if we are dealing with a manufactured item. (See Chapter 14 if you need help in determining the manufacturing cost.) In determining purchase price, do not become overly concerned about price breaks. You know at approximately what quantities you will be purchasing and that is the price you should use for these calculations. If you want to check out a price break, plug that "Q" value (quantity that must be ordered to achieve the price break) into the total cost formula along with the reduced price and compare the total cost at the price break with the total cost at the recommended EOQ value.

The remaining two variables (A and R) require a little analysis. Looking first at "A," we see in Chart 11.3, Part A, an example of the calculation of "A" for both a manufactured and a purchased item. Next, look at Chart 11.3, Part B, to see an example of the calculation of the holding rate. Note that these values are percentages. Also note that the higher rates should be chosen. For example, if the interest rate at which you are financing your money is 10 percent, but the opportunity cost[2] that you are giving up is 20 percent, use the 20 percent value.

As we evaluate and calculate the values for "A" and "R" we have to be careful and remember that only those components that vary based on the order size should be considered. For example, in the evaluation of "R," we have taxes. A sales tax is the same regardless of how large

[1] If you don't feel comfortable with this assumption of equality, which doesn't commonly appear in the textbooks, read my article "Bottleneck Scheduling for an Unlimited Number of Products," *Journal of Manufacturing Systems,* Vol. 9, No. 4, pp. 324–331, which proves this equality using geometric programming.

[2] An opportunity cost is the interest rate you could be earning by investing this same money in some other way. For example, if you were to use $10,000 that is currently tied up in inventory to do a plant expansion, and you anticipate that this expansion will earn a 20 percent return, then the 20 percent value is the opportunity cost that you are giving up by leaving the money tied up in inventory. This 20 percent is what should be used for "R."

CHART 11.3 Ordering Cost (A) Breakdown, Part A

(These are examples only and are not to be considered all-inclusive.)

Ordering costs for a purchased item:
- Labor, equipment, and materials
- Preparation of purchase order includes paperwork and phone calling
- Transportation costs
- Receiving and inspection
- Preparation of payment documents
- Interplant transportation
- Expediting costs
- Postage costs

Ordering costs for a manufactured item:
- Preparation of production order
- Materials picking costs
- Inspection costs
- Interplant transportation
- Expediting costs
- Machine setup and cleanup costs
- Receiving back into inventory

CHART 11.3 *(continued)* **Carrying Cost (R) Breakdown, Part B**

(These are examples only and are not to be considered all-inclusive.)

Carrying costs (percent)
- Loss due to inability to invest funds in profit-making ventures (opportunity costs or interest rate, whichever is higher)
- Cost of replacing inventory
- Inventory obsolescence
- Deterioration of inventory
- Handling and distribution
- Taxes
- Storage
- Pilferage
- General supplies
- Insurance

our order size is or how long we keep the items in inventory before we sell the product. But an inventory holding tax is affected by our average inventory level, which is affected by our "Q" size. Therefore, the sales tax would be part of the fixed cost (FC) component, whereas the inventory tax would be a part of the carrying cost (CC) component and will be added to "R." This type of thinking should go into each of the incremental values used in the development of either "R" or "A."

EOQ Equation

At this point we know how to come up with "A," "D," "V," and "R" for any one particular item in our production shop. This process needs to occur for every item that we have in our shop, regardless of whether it is a raw material, work-in-process item, or a finished goods item. After we have calculated these variables, we are now ready to calculate the optimal "Q" value for the purchased items using the equation of "Q." To help you do this, use Chart 11.4, Part A. We are not yet ready to calculate the optimal "Q" value for manufactured items. That process has an additional kink and will be discussed next.

Chart 11.4, Part B, is an example of how to calculate the EOQ value. Values are plugged in for "D," "A," "V," and "R" and then dem-

CHART 11.4 EOQ Calculations for Purchased Items, Part A

$$Q = \sqrt{\frac{2 \times A \times D}{V \times R}}$$

Product Number	Annual Demand (D)	Cost of Placing an Order (A)	Item Price (V)	Carrying Rate (R)	EOQ (Q)

CHART 11.4 *(continued)* **EOQ Calculations for Purchased Items—Example, Part B**

$$Q = \sqrt{\frac{2 \times A \times D}{V \times R}}$$

Product Number	Annual Demand (D)	Cost of Placing an Order (A)	Item Price (V)	Carrying Rate (R)	EOQ (Q)
AXRFT	2,000	$35.00	$70.00	20%	100

$$Q = \sqrt{\frac{2 \times A \times D}{V \times R}} = \sqrt{\frac{2 \times (35.00) \times (2{,}000)}{(70.00) \times (0.20)}} = \sqrt{10{,}000} = 100$$

Product Number	Annual Demand (D)	Cost of Placing an Order (A)	Item Price (V)	Carrying Rate (R)	EOQ (Q)
QRSTUV	10,000	$75.00	$50.00	15%	447.2

$$Q = \sqrt{\frac{2 \times A \times D}{V \times R}} = \sqrt{\frac{2 \times (75.00) \times (10{,}000)}{(50.00) \times (0.15)}} = \sqrt{200{,}000} = 447.2$$

Product Number	Annual Demand (D)	Cost of Placing an Order (A)	Item Price (V)	Carrying Rate (R)	EOQ (Q)
XOYOP	11,111	$75.75	$51.13	17.5%	433.74

$$Q = \sqrt{\frac{2 \times A \times D}{V \times R}} = \sqrt{\frac{2 \times (75.75) \times (11{,}111)}{(51.13) \times (0.175)}} = \sqrt{188{,}127} = 433.74$$

(continued)

CHART 11.4 *(continued)* **EOQ Calculations for Purchased Items Using a Spreadsheet, Part C**

	A	B	C	D	E	F	G
1							
2	EOQ Calculations for Purchased Items						
3							
4		Annual	Cost of	Item	Carrying		
5	Product	Demand	Placing an	Price	Rate	EOQ	
6	Number	(D)	Order (A)	(V)	(R)	(Q)	
7	AXRFT	2000	35	70	20	100	
8	QRSTUV	10000	75	50	15	447.2136	
9	XOYOP	11111	75.75	51.13	17.5	433.7365	
10							

CHART 11.4 *(concluded)* **EOQ Calculations for Purchased Items Using a Spreadsheet and Showing Calculations, Part D**

	A	B	C	D	E	F	G	H
1								
2	EOQ Calculations for Purchased Items							
3								
4		Annual	Cost of	Item	Carrying			
5	Product	Demand	Placing an	Price	Rate	EOQ		
6	Number	(D)	Order (A)	(V)	(R)	(Q)		
7	AXRFT	2000	35	70	20	SQRT(2×C7×B7/(D7×E7/100))		
8	QRSTUV	10000	75	50	15	SQRT(2×C8×B8/(D8×E8/100))		
9	XOYOP	11111	75.75	51.13	17.5	SQRT(2×C9×B9/(D9×E9/100))		
10								

onstrate the calculation process. Chart 11.4, Part C, shows this same calculation process using a simple spreadsheet package, Supercalc.[3] Chart 11.4, Part D, shows the formulas that correspond to the spreadsheet process of Part C.

Manufacturing EOQs

Manufacturing EOQs are slightly more complicated than purchasing EOQs. One of two situations may exist with the manufactured product. These are:

1. If the manufactured product is produced in a batch and the entire batch is delivered to the stockroom after the manufacturing process has been completed, then the EOQ formula is the same as for a purchased item.
2. If the manufactured product is produced and delivered into inventory as it is produced, over a period of time, then an additional variable comes into the calculation. The sawtooth diagram for this model would look like Chart 11.5.

[3] Supercalc is an easy to use spreadsheet package offered by Computer Associates. Their national marketing office can be reached at (516)227-3300.

CHART 11.5 Production Inventory Sawtooth

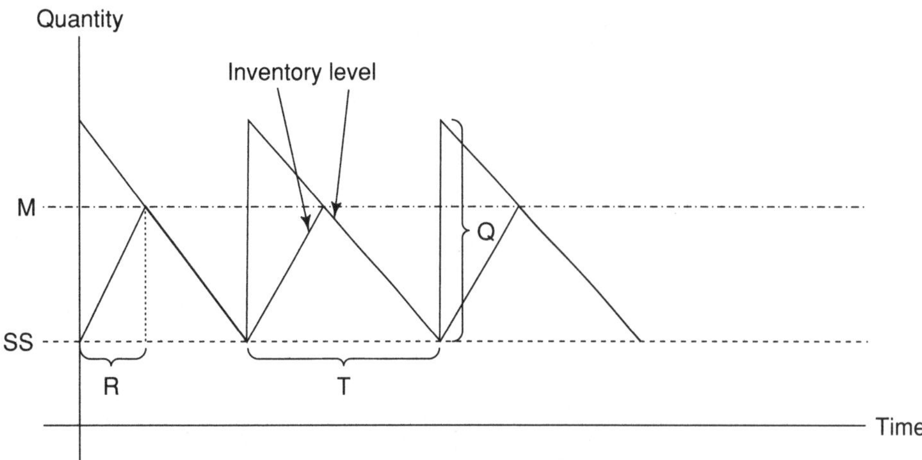

In Chart 11.5 we see "R," which is the amount of time it takes to build "Q" items. As we are building inventory, we are also using it up. Unlike the purchasing model where we receive all "Q" materials into inventory in one surge, in this production model it takes "R" days for us to receive "Q" items, during which time we have already used up some of the items. We will never have the full "Q" items in inventory. The maximum level of inventory (M) is therefore lower than in the purchasing model, which means that the average inventory level will be lower. The result is a new total cost equation (TC) that adjusts for this reduction in average inventory level. The new "TC" equation starts with the same basic form:

$$TC = FC + OC + CC$$

Fixed costs (FC) will again fall out of the evaluation process as they did under the purchasing model because they have no influence on the size of "Q" (see Chart 11.2). Ordering cost (OC) also remains the same as far as the formula goes, even though the calculation of "A" varies slightly (see Chart 11.3, Part A). It is the carrying cost that has changed. The original form of the equation was:

$$CC = I \times X$$

Now we need to add an adjustment to the average inventory term. Average inventory level "X" is no longer just the order size "Q" divided by 2; it also has an adjustment factor:

$$\left(1 - \frac{D}{P}\right)$$

where

P = The production rate. In other words, what is the total number of units that could be produced over a year's time using the same process that you would normally use? If, for example, you use a certain machine to build this product normally, what would be the annual production rate if you used that same machine to produce that product for a full year?

The full evaluation of the carrying cost (CC) would be:

$$CC = I \times X = (V \times R) \times \left(\frac{Q}{2}\right) \times \left(1 - \frac{D}{P}\right)$$

Finally, the new total cost equation would be:

$$TC = (SSC + PC + QC) + \left(A \times \frac{D}{Q}\right) + \left(V \times R \times \frac{Q}{2}\right) \times \left(1 - \frac{D}{P}\right)$$

Following the same procedure as previously, we would set the carrying cost (CC) equal to the ordering cost (OC) and solve for "Q." The result would be:

$$Q = \sqrt{\frac{2 \times A \times D}{V \times R} \times \frac{P}{P - D}}$$

Chart 11.6, Part A, is the worksheet for calculating production EOQs. Chart 11.6, Part B, is an example of the calculations used in Part A. Chart 11.6, Part C, shows how these calculations can be done on a spreadsheet, and Part D shows the formulas that correspond to the Part C spreadsheet.

Reorder Point Calculations

Reflecting back on the previous chapters on inventory planning and control (Chapters 8 and 9), we stated that there were two key fields that were needed for a fixed quantity ordering system: EOQ and ROP. ROP

CHART 11.6 EOQ Calculations for Production Items, Part A

$$Q = \sqrt{\frac{2 \times A \times D}{V \times R} \times \frac{P}{P - D}}$$

Product Number	Annual Demand (D)	Cost of Placing an Order (A)	Item Price (V)	Carrying Rate (R)	Annual Production (P)	EOQ (Q)

CHART 11.6 *(continued)* **EOQ Calculations for Production Items—Example, Part B**

$$Q = \sqrt{\frac{2 \times A \times D}{V \times R} \times \frac{P}{P - D}}$$

Product Number	Annual Demand (D)	Cost of Placing an Order (A)	Item Price (V)	Carrying Rate (R)	Annual Production (P)	EOQ (Q)
AXRFT	2,000	$35.00	$70.00	20%	10,000	111.8

$$Q = \sqrt{\frac{2 \times A \times D}{V \times R} \times \frac{P}{P - D}} = \sqrt{\frac{2 \times (35.00) \times (2{,}000)}{(70.00) \times (0.20)} \times \frac{(10{,}000)}{(10{,}000) - (2{,}000)}}$$
$$= \sqrt{(12{,}500)} = 111.8$$

Product Number	Annual Demand (D)	Cost of Placing an Order (A)	Item Price (V)	Carrying Rate (R)	Annual Production (P)	EOQ (Q)
QRSTUV	10,000	$75.00	$50.00	15%	20,000	632.46

$$Q = \sqrt{\frac{2 \times A \times D}{V \times R} \times \frac{P}{P - D}} = \sqrt{\frac{2 \times (75.00) \times (10{,}000)}{(50.00) \times (0.15)} \times \frac{(20{,}000)}{(20{,}000) - (10{,}000)}}$$
$$= \sqrt{(400{,}000)} = 632.46$$

Product Number	Annual Demand (D)	Cost of Placing an Order (A)	Item Price (V)	Carrying Rate (R)	Annual Production (P)	EOQ (Q)
XOYOP	11,111	$75.75	$51.13	17.5%	100,000	460

$$Q = \sqrt{\frac{2 \times A \times D}{V \times R} \times \frac{P}{P - D}} = \sqrt{\frac{2 \times (75.75) \times (11{,}111)}{(51.13) \times (0.175)} \times \frac{(100{,}000)}{(100{,}000) - (11{,}111)}}$$
$$= \sqrt{(211{,}643)} = 460$$

CHART 11.6 *(continued)* **EOQ Calculations for Production Items Using a Spreadsheet, Part C**

	A	B	C	D	E	F	G	H
1								
2	EOQ Calculations for Production Items							
3								
4	Product	Annual	Cost of	Item	Carrying	Annual	EOQ	
5	Number	Demand	Placing an	Price	Rate	Production	(Q)	
6		(D)	Order (A)	(V)	(R)	(P)		
7	AXRFT	2000	35	70	20	10000	111.8034	
8	QRSTUV	10000	75	50	15	20000	632.4555	
9	XOYOP	11111	75.75	51.13	17.5	100000	460.0467	
10								

CHART 11.6 *(concluded)* **EOQ Calculations for Production Items Using a Spreadsheet and Showing Calculations, Part D**

	A	B	C	D	E	F	G	H	I	J	K
1											
2	EOQ Calculations for Purchased Items										
3											
4	Product	Annual	Cost of	Item	Carrying	Annual	EOQ				
5	Number	Demand	Placing an	Price	Rate	Production	(Q)				
6		(D)	Order (A)	(V)	(R)	(P)					
7	AXRFT	2000	35	70	20	10000	SQRT((2×C7×B7/(D7×E7/100))×F7/(F7−B7))				
8	QRSTUV	10000	75	50	15	20000	SQRT((2×C8×B8/(D8×E8/100))×F8/(F8−B8))				
9	XOYOP	11111	75.75	51.13	17.5	100000	SQRT((2×C9×B9/(D9×E9/100))×F9/(F9−B9))				
10											

CHART 11.7 Fixed Quantity Ordering System

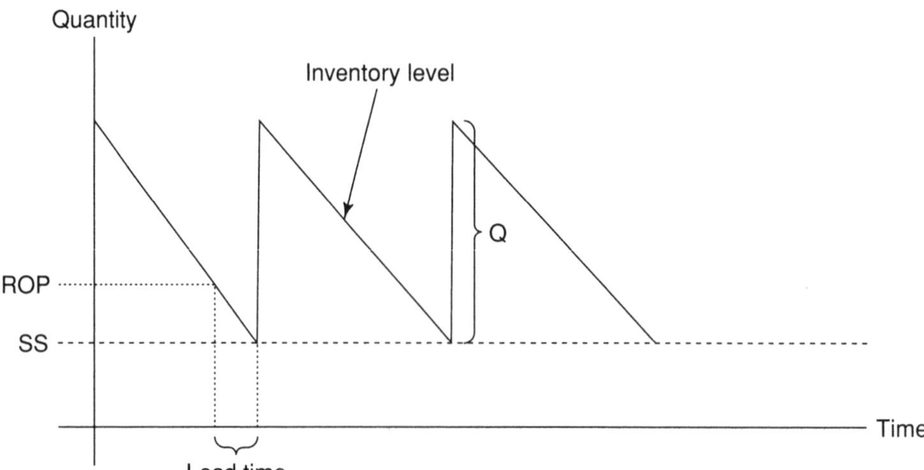

told us when to order, and EOQ told us how much to order. At this point we are able to calculate the EOQs for both the production and the purchasing models. The next calculation that is important to us is the reorder point (ROP). Chart 11.7 (redrawn from Chart 8.5) shows us graphically how the ROP works.

From Chart 11.7 we see that there is a lead time that ends at the point where the inventory level hits safety stock. Lead time is calculated backward from this point. Based on the lead time discussion in Chapter 10, if this is a purchasing lead time, the lead time would start at the time the phone call is made to place the order. It would end when the items are stored in inventory, which should correspond with the point in time when the inventory level hits safety stock. The point

CHART 11.8 ROP Calculations, Part A

$$ROP = \frac{D}{DW} \times LT$$

Product Number	Annual Demand (D)	Days Worked (DW)	Lead Time (LT)	Reorder Point (ROP)	Safety Stock (SS)

CHART 11.8 *(continued)* **ROP Calculations—Example, Part B**

$$ROP = \frac{D}{DW} \times LT$$

Product Number	Annual Demand (D)	Days Worked (DW)	Lead Time (LT)	Reorder Point (ROP)	Safety Stock (SS)
AXRFT	2,000	300	3 days	20	20

$$ROP = \frac{D}{DW} \times LT = \frac{(2{,}000)}{(300)} \times (3) = 20$$

This product is highly critical with extensive demand fluctuation. Therefore, based on Chart 11.9, SS = ROP.

Product Number	Annual Demand (D)	Days Worked (DW)	Lead Time (LT)	Reorder Point (ROP)	Safety Stock (SS)
QRSTUV	10,000	350	15 days	429	429

$$ROP = \frac{D}{DW} \times LT = \frac{(10{,}000)}{(350)} \times (15) = 429$$

This product is moderately critical with a long lead time. Therefore, based on Chart 11.9, SS = ROP.

Product Number	Annual Demand (D)	Days Worked (DW)	Lead Time (LT)	Reorder Point (ROP)	Safety Stock (SS)
XOYOP	11,111	240	8 days	370	165

$$ROP = \frac{D}{DW} \times LT = \frac{(11{,}111)}{(240)} \times (8) = 370$$

This product is moderately critical with minimal demand fluctuation. Therefore, based on Chart 11.9, SS = half of ROP.

CHART 11.8 *(continued)* **ROP Calculations Using a Spreadsheet, Part C**

	A	B	C	D	E	F	G
1							
2	ROP Calculations						
3							
4	Product	Annual	Days	Lead	Reorder	Safety	
5	Number	Demand	Worked	Time	Point	Stock	
6		(D)	(DW)	(LT)	(ROP)	(SS)	
7	AXRFT	2000	300	3	20	20	
8	QRSTUV	10000	350	15	428.5714	429	
9	XOYOP	11111	240	8	370.3667	165	
10							

CHART 11.8 *(concluded)* **ROP Calculations Using a Spreadsheet and Showing Calculations, Part D**

	A	B	C	D	E	F	G
1							
2	ROP Calculations						
3							
4	Product	Annual	Days	Lead	Reorder	Safety	
5	Number	Demand	Worked	Time	Point	Stock	
6		(D)	(DW)	(LT)	(ROP)	(SS)	
7	AXRFT	2000	300	3	B7×D7/C7	20	
8	QRSTUV	10000	350	15	B8×D8/C8	429	
9	XOYOP	11111	240	8	B9×D9/C9	165	
10							

when this lead time starts, corresponds to an inventory level, and this level of inventory is called the reorder point (ROP).

To calculate the reorder point (ROP), we need to know two things:

DU = the daily usage of parts
LT = the lead time in work days

The formula for the reorder point would then be:

$$\text{ROP} = \text{DU} \times \text{LT}$$

Daily usage (DU) is calculated by looking at the total demand for the year (D) and dividing it by the number of working days in the year (DW). Then the formula for reorder point becomes:

$$\text{ROP} = \text{DU} \times \text{LT} = \frac{\text{D}}{\text{DW}} \times \text{LT}$$

If safety stock exists, then it may be necessary to add safety stock to calculate the total inventory level of the ROP (see the process for calculating total ROP in Chapter 9; also see Chart 9.8). The calculation of ROP is independent of EOQ; therefore, the calculation for ROP is the same regardless of whether you are using the purchasing or the production model. The worksheet for calculating ROP can be found in Chart 11.8, Part A. (*Note:* Ignore the safety stock calculation for now. It will be explained later in this chapter.)

Once again, an example of how to make the calculations of Chart 11.8, Part A, is given in Part B. Chart 11.8, Part C, is the spreadsheet version of Part A and Part D has the formulas that were used for Part C.

Safety Stock

At this point we have all the basic information we need to run an EOQ production planning system. We monitor our perpetual inventory system and we order "Q" parts every time our inventory level reaches the "ROP" level (see the section in Chapter 9 on inventory ledger cards). However, we have one additional concern: What is an appropriate level of safety stock, considering that the best inventory is no inventory? If the product that we are calculating safety stock for is not critical to production, and if a shortage will not seriously disrupt our production process, then the best safety stock is no safety stock. Inventory is just an inefficient way of tying up money.

There are a lot of sophisticated statistical ways of calculating safety stock. We will avoid these and give you some simple rules of thumb:

1. As already stated, if the item is not critical to production, or if the item can quickly be replaced (in a matter of hours), and running out of the item will not seriously hamper production, then the safety stock should be 0.

CHART 11.9 Safety Stock Planning Chart

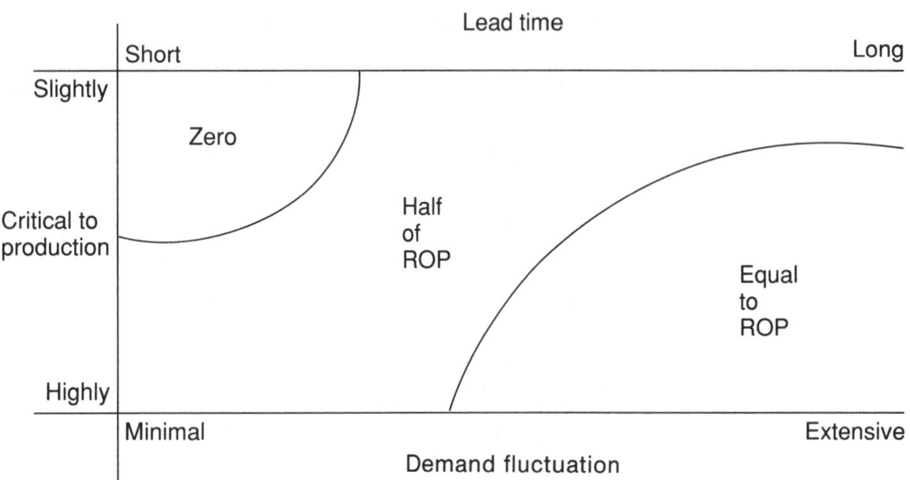

2. If the item is critical to the production process, then we need to determine how critical it is. The more critical it is, the more safety stock we want.
3. If the item is critical to production, we also need to look at the lead time of the product. The longer the lead time, the higher the level of safety stock we should have.

Chart 11.9 is a planning chart for safety stock. Do not consider this chart to be the last word on what your safety stock level should be. If you find a safety stock level to be inadequate because of the demand fluctuations or poor supplier reliability, increase the safety stock. If, however, you find that you rarely dip into the safety stock, and that when you do it is only minor, reduce the safety stock level. Safety stock should be monitored to keep it at a minimum. The inventory status report of Chart 9.15 will help you monitor your safety stock level.

Looking at Chart 11.9, we see that the reorder point is our determinant of how much we should have in safety stock. The idea is that if the day came when the order was due, and it didn't arrive, we would have enough inventory for another full order to be placed. It is possible that on occasions you may want even more inventory, perhaps two times ROP. These situations, however, should be the exceptions rather than the rule. In most cases we should have a safety stock somewhere around half of the reorder point level.

Take a quick look back at Chart 9.8 to the inventory ledger card. If our ROP was 50, and we decide to keep half the ROP in safety stock, then the total ROP should be 75 (50 + 50/2). Then, every time the inventory level reached 75 we would place an order for EOQ parts. Chart 11.8, Part A, allows for the calculation of safety stock next to the ROP calculation.

Fixed Time Ordering Systems

We need to consider one additional twist to EOQ planning. If, for example, you do not have a perpetual inventory system, you can still use EOQ inventory planning. This type of system is called a *fixed period ordering system*. Chart 11.10 (taken from Chart 8.6) shows how a fixed-period ordering system would look graphically. The key elements in this system are time (T) and the maximum level of inventory (M). The idea is that if you don't have a perpetual inventory system that would track inventory level, you would track time instead. Every "T" days you would go out into inventory and count how many parts you have of a certain product. Then you would order the difference between "M" and the current inventory balance.

The calculations for a fixed period ordering system are the same as for the EOQ of a fixed quantity ordering system. The only important consideration is that the time period between orders (T) must equal the size of an order (Q) over the total demand for the year (D). In other words, what portion of a year does it take to use up "Q" parts? The equation would be:

$$T = \frac{Q}{D}$$

If we substitute for "Q" in the total cost equation we would end up with:

$$TC = (SSC + PC + QC) + \left(\frac{A}{T}\right) + \left(V \times R\,\frac{D \times T}{2}\right)$$

Again, we drop the fixed cost components and set the carrying cost (CC) equal to the ordering cost (OC). Then solving for "T" we get:

$$T = \sqrt{\frac{2 \times A}{D \times V \times R}}$$

The "M" level for the purchasing model would be:

$$M = SS + (T \times D)$$

CHART 11.10 Fixed Period Ordering System

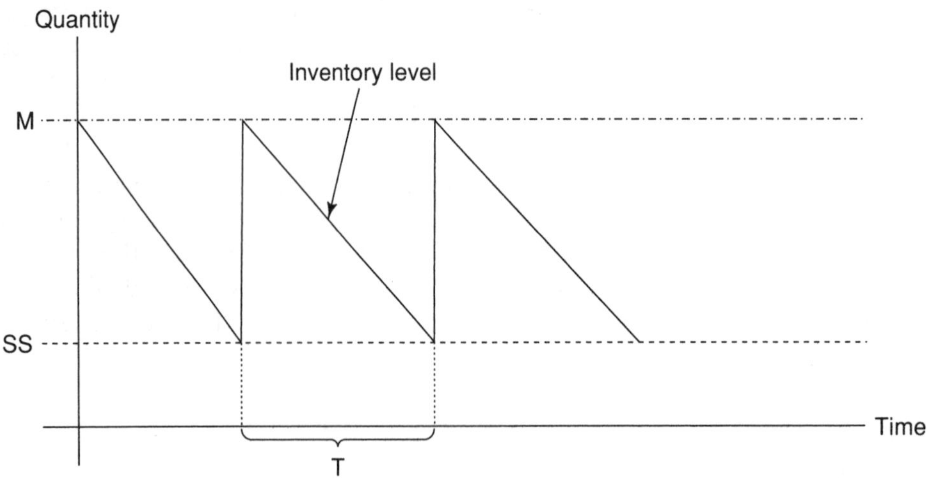

The input document for the fixed time period purchasing model is shown in Chart 11.11, Part A.

For the production model, using the fixed time period model would give us the following "T":

$$T = \sqrt{\frac{2 \times A}{D \times V \times R} \times \frac{P}{P - D}}$$

The "M" level for the production model would be:

$$M = SS + (T \times D) \times \left(1 - \frac{D}{P}\right)$$

The input document for the fixed time period production model is shown in Chart 11.11, Part E.

Chart 11.11, Part B, is an example of how to use Part A, including an example of how the calculations are made. Chart 11.11, Part C, demonstrates what a spreadsheet version of Part A would look like using the example of Part B. Chart 11.11, Part D, shows the formulas that went into Part C.

Chart 11.11, Part F, is an example of the use and calculations of Chart 11.11, Part E. Part G of Chart 11.11 is an example of the spreadsheet version of Part E using the data of Part F. Chart 11.11, Part H, shows the formulas used in Part G.

Note that the "T" value is given in terms of years. A "T" value in terms of working days is much more practical. To obtain this value, multiply the number of days worked (DW) in the year times the "T" value. This can be done using Chart 11.12, Parts A and E, the same chart that is used to calculate the "M" values.

Times As Days = (T × DW)

Chart 11.12, Part B, is an example of how to use Part A. Chart 11.12, Part C, is the spreadsheet version of how to process Part A using

CHART 11.11 Fixed-Time-Period Calculations for Purchased Items, Part A

$$T = \sqrt{\frac{2 \times A}{D \times V \times R}}$$

Product Number	Annual Demand (D)	Cost of Placing an Order (A)	Item Price (V)	Carrying Rate (R)	Time Period (T)

CHART 11.11 *(continued)* **Fixed-Time-Period Calculations for Purchased Items—Example, Part B**

$$T = \sqrt{\frac{2 \times A}{D \times V \times R}}$$

Product Number	Annual Demand (D)	Cost of Placing an Order (A)	Item Price (V)	Carrying Rate (R)	Time Period (T)
AXRFT	2,000	$35.00	$70.00	20%	0.05

$$T = \sqrt{\frac{2 \times A}{D \times V \times R}} = \sqrt{\frac{2 \times (35.00)}{(2{,}000) \times (70.00) \times (0.20)}} = \sqrt{0.0025} = 0.05$$

Product Number	Annual Demand (D)	Cost of Placing an Order (A)	Item Price (V)	Carrying Rate (R)	Time Period (T)
QRSTUV	10,000	$75.00	$50.00	15%	0.04472

$$T = \sqrt{\frac{2 \times A}{D \times V \times R}} = \sqrt{\frac{2 \times (75.00)}{(10{,}000) \times (50.00) \times (0.15)}} = \sqrt{0.002} = 0.04472$$

Product Number	Annual Demand (D)	Cost of Placing an Order (A)	Item Price (V)	Carrying Rate (R)	Time Period (T)
XOYOP	11,111	$75.75	$51.13	17.5%	0.03904

$$T = \sqrt{\frac{2 \times A}{D \times V \times R}} = \sqrt{\frac{2 \times (75.75)}{(11{,}111) \times (51.13) \times (0.175)}} = \sqrt{0.00155} = 0.03904$$

CHART 11.11 *(continued)* **Fixed-Time-Period Calculations for Purchased Items Using a Spreadsheet, Part C**

	A	B	C	D	E	F	G
1							
2	Fixed-Time-Period Calculations for Purchased Items						
3							
4	Product	Annual	Cost of	Item	Carrying	Time	
5	Number	Demand	Placing an	Price	Rate	Period	
6		(D)	Order (A)	(V)	(R)	(T)	
7	AXRFT	2000	35	70	20	.05	
8	QRSTUV	10000	75	50	15	.0447214	
9	XOYOP	11111	75.75	51.13	17.5	.0390367	
10							

CHART 11.11 *(continued)* **Fixed-Time-Period Calculations for Purchased Items Using a Spreadsheet and Showing Calculations, Part D**

	A	B	C	D	E	F	G	H
1								
2	Fixed-Time-Period Calculations for Purchased Items							
3								
4	Product	Annual	Cost of	Item	Carrying	Time		
5	Number	Demand	Placing an	Price	Rate	Period		
6		(D)	Order (A)	(V)	(R)	(T)		
7	AXRFT	2000	35	70	20	SQRT(2×C7/(B7×D7×E7/100))		
8	QRSTUV	10000	75	50	15	SQRT(2×C8/(B8×D8×E8/100))		
9	XOYOP	11111	75.75	51.13	17.5	SQRT(2×C9/(B9×D9×E9/100))		
10								

CHART 11.11 *(continued)* **Fixed-Time-Period Calculations for Production Items, Part E**

$$T = \sqrt{\frac{2 \times A}{D \times V \times R} \times \frac{P}{P - D}}$$

Product Number	Annual Demand (D)	Cost of Placing an Order (A)	Item Price (V)	Carrying Rate (R)	Annual Production (P)	Time Period (T)

CHART 11.11 *(continued)* **Fixed-Time-Period Calculations for Production Items—Example, Part F**

$$T = \sqrt{\frac{2 \times A}{D \times V \times R} \times \frac{P}{P - D}}$$

Product Number	Annual Demand (D)	Cost of Placing an Order (A)	Item Price (V)	Carrying Rate (R)	Annual Production (P)	Time Period (T)
AXRFT	2,000	$35.00	$70.00	20%	10,000	0.0559

$$T = \sqrt{\frac{2 \times A}{D \times V \times R} \times \frac{P}{(P - D)}} = \sqrt{\frac{2 \times (35.00)}{(2{,}000) \times (70.00) \times (0.20)} \times \frac{(10{,}000)}{(10{,}000) - (2{,}000)}}$$
$$= \sqrt{0.003125} = 0.0559$$

Product Number	Annual Demand (D)	Cost of Placing an Order (A)	Item Price (V)	Carrying Rate (R)	Annual Production (P)	Time Period (T)
QRSTUV	10,000	$75.00	$50.00	15%	20,000	0.06325

$$T = \sqrt{\frac{2 \times A}{D \times V \times R} \times \frac{P}{(P - D)}}$$
$$= \sqrt{\frac{2 \times (75.00)}{(10{,}000) \times (50.00) \times (0.15)} \times \frac{(20{,}000)}{(20{,}000) - (10{,}000)}} = \sqrt{0.004} = 0.06325$$

Product Number	Annual Demand (D)	Cost of Placing an Order (A)	Item Price (V)	Carrying Rate (R)	Annual Production (P)	Time Period (T)
XOYOP	11,111	$75.75	$51.13	17.5%	100,000	0.0414

$$T = \sqrt{\frac{2 \times A}{D \times V \times R} \times \frac{P}{(P - D)}}$$
$$= \sqrt{\frac{2 \times (75.75)}{(11{,}111) \times (51.13) \times (0.175)} \times \frac{(100{,}000)}{(100{,}000) - (11{,}111)}} = \sqrt{0.001714} = 0.0414$$

(continued)

CHART 11.11 *(continued)* **Fixed-Time-Period Calculations for Production Items Using a Spreadsheet, Part G**

	A	B	C	D	E	F	G	H
1								
2	Fixed-Time-Period Calculations for Production Items							
3								
4	Product	Annual	Cost of	Item	Carrying	Annual	Time	
5	Number	Demand	Placing an	Price	Rate	Produc.	Period	
6		(D)	Order (A)	(V)	(R)	(P)	(T)	
7	AXRFT	2000	35	70	20	10000	.0559017	
8	QRSTUV	10000	75	50	15	20000	.0632456	
9	XOYOP	11111	75.75	51.13	17.5	100000	.0414046	
10								

CHART 11.11 *(concluded)* **Fixed-Time-Period Calculations for Production Items Using a Spreadsheet and Showing Calculations, Part H**

	A	B	C	D	E	F	G	H	I	J	K
1											
2	Fixed-Time-Period Calculations for Production Items										
3											
4	Product	Annual	Cost of	Item	Carrying	Annual	Time				
5	Number	Demand	Placing an	Price	Rate	Produc.	Period				
6		(D)	Order (A)	(V)	(R)	(P)	(T)				
7	AXRFT	2000	35	70	20	10000	SQRT((2×C7/(B7×D7×E7/100))×F7/(F7−B7))				
8	QRSTUV	10000	75	50	15	20000	SQRT((2×C8/(B8×D8×E8/100))×F8/(F8−B8))				
9	XOYOP	11111	75.75	51.13	17.5	100000	SQRT((2×C9/(B9×D9×E9/100))×F9/(F9−B9))				
10											

CHART 11.12 Maximum Inventory Level Calculations for Purchased Items, Part A

M = SS + (T × D)
Time as Days = (T × DW)

Product Number	Safety Stock (SS)	Annual Demand (D)	Annual Time Period (T)	Days Worked (DW)	Maximum Inventory (M)	Time as Days

CHART 11.12 *(continued)* **Maximum Inventory Level Calculations for Purchased Items—Example, Part B**

M = SS + (T × D)
Time as Days = (T × DW)

Product Number	Safety Stock (SS)	Annual Demand (D)	Annual Time Period (T)	Days Worked (DW)	Maximum Inventory (M)	Time as Days
AXRFT	20	2,000	0.05	300	120	15
M = SS + (T × D) = 20 + (0.05 × 2,000) = 120 Time as Days = (T × DW) = (0.05 × 300) = 15 Days						
QRSTUV	429	10,000	0.04472	350	876	15.7
M = SS + (T × D) = 429 + (0.04472 × 10,000) = 876 Time as Days = (T × DW) = (0.04472 × 350) = 15.7 Days						
XOYOP	165	11,111	0.03904	240	599	9.4
M = SS + (T × D) = 165 + (0.03904 × 11,111) = 599 Time as Days = (T × DW) = (0.03904 × 240) = 9.4 Days						

CHART 11.12 *(continued)* **Maximum Inventory Level Calculations for Purchased Items Using a Spreadsheet, Part C**

	A	B	C	D	E	F	G	H
1								
2	Maximum Inventory Level Calculations for Purchased Items							
3								
4	Product	Safety	Annual	Annual	Days	Maximum	Time	
5	Number	Stock	Demand	Time (T)	Worked	Inventory	As	
6		(SS)	(D)	Period	(DW)	(M)	Days	
7	AXRFT	20	2000	.05	300	120	15	
8	QRSTUV	429	10000	.04472	350	876.2	15.652	
9	XOYOP	165	11111	.03904	240	598.7734	9.3696	
10								

CHART 11.12 *(continued)* **Maximum Inventory Level Calculations for Purchased Items Using a Spreadsheet and Showing Calculations, Part D**

	A	B	C	D	E	F	G
1							
2	Maximum Inventory Level Calculations for Purchased Items						
3							
4	Product	Safety	Annual	Annual	Days	Maximum	Time
5	Number	Stock	Demand	Time (T)	Worked	Inventory	As
6		(SS)	(D)	Period	(DW)	(M)	Days
7	AXRFT	20	2000	.05	300	B7+C7×D7	D7×E7
8	QRSTUV	429	10000	.04472	350	B8+C8×D8	D8×E8
9	XOYOP	165	11111	.03904	240	B9+C9×D9	D9×E9
10							

(continued)

CHART 11.12 *(continued)* **Maximum Inventory Level Calculations for Production Items, Part E**

$$M = SS + (T \times D) \times \left(1 - \frac{D}{P}\right)$$

Time as Days = (T × DW)

Product Number	Safety Stock (SS)	Annual Demand (D)	Annual Time Period (T)	Days Worked (DW)	Annual Prod. (P)	Maximum Inventory (M)	Time as Days

CHART 11.12 *(continued)* **Example of Maximum Inventory Level Calculations for Production Items—Example, Part F**

$$M = SS + (T \times D) \times \left(1 - \frac{D}{P}\right)$$

Time as Days = (T × DW)

Product Number	Safety Stock (SS)	Annual Demand (D)	Annual Time Period (T)	Days Worked (DW)	Annual Prod. (P)	Maximum Inventory (M)	Time as Days
AXRFT	20	2,000	0.0559	300	10,000	109.44	16.8

$$M = SS + (T \times D) \times \left(1 - \frac{D}{P}\right) = 20 + (0.0559 \times 2{,}000) \times \left[1 - \frac{(2{,}000)}{(10{,}000)}\right] = 109.4$$

Time as Days = (T × DW) = (0.0559 × 300) = 16.8 Days

Product Number	Safety Stock (SS)	Annual Demand (D)	Annual Time Period (T)	Days Worked (DW)	Annual Prod. (P)	Maximum Inventory (M)	Time as Days
QRSTUV	429	10,000	0.06325	350	20,000	745	22

$$M = SS + (T \times D) \times \left(1 - \frac{D}{P}\right) = 429 + (0.06325 \times 10{,}000) \times \left[1 - \frac{(10{,}000)}{(20{,}000)}\right] = 745$$

Time as Days = (T × DW) = (0.06325 × 350) = 22 Days

Product Number	Safety Stock (SS)	Annual Demand (D)	Annual Time Period (T)	Days Worked (DW)	Annual Prod. (P)	Maximum Inventory (M)	Time as Days
XOYOP	165	11,111	0.0414	240	100,000	574	10

$$M = SS + (T \times D) \times \left(1 - \frac{D}{P}\right) = 165 + (0.0414 \times 11{,}111) \times \left[1 - \frac{(11{,}111)}{(100{,}000)}\right] = 574$$

Time as Days = (T × DW) = (0.0414 × 240) = 10 Days

CHART 11.12 *(continued)* **Maximum Inventory Level Calculations for Production Items Using a Spreadsheet, Part G**

	A	B	C	D	E	F	G	H
1								
2	Maximum Inventory Level Calculations for Purchased Items							
3								
4	Product	Safety	Annual	Annual	Days	Annual	Maximum	Time
5	Number	Stock	Demand	Time	Worked	Produc.	Inventory	as
6		(SS)	(D)	Period (T)	(DW)	(P)	(M)	Days
7	AXRFT	20	2000	.0559	300	10000	109.44	16.77
8	QRSTUV	429	10000	.06325	350	20000	745.25	22.1375
9	XOYOP	165	11111	.0414	240	100000	573.8853	9.936
10								

CHART 11.12 *(concluded)* **Maximum Inventory Level Calculations for Production Items Using a Spreadsheet and Showing Calculations, Part H**

	A	B	C	D	E	F	G	H
1								
2	Maximum Inventory Level Calculations for Production Items							
3								
4	Product	Safety	Annual	Annual	Days	Annual	Maximum	Time
5	Number	Stock	Demand	Time	Worked	Produc.	Inventory	as
6		(SS)	(D)	Period (T)	(DW)	(P)	(M)	Days
7	AXRFT	20	2000	.0559	300	10000	B7+C7×D7×(1−C7/F7)	D7×E7
8	QRSTUV	429	10000	.06325	350	20000	B8+C8×D8×(1−C8/F8)	D8×E8
9	XOYOP	165	11111	.0414	240	100000	B9+C9×D9×(1−C9/F9)	D7×E9
10								

the data of Part B. Chart 11.12, Part D, shows the formulas of Part C. Similarly, Part F of Chart 11.12 is an example of how to use Part E, and Part G is the spreadsheet version of Part E using the data of part F. Last of all, Chart 11.12, Part H, shows the formulas of Part G.

A fixed period ordering system is much riskier than a fixed quantity ordering system because you are not monitoring inventory balance. A sudden surge in demand may leave you out of inventory. But a fixed period ordering system is still better than no system. Then when you get the perpetual inventory system installed, switch to a fixed quantity ordering system.

Two-Bin System

Many parts used in the production process are just not worth a tight control system. Things such as washers, nuts, bolts, spacers, paper, etc., do not need an EOQ level of control. For these items we use a two-bin control system, as explained in Chapters 8 and 9. We would receive these items into the stockroom and route them through the stockroom just like all other parts so that we can keep control of them. In this way, we could record the receipt of these items into inventory. We would immediately reissue most of these items back out to the factory floor.

We would only keep enough of them in inventory so that when someone comes to us and says that they have run out of the part, we can issue this small batch out to the factory floor and place an appropriate production or purchase order for more parts. The amount we keep in the stockroom is the reorder point (ROP) plus the safety stock (SS) (which equals total ROP) quantity. The quantity that is kept in the stockroom is the second bin of the two-bin system.

Use and Abuse of an EOQ System

I want to remind you once again of the appropriate use and abuse of an EOQ system. An EOQ system assumes that demand is fixed and constant. Therefore, if you have sporadic and intermittent demand, you need something better, such as MRP (see the next chapter). Also, the value calculated for EOQ isn't any better than the data used to calculate the numbers. Poor estimates of the variables, such as "D," "A," "V," or "R," lead to resulting calculations that are worthless. Follow the procedures for calculating these numbers very carefully.

The Flow of It All

As a final step, let's tie it all together. Here is how EOQ production planning works. We start with the primary input into production planning, the master production schedule, which tells us what the total demand of the end items is. From this we can do one of two things:

1. **MPS–EOQ:** We can plan out production of the end items based entirely on the master production schedule. This production load takes advantage of the efficiencies that we calculated in the aggregate production scheduling process. To do this, we follow the master production schedule exactly.
2. **EOQ–End Item Planning:** We can average out the production requirements for each end item over the entire year and schedule the end items based on an EOQ–ROP system.

Let me explain each process.

MPS–EOQ

The first process has us start with the master production schedule for our end items. These data are displayed in Chart 11.13. If this process is to function, we would order the specific number of end items needed for each type of production. For example, in the first month we would place the production orders listed in Chart 11.14.

The perpetual inventory system is still used to track inventory levels for all items including finished goods. But the finished goods items do not have an ROP, EOQ, safety stock, or total ROP. In the case of finished goods, production orders are not generated by the stockroom using the perpetual inventory system, although they still are in the case of work-in-process items.

For work-in-process items and raw material items, we calculate and use the EOQ and ROP process discussed in this chapter. Then, as the

CHART 11.13 Master Production Schedule

		Mountain Bikes					
Month	Family	MB–E	MB–E–SP	MB–HD	MB–HD–SP	MB–SLW	MB–SLW–SP
1	100	45	5	27	6	14	3
2	50	23	3	13	3	7	1
3	50	22	2	14	3	7	2
4	100	45	5	27	6	14	3
5	100	45	5	27	6	14	3
6	150	67	8	41	9	21	4
7	200	90	10	54	13	28	5
8	150	68	7	40	10	21	4
9	50	23	2	13	3	7	2
10	50	22	3	14	3	7	1
11	75	34	4	20	5	10	2
12	250	113	12	68	16	35	6
Total	1,325	597	66	358	83	185	36

		Ten-speed Bikes			
Month	Family	TS–M	TS–M–SP	TS–W	TS–W–SP
1	200	100	13	80	7
2	50	25	3	20	2
3	50	25	3	20	2
4	100	50	6	40	4
5	200	100	13	80	7
6	200	100	12	80	8
7	200	100	13	80	7
8	200	100	12	80	8
9	100	50	6	40	4
10	50	25	3	20	2
11	230	115	15	92	8
12	120	60	8	48	4
Total	1,700	850	107	680	63

		Tricycles	
Month	Family	TRI	TRI–SP
1	150	143	7
2	50	47	3
3	75	71	4
4	134	127	7
5	200	190	10
6	133	126	7
7	0	0	0
8	133	126	7
9	50	48	2
10	207	197	10
11	193	183	10
12	0	0	0
Total	1,325	1,258	67

CHART 11.14 First Month's Production Orders Based on the Master Production Schedule

MB–E	45
MB–E–SP	5
MB–HD	27
MB–HD–SP	6
MB–SLW	14
MB–SLW–SP	3
TS–M	100
TS–M–SP	13
TS–W	80
TS–W–SP	7
TRI	143
TRI–SP	7

production process for the finished goods generates parts issues, it uses up work-in-process and raw materials items. As the inventory levels fall below ROP in the work-in-process and raw materials items, the EOQ ordering process will kick in and orders will be placed. It is just the finished goods that are handled differently in this process.

EOQ–End Item Planning

The second finished goods scheduling system suggests that we average the production requirements for each end item over the entire year and schedule the end items based on an EOQ-ROP system. To do this, we would look at the annual requirement of each product and calculate the EOQ and ROP for each of these items based on their annual demand. From Chart 11.13 we can see the total annual demand for each item. Using Chart 11.6, Part A, we would calculate the EOQ for each of these items. Then using Chart 11.8, Part A, we would calculate the ROP for each item. We may or may not want to have a safety stock for each of these items based on Chart 11.9. The last field that we need to develop is the anticipation inventory. Chart 11.15 shows the averaged production load for each end item by month. Chart 11.15 also shows what the demand (forecast) is for each month. The cumulative difference between the anticipated work load and the forecast is the anticipation inventory level. Looking at mountain bikes, the anticipation inventory for month 1 is 110 minus 100 equals 10. For the second month it starts with the 10 from the previous month and adds the "month 2" production of 110 to it. Then it subtracts the "month 2" forecast of 50 from it giving a net of 70 ($10 + 110 - 50 = 70$). A worksheet for calculating anticipation inventory can be found in Chart 11.16.

At this point we need to break down the production loads for each product family into specific product lines. To do this we use the same percentages we used in the planning bill of materials. Chart 11.17 is the partial production load for the EOQ production planning method using EOQ planning for the end items (not all months are calculated because it isn't necessary to demonstrate the process). Chart 11.17 also shows the anticipation inventory level calculation by product. This is

CHART 11.15 Anticipation Inventory Level for EOQ Production Planning
(Taken from Chart 11.13)

Mountain Bikes

Month	Family Production	Forecast	Anticipation Inventory
1	110	100	10
2	110	50	70
3	110	50	130
4	110	100	140
5	111	100	151
6	111	150	112
7	111	200	23
8	111	150	−16
9	110	50	44
10	110	50	104
11	110	75	139
12	111	250	0
Total	1,325		

Ten-speed Bikes

Month	Family Production	Forecast	Anticipation Inventory
1	142	200	−58
2	141	50	33
3	142	50	125
4	141	100	166
5	142	200	108
6	142	200	50
7	142	200	− 8
8	142	200	−66
9	142	100	−24
10	141	50	67
11	142	50	159
12	141	300	0
Total	1,700		

Tricycles

Month	Family Production	Forecast	Anticipation Inventory
1	111	150	−39
2	110	50	21
3	110	75	56
4	110	100	66
5	111	100	77
6	111	100	88
7	110	150	48
8	110	150	8
9	110	50	68
10	110	50	128
11	111	50	189
12	111	300	0
Total	1,325		

CHART 11.16 Anticipation Inventory Level Worksheet

Product Line ______________________ Date ____/____/____

Month	Family Production Level	Forecast	Difference	Anticipation Inventory Level

necessary in controlling the appropriate total reorder point inventory levels.

At this point we are ready to plan production based on EOQ production planning of the end products. This is the procedure that we would use. At every month end, we would complete an inventory status report, at which time we would also update our inventory ledger cards (this procedure is outlined for you in Chapter 9). For finished goods items, the inventory ledger card information needs to be updated each month. The EOQ, safety stock, and ROP would stay the same, but the anticipation inventory level would change, causing the calculation for the total ROP to change. The new total ROP may fall below the balance and trigger a production requisition (this would only happen if on the old card we were not yet below the total ROP level).

A word of caution on negative anticipation inventories is necessary. A negative anticipation inventory may cause a negative total ROP to be lower than the ROP. In this case, use the ROP value for the total ROP. In other words, never let the total ROP be lower than the ROP.

The steps for updating the finished goods inventory ledger card (Chart 9.8) are listed in Chart 11.18.

With an updated inventory ledger card for finished goods, we simply follow the EOQ–ROP planning procedure for all items in inventory. This procedure is simply that if the inventory balance falls below the reorder point, place an order for the economic order quantity (EOQ or Q) parts. This procedure is followed for all parts, including the finished goods items. Therefore, all production and purchase orders are generated out of the inventory stores area.

CHART 11.17 Monthly EOQ Production Plan Using EOQ Planning for End Items
(Taken from Chart 11.8, Part D)

		Mountain Bikes					
Month	Family	MB–E	MB–E–SP	MB–HD	MB–HD–SP	MB–SLW	MB–SLW–SP
		45%	5%	27%	6.3%	14%	2.7%
1	110	49	6	30	7	15	3
5	111	50	6	30	7	15	3

(Use a similar process for each month, making sure the total for each month adds up to the family total.)

		Mountain Bikes—Anticipation Inventories					
Month	Family	MB–E	MB–E–SP	MB–HD	MB–HD–SP	MB–SLW	MB–SLW–SP
		45%	5%	27%	6,3%	14%	2.7%
1	10	4	1	3	1	1	0
2	70	31	4	19	4	10	2
3	130	59	6	35	8	18	4

(Use a similar process for each month, making sure the total for each month adds up to the family total.)

		Ten-speed Bikes			
Month	Family	TS–M	TS–M–SP	TS–W	TS–W–SP
		50%	6.3%	40%	3.7%
1	142	71	9	57	5
2	141	70	9	57	5

		Ten-speed Bikes—Anticipation Inventories			
Month	Family	TS–M	TS–M–SP	TS–W	TS–W–SP
		50%	6.3%	40%	3.7%
1	−58	−29	−4	−23	−2
2	33	17	2	13	1
3	125	63	8	50	4

		Tricycles	
Month	Family	TRI	TRI–SP
		95%	5%
1	111	105	6
2	110	105	5

		Tricycles—Anticipation Inventory	
Month	Family	TRI	TRI–SP
		95%	5%
1	−39	−37	−2
2	21	20	1
3	56	53	3

CHART 11.18 Steps for Updating the Finished Goods Inventory Ledger Cards When Using EOQ Planning for End Items

1. Pull the old ledger card.
2. Post the month's activity to the inventory status report.
3. Create a new ledger card:
   Transfer the balance forward.
   Transfer the heading information except for the anticipation inventory and the Total ROP values.
4. Post the anticipation inventory value for the upcoming month.
5. Calculate the Total ROP:

   Total ROP = ROP + Safety Stock + Anticipation Inventory

   If Total ROP is less than ROP, use the ROP value.
6. Check if the balance is less than the Total ROP this month. If it is, check the following: If the balance at the end of last month was greater than the Total ROP of last month, place a production order for EOQ parts. The function of the Total ROP adjustments and the anticipation inventory calculation is to control inventory buildups and avoid inventory shortages.

CHART 11.19 Comparing the MPS–EOQ System with the EOQ–End Items System

Method 1—MPS–EOQ
- Advantages
  - Build products to match demand
  - Minimize excess finished goods inventory by taking advantage of the aggregate production scheduling efficiencies
- Disadvantages
  - Unleveled production load
  - Finished goods are not scheduled in economic lot sizes

Method 2—EOQ–End Item Planning
- Advantages
  - Levelized production load
- Disadvantages
  - Demand shortages (negative anticipation inventory)
  - Inventory buildup and storage in finished goods

Comparing the MPS–EOQ and EOQ–End Item Systems

The two EOQ production planning systems differ only in the manner in which end items are scheduled. All other items (work-in-process and raw materials) are handled the same way in both systems. A comparison between the two systems is made in Chart 11.19.

Summary

This is exciting. We have made it through our first production planning system and we still haven't given up! But that's one of the advantages of the EOQ system: It is simple to operate and easy to use. The next system, MRP, is a lot better for scheduling sporadic demand. However, it is a lot more complicated to calculate. But if you want to reduce your inventory levels and improve the accuracy of your production scheduling, MRP is for you. The next few chapters discuss this second most popular production planning system, material requirements planning.

Chapter

12 Material Requirements Planning

MRP versus EOQ

The biggest difference between material requirements planning (MRP) and economic order quantity (EOQ) production planning is that MRP looks at the three primary resources (materials, labor, and machinery) when it plans production, whereas EOQ looks only at materials. This three-dimensional perspective makes MRP three times as complicated. However, the benefits of MRP over a straight EOQ planning process are also three times as great, primarily in the areas of inventory reduction and on-time customer delivery.

Chapter 10 has already compared the two production planning philosophies, MRP and EOQ (see Chart 10.2). This chapter gives more details on how MRP works. It starts with a review of the total information flow diagram. A look at this diagram will help us remember how MRP fits into the total picture. Chart 12.1 is redrawn from Chart 4.9. Starting at the top, the business plan defines the long-range goals and objectives of the organization. The forecast quantifies these goals in terms of sales over the next couple of years. The customer orders relieve (replace) the forecast. Eventually you would like to have all customer orders and no forecast, because the forecast is an estimate and the customer order is the real thing (a sale). The sum of the forecast and the customer orders is the total demand for resources being placed on the factory for the three M's. The rough-cut capacity (RCC) is the available

CHART 12.1 The Production Information Flow Diagram

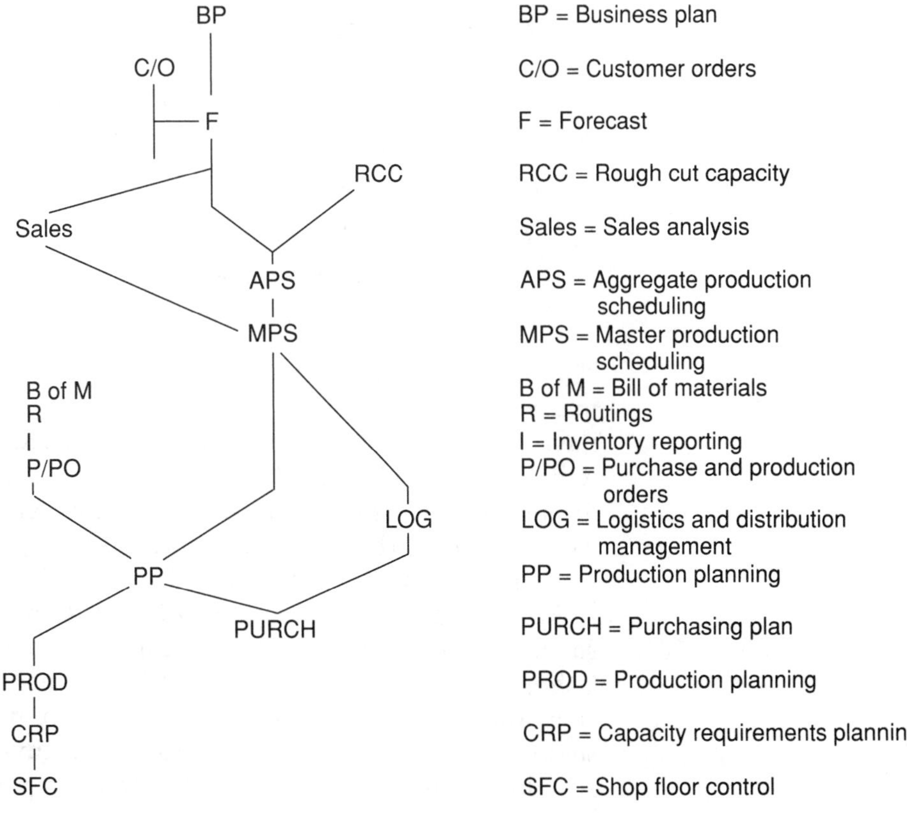

capacity for the three M's. The balancing act between the RCC and the forecast (F) plus customer orders (C/O) creates the aggregate production schedule. The planning bill of materials converts the APS into a master production schedule. At this point we are ready for a production planning system (Chapter 10).

We have already discussed the first of the two forms of production planning that will be covered in this book. We have covered economic order quantity (Chapter 11), a system that required two inputs, the MPS and the inventory reporting or perpetual inventory system (Chapters 8 and 9). The output from the EOQ production planning process included purchasing and production orders.

The second form of production planning to be discussed in this book is the material requirements planning system. Since MRP schedules all three of the resource areas, we will need additional inputs. Also because MRP plans only *what* we need, *when* we need it, we will need to know more about the specific materials and production requirements of the products that we are going to produce.

The additional inputs that we need to discuss include a bill of materials (Chapter 13). This bill of materials describes the part breakdown (material requirements) of the product to be manufactured. Another input is the routing (Chapter 14). The routings describe the production steps (labor and machinery) needed to produce the product. The last of the additional inputs is the purchase and production orders (P/PO). These P/POs are part of the feedback mechanism that reports on the performance of the shop floor (Chapter 19). The shop floor gets purchase and production orders that are generated by the MRP system, and the feedback loop reports on how the shop floor is performing on these orders. For example, are they on time, have they had a lot of breakages, etc.

We have a total of five inputs into MRP:

Master production schedule

Bill of materials (Chapter 13)

Routings (Chapter 14)

Inventory (Chapters 8 and 9)

Purchase and production orders (Chapter 19)

The next couple of chapters will help in the understanding of the bill of materials and routings. The inventory and master production schedule have already been discussed, and the purchase and production orders will be discussed as part of shop floor control. In Chapter 15 we will discuss how some of these inputs were developed. Then in Chapter 16 we will discuss the actual calculations that go into MRP planning and we will describe the outputs of the system.

The primary advantage of MRP is its ability to manage three resources. This gives us better planning and reduced inventory levels. Other advantages include its ability to schedule purchase and production orders so that they only occur when you need them and as you need them. In this way, MRP avoids excessive inventories. MRP is good for scheduling lumpy demands and expensive parts.

The primary disadvantages of MRP include its complexity, its need for highly accurate data (90+ percent accuracy), and its need for computer power to generate the schedules. We will now cover a few definitions about MRP and then we will be ready to study the bill of materials and the routings.

Definitions

Regeneration: A regeneration is the taking of all five inputs and running them through the MRP scheduler. This process occurs once a week and sets the schedules for the following week.

Net change: A net change MRP system is one that adjusts the schedules every time there is a change to one of the inputs. Although in theory this sounds exciting, it's actually a nuisance for the production floor because it is constantly changing their direction. The shop floor needs more consistency than a net change system can offer. My recommendation is that unless you have extremely high data accuracy (more than 95 percent), stick with a weekly regeneration process. Net change will give you nothing but headaches.

Independent vs. dependent demand: The items that are on the master schedule, which includes anything that we sell, such as end items or replacement parts, are considered independent demand items. The component parts that make up these independent items have schedules that are dependent on the number of independent items we sell. In other words, the number of wheels (dependent item) we buy or build is dependent on the number of bicycles (independent item) we plan to make.

How to Select MRP Software

This book demonstrates MRP with a spreadsheet and a very simplistic IBM-PC software package.[1] This is not necessarily recommended for your factory. Every factory has different needs. However, if MRP is new to you, you may want to try one of these easy methods before you purchase some package that overwhelms you with unnecessary bells and whistles. As you get ready to search for the specific MRP package that will fit your needs, go to APICS, in particular their monthly magazine, *APICS—The Performance Advantage*. They publish regular evaluations of available software solutions. Another good source is the APICS annual conference. Here you can actually see the software op-

[1] The spreadsheet I am using is "Supercalc" and the MRP planner is part of an operations package called "QS—Quant Systems" published by Prentice Hall, Englewood Cliffs, NJ. The authors are Chang and Sullivan, 1991, ISBN #0-13-747205-6.

tions available in operation at vendor booths. You can do an awful lot of software shopping in one place.[2]

As you use some of the simplistic MRP methods shown in this book, watch for features and functions that are important to you. Write down these features. Then when you shop for software, you can focus on these needs. Additionally, it is strongly recommended that you actually do a trial run of one of your schedules on the software package that you are considering. You'd be surprised how complicated a very simple process can become if the software package is an overkill for your needs. Overkill in MRP packages is wasteful. Simplicity and efficiency are much more important.

The First Three Inputs

To demonstrate the operation of a material requirements planning system, sample data are needed. For my master production schedule we will use the master production schedule of tricycles (TRI) and tricycle spare parts (TRI–SP). All the products that have master production schedules will be scheduled similarly to the way the first six months of tricycles are done, but we shouldn't get too carried away in the complexity of the example of MRP production planning. The MPS data used in this example are shown in Chart 12.2. Chart 12.2 breaks the production requirements down by week. In this example the total number of units produced in the month is equal to the sum of the production requirements for the four weeks in the month.

The second input into the MRP system is the inventory data. Inventory data come from the perpetual inventory system and represent the inventory on-hand balance of all the items in inventory. For purposes of this example, some inventory balances were generated as shown in Chart 12.3.

The third input into the MRP system is the purchase and production orders. These are actual purchase and production orders that are in process or are being routed to our inventory storage location. They are tracked by the shop floor control system (Chapter 19). They may consist of purchase orders just placed, or they may consist of purchased products that are already in our plant but have not yet been inspected and placed into inventory. Either way, they are in-process purchase orders and are a part of this third input.

If the product with an outstanding purchase/production order is a produced item, the production order quantity is the number of units that are anticipated to be completed and the date by which they should be completed. Chart 12.4 is the production and purchase order data that will be used for the MRP example.

[2] For information about the APICS magazine or APICS conferences, contact APICS at 1-800-444-2742 or write APICS, 500 W. Annandale Road, Falls Church, VA 22046, USA. There are APICS chapters all around the world. The U.S. headquarters of APICS can help you find your local APICS organization.

CHART 12.2 Master Production Scheduling Data for the MRP Example

Month/Week	Tricycles (TRI) Quantity	Tricycle Spare Parts (TRI–SP) Quantity
1/1	38	
1/2	30	7
1/3	38	
1/4	37	
2/1	13	
2/2	9	3
2/3	13	
2/4	12	
3/1	15	4
3/2	19	
3/3	19	
3/4	18	
4/1	27	7
4/2	33	
4/3	34	
4/4	33	
5/1	40	10
5/2	50	
5/3	50	
5/4	50	
6/1	26	7
6/2	33	
6/3	34	
6/4	33	

CHART 12.3 Inventory On-Hand Balance Data for the MRP Example

Product Number	Balance
TRI	121
TRI–SP	6
BBBB	45
CCCC	4
ABCD	5
DDDD	10
AABB	15
AACC	6
A4B4	200
ACAC	20
A5B5	23
A555	40
B555	7

CHART 12.4 Purchase and Production Order Data for the MRP Example

Product Number	Balance	Week of Arrival
TRI	21	1/1
TRI–SP	6	1/1
BBBB	100	1/2
CCCC	4	1/1
ABCD	5	1/3
DDDD	10	1/2
AABB	15	1/3
AACC	20	1/2
A4B4	400	1/1
ACAC	20	1/2
A5B5	23	1/3
A555	300	1/2
B555	20	1/1

There are two remaining inputs into an MRP system. Sample data for these other two inputs, bill of materials and routings, will be given to us in their respective chapters.

Summary

We are now ready to move forward with our study of the last two inputs into the MRP system. First we will look at the bill of materials, then at the routings. With a clear understanding of these inputs, we will then be ready to move forward with the calculation of a material requirements plan.

Chapter

13 Bill of Materials

Before we can make proper production planning decisions, we need to prepare our inputs appropriately. We have already covered three of these inputs in the last chapter. In this chapter we will discuss the fourth, the bill of materials.

Definitions

The bill of materials is a list of the component parts needed to make our product. This list is created by the product engineers when they design the product (see Chapter 15). For example, Chart 13.1 shows the bill of materials for a simple pen. From this chart we learn several things. But before we look at these, let's list a few definitions:

Purchased items or raw materials items are any items that do not have a structure below them. The purchased items in this structure are:

Cap
Head
Body
Cartridge
Clip
Rings
Plastic cap

Production items are products we produce in our plant. These items have a structure below them. They are:

Pen
Body assembly
Cover

Finished goods items (also known as independent demand items or forecast items) are products that are completed and ready for sale. In this structure we are not selling components like the cover, which could be both a component to the pen and an independent demand item that is sold. In this structure the finished goods item is:

Pen

Work-in-process items or subassemblies are products that we produce but are not yet ready for sale. They are:

Body assembly
Cover

End items are any items that are completed and sold. These are not components for other products. In this structure the end item is:

Pen

The bill of materials for the pen, also known as a *product structure* (in Chart 13.1), shows us where production is performed. Production occurs at several stages. First, we purchase all the necessary materials (purchased items): the cap, head, body, cartridge, clip, rings, and plastic cap. These items go through the purchasing process and are placed into

CHART 13.1 Pen Bill of Materials

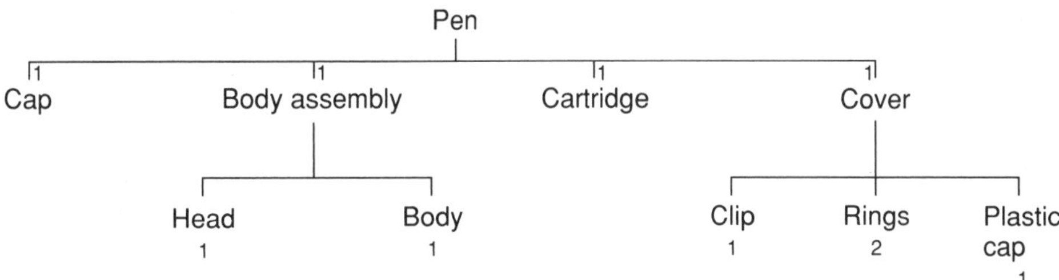

inventory. Next, we pull the head and body out of inventory and make the first subassembly called the body assembly. After production we place the completed body assembly back into inventory. Then we build the second subassembly, which is the cover. To do this, we pull one clip, one plastic cap, and two rings out of inventory. We assemble the cover. Then we place the completed cover back into inventory.

Now we are ready to do the final assembly. We go to inventory and pull one cap, one body assembly, one cartridge, and one cover out of inventory. We assemble these and return them to inventory as a finished goods item called a pen. The pen is now ready for sale.

The bill of materials is an invaluable tool for planning the materials requirements. Using Chart 13.1 we can calculate how many of each item we need to purchase and to build. This calculation can occur as soon as we know our requirements for end items. For example, if we want to make 100 pens, we would place a purchase order for each of the following in the following quantities (note that we need two rings for every cover and one cover for every pen):

Cap	100
Head	100
Body	100
Cartridge	100
Clip	100
Rings	200
Plastic cap	100

Then we would place production orders for each of the following subassemblies in the following quantities:

Body assembly	100
Cover	100

Last of all we would place a production order for our end item, the pen, for 100 units. Notice we started the production and purchasing planning process at the bottom of the bill of materials and worked our way to the top one step at a time.

At this point we are ready to look at a more complex bill of materials structure. Chart 13.2 is the structure of the tricycle (TRI) that we will be planning in our MRP planning process.

In this structure of Chart 13.2, we see the same raw material (purchased item) at several locations in the structure. For example, BBBB

CHART 13.2 Bill of Material for Tricycles

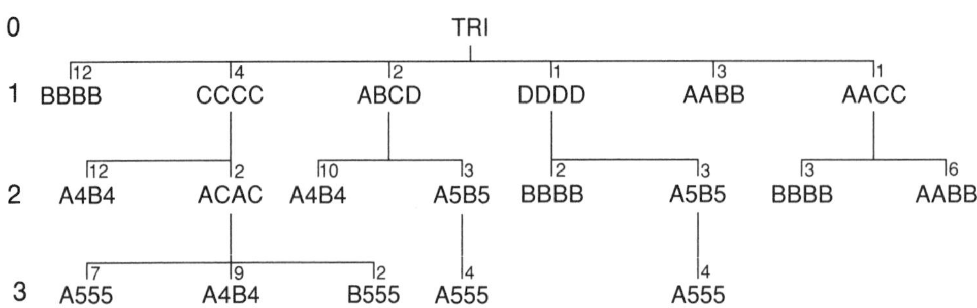

is used in three different places. It is used in the final assembly of TRI, and it is used to build subassemblies DDDD and AACC. Similarly, we see A4B4 used to build CCCC, ABCD, and ACAC.

Exploding

Exploding the tricycle bill of materials would work as follows. To determine how many BBBBs are needed to build one tricycle, the calculation would be as follows:

12 BBBBs for every TRI

2 BBBBs for every DDDD
  1 DDDD for every TRI

3 BBBBs for every AACC
  1 AACC for every TRI

We end up with:

$12 + (2 \times 1) + (3 \times 1) = 17$ BBBBs for every TRI

A slightly more complicated example would be to explode the bill of materials for A4B4. The calculation would be as follows:

10 A4B4s for every ABCD
  2 ABCDs for every TRI

12 A4B4s for every CCCC
  4 CCCCs for every TRI

9 A4B4s for every ACAC
  2 ACACs for every CCCC
    4 CCCCs for every TRI

We end up with:

$(10 \times 2) + (12 \times 4) + (9 \times 2 \times 4)$
  $= 140$ A4B4s for every TRI

To calculate how many A555s are needed in order to make 10 TRIs, the calculation would be as follows:

4 A555s for every A5B5
3 A5B5s for every ABCD
2 ABCDs for every TRI
10 TRIs
4 A555s for every A5B5
3 A5B5s for every DDDD
1 DDDD for every TRI
10 TRIs
7 A555s for every ACAC
2 ACACs for every CCCC
4 CCCCs for every TRI
10 TRIs

We end up with:

$$(4 \times 3 \times 2 \times 10) + (4 \times 3 \times 1 \times 10) + (7 \times 2 \times 4 \times 10) = 920 \text{ A4B4s for 10 TRIs}$$

Low-Level Coding

Low-level coding is important in determining a sequence in which to schedule our production parts. The numbers along the left-hand side of Chart 13.2 are the level numbers. TRI is a level 0 item. On level 1 we have BBBB, CCCC, ABCD, DDDD, AABB, and AACC, and so on. As we mentioned earlier, some of these products appear in multiple places. We need to identify a low-level code for each product. This low-level code is the lowest (physically, not numerically) place that the product appears in the product structure. For example, BBBB appears at level 1 and in two places at level 2. The low-level code for BBBB is 2. Another example would be A4B4. It appears at two places in level 2 and in one place in level 3. The low-level code for A4B4 is 3. Some other low-level code examples would be:

AABB low level code is 2

AACC low level code is 1

A555 low level code is 3

When we develop our schedules for our MRP process we will schedule all the low-level code 0's first, then all the low-level code 1's next, then the 2's, and last the 3's (see Chapter 16 for these calculations).

Indented Listing

An *indented listing* of a bill of materials is another way of looking at Chart 13.2. Chart 13.3 is the indented listing of Chart 13.2. This is the way a computer would display this bill of materials chart. All the same

CHART 13.3 Indented Bill of Materials Listing
(Taken from the data in Chart 13.2)

Levels—0	1	2	3	Quantities Per
TRI				
	BBBB			12
	CCCC			4
		A4B4		12
		ACAC		2
			A555	7
			A4B4	9
			B555	2
	ABCD			2
		A5B5		3
			A555	4
		A4B4		10
	DDDD			1
		BBBB		2
		A5B5		3
			A555	4
	AACC			1
		BBBB		3
		AABB		6
	AABB			

information appears on the indented listing of Chart 13.3 as appears on the graphical display of Chart 13.2.

"Where Used" or Pegging Report

Another valuable report that can be generated using the bill of materials information is the *"where used" or pegging report*. An example of this report can be seen in Chart 13.4. This report lists every place in which a part is used. This is valuable information if you are having trouble with a part and you need to see who will be affected by a delay in production. It also helps to define what products will be affected by an engineering change (see Chapter 15).

Chart 13.5 gives a multilevel "where used" or pegging report. With this report we can trace several levels—all the way to the end item if necessary—to see what the effects would be of any problems with this component.

Scrap and Wastage Factors

Scrap and wastage factors are something we do not like to talk about but are necessary in our calculations. The scrap factors are built into the unit requirements for a particular product. For example, if A5B5 is manufactured from a 3-inch piece of bar steel (A555), but we waste 1 inch of steel every time we cut it, then the bill of materials require-

CHART 13.4 "Where Used" or Pegging Report
(Taken from the data in Chart 13.2)

		Quantity Needed
BBBB		
	TRI	12
	DDDD	2
	AACC	3
CCCC		
	TRI	4
ABCD		
	TRI	2
DDDD		
	TRI	1
AABB		
	TRI	3
	AACC	6
AACC		
	TRI	1
A4B4		
	CCCC	12
	ABCD	10
	ACAC	9
ACAC		
	CCCC	2
A5B5		
	ABCD	3
	DDDD	3
A555		
	ACAC	7
	A5B5	4
B555		
	ACAC	2

ments for steel (A555) is 4 inches. Another example would be if we actually use 11 A4B4s in a CCCC, but on the average we break one A4B4 every time we build a CCCC, then our bill of materials should reflect a demand of 12 A4B4s for every CCCC we build because that is the actual quantity we should purchase. Additionally, when we cost out the price of TRI we need to include the scrap and wastage costs (product costing will be discussed more in Chapter 14).

Spare Parts

Tricycle Spare Parts (TRI–SP) is a second bill of materials that we need in order to complete the MRP production planning process of Chapter 16. This bill of materials is listed in Chart 13.6. It is composed of the average number of spare parts needed for bicycles already in use. All the level 1 items are sold as spare parts. In some cases we do not sell an assembly as a spare part, for example, AACC, but we do sell the parts that make up AACC, which are BBBB and AABB (see Chart 13.2).

CHART 13.5 Multilevel "Where Used" or Pegging Report
(Taken from the data in Chart 13.2)

Levels—	1	2	3	Quantity Needed
BBBB				
	TRI			12
	DDDD			2
		TRI		1
	AACC			3
		TRI		1
CCCC				
	TRI			4
ABCD				
	TRI			2
DDDD				
	TRI			1
AABB				
	TRI			3
	AACC			6
		TRI		1
AACC				
	TRI			1
A4B4				
	CCCC			12
		TRI		4
	ABCD			10
		TRI		2
	ACAC			9
		CCCC		4
			TRI	4
ACAC				
	CCCC			2
		TRI		4
A5B5				
	ABCD			3
		TRI		2
	DDDD			3
		TRI		1
A555				
	ACAC			7
		CCCC		4
			TRI	4
	A5B5			4
		ABCD		3
			TRI	2
		DDDD		3
			TRI	1
B555				
	ACAC			2
		CCCC		4
			TRI	4

CHART 13.6 Tricycles Spare Parts Bill of Materials

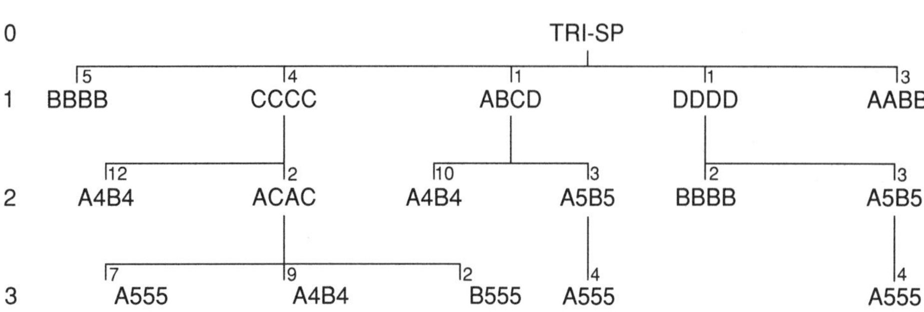

Summary

The bill of materials is a critical tool in identifying the materials components of a manufactured product. With the bill of materials we can calculate exactly how many purchased and manufactured materials we need in order to build a product. The next chapter on routings will tell us when to order these materials so that we will have them when we need them. The ultimate objective is to get the right materials, at the right time, thereby minimizing our materials inventories.

Chapter

14 Routings

Manufacturing routings list the step-by-step procedure necessary to build a product. After product engineering has completed the design of the product, process engineering determines the production procedure that will be necessary in order to build the product (see Chapter 15). There are two areas of process engineering that get involved in defining this procedure. The first is manufacturing engineering. These individuals determine which machines should be used and what tools, jigs, and dies should be used in order to manufacture the product. The second engineering group is the industrial engineers group, which determines the labor steps necessary in order to build the product. From this we see that the routings contain both the labor and the machine requirements for manufacturing.

Production Lead Time

A routing serves several purposes. One is that it is used to develop the job traveler that will travel with the production job around the factory floor (see Chapter 19 for more information about travelers). Another purpose for the routing is to calculate production lead time. By accumulating the production time at each step, we can calculate the lead time necessary to build the product. Note that the lead times are the production time needed to produce a standard batch (EOQ batch) of the product. A lot of the time spent in production is travel time, setup time, and wait time, and these numbers are calculated by the batch. The assumption is that even if the actual production batch size is significantly smaller (or larger) than the normal standard batch size, these differences will have a minor and insignificant effect when compared to the other factors that affect lead time.

Production lead time was discussed briefly in Chapter 10. Expanding slightly on this discussion, Chart 14.1 lists the elements that make up production lead time and Chart 14.2 demonstrates the calculation process for production lead time for each step in the production process.

Production Routing

Chart 14.3 is a sample production routing. The routing tells us who does the job ("Labor Code"), where the job is done ("Department"), what machine is used to do the job ("Machine"), and in what sequence the steps should be done ("Routing Step #"). It also gives us a standard in which to measure ourselves in both setup time and run time. The run time per unit is simply the total run time divided by the standard lot size. For example, the run time per unit for step 10 is 2 hours divided by 50 standard units or 2.4 minutes. From this we know that the run time for any quantity, for example, 45 units, would be 45 times the 2.4 minutes or 108 minutes (45 units × 2.4 minutes = 108 minutes =

CHART 14.1 Production Lead Time Calculation

(Not every one of these occurs during every production step.)

Production order time: The time it takes to make the order and start the production process on the floor (this entry would only occur in the first step of a routing)

Inventory picking time: The time it takes to pick the raw materials (this may not affect the production time, it may occur as a separate process; only include it if it does affect production time)

Product move time: The amount of time it takes to transfer the materials from one work station to the next (or from inventory stores to the first work station)

Wait time: The average amount of time the materials wait in front of the work station before actually being worked on

Machine setup time: The time it takes to prepare the machine for the production process

Product cycle time: The amount of time it takes to run a standard lot size (EOQ batch size) through a production run

Inspection time: The amount of time it takes to check quality

Transfer to stores: The amount of time it takes to transfer the finished product back into stores (this is only included in the last step of the production process)

CHART 14.2 Production Lead Time Calculation—Example

Production order time	2 hours	
Inventory picking time	3 hours	
Product move time	2 days	
Wait time	3 days	
Machine setup time	3 hours	
Product cycle time	2 hours	
Inspection time	2 hours	
Transfer to stores	3 hours	
Total	8 days	(assume 5 productive hours in a day)

CHART 14.3 Sample Production Routing

Product number CCCC Standard lot size 50

Routing Step #	Department	Machine	Labor Code	Setup Time	Run Time	Lead Time (total)
10	Cutting	X40	L35	2 hrs.	2 hrs.	6 hrs.
20	Grinding	RV282	L40	1 hr.	1 hr.	2 days
30	Stamping	Brilton	L35	10 min.	1 hr.	9 hrs.
40	Plating	Stall	L50	2 hrs.	3 hrs.	1 day
50	Inspection		I20		3 hrs.	2 days
					Total lead time =	8 days

1 hour and 48 minutes). This information is used for measuring the efficiency of individual employees.

Note that the total lead time does not add up to the sum of the setup time plus the run time. That is because all the other factors listed in Chart 14.1 are also included in this calculation (see Charts 14.4 and 14.5). The total lead time is the value that is used to determine the total production lead time for a product. In this example, the total lead time

CHART 14.4 Routing Development Worksheet

Date ___/___/___ Product number ________ Product name ________________ Standard batch size ________

Routing Step #	Department	Machine	Labor Code	Setup Time	Run Time (per unit)	Run Time (std. batch)	Lead Times							
							Order	Picking	Move	Wait	Inspection	Transfer	Other	Total
													Total	

CHART 14.5 Routing Development Worksheet—Example

Date 1 / 1 /1992 Product number CCCC Product name Wheel Standard batch size 50

Routing Step #	Department	Machine	Labor Code	Setup Time	Run Time (per unit)	Run Time (std. batch)	Lead Times: Order	Picking	Move	Wait	Inspection	Transfer	Other	Total
10	Cutting	X40	L35	2 hrs.	1.2 min.	2 hrs.	1 hr.		1 hr.					6 hrs.
20	Grinding	RV282	L40	1 hr.	.6 min.	1 hr.		1 day	1 hr.	2 hr.				2 days
30	Stamping	Brilton	L35	10 min.	.6 min.	1 hr.			1 hr.	5 hr.	50 min.	1 hr.		9 hrs.
40	Plating	Stall	L50	2 hrs.	1.8 min.	3 hrs.								1 day
50	Inspection		I20	0	1.8 min.	3 hrs.				3 hrs.	2 hrs.	2 hrs.		2 days
													Total	8 days

to place an order for CCCC, to pull its components A4B4 and ACAC, to manufacture the product, to inspect it, and to return the finished product to inventory, is eight days (assuming five productive hours in a day).

Chart 14.4 is the worksheet that will help you create a routing and calculate the lead times. Chart 14.5 is an example of the worksheet that was used to create the summary of Chart 14.3. The calculation of run time for the standard batch is performed by looking at the production runs for this product over several cycles and calculating the per unit run time. Then, by multiplying the per unit run time times the standard batch size, we can calculate the run time for the standard batch. The total lead time for each step is calculated by summing up all the incremental lead time components, except for the run time per unit value. The total lead time is calculated assuming five productive hours per working day.

Purchasing Lead Time

Purchasing lead time (see Chapter 10) is not quite as complicated to calculate as production lead time. Purchasing lead time is simply the time from when we place the order until we receive the materials into stores. Chart 14.6 lists the components included in purchasing lead time, and Chart 14.7 is an example of a purchasing lead time calculation.

Chart 14.8 lists the lead times for all the parts that we will be considering for production in our MRP production planning example (see Chapter 16).

Time Phased Bill of Materials

Now we will look at an example of the power of lead time planning. The diagram in Chart 14.9 is called a *time phased bill of materials.* It is created using the bill of materials for the tricycles (Chart 13.2), turning

CHART 14.6 Purchasing Lead Time Calculation

(Not every one of these occurs for every product.)

Purchase order creation time: The time it takes to make the order including the paperwork and placing the phone call
Inventory picking, packing, and loading time at the vendor: The time it takes at the vendor's shop to get the materials from their inventory stores onto a truck
Shipping time: The time required to transfer the product to your factory
Unloading time: The time required to unload the product and accept it into our plant
Wait time: The average amount of time it takes before the materials are inspected
Inspection time: The amount of time it takes to check quality
Transfer to stores: The amount of time it takes to transfer the inspected product to inventory stores

CHART 14.7 Purchasing Lead Time Calculation—Example

Purchase order creation time	3 hours
Inventory picking, packing, and loading time at the vendor	2 days
Shipping time	3 days
Unloading time	3 hours
Wait time	2 days
Inspection time	3 hours
Transfer to stores	2 days
Total	10.8 days

CHART 14.8 Purchasing and Production Lead Times

	Product	Lead Time (in days)
Production items—	TRI	3
	TRI–SP	1
	CCCC	8
	ABCD	4
	DDDD	9
	AACC	14
	A5B5	1
	ACAC	6
Purchased items—	BBBB	6
	AABB	3
	A4B4	4
	A555	2
	B555	1

this bill of materials chart sideways and using the lead times from Chart 14.8 to graph out the production and purchasing schedules. Look at both Chart 13.2 and Chart 14.8 as we discuss Chart 14.9. The time phase bill of materials for TRI starts at the right and moves toward the left. At the right end we see TRI, the end product that we are trying to produce. Looking at Chart 14.8, we see that the lead time for TRI is three days, which means that in order to complete TRI on time, we would need to start the production of TRI three days earlier. That is what the "3" on the time phased bill of materials is trying to tell us. We need to start TRI three days before the TRI due date of "0." This also means that all the components that are used to build TRI need to be ready for us on day 3. For example, the purchased parts BBBB and AABB (taken from Chart 13.2) need to be in our inventory stores area on day 3, and the manufactured products CCCC, ABCD, DDDD, and AACC (taken from Chart 13.2) need to be completed and in stores by day 3. To achieve this, BBBB will need to start the ordering process six days (taken from Chart 14.8) before the day 3 due date or on day 9. Similarly, the production order for CCCC will need to be released eight days before the day 3 due date or on day 11. We repeat this "time phasing" process for all the parts in the Bill of Materials (Chart 13.2) using the lead times of Chart 14.8 until we have the completed time phased bill of materials for product TRI as shown on Chart 14.9.

CHART 14.9 Time Phased Bill of Materials

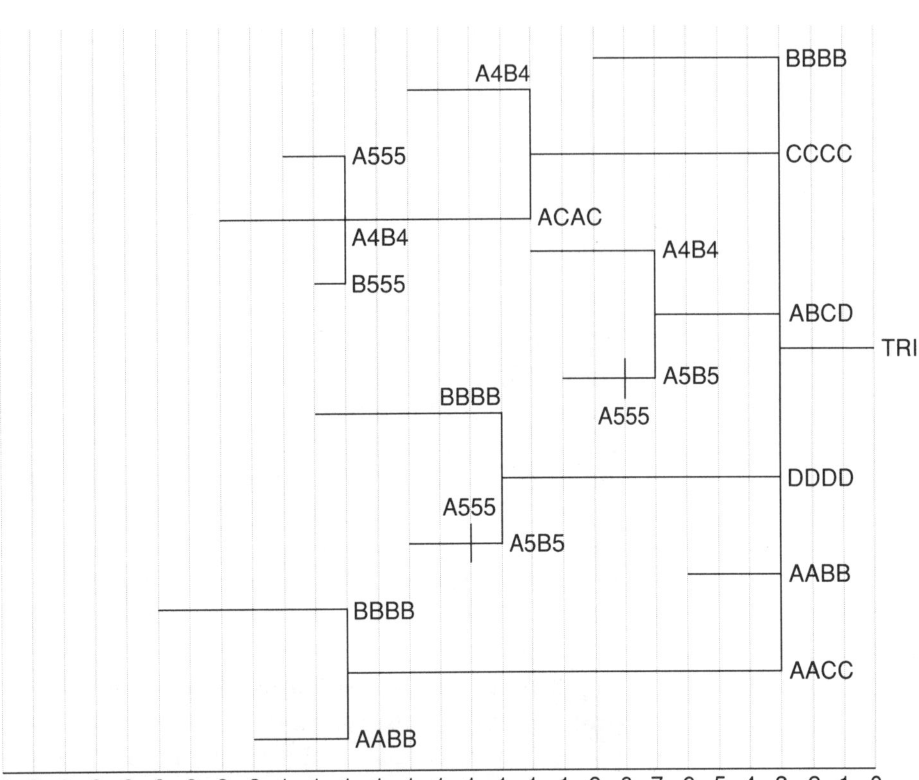

Once we have created Chart 14.9, we can ask some interesting questions about the production and purchasing time that it takes to build these products. For example:

> What is the total amount of time required to build the product?
> *Answer:* 17 days (note that purchasing lead time is not part of the production or "build" time)
>
> How many days before the final delivery of the product must the first order for parts be placed?
> *Answer:* 23 days
>
> How many days before the final delivery of the product must the first order for AABB parts be placed?
> *Answer:* 20 days

As you can see, with the time phased bill of materials, we can calculate when each phase of the production process should begin and end. Combining this with the ability to calculate how many we should order (Chapter 13), we are now ready to perform our MRP calculations.

Alternate Routings

An alternate routing is a routing that is set up as a secondary way to run an already existing production process. It is usually a less efficient or less desirable way to build the same product. Alternate routings can be helpful if some part of the primary or original routing becomes disabled, for example, if a machine breaks down. Having the alternate routing prepared would save having to wonder how you should build the product at the last minute.

Planning Horizon

The planning horizon of a product is an estimate of how far out we need to plan the product before we get into trouble in our scheduling. Looking at the time phased bill of materials (Chart 14.9), we see that the first action that needs to be taken on a product is 23 days before the due date. Assuming a five-day work week, this would be 4.6 weeks before the final due date. The planning horizon that we use in planning our product should give us a perspective that is out at least two or three times the planning horizon. In this way, we can watch new product schedules interact with our existing product schedules and we can properly prepare for them. For TRI the planning horizon should be about 3.5 to 4 months.

If we have multiple products, as we would have in a more complicated factory than our example, we would have a variety of products with a variety of planning horizons. Select the longest of these product lead times in your calculation of the planning horizon.

Lead Time Risks

Lead time is too easy to inflate. You received a strong warning against safety stock in the chapter on EOQ (Chapter 11), and the same strong warning applies to lead time in this chapter. Lead time is inventory, and inventory has to be financed, which means that inventory costs you interest, and interest is wasted money. Lead time is inventory because long lead times are primarily composed of long wait or move times (see Charts 14.1 and 14.6). These wait or move times are times when we are not adding any value to the materials. The materials are just sitting around doing nothing but collecting dust and costing us interest—which has to be one of the biggest wastes in American industry. When inflation hit, and the American car market was seriously hurt by the cheaper Japanese cars, the primary reason was the interest costs we had to pay for financing inventory. These interest costs jumped by about $2,000 per car, and that ruined our competitiveness. If you have excessive lead times in your plant, analyze how much it is costing you in interest per day (see the section near the end of this chapter titled "Cost of Work-in-Process Inventory"). Then reestimate how much you would be paying in interest if this lead time were cut in half. The difference, which would be a direct increase to your profit line, will amaze you. These lead times can be reduced by proper planning of material movement and production efficiencies.

Lead time reduction is the focus of other books that can be used after you have the concepts of this book implemented. But even without that supplement, if you get serious about lead time reduction in your plant, you can make immediate and dramatic changes. Just do some of the obvious, simple things first, such as don't start jobs just because someone feels like having something to do. It's OK if everyone is not constantly working like crazy. In fact, it would be cheaper for you to let someone play checkers, and pay them for it, than to have them build inventory that you won't be using for one month and have to pay interest on that inventory. Calculate it for yourself. To reduce work-in-process inventory immediately, try this: Temporarily slow down the number of job starts for the products at the bottom of your bill of materials. Let everyone else (higher level components or end products) work at their regular pace. You'd be amazed at how work-in-process inventory will be reduced.

Product Cost Calculations

At this point, we are ready to calculate product cost. Realize, however, that we are only looking at three resources (materials, labor, and machinery) and that there are more than 20 resources in your factory. But these three are the key resources. From Chart 13.2 we can determine all the purchased material costs for each purchased item. The purchased materials costs are estimated on Chart 14.10 as an example of

CHART 14.10 Purchased Materials Costs

Product Produced	Product Component	Quantity Required	Cost Per Unit	Extended Cost	Other Subassemblies
TRI					CCCC, ABCD, DDDD, and AACC
	BBBB	12	0.025	0.30	
	AABB	3	0.07	0.21	
TRI–SP					CCCC, ABCD, DDDD
	BBBB	5	0.025	0.125	
	AABB	3	0.07	0.21	
ACAC					
	A4B4	9	0.03	0.27	
	A555	7	0.015	0.105	
	B555	2	0.07	0.14	
CCCC					ACAC
	A4B4	12	0.03	0.36	
A5B5					
	A555	4	0.015	0.06	
ABCD					A5B5
	A4B4	10	0.03	0.30	
DDDD					A5B5
	BBBB	2	0.025	0.05	
AACC					
	BBBB	3	0.025	0.075	
	AABB	6	0.07	0.42	

how this materials costing process would work. Of the seven products listed in Chart 14.10, three of them are only composed of raw materials items (see Chart 13.2). These are ACAC, A5B5, and AACC. The other four manufactured items also have components that are manufactured in our plant. These materials costs will need to be accumulated as they are computed. This process of calculating the costs of the lower items and then building these costs up into the higher items is called a *cost roll*. To perform the total cost roll for TRI, we would first need to calculate the production costs of ACAC, A5B5, and AACC. Then we could "roll" these costs into a calculation of the costs for CCCC, ABCD, and DDDD. Having completed this step in the cost roll, we can now roll (accumulate) the costs for TRI.

Manufacturing costs are calculated by looking at the routing for each manufactured product (see Chart 14.3). We need to calculate a labor cost component by multiplying the run time times the labor rate for the labor code. We also need to multiply the setup time times the labor rate for the individual doing the setup process. Last of all we need to calculate machine costs by multiplying the machine rate times the sum of the setup time plus the run time. Most companies do not calculate the machine costs because they assume these costs to be trivial. However, machine costs are often not trivial and can be much higher than the labor costs. In these nontrivial cases, calculate a machine rate by dividing the annual cost of the machine, which includes depreciation, maintenance, etc., by the total production and setup hours for which the machine is used during the year. This gives us a machine cost rate that we can use in these calculations. Chart 14.11 gives an example of the calculation of labor and machine costs using the routing shown in Chart 14.3. Note that all calculations are based on the standard lot size. Once the costs for running this lot have been calculated, we can divide the total costs through by the lot size, which in this case is 50 units, and determine a per unit cost of production.

Chart 14.12 lists the costs of production for each of the manufactured products. Chart 14.13 accumulates the costs of production and combines them with the costs of raw materials in a cost roll. Note that

CHART 14.11 Sample Production Cost Calculation

Product number CCCC | Standard lot size 50

Routing Step #	Machine	Labor Code	Setup Time	Run Time	Labor Rate	Labor Cost	Machine Rate	Machine Cost
10	X40	L35	2 hrs.	2 hrs.	4.50	18.00	3.00	12.00
20	RV282	L40	1 hr.	1 hr.	5.00	10.00	4.00	8.00
30	Brilton	L35	10 min.	1 hr.	6.70	7.82	8.00	9.33
40	Stall	L50	2 hrs.	3 hrs.	5.00	25.00	1.00	5.00
50		I20		3 hrs.	8.00	24.00	0.50	1.50
				Totals		84.82		35.83
				Unit cost		1.70		0.72

CHART 14.12 Costs of Production

(All costs are per unit costs.)

Product Number	Labor Costs	Machine Costs	Total Costs
TRI	2.10	1.10	3.20
TRI–SP	0.10		0.10
CCCC	1.70	0.72	2.42
ABCD	0.75	0.43	1.18
DDDD	0.25	0.33	0.58
AACC	2.30	1.20	3.50
A5B5	0.09	0.08	0.17
ACAC	0.22	0.12	0.34

in Chart 14.13, the cost roll "burden" has not been included, which is also referred to as "overhead." This is a number that you may or may not want as part of your product cost calculation process. It is an averaged number that covers all administrative and other costs and spreads these costs over all the products. The difficult part is deciding what the spreading process should be, which should be left up to your accountant. However, the cost roll is just as meaningful (and often more meaningful) without this "averaging" process, which often distorts the profitability of a product. I once worked with a factory that made rubber cords along with numerous other rubber products. Their costing system applied burden to all the products based on labor hours (the standard basis for spreading these costs). This factory was selling these rubber cords like crazy. Unfortunately, quick calculations demonstrated that because there was very little labor in the cord, they were costing the product wrong, and they were actually selling the product for less than it cost them to make it.

The application of burden and overhead can be done later by the accountants if they are inclined to do so. Using the costs as they were calculated in Chart 14.13 is just as helpful for production planning purposes in determining the profitability of the product because we have the primary resources covered in the calculation.

Worksheets for the cost roll are included in this section. Chart 14.14 is the worksheet for purchased materials cost calculations as demonstrated in Chart 14.10. Chart 14.15 is the worksheet for the production cost calculations as demonstrated in Charts 14.11 and 14.12. Chart 14.16 shows how Chart 14.15 would have been used to calculate the information on Charts 14.11 and 14.12. Note that the run calculations have been broken out separately from the setup calculations. This is in case a different individual does the setup than does the run. These different individuals may have different labor rates. Chart 14.17 is the worksheet for the cost roll as demonstrated in Chart 14.13.

Having calculated the cost of our product, we can now move forward and estimate a selling price. Realize that if you haven't "loaded" your cost numbers with burden and overhead prior to this, you may want to

CHART 14.13 Cost Roll
(Combining Charts 14.10 and 14.12)

(All costs are per unit costs.)

Product Produced	Product Component	Quantity Required	Cost Per Unit	Extended Cost	Total Cost
First Step in the Roll					
ACAC					
	A4B4	9	0.03	0.27	
	A555	7	0.015	0.105	
	B555	2	0.07	0.14	
	Manufacturing cost			0.34	0.855
A5B5					
	A555	4	0.015	0.06	
	Manufacturing cost			0.17	0.23
AACC					
	BBBB	3	0.025	0.075	
	AABB	6	0.07	0.42	
	Manufacturing cost			3.50	3.995
Second Step in the Roll					
CCCC					
	A4B4	12	0.03	0.36	
	Manufacturing cost			2.42	
	ACAC	2	0.855	1.71	4.49
ABCD					
	A4B4	10	0.03	0.30	
	Manufacturing cost			1.18	
	A5B5	3	0.23	0.69	2.17
DDDD					
	BBBB	2	0.025	0.05	
	Manufacturing cost			0.58	
	A5B5	3	0.23	0.69	1.32
Final Step in the Roll					
TRI					
	BBBB	12	0.025	0.30	
	AABB	3	0.07	0.21	
	Manufacturing cost			3.20	
	CCCC	4	4.49	17.96	
	ABCD	2	2.17	4.34	
	DDDD	1	1.32	1.32	
	AACC	1	3.995	3.995	31.325
TRI–SP					
	BBBB	5	0.025	0.125	
	AABB	3	0.07	0.21	
	Manufacturing cost			0.10	
	CCCC	4	4.49	17.96	
	ABCD	1	2.17	2.17	
	DDDD	1	1.32	1.32	21.885

CHART 14.14 Purchased Materials Costs Worksheet

Date _____/_____/_____

Product Produced	Product Component	Quantity Required	Cost Per Unit	Extended Cost	Other Subassemblies

CHART 15.15 Production Cost Worksheet

Date ___/___/___ Product number __________ Product name ______________________ Standard lot size __________

		Labor Costs									Machine Costs			Per Unit Costs		
Routing Step #	Machine	Labor Code	Labor Rate	Run Time	Run Cost	Setup Code	Setup Rate	Setup Time	Setup Cost	Labor Cost	Machine Rate	Machine Time	Machine Cost	Labor Costs	Machine Costs	Total Costs
								Totals								

CHART 14.16 Example of Production Cost Worksheet
(Example using the Data from Chart 14.11 and 14.12)

Date 1 / 1 /1992 Product number CCCC Product name Wheel Standard lot size 50

		Labor Costs									Machine Costs			Per Unit Costs		
Routing Step #	Machine	Labor Code	Labor Rate	Run Time	Run Cost	Setup Code	Setup Rate	Setup Time	Setup Cost	Labor Cost	Machine Rate	Machine Time	Machine Cost	Labor Costs	Machine Costs	Total Costs
10	X40	L35	4.50	2 hrs.	9.00	L35	4.50	2 hrs.	9.00	18.00	3.00	4 hrs.	12.00			
20	RV282	L40	5.00	1 hr.	5.00	L40	5.00	1 hr.	5.00	10.00	4.00	2 hrs.	8.00			
30	Brilton	L35	6.70	1 hr.	6.70	L35	6.70	10 min.	1.12	7.82	8.00	1.17 hr.	9.33			
40	Stall	L50	5.00	3 hrs.	15.00	L50	5.00	2 hrs.	10.00	25.00	1.00	5 hrs.	5.00			
50		I20	8.00	3 hrs.	24.00		8.00			24.00	0.50	3 hrs.	1.50			
								Totals		84.82			35.83	1.70	.72	2.42

CHART 14.17 Cost Roll Worksheet

Date / /

Product Produced	Product Component	Quantity Required	Cost Per Unit	Extended Cost	Total Cost
	Manufacturing costs				

do so now. Then you can compare this total cost with the cost of manufacturing to see if you are actually making any money on your product.

Cost of Work-in-Process Inventory

This section of the chapter is not critical in controlling your operations. The report we generate here is primarily informational. However, it is often shocking for production personnel to realize how much money they are wasting on work-in-process inventory that is sitting on the production floor. This does not include inventory in the stockroom. We have already discussed safety stock methods that would minimize stockroom inventory. At this point you already have all the information you need to make the necessary calculations for the work-in-process inventory costs tied up on the production floor.

What we are trying to do with this calculation is look at each of the manufactured components of our product, determine how much that component costs, determine how long we keep that product on the factory floor, and figure out how much it costs us to keep this inventory on the floor. If we multiply this number times the number of units we are producing, we calculate our cost of carrying inventory for production work-in-process.

To perform this calculation, follow along on Chart 14.18. We start by looking at what the manufactured products are. This information comes from Chart 14.13. Next we look at one month of TRI and its corresponding TRI–SP. We know how many units we plan to produce in the first month, because we can get this information from Chart 12.2. We plan to build 143 TRIs and 7 TRI–SPs. We explode the requirements for each of the other manufactured products by looking at their bills of materials (Charts 13.2 and 13.6). (The process of exploding these

CHART 14.18 Cost of Carrying Work-in-Process Inventory on the Factory Floor
(Combining Charts 12.2, 14.13, 11.4, 13.2, 13.6, and 14.8)

Opportunity cost rate = 20%
Total working days in the year = 300

$$(\text{IHC}) = (\text{QP}) \times (\text{OCR}) \times (\text{MC}) \times \frac{(\text{TMLT})}{(\text{TWDY})}$$

Product Produced	Quantity Produced	Manufacturing Cost	Total Manufacturing Lead Time	Inventory Holding Cost
ACAC	1200	.855	6 days	4.10
A5B5	1329	.23	1	.20
AACC	143	3.995	14	5.33
CCCC	600	4.49	8	14.37
ABCD	293	2.17	4	1.70
DDDD	150	1.32	9	1.19
TRI	143	31.325	3	8.96
TRI–SP	7	21.885	1	.10
			Total Cost	35.95

requirements is explained in Chapter 13.) An example of an exploded calculation is:

Quantity ACAC Produced =
2 ACAC for every CCCC
4 CCCC for every TRI–SP
7 TRI–SP produced
2 ACAC for every CCCC
4 CCCC for every TRI
143 TRI produced
$= 2 \times 4 \times 7 + 2 \times 4 \times 143 = 1{,}200$

We know what the work-in-process manufacturing cost values of each of the manufactured components for TRI and TRI–SP are. This information comes from Chart 14.13. The next value we need is the interest rate (or opportunity cost) for the money we have tied up in inventory. This calculation was discussed in detail in Chapter 11 (see Chart 11.3, Part B). Chart 14.8 gives us the manufacturing lead time of each of the manufactured products. The number of working days comes from the calendar. The formula for calculating the inventory holding cost is:

$$\text{IHC} = \text{QP} \times \text{OCR} \times \text{MC} \times \frac{\text{TMLT}}{\text{TWDY}}$$

where:

IHC = inventory holding cost
QP = quantity produced
OCR = opportunity cost rate
MC = manufacturing cost
TMLT = total manufacturing lead time (in days)
TWDY = total working days in the year

As an example of how to calculate the inventory holding cost, we will use ACAC. The calculations are as follows:

(ACAC Inventory Holding Cost)

$$= (1{,}200) \times (0.20) \times (0.855) \times \frac{(6)}{(300)}$$

After calculating the inventory holding cost of each manufactured item, we sum these total costs. Realize that in my example we are dealing with only one product (and its spare parts), and we are dealing with only one month. If you did this for your entire product line for the full year, the number could be enormous. Additionally, my example here is a very inexpensive product, and my example is a little more idealistic than your operation may be.

What we learn from the calculations of Chart 14.18 is how much our manufacturing lead time is costing us (remember the discussion earlier in this chapter on lead time risks). I've seen some rather large numbers come out of the calculation process of Chart 14.18. Reducing this lead time in half would add half of this cost directly back into the profit line. How's that for motivation?

Summarization by Family for Aggregate Production Scheduling

In an earlier chapter we looked at the manufacturing resource requirements for products we manufacture. At that time we mentioned that the resource requirements are calculated from the routings. Now we discuss the basic procedure for calculating these resource requirements by manufactured product. We start with the routing for each of the manufactured components. Then we summarize each of these routings

CHART 14.19 Product Resource Requirements for CCCC
(Combining information from Charts 14.3 and 14.10)

Purchase materials costs	$0.36
Manufacturing costs (run plus setup time)	
Machinery	
Lathe category	
X40 + Brilton	(5 hours, 10 min.) for 50 equals 6.2 minutes each
Drill press category	
RV282 + Stall	7 hours for 50 equals 8.4 minutes each
Labor	
Painting	0
Assembly	0
Welding	0
Grinding	(12 hours, 10 min.) for 50 equals 14.6 minutes each

CHART 14.20 Product Resource Requirements Worksheet

Date ___/___/___ Product # ________

	Materials			Machinery		Manpower			
Product Number	Bar Stock	Purchased Parts	Sheet Metal	Lathe	Drill Press	Painting	Assembly	Welding	Grinding

CHART 14.21 Extended Product Resource Requirements Worksheet

Date ____/____/____ Product # __________

Product Number	Quantity Per	Materials: Bar Stock	Materials: Purchased Parts	Materials: Sheet Metal	Machinery: Lathe	Machinery: Drill Press	Manpower: Painting	Manpower: Assembly	Manpower: Welding	Manpower: Grinding
Totals										

CHART 14.22 Tricycle Example of a Product Resource Requirements Worksheet

Date 1 / 1 /1992 Product # TRI

Product Number	Materials: Bar Stock	Materials: Purchased Parts	Materials: Sheet Metal	Machinery: Lathe	Machinery: Drill Press	Manpower: Painting	Manpower: Assembly	Manpower: Welding	Manpower: Grinding
ACAC	6 in.	$ .25	0	5 min.	20 min.	0	0	10 min.	0
A5B5	8 in.	.30	0	2	6	0	0	4.4 min.	0
AACC	0	1.10	6 sq ft.	7.2	25	0	0	0	1.6 min.
CCCC	0	.36	0	6.2	8.4	0	0	0	14.6 min.
ABCD	0	.55	0	20	0	0	.125 hr.	0	0
DDDD	0	2.66	0	10	27.4	0	.25 hr.	0	0
TRI	0	4.00	4 sq ft.	0	0	.25 hr.	1.0 hr.	0	0

CHART 14.23 Tricycle Example of an Extended Product Resource Requirements Worksheet

Date 1 / 1 /1992 Product # TRI

		Materials			Machinery		Manpower			
Product Number	Quantity Per	Bar Stock	Purchased Parts	Sheet Metal	Lathe	Drill Press	Painting	Assembly	Welding	Grinding
ACAC	8	4 ft.	$ 2.00	0	40 min.	160 min.	0	0	80 min.	0
A5B5	9	6 ft.	2.70	0	18	54	0	0	40 min.	0
AACC	1	0	1.20	6 sq ft.	7.2	25	0	0	0	1.6 min.
CCCC	4	0	1.44	0	24.8	33.6	0	0	0	58.4 min.
ABCD	2	0	1.10	0	20	0	0	.25 hr.	0	0
DDDD	1	0	2.66	0	10	27.4	0	.25 hr.	0	0
TRI	1	0	4.00	4 sq ft.	0	0	.25 hr.	1.0 hr.	0	0
Totals		10 ft.	$15.00	10 sq ft.	2 hrs.	5 hrs.	.25 hr.	1.5 hrs.	2 hrs.	1 hr.

into the same categories that we used in our product resource requirements list. As an example of how this summarization process would occur, let's look at the manufactured product CCCC. From Chart 14.3 we get the labor and machinery requirements of CCCC, and from Chart 14.10 we get the materials purchase parts cost requirements. Chart 14.19 shows how these costs and capacity requirements would be summarized for CCCC. Note that some areas, like inspection time, are not evaluated for capacity. The summarization process that occurs in Chart 14.19 needs to occur for each manufactured product. The result would be similar to using the worksheet of Chart 14.20 for tricycles (see Chart 14.22). The values used in Chart 14.20 come directly from the work done in Chart 14.19 (see the CCC line in Chart 14.22). Chart 14.21 multiplies the unit requirements for each product listed in Chart 14.20 and sums up the total requirements. The "Quantity Per" information for Chart 14.21 comes from exploding the bill of materials for the manufactured components of that product (note that the "Quantity Per" line of Chart 14.23 comes from exploding the TRI bill of materials of Chart 13.2). The tricycle example is calculated in Chart 14.22, which is an example of Chart 14.20, and Chart 14.23, which is an example of Chart 14.21. These total requirements of Chart 14.23 correspond to the "Product Resource Requirements" for tricycles.

Summary

We have conquered the inputs into an MRP system. The next chapter will describe how some of the numbers from this chapter on routings and from the last chapter on the bill of materials were developed. Chapter 15 also discusses the engineering connection and how it functions in relation to the product we are developing. Then we will do an MRP calculation (Chapter 16).

Chapter

15 Engineering

Steps in New Product Development

We keep hearing about how our society is becoming more of a service-oriented society and less of an industrial society. More and more of our work force is working in service areas and less in our factories. This is because more of our factories are being moved overseas. We need to rebuild our industry to its previous dominating strength. One of the first steps toward doing this is in the area of engineering. Currently, the engineering departments of most companies are "over the wall" departments—departments that draw up the product and "throw the drawing over the wall" to the Production Department hoping to never see it again.

American products need to have higher quality and at the same time be easier to build. This would increase productivity and competitiveness. This involves all levels of engineering, from product engineering to process engineering.

To improve engineering, some organizations have taken radical, but successful steps. In those few companies where these steps have been used, it has demonstrated to be very successful. These steps are:

1. Product, manufacturing, and industrial engineers design the new product or the product modification.

2. These engineers work on the factory floor for a few days to a week. They will work directly on the production line building the product that they have just designed. They will be working side-by-side with the shop floor employees who will later be responsible for building the product. These shop floor employees will be encouraged to give their comments and recommendations.

3. The engineers can then return to their drawing boards and redo the design of the product. The product will be much more easily built and will be of a better quality.

Experiment with this three-step plan on some existing product about which you have concerns. You'll be amazed at the improvement.

I also highly recommend a similar three-step plan for your engineers working at the customer site or using the produced product. Have your engineers work with the users and listen to their comments. This will be one of the best investments you will ever make toward product quality and increased sales.

In Chapter 5 we discussed the role of engineering in product development. We need to remember this emphasis in the development of the inputs into an MRP system.

Product engineering designed the product. They defined the components of the product on drawings that will be used in the manufacturing process. From these drawings they were able to develop a bill of materials (Chapter 13), which defined the components of the product. At this point, manufacturing engineering takes over. It is the responsibility of these individuals to know the equipment and the employees of the factory. These engineers define the steps that will go into the manufacturing process. They describe the step-by-step procedure necessary for making the product. This is called the routing (Chapter 14). They also make modifications to the lower levels of the bill of materials, defining what components can be made in-house and what materials will need to be purchased.

The last engineering step is done by the industrial engineers who define the labor components of the production process. They define who does what and how long each step should take. This information is also included in the routing and helps define the total lead time for the manufacture of the product.

Engineering Change Orders

As the product goes through its life cycle, changes are made. These changes are called *engineering change orders* (ECOs). ECOs occur because of improvements or technological changes to the product. ECOs can be a nightmare for production planning if they are not handled correctly. The key to understanding how ECOs should be processed is in determining the urgency of the change. If the change requires immediate implementation because of a design defect, then we will probably need to place some emergency purchase or production orders in order to compensate for the need for corrective materials. The bill of materials and routings will need to be immediately modified. Obsolete inventory will necessarily result.

However, if the change does not require immediate implementation, then we may want to use up all the "old" materials first before they become obsolete. The trick here is in determining how many end products we can make with the existing materials. Then we would release a production order for as many of the "old design" products as we can make. After this, we would modify the bill of materials and the routings and release all new production orders for the "new design" products.

It is the timing of when to release "new" versus "old" design production orders that makes this process tricky. The easiest solution is to have an "old" and a "new" product number. Often this is done by having the same product number but modifying the model number. This would in effect require the use of the model number as a suffix to the product number. By changing the number you will be able to have two separate bills of materials and two separate routings. Production scheduling would then be performed under these two separate numbers. We would use up all of the inventory under the old number and then start scheduling under the new number. This separated information may be helpful if at some future date you need to refer back to see how you manufactured an earlier model.

Standards

The development of standards is originally performed by engineering when a new product is being introduced. These standards are developed based on time and motion studies and manufacturing experimentation. For modifications of products or for planning similar products, many of these estimates are developed based on the estimates used for the similar products.

After we have some history of actual manufacturing data, we can use these data to update the standards. History of activity allows us to take averages of "what it really takes" to produce the product. In Chapter 19 we will discuss the job sheet, which is the source document for the data collection process that builds this history. These averages become our updated standards, both for materials usage and for machine and labor time.

Learning Curves

Employees do not always do the same function at the same rate of speed. As new employees are hired, they will experience a learning curve. Also, as new manufacturing processes are introduced into the plant, it will take a little time before the employees become proficient at the process. These are all different forms of learning curves. The learning curve helps us in operations by giving us a feeling for how an employee will be performing after they have learned the new process. Here is how it works:

1. Determine the amount of time it takes to produce the first unit (A).
2. Estimate a rate of learning (R). This is difficult. Some employees learn faster than others. However, after you have used the learning

CHART 15.1 Learning Curve Matrix—0.1 to 0.9

A	B	C	D	E	F	G	H	I	J	K
Learning Curve Matrix										
				Rate of Learning						
Xth Time	.1	.2	.3	.4	.5	.6	.7	.8	.9	
1	1	1	1	1	1	1	1	1	1	
2	.1	.2	.3	.4	.5	.6	.7	.8	.9	
3	.0260038	.0780115	.1483395	.2340346	.3333333	.4450185	.5681803	.7021037	.8462060	
4	.01	.04	.09	.16	.25	.36	.49	.64	.81	
5	.0047651	.0238255	.0610820	.1191275	.2	.3054099	.4368464	.5956373	.7829867	
6	.0026004	.0156023	.0445018	.0936138	.1666667	.2670111	.3977262	.5616830	.7615854	
7	.0015583	.0109079	.0340482	.0763556	.1428571	.2383372	.3673967	.5344895	.7439478	
8	.001	.008	.027	.064	.125	.216	.343	.512	.729	
9	.0006762	.0060858	.0220046	.0547722	.1111111	.1980415	.3228289	.4929496	.7160646	
10	.0004765	.0047651	.0183246	.0476510	.1	.1832460	.3057925	.4765099	.7046880	
11	.0003472	.0038191	.0155288	.0420101	.0909091	.1708163	.2911570	.4621111	.6945525	
12	.0002600	.0031205	.0133506	.0374455	.0833333	.1602067	.2784084	.4493464	.6854268	
13	.0001993	.0025912	.0116177	.0336858	.0769231	.1510296	.2671743	.4379155	.6771380	
14	.0001558	.0021816	.0102145	.0305423	.0714286	.1430023	.2571777	.4275916	.6695531	
15	.0001239	.0018587	.0090609	.0278799	.0666667	.1359131	.2482076	.4181992	.6625681	
16	.0001	.0016	.0081	.0256	.0625	.1296	.2401	.4096	.6561	
17	.0000818	.0013899	.0072904	.0236284	.0588235	.1239371	.2327255	.4016834	.6500817	
18	.0000676	.0012172	.0066014	.0219089	.0555556	.1188249	.2259802	.3943597	.6444581	
19	.0000565	.0010736	.0060096	.0203976	.0526316	.1141833	.2197798	.3875550	.6391834	
20	.0000477	.0009530	.0054974	.0190604	.05	.1099476	.2140547	.3812079	.6342192	

curve for a while, you will get a feel for the rate of learning of certain employees. For example, looking at Charts 15.1 and Chart 15.2 we see what the improvement effect of repeated tries at building a product will be. After 10 tries (left-hand column), an individual with a learning rate of 0.9 (across the top) will take 70.47 percent as long as it took the first time (find 0.7046880 at the intersection of 10 and 0.9). The tenth try of an employee with a 0.8 rate of learning will take 47.65 percent as long. Chart 15.2 has a more reasonable range of learning rates.

3. Determine how many units you want to have the employee produce (X). For example, do you want to know how fast the employee will produce the tenth item?
4. Use Chart 15.1 or Chart 15.2 to look up the "F" factor using "R" and "X." Note that you can build your own learning curve matrix charts, just like those of Chart 15.1 or 15.2 by using the spreadsheet formula example of Chart 15.3. By building your own learning curve matrix you can investigate the rates of learning that fit your company the best.
5. Calculate how long it will take your employee to produce the Xth item using the following formula:

$$\text{Time Taken to Produce Xth Item} = F \times A$$

CHART 15.2 Learning Curve Matrix—0.91 to 0.99

	A	B	C	D	E	F	G	H	I	J	K
26											
27											
28											
29											
30											
31	Learning Curve Matrix										
32						Rate of Learning					
33	Xth Time	.91	.92	.93	.94	.95	.96	.97	.98	.99	
34	1	1	1	1	1	1	1	1	1	1	
35	2	.91	.92	.93	.94	.95	.96	.97	.98	.99	
36	3	.8611566	.8762037	.8913467	.9065853	.9219190	.9373474	.9528701	.9684867	.9841968	
37	4	.8281	.8464	.8649	.8836	.9025	.9216	.9409	.9604	.9801	
38	5	.8033357	.8239824	.8449279	.8661733	.8877196	.9095678	.9317189	.9541740	.9769340	
39	6	.7836525	.8061074	.8289524	.8521901	.8758230	.8998535	.9242840	.9491170	.9743548	
40	7	.7673874	.7912971	.8156812	.8405438	.8658891	.8917211	.9180441	.9448622	.9721795	
41	8	.753571	.778688	.804357	.830584	.857375	.884736	.912673	.941192	.970299	
42	9	.7415907	.7677329	.7944989	.8218968	.8499346	.8786201	.9079614	.9379665	.9686433	
43	10	.7310355	.7580638	.7857830	.8142029	.8433336	.8731851	.9037674	.9350905	.9671647	
44	11	.7216166	.7494220	.7779809	.8073050	.8374065	.8682975	.8999901	.9324965	.9658290	
45	12	.7131238	.7416188	.7709258	.8010587	.8320319	.8638593	.8965555	.9301346	.9646113	
46	13	.7053995	.7345122	.7644922	.7953554	.8271181	.8597967	.8934075	.9279672	.9634924	
47	14	.6983225	.7279933	.7585835	.7901112	.8225946	.8560523	.8905028	.9259650	.9624577	
48	15	.6917978	.7219764	.7531237	.7852600	.8184055	.8525810	.8878071	.9241048	.9614953	
49	16	.6857496	.7163930	.7480520	.7807490	.8145063	.8493466	.8852928	.9223682	.9605960	
50	17	.6801163	.7111875	.7433190	.7765351	.8108603	.8463195	.8829375	.9207398	.9597520	
51	18	.6748476	.7063142	.7388840	.7725830	.8074379	.8434753	.8807226	.9192071	.9589569	
52	19	.6699013	.7017353	.7347132	.7688632	.8042137	.8407938	.8786325	.9177597	.9582054	
53	20	.6652423	.6974187	.7307782	.7653508	.8011669	.8382577	.8766543	.9163887	.9574930	
54											
55											

CHART 15.3 Learning Curve Matrix—Spreadsheet Formulas

	A	B	C	D	E	F	G	H
1								
2	Learning Curve Matrix							
3					Rate of Learning			
4	Xth Time	1	.2	.3	.4	.5	.6	.7
5	1	A5××(LOG(B4)/LOG(2))	A5××(LOG(C4)/LOG(2))	A5××(LOG(D4)/LOG(2))	A5××(LOG(E4)/LOG(2))	A5××(LOG(F4)/LOG(2))	A5××(LOG(G4)/LOG(2))	A5××(LOG(H4)/LOG(2))
6	2	A6××(LOG(B4)/LOG(2))	A6××(LOG(C4)/LOG(2))	A6××(LOG(D4)/LOG(2))	A6××(LOG(E4)/LOG(2))	A6××(LOG(F4)/LOG(2))	A6××(LOG(G4)/LOG(2))	A6××(LOG(H4)/LOG(2))
7	3	A7××(LOG(B4)/LOG(2))	A7××(LOG(C4)/LOG(2))	A7××(LOG(D4)/LOG(2))	A7××(LOG(E4)/LOG(2))	A7××(LOG(F4)/LOG(2))	A7××(LOG(G4)/LOG(2))	A7××(LOG(H4)/LOG(2))
8	4	A8××(LOG(B4)/LOG(2))	A8××(LOG(C4)/LOG(2))	A8××(LOG(D4)/LOG(2))	A8××(LOG(E4)/LOG(2))	A8××(LOG(F4)/LOG(2))	A8××(LOG(G4)/LOG(2))	A8××(LOG(H4)/LOG(2))
9	5	A9××(LOG(B4)/LOG(2))	A9××(LOG(C4)/LOG(2))	A9××(LOG(D4)/LOG(2))	A9××(LOG(E4)/LOG(2))	A9××(LOG(F4)/LOG(2))	A9××(LOG(G4)/LOG(2))	A9××(LOG(H4)/LOG(2))
10	6	A10××(LOG(B4)/LOG(2))	A10××(LOG(C4)/LOG(2))	A10××(LOG(D4)/LOG(2))	A10××(LOG(E4)/LOG(2))	A10××(LOG(F4)/LOG(2))	A10××(LOG(G4)/LOG(2))	A10××(LOG(H4)/LOG(2))
11	7	A11××(LOG(B4)/LOG(2))	A11××(LOG(C4)/LOG(2))	A11××(LOG(D4)/LOG(2))	A11××(LOG(E4)/LOG(2))	A11××(LOG(F4)/LOG(2))	A11××(LOG(G4)/LOG(2))	A11××(LOG(H4)/LOG(2))
12	8	A12××(LOG(B4)/LOG(2))	A12××(LOG(C4)/LOG(2))	A12××(LOG(D4)/LOG(2))	A12××(LOG(E4)/LOG(2))	A12××(LOG(F4)/LOG(2))	A12××(LOG(G4)/LOG(2))	A12××(LOG(H4)/LOG(2))
13	9	A13××(LOG(B4)/LOG(2))	A13××(LOG(C4)/LOG(2))	A13××(LOG(D4)/LOG(2))	A13××(LOG(E4)/LOG(2))	A13××(LOG(F4)/LOG(2))	A13××(LOG(G4)/LOG(2))	A13××(LOG(H4)/LOG(2))
14	10	A14××(LOG(B4)/LOG(2))	A14××(LOG(C4)/LOG(2))	A14××(LOG(D4)/LOG(2))	A14××(LOG(E4)/LOG(2))	A14××(LOG(F4)/LOG(2))	A14××(LOG(G4)/LOG(2))	A14××(LOG(H4)/LOG(2))
15	11	A15××(LOG(B4)/LOG(2))	A15××(LOG(C4)/LOG(2))	A15××(LOG(D4)/LOG(2))	A15××(LOG(E4)/LOG(2))	A15××(LOG(F4)/LOG(2))	A15××(LOG(G4)/LOG(2))	A15××(LOG(H4)/LOG(2))
16	12	A16××(LOG(B4)/LOG(2))	A16××(LOG(C4)/LOG(2))	A16××(LOG(D4)/LOG(2))	A16××(LOG(E4)/LOG(2))	A16××(LOG(F4)/LOG(2))	A16××(LOG(G4)/LOG(2))	A16××(LOG(H4)/LOG(2))
17	13	A17××(LOG(B4)/LOG(2))	A17××(LOG(C4)/LOG(2))	A17××(LOG(D4)/LOG(2))	A17××(LOG(E4)/LOG(2))	A17××(LOG(F4)/LOG(2))	A17××(LOG(G4)/LOG(2))	A17××(LOG(H4)/LOG(2))
18	14	A18××(LOG(B4)/LOG(2))	A18××(LOG(C4)/LOG(2))	A18××(LOG(D4)/LOG(2))	A18××(LOG(E4)/LOG(2))	A18××(LOG(F4)/LOG(2))	A18××(LOG(G4)/LOG(2))	A18××(LOG(H4)/LOG(2))
19	15	A19××(LOG(B4)/LOG(2))	A19××(LOG(C4)/LOG(2))	A19××(LOG(D4)/LOG(2))	A19××(LOG(E4)/LOG(2))	A19××(LOG(F4)/LOG(2))	A19××(LOG(G4)/LOG(2))	A19××(LOG(H4)/LOG(2))
20	16	A20××(LOG(B4)/LOG(2))	A20××(LOG(C4)/LOG(2))	A20××(LOG(D4)/LOG(2))	A20××(LOG(E4)/LOG(2))	A20××(LOG(F4)/LOG(2))	A20××(LOG(G4)/LOG(2))	A20××(LOG(H4)/LOG(2))
21	17	A21××(LOG(B4)/LOG(2))	A21××(LOG(C4)/LOG(2))	A21××(LOG(D4)/LOG(2))	A21××(LOG(E4)/LOG(2))	A21××(LOG(F4)/LOG(2))	A21××(LOG(G4)/LOG(2))	A21××(LOG(H4)/LOG(2))
22	18	A22××(LOG(B4)/LOG(2))	A22××(LOG(C4)/LOG(2))	A22××(LOG(D4)/LOG(2))	A22××(LOG(E4)/LOG(2))	A22××(LOG(F4)/LOG(2))	A22××(LOG(G4)/LOG(2))	A22××(LOG(H4)/LOG(2))
23	19	A23××(LOG(B4)/LOG(2))	A23××(LOG(C4)/LOG(2))	A23××(LOG(D4)/LOG(2))	A23××(LOG(E4)/LOG(2))	A23××(LOG(F4)/LOG(2))	A23××(LOG(G4)/LOG(2))	A23××(LOG(H4)/LOG(2))
24	20	A24××(LOG(B4)/LOG(2))	A24××(LOG(C4)/LOG(2))	A24××(LOG(D4)/LOG(2))	A24××(LOG(E4)/LOG(2))	A24××(LOG(F4)/LOG(2))	A24××(LOG(G4)/LOG(2))	A24××(LOG(H4)/LOG(2))
25								

Calculation Example: If we had a job that takes three hours to do and we want to see what it will take after 15 tries with an employee that has a 0.92 learning curve we would first look up the "F" value on Chart 15.2, which is 0.7219764. Then we would use the formula to get:

$$\text{Time Taken to Produce 15th Item} = F \times A$$
$$= (0.7219764) \times (3 \text{ hours}) = 2.1659 \text{ hours} = 2 \text{ hours, } 10 \text{ minutes}$$

Working backwards, we can estimate the rate of learning for an employee. For example, if an employee takes 5 hours to do a job the first time, and 4.22 hours to complete the same job after the tenth try, we can divide the tenth try by the first try as follows:

$$\frac{(\text{Time for Tenth Try})}{(\text{Time for First Try})} = \frac{(4.22 \text{ hours})}{(5 \text{ hours})} = 0.844$$

The calculated value of 0.844 is used to look across the row of the table that has 10 tries. We find that the closest value is 0.8433336, which lies in the 0.95 rate of learning column. Based on this analysis, the rate of learning for this employee is about 0.95. This "R" value can then be used in future learning curve calculations.

Summary

This chapter gave us a brief explanation of how the routing and bill of materials inputs are developed. It also discussed the importance of handling engineering changes correctly. Now we can move forward and calculate MRP schedules, which is the subject of the next chapter.

Chapter

16 Material Requirements Planning Outputs

MRP Inputs

In Chapter 11 we discussed EOQ production planning. The intent of this chapter is to try to make everyone even better production planners by helping them understand how the production planning process works using MRP (material requirements planning).

We have already discussed the inputs into MRP. These were:

Master production scheduling

Bill of materials (Chapter 13)

Routings (Chapter 14)

Inventory (Chapters 8, 9, and 12)

Purchase and production orders (Chapters 12 and 19)

Chart 16.1 focuses on the inputs and outputs of an MRP production planning system. This chart diagrams the inputs listed above. The primary outputs of MRP are production orders (Chapter 19) and purchasing orders.

We are now ready to start generating production schedules. This part is exciting because we need to start flipping back and forth between each of the five inputs. We perform the scheduling process by planning the products one at a time. We use the bill of materials (Charts 13.2 and 13.6) to calculate the low-level codes for each of the products to be scheduled. The low-level codes for these products are

CHART 16.1 MRP Information Flow

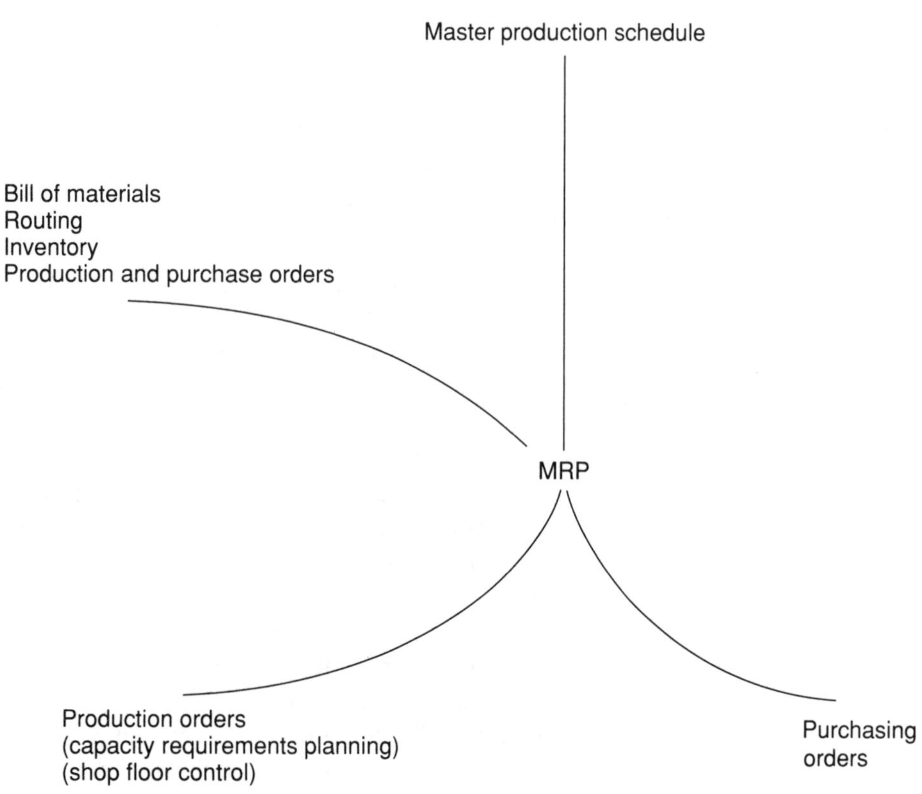

CHART 16.2 The Inputs into MRP
(Taken from Charts 12.2, 12.4, 13.2, 13.6, and 14.8)

Product Number	Inventory On-Hand Balance	Purchase & Production Orders Balance	Week	Lead Time	Low-Level Codes
TRI	121	21	1/1	3	0
TRI–SP	6	6	1/1	1	0
BBBB	45	100	1/2	6	2
CCCC	4	4	1/1	8	1
ABCD	5	5	1/3	4	1
DDDD	10	10	1/2	9	1
AABB	15	15	1/3	3	1
AACC	6	20	1/2	14	1
A4B4	200	400	1/1	4	3
ACAC	20	20	1/2	6	2
A5B5	23	23	1/3	1	2
A555	40	300	1/2	2	3
B555	7	20	1/1	1	3

shown on Chart 16.2 (see Chapter 13 for instructions on how to calculate low-level codes). We use the low-level codes to determine what the sequence for scheduling the parts should be. Those parts with the lowest code are scheduled first; in Chart 16.2, this would be TRI and TRI–SP, which have low-level codes of 0. Next, the low level 1 coded items are scheduled, which are CCCC, ABCD, DDDD, AABB, and AACC. Next the low-level 2 coded items are scheduled, which are BBBB, ACAC, and A5B5. And last the low-level 3 coded items are scheduled, which are A4B4, A555, and B555. Additionally, Chart 16.2 summarizes three of the inputs into MRP. It includes the routings, inventory, and purchase and production order inputs.

MRP Worksheet and Calculations

Chart 16.3 is the scheduling worksheet that is used for generating the MRP schedules. Chart 16.4 shows an example of how to calculate the MRP schedules using the information from Charts 16.2, 12.2, 13.2, and 13.6. Looking at Chart 16.4, we schedule the level 0 items first. These are finished goods items that have a master production schedule. Note that spare parts may also have gross requirements coming in from the master production schedule. However, spare parts will be scheduled based on their low-level code, which is the lowest code at which they occur in any of the bill of materials. This will be something lower than level 0.

The gross requirements for all the level 0 items come from the master production schedule (Chart 12.2). Level 0 items may also have anticipation inventory. This is inventory that is prebuilt anticipating future sales. The anticipation inventory level for tricycles for the first six months was calculated in Chart 8.3. The anticipation inventory

CHART 16.3 Material Requirements Planning Worksheet

Date ______/______/______

Startup Inventory Values
Lead Time___ Inventory Balance____ − Anticipation Inventory___ − Safety Stock___ = Week Zero Inventory Balance____

Product #________	0	1	2	3	4	5	6	7	8	9	10	11	12	13	14	15	16	17	18	19	20	21	22	23	24	25	26	27	28
Week																													
Gross requirements																													
Scheduled receipts																													
Anticipation inventory or SS changes																													
On hand																													
Net requirements																													
Planned receipts																													
Planned releases																													

Startup Inventory Values
Lead Time___ Inventory Balance____ − Anticipation Inventory___ − Safety Stock___ = Week Zero Inventory Balance____

Product #________	0	1	2	3	4	5	6	7	8	9	10	11	12	13	14	15	16	17	18	19	20	21	22	23	24	25	26	27	28
Week																													
Gross requirements																													
Scheduled receipts																													
Anticipation inventory or SS changes																													
On hand																													
Net requirements																													
Planned receipts																													
Planned releases																													

CHART 16.4 Material Requirements Planning Worksheet—Example of Level 0 Items

Date 1 / 1 / 1992

Product # TRI   Lead Time 3

Startup Inventory Values
Inventory Balance 121 – Anticipation Inventory 0 – Safety Stock 0 = Week Zero Inventory Balance 121

	0	1	2	3	4	5	6	7	8	9	10	11	12	13	14	15	16	17	18	19	20	21	22	23	24	25	26	27	28	
Week		1/1	1/2	1/3	1/4	2/1	2/2	2/3	2/4	3/1	3/2	3/3	3/4	4/1	4/2	4/3	4/4	5/1	5/2	5/3	5/4	6/1	6/2	6/3	6/4					
Gross requirements		38	30	38	37	13	9	13	12	15	19	19	18	27	33	34	33	40	50	50	50	26	33	34	33					Friday due dates
Scheduled receipts		21																												
Anticipation inventory or SS changes														8	8	8	8	24	24	24	23	8	8	8	8					
On hand	121	104	74	36																										
Net requirements					1	13	9	13	12	15	19	19	18	35	41	42	41	64	74	74	73	34	41	42	41					
Planned receipts					1	13	9	13	12	15	19	19	18	35	41	42	41	64	74	74	73	34	41	42	41					Friday due dates
Planned releases					1	13	9	13	12	15	19	19	18	35	41	42	41	64	74	74	73	34	41	42	41					Tuesday start dates

Product # TRI–SP   Lead Time 1

Startup Inventory Values
Inventory Balance 6 – Anticipation Inventory 0 – Safety Stock 0 = Week Zero Inventory Balance 6

	0	1	2	3	4	5	6	7	8	9	10	11	12	13	14	15	16	17	18	19	20	21	22	23	24	25	26	27	28	
Week		1/1	1/2	1/3	1/4	2/1	2/2	2/3	2/4	3/1	3/2	3/3	3/4	4/1	4/2	4/3	4/4	5/1	5/2	5/3	5/4	6/1	6/2	6/3	6/4					
Gross requirements			7				3			4				7				10				7								Friday due dates
Scheduled receipts		6																												
Anticipation inventory or SS changes														2				7				8								
On hand	6	12	5	5	5	5	2	2	2																					
Net requirements										2				9				17				15								
Planned receipts										2				9				17				15								Friday due dates
Planned releases										2				9				17				15								Thursday release dates

levels are redisplayed in Chart 16.5, breaking down the tricycle family into its specific components using the planning bill of material ratios.

Inventory items that do not occur on the master production schedule should not have anticipation inventory. Because spare parts may occur on the master production schedule, they may have anticipation inventory even though they are not scheduled with the level 0 parts. For example, CCCC in the bill of materials of Chart 13.2 may be sold as a spare part, placing it on level 0, but since it is also a component into TRI it is placed with the low-level code 1 items for scheduling purposes. For the examples we are scheduling in this chapter, we are not selling spare parts individually, such as CCCC. Rather, we sell a spare parts kit labeled with the finished goods part number TRI–SP.

Chart 16.4 demonstrates how the level 0 products are planned. Across the top we put in the following information:

Product #

Lead time (Chart 16.2)

Inventory balance (Chart 16.2)

Anticipation inventory (Chart 16.5)

Safety stock (based on Chart 11.9)

From these values we are able to calculate the starting inventory balance for week zero (week 0). For "TRI" we have 121 units in inventory and no anticipation inventory or safety stock, leaving a starting inventory balance of 121 units.

The "Week" row is where you record the starting date for each week in the future. Week 0 is the current week. Week 1 is next week, and so on. The "Gross Requirements" amount for level 0 items is taken from the master production schedule (Chart 12.2).

The "Scheduled Receipts" are taken from existing purchase and production orders (Chart 16.2). For "TRI" we have a production order for 21 units. This order is in process and will be completed during month 1, week 1.

The "Anticipation Inventory or Safety Stock Changes" row is where we report anticipated changes to either of these inputs. Only level 0 items or spare part items that have a master production schedule will have anticipation inventory and, hence, changes to the anticipation inventory level. Looking at Chart 16.5, we see that the anticipation inventory level for "TRI" is currently at 0 at the start of month 1, week

CHART 16.5 Anticipation Inventory for Tricycles
(Taken from Charts 16.3 and 8.3)

Month	Family	TRI (95%)	TRI-SP (5%)
1	0	0	0
2	0	0	0
3	0	0	0
4	34	32	2
5	134	127	7
6	167	159	8

1. It stays at that level until month 4 where it jumps to 32 units. Therefore, there is a 32-unit positive increase to the anticipation inventory level in month 4, which is broken up into four components, one for each week in the month. Month 4, week 1, gets an 8-unit increase, and so does each of weeks 2, 3, and 4. The total of the four increases is the required 32-unit jump. Similarly, in month 5, the "TRI" anticipation inventory level jumps up to 127 units, which is a 95-unit increase over month 4. These 95 units are broken up over the four weeks of month 5 in the following quantities: 24, 24, 24, and 23.

By dividing the anticipation inventory into weekly incremental jumps, we don't dump the entire work load into one week. However, these anticipation inventory changes should be handled in whatever way is most appropriate for your production environment. For example, for TRI–SP all of the anticipation inventory jumps for each month were entered into the only week where there was any production scheduled.

Drops in anticipation are handled the same way as increases. If the anticipation inventory level were to drop from 200 units to 120 units, we would have an 80-unit drop and this would be reported as a −80 in the "Anticipation Inventory or Safety Stock Changes" row of the worksheet.

Changes in the safety stock level can occur because of seasonal effects on demand. If safety stock levels change, these changes are handled in the same way as anticipation inventory level changes. The only difference is that safety stock can change at any low-level code, not just at the level 0 codes or for spare parts.

The "On Hand" inventory column starts in week 0 with the "Week Zero Inventory Balance" figure taken from the top of the schedule. For TRI this level is 121 units. For month 1, week 1, and beyond, we calculate the "On Hand" level for each week. The procedure is as follows:

"On Hand" inventory level from previous week

(−) "Gross Requirements" for current week

(+) "Scheduled Receipts" for current week

(−) "Anticipation inventory or Safety Stock Changes" for current week

(=) "On Hand" Inventory level for current week

If the current "On Hand" is negative do the following:

1. Place the absolute value of the "On Hand" inventory level in the "Net Requirements" column under the current week.
2. Zero out the "On Hand" value for the current week.

Using TRI as the example (Chart 16.4), the calculations would be as follows:

For month 1, week 1:
Week 0 "On Hand" is 121
(−) "Gross Requirements" of 38
(+) "Scheduled Receipts" of 21
(−) "Anticipation Inventory or SS Changes" of 0
(=) current "On Hand" of
$121 - 38 + 21 - 0 = 104$

For month 1, week 2:
1/1 "On Hand" is 104
(−) "Gross Requirements" of 30
(+) "Scheduled Receipts" of 0
(−) "Anticipation Inventory or SS Changes" of 0
(=) current "On Hand" of
$104 - 30 + 0 - 0 = 74$

For month 1, week 3:
1/2 "On Hand" is 74
(−) "Gross Requirements" of 38
(+) "Scheduled Receipts" of 0
(−) "Anticipation Inventory or SS Changes" of 0
(=) current "On Hand" of
$74 - 38 + 0 - 0 = 36$

For month 1, week 4:
1/3 "On Hand" is 36
(−) "Gross Requirements" of 37
(+) "Scheduled Receipts" of 0
(−) "Anticipation Inventory or SS Changes" of 0
(=) current "On Hand" of
$36 - 37 + 0 - 0 = -1$

Since "On Hand" is negative we:

1. Put "1" (the absolute value of −1) into the "Net Requirements" row
2. Put "0" into the "On Hand" row

For month 2, week 1:
1/4 "On Hand" is 0
(−) "Gross Requirements" of 13
(+) "Scheduled Receipts" of 0
(−) "Anticipation Inventory or SS Changes" of 0
(=) current "On Hand" of
$0 - 13 + 0 - 0 = -13$

Since "On Hand" is negative we:

1. Put "13" (the absolute value of −13) into the "Net Requirements" row
2. Put "0" into the "On Hand" row

This should be enough examples to make you feel comfortable with the calculation process. This process repeats itself all the way across the chart.

The "Net Requirements" row shows us what we need to build or buy. In the TRI example, we have a manufactured product so the net requirements are those products that we need to build. Then, these units that we build, in combination with our on hand and our scheduled receipts, should satisfy our gross requirements.

The "Planned Receipts" line is identical to the "Net Requirements" line in the TRI example. This is because we are using the lot-for-lot method as our lot sizing technique. The lot-for-lot method suggests that we order only what we need and nothing more. However, the "Planned Receipts" line does not always have to be equal to the "Net Requirements" line. In the next chapter (Chapter 17) we discuss lot sizing to explain this concept further and give you some other alternatives. For now, in the next few examples, we will use lot-for-lot as the lot sizing technique.

The "Planned Releases" identifies when an order has to be released in order to get it completed (planned order receipt or "Planned Receipts" line) on time. For TRI we have a lead time of three days (from top of chart). This means that if we plan to complete the production of TRI on Friday, we need to start it three days earlier or Tuesday (assume middle of day to middle of day for each increment of a day). This lead time planning for the entire TRI product structure can be seen on the time phased bill of materials diagram of Chart 14.9. In all the examples we are working with here we assume a five-day work week.

Some lead time shift examples can be seen on Chart 16.6. For example, TRI is shifting back from the planned receipts due date of Friday to start the production planned release on Tuesday of the same week. In other words, we start working on TRI on Tuesday (planned release) and we get done working on it on Friday (planned receipt) of the same week.

Chart 16.6 also shows how TRI–SP is similarly scheduled backward from its due date of Friday to a production start date of Thursday. From the bill of materials chart (Chart 13.2) we see that CCCC is a component into TRI. Similarly, from Chart 13.6 we see that CCCC is a component of TRI–SP. However, for TRI we need the CCCCs on Tuesday to start the TRI production process and for TRI-SP we need the CCCCs on

CHART 16.6 Lead Time Adjusments

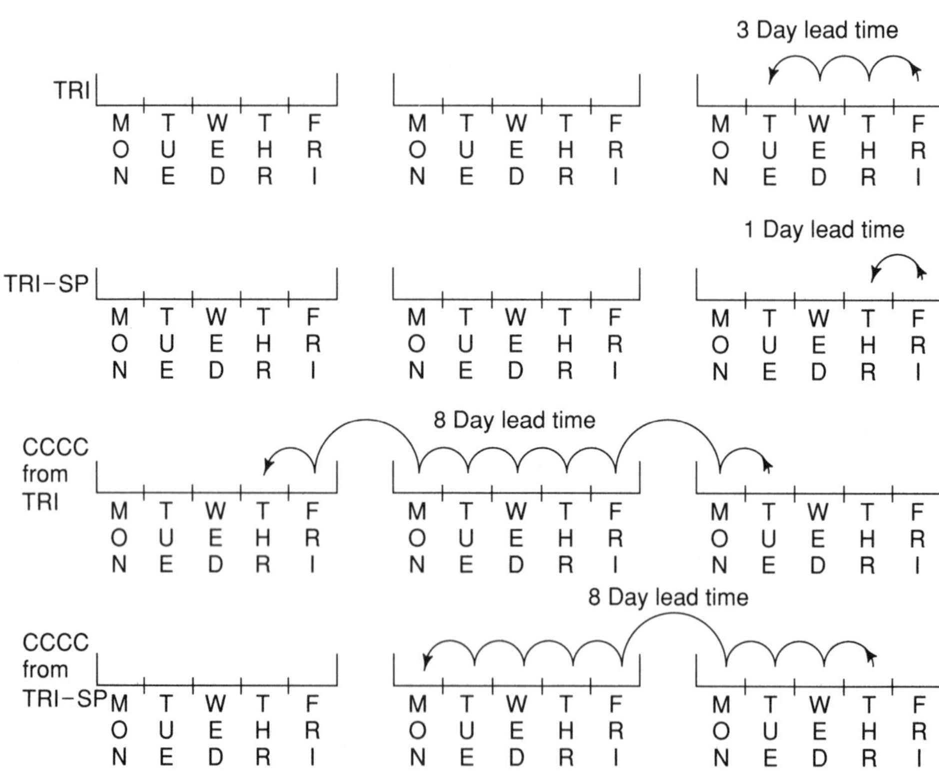

CHART 16.7 Material Requirements Planning Gross Requirements Worksheet

Date ____/____/____

Product # ________

	0	1	2	3	4	5	6	7	8	9	10	11	12	13	14	15	16	17	18	19	20	21	22	23	24	25	26	27	28
Week																													
Source product ____ Quantity per ____																													
Source product ____ Quantity per ____																													
Source product ____ Quantity per ____																													
Source product ____ Quantity per ____																													
Total gross requirements																													

Product # ________

	0	1	2	3	4	5	6	7	8	9	10	11	12	13	14	15	16	17	18	19	20	21	22	23	24	25	26	27	28
Week																													
Source product ____ Quantity per ____																													
Source product ____ Quantity per ____																													
Source product ____ Quantity per ____																													
Source product ____ Quantity per ____																													
Total gross requirements																													

CHART 16.8 Material Requirements Planning Gross Requirements Worksheet—Example of Level 1 Items

Date 1 / 1 / 1992

Product # CCCC

	0	1	2	3	4	5	6	7	8	9	10	11	12	13	14	15	16	17	18	19	20	21	22	23	24	25	26	27	28
Week		1/1	1/2	1/3	1/4	2/1	2/2	2/3	2/4	3/1	3/2	3/3	3/4	4/1	4/2	4/3	4/4	5/1	5/2	5/3	5/4	6/1	6/2	6/3	6/4				
Source product TRI Quantity per 4					4	52	36	52	48	60	76	76	72	140	164	168	164	256	296	296	292	136	164	168	164				
Source product TRI–SP Quantity per 4										8				36				68				60							
Total gross requirements					4	52	36	52	48	68	76	76	72	176	164	168	164	324	296	296	292	196	164	168	164				

Product # ABCD

	0	1	2	3	4	5	6	7	8	9	10	11	12	13	14	15	16	17	18	19	20	21	22	23	24	25	26	27	28
Week		1/1	1/2	1/3	1/4	2/1	2/2	2/3	2/4	3/1	3/2	3/3	3/4	4/1	4/2	4/3	4/4	5/1	5/2	5/3	5/4	6/1	6/2	6/3	6/4				
Source product TRI Quantity per 2					2	26	18	26	24	30	38	38	36	70	82	84	82	128	148	148	146	68	82	84	82				
Source product TRI–SP Quantity per 1										2				9				17				15							
Total gross requirements					2	26	18	26	24	32	38	38	36	79	82	84	82	145	148	148	146	83	82	84	82				

Product # DDDD	0	1	2	3	4	5	6	7	8	9	10	11	12	13	14	15	16	17	18	19	20	21	22	23	24	25	26	27	28
Week		1/1	1/2	1/3	1/4	2/1	2/2	2/3	2/4	3/1	3/2	3/3	3/4	4/1	4/2	4/3	4/4	5/1	5/2	5/3	5/4	6/1	6/2	6/3	6/4				
Source product TRI Quantity per 1					1	13	9	13	12	15	19	19	18	35	41	42	41	64	74	74	73	34	41	42	41				
Source product TRI–SP Quantity per 1										2				9				17				15							
Total gross requirements					1	13	9	13	12	17	19	19	18	44	41	42	41	81	74	74	73	49	41	42	41				

Product # AABB	0	1	2	3	4	5	6	7	8	9	10	11	12	13	14	15	16	17	18	19	20	21	22	23	24	25	26	27	28
Week		1/1	1/2	1/3	1/4	2/1	2/2	2/3	2/4	3/1	3/2	3/3	3/4	4/1	4/2	4/3	4/4	5/1	5/2	5/3	5/4	6/1	6/2	6/3	6/4				
Source product TRI Quantity per 3					3	39	27	39	36	45	57	57	54	105	123	126	123	192	222	222	219	102	123	126	123				
Source product TRI–SP Quantity per 3										6				27				51				45							
Total gross requirements					3	39	27	39	36	51	57	57	54	132	123	126	123	243	222	222	219	147	123	126	123				

Product # AACC	0	1	2	3	4	5	6	7	8	9	10	11	12	13	14	15	16	17	18	19	20	21	22	23	24	25	26	27	28
Week		1/1	1/2	1/3	1/4	2/1	2/2	2/3	2/4	3/1	3/2	3/3	3/4	4/1	4/2	4/3	4/4	5/1	5/2	5/3	5/4	6/1	6/2	6/3	6/4				
Source product TRI Quantity per 1					1	13	9	13	12	15	19	19	18	35	41	42	41	64	74	74	73	34	41	42	41				
Total gross requirements					1	13	9	13	12	15	19	19	18	35	41	42	41	64	74	74	73	34	41	42	41				

CHART 16.9 Material Requirements Planning Worksheet—Example of Level 1 Items

Date 1 / 1 / 1992

Product # CCCC Lead Time 8

Startup Inventory Values
Inventory Balance 4 − Anticipation Inventory 0 − Safety Stock 3 = Week Zero Inventory Balance 1

	0	1	2	3	4	5	6	7	8	9	10	11	12	13	14	15	16	17	18	19	20	21	22	23	24	25	26	27	28
Week		1/1	1/2	1/3	1/4	2/1	2/2	2/3	2/4	3/1	3/2	3/3	3/4	4/1	4/2	4/3	4/4	5/1	5/2	5/3	5/4	6/1	6/2	6/3	6/4				
Gross requirements					4	52	36	52	48	68	76	76	72	176	164	168	164	324	296	296	292	196	164	168	164				
Scheduled receipts		4																											
Anticipation inventory or SS changes																													
On hand	1	5	5	5	1																								
Net requirements						51	36	52	48	68	76	76	72	176	164	168	164	324	296	296	292	196	164	168	164				
Planned receipts						51	36	52	48	68	76	76	72	176	164	168	164	324	296	296	292	196	164	168	164				
Planned releases				51	36	52	48	68	76	76	72	176	164	168	164	324	296	296	292	196	164	168	164						

Product # ABCD Lead Time 4

Startup Inventory Values
Inventory Balance 5 − Anticipation Inventory 0 − Safety Stock 3 = Week Zero Inventory Balance 2

	0	1	2	3	4	5	6	7	8	9	10	11	12	13	14	15	16	17	18	19	20	21	22	23	24	25	26	27	28
Week		1/1	1/2	1/3	1/4	2/1	2/2	2/3	2/4	3/1	3/2	3/3	3/4	4/1	4/2	4/3	4/4	5/1	5/2	5/3	5/4	6/1	6/2	6/3	6/4				
Gross requirements					2	26	18	26	24	32	38	38	36	79	82	84	82	145	148	148	146	83	82	84	82				
Scheduled receipts				5																									
Anticipation inventory or SS changes																													
On hand	2	2	2	7	5																								
Net requirements						21	18	26	24	32	38	38	36	79	82	84	82	145	148	148	146	83	82	84	82				
Planned receipts						21	18	26	24	32	38	38	36	79	82	84	82	145	148	148	146	83	82	84	82				
Planned releases					21	18	26	24	32	38	38	36	79	82	84	82	145	148	148	146	83	82	84	82					

Product # DDDD Lead Time 9

Startup Inventory Values
Inventory Balance 10 − Anticipation Inventory 0 − Safety Stock 5 = Week Zero Inventory Balance 5

	0	1	2	3	4	5	6	7	8	9	10	11	12	13	14	15	16	17	18	19	20	21	22	23	24	25	26	27	28
Week		1/1	1/2	1/3	1/4	2/1	2/2	2/3	2/4	3/1	3/2	3/3	3/4	4/1	4/2	4/3	4/4	5/1	5/2	5/3	5/4	6/1	6/2	6/3	6/4				
Gross requirements					1	13	9	13	12	17	19	19	18	44	41	42	41	81	74	74	73	49	41	42	41				

	0	1	2	3	4	5	6	7	8	9	10	11	12	13	14	15	16	17	18	19	20	21	22	23	24	25	26	27	28
Scheduled receipts			10																										
Anticipation inventory or SS changes																													
On hand	5	5	15	15	14	1																							
Net requirements							8	13	12	17	19	19	18	44	41	42	41	81	74	74	73	49	41	42	41				
Planned receipts							8	13	12	17	19	19	18	44	41	42	41	81	74	74	73	49	41	42	41				
Planned releases					8	13	12	17	19	19	18	44	41	42	41	81	74	74	73	49	41	42	41						

Product # AABB Lead Time 3

Startup Inventory Values
Inventory Balance 15 − Anticipation Inventory 0 − Safety Stock 5 = Week Zero Inventory Balance 10

	0	1	2	3	4	5	6	7	8	9	10	11	12	13	14	15	16	17	18	19	20	21	22	23	24	25	26	27	28
Week		1/1	1/2	1/3	1/4	2/1	2/2	2/3	2/4	3/1	3/2	3/3	3/4	4/1	4/2	4/3	4/4	5/1	5/2	5/3	5/4	6/1	6/2	6/3	6/4				
Gross requirements					3	39	27	39	36	51	57	57	54	132	123	126	123	243	222	222	219	147	123	126	123				
Scheduled receipts				15																									
Anticipation inventory or SS changes																													
On hand	10	10	10	25	22																								
Net requirements						17	27	39	36	51	57	57	54	132	123	126	123	243	222	222	219	147	123	126	123				
Planned receipts						17	27	39	36	51	57	57	54	132	123	126	123	243	222	222	219	147	123	126	123				
Planned releases					17	27	39	36	51	57	57	54	132	123	126	123	243	222	222	219	147	123	126	123					

Product # AACC Lead Time 14

Startup Inventory Values
Inventory Balance 6 − Anticipation Inventory 0 − Safety Stock 3 = Week Zero Inventory Balance 3

	0	1	2	3	4	5	6	7	8	9	10	11	12	13	14	15	16	17	18	19	20	21	22	23	24	25	26	27	28
Week		1/1	1/2	1/3	1/4	2/1	2/2	2/3	2/4	3/1	3/2	3/3	3/4	4/1	4/2	4/3	4/4	5/1	5/2	5/3	5/4	6/1	6/2	6/3	6/4				
Gross requirements					1	13	9	13	12	15	19	19	18	35	41	42	41	64	74	74	73	34	41	42	41				
Scheduled receipts			20																										
Anticipation inventory or SS changes																													
On hand	3	3	23	23	22	9																							
Net requirements								13	12	15	19	19	18	35	41	42	41	64	74	74	73	34	41	42	41				
Planned receipts								13	12	15	19	19	18	35	41	42	41	64	74	74	73	34	41	42	41				
Planned releases					13	12	15	19	19	18	35	41	42	41	64	74	74	73	34	41	42	41							

Thursday. CCCC has an eight-day lead time. The CCCC demands for TRI need to be ordered on Thursday, two weeks back, and the CCCC demands for TRI–SP need to be ordered on Monday of the previous week (see Chart 16.6). This type of time phasing was demonstrated on Chart 14.9 and will occur for every MRP schedule we generate (see Chart 16.4). The due date of the materials is always the "Planned Receipts" line, and the order date is always the "Planned Releases" line.

Going back to the Chart 16.4, we see that in the TRI schedule the planned releases are in the same week as the planned receipts. However, as demonstrated by Chart 16.6, they occur on different days.

At this point you should be comfortable with the TRI material requirements schedule of Chart 16.4. If you have any questions about what the numbers mean, reread the last few pages. You need to understand this schedule before you continue or the MRP discussion will only get more confusing.

Having scheduled TRI, we now schedule TRI–SP. This is also done in Chart 16.4. Having done this we have now scheduled all the low-level code 0 items and are now ready to move on to the low-level code 1 items (see Chart 16.2). As mentioned earlier, we have five low-level code 1 items:

CCCC ABCD DDDD AABB AACC

Before we can schedule these items, we need to calculate the gross requirements for each. To do this we need a special worksheet that will facilitate this accumulation. The gross requirements worksheet is shown in Chart 16.7. An example of how to use this sheet is given in Chart 16.8.

Referring back to the bill of materials of TRI and TRI–SP (Charts 13.2 and 13.6), we see that CCCC gets requirements from both TRI and TRI–SP. This is also true for ABCD, DDDD, and AABB. Part AACC only gets requirements from TRI. On the left-hand side of Chart 16.7 we put in the source products. For part CCCC these are TRI and TRI–SP (see Chart 16.8). From the bill of materials charts we also determine the quantity of CCCCs per each TRI or TRI–SP that we will need. In this case we need four CCCCs for every TRI and four CCCCs for every TRI–SP. We multiply the numbers on the "Planned Release" line of TRI times four (the quantity per) and place these values into the appropriate columns of Chart 16.7 (see the example of Chart 16.8). Similarly, we multiply the values taken from the "Planned Release" line of TRI–SP times four and record them on the chart. Having calculated the individual gross requirements, we then sum up each column to get the total gross requirements for CCCCs.

We similarly calculate the total gross requirements for each of the low-level 1 items. These calculations are also shown on Chart 16.8.

Now we are ready to calculate the MRP schedules for all the low-level 1 items. The gross requirements come from Chart 16.8. The remaining calculations are shown in Chart 16.9 (using the input format of Chart 16.3) and, except for the source of the gross requirements, the procedure is similar to the calculations of Chart 16.4.

CHART 16.10 Material Requirements Planning Gross Requirements Worksheet—Example of Level 2 Items

Date 1 / 1 / 1992

Product # BBBB

	0	1	2	3	4	5	6	7	8	9	10	11	12	13	14	15	16	17	18	19	20	21	22	23	24	25	26	27	28
Week		1/1	1/2	1/3	1/4	2/1	2/2	2/3	2/4	3/1	3/2	3/3	3/4	4/1	4/2	4/3	4/4	5/1	5/2	5/3	5/4	6/1	6/2	6/3	6/4				
Source product TRI Quantity per 12					12	156	108	156	144	180	228	228	216	420	492	504	492	768	888	888	876	408	492	504	492				
Source product TRI–SP Quantity per 5										10				45				85				75							
Source product DDDD Quantity per 2				82	72	104	96	136	152	152	144	352	328	336	328	648	592	592	584	392	328	336	328						
Source product AACC Quantity per 3			99	108	156	144	180	228	228	216	420	492	504	492	768	888	888	876	408	492	504	492							
Total gross requirements			99	190	240	404	384	520	524	558	792	1072	1048	1293	1588	2040	1972	2321	1880	1772	1708	1311	820	504	492				

Product # ACAC

	0	1	2	3	4	5	6	7	8	9	10	11	12	13	14	15	16	17	18	19	20	21	22	23	24	25	26	27	28
Week		1/1	1/2	1/3	1/4	2/1	2/2	2/3	2/4	3/1	3/2	3/3	3/4	4/1	4/2	4/3	4/4	5/1	5/2	5/3	5/4	6/1	6/2	6/3	6/4				
Source product CCCC Quantity per 2				102	72	104	96	136	152	152	144	352	328	336	328	648	592	592	584	392	328	336	328						
Total gross requirements				102	72	104	96	136	152	152	144	352	328	336	328	648	592	592	584	392	328	336	328						

Product # A5B5

	0	1	2	3	4	5	6	7	8	9	10	11	12	13	14	15	16	17	18	19	20	21	22	23	24	25	26	27	28
Week		1/1	1/2	1/3	1/4	2/1	2/2	2/3	2/4	3/1	3/2	3/3	3/4	4/1	4/2	4/3	4/4	5/1	5/2	5/3	5/4	6/1	6/2	6/3	6/4				
Source product ABCD Quantity per 3				3	312	216	312	288	384	456	456	432	948	1008	984	984	1740	1776	1776	1752	996	984	1008	984					
Source product DDDD Quantity per 3				123	108	156	144	204	228	228	216	528	492	504	492	972	888	888	876	588	492	504	492						
Total gross requirements				126	420	372	456	492	612	684	672	960	1440	1488	1500	1956	2628	2664	2652	2340	1488	1488	1500	984					

CHART 16.11 Material Requirements Planning Worksheet—Example of Level 2 Items

Date 1 / 1 / 1992

Product # BBBB Lead Time 6

Startup Inventory Values
Inventory Balance 45 − Anticipation Inventory 0 − Safety Stock 15 = Week Zero Inventory Balance 30

	0	1	2	3	4	5	6	7	8	9	10	11	12	13	14	15	16	17	18	19	20	21	22	23	24	25	26	27	28
Week		1/1	1/2	1/3	1/4	2/1	2/2	2/3	2/4	3/1	3/2	3/3	3/4	4/1	4/2	4/3	4/4	5/1	5/2	5/3	5/4	6/1	6/2	6/3	6/4				
Gross requirements			99	190	240	404	384	520	524	558	792	1072	1048	1293	1588	2040	1972	2321	1880	1772	1708	1311	820	504	492				
Scheduled receipts			100																										
Anticipation inventory or SS changes																													
On hand	30	30	31																										
Net requirements				159	240	404	384	520	524	558	792	1072	1048	1293	1588	2040	1972	2321	1880	1772	1708	1311	820	504	492				
Planned receipts				159	240	404	384	520	524	558	792	1072	1048	1293	1588	2040	1972	2321	1880	1772	1708	1311	820	504	492				
Planned releases			159	240	404	384	520	524	558	792	1072	1048	1293	1588	2040	1972	2321	1880	1772	1708	1311	820	504	492					

Product # ACAC Lead Time 6

Startup Inventory Values
Inventory Balance 20 − Anticipation Inventory 0 − Safety Stock 10 = Week Zero Inventory Balance 10

	0	1	2	3	4	5	6	7	8	9	10	11	12	13	14	15	16	17	18	19	20	21	22	23	24	25	26	27	28
Week		1/1	1/2	1/3	1/4	2/1	2/2	2/3	2/4	3/1	3/2	3/3	3/4	4/1	4/2	4/3	4/4	5/1	5/2	5/3	5/4	6/1	6/2	6/3	6/4				
Gross requirements				102	72	104	96	136	152	152	144	352	328	336	328	648	592	592	584	392	328	336	328						

Scheduled receipts			20																										
Anticipation inventory or SS changes																													
On hand	10	10	30																										
Net requirements				72	72	104	96	136	152	152	144	352	328	336	328	648	592	592	584	392	328	336	328						
Planned receipts				72	72	104	96	136	152	152	144	352	328	336	328	648	592	592	584	392	328	336	328						
Planned releases			72	72	104	96	136	152	152	144	352	328	336	328	648	592	592	584	392	328	336	328							

Product # A5B5 Lead Time 1

Startup Inventory Values
Inventory Balance 23 − Anticipation Inventory 0 − Safety Stock 10 = Week Zero Inventory Balance 13

	0	1	2	3	4	5	6	7	8	9	10	11	12	13	14	15	16	17	18	19	20	21	22	23	24	25	26	27	28
Week		1/1	1/2	1/3	1/4	2/1	2/2	2/3	2/4	3/1	3/2	3/3	3/4	4/1	4/2	4/3	4/4	5/1	5/2	5/3	5/4	6/1	6/2	6/3	6/4				
Gross requirements				126	420	372	456	492	612	684	672	960	1440	1488	1500	1956	2628	2664	2652	2340	1488	1488	1500	984					
Scheduled receipts				23																									
Anticipation inventory or SS changes																													
On hand	13	13	13																										
Net requirements				90	420	372	456	492	612	684	672	960	1440	1488	1500	1956	2628	2664	2652	2340	1488	1488	1500	984					
Planned receipts				90	420	372	456	492	612	684	672	960	1440	1488	1500	1956	2628	2664	2652	2340	1488	1488	1500	984					
Planned releases				90	420	372	456	492	612	684	672	960	1440	1488	1500	1956	2628	2664	2652	2340	1488	1488	1500	984					

CHART 16.12 Material Requirements Planning Gross Requirements Worksheet—Example of Level 3 Items

Date 1/1/1992

Product # A4B4

	0	1	2	3	4	5	6	7	8	9	10	11	12	13	14	15	16	17	18	19	20	21	22	23	24	25	26	27	28
Week		1/1	1/2	1/3	1/4	2/1	2/2	2/3	2/4	3/1	3/2	3/3	3/4	4/1	4/2	4/3	4/4	5/1	5/2	5/3	5/4	6/1	6/2	6/3	6/4				
Source product CCCC Quantity per 12				612	432	624	576	816	912	912	864	2112	1968	2016	1968	3888	3552	3552	3504	2352	1968	2016	1968						
Source product ABCD Quantity per 10				10	1040	720	1040	960	1280	1520	1520	1440	3160	3280	3360	3280	5800	5920	5920	5840	3320	3280	3360	3280					
Source product ACAC Quantity per 9			648	648	936	864	1224	1368	1368	1296	3168	2952	3024	2952	5832	5328	5328	5256	3528	2952	3024	2952							
Total gross requirements			648	1270	2408	2208	2840	3144	3560	3728	5552	6504	8152	8248	11160	12496	14680	14728	12952	11144	8312	8248	5328	3280					

Product # A555

	0	1	2	3	4	5	6	7	8	9	10	11	12	13	14	15	16	17	18	19	20	21	22	23	24	25	26	27	28
Week		1/1	1/2	1/3	1/4	2/1	2/2	2/3	2/4	3/1	3/2	3/3	3/4	4/1	4/2	4/3	4/4	5/1	5/2	5/3	5/4	6/1	6/2	6/3	6/4				
Source product ACAC Quantity per 7			504	504	728	672	952	1064	1064	1008	2464	2296	2352	2296	4536	4144	4144	4088	2744	2296	2352	2296							
Source product B555 Quantity per 4				360	1680	1488	1824	1968	2448	2736	2688	3840	5760	5952	6000	7824	10512	10656	10608	9360	5952	5952	6000	3936					
Total gross requirements			504	864	2408	2160	2776	3032	3512	3744	5152	6136	8112	8248	10536	11968	14656	14744	13352	11656	8304	8248	6000	3936					

Product # B555

	0	1	2	3	4	5	6	7	8	9	10	11	12	13	14	15	16	17	18	19	20	21	22	23	24	25	26	27	28
Week		1/1	1/2	1/3	1/4	2/1	2/2	2/3	2/4	3/1	3/2	3/3	3/4	4/1	4/2	4/3	4/4	5/1	5/2	5/3	5/4	6/1	6/2	6/3	6/4				
Source product ACAC Quantity per 2			144	144	208	192	272	304	304	288	704	656	672	656	1296	1184	1184	1168	784	656	672	656							
Total gross requirements			144	144	208	192	272	304	304	288	704	656	672	656	1296	1184	1184	1168	784	656	672	656							

Now we are ready to calculate the MRP schedules for the low-level code 2 items, which are:

BBBB ACAC A5B5

The total gross requirements are again calculated using Chart 16.7. However, this time the sources of the requirements are more difficult. Looking back at the bill of materials charts (Chart 13.2 and Chart 13.6) we see that BBBB gets requirements from several sources. These are:

TRI	12 BBBBs for each TRI
TRI-SP	5 BBBBs for each TRI-SP
DDDD	2 BBBBs for each DDDD
AACC	3 BBBBs for each AACC

Similarly, ACAC gets requirements from CCCC and A5B5 gets requirements from ABCD and DDDD. Each time, we multiply the "Planned Releases" line of the product generating the demand by the quantity required to generate the individual gross requirements. These individual gross requirements are then accumulated to get the total gross requirements for each product. These calculations can be seen on Chart 16.10. We then generate the MRP schedules for these low-level code 2 products. These calculations are performed again using the worksheet from Chart 16.3 and the gross requirements from Chart 16.10. The calculations are done on Chart 16.11.

We are now ready to calculate the MRP schedules for the last level of production, level 3. But first we need to generate the total gross requirements. This is done on Chart 16.12 using the form in Chart 16.7. The MRP schedules for these products can be found on Chart 16.13 using the form of Chart 16.3.

Appendix 6.A gives an example of how to execute the MRP process on a computer using a simple spreadsheet. There are also numerous computer packages available that integrate MRP with some of the other information flow pieces. However, as previously stated, it is helpful to run MRP manually or using the spreadsheet for a little while until you see what your organization requires from an MRP package so that you don't invest in a mistake.

At this point you are an expert MRP scheduler. Reread this chapter and it will make even more sense the second or third time around. Now that you have reached this point, let me make some sense of what these schedules tell you.

Output Reports

At this point we have generated an MRP schedule for each of the products we produce or purchase. Next we need to determine what all these charts tell us. The first thing we do is separate the purchase schedules from the production schedules. We know which products are purchased and which are manufactured by looking back at the bill of

CHART 16.13 Material Requirements Planning Worksheet—Example of Level 3 Items

Date 1/1/1992

Product # A4B4 — Lead Time 4

Startup Inventory Values
Inventory Balance 200 − Anticipation Inventory 0 − Safety Stock 50 = Week Zero Inventory Balance 150

	0	1	2	3	4	5	6	7	8	9	10	11	12	13	14	15	16	17	18	19	20	21	22	23	24	25	26	27	28
Week		1/1	1/2	1/3	1/4	2/1	2/2	2/3	2/4	3/1	3/2	3/3	3/4	4/1	4/2	4/3	4/4	5/1	5/2	5/3	5/4	6/1	6/2	6/3	6/4				
Gross requirements			648	1270	2408	2208	2840	3144	3560	3728	5552	6504	8152	8248	11160	12496	14680	14728	12952	11144	8312	8248	5328	3280					
Scheduled receipts		400																											
Anticipation inventory or SS changes																													
On hand	150	550																											
Net requirements			98	1270	2408	2208	2840	3144	3560	3728	5552	6504	8152	8248	11160	12496	14680	14728	12952	11144	8312	8248	5328	3280					
Planned receipts			98	1270	2408	2208	2840	3144	3560	3728	5552	6504	8152	8248	11160	12496	14680	14728	12952	11144	8312	8248	5328	3280					
Planned releases		98	1270	2408	2208	2840	3144	3560	3728	5552	6504	8152	8248	11160	12496	14680	14728	12952	11144	8312	8248	5328	3280						

Product # A555 — Lead Time 2

Startup Inventory Values
Inventory Balance 40 − Anticipation Inventory 0 − Safety Stock 10 = Week Zero Inventory Balance 30

	0	1	2	3	4	5	6	7	8	9	10	11	12	13	14	15	16	17	18	19	20	21	22	23	24	25	26	27	28
Week		1/1	1/2	1/3	1/4	2/1	2/2	2/3	2/4	3/1	3/2	3/3	3/4	4/1	4/2	4/3	4/4	5/1	5/2	5/3	5/4	6/1	6/2	6/3	6/4				
Gross requirements			504	864	2408	2160	2776	3032	3512	3744	5152	6136	8112	8248	10536	11968	14656	14744	13352	11656	8304	8248	6000	3936					
Scheduled receipts		300																											

Anticipation inventory or SS changes																													
On hand	30	30																											
Net requirements			174	864	2408	2160	2776	3032	3512	3744	5152	6136	8112	8248	10536	11968	14656	14744	13352	11656	8304	8248	6000	3936					
Planned receipts			174	864	2408	2160	2776	3032	3512	3744	5152	6136	8112	8248	10536	11968	14656	14744	13352	11656	8304	8248	6000	3936					
Planned releases			174	864	2408	2160	2776	3032	3512	3744	5152	6136	8112	8248	10536	11968	14656	14744	13352	11656	8304	8248	6000	3936					

Startup Inventory Values

Product # B555 **Lead Time 1** **Inventory Balance 7 − Anticipation Inventory 0 − Safety Stock 5 = Week Zero Inventory Balance 2**

	0	1	2	3	4	5	6	7	8	9	10	11	12	13	14	15	16	17	18	19	20	21	22	23	24	25	26	27	28
Week		1/1	1/2	1/3	1/4	2/1	2/2	2/3	2/4	3/1	3/2	3/3	3/4	4/1	4/2	4/3	4/4	5/1	5/2	5/3	5/4	6/1	6/2	6/3	6/4				
Gross requirements			144	144	208	192	272	304	304	288	704	656	672	656	1296	1184	1184	1168	784	656	672	656							
Scheduled receipts		20																											
Anticipation inventory or SS changes																													
On hand	2	22																											
Net requirements			122	144	208	192	272	304	304	288	704	656	672	656	1296	1184	1184	1168	784	656	672	656							
Planned receipts			122	144	208	192	272	304	304	288	704	656	672	656	1296	1184	1184	1168	784	656	672	656							
Planned releases			122	144	208	192	272	304	304	288	704	656	672	656	1296	1184	1184	1168	784	656	672	656							

materials schedules. (See Charts 13.2 and 13.6. Review Chapter 13 if you need further explanation.) Once these have been separated, we are ready to generate a series of reports.

Planned Order Release Report

There are two planned order release reports, one for purchased parts and one for manufactured parts. They are both generated the same way, however, one uses the purchased MRP schedules and one uses the manufacturing part schedules. Once the two reports have been generated, the purchasing planned order report goes to the Purchasing De-

CHART 16.14 Production Planned Order Releases for the Next Two Months
(Taken from the planned release lines of the MRP schedules of Charts 16.4, 16.9, 16.11, and 16.13)

Product Number	Date	Quantity
TRI	1/4	1
	2/1	13
	2/2	9
	2/3	13
	2/4	12
TRI–SP	None	
CCCC	1/3	51
	1/4	36
	2/1	52
	2/2	48
	2/3	68
	2/4	76
ABCD	1/4	21
	2/1	18
	2/2	26
	2/3	24
	2/4	32
DDDD	1/4	8
	2/1	13
	2/2	12
	2/3	17
	2/4	19
AACC	1/4	13
	2/1	12
	2/2	15
	2/3	19
	2/4	19
ACAC	1/2	72
	1/3	72
	1/4	104
	2/1	96
	2/2	136
	2/3	152
	2/4	152
A5B5	1/3	90
	1/4	420
	2/1	327
	2/2	456
	2/3	492
	2/4	612

partment and the production planned order report goes to the Production Scheduling Department (see Chapter 19).

To generate the planned order release report we look at the Chart 16.3 schedules. For the example we have been working on, these schedules are found in Chart 16.4 (level 0), Chart 16.9 (level 1), Chart 16.11 (level 2), and Chart 16.13 (level 3). The manufactured components are:

TRI	TRI–SP	CCCC	ABCD
DDDD	AACC	ACAC	A5B5

The purchased components are:

BBBB	AABB	A4B4	A555
B555			

The manufacturing planned order release report lists all of the orders that need to be planned over the next couple of months. This information comes from the "Planned Releases" line of each production schedule. The planned order report for our example products is shown in Chart 16.14.

The planned order purchasing report is shown in Chart 16.15. This report lists the planned purchase order releases that should occur over the next two months. This information would be extremely helpful to your vendors so that they can plan appropriately to meet your needs.

Order Release Report

At this point we know what our production orders and purchase orders will be for the next couple of months. Next we need to take action on these planned orders. If there are any orders that are in time period zero, they are probably late and action needs to be taken to release them immediately. These orders are probably the result of a change to one of the inputs. A listing of these urgent items is called an order release report. This report is usually in the form of a memo indicating urgent items, rather than in the form of a report. It needs to be sent to their corresponding purchasing or production scheduling departments.

Cancellations or Reschedulings Report

Occasionally, due to changes in the inputs, an outstanding order is no longer needed as early as it was previously. Or perhaps the order is now more urgent than it was before. Or the order may no longer be needed at all. We need to generate a list of changes of this type to the existing orders. This report is called a cancellations or reschedulings report. This report is also more of a memo than a report. The change information needs to be sent to the corresponding purchasing or production departments as needed.

Chart 16.16 gives an example of a cancellations or reschedulings report based on the sample MRP schedule data of Charts 16.4, 16.9, 16.11, and 16.13. Only a few examples have been included to demonstrate how it would work. You will need to refer back to the MRP

CHART 16.15 Purchasing Planned Order Releases for the Next Two Months
(Taken from the planned release lines of the MRP schedules of Charts 16.9, 16.11, and 16.13)

Product Number	Date	Quantity
AABB	1/4	17
	2/1	27
	2/2	39
	2/3	36
	2/4	51
BBBB	1/2	159
	1/3	240
	1/4	404
	2/1	348
	2/2	520
	2/3	524
	2/4	558
A4B4	1/1	98
	1/2	1270
	1/3	2408
	1/4	2208
	2/1	2840
	2/2	3144
	2/3	3560
	2/4	3728
A555	1/2	174
	1/3	864
	1/4	2408
	2/1	2160
	2/2	2776
	2/3	3032
	2/4	3512
B555	1/2	122
	1/3	144
	1/4	208
	2/1	192
	2/2	272
	2/3	304
	2/4	304

scheduling charts to see which "Scheduled Receipts" items have been rescheduled.

Firm Planned Order Report

Many of the orders that are listed on the planned order report (see Charts 16.14 and 16.15) will need to be "firmed up." In other words, they will need to become permanently scheduled so that they will appear as "Scheduled Receipts" even though they have not yet been placed (released), because they have not yet become current. This should happen to orders that are due for release over the next couple of weeks. We would select the appropriate orders and create a "firm planned order" report for each of purchasing and production scheduling so they can plan for these orders. A sample firm planned order list for the sample MRP schedule data of Charts 16.4, 16.9, 16.10, 16.11, 16.12, and 16.13 is shown on Chart 16.17.

CHART 16.16 Cancellations or Reschedulings Report for the Next Two Months
(Taken from the planned release lines of the MRP schedules of Charts 16.4, 16.9, 16.11, and 16.13)

Production Items Product Number	Date	Quantity
TRI	Due 1/1	21
	Reschedule to be due 1/4 and change quantity to 22.	
TRI–SP	Due 1/1	6
	Reschedule to be due 2/2	
CCCC	Due 1/1	4
	Reschedule to be due 1/4	
ABCD	Due 1/4	5
	Reschedule to be due 2/1	
DDDD	Due 1/2	10
	Reschedule to be due 2/1	
AACC	Due 1/2	20
	Reschedule to be due 2/1	
ACAC	Due 1/2	20
	Reschedule to be due 1/3 and combine with planned order due 1/3 for 72	

Purchasing Items Product Number	Date	Quantity
AABB	Due 1/3	15
	Reschedule to be due 2/1 and combine with planned order due 2/1 for 17	
A4B4	Due 1/1	400
	Reschedule to be due 1/2	
B555	Due 1/1	20
	Reschedule to be due 1/2	

CHART 16.17 Firmed Planned Order Report for the Next Couple of Weeks
(Taken from the planned release lines of the MRP schedules of Charts 16.4, 16.9, 16.11, and 16.13; also taken from Charts 16.14 and 16.15)

Production Items Product Number	Date	Quantity
ACAC	1/2	72

Purchasing Items Product Number	Date	Quantity
BBBB	1/2	159
A4B4	1/1	98
	1/2	1270
A555	1/2	174
B555	1/2	122

CHART 16.18 Material Requirements Planning Worksheet After MRP Output Adjustments (Compare with Charts 16.11 and 16.13)

Date 1 / 1 / 1992

Product # ACAC Lead Time 6

Startup Inventory Values
Inventory Balance 20 − Anticipation Inventory 0 − Safety Stock 10 = Week Zero Inventory Balance 10

	0	1	2	3	4	5	6	7	8	9	10	11	12	13	14	15	16	17	18	19	20	21	22	23	24	25	26	27	28
Week		1/1	1/2	1/3	1/4	2/1	2/2	2/3	2/4	3/1	3/2	3/3	3/4	4/1	4/2	4/3	4/4	5/1	5/2	5/3	5/4	6/1	6/2	6/3	6/4				
Gross requirements				102	72	104	96	136	152	152	144	352	328	336	328	648	592	592	584	392	328	336	328						
Scheduled receipts				92																									
Anticipation inventory or SS changes																													
On hand	10	10	10																										
Net requirements					72	104	96	136	152	152	144	352	328	336	328	648	592	592	584	392	328	336	328						
Planned receipts					72	104	96	136	152	152	144	352	328	336	328	648	592	592	584	392	328	336	328						
Planned releases				72	104	96	136	152	152	144	352	328	336	328	648	592	592	584	392	328	336	328							

Product # A4B4 Lead Time 4

Startup Inventory Values
Inventory Balance 200 − Anticipation Inventory 0 − Safety Stock 50 = Week Zero Inventory Balance 150

	0	1	2	3	4	5	6	7	8	9	10	11	12	13	14	15	16	17	18	19	20	21	22	23	24	25	26	27	28
Week		1/1	1/2	1/3	1/4	2/1	2/2	2/3	2/4	3/1	3/2	3/3	3/4	4/1	4/2	4/3	4/4	5/1	5/2	5/3	5/4	6/1	6/2	6/3	6/4				
Gross requirements			648	1270	2408	2208	2840	3144	3560	3728	5552	6504	8152	8248	11160	12496	14680	14728	12952	11144	8312	8248	5328	3280					
Scheduled receipts			498	1270																									
Anticipation inventory or SS changes																													
On hand	150	150																											
Net requirements					2408	2208	2840	3144	3560	3728	5552	6504	8152	8248	11160	12496	14680	14728	12952	11144	8312	8248	5328	3280					
Planned receipts					2408	2208	2840	3144	3560	3728	5552	6504	8152	8248	11160	12496	14680	14728	12952	11144	8312	8248	5328	3280					
Planned releases				2408	2208	2840	3144	3560	3728	5552	6504	8152	8248	11160	12496	14680	14728	12952	11144	8312	8248	5328	3280						

Using the MRP Output Reports

At this point we have a collection of reports used by purchasing and production scheduling to plan the production process in the factory. In priority sequence they are:

Order Releases: orders that need to be released immediately

Cancellations and Reschedulings: orders that need to be changed

Firm Planned Orders: orders that need to be scheduled but are not due to start for another week or two

Planned Orders: orders that are coming up over the next couple of months

The planned orders report is the only report that is strictly informational. The other three reports will affect the scheduling process because these are scheduled orders that are either set up or modified. Chart 16.18 demonstrates what the new MRP schedules would look like for products ACAC and A4B4. In implementing these changes we assume that no other products were changed. Note that when a level 0 product is changed, it affects all the products below it in the bill of materials product structure. This is similarly true for all products at all levels. Chart 16.18 demonstrates what happened to these two products as a result of their specific changes without considering any other changes at any other levels.

Note that after applying the cancellations and reschedulings, and the firm planned orders to products ACAC and A4B4, we have all the production and purchase order releases scheduled through week 1/2, which shows that the planning and control employees are tracking the production and purchasing needs of the factory appropriately.

Customer Orders and the "Build-to-Order" Environment

In some types of manufacturing we "build to order" rather than "build to forecast," as this book has been demonstrating. The "build-to-order" process is actually scheduled in a similar manner. Most of the procedures up to this point are still basically the same. For example, the forecasting still needs to be done in order to estimate the load that will be placed on your facility. Rough-cut capacity is needed for planning and building an aggregate production schedule. This gives us "available to promise" information for planning customer orders, and from this we can generate the master production schedule.

The big difference between "build to forecast" (also known as "make to stock") and "build to order" is that the customer order replaces the firm planned order. For example, if a customer order comes in, we check to make sure we have the capacity to build the order using the "available to promise" report just as we did in the "build-to-stock" environment. Then we schedule the order using the firm planned order (or

CHART 16.19 Make-to-Order Master Production Scheduling for TRI

Date	Master Schedule	Customer Order	Planned Orders
1/1	38	30	8
1/2	30	30	0
1/3	38	15	23
1/4	37	20	17
2/1	13	0	13
2/2	9	5	4
2/3	13	0	13
2/4	12	10	2

order release if the order needs to be started immediately) process that we just discussed. After it has been scheduled, the customer order works the same way as the firm planned order or order release and gets scheduled in the MRP system. Therefore, except for the labeling of the order as a firm planned order or as a customer order, everything else in the scheduling process works the same.

Customer orders are initiated by the Sales Department. When they come to the Production Scheduling Department they are released as production orders and they eliminate (replace) a corresponding planned order. This procedure only occurs for products that appear on the master production schedule. All other component parts are still scheduled based on these end item demands, just as we have done previously in this chapter. Chart 16.19 demonstrates how customer orders could come in and "replace" part of a master production schedule requirement. Note that the total demanded quantity (customer order plus planned orders) is still the same as the master schedule quantity. It is useful to track what portion of the master schedule has not yet been committed to a specific customer order. This is considered a master scheduling "available to promise" report, as demonstrated in Chart 16.19. The master schedule "available to promise" amount is the planned order amount. This is how much capacity is available to be promised or committed to a customer.

Another difference may occur between the "make-to-order" and the "build-to-forecast" environments, and that is that if a customer order does not exist, we don't work. In other words, we never release anything but customer orders. However, in most cases, rather than wasting this productive capacity, a "make-to-stock" product is substituted to fill the underutilized capacity. These products would be scheduled as firm planned orders or order releases for the quantity of the planned order amount of Chart 16.19.

Net Change versus Regenerative MRP

There are two types of MRP. The first is *regenerative MRP*, which is the type we have been using throughout this chapter. In regenerative ("Regen" for short) MRP, we recalculate the MRP schedules once a week.

CHART 16.20 Regen vs. Net Change MRP

	Regen	Net Change
Data accuracy	90%	95%
Response time	Weekly	Daily
Computer requirement	Helpful	Extensive and required
Most sensitive to errors		X
Most preferred	X	

MRP planning on a weekly basis is considered adequate. The second type of MRP is *net change MRP*. In net change MRP, we are assuming that we want the MRP system to react every time there is a change to one of the inputs to the system. Chart 16.20 draws a comparison between the two MRP types. Note that Regen is the most preferred. This is because the normal factory floor doesn't like being rescheduled on a daily basis. And when an error occurs with one of the inputs of a net change system, the entire factory feels the effects of the error. A large number of factories in Europe that started out with net change MRP have switched to Regen MRP for this reason. Regen MRP, although it is not as hi-tech as net change MRP, is by far the easiest of the two types to use.

MRP Schedules Using a Computer Software Package

The appendix at the end of this chapter shows how to generate the MRP schedules using a spreadsheet package. This software package will greatly simplify the calculation process.

There are dozens of comprehensive MRP software packages available that all claim to be the best when it comes to MRP scheduling. It is dangerous to purchase an MRP package based on some sales claim before you truly have a feel for what it is you need. By understanding the basics of this chapter, you are now better able to determine what your MRP requirements are, and you will find that all MRP packages do not meet these requirements.

If you still do not feel that you are ready to select a computerized MRP package, let me suggest one additional interim step. Purchase an educational MRP software package, such as *QS*[1] and use it to experiment with a computerized MRP software package. This will again help you to recognize your MRP requirements. In fact, you may find that QS is all you need as an MRP scheduler and you may not need to go any further in your MRP search.

[1] QS, by Yin-Long Chang and Robert S. Sullivan, is sold as a textbook by Prentice Hall, Englewood Cliffs, NJ (ISBN 0-13-747205-6). It offers some basic operations management tools such as MRP and inventory control for under $100. This will allow you to experiment with computerized MRP without incurring a high cost.

Good luck installing MRP. If you don't see major inventory improvements, go back to the drawing board and reread this book to find out what step you're leaving out (assuming you're the average factory). If everything's working right, you should be pleasantly surprised.

Summary

We've done it. We've generated an MRP schedule. Now we have a set of production and purchasing orders that we can release on time. The schedules will now allow us to build and buy what we need, when we need it, and in the amounts that we need. This is about as far as we need to go in the planning process, with the exception of capacity requirements planning (Chapter 18). However, we do have one additional chapter to study that affects the MRP schedules. This is Chapter 17, which discusses lot sizing, a technique for lumping requirements together.

After Chapters 17 and 18 the rest of the production planning and control flow becomes primarily a control process. We need to control the production (Chapter 19) and purchase orders, making sure that they arrive into inventory when they were scheduled. If they don't, we need to find out why. So let's charge forward and implement capacity requirements planning and shop floor control.

CHART 16.A1 Material Requirements Planning Using the Spreadsheet—Example of Level 0 Items

	A	B	C	D	E	F	G	H	I	J	K	L	M	N	O
1															
2	Material Requirements Planning				Jan. 1, 1992										
3															
4	Level 0 Analysis														
5															
6	Product TRI		Startup Inventory Values												
7			Inventory Balance		121		Anticipation Inventory			0		Safety Stock		0	
8															
9	Week		0	1	2	3	4	5	6	7	8	9	10	11	12
10	Month/Week			Jan/1	Jan/2	Jan/3	Jan/4	Feb/1	Feb/2	Feb/3	Feb/4	Mar/1	Mar/2	Mar/3	Mar/4
11	Gross requirements			38	30	38	37	13	9	13	12	15	19	19	18
12	Scheduled receipts			21											
13	Anticipated inventory or SS change														
14	On hand		121	104	74	36	0	0	0	0	0	0	0	0	0
15	Net requirements			0	0	0	1	13	9	13	12	15	19	19	18
16	Planned receipts			0	0	0	1	13	9	13	12	15	19	19	18
17	Planned releases			0	0	0	1	13	9	13	12	15	19	19	18
18															
19	Product TRI–SP		Startup Inventory Values												
20			Inventory Balance		6		Anticipation Inventory			0		Safety Stock		0	
21															
22	Week		0	1	2	3	4	5	6	7	8	9	10	11	12
23	Month/Week			Jan/1	Jan/2	Jan/3	Jan/4	Feb/1	Feb/2	Feb/3	Feb/4	Mar/1	Mar/2	Mar/3	Mar/4
24	Gross requirements			0	7	0	0	0	3	0	0	4	0	0	0
25	Scheduled receipts			6											
26	Anticipated inventory or SS change														
27	On hand		6	12	5	5	5	5	2	2	2	0	0	0	0
28	Net requirements			0	0	0	0	0	0	0	0	2	0	0	0
29	Planned receipts			0	0	0	0	0	0	0	0	2	0	0	0
30	Planned releases			0	0	0	0	0	0	0	0	2	0	0	0
31															

APPENDIX 16.A: MRP Schedules Using a Spreadsheet Package

This appendix demonstrates how to construct the MRP schedules using a spreadsheet. The procedure is the same as that discussed for Charts 16.3 and 16.7. We start with the level 0 products, as demonstrated in Chart 16.4. The spreadsheet version of Chart 16.4 is shown as Chart 16.A1. Then we proceed to accumulate the gross requirements for the level 1 items. This procedure was carried out using Chart 16.7 and demonstrated in Chart 16.8. After the level 1 gross requirements were accumulated, the level 1 products were scheduled. This scheduling occurred on Chart 16.9. When we consider the spreadsheet versions of Charts 16.8 and 16.9, we find that both steps can be consolidated into one spreadsheet. The example of this can be seen in Chart 16.A2. Here we see the accumulation of the gross requirements followed immediately by the generation of the MRP schedule.

The next step is to schedule the level 2 items. First we needed to accumulate the gross requirements and this occurred in Chart 16.10. This was followed by the generation of the MRP schedules, which occurred in Chart 16.11. Once again, for the spreadsheet version, we are able to combine these two steps. The result was Chart 16.A3. The "Planned Releases" requirements for all the level 0 and level 1 parts have been summarized at the start of the spreadsheet. Then it is possible to calculate the requirements for each of the level 2 items.

P	Q	R	S	T	U	V	W	X	Y	Z	AA	AB	AC	AD	AE	AF	AG
Lead Time	3																
13	14	15	16	17	18	19	20	21	22	23	24	25	26	27	28	29	30
Apr/1	Apr/2	Apr/3	Apr/4	May/1	May/2	May/3	May/4	June/1	June/2	June/3	June/4						
27	33	34	33	40	50	50	50	26	33	34	33						
8	8	8	8	24	24	24	23	8	8	8	8						
0	0	0	0	0	0	0	0	0	0	0	0	0	0	0	0	0	0
35	41	42	41	64	74	74	73	34	41	42	41	0	0	0	0	0	0
35	41	42	41	64	74	74	73	34	41	42	41	0	0	0	0	0	0
35	41	42	41	64	74	74	73	34	41	42	41	0	0	0	0	0	0
Lead Time	1																
13	14	15	16	17	18	19	20	21	22	23	24	25	26	27	28	29	30
Apr/1	Apr/2	Apr/3	Apr/4	May/1	May/2	May/3	May/4	June/1	June/2	June/3	June/4						
7	0	0	0	10	0	0	0	7	0	0	0						
2				7				8									
0	0	0	0	0	0	0	0	0	0	0	0	0	0	0	0	0	0
9	0	0	0	17	0	0	0	15	0	0	0	0	0	0	0	0	0
9	0	0	0	17	0	0	0	15	0	0	0	0	0	0	0	0	0
9	0	0	0	17	0	0	0	15	0	0	0	0	0	0	0	0	0

CHART 16.A2 Material Requirements Planning Using the Spreadsheet—Example of Level 1 Items

	A	B	C	D	E	F	G	H	I	J	K	L	M	N	O
32	Level 1 Analysis														
33															
34	Product	CCCC	Startup Inventory Values												
35			Inventory Balance		4	Anticipation Inventory				0	Safety Stock			3	
36															
37		Week	0	1	2	3	4	5	6	7	8	9	10	11	12
38		Month/Week		Jan/1	Jan/2	Jan/3	Jan/4	Feb/1	Feb/2	Feb/3	Feb/4	Mar/1	Mar/2	Mar/3	Mar/4
39	Source	quantity													
40	Product	per													
41	TRI	4	0	0	0	0	4	52	36	52	48	60	76	76	72
42	TRI–SP	4	0	0	0	0	0	0	0	0	0	8	0	0	0
43															
44	Gross requirements		0	0	0	0	4	52	36	52	48	68	76	76	72
45	Scheduled receipts			4											
46	Anticipated inventory or SS change														
47	On hand		1	5	5	5	1	0	0	0	0	0	0	0	0
48	Net requirements			0	0	0	0	51	36	52	48	68	76	76	72
49	Planned receipts			0	0	0	0	51	36	52	48	68	76	76	72
50	Planned releases		0	0	0	51	36	52	48	68	76	76	72	176	164
51															
52	Product	ABCD	Startup Inventory Values												
53			Inventory Balance		5	Anticipation Inventory				0	Safety Stock			3	
54															
55		Week	0	1	2	3	4	5	6	7	8	9	10	11	12
56		Month/Week		Jan/1	Jan/2	Jan/3	Jan/4	Feb/1	Feb/2	Feb/3	Feb/4	Mar/1	Mar/2	Mar/3	Mar/4
57	Source	quantity													
58	Product	per													
59	TRI	2	0	0	0	0	2	26	18	26	24	30	38	38	36
60	TRI–SP	1	0	0	0	0	0	0	0	0	0	2	0	0	0
61															
62	Gross requirements		0	0	0	0	2	26	18	26	24	32	38	38	36
63	Scheduled receipts					5									
64	Anticipated inventory or SS change														
65	On hand		2	2	2	7	5	0	0	0	0	0	0	0	0
66	Net requirements			0	0	0	0	21	18	26	24	32	38	38	36
67	Planned receipts			0	0	0	0	21	18	26	24	32	38	38	36
68	Planned releases		0	0	0	0	21	18	26	24	32	38	38	36	79
69															
70	Product	DDDD	Startup Inventory Values												
71			Inventory Balance		10	Anticipation Inventory				0	Safety Stock			5	
72															
73		Week	0	1	2	3	4	5	6	7	8	9	10	11	12
74		Month/Week		Jan/1	Jan/2	Jan/3	Jan/4	Feb/1	Feb/2	Feb/3	Feb/4	Mar/1	Mar/2	Mar/3	Mar/4
75	Source	quantity													
76	Product	per													
77	TRI	1	0	0	0	0	1	13	9	13	12	15	19	19	18
78	TRI–SP	1	0	0	0	0	0	0	0	0	0	2	0	0	0
79															
80	Gross requirements		0	0	0	0	1	13	9	13	12	17	19	19	18
81	Scheduled receipts				10										
82	Anticipated inventory or SS change														
83	On hand		5	5	15	15	14	1	0	0	0	0	0	0	0
84	Net requirements			0	0	0	0	0	8	13	12	17	19	19	18
85	Planned receipts			0	0	0	0	0	8	13	12	17	19	19	18
86	Planned releases		0	0	0	0	8	13	12	17	19	19	18	44	41
87															
88	Product	AABB	Startup Inventory Values												
89			Inventory Balance		15	Anticipation Inventory				0	Safety Stock			5	
90															
91		Week	0	1	2	3	4	5	6	7	8	9	10	11	12
92		Month/Week		Jan/1	Jan/2	Jan/3	Jan/4	Feb/1	Feb/2	Feb/3	Feb/4	Mar/1	Mar/2	Mar/3	Mar/4
93	Source	quantity													
94	Product	per													
95	TRI	3	0	0	0	0	3	39	27	39	36	45	57	57	54
96	TRI–SP	3	0	0	0	0	0	0	0	0	0	6	0	0	0
97															
98	Gross requirements		0	0	0	0	3	39	27	39	36	51	57	57	54
99	Scheduled receipts					15									
100	Anticipated inventory or SS change														
101	On hand		10	10	10	25	22	0	0	0	0	0	0	0	0
102	Net requirements			0	0	0	0	17	27	39	36	51	57	57	54
103	Planned receipts			0	0	0	0	17	27	39	36	51	57	57	54
104	Planned releases		0	0	0	0	17	27	39	36	51	57	57	54	132
105															
106	Product	AACC	Startup Inventory Values												
107			Inventory Balance		6	Anticipation Inventory				0	Safety Stock			3	
108															
109		Week	0	1	2	3	4	5	6	7	8	9	10	11	12
110		Month/Week		Jan/1	Jan/2	Jan/3	Jan/4	Feb/1	Feb/2	Feb/3	Feb/4	Mar/1	Mar/2	Mar/3	Mar/4
111	Source	quantity													
112	Product	per													
113	TRI	1	0	0	0	0	1	13	9	13	12	15	19	19	18
114															
115	Gross requirements		0	0	0	0	1	13	9	13	12	15	19	19	18
116	Scheduled receipts				20										
117	Anticipated inventory or SS change														
118	On hand		3	3	23	23	22	9	0	0	0	0	0	0	0
119	Net requirements			0	0	0	0	0	0	13	12	15	19	19	18
120	Planned receipts			0	0	0	0	0	0	13	12	15	19	19	18
121	Planned releases		0	0	0	0	13	12	15	19	19	18	35	41	42
122															

P	Q	R	S	T	U	V	W	X	Y	Z	AA	AB	AC	AD	AE	AF	AG
Lead Time																	
13	14	15	16	17	18	19	20	21	22	23	24	25	26	27	28	29	30
Apr/1	Apr/2	Apr/3	Apr/4	May/1	May/2	May/3	May/4	June/1	June/2	June/3	June/4						
140	164	168	164	256	296	296	292	136	164	168	164	0	0	0	0	0	0
36	0	0	0	68	0	0	0	60	0	0	0	0	0	0	0	0	0
176	164	168	164	324	296	296	292	196	164	168	164	0	0	0	0	0	0
0	0	0	0	0	0	0	0	0	0	0	0	0	0	0	0	0	0
176	164	168	164	324	296	296	292	196	164	168	164	0	0	0	0	0	0
176	164	168	164	324	296	296	292	196	164	168	164	0	0	0	0	0	0
168	164	324	296	296	292	196	164	168	164	0	0	0	0	0	0	0	0
Lead Time	4																
13	14	15	16	17	18	19	20	21	22	23	24	25	26	27	28	29	30
Apr/1	Apr/2	Apr/3	Apr/4	May/1	May/2	May/3	May/4	June/1	June/2	June/3	June/4						
70	82	84	82	128	148	148	146	68	82	84	82	0	0	0	0	0	0
9	0	0	0	17	0	0	0	15	0	0	0	0	0	0	0	0	0
79	82	84	82	145	148	148	146	83	82	84	82	0	0	0	0	0	0
0	0	0	0	0	0	0	0	0	0	0	0	0	0	0	0	0	0
79	82	84	82	145	148	148	146	83	82	84	82	0	0	0	0	0	0
79	82	84	82	145	148	148	146	83	82	84	82	0	0	0	0	0	0
82	84	82	145	148	148	146	83	82	84	82	0	0	0	0	0	0	0
Lead Time	9																
13	14	15	16	17	18	19	20	21	22	23	24	25	26	27	28	29	30
Apr/1	Apr/2	Apr/3	Apr/4	May/1	May/2	May/3	May/4	June/1	June/2	June/3	June/4						
35	41	42	41	64	74	74	73	34	41	42	41	0	0	0	0	0	0
9	0	0	0	17	0	0	0	15	0	0	0	0	0	0	0	0	0
44	41	42	41	81	74	74	73	49	41	42	41	0	0	0	0	0	0
0	0	0	0	0	0	0	0	0	0	0	0	0	0	0	0	0	0
44	41	42	41	81	74	74	73	49	41	42	41	0	0	0	0	0	0
44	41	42	41	81	74	74	73	49	41	42	41	0	0	0	0	0	0
42	41	81	74	74	73	49	41	42	41	0	0	0	0	0	0	0	0
Lead Time	3																
13	14	15	16	17	18	19	20	21	22	23	24	25	26	27	28	29	30
Apr/1	Apr/2	Apr/3	Apr/4	May/1	May/2	May/3	May/4	June/1	June/2	June/3	June/4						
105	123	126	123	192	222	222	219	102	123	126	123	0	0	0	0	0	0
27	0	0	0	51	0	0	0	45	0	0	0	0	0	0	0	0	0
132	123	126	123	243	222	222	219	147	123	126	123	0	0	0	0	0	0
0	0	0	0	0	0	0	0	0	0	0	0	0	0	0	0	0	0
132	123	126	123	243	222	222	219	147	123	126	123	0	0	0	0	0	0
132	123	126	123	243	222	222	219	147	123	126	123	0	0	0	0	0	0
123	126	123	243	222	222	219	147	123	126	123	0	0	0	0	0	0	0
Lead Time	14																
13	14	15	16	17	18	19	20	21	22	23	24	25	26	27	28	29	30
Apr/1	Apr/2	Apr/3	Apr/4	May/1	May/2	May/3	May/4	June/1	June/2	June/3	June/4						
35	41	42	41	64	74	74	73	34	41	42	41	0	0	0	0	0	0
35	41	42	41	64	74	74	73	34	41	42	41	0	0	0	0	0	0
0	0	0	0	0	0	0	0	0	0	0	0	0	0	0	0	0	0
35	41	42	41	64	74	74	73	34	41	42	41	0	0	0	0	0	0
35	41	42	41	64	74	74	73	34	41	42	41	0	0	0	0	0	0
41	64	74	74	73	34	41	42	41	0	0	0	0	0	0	0	0	0

CHART 16.A3 Material Requirements Planning Using the Spreadsheet—Example of Level 2 Items

	A	B	C	D	E	F	G	H	I	J	K	L	M	N	O
1															
2	Material Requirements Planning			Jan. 1, 1992											
3															
4	Planned Order Releases for Level 0 and Level 1 Items														
5															
6		Week	0	1	2	3	4	5	6	7	8	9	10	11	12
7		Month/Week		Jan/1	Jan/2	Jan/3	Jan/4	Feb/1	Feb/2	Feb/3	Feb/4	Mar/1	Mar/2	Mar/3	Mar/4
8	TRI						1	13	9	13	12	15	19	19	
9	TRI–SP											2			
10	CCCC					51	36	52	48	68	76	76	72	176	164
11	ABCD					1	104	72	104	96	128	152	152	144	316
12	DDDD					41	36	52	48	68	76	76	72	176	164
13	AABB						143	108	156	144	204	228	228	216	528
14	AACC				33	36	52	48	60	76	76	72	140	164	168
15															
16	Level 2 Analysis														
17															
18	Product BBBB		Startup Inventory Values												
19			Inventory Balance		45	Anticipation Inventory			0		Safety Stock		15		
20															
21		Week	0	1	2	3	4	5	6	7	8	9	10	11	12
22		Month/Week		Jan/1	Jan/2	Jan/3	Jan/4	Feb/1	Feb/2	Feb/3	Feb/4	Mar/1	Mar/2	Mar/3	Mar/4
23	Source	quantity													
24	Product	per													
25	TRI	12	0	0	0	0	12	156	108	156	144	180	228	228	216
26	TRI–SP	5	0	0	0	0	0	0	0	0	0	10	0	0	0
27	DDDD	2	0	0	0	82	72	104	96	136	152	152	144	352	328
28	AACC	3	0	0	99	108	156	144	180	228	228	216	420	492	504
29															
30	Gross requirements		0	0	99	190	240	404	384	520	524	558	792	1072	1048
31	Scheduled receipts				100										
32	Anticipated inventory or SS change														
33	On hand		30	30	31	0	0	0	0	0	0	0	0	0	0
34	Net requirements			0	0	159	240	404	384	520	524	558	792	1072	1048
35	Planned receipts			0	0	159	240	404	384	520	524	558	792	1072	1048
36	Planned releases		0	0	159	240	404	384	520	524	558	792	1072	1048	1293
37															
38	Product ACAC		Startup Inventory Values												
39			Inventory Balance		20		Anticipation Inventory			0		Safety Stock		10	
40															
41		Week	0	1	2	3	4	5	6	7	8	9	10	11	12
42		Month/Week		Jan/1	Jan/2	Jan/3	Jan/4	Feb/1	Feb/2	Feb/3	Feb/4	Mar/1	Mar/2	Mar/3	Mar/4
43	Source	quantity													
44	Product	per													
45	CCCC	2	0	0	0	102	72	104	96	136	152	152	144	352	328
46															
47	Gross requirements		0	0	0	102	72	104	96	136	152	152	144	352	328
48	Scheduled receipts				20										
49	Anticipated inventory or SS change														
50	On hand		10	10	30	0	0	0	0	0	0	0	0	0	0
51	Net requirements			0	0	72	72	104	96	136	152	152	144	352	328
52	Planned receipts			0	0	72	72	104	96	136	152	152	144	352	328
53	Planned releases		0	0	72	72	104	96	136	152	152	144	352	328	336
54															
55	Product A5B5		Startup Inventory Values												
56			Inventory Balance		23		Anticipation Inventory			0		Safety Stock		10	
57															
58		Week	0	1	2	3	4	5	6	7	8	9	10	11	12
59		Month/Week		Jan/1	Jan/2	Jan/3	Jan/4	Feb/1	Feb/2	Feb/3	Feb/4	Mar/1	Mar/2	Mar/3	Mar/4
60	Source	quantity													
61	Product	per													
62	ABCD	3	0	0	0	3	312	216	312	288	384	456	456	432	948
63	DDDD	3	0	0	0	123	108	156	144	204	228	228	216	528	492
64															
65	Gross requirements		0	0	0	126	420	372	456	492	612	684	672	960	1440
66	Scheduled receipts					23									
67	Anticipated inventory or SS change														
68	On hand		13	13	13	0	0	0	0	0	0	0	0	0	0
69	Net requirements			0	0	90	420	372	456	492	612	684	672	960	1440
70	Planned receipts			0	0	90	420	372	456	492	612	684	672	960	1440
71	Planned releases			0	0	90	420	372	456	492	612	684	672	960	1440
72															

P	Q	R	S	T	U	V	W	X	Y	Z	AA	AB	AC	AD	AE	AF	AG
13	14	15	16	17	18	19	20	21	22	23	24	25	26	27	28	29	30
Apr/1	Apr/2	Apr/3	Apr/4	May/1	May/2	May/3	May/4	June/1	June/2	June/3	June/4						
						74	73	34	41	42	41						
9				17				15									
168	164	324	296	296	292	196	164	168	164								
328	336	328	580	592	592	584	332	328	336	328							
168	164	324	296	296	292	196	164	168	164								
492	504	492	972	888	888	876	588	492	504	492							
164	256	296	296	292	136	164	168	164									

Lead Time 6

13	14	15	16	17	18	19	20	21	22	23	24	25	26	27	28	29	30
Apr/1	Apr/2	Apr/3	Apr/4	May/1	May/2	May/3	May/4	June/1	June/2	June/3	June/4						
420	492	504	492	768	888	888	876	408	492	504	492	0	0	0	0	0	0
45	0	0	0	85	0	0	0	75	0	0	0	0	0	0	0	0	0
336	328	648	592	592	584	392	328	336	328	0	0	0	0	0	0	0	0
492	768	888	888	876	408	492	504	492	0	0	0	0	0	0	0	0	0
1293	1588	2040	1972	2321	1880	1772	1708	1311	820	504	492	0	0	0	0	0	0
0	0	0	0	0	0	0	0	0	0	0	0	0	0	0	0	0	0
1293	1588	2040	1972	2321	1880	1772	1708	1311	820	504	492	0	0	0	0	0	0
1293	1588	2040	1972	2321	1880	1772	1708	1311	820	504	492	0	0	0	0	0	0
1588	2040	1972	2321	1880	1772	1708	1311	820	504	492	0	0	0	0	0	0	0

Lead Time 6

13	14	15	16	17	18	19	20	21	22	23	24	25	26	27	28	29	30
Apr/1	Apr/2	Apr/3	Apr/4	May/1	May/2	May/3	May/4	June/1	June/2	June/3	June/4						
336	328	648	592	592	584	392	328	336	328	0	0	0	0	0	0	0	0
336	328	648	592	592	584	392	328	336	328	0	0	0	0	0	0	0	0
0	0	0	0	0	0	0	0	0	0	0	0	0	0	0	0	0	0
336	328	648	592	592	584	392	328	336	328	0	0	0	0	0	0	0	0
336	328	648	592	592	584	392	328	336	328	0	0	0	0	0	0	0	0
328	648	592	592	584	392	328	336	328	0	0	0	0	0	0	0	0	0

Lead Time 1

13	14	15	16	17	18	19	20	21	22	23	24	25	26	27	28	29	30
Apr/1	Apr/2	Apr/3	Apr/4	May/1	May/2	May/3	May/4	June/1	June/2	June/3	June/4						
984	1008	984	1740	1776	1776	1752	996	984	1008	984	0	0	0	0	0	0	0
504	492	972	888	888	876	588	492	504	492	0	0	0	0	0	0	0	0
1488	1500	1956	2628	2664	2652	2340	1488	1488	1500	984	0	0	0	0	0	0	0
0	0	0	0	0	0	0	0	0	0	0	0	0	0	0	0	0	0
1488	1500	1956	2628	2664	2652	2340	1488	1488	1500	984	0	0	0	0	0	0	0
1488	1500	1956	2628	2664	2652	2340	1488	1488	1500	984	0	0	0	0	0	0	0
1488	1500	1956	2628	2664	2652	2340	1488	1488	1500	984	0	0	0	0	0	0	0

CHART 16.A4 Material Requirements Planning Using the Spreadsheet—Example of Level 3 Items

	A	B	C	D	E	F	G	H	I	J	K	L	M	N	O
1															
2	Material Requirements Planning				Jan. 1, 1992										
3															
4	Planned Order Releases for Level 0, Level 1, and Level 2 Items														
5															
6		Week	0	1	2	3	4	5	6	7	8	9	10	11	12
7		Month/Week		Jan/1	Jan/2	Jan/3	Jan/4	Feb/1	Feb/2	Feb/3	Feb/4	Mar/1	Mar/2	Mar/3	Mar/4
8	TRI						1	13	9	13	12	15	19	19	18
9	TRI–SP											2			
10	CCCC					51	36	52	48	68	76	76	72	176	164
11	ABCD					1	104	72	104	96	128	152	152	144	316
12	DDDD					41	36	52	48	68	76	76	72	176	164
13	AABB						143	108	156	144	204	228	228	216	528
14	AACC				33	36	52	48	60	76	76	72	140	164	168
15	BBBB				159	240	404	384	520	524	558	792	1072	1048	1293
16	ACAC				72	72	104	96	136	152	152	144	352	328	336
17	A5B5					90	420	372	456	492	612	684	672	960	1440
18															
19	Level 3 Analysis														
20															
21	Product A4B4		Startup Inventory Values												
22			Inventory Balance		200		Anticipation Inventory			0		Safety Stock		50	
23															
24		Week	0	1	2	3	4	5	6	7	8	9	10	11	12
25		Month/Week		Jan/1	Jan/2	Jan/3	Jan/4	Feb/1	Feb/2	Feb/3	Feb/4	Mar/1	Mar/2	Mar/3	Mar/4
26	Source	quantity													
27	Product	per													
28	CCCC	12	0	0	0	612	432	624	576	816	912	912	864	2112	1968
29	ABCD	10	0	0	0	10	1040	720	1040	960	1280	1520	1520	1440	3160
30	ACAC	9	0	0	648	648	936	864	1224	1368	1368	1296	3168	2952	3024
31															
32	Gross requirements		0	0	648	1270	2408	2208	2840	3144	3560	3728	5552	6504	8152
33	Scheduled receipts			400											
34	Anticipated inventory or SS change														
35	On hand		150	150	0	0	0	0	0	0	0	0	0	0	0
36	Net requirements			0	98	1270	2408	2208	2840	3144	3560	3728	5552	6504	8152
37	Planned receipts			0	98	1270	2408	2208	2840	3144	3560	3728	5552	6504	8152
38	Planned releases		0	98	1270	2408	2208	2840	3144	3560	3728	5552	6504	8152	8248
39															
40	Product A555		Startup Inventory Values												
41			Inventory Balance		40		Anticipation Inventory			0		Safety Stock		10	
42															
43		Week	0	1	2	3	4	5	6	7	8	9	10	11	12
44		Month/Week		Jan/1	Jan/2	Jan/3	Jan/4	Feb/1	Feb/2	Feb/3	Feb/4	Mar/1	Mar/2	Mar/3	Mar/4
45	Source	quantity													
46	Product	per													
47	ACAC	7	0	0	504	504	728	672	952	1064	1064	1008	2464	2296	2352
48	A5B5	4	0	0	0	360	1680	1488	1824	1968	2448	2736	2688	3840	5760
49															
50	Gross requirements		0	0	504	864	2408	2160	2776	3032	3512	3744	5152	6136	8112
51	Scheduled receipts				300										
52	Anticipated inventory or SS change														
53	On hand		30	30	0	0	0	0	0	0	0	0	0	0	0
54	Net requirements			0	174	864	2408	2160	2776	3032	3512	3744	5152	6136	8112
55	Planned receipts			0	174	864	2408	2160	2776	3032	3512	3744	5152	6136	8112
56	Planned releases			0	174	864	2408	2160	2776	3032	3512	3744	5152	6136	8112
57															
58	Product B555		Startup Inventory Values												
59			Inventory Balance		7		Anticipation Inventory			0		Safety Stock		5	
60															
61		Week	0	1	2	3	4	5	6	7	8	9	10	11	12
62		Month/Week		Jan/1	Jan/2	Jan/3	Jan/4	Feb/1	Feb/2	Feb/3	Feb/4	Mar/1	Mar/2	Mar/3	Mar/4
63	Source	quantity													
64	Product	per													
65	ACAC	2	0	0	144	144	208	192	272	304	304	288	704	656	672
66															
67	Gross requirements		0	0	144	144	208	192	272	304	304	288	704	656	672
68	Scheduled receipts				20										
69	Anticipated inventory or SS change														
70	On hand		2	22	0	0	0	0	0	0	0	0	0	0	0
71	Net requirements			0	122	144	208	192	272	304	304	288	704	656	672
72	Planned receipts			0	122	144	208	192	272	304	304	288	704	656	672
73	Planned releases			0	122	144	208	192	272	304	304	288	704	656	672

P	Q	R	S	T	U	V	W	X	Y	Z	AA	AB	AC	AD	AE	AF	AG
13	14	15	16	17	18	19	20	21	22	23	24	25	26	27	28	29	30
Apr/1	Apr/2	Apr/3	Apr/4	May/1	May/2	May/3	May/4	June/1	June/2	June/3	June/4						
35	41	42	41	64	74	74	73	34	41	42	41						
9				17				15									
168	164	324	296	296	292	196	164	168	164								
328	336	328	580	592	592	584	332	328	336	328							
168	164	324	296	296	292	196	164	168	164								
492	504	492	972	888	888	876	588	492	504	492							
164	256	296	296	292	136	164	168	164									
1588	2040	1972	2321	1880	1772	1708	1311	820	504	492							
328	648	592	592	584	392	328	336	328									
1488	1500	1956	2628	2664	2652	2340	1488	1488	1500	984							

Lead Time 4

13	14	15	16	17	18	19	20	21	22	23	24	25	26	27	28	29	30
Apr/1	Apr/2	Apr/3	Apr/4	May/1	May/2	May/3	May/4	June/1	June/2	June/3	June/4						
2016	1968	3888	3552	3552	3504	2352	1968	2016	1968	0	0	0	0	0	0	0	0
3280	3360	3280	5800	5920	5920	5840	3320	3280	3360	3280	0	0	0	0	0	0	0
2952	5832	5328	5328	5256	3528	2952	3024	2952	0	0	0	0	0	0	0	0	0
8248	11160	12496	14680	14728	12952	11144	8312	8248	5328	3280	0	0	0	0	0	0	0
0	0	0	0	0	0	0	0	0	0	0	0	0	0	0	0	0	0
8248	11160	12496	14680	14728	12952	11144	8312	8248	5328	3280	0	0	0	0	0	0	0
8248	11160	12496	14680	14728	12952	11144	8312	8248	5328	3280	0	0	0	0	0	0	0
11160	12496	14680	14728	12952	11144	8312	8248	5328	3280	0	0	0	0	0	0	0	0

Lead Time 2

13	14	15	16	17	18	19	20	21	22	23	24	25	26	27	28	29	30
Apr/1	Apr/2	Apr/3	Apr/4	May/1	May/2	May/3	May/4	June/1	June/2	June/3	June/4						
2296	4536	4144	4144	4088	2744	2296	2352	2296	0	0	0	0	0	0	0	0	0
5952	6000	7824	10512	10656	10608	9360	5952	5952	6000	3936	0	0	0	0	0	0	0
8248	10536	11968	14656	14744	13352	11656	8304	8248	6000	3936	0	0	0	0	0	0	0
0	0	0	0	0	0	0	0	0	0	0	0	0	0	0	0	0	0
8248	10536	11968	14656	14744	13352	11656	8304	8248	6000	3936	0	0	0	0	0	0	0
8248	10536	11968	14656	14744	13352	11656	8304	8248	6000	3936	0	0	0	0	0	0	0
8248	10536	11968	14656	14744	13352	11656	8304	8248	6000	3936	0	0	0	0	0	0	0

Lead Time 1

13	14	15	16	17	18	19	20	21	22	23	24	25	26	27	28	29	30
Apr/1	Apr/2	Apr/3	Apr/4	May/1	May/2	May/3	May/4	June/1	June/2	June/3	June/4						
656	1296	1184	1184	1168	784	656	672	656	0	0	0	0	0	0	0	0	0
656	1296	1184	1184	1168	784	656	672	656	0	0	0	0	0	0	0	0	0
0	0	0	0	0	0	0	0	0	0	0	0	0	0	0	0	0	0
656	1296	1184	1184	1168	784	656	672	656	0	0	0	0	0	0	0	0	0
656	1296	1184	1184	1168	784	656	672	656	0	0	0	0	0	0	0	0	0
656	1296	1184	1184	1168	784	656	672	656	0	0	0	0	0	0	0	0	0

CHART 16.A5 Material Requirements Planning Using the Spreadsheet and Showing Calculations

	A	B	C	D	E
1					
2	Material requirements planning				Jan. 1, 1992
3					
4	Level 0 Analysis				
5					
6	Product	TRI	Startup Inventory Values		
7			Inventory balance		121
8					
9	Week		0	1	2
10	Month/Week			Jan/1	Jan/2
11	Gross requirements			38	30
12	Scheduled receipts			21	
13	Anticipated inventory or SS change				
14	On hand		E7-J7-N7	IF(C14-D11+D12-D13<0,0,C14-D11+D12-D13)	IF(D14-E11+E12-E13<0,0,D14-E11+E12-E13)
15	Net requirements			IF(C14-D11+D12-D13<0,D11-D12+D13-C14,0)	IF(D14-E11+E12-E13<0,E11-E12+E13-D14,0)
16	Planned receipts			D15	E15
17	Planned releases			D16	E16
18					
19	Product	TRI-SP	Startup inventory values		
20			Inventory balance		6
21					
22	Week		0	1	2
23	Month/Week			Jan/1	Jan/2
24	Gross requirements			0	7
25	Scheduled receipts			6	
26	Anticipated Invenory or SS change				
27	On hand		E20-J20-N20	IF(C27-D24+D25-D26<0,0,C27-D24+D25-D26)	IF(D27-E24+E25-E26<0,0,D27-E24+E25-E26)
28	Net requirements			IF(C27-D24+D25-D26<0,D24-D25+D26-C27,0)	IF(D27-E24+E25-E26<0,E24-E25+E26-D27,0)
29	Planned receipts			D28	E28
30	Planned releases			D29	E29
31					
32	Level 1 Analysis				
33					
34	Product	CCCC	Startup Inventory Values		
35			Inventory Balance		4
36					
37		Week	0	1	2
38		Month/week		Jan/1	Jan/2
39	Source	Quantity			
40	Product	per			
41	TRI	4	C17×B41	D17×B41	E17×B41
42	TRI-SP	4	C30×B42	D30×B42	E30×B42
43					
44	Gross requirements		C41+C42	D41+D42	E41+E42
45	Scheduled receipts			4	
46	Anticipated inventory or SS change				
47	On hand		E35-J35-N35	IF(C47-D44+D45-D46<0,0,C47-D44+D45-D46)	IF(D47-E44+E45-E46<0,0,D47-E44+E45-E46)
48	Net requirements			IF(C47-D44+D45-D46<0,D44-D45+D46-C47,0)	IF(D47-E44+E45-E46<0,E44-E45+E46-D47,0)
49	Planned receipts			D48	E48
50	Planned releases		D49+E49	F49	G49
51					

F	G
	Anticipation inventory
3	4
Jan/3	Jan/4
38	37
IF(E14−F11+F12−F13<0,0,E14−F11+F12−F13)	IF(F14−G11+G12−G13<0,0,F14−G11+G12−G13)
IF(E14−F11+F12−F13<0,F11−F12+F13−E14,0)	IF(F14−G11+G12−G13<0,G11−G12+G13−F14,0)
F15	G15
F16	G16
	Anticipation inventory
3	4
Jan/3	Jan/4
0	0
IF(E27−F24+F25−F26<0,0,E27−F24+F25−F26)	IF(F27−G24+G25−G26<0,0,F27−G24+G25−G26)
IF(E27−F24+F25−F26<0,F24−F25+F26−E27,0)	IF(F27−G24+G25−G26<0,G24−G25+G26−F27,0)
F28	G28
G29	G29
	Anticipation Inventory
3	4
Jan/3	Jan/4
F17×B41	G17×B41
F30×B42	G30×B42
F41+F42	G41+G42
IF(E47−F44+F45−F46<0,0,E47−F44+F45−F46)	IF(F47−G44+G45−G46<0,0,F47−G44+G45−G46)
IF(E47−F44+F45−F46<0,F44−F45+F46−E47,0)	IF(F47−G44+G45−G46<0,G44−G45+G46−F47,0)
F48	G48
H49	I49

(*continued*)

CHART 16.A5 *(continued)*

	H	I
1		
2		
3		
4		
5		
6		
7		
8		
9	5	6
10	Feb/1	Feb/2
11	13	9
12		
13		
14	IF(G14−H11+H12−H13<0,0,G14−H11+H12−H13)	IF(H14−I11+I12−I13<0,0,H14−I11+I12−I13)
15	IF(G14−H11+H12−H13<0,H11−H12+H13−G14,0)	IF(H14−I11+I12−I13<0,I11−I12+I13−H14,0)
16	H15	I15
17	H16	I16
18		
19		
20		
21		
22	5	6
23	Feb/1	Feb/2
24	0	3
25		
26		
27	IF(G27−H24+H25−H26<0,0,G27−H24+H25−H26)	IF(H27−I24+I25−I26<0,0,H27−I24+I25−I26)
28	IF(G27−H24+H25−H26<0,H24−H25+H26−G27,0)	IF(H27−I24+I25−I26<0,I24−I25+I26−H27,0)
29	H28	I28
30	H29	I29
31		
32		
33		
34		
35		
36		
37	5	6
38	Feb/1	Feb/2
39		
40		
41	H17×B41	I17×B41
42	H30×B42	I30×B42
43		
44	H41+H42	I41+I42
45		
46		
47	IF(G47−H44+H45−H46<0,0,G47−H44+H45−H46)	IF(H47−I44+I45−I46<0,0,H47−I44+I45−I46)
48	IF(G47−H44+H45−H46<0,H44−H45+H46−G47,0)	IF(H47−I44+I45−I46<0,I44−I45+I46−H47,0)
49	H48	I48
50	J49	K49
51		

J	K
0	
7	8
Feb/3	Feb/4
13	12
IF(I14−J11+J12−J13<0,0,I14−J11+J12−J13)	IF(J14−K11+K12−K13<0,0,J14−K11+K12−K13)
IF(I14−J11+J12−J13<0,J11−J12+J13−I14,0)	IF(J14−K11+K12−K13<0,K11−K12+K13−J14,0)
J15	K15
J16	K16
0	
7	8
Feb/3	Feb/4
0	0
IF(I27−J24+J25−J26<0,0,I27−J24+J25−J26)	IF(J27−K24+K25−K26<0,0,J27−K24+K25−K26)
IF(I27−J24+J25−J26<0,J24−J25+J26−I27,0)	IF(J27−K24+K25−K26<0,K24−K25+K26−J27,0)
J28	K28
J29	K29
0	
7	8
Feb/3	Feb/4
J17×B41	K17×B41
J30×B42	K30×B42
J41+J42	K41+K42
IF(I47−J44+J45−J46<0,0,I47−J44+J45−J46)	IF(J47−K44+K45−K46<0,0,J47−K44+K45−K46)
IF(I47−J44+J45−J46<0,J44−J45+J46−I47,0)	IF(J47−K44+K45−K46<0,K44−K45+K46−J47,0)
J48	K48
L49	M49

(continued)

CHART 16.A5 *(concluded)*

	L	M
1		
2		
3		
4		
5		
6		
7	Safety stock	
8		
9	9	10
10	Mar/1	Mar/2
11	15	19
12		
13		
14	IF(K14−L11+L12−L13<0,0,K14−L11+L12−L13)	IF(L14−M11+M12−M13<0,0,L14−M11+M12−M13)
15	IF(K14−L11+L12−L13<0,L11−L12+L13−K14,0)	IF(L14−M11+M12−M13<0,M11−M12+M13−L14,0)
16	L15	M15
17	L16	M16
18		
19		
20	Safety stock	
21		
22	9	10
23	Mar/1	Mar/2
24	4	0
25		
26		
27	IF(K27−L24+L25−L26<0,0,K27−L24+L25−L26)	IF(L27−M24+M25−M26<0,0,L27−M24+M25−M26)
28	IF(K27−L24+L25−L26<0,L24−L25+L26−K27,0)	IF(L27−M24+M25−M26<0,M24−M25+M26−L27,0)
29	L28	M28
30	L29	M29
31		
32		
33		
34		
35	Safety stock	
36		
37	9	10
38	Mar/1	Mar/2
39		
40		
41	L17×B41	M17×B41
42	L30×B42	M30×B42
43		
44	L41+L42	M41+M42
45		
46		
47	IF(K47−L44+L45−L46<0,0,K47−L44+L45−L46)	IF(L47−M44+M45−M46<0,0,L47−M44+M45−M46)
48	IF(K47−L44+L45−L46<0,L44−L45+L46−K47,0)	IF(L47−M44+M45−M46<0,M44−M45+M46−L47,0)
49	L48	M48
50	N49	O49
51		

N	O
0	
11	12
Mar/3	Mar/4
19	18
IF(M14−N11+N12−N13<0,0,M14−N11+N12−N13)	IF(N14−O11+O12−O13<0,0,N14−O11+O12−O13)
IF(M14−N11+N12−N13<0,N11−N12+N13−M14,0)	IF(N14−O11+O12−O13<,O11−O12+O13−N14,0)
N15	O15
N16	O16
0	
11	12
Mar/3	Mar/4
0	0
IF(M27−N24+N25−N26<0,0,M27−N24+N25−N26)	IF(N27−O24+O25−O26<0,0,N27−O24+O25−O26)
IF(M27−N24+N25−N26<0,N24−N25+N26−M27,0)	IF(N27−O24+O25−O26<0,O24−O25+O26−N27,0)
N28	O28
N29	O29
3	
11	12
Mar/3	Mar/4
N17×B41	O17×B41
N30×B42	O30×B42
N41+N42	O41+O42
IF(M47−N44+N45−N46<0,0,M47−N44+N45−N46)	IF(N47−O44+O45−O46<0,0,N47−O44+O45−O46)
IF(M47−N44+N45−N46<0,N44−N45+N46−M47,0)	IF(N47−O44+O45−O46<0,O44−O45+O46−N47,0)
N48	O48
P49	Q49

We are now ready to calculate the MRP schedules for the last level, the level 3 parts. Chart 16.12 shows the accumulation of the gross requirements, and Chart 16.13 shows the MRP schedules. The spreadsheet version can be found in Chart 16.A4.

With the spreadsheet software package, the generation of MRP schedules has been greatly simplified. An example of the calculations that would go into the spreadsheet has been included and can be found in Chart 16.A5. This demonstrates the calculations that went into Chart 16.A1 and the upper left-hand corner of Chart 16.A2. This example is sufficient to allow you to build all of the Appendix 16.A MRP schedules since the remainder of the calculations in all the schedules are repetitions of these initial calculations.

Chapter

17 Lot Sizing Techniques

Inventory is probably your most expensive resource. In this chapter we will discuss methods for lumping purchase or production orders, which generates inventory. Be careful how these techniques are used because only the lot-for-lot technique minimizes inventories.

Lot-for-Lot Lot Sizing

The MRP scheduling examples that we have considered in the previous chapter have used the lot-for-lot planning method. The lot-for-lot method states that we order only what we need when we need it. This means that for Chart 16.3, the "Net Requirements" line is the same as the "Planned Receipts" line. Lot-for-lot is the best lot sizing strategy for any factory, especially for those items that are manufactured. However, occasionally some purchased or manufactured components are just too much trouble to order only "just what you need when you need it." I'm talking about things like nails, nuts, washers, etc.

For the scheduling of cheap items, three other lot sizing techniques will be discussed. These methods are variations of the EOQ model discussed in earlier chapters (see Chapter 11). The first lot sizing model is called *EOQ lot sizing*. For this model we use EOQ to determine what quantity you should order. The second new model is called *discrete period EOQ*. For this model we used the EOQ value to estimate or approximate the quantity we should order. The last model is called *fixed order interval lot sizing*. Here we use the time period calculation "T" of the fixed time period model of EOQ to estimate how much we should order.

The EOQ calculations required for these models (EOQ and T) can be found in Chapter 11. Let me demonstrate how each of these processes works.

EOQ Lot Sizing

Charts 17.1 and 17.2 show examples of the "Net Requirements" line generated by an MRP scheduling system. In Chart 17.1 we see how lot-for-lot would schedule these items and generate a "Planned Receipts" line that is the same as the "Net Requirements" line. Chart 17.2 starts with the same "Net Requirements" line as in Chart 17.1. In this example we have calculated EOQs for this product. This is a cheap product and carrying a little inventory is not too damaging to the budget.

CHART 17.1 Lot-for-Lot Lot Sizing Example

Period	1	2	3	4	5	6	7	8	9	10	11	12
Net requirements	0	25	70	30	45	60	77	82	40	0	40	50
Planned receipts	0	25	70	30	45	60	77	82	40	0	40	50

CHART 17.2 EOQ Lot Sizing Example

EOQ = 150

Period	1	2	3	4	5	6	7	8	9	10	11	12	
Net requirements	0	25	70	30	45	60	77	82	40	0	40	50	
Planned receipts	0	150	0	0	150	0	150	0	0	0	150	0	81 extra units left over

EOQ = 200

Period	1	2	3	4	5	6	7	8	9	10	11	12	
Net requirements	0	25	70	30	45	60	77	82	40	0	40	50	
Planned receipts	0	200	0	0	0	200	0	0	200	0	0	0	81 extra units left over

EOQ = 250

Period	1	2	3	4	5	6	7	8	9	10	11	12	
Net requirements	0	25	70	30	45	60	77	82	40	0	40	50	
Planned receipts	0	250	0	0	0	0	250	0	0	0	0	250	231 extra units left over

Chart 17.2 provides examples of three different EOQ values. The first example shows what would happen with an EOQ of 150. The first time there is a demand for parts (period 2) we order an EOQ quantity of parts (150 in the planned receipts). This order of 150 will satisfy the 25 units required in period 2, the 70 units required in period 3, the 30 units required in period 4, and 25 of the 45 units required in period 5. We still need another 20 units to satisfy completely the demand of period 5 and so we order another EOQ of parts. Of the 150 units ordered in period 5, 20 of them are used up in period 5. Another 60 are used up in period 6 and the remaining 70 are used up in period 7.

Period 7 still has a shortage of 7 units, so we place another order for the EOQ quantity of 150 in period 7. This order also satisfies the need for 82 in period 8 and the demand for 40 in period 9, leaving 21 for period 11. Period 11 needs 19 additional units and so we place another order for 150 in period 11. This order also satisfies the demand for 50 in period 12 and leaves 81 units left over.

This same procedure is used for the other two examples of Chart 17.2 where we have EOQs of 200 and 250. After studying these examples you should now be able to calculate your own EOQ lot sizing quantities. Remember that this process occurs while you are calculating the MRP schedules of Chart 16.3. The step from the net requirements to the planned receipts is where the EOQ order consolidations would occur. It has to be done at this time because, if this is a manufactured product, you may have future requirements for lower level products that are affected by this consolidation.

Chart 17.3 demonstrates how this EOQ lot sizing process would look using a spreadsheet. Chart 17.4 shows the calculations that went into the spreadsheet of Chart 17.3. These calculations would be included as part of the MRP schedules demonstrated in the previous chapter.

Discrete Period EOQ Lot Sizing

A third lot sizing technique is the discrete period EOQ lot sizing technique. This lot sizing method attempts to eliminate one of the main disadvantages of EOQ lot sizing, which is that excessive inventory may

CHART 17.3 EOQ Lot Sizing Example Using a Spreadsheet

	A	B	C	D	E	F	G	H	I	J	K	L	M	N
1														
2	EOQ lot sizing example				EOQ = 150									
3														
4	Period		1	2	3	4	5	6	7	8	9	10	11	12
5														
6	Net requirements		0	25	70	30	45	60	77	82	40	0	40	50
7	Planned receipts		0	150	0	0	150	0	150	0	0	0	150	0
8														

CHART 17.4 EOQ Lot Sizing Example Using a Spreadsheet and Showing Calculations

	A	B	C	D	E	F	G
1							
2	EOQ lot sizing example				EOQ = 150		
3							
4	Period		1	2	3	4	5
5							
6	Net requirements		0	25	70	30	45
7	Planned receipts		IF(C6=0,0,F2)	IF(C6+D6>C7,F2,0)	IF(C6+D6+E6>C7+D7,F2,0)	IF(C6+D6+E6+F6>C7+D7+E7,F2,0)	IF(C6+D6+E6+F6+G6>C7+D7+E7+F7,F2,0)
8							

CHART 17.5 Discrete Period EOQ Lot Sizing Example

EOQ = 150

Period	1	2	3	4	5	6	7	8	9	10	11	12
Net requirements	0	25	70	30	45	60	77	82	40	0	40	50
Planned receipts	0	170	0	0	0	137	0	162	0	0	0	50

EOQ = 200

Period	1	2	3	4	5	6	7	8	9	10	11	12
Net requirements	0	25	70	30	45	60	77	82	40	0	40	50
Planned receipts	0	170	0	0	0	219	0	0	130	0	0	0

EOQ = 250

Period	1	2	3	4	5	6	7	8	9	10	11	12
Net requirements	0	25	70	30	45	60	77	82	40	0	40	50
Planned receipts	0	230	0	0	0	0	239	0	0	0	0	50

be ordered and not used for long periods of time (refer back to the assumptions EOQ makes in Chapter 11). In discrete period EOQ lot sizing we attempt to take advantage of some of the benefits of EOQ orders, such as quantity discounts, while at the same time ordering only what we need when we need it, which takes advantage of a benefit of the lot-for-lot philosophy.

In discrete period EOQ we calculate the EOQ for the product just as we did with EOQ lot sizing. Then we use this EOQ value to approximate our order size. We order the quantity of product that most closely matches our EOQ lot size. For example, in Chart 17.5 we see the same data used for Chart 17.2. Again, this time we place an order the first time we have a need for parts, which occurs in period 2. Then we order one of the following:

One period's worth of parts
period 2 only = 25 parts

Two periods' worth of parts
period 2 and period 3 = 95 parts

Three periods' worth of parts
periods 2, 3, and 4 = 125 parts

Four periods' worth of parts
periods 2, 3, 4, and 5 = 170 parts

The three periods' worth of parts is 25 units away from our EOQ of 150. The four periods' worth of parts is 20 units away from our EOQ. Since the four periods' worth is closer to the EOQ than the three periods' worth (or any other group of periods for that matter), we order four periods' worth of parts in period 2. As you can see from the example, we ordered 170 parts in period 2.

Then we start this process over again. We look at the following alternatives:

One period's worth of parts
period 6 only = 60 parts

Two periods' worth of parts
period 6 and period 7 = 137 parts

Three periods' worth of parts
periods 6, 7, and 8 = 219 parts

This time two periods' worth of parts is 13 units away from the EOQ of 150 and three periods' worth of parts is 69 units away from the EOQ. The closest is two periods' worth, so we order 137 units in period 6.

Repeating this process again gives us:

One period's worth of parts
period 8 only = 82 parts

Two periods' worth of parts
period 8 and period 9 = 122 parts

Three periods' worth of parts
periods 8, 9, and 10 = 122 parts

Four periods' worth of parts
periods 8, 9, 10, and 11 = 162 parts

This time three periods' worth is 28 units away from the EOQ of 150 and four periods' worth is 12 units away from the EOQ so we order 162 units in period 8.

The process repeats itself over and over again until all orders are calculated. The same process is demonstrated using these data for the EOQ levels of 200 or 250, as shown in the example of Chart 17.5.

Fixed Order Interval Lot Sizing

In fixed order interval lot sizing we become concerned about large gaps between demands. For example, if we have several weeks with 0 demand we don't want to order quantities for periods after these intervals just because the total is closer to the EOQ value, as discrete period EOQ or EOQ lot sizing would have you do. What we do differently here is we order all the requirements for a fixed interval of time.

The equation for determining the interval of time used for the ordering process is found in Chapter 11 under the discussion of fixed time period calculations for purchased items (see Chart 11.11). Using this formula we calculate a T value, which states how often we should place an order. However, T is given in terms of years and we need to multiply it times 52 weeks per year to get the number of weeks between orders (in Chapter 11 we multiplied T times working days to get the number of days between orders). You may get a fraction of weeks and you will need to round off to the nearest week. Once we have calculated T in terms of weeks we can demonstrate how fixed order interval lot sizing works.

An example of fixed order interval lot sizing is shown in Chart 17.6. The procedure is as follows: The first time there is a demand for parts,

CHART 17.6 Fixed Order Interval Lot Sizing Example

T = 4 weeks

Period	1	2	3	4	5	6	7	8	9	10	11	12
Net requirements	0	25	70	30	45	60	77	82	40	0	40	50
Planned receipts	0	170	0	0	0	259	0	0	0	0	90	0

T = 5 weeks

Period	1	2	3	4	5	6	7	8	9	10	11	12
Net requirements	0	25	70	30	45	60	77	82	40	0	40	50
Planned receipts	0	230	0	0	0	0	239	0	0	0	0	50

T = 4 weeks

Period	1	2	3	4	5	6	7	8	9	10	11	12
Net requirements	0	25	70	30	45	0	0	0	60	89	40	50
Planned receipts	0	170	0	0	0	0	0	0	239	0	0	0

order the next T weeks' worth of parts in one order. Then we again look for the next time where there is a need for parts (there may be zero demand and these weeks are skipped; see the third example) and then we accumulate T periods' worth of parts and order them. Three different examples of the fixed order interval lot sizing model are shown in Chart 17.6. These should help you get a feel for how this simple model functions.

Summary

Lot sizing policies are techniques for summarizing the order quantities of cheap parts into economic batch sizes. Lot-for-lot, which says that you should order only what you need when you need it, should be your most commonly used technique. But other techniques have been presented to help you with the inexpensive parts that you purchase. Now we will move forward to initiate the production orders we have generated. This process occurs in the next two chapters where we will plan departmental capacity (Chapter 18) and then release and track production orders (Chapter 19).

Chapter

18 Capacity Requirements Planning

CRP Explained

Behind every balanced Shop Department is a surprised shop steward. What is a balanced Shop Department? It is one where the work load expected of the department is exactly what the capacity of the department has available.

Capacity requirements planning (CRP) takes the production orders and determines what the production load generated by these production orders would be. For many plants this analysis is more trouble than it's worth. Specifically, if your production lead time is very short and the product you produce is very repetitive, then the production load placed on your facility will be approximately the same each day. Going through all the trouble of working out a capacity load for each department is more trouble than it's worth.

However, if your production lead time is long, and if there is a significant variability in the product mix that you produce, then capacity requirements planning can be very helpful. You must decide whether you need the tools offered in this chapter or not.

Inputs into CRP

At this point in our planning process, we have a list of production orders that have either been released or are firm planned orders (refer to Chart 16.1 for the production order output of the MRP system). Each of these orders requires a specific amount of hours to produce and these hours are disbursed among several departments. We need to determine what the hour demand of each of the departments will be. Referring to the MRP schedules of Chapter 16, we have the open production orders listed in Chart 18.1. These orders are a combination of the existing orders (Chart 16.2), the cancellations and reschedulings (Chart 16.16), the order releases (there weren't any in this example), and the firm planned orders (Chart 16.17). This comprises all of the adjusted outstanding orders (cancellations and reschedulings have made some adjustments) and Chart 18.1 shows these orders along with their start and due dates.

CHART 18.1 Production Order Inputs into CRP (Taken from Charts 16.2, 16.16, and 16.17)

Product Number	Quantity	Start Date	Due Date
TRI	22	1/4	1/4
TRI–SP	6	2/2	2/2
CCCC	4	1/3	1/4
ABCD	5	1/4	2/1
DDDD	10	1/3	2/1
AACC	20	1/3	2/1
ACAC	92	1/2	1/3
A5B5	23	1/3	1/3

The next step in determining what the work load is for each department is to determine what each of the manufactured products in Chart 18.1 requires from each department. This information comes from the routings (Chapter 14). Chart 14.5 was a sample routing for product CCCC. From Chart 14.5 we learned that CCCC requires loads from each of these departments as summarized in Chart 18.2. Since the CCCC batch size is four units, we have extended the total hours demanded for each department by the amount of this batch size.

Using the same principles that were used to generate Chart 18.2, we have generated Chart 18.3, which shows the extended department demand for each of the manufactured products that have been scheduled (Chart 18.1).

The next step is to define in which time periods these demands fall. We use the information from Chart 18.1 and break out each of these demands into a time period. For example, TRI is done completely in week 1/4 so the entire demand for TRI is placed into week 1/4. But CCCC appears in week 1/3 and week 1/4. The first half of its demand is placed in week 1/3 (the department functions of cutting, grinding, and drilling), and the last half of its demand is placed in week 1/4 (stamping, heat treatment, plating, and inspection). The demand, broken down by week, is shown in Chart 18.4. Note that the capacity requirements seem rather weak for this factory. We would expect the plant to have a heavy load. However, this factory doesn't look very busy. That is

CHART 18.2 Load Requirements for Product CCCC at a Batch Quantity of Four (Taken from Charts 14.5 and 18.1)

Department	Labor Time		Total Time Required
	Set-up	Run	
Cutting	2 hrs.	1.2 min.	124.8 min.
Grinding	1 hr.	0.6 min.	62.4 min.
Stamping	10 min.	0.6 min.	12.4 min.
Plating	2 hrs.	1.8 min.	127.2 min.
Inspection	0	1.8 min.	7.2 min.

CHART 18.3 Total Load Requirements for All Products at Their Planned Batch Quantities (in minutes) (Taken from Chart 18.1)

Department	Total Extended Times Quantity Demanded							
	TRI	TRI–SP	CCCC	ABCD	DDDD	AACC	ACAC	A5B5
Cutting	300	0	125	50	100	300	2000	350
Grinding	400	0	62	100	200	4000	6000	1000
Drilling	400	0	0	75	200	700	900	300
Stamping	150	20	12	0	50	0	100	0
Heat treat	0	0	0	100	150	1000	900	350
Plating	100	0	127	0	50	0	50	0
Inspection	200	20	7	0	10	0	20	0

CHART 18.4 Load Requirements for All Products at Their Planned Batch Quantities Broken Down by Week (in minutes) (Taken from Charts 18.1 and 18.2)

Week 1/2

Department	TRI	TRI–SP	CCCC	ABCD	DDDD	AACC	ACAC	A5B5
Cutting	0	0	0	0	0	0	2000	0
Grinding	0	0	0	0	0	0	6000	0
Drilling	0	0	0	0	0	0	900	0
Stamping	0	0	0	0	0	0	0	0
Heat treat	0	0	0	0	0	0	0	0
Plating	0	0	0	0	0	0	0	0
Inspection	0	0	0	0	0	0	0	0

Week 1/3

Department	TRI	TRI–SP	CCCC	ABCD	DDDD	AACC	ACAC	A5B5
Cutting	0	0	125	0	100	300	0	350
Grinding	0	0	62	0	200	4000	0	1000
Drilling	0	0	0	0	0	0	0	300
Stamping	0	0	0	0	0	0	100	0
Heat treat	0	0	0	0	0	0	900	350
Plating	0	0	0	0	0	0	50	0
Inspection	0	0	0	0	0	0	20	0

Week 1/4

Department	TRI	TRI–SP	CCCC	ABCD	DDDD	AACC	ACAC	A5B5
Cutting	300	0	0	50	0	0	0	350
Grinding	400	0	0	100	0	0	0	1000
Drilling	400	0	0	75	200	700	0	300
Stamping	150	0	12	0	50	0	0	0
Heat treat	0	0	0	0	0	0	0	350
Plating	100	0	127	0	0	0	0	0
Inspection	200	0	7	0	0	0	0	0

Week 2/1

Department	TRI	TRI–SP	CCCC	ABCD	DDDD	AACC	ACAC	A5B5
Cutting	0	0	0	0	0	0	0	0
Grinding	0	0	0	0	0	0	0	0
Drilling	0	0	0	0	0	0	0	0
Stamping	0	0	0	0	0	0	0	0
Heat treat	0	0	0	100	150	1000	0	0
Plating	0	0	0	0	50	0	0	0
Inspection	0	0	0	0	10	0	0	0

Week 2/2

Department	TRI	TRI–SP	CCCC	ABCD	DDDD	AACC	ACAC	A5B5
Cutting	0	0	0	0	0	0	0	0
Grinding	0	0	0	0	0	0	0	0
Drilling	0	0	0	0	0	0	0	0
Stamping	0	20	0	0	0	0	0	0
Heat treat	0	0	0	0	0	0	0	0
Plating	0	0	0	0	0	0	0	0
Inspection	0	20	0	0	0	0	0	0

CHART 18.5 Capacity and Weekly Demands for Three Departments (in minutes) (Taken from Chart 18.4)

Capacity	Cutting 2000	Grinding 5000	Drilling 1500
Week 1/2	2000	6000	900
Week 1/3	875	5262	300
Week 1/4	700	1500	1675

because, in order to keep this example simple, we have not scheduled the requirements for the mountain bikes or the ten-speed bikes.

Now that we have calculated the demand for each department by week, we can analyze the weekly demand by department and compare it to the capacity for each department. The weekly capacity for each department is calculated, except here we want the capacity available for a one-week increment. Chart 18.5 shows the weekly demands and capacities for the first three departments. In this chart we see that cutting is within capacity while grinding and drilling fall out of capacity. Using a piece of graph paper it is very easy to plot this information graphically. A visual picture can be very helpful. Chart 18.6 shows how a graph of the Grinding and Drilling departments would look.

Since we have only scheduled one product in this example, the capacity does not look very evenly loaded. However, since we planned a somewhat level loaded aggregate production schedule, the overall load should be level. Also, with the aid of a computerized MRP and CRP system, this load can be displayed on a daily basis, giving even more load detail if necessary.

In a computerized system, the graph can distinguish between what part of the load is caused by customer or open orders, what part is caused by firm planned orders, and what part is caused by planned orders (planned orders are not plotted in the manual graph of Chart 18.6). This additional information will help in recognizing which orders are the most critical (the ones that affect the customer).

CHART 18.6 Capacity Requirements Planning

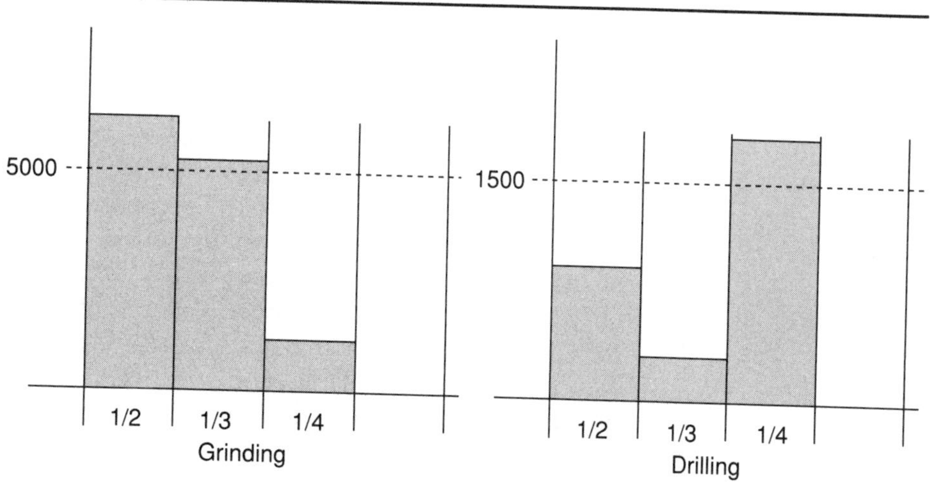

A computerized system will also be able to give you a list of jobs for each day. This allows you to identify what specific jobs make up the day's production load. This level of detail may not be important to you. I'm not trying to talk you into a computerized CRP system. However, if this level of detail is helpful, then a computerized system may be what you need. But for now anyway, a weekly load report like the one shown in Chart 18.6 should be adequate for your needs.

Infinite, Finite, Forward, and Backward Loading

Using the example of Chart 18.6 we can see how it may be helpful to shift some of the overloads into weeks where we have a shortage. There are three basic concepts to shifting this load. They are:

Infinite Loading: This is where the load is not shifted. Infinite capacity is assumed. If any shifting is to be done it will have to be done on the factory floor.

Finite Forward Loading: This is where any overloads are shifted forward. For example, looking at Chart 18.6, the overload for Grinding in weeks 1/2 and 1/3 will be shifted to week 1/4. The new loads would be:

1/2 is 5,000 units
1/3 is 5,000 units
1/4 is 2,762 units

Finite Backward Loading: This is where any overloads are shifted backward. Again, looking at Chart 18.6, the overload for drilling in week 1/4 is shifted back into the previous week. The new loads would be:

1/2 is 900 units
1/3 is 475 units
1/4 is 1,500 units

Input/Output Control

Input/output control is a system that investigates bottlenecks within a factory. These bottlenecks may be real, for example, due to a machine capacity restriction, or they may be what is referred to as a *wandering bottleneck*. This latter type of bottleneck is caused by a production wave that flows through the shop. If you've worked on the shop floor you understand the wave. The way to control these bottlenecks is by means of *input/output analysis*. Very simply, what this means is that you are only allowed a certain number of hours of work within your work center. You can't receive any more work in than what you've shipped out. You monitor your output, and you limit your input based on this output. By doing this, any department that comes before you that would

CHART 18.7 Input/Output Analysis Control Form

Que size limit ______________________ Department __________

Work Inflow	Work Outflow	Work Que	Job Number	Date

CHART 18.8 Input/Output Analysis Control Form—Example

Que size limit 600 hours Department Cutting

Work Inflow	Work Outflow	Work Que	Job Number	Date
Balance forward		500		
75		575	1234	1/1/91
	200	375	2222	1/2/91
150		525	1212	1/2/91
	100	425	1333	1/3/91
	100	325	1414	1/3/91
250		575	1122	1/5/91

like to ship you an overload of work can't—it has to keep it until you're ready. Since this previous department is also on an input/output control system, they are also restricted in receiving new work until they transfer this job to you. This restriction of work inflow vibrates all the way through the factory. Input/output analysis attempts to keep the factory balanced, thereby avoiding a buildup of work in process inventory.

The type of document used to control input/output work flows can be seen in Chart 18.7. As a job flows out, the que is reduced. Then, when a job comes in, the que is increased. But the que is never allowed to go over the limit. Chart 18.8 gives an example of how this process should work.

Summary

We have now done all the planning for the work flows that will occur on the shop floor. We are now ready to monitor and control the shop floor activity. This is an important part of the feedback mechanism that tells the production control system how we are performing on our production orders. So let's move forward to Chapter 19, Shop Floor Control.

Chapter

19 Shop Floor Control

Shop floor control is a world of fighting fires. We often get so wrapped up in the symptoms that we don't have enough time to look for problems. For example, we get wrapped up in collecting data about every movement that our employees' make in an attempt to make sure that they are busy, but we don't measure the materials scrap and wastage that is costing us four to six times as much as labor inefficiencies.

Operator Errors

Another example is the "operator error" cop-out. Nearly every error that occurs on the production floor is blamed on the all-encompassing "operator error." Even the Chernobyl nuclear plant accident in Russia was blamed on "operator error." We would have a perfect world if not for all those fool operators. This sarcasm is attempting to make the point that if the product engineering and process engineering designs are so lousy and complicated that even a Ph.D. can't figure it out, can we expect anything but operator errors? For example, if engineers build a nuclear plant, but don't consider safeguards for operator errors, then who is to blame when an error occurs? The operator, of course, because the engineer told him how to do it right.

Here is an appropriate time to reinforce a strong statement. *If an engineer hasn't built his or her own designs, the engineer is worthless!* Take your engineers, put them on the shop floor, and make them build their own designs for a few days. Stress that the engineers should look for ways to prevent errors and improve quality. You'll be amazed at how much they'll learn about designing a product once they've built it. This is good for the engineers, for the shop floor worker, and for the plant overall. It will reduce operator errors.

Another important issue is "focus." As discussed in previous chapters, after we have defined our goal, we need to focus on the resource that is the most critical in the achievement of the goal. Once we have identified this critical resource, we need to develop a measurement system that focuses on that resource and, hence, on the goal.

For example, if you are the typical discrete U.S. factory, your goal would be to make a profit. Next, focusing on resources, the value-added components of those resources would break down something like:

Labor	10% of the value-added cost
Materials	50% of the value-added cost
Machinery	15% of the value-added cost
Overhead	25% of the value-added cost

Using this example, the resource that is the most critical in achieving the goal of increased profits is materials. Labor is the least important. Therefore, based on these numbers, we should focus on measuring the materials usage, scrap, and breakage so we can determine what areas of materials usage need improvement. A 10 percent improvement in materials usage will give you five times the benefits (profit increases) of a 10 percent improvement in labor costs. Your shop floor control system should be "focused" on these types of improvements.

What happens in the area of information flow on the shop floor? We'll start by discussing how orders are released and controlled, and how the feedback process works. Next, we will discuss a number of shop floor considerations that need to be incorporated into the flow. We will also discuss the feedback reports and how they are used.

Order Releases, Changes, and Reschedulings

The flow chart in Chart 19.1 diagrams the steps in production shop floor control. Chart 19.2 summarizes the steps in Chart 19.1 for easy reference. In Charts 19.1 and 19.2 several documents are referenced. The first of these, the production traveler, is shown in Chart 19.3. The basic information that is reported on the traveler is a summary of the information that comes from the routings (Chapter 14) and the bill of materials (Chapter 13). The traveler also reports the desired quantity, the due date, the performance of each step, scrap or wastage, the completion date, and the actual quantity produced. This document is used later to review job performance or employee efficiency information (see some of the output reports demonstrated later in this chapter). This traveler was generated with the assumption that employee time is our

CHART 19.1 Shop Order Information Flow

Production Planning Department

Production orders are triggered by either of the following:
1. The MRP system has supplied order release information and based on this we need to release a production order (Chapter 16), or,
2. The EOQ system that is tracking inventory levels in the stockroom has reached its reorder point and we have received a production order for EOQ parts (Chapters 8, 9, and 11)
Step 1

Production Planning and Scheduling Department

A production packet is prepared that contains:
1. A job traveler, which is a routing sheet showing the steps that the job is routed through. This is also used to monitor progress since steps completed are reported on this form (see Chart 19.3). This form indicates the quantity to be produced and the due date.
2. Engineering drawings showing the product to be made.
Step 2

(continued)

Shop Floor Supervisor and Production Scheduling

The following steps occur on the production release date:
1. The shop floor supervisor gets the production packets and records the job on his/her "big" sheet. This sheet is a listing of what jobs are "open" on the production floor. The jobs are usually categorized by what type of job they are, when they are due, and what quantity is required. See the example on Chart 19.5.
2. The job packet is sent on to the first department required to work on the job.
3. A pick list is generated and sent to the Inventory Stores Department. This is a list of what materials will be required for the production process. This is an optional, time-saving step. The idea is that if the Inventory Department knows what materials will be needed for this job before the shop floor employees actually come to pick those materials up, they can prepare early. They can have all these materials picked so that when the shop floor employee shows up they won't have to wait around while the stockroom personnel "pick" the materials. See the example on Chart 19.7.
4. If we are using an MRP system we will need to report this production order release back to the production control system so that the MRP system knows about the pending production order receipt. See the section on production orders in Chapter 12 and the inputs into MRP in Chart 16.2.

Step 3

Shop Floor Department

When the packet arrives into the department we schedule it in with the other packets that are currently in the department. Later in this chapter we will discuss shop floor job prioritization where we will look at several alternatives for sequencing these jobs. When the job is completed it is transferred to the next department listed in the traveler.

Step 4

Shop Floor Department and Shop Floor Supervisor

Upon completion of all the steps identified in the production traveler, the following occurs:
1. The completed materials are delivered to the stockroom and added to inventory.
2. The completing department returns the completed paperwork (drawing and production traveler) to the shop floor supervisor. This individual takes the job off of the "big" sheet and returns the paperwork to the Production Planning and Scheduling Department.

Step 5

Production Planning and Scheduling

When Production Planning and Scheduling receives the paperwork they adjust the MRP system by closing down the production order and adjusting inventory (the inventory adjustment should have already occurred through the stockroom). If you are running EOQ production scheduling, the adjustments occur automatically when you receive the completed materials into inventory.

Step 6

CHART 19.2 Shop Order Information Flow Chart Summary
(Taken from Chart 19.1)

Production order release date

Production Planning Department

Production orders are triggered by:
1. The MRP order releases
2. The EOQ reorder points

Step 1

Production Planning and Scheduling Department

A production packet is prepared that contains:
1. A job traveler (Chart 19.3)
2. Engineering drawings

Step 2

Shop Floor Supervisor and Production Scheduling

On production release date the following happens:
1. The shop floor supervisor gets the production packets and records the job on his/her "big" sheet (Chart 19.5).
2. The job packet is sent on to the first department that will be required to work on the job.
3. A pick list is generated and sent to the Inventory Stores Department (Chart 19.7).
4. If we are using an MRP system, report this production order release to production control.

Step 3

Step 4 repeats itself until all steps in the production process are completed.

Shop Floor Department

Schedule the job in your department. When the job is completed it is transferred to the next department listed in the production traveler.

Step 4

(*continued*)

CHART 19.2 *(concluded)*

Upon completion of all steps:

Shop Floor Department and Shop Floor Supervisor

Upon completion:
1. The completed materials are delivered to the stockroom and added to inventory.
2. The completing department returns the completed paperwork to the shop floor supervisor.
Step 5

Production Planning and Scheduling

Adjust the MRP system
Step 6

critical resource. This assumption is made not because it is truly your critical resource, but because most companies operate under this assumption (see the discussion at the beginning of this chapter).

The production traveler can be generated easily by computer if you have an MRP system. However, Chart 19.3 is the form that can be used to generate a production traveler manually. Chart 19.4 demonstrates how this document would look for product CCCC if it is filled out using the information from Chart 14.5 for routings and Chart 13.2 for Bill of Materials.

Note that the job number is not included on the traveler. Normally the "Product Number," "Due Date," and "Quantity" are enough information to identify the job. These three together could be used as a job number if desired. However, if you have multiple runs for the same product due on the same day, you may want to add a run number to the end of this identifier, for example, Product Number/Due Date/Run Number, and use this as your job identifier. A third alternative for identifying each job is to develop a totally unique job number for every job in the shop. The purpose of the job number is to track each job as it progresses through the shop.

The production big sheet planner (Chart 19.5) is used by the shop floor supervisor and other personnel throughout the shop floor who track jobs. The best way to use this is to make a pad of them and each day rip off the top sheet and file it somewhere for future reference. At the start of the day you transfer any open or pending jobs (jobs without a completion date) onto the new sheet for the day. Then you add the new jobs as they come in during the day. As jobs are completed you post

CHART 19.3 Production Traveler

Due Date _____/_____/_____ Product Number ____________ Product Name ____________________ Batch Size __________

Routing Step #	Department	Machine	Labor Code	Setup Time	Run Time (per batch)	Component---------- Item #	Quantity	Actual production----> Date	Start	Stop	Lapse	Quantity Used	Quantity Scrapped	Output Quantity	Employee Initials

CHART 19.4 Production Traveler—Example (Example of Chart 19.3)

Date 1 / 1 / 1992 Product Number CCCC Product Name Wheel Batch Size 50

Routing Step #	Department	Machine	Labor Code	Setup Time	Run Time (per batch)	Item #	Component Quantity	Actual Date	production-> Start	Stop	Lapse	Quantity Used	Quantity Scrapped	Output Quantity	Employee Initials
						A4B4	600								
						ACAC	100								
10	Cutting	X40	L35	2 hrs.	2 hrs.										
20	Grinding	RV282	L40	1 hr.	1 hr.										
30	Stamping	Brilton	L35	10 min.	1 hr.										
40	Plating	Stall	L50	2 hrs.	3 hrs.										
50	Inspection		I20	0	3 hrs.										

CHART 19.5 Production Big Sheet Planner

Due Date ______/______/______

Job Identifier			Completion		Job Identifier			Completion		Job Identifier			Completion	
Product #	Due Date	Quantity	Date	Quantity	Product #	Due Date	Quantity	Date	Quantity	Product #	Due Date	Quantity	Date	Quantity

CHART 19.6 Production Big Sheet Planner—Example (Example of Chart 19.5)

Date 1 / 1 /1992

Job Identifier			Completion		Job Identifier			Completion		Job Identifier			Completion	
Product #	Due Date	Quantity	Date	Quantity	Product #	Due Date	Quantity	Date	Quantity	Product #	Due Date	Quantity	Date	Quantity
CCCC	1 / 1 / 1992	50	1 / 1 / 1992	51		/ /		/ /			/ /		/ /	
BBBB	1 / 5 / 1992	150	/ /			/ /		/ /			/ /		/ /	
BBBB	1 / 10 / 1992	200	/ /			/ /		/ /			/ /		/ /	

the completion date and the actual end quantity produced and proceed with the other functions listed in step 5 of Chart 19.1.

When filling out the big sheet, attempt to group similar products. This will give you a feel for which areas of the shop floor are getting an overload or underload of work. For example, in the first column list all parts of a certain type, in the second column list all the parts of another category, and so on.

One important part of the big sheet is the control aspect. As we rewrite the schedule each day, we watch for jobs that are due to be completed today, or even worse, jobs that are overdue. Then we monitor these jobs to see why they are not complete (if late) and to make sure they get completed quickly. Chart 19.6 shows an example of a filled-out big sheet.

The big sheet of Chart 19.5, or something similar to it, is useful at the department and possibly even at the machine level for tracking jobs. Sometimes a blackboard or a scribble pad is all that is needed at this level. You will need to determine which method works best at each of these levels.

The pick list mentioned in step 3 of Chart 19.1 can be found in Chart 19.7. The function of the pick list is to give the Inventory Department an early warning that a shop order is being started and that they need to get the materials ready for the order. The pick list is simply the materials list shown on the production traveler. The Inventory Department will "pick" these materials and package them together as a "kit." That kit will be picked up by the production worker when he/she is ready to start working on the job. An example of Chart 19.7, using the data of Chart 19.4, is shown in Chart 19.8.

Note that there is a difference between the pick list used for customer shipments and the pick list of Chart 19.7, which is for work-in-process picking. The customer shipment pick list allows for back orders, whereas the production order pick list does not. The assumption is that if you are trying to produce a part and you don't have all the necessary pieces, then production is delayed.

CHART 19.7 Pick List

Due Date ____/____/____ Product Number ________________
Product Name ________________ Batch Size ________

	Component	
Item #	Description	Quantity

CHART 19.8 Pick List Example

Due Date 1 / 1 / 1992 Product Number CCC
Product Name ______ Batch Size 50

Item #	Component Description	Quantity
A4B4		600
ACAC		100

Production Flow Through a Departmental Discrete Manufacturing Plant

Chart 19.9, Part A, diagrams a typical departmental discrete manufacturing facility. We have a series of functional departments, each specializing in a certain process. Aisle space is available for the transfer of products and there is an inventory storage area. The production planning process occurs in a front office. We have a shop floor supervisor on the factory floor where the big sheet is located. The shop floor will be discussed in two ways. First the sequence of materials movement will be discussed (Chart 19.9, Parts B through F). Then the paperwork flow will be discussed (Chart 19.9, Parts G and H).

CHART 19.9 Plant Layout, Part A

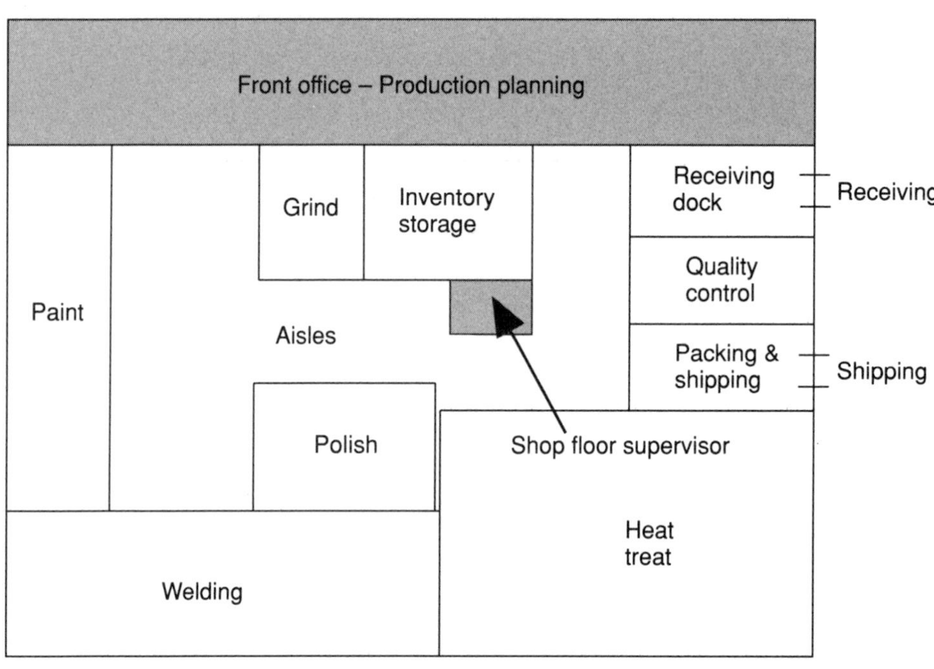

CHART 19.9 Receiving to Inspection, Part B

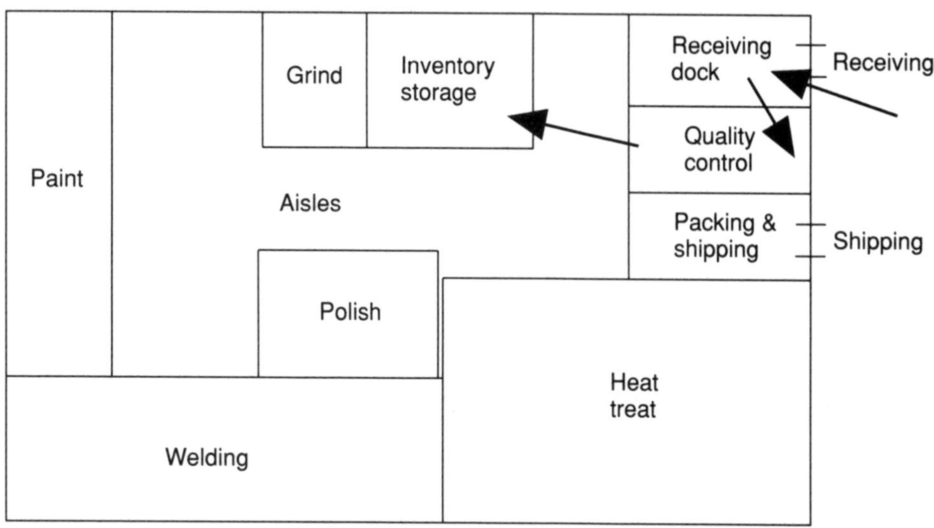

CHART 19.9 Starting a Production Order, Part C

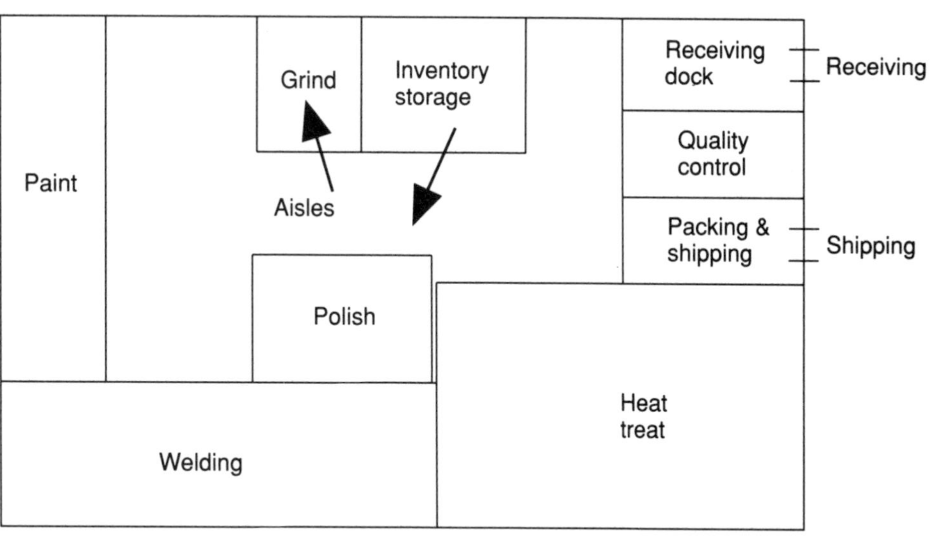

(continued)

CHART 19.9 Routing the Production Order Through the Factory, Part D

Receiving dock
Receiving
Grind
Inventory storage
Quality control
Paint
Aisles
Packing & shipping
Shipping
Polish
Heat treat
Welding

CHART 19.9 Routing the Completed Production Order Back to Inventory, Part E

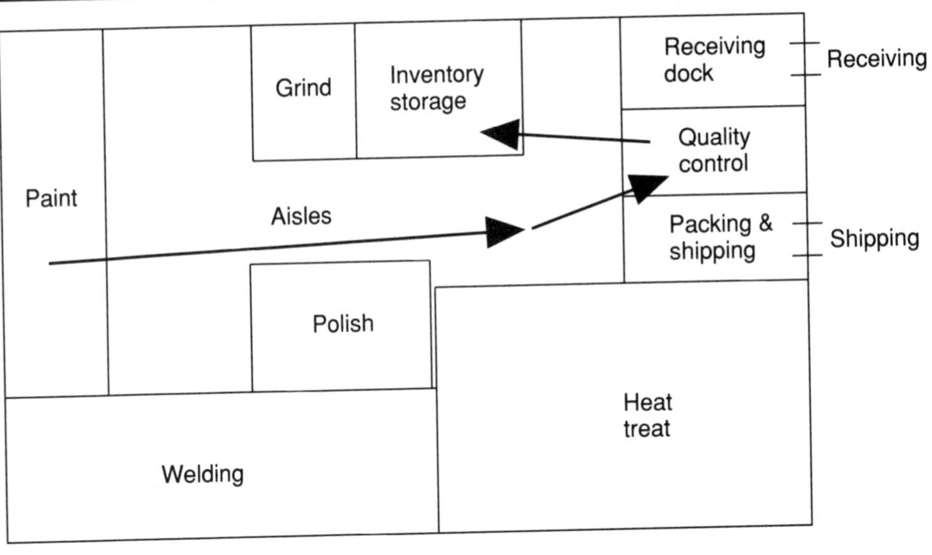

CHART 19.9 Shipping the Finished Product, Part F

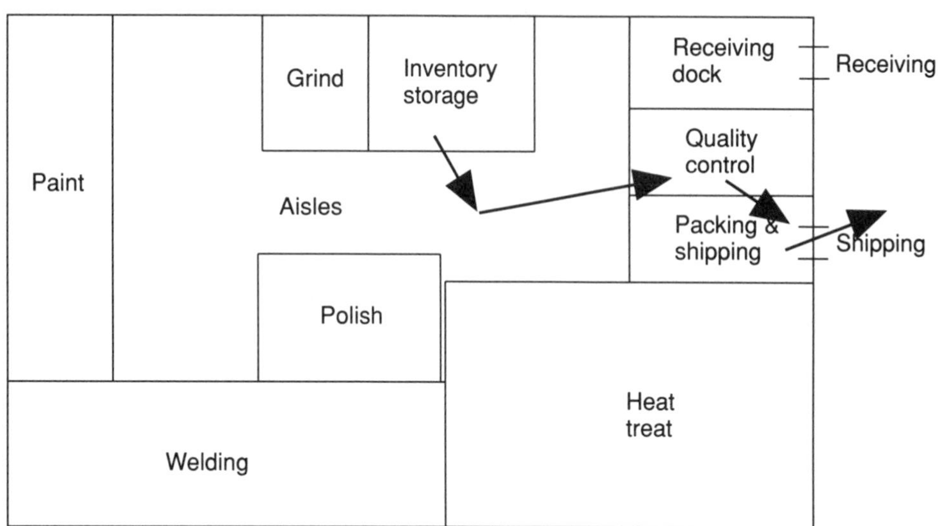

CHART 19.9 Paperwork Flow at the Start of a Production Order, Part G

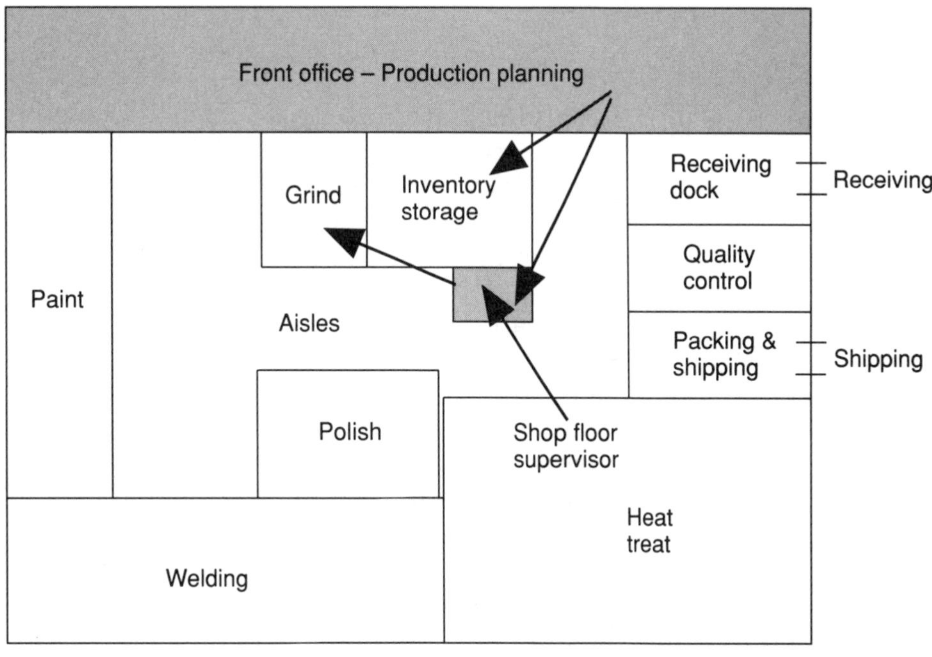

(*continued*)

CHART 19.9 **Paperwork Flow at the Completion of a Production Order, Part H**

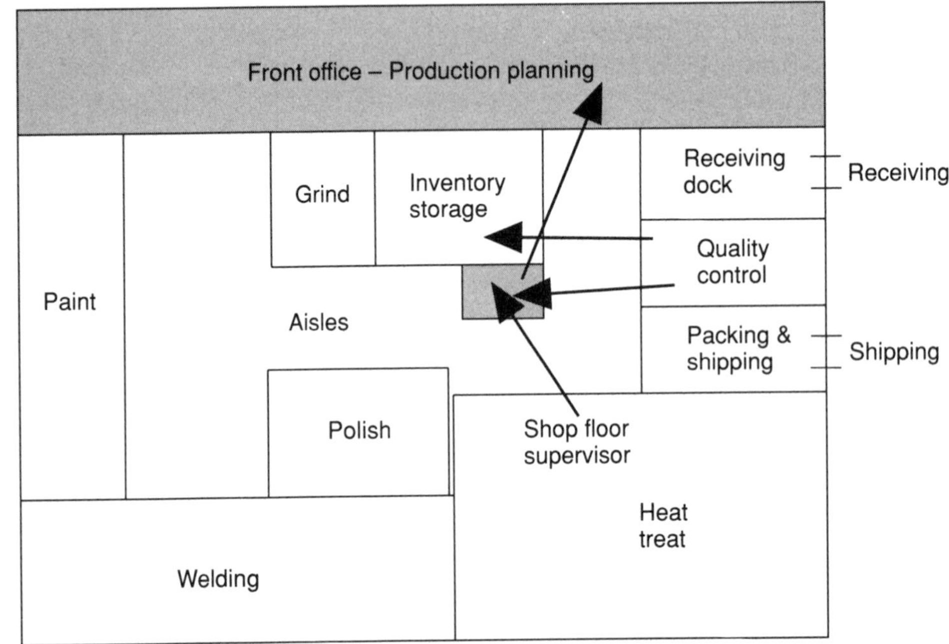

Receiving Raw Materials. In discussing the movement of materials on the factory floor, we need first to discuss the receipt of purchased goods (Chart 19.9, Part B). We start by receiving raw materials into the factory at the receiving dock. The materials are unpacked and then transferred to the Quality Control Department for inspection. After they are inspected, the materials are transferred to the inventory storage area where they are counted, reported to the perpetual inventory system (Chapters 8 and 9), and stored.

Production Order Flow. The next phase of our materials movement discussion starts when a production order is initiated. To start the production process, we pull the necessary materials from inventory and transfer them to the first department, which in this example happens to be the Grinding Department (see Chart 19.9, Part C). When we take items out of inventory, the perpetual inventory control system is reduced by the quantity of goods taken.

As production continues, the batch of materials is moved from one department to the next until all the production steps have been completed (see Chart 19.9, Part D). In this example the materials move from grinding to welding, then back to grinding, then to heat treatment, then to polishing, and finally to painting.

The final step in the production process is a move from the last work station, which is painting, to the Quality Department where the product is inspected (see Chart 19.9, Part E). If there are any repairable problems, they are fixed at this point. Then the finished, quality products are transferred to inventory storage where they are counted, reported to the perpetual inventory system, and stored. This completes the flow of materials for a production order.

Finished Goods Shipping. For a customer shipment, the flow starts with the picking of materials from the inventory storage area. These materials are transferred to the quality control area for one final inspection before shipment (see Chart 19.9, Part F). The inventory stores personnel reduce the count in the perpetual inventory system by the number of units of product shipped. The Quality Department then transfers the materials to the packaging and shipping area, which is part of the shipping dock where the product is loaded and shipped.

Production Order Paperwork Flow. The discussion of the paperwork flow for a production order, for the factory in Chart 19.9, Part A, starts with the release of the production order. The released order along with the appropriate drawings (see step 2 in Chart 19.1) are transferred to the shop floor supervisor (see Chart 19.9, Part G). The shop floor supervisor reports the order on the big sheet and then forwards the packet to the first department, which in this example happens to be grinding.

As part of this production order initiating process, the inventory storage area also gets a pick list, which lists all the parts that are needed for this production order. The inventory area can then pick the appropriate materials and prepare a kit of these parts so that when the shop floor employee from grinding comes to pick up the parts they will be ready.

The paperwork (traveler packet) stays with the materials as they move throughout the production process. This follows the same route as shown in Chart 19.9, Part D. After finishing the last step in the process, which is painting (see Chart 19.9, Part E), the materials and the packet are transferred to the quality control area for inspection. After inspection, the materials are transferred to inventory and counted (see Chart 19.9, Part H). The new count is reported to the perpetual inventory system. At the same time, this count is reported on the traveler (see Chart 19.3 or 19.4) and the traveler is given to the shop floor supervisor. The supervisor will then report the job completion date and the quantity completed on the big sheet and forward the completed packet to the production planning office. The production planning office will then close the production order.

EOQ-Related Issues

Feedback. The feedback mechanism in EOQ is contained in the perpetual inventory system (see Chapters 8, 9, and 11). As we learned from these previous chapters, when a production order is needed, the reorder point triggers it. When the completed order is received into inventory, the perpetual inventory system updates the count of the goods produced. The perpetual inventory system is the control and feedback mechanism for EOQ production planning.

Product Changes—Engineering Change Orders. In EOQ, changes to the product are taken care of as a new production order for the product is released. The change is processed by issuing both an updated traveler and an updated drawing. The only thing that we need to be concerned about is obsolescence, which occurs if we have eliminated the need for a component part that in the past was kept in inventory. This part will need to have its demand reduced and its EOQ recalculated (see Chapter 11). The inventory reports of Chapter 9 will also help track these obsolescence situations.

MRP-Related Issues

Feedback. The shop floor control process reports the status of the jobs that have been started. This feedback is then recorded in the MRP system so that the job can be listed as a scheduled receipt. This feedback keeps the MRP from generating new planned orders or order releases for products that are already being produced (see Chapter 16).

Planned Order Releases. The planned order releases that were generated by the MRP system do not get released onto the production floor because they are out in the future. Only the order releases get released because they affect the current period. The planned order releases may get firmed up and become firm planned orders as they get close to their release date, but the firming up process would happen in the Production Scheduling Department. Then, as these firm planned orders become current, they are released into production.

Product Changes—Engineering Change Orders. When product changes occur in an MRP environment we need to be careful to track the effective change date of the change. Generally three different methods are used to implement these changes:

1. *Immediate change* occurs when the change needs to be implemented immediately. This happens when customer safety is involved. In this case we would modify the bill of materials (see Chapter 13) and routings (see Chapter 14) appropriately. We would also go out on the factory floor and change any production packets that are in process. This type of a change has a rippling effect in that it changes component production orders and purchase orders as well. The rippled effects that will be felt by these other orders will need to be corrected within the system.

2. *Timed change* is when a specific change needs to be implemented on a specific date. This occurs when we are changing the product for the new model year. In this case we may need to have two bill of materials entries identified by part number and model number. We

would release orders under the old number until we hit the point where the changeover date occurs. Then we would start issuing production orders based on the new number. The MRP planning system can adjust for a time phased change of this type because the master production schedule would contain two entries, one for the old number, and one for the new product–model number.

3. *Inventory depletion* occurs when we decide that we want to make the change when all the old parts are used. This occurs when the new part is a different type, or made from a different material, than the old part. The procedure would be similar to that of the second type of change. We should set up two-part model numbers. The first would schedule enough volume to use up the remaining old inventory. The new part number would be triggered when the old inventory is used.

Alternate Routings. In our routing system we have established a standard routing for each manufactured item. However, occasionally there are breakdowns or capacity buildups that would make it desirable to build the part in an "alternate" way. This secondary build sequence is called an *alternate routing*. All production planning is developed based on the primary routing; however, if a disruption occurs, it is helpful for the employees on the shop floor to be aware of alternative ways in which the same functions can be performed. Therefore, establishing alternate routings and having them available to the shop floor employees helps avoid confusion and mistakes if disruptions occur.

Low-Efficiency Situations. Occasionally, the employee that has been assigned to do a job has a much lower level of efficiency than the "standard" employee (see Chapter 14). This would delay the production process. In most plants this will not be a problem in meeting total production lead time because the largest component of this lead time is the wait or que times. These times are buffered for just such a situation. If a low-efficiency problem is anticipated, it is helpful to monitor the progress of the jobs through the shop floor and hurry them along especially if it looks like they may be late.

Bottlenecks

A bottleneck is an area in the factory that does not have the capacity to produce the total amount of output desired. For example, in the factory of Chart 19.9, Part A, the heat treatment area may be a bottleneck if we have more demand for heat treatment than we have capacity available to handle the demand. Bottlenecks should have been identified when we did our aggregate planning. If a bottleneck exists, then we need to optimize the flow through the bottleneck. Here are some general guidelines to follow:

1. Setup time on the bottleneck needs to be minimized. By minimizing setup you will maximize the amount of time available for throughput.

2. A buffer needs to be established in front of the bottleneck in terms of inventory and capacity so that there will always be plenty for the bottleneck to do. It would be foolish for the bottleneck machine to be sitting idle.
3. Priority should be given to the products that offer the most profitability. We should focus on those products that will give our plant the most bang for the buck.

There are two types of bottlenecks, real and wandering. A real bottleneck is like the heat treatment machine in our example. A false bottleneck, or wandering bottleneck, is one that is caused by production inefficiencies. For example, a machine breakdown would cause a temporary false (wandering) bottleneck.

Another example of a wandering bottleneck is the production wave. Employees who work inefficiently will affect the ability for employees further down the production sequence to complete their jobs on time. This causes a wave effect that runs throughout the factory. The result is a false bottleneck.

From a shop floor perspective, we need to understand the importance of the bottleneck. The bottleneck controls the total throughput of the factory. Failure to optimize the bottleneck results in less than optimal profitability for the entire factory.

Costing

Job costing is used to compute actual costs. It can be done for every job that is performed on the factory floor. Normally this type of effort is unnecessary because a good estimate of product cost can be achieved by using a cost roll (see Chapter 14). One job run may be more expensive than another, but on the average, we should achieve the numbers we are using for our standards (this is called standard costing).

If job costing is desirable, the information necessary for performing the costing is available on the completely filled out traveler. Chart 19.3 is the initial blank traveler sheet. Chart 19.4 is the traveler in the format that it would be released to the shop floor. Chart 19.10 is the traveler as it would be returned to the shop floor supervisor and then back to production planning. It is the Chart 19.10 version that would be used for calculating actual job costs. The accounting interfaces, including job costing, will be discussed in more detail in a later chapter.

The information on Chart 19.10 is also used for updating standards, because the standards we use in our routing occasionally become outdated. For example, equipment improvements or employee changes may make the old standards so inaccurate that the product costing may be wrong. What we need to do is occasionally update these standards based on the travelers that we have used through the year. We collect all the travelers for a particular job and then calculate the average actual for each operation of the product (see Chart 19.11). Then we would compare it with the current standard to see if there is a signifi-

CHART 19.10 Production Traveler—Example After It Was Filled Out

Date 1 / 1 /1992 Product number CCCC Product name Wheel Standard batch size 50

Routing Step #	Department	Machine	Labor Code	Setup Time	Run Time (per batch)	Component		Actual Production				Quantity Used	Quantity Scrapped	Output Quantity	Employee Initials
						Item #	Quantity	Date	Start	Stop	Lapse				
						A4B4	600					605			GJP
						ACAC	100					101			GJP
10	Cutting	X40	L35	2 hrs.	2 hrs.			12/19/91	8 AM	12:20 PM	260 min.		2	55	RSP
20	Grinding	RV282	L40	1 hr.	1 hr.			12/23/91	10 AM	11:50 AM	110 min.		1	54	NIP
30	Stamping	Brilton	L35	10 min.	1 hr.			12/24/91	10:30 AM	11:40 AM	70 min.			54	JJP
40	Plating	Stall	L50	2 hrs.	3 hrs.			12/30/91	8 AM	1:20 PM	320 min.		2	52	ZJP
50	Inspection		I20	0	3 hrs.			1/1/92	2 PM	5 PM	180 min.		1	51	CJP

CHART 19.11 Standards Updating (Data taken from Chart 19.10)

Product CCCC Routing Step #10 Department Cutting
Machine X40 Current Standard = 120 min./50 = 2.4 min.

Date	Actual Quantity	Lapse	Setup	Run	Per Piece
1/1/92	51	260 min.	120 min.	140 min.	2.8 min.
3/1/92	49	265 min.	120 min.	145 min.	2.96 min.
5/1/92	53	250 min.	120 min.	130 min.	2.45 min.
7/1/92	54	260 min.	120 min.	140 min.	2.59 min.
			Overall average:		2.7 min.

cant difference. The data of Chart 19.11 are an example of four jobs that have been run. We are only looking at one step in the routing, step 10. In the four jobs that have been run, we get an average run time of 2.7 minutes for step 10. The current standard for step 10 is 2.4 minutes. It would appear, based on the actual data, that our standard for step 10 is slightly low. We should probably raise the standard to 2.7 minutes run time duration per piece produced.

About once every year, usually at year end, it would be helpful to perform an analysis similar to that of Chart 19.11. This would validate the standards that you use and thereby assure correct product costing. The corrected standards would then be used to update the routing lead times.

Feedback Reports

We can generate a number of reports that would help in monitoring the performance of the shop floor. Most of these would be generated from the completed travelers (Chart 19.10).

Efficiency Reports. Efficiency reports can be run to validate the performance of any of the resources that we are monitoring on our travelers. Often an efficiency report is thought of as an employee efficiency report, but a materials or machine efficiency report would be just as valuable, as long as you collect the necessary data on the traveler. Employee efficiency reporting will be discussed first. Then, in the next section, using scrap/rework and pilferage reporting we can take a look at materials efficiency reporting.

Using the data from Chart 19.10, the report on Chart 19.12 can be generated. This report shows the performance of each of the employees who worked. Normally we would be interested in checking the performance of an employee over several jobs, not just one. An efficiency value of under 100% means that it is taking longer than the standard says it should take. Employee RSP in Chart 19.12 is being 11.7 percent inefficient (100% − 88.3% = 11.7%).

CHART 19.12 Employee Efficiency Reporting (Data taken from Charts 19.10 and 19.11)

Employee—RSP Product	Date	Standard	Actual	Efficiency
CCCC	12/19/92	2.4 min.	2.8 min.	85.7%
CCCC	2/21/92	2.4 min.	2.96 min.	81.1%
CCCC	4/25/92	2.4 min.	2.45 min.	98.0%
	Average percentage efficiency			88.3%

CHART 19.13 Scrap/Rework/Pilferage Report (Data taken from Chart 19.10)

Product CCCC

Material A4B4 — Standard Usage = 12

Job Date	Job Quantity	Actual Usage	Quantity Completed	Average Actual
1/1/92	50	605	51	11.86
3/1/92	50	610	49	12.45
5/1/92	50	610	53	11.51
		Overall average actual:		11.94
		Overall efficiency:		100.5%

Material ACAC — Standard Usage = 2

Job Date	Job Quantity	Actual Usage	Quantity Completed	Average Actual
1/1/92	50	101	51	1.98
3/1/92	50	102	49	2.08
5/1/92	50	102	53	1.92
		Overall average actual:		1.99
		Overall efficiency:		100.5%

Similarly, if machine time was reported on the traveler, then we could run a report on machine efficiency. This is helpful when trying to determine if a machine is getting old and having efficiency problems.

Scrap/Rework and Pilferage Reporting. Chart 19.13 uses the data from Chart 19.10 to demonstrate a materials efficiency report. This report demonstrates that the material usage standards are pretty close to reality. We are slightly more efficient than the standard in both examples (efficiency is less than 100).

Order Status Reporting. With order status reporting, we are trying to check the shop floor's performance on the production plan. An order status report would report what jobs have recently been completed, what jobs are pending, and what the current inventory balance is for a product. The order status report is something we would run occasionally as we check on a product that may be giving us difficulty. It would look like Chart 19.14. From this example we can see that we were late

CHART 19.14 Order Status Report (Data taken from Chart 19.10)

Date 9/2/92

Product CCCC
Inventory Balance 4

	Due Date	Completion Date	Due Quantity	Completion Quantity
Orders Completed				
	1/1/92	1/1/92	50	51
	3/1/92	3/2/91	50	49
	5/1/92	5/2/91	50	53
Orders in Process				
	9/1/92		50	*** Overdue ***
	11/1/92		50	

twice and that once we produced less than the required amount, but on the average we produce approximately the right amount. We also see that one in-process order is overdue.

Time Cards

Time cards are the device that we use to pay the employees. The employee would clock in at the start of the day, clock out for lunch, clock back in after lunch, and clock out at the end of the day. With these time values we can then calculate the amount of hours worked and calculate

CHART 19.15 Time Cards

Employee # ________ Employee name ____________________

Date	Time In	Time Out	Date	Time In	Time Out

Approvals ____________________ ____________________ ____________________ a paycheck. Time cards are kept entirely separate from the job traveler. We cannot calculate pay from the traveler because it would delay paycheck processing. The time card and the time clock are kept at some central location, normally by the door where the employee typically enters the plant. A typical time card would look like Chart 19.15.

Often there is a tendency to report excessively all the activity that occurs during the working day on the time card. If this is the tendency in your factory, review the start of this chapter, which discusses the priorities that need to be placed on the data collection process. Data need to be collected on the most critical resources, which are those resources that will give you the most improvement. This is usually not labor. Be careful to build a meaningful data collection system that sends the correct message to the employees.

Expediters

An expediter is a parts chaser. This is an individual that runs around the factory trying to find out what the status of some "urgent" job is and tries to hurry it up. The use of expediters suggests that you have production planning problems. If your production schedules are correct, you shouldn't need expediters. Realize that every time an expediter rushes one job through, another job gets delayed. In the end, an expediter does more damage to the production schedules than good. However, until you get your production schedules refined, you may still need an expediter. Just remember, the sooner you can get rid of your dependence on expediters, the sooner you will be demonstrating that you have control of your production schedules and that they are accurate.

Shop Floor Job Prioritization

As we release production orders we end up with a series of jobs in front of each work station. We need some process that helps us select which jobs should be done first. There are literally hundreds of methods for accomplishing this. However, in this segment we will discuss just a few, the few that get the most use. The methods discussed will be categorized into two groups, those where each department is scheduled independently and those where two or more department functions are dependent on each other.

Independent Departments. If each department is scheduled independently then we look for methods that will maximize the performance of the individual department. One of the most common measures of performance is to calculate how many "days (or hours) late" your jobs are. The procedure is that we schedule the jobs four different ways, then we look to see which of these schedules will minimize the number of

CHART 19.16 Shop Floor Job Prioritization Data

Date 1/1/92

Job: Product / Date / Quantity	Processing Time
CCCC / 1/1/92 / 50	4 hours
CCCC / 1/10/92 / 50	4 hours
R2D2 / 1/5/92 / 100	10 hours
A4F2 / 1/7/92 / 200	15 hours
AAAA / 1/5/92 / 200	30 hours
ABAB / 1/6/92 / 150	15 hours

Assume six hours' capacity per day

days late. Then from this analysis we select the scheduling method that we use for all job loads for the department. Chart 19.16 lists some sample data for an analysis of this type.

Chart 19.17 analyzes the data of Chart 19.16 using four different scheduling methods. These are:

1. *First Come-First Serve (FCFS):* In this method we run the jobs in the sequence in which they arrive into our work area. The jobs listed in Chart 19.16 would be processed exactly in the sequence that they are listed.

2. *Shortest Processing Time (SPT):* In this method we run the shortest jobs first (secondarily sort on due date). The jobs in Chart 19.16 would be processed in the following sequence:

CCCC / 1/ 1/92 / 50	4 hours
CCCC / 1/10/92 / 50	4 hours
R2D2 / 1/ 5/92 / 100	10 hours
A4F2 / 1/ 7/92 / 200	15 hours
ABAB / 1/ 6/92 / 150	15 hours
AAAA / 1/ 5/92 / 200	30 hours

3. *Due Date (DD):* In this method we run the jobs in due date order (secondarily sort on processing time). The jobs of Chart 19.16 would be processed in the following sequence:

CCCC / 1/ 1/92 / 50	4 hours
R2D2 / 1/ 5/92 / 100	10 hours
AAAA / 1/ 5/92 / 200	30 hours
ABAB / 1/ 6/92 / 150	15 hours
A4F2 / 1/ 7/92 / 200	15 hours
CCCC / 1/10/92 / 50	4 hours

4. *Slack Per Operation (S/O):* In this method we calculate the slack of each activity and run the jobs in sequence from shortest to longest slack. The jobs of Chart 19.16 would be processed in the following sequence:

Job #	Processing Time	Slack
AAAA / 1/5/92 / 200	30 hours	−12
Due in three working days and it takes 30 hours to do the job so the difference is 3 × 6 − 30 = −12 hours (6 is the number of hours in a day).		
CCCC / 1/1/92 / 50	4 hours	0
Due today so "0" slack		
R2D2 / 1/5/92 / 100	10 hours	8
Due in three working days and it takes 10 hours to do the job so the difference is 3 × 6 − 10 = 8 hours		
ABAB / 1/6/92 / 150	15 hours	9
Due in four working days and it takes 15 hours to do the job so the difference is 4 × 6 − 15 = 9 hours.		
A4F2 / 1/7/92 / 200	15 hours	15
Due in five working days and it takes 15 hours to do the job so the difference is 5 × 6 − 15 = 15 hours.		
CCCC / 1/10/92 / 50	4 hours	32
Due in six working days and it takes 4 hours to do the job so the difference is 6 × 6 − 4 = 32 hours.		

The calculations of Chart 19.17 are as follows (using first come–first serve as the example):

Flow Time. When will the job be done? The first job's flow time is equal to the processing time. Each succeeding job's flow time is equal to the previous job's flow time plus its own processing time. In our example, the flow time for job {CCCC / 1/1/92 / 50} is equal to the processing time (4 hours). The flow time for job {CCCC / 1/10/92 / 50} is equal to the processing time of this job plus the flow time of the previous job (4 hours processing time plus 4 hours flow time = 8 hours). Repeating this same procedure, the flow time for job {R2D2 / 1/5/92 / 100} is equal to 10 hours processing time plus the previous job's 8 hours flow time = 18 hours.

Due Date in Hours. This is simply the number of working days times six hours per day. For 1/1/91 the due date in hours is eight. For 1/5/92, because of a weekend, the due date in hours is three days out or 18 hours. And so on.

Hours Late. The hours late is 0 if the job is done on time or early. However, if the job is late, the hours late calculation is the number of hours the job is late. For example, for jobs {CCCC / 1/1/92 / 50}, {CCCC / 1/10/92 / 50}, and {R2D2 / 1/5/92 / 100} the flow time is less than or equal to the due date in hours. Therefore, for these jobs the hours late is 0. For the other three jobs the flow time is greater than the due date in hours so the hours late is the difference of the two values.

Looking at Chart 19.17 and looking only at total hours late would cause us to select the shortest processing time as the best planning method for this factory. However, looking slightly closer at the data

CHART 19.17 Shop Floor Job Prioritization Data Analyzed Four Different Ways

Date 1/1/92

First Come First Serve

Job Product / Date / Quantity	Processing Time	Flow Time	Due Date in Hours	Hours Late
CCCC / 1/1/92 / 50	4 hours	4 hours	6 hours	0
CCCC / 1/10/92 / 50	4 hours	8 hours	36 hours	0
R2D2 / 1/5/92 / 100	10 hours	18 hours	18 hours	0
A4F2 / 1/7/92 / 200	15 hours	33 hours	30 hours	3
AAAA / 1/5/92 / 200	30 hours	63 hours	18 hours	45
ABAB / 1/6/92 / 150	15 hours	78 hours	24 hours	54
			Total hours late:	102

Shortest Processing Time

Job Product / Date / Quantity	Processing Time	Flow Time	Due Date in Hours	Hours Late
CCCC / 1/1/92 / 50	4 hours	4 hours	6 hours	0
CCCC / 1/10/92 / 50	4 hours	8 hours	36 hours	0
R2D2 / 1/5/92 / 100	10 hours	18 hours	18 hours	0
A4F2 / 1/7/92 / 200	15 hours	33 hours	30 hours	3
ABAB / 1/6/92 / 150	15 hours	48 hours	24 hours	24
AAAA / 1/5/92 / 200	30 hours	78 hours	18 hours	60
			Total hours late:	87

Due Date

Job Product / Date / Quantity	Processing Time	Flow Time	Due Date in Hours	Hours Late
CCCC / 1/1/92 / 50	4 hours	4 hours	6 hours	0
R2D2 / 1/5/92 / 100	10 hours	14 hours	18 hours	0
AAAA / 1/5/92 / 200	30 hours	44 hours	18 hours	26
ABAB / 1/6/92 / 150	15 hours	59 hours	24 hours	35
A4F2 / 1/7/92 / 200	15 hours	74 hours	30 hours	44
CCCC / 1/10/92 / 50	4 hours	78 hours	36 hours	42
			Total hours late:	147

Slack Per Operation

Job Product / Date / Quantity	Processing Time	Flow Time	Due Date in Hours	Hours Late
AAAA / 1/5/92 / 200	30 hours	30 hours	18 hours	12
CCCC / 1/1/92 / 50	4 hours	34 hours	6 hours	28
R2D2 / 1/5/92 / 100	10 hours	44 hours	18 hours	26
ABAB / 1/6/92 / 150	15 hours	59 hours	24 hours	35
A4F2 / 1/7/92 / 200	15 hours	74 hours	30 hours	44
CCCC / 1/10/92 / 50	4 hours	78 hours	36 hours	42
			Total hours late:	187

would reveal that although the shortest processing time is best in total hours late, the jobs that are late under this method are very late. In other words, the shortest processing time gives you the fewest late jobs, but those that are late are extremely late. Due date and slack per operation tend to spread out the lateness. In slack per operation, all jobs are late but approximately equally late. So you need to select what is most important to you: Do you prefer having a few mad customers, but those that are mad are really mad (shortest processing), or do you prefer to have them all equally mad? Good luck in making your decision. However, once you have made this decision, you don't need to repeat this calculation process. Simply use this same sequencing method each day with the jobs that you have in your department.

Dependent Departments. In discussing dependent departments we start with the most simple example first. In the next section on assembly line balancing we will be able to define flows through a series of balanced work centers.

In this section we will discuss a situation where there are two departments, Departments A and B. All jobs go through Department A first, then through Department B. The objective is to minimize the total amount of processing time required for all jobs to go through both departments. Chart 19.18 provides the data used for this example. Six jobs exist, all of which need to be processed through the two departments in sequence.

To determine what the optimal sequence for the jobs in Chart 19.18 would be, we apply Johnson's rule. Here is how it works. We look at all the processing times for both departments and we identify the smallest of these times. The smallest is 2 hours in Department B for job {AXF2 / 1/7/92 / 200}. Since this time was in Department B, this job will be scheduled last. We have now scheduled this job and eliminated it from further consideration. We have six slots in which we want to schedule jobs and the first is now filled:

slot 1 =
slot 2 =
slot 3 =
slot 4 =
slot 5 =
slot 6 = AXF2 / 1/7/92 / 200

The next smallest time is 4 hours in Department A for job {CXCC / 1/1/92 / 50}. Since this time was in Department A, we schedule this job first. Now this job has been eliminated from further consideration:

slot 1 = CXCC / 1/1/92 / 50
slot 2 =
slot 3 =
slot 4 =
slot 5 =
slot 6 = AXF2 / 1/7/92 / 200

CHART 19.18 Two-Department Shop Floor Job Prioritization Data

Date 1/1/92

Job			Processing Time	
Product /	Date	/ Quantity	Department A	Department B
CXCC	/ 1/1/92 /	50	4 hours	6 hours
CXCC	/ 1/10/92 /	50	5 hours	8 hours
RXD2	/ 1/5/92 /	100	10 hours	12 hours
AXF2	/ 1/7/92 /	200	17 hours	2 hours
AXAA	/ 1/5/92 /	200	30 hours	20 hours
AXAB	/ 1/6/92 /	150	18 hours	16 hours

The next smallest time is in Department A for 5 hours for job {CXCC / 1/10/92 / 50}. Because it is in Department A, we schedule this job toward the front but it will be second to job {CXCC / 1/1/92 / 50}:

slot 1 = CXCC / 1/1/92 / 50
slot 2 = CXCC / 1/10/92 / 50
slot 3 =
slot 4 =
slot 5 =
slot 6 = AXF2 / 1/7/92 / 200

The next job to be scheduled is {RXD2 / 1/5/92 / 100} because it has the next smallest remaining time of 10 hours in Department A. Because we are in Department A, this job will be scheduled toward the front and will be the third job in the que:

slot 1 = CXCC / 1/1/92 / 50
slot 2 = CXCC / 1/10/92 / 50
slot 3 = RXD2 / 1/5/92 / 100
slot 4 =
slot 5 =
slot 6 = AXF2 / 1/7/92 / 200

The next job to be scheduled is {AXAB / 1/6/92 / 150}, which will be scheduled second from the last because its smallest value is in Department B:

slot 1 = CXCC / 1/1/92 / 50
slot 2 = CXCC / 1/10/92 / 50
slot 3 = RXD2 / 1/5/92 / 100
slot 4 =
slot 5 = AXAB / 1/6/92 / 150
slot 6 = AXF2 / 1/7/92 / 200

This leaves only job {AXAA / 1/5/92 / 200}, which will be scheduled in the remaining slot:

slot 1 = CXCC / 1/1/92 / 50
slot 2 = CXCC / 1/10/92 / 50
slot 3 = RXD2 / 1/5/92 / 100
slot 4 = AXAA / 1/5/92 / 200
slot 5 = AXAB / 1/6/92 / 150
slot 6 = AXF2 / 1/7/92 / 200

Note that in this sequencing process we assume that all jobs need to be completed as soon as possible. Due date does not become part of the analysis process. Now that we have the sequence of these jobs analyzed, the next step is to analyze what the total processing time of these jobs will be. Chart 19.19 shows a time line for these jobs. This time line shows job A starting immediately and taking 4 hours in Department A. Job A is immediately followed by job B, and so on. Department A runs all the jobs back-to-back and it takes 84 hours. In Department B job A starts immediately after Department A is done with it. Job A then runs for 6 hours in Department B, ending 10 hours out. Then job B can start, which runs for 8 hours, ending 18 hours out. Job C did not end in Department A until 19 hours out, so it could not start in Department B until then. That delay causes a 1-hour gap between the end of job B and the start of job C in Department B. The same thing happens again between job C and job D in Department B. In the end, Department B is completely done with all jobs 87 hours out.

CHART 19.19 Two-Department Shop Floor Prioritization Time Line—First Example

Job A = CXCC / 1/1/92 / 50
Job B = CXCC / 1/10/92 / 50
Job C = RXD2 / 1/5/92 / 100
Job D = AXAA / 1/5/92 / 200
Job E = AXAB / 1/6/92 / 150
Job F = AXF2 / 1/7/92 / 200

Slack in Department A = 3 hours
Slack in Department B = 4 +1+18 = 23 hours
Total time required to run all jobs through both departments = 87 hours

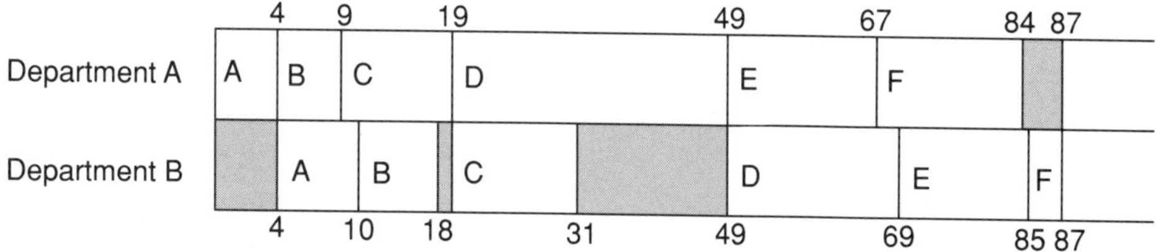

Department B consolidation

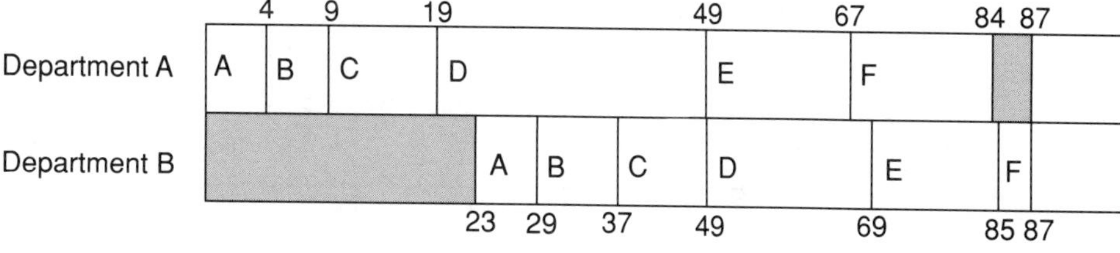

The slack time in Department A occurs between the time when Department A is finished (84 hours out) and when Department B is finished (87 hours out). The slack time for Department B occurs every time Department B is waiting for Department A to transfer work to it. This occurs between 0 and 4 hours out, 18 and 19 hours out, and 31 to 49 hours out. The total slack time for Department B is 23 hours. To keep Department B working efficiently, it would be best for Department B to start operation 23 hours late, thereby consolidating all the slack times (see the second time line on Chart 19.19).

Johnson's rule has minimized the total processing time required to run all the jobs through both departments. It has also provided a schedule that maximizes schedule efficiency. Let me give you a second example of how this process works. The data for this second example are found in Chart 19.20.

To determine what the optimal sequence for the jobs in Chart 19.20 would be, we apply Johnson's rule. Again, we look at all the processing times for both departments and we identify the smallest of these times. The smallest is two hours in Department B for job J. Since this time was in Department B, this job will be scheduled last. We have now scheduled this job and eliminated it from further consideration. We have 12 slots (because there are 12 jobs) in which we want to schedule jobs and the first is now filled.

_ _ _ _ _ _ _ _ _ _ _ J

The next smallest time is three hours in Department B for job A. Since this was in Department B, we schedule this job toward the end. Now this job has been eliminated from further consideration.

_ _ _ _ _ _ _ _ _ _ A J

The next smallest time is four hours, of which we have one in Department A (job G) and one in Department B (job I). The Department A one

CHART 19.20 Two-Department Shop Floor Job Prioritization Data—Second Example

	Processing Time	
Job	Department A	Department B
A	8 hours	3 hours
B	15 hours	5 hours
C	9 hours	7 hours
D	17 hours	11 hours
E	10 hours	10 hours
F	8 hours	16 hours
G	4 hours	6 hours
H	5 hours	8 hours
I	6 hours	4 hours
J	7 hours	2 hours
K	9 hours	9 hours
L	8 hours	12 hours

is scheduled toward the front and the Department B job is scheduled toward the back.

G _ _ _ _ _ _ _ _ I A J

There is also a duplication at five hours. Job H has five hours in Department A and job B has five hours in Department B. We now schedule these appropriately.

G H _ _ _ _ _ _ B I A J

The next job to be scheduled is C, which will be scheduled toward the end because its smallest value (seven hours) is in Department B.

G H _ _ _ _ _ C B I A J

Now we have another interesting problem. Two jobs require eight hours each (the next lowest time), but they are both in Department A. These are jobs F and L. Since L has the smallest Department B time of these two, it will be scheduled before job F, but both will still be scheduled toward the front.

G H L F _ _ _ C B I A J

Now we have a job (job K) that has the next lowest time (nine hours) in both departments. In this case we can schedule this job toward either end. Either option will give the same minimum processing time. In this example we have placed the job toward the front.

G H L F K _ _ C B I A J

Similarly, job E has the next lowest time of 10 hours in both departments. This job is also scheduled toward the front.

G H L F K E _ C B I A J

This leaves only job D, which will be scheduled in the remaining slot.

G H L F K E D C B I A J

Now that we have the sequence of these jobs analyzed, the next step is to analyze what the total processing time of these jobs will be. Looking at Chart 19.21, we see a time line for these jobs. The time line shown in Chart 19.21 shows that it takes 108 hours to process all jobs through both departments. Department A has 2 hours of slack time between 106 and 108, and Department B has 15 hours of slack time, between 0 and 4, between 83 and 85, between 90 and 91, between 95 and 99, and between 102 and 106 (4 + 2 + 1 + 4 + 4 = 15).

There are more complex models that schedule multiple departments and in any combination of sequences. However, none of these models offer an optimal solution. If you use the principles and methods that have been presented here, you'll get about as good a schedule as any of the more complicated methods will give you.

CHART 19.21 Two-Department Shop Floor Prioritization Time Line—Second Example

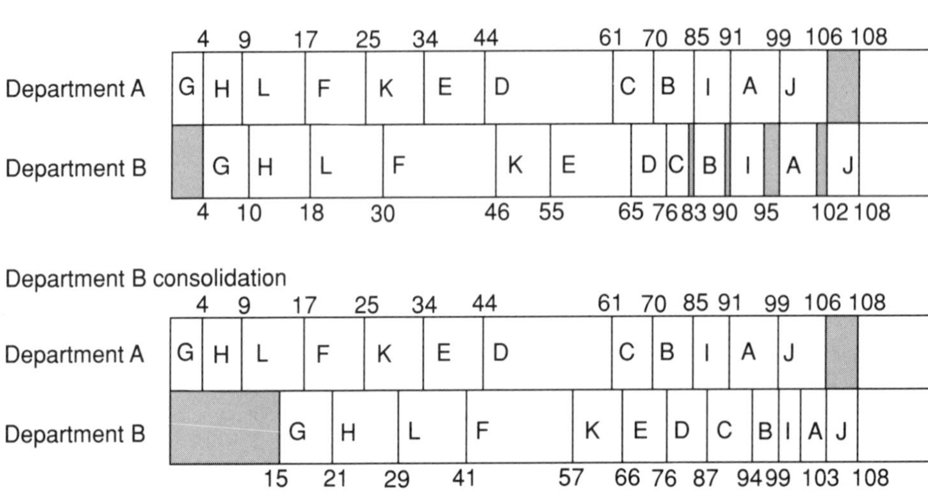

Assembly Line Balancing

If the product we produce is extremely repetitive to the point at which we can produce it on an assembly line, we need to analyze the assembly line to assure its maximum efficiency. The objective in this type of environment is materials movement. We want to be able to move the materials through the production process so quickly and efficiently that there is effectively no work-in-process inventory. The line balancing process is called assembly line balancing. Let's take a look at an example of an assembly line in Chart 19.22, Part A. Here we see the flow of the production process through a series of machines that have been placed in sequence with the way the product is actually produced.

The focus of assembly line balancing is to balance the work loads of the work centers on the line. In this process we are looking for ways to group the work so that each of the work centers is equally busy. Looking at the example of Chart 19.22, Part A, we see that the total production time required is 9 minutes (the sum of the times for all the tasks). If we anticipate a demand of 200 units, and we want to produce these 200 units in one shift (assume six productive hours in an eight-hour shift), then we would have 360 minutes in which to produce all 200 units. From this information we can calculate the cycle time, which is how often a finished product would need to come rolling off the end of the production line. The calculation is:

$$\text{Cycle Time} = \frac{\text{Total Available Time}}{\text{Total Units Produced}} = \frac{360 \text{ minutes}}{200 \text{ units}}$$
$$= 1.8 \text{ minutes per unit}$$

The cycle time is 1.8 minutes or 108 seconds, which means that every 108 seconds we need to have produced a finished product. Next, we need to determine how many work centers will be needed in order to achieve these results. The minimum number of work centers that will be required is:

$$\text{Minimum Work Centers} = \frac{\text{Total Production Time}}{\text{Cycle Time}} = \frac{9 \text{ minutes}}{1.8 \text{ minutes}}$$
$$= 5 \text{ Work Centers}$$

In this example we calculated that exactly five work centers were needed. If the answer came out as a fraction, for example, 6.1, we would always round up, in this case to 7.

Five work centers is the minimum number (the ideal number) of work centers. What we need to do now is draw little circles around the tasks of Chart 19.22, Part A, to see if we can group these work centers into groups that will not take longer than 1.8 minutes (cycle time) and still minimize the number of work centers. A few examples are demonstrated in Chart 19.22, Parts B and C.

It is impossible to balance the assembly line process of Chart 19.22, Part A, out to exactly five work centers because each work center would have to have exactly 1.8 minutes of work. An example of six work centers is shown in Chart 19.22, Part B. In this example we have work centers loaded with as much as 1.8 minutes and as little as 1.2 minutes of work. If we look at the efficiency of this assembly line we would see:

$$\text{Efficiency} = \frac{\text{Demand on Time}}{\text{Available Capacity}}$$
$$= \frac{(9 \text{ minutes}) \times (200 \text{ units})}{(6 \text{ work stations}) \times (360 \text{ minutes per day})}$$
$$= 83.3\% \text{ efficiency}$$

A second example of the assembly line balance of Chart 19.22, Part A, can be seen in Chart 19.22, Part C. In this example we have established seven work centers but the range of work loads is not as widespread (between 1.1 and 1.5 minutes). The efficiency of this example is:

$$\text{Efficiency} = \frac{\text{Demand on Time}}{\text{Available Capacity}}$$
$$= \frac{(9 \text{ minutes}) \times (200 \text{ units})}{(7 \text{ work stations}) \times (360 \text{ minutes per day})}$$
$$= 71.4\% \text{ efficiency}$$

The level of efficiency has dropped significantly by adding the extra work center. So, in spite of the fact that example 19.22 (Part B) shows a higher variation in the work loads, it is the more cost-effective program with which we should work.

CHART 19.22 Assembly Line Balancing—First Example, Part A

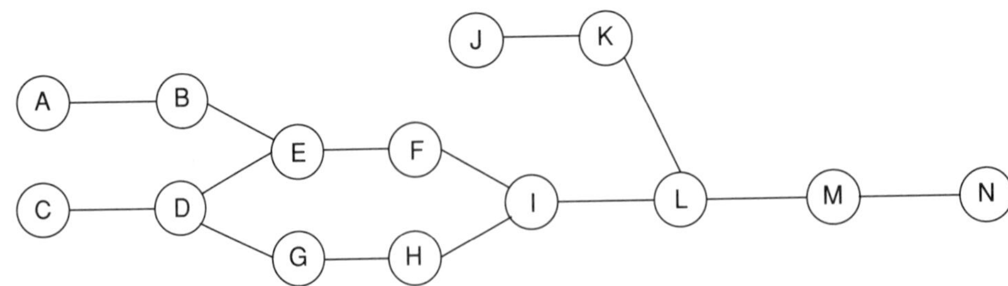

Tasks and durations (in minutes)

A - .5	F - .9	K - .5
B - .6	G - .4	L - .8
C - .2	H - 1.2	M - 1.4
D - .4	I - .6	N - .5
E - .3	J - .7	

CHART 19.22 Assembly Line Balancing—Try #1—First Example, Part B

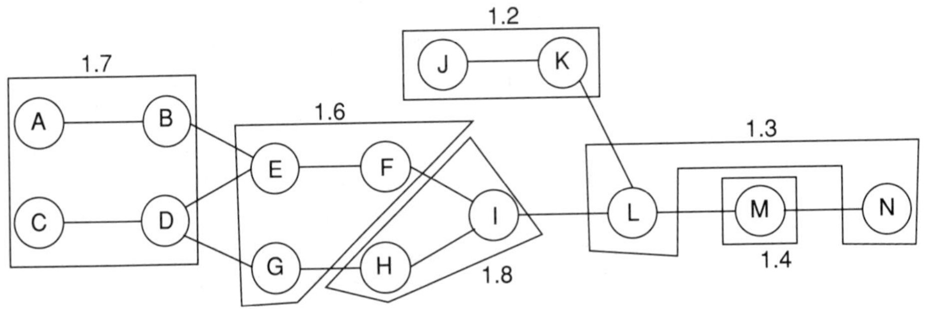

Tasks and durations (in minutes)

A - .5	F - .9	K - .5
B - .6	G - .4	L - .8
C - .2	H - 1.2	M - 1.4
D - .4	I - .6	N - .5
E - .3	J - .7	

CHART 19.22 Assembly Line Balancing—Try #2—First Example, Part C

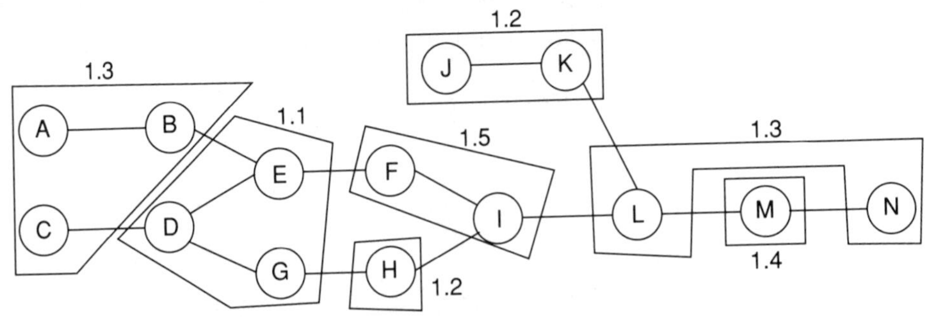

Tasks and durations (in minutes)

A - .5	F - .9	K - .5
B - .6	G - .4	L - .8
C - .2	H - 1.2	M - 1.4
D - .4	I - .6	N - .5
E - .3	J - .7	

A second, more complicated example of assembly line balancing is shown in Chart 19.23, Part A, where we see that the total production time required is 17.7 minutes (the sum of the times for all the tasks). If we anticipate a demand of 100 units, and we want to produce these 100 units in one shift (assume six productive hours in an eight-hour shift), then we would have 360 minutes in which to produce all 100 units. From this information we can calculate the cycle time:

$$\text{Cycle Time} = \frac{\text{Total Available Time}}{\text{Total Units Produced}} = \frac{\text{360 minutes}}{\text{100 units}}$$

$$= \text{3.6 minutes per unit}$$

The cycle time is 3.6 minutes. That means that every 3.6 minutes we need to have a finished product rolling off the end of the production line. Next, we need to determine how many work centers will be needed in order to achieve these results. The minimum number of work centers required is:

$$\text{Minimum Work Centers} = \frac{\text{Total Production Time}}{\text{Cycle Time}} = \frac{\text{17.7 minutes}}{\text{3.6 minutes}}$$

$$= \text{4.92 Work Centers}$$

In this example we calculated that 4.92 work centers were needed. This would be rounded up to five work centers, which is the minimum number (the ideal number) of work centers. What we need to do now is to draw little circles around the tasks of Chart 19.23, Part A, to see if we can group these work centers into groups that will not take longer than 3.6 minutes and still minimize the number of work centers.

It is impossible to balance out the assembly line process of Chart 19.22, Part A, to exactly five work centers because each work center would have to have exactly 3.6 (cycle time) minutes of work on each product. This means that we would have to be able to add up five combinations of tasks that equaled 3.6 minutes or less each.

Examples of six work centers are shown in Chart 19.23, Parts B and C. In the first example we have work centers loaded with as much as 3.5 minutes and as little as 2.1 minutes of work. This shows quite an imbalance in the work center work loads. In the second example (Chart 19.23, Part C), the variance is from 2.8 to 3.2. The balance is much better. Unfortunately, in the second example we have a rather disjointed work center, the one that does tasks F, G, K, and O. This disjointed arrangement is often not practical and so Chart 19.23, Part B, in spite of its imbalance, is more desirable because it has a better materials flow through the departments. The disjointed flow may also cause trouble in the previous examples of Chart 19.22, Parts B and C.

If we look at the efficiency of the assembly line for either the example in Chart 19.23, Part B or C, we would see that they have the same efficiency because they have the same number of work centers:

$$\text{Efficiency} = \frac{\text{Demand on Time}}{\text{Available Capacity}}$$

$$= \frac{\text{(17.7 minutes)} \times \text{(100 units)}}{\text{(6 work stations)} \times \text{(360 minutes per day)}}$$

$$= \text{81.9\% efficiency}$$

CHART 19.23 Assembly Line Balancing—Second Example, Part A

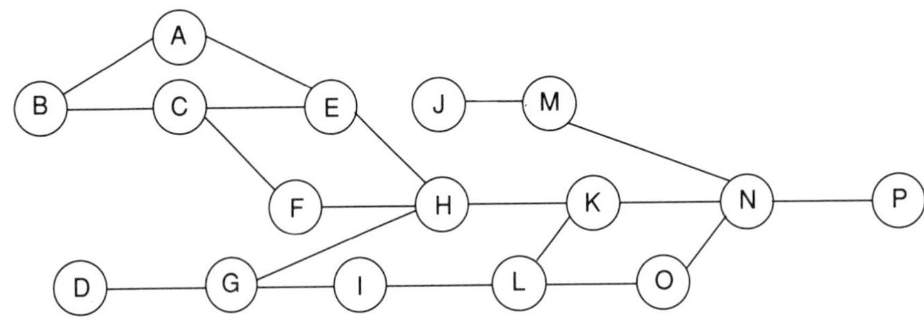

Tasks and durations (in minutes)

A - .7	G - .8	M - 1.8
B - .9	H - 1.2	N - .7
C - 2.0	I - .7	O - 1.2
D - 2.1	J - .3	P - .4
E - 1.6	K - .2	
F - .7	L - 2.4	

CHART 19.23 Assembly Line Balancing—Try #1—Second Example, Part B

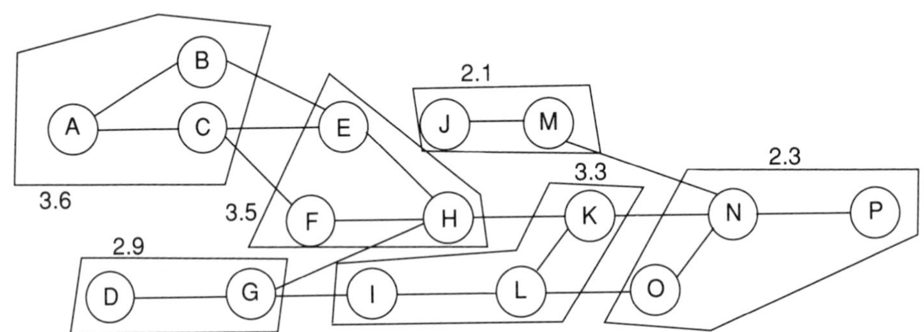

Tasks and durations (in minutes)

A - .7	G - .8	M - 1.8
B - .9	H - 1.2	N - .7
C - 2.0	I - .7	O - 1.2
D - 2.1	J - .3	P - .4
E - 1.6	K - .2	
F - .7	L - 2.4	

From these examples we can establish the most efficient assembly line flow. To balance this flow, we will need to look for improvements in those work centers that are overloaded. These improvements include setup time reductions, automation, product engineering changes, and production modifications. As we chip away the processing time with improvements, we will end up improving the total production time and end up reducing and improving on the number of work centers. The better the balance we achieve, the better the inventory flow, and the better the throughput.

CHART 19.23 Assembly Line Balancing—Try #2—Second Example, Part C

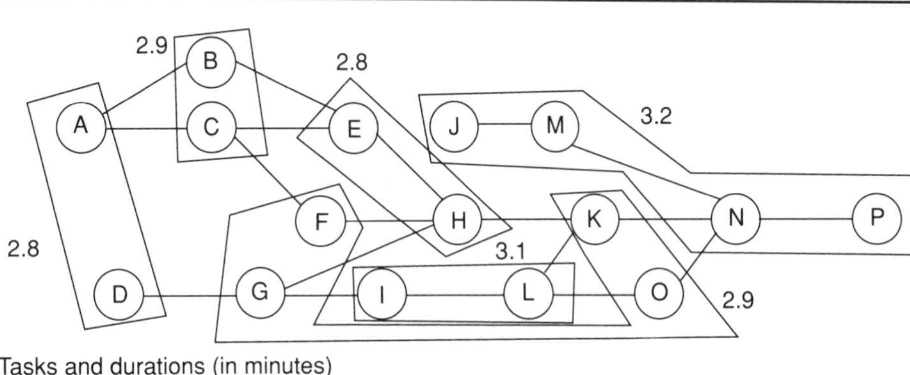

Tasks and durations (in minutes)

A - .7	G - .8	M - 1.8
B - .9	H - 1.2	N - .7
C - 2.0	I - .7	O - 1.2
D - 2.1	J - .3	P - .4
E - 1.6	K - .2	
F - .7	L - 2.4	

Resource Focus

In earlier chapters we discussed the need to establish simple, measurable, and meaningful goals. We also discussed the need to identify the resources that are the most influential in achieving this goal. Then we stressed the development of a measurement system around which we can make sure we are achieving our desired goal. We need to be reminded of this fact because it is in shop floor control that we get carried away with data collection. It is here where we lose focus and start nitpicking. The measurement system is the means by which we transmit our goals to our employees. If we focus on measuring employee times, then we will get a shop floor focus on employee efficiency. If we measure materials usage, then we will get a focus on materials efficiency, etc. So we need to identify what it is we are trying to achieve and develop a measurement system that satisfies that need.

Once we have identified the appropriate goal, focused on the critical resource, and established an appropriate and meaningful measurement system that focuses on this resource, then we can monitor our progress toward achieving the goal. The risk that we run into is that rather than focusing on one or two critical resources, we tend to focus on and measure all resources hoping we will somehow be able to stay on top of everything that happens. This is not true. By measuring everything, you will only succeed in confusing the shop floor employees. They will tend to become confused about what is important and may end up focusing on the wrong things. The second risk that you run by getting excessive in the data collection process is that you will be wasting an excessive amount of time collecting worthless data. These data are worthless because they don't focus on the critical resource. If you make changes in the critical resource, it is highly likely that much of what happens with the secondary resources will also change. In other words, understanding how a secondary resource performed prior to changes to the primary resource will probably not be useful after the changes. So don't waste time and money collecting it.

Shop Floor Layout Planning

The question is often asked, "What is the best way to organize my shop floor or my office?" Numerous ways exist for analyzing optimal shop floor layouts. The most common process is to lay out the factory floor in such a way as to minimize the travel time between departments. To do this we would establish a linear programming model to perform this minimization. Using the "Facility Layout" module of the QS software package that was discussed earlier will demonstrate how this process works. For my first example look at Chart 19.24, Part A, which shows an initial plant layout. Corresponding to Chart 19.24, Part A, there is a trip or contact chart. This chart identifies the number of contacts that occurs between any combinations of departments. The contact chart is found in Chart 19.25.

Using the QS (Quant Systems software package—check previous chapters for full reference) plant layout module, we attempt to minimize the amount of travel distance based on the number of contacts required (Chart 19.25). We input the layout (Chart 19.24, Part A) and the contact data into the QS "Facility Layout" module and calculate the solution. Several different calculation options are available. After pro-

CHART 19.24 Plant Layout Example #1, Part A

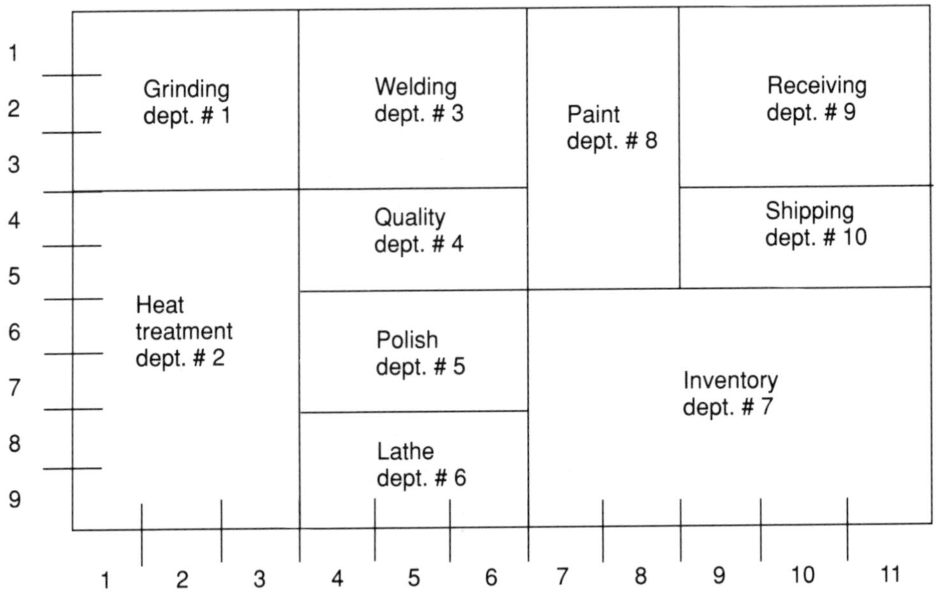

Grinding dept. # 1
Welding dept. # 3
Paint dept. # 8
Receiving dept. # 9
Quality dept. # 4
Shipping dept. # 10
Heat treatment dept. # 2
Polish dept. # 5
Inventory dept. # 7
Lathe dept. # 6
1 2 3 4 5 6 7 8 9
1 2 3 4 5 6 7 8 9 10 11

CHART 19.24 Plant Layout Example #1 Solution, Part B

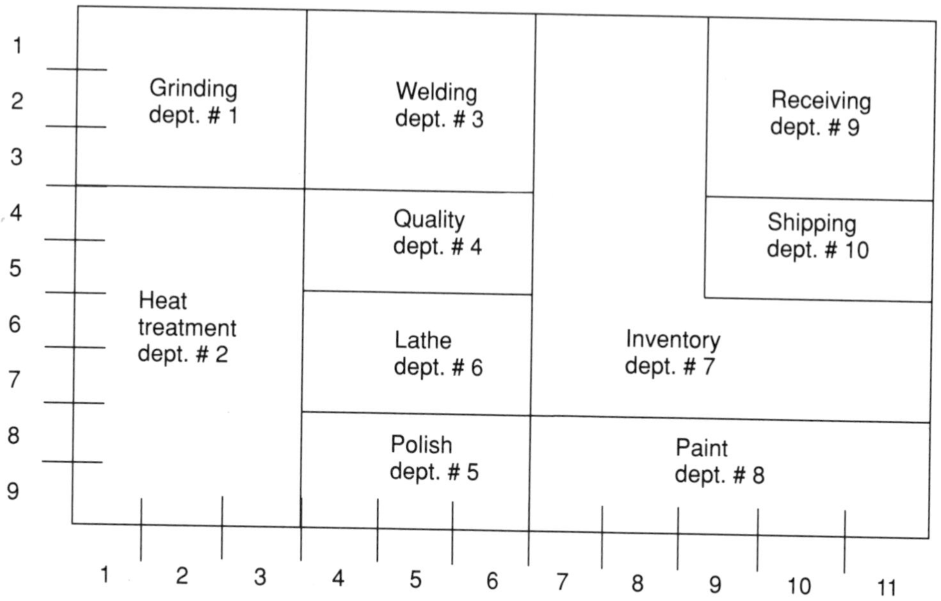

Grinding dept. # 1
Welding dept. # 3
Receiving dept. # 9
Quality dept. # 4
Shipping dept. # 10
Heat treatment dept. # 2
Lathe dept. # 6
Inventory dept. # 7
Polish dept. # 5
Paint dept. # 8

1 2 3 4 5 6 7 8 9

1 2 3 4 5 6 7 8 9 10 11

CHART 19.25 Contact Chart for First Factory Shop Floor Example

Number of Contacts Per Day

To Department	From Department									
	Gr.	HT	W.	Q.	Pol.	Lay.	Inv.	Pnt.	Rcv.	Ship.
Grinding	0	5	20	0	0	5	5	0	0	0
Heat treat	20	0	5	5	0	20	0	0	0	0
Welding	20	0	0	0	0	3	20	0	0	0
Quality	5	3	0	0	10	5	15	20	15	0
Polish	10	15	2	0	0	3	5	0	0	0
Lathe	10	0	8	0	0	0	9	0	0	0
Inventory	0	0	0	30	0	0	0	0	0	0
Paint	5	10	0	0	15	2	0	0	0	0
Receiving	0	0	0	0	0	0	0	0	0	0
Shipping	0	0	0	25	0	0	0	0	0	0

cessing several of them, the most optimal solution took the Inventory Department and spread it out into several small inventory departments all over the factory. Since this was not feasible, we would analyze solutions that were less and less optimal until one was found that worked. This solution is displayed in Chart 19.24, Part B.

As a second example of shop floor layout planning we will use the shop floor layout of Chart 19.9, Part A. To simplify the input of the problem, the layout was reformatted into the form of Chart 19.26, Part A. Using the format of Chart 19.26, Part A, allows me to input each of the departments as a rectangular area. The software package needs to know how many squares (in this case squares of 10 feet by 10 feet) each department requires. Also, in the format of problem 19.26, (Part A),

CHART 19.26 Plant Layout—Example #2, Part A

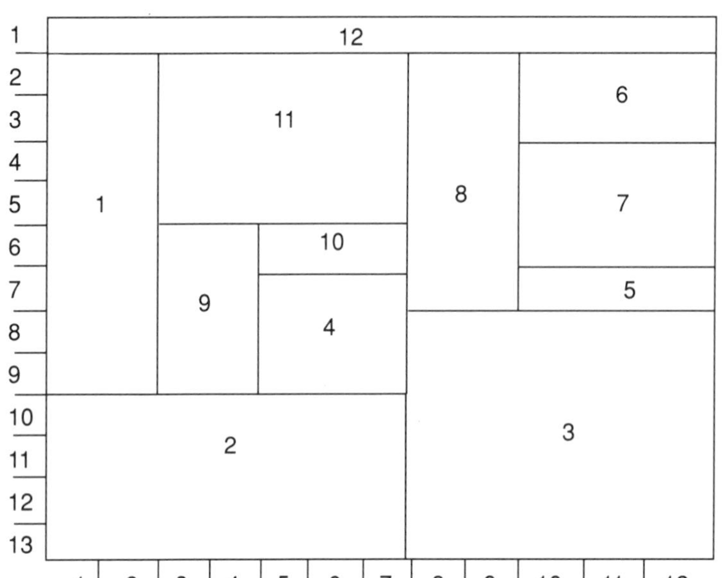

Departments:
1 - Painting
2 - Welding
3 - Heat treatment
4 - Polish
5 - Shipping
6 - Receiving
7 - Quality
8 - Inventory
9 - Grinding
10 - Supervisor
11 - Aisles
12 - Front office

CHART 19.26 Plant Layout—Example #2—Computer Solution, Part B

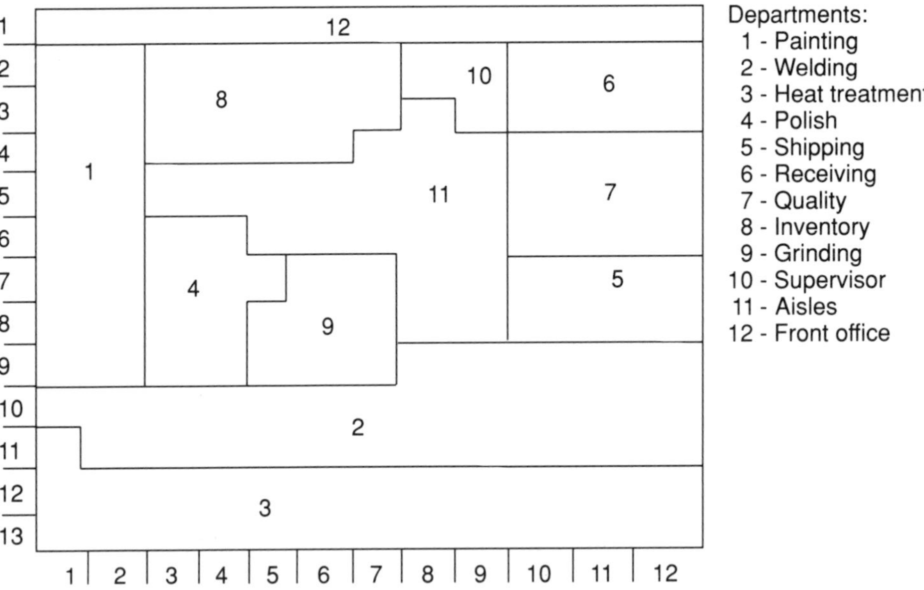

Departments 6 (Receiving), 12 (Front Office), and 5 (Shipping) were fixed.

The frequency of transfers is shown in Chart 19.27. Note that all interaction with the aisle is set very high (99) to assure that there is an aisle connection with each department. Also note that this chart counts paperwork interactions as well as materials flow interactions. Often the materials flow interactions will be weighted heavier than the pa-

CHART 19.26 Plant Layout—Example #2—Solution, Part C

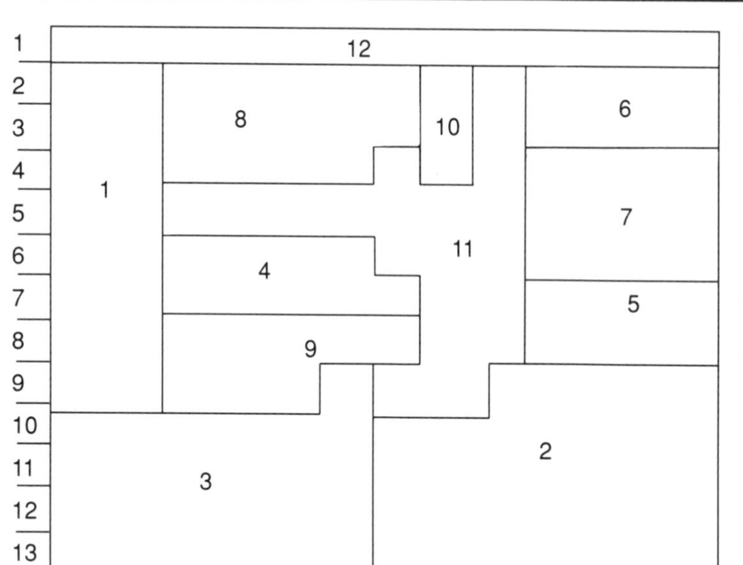

Departments:
1 - Painting
2 - Welding
3 - Heat treatment
4 - Polish
5 - Shipping
6 - Receiving
7 - Quality
8 - Inventory
9 - Grinding
10 - Supervisor
11 - Aisles
12 - Front office

CHART 19.27 Contact Chart for Second Factory Shop Floor Example
(Department numbers are the same as in Chart 19.26, Part A)

Number of Materials and Paperwork Contacts Per Day

To Department	From Department											
	1	2	3	4	5	6	7	8	9	10	11	12
1	0	0	3	20	0	0	0	3	10	0	99	0
2	0	0	5	0	0	0	0	10	5	5	99	0
3	0	15	0	0	0	0	0	10	15	5	99	0
4	0	3	10	0	0	0	0	5	30	0	99	0
5	0	0	0	0	0	0	30	5	0	0	99	0
6	0	0	0	0	0	0	0	0	0	0	99	0
7	15	0	5	10	0	30	0	30	5	0	99	0
8	3	10	10	5	0	0	30	0	7	0	99	10
9	0	20	7	0	0	0	0	7	0	15	99	0
10	0	0	0	0	0	0	40	0	0	0	99	30
11	99	99	99	99	99	99	99	99	99	99	0	99
12	0	0	0	0	0	0	10	0	0	30	30	0

perwork flow interactions. The department numbers of Chart 19.27 are the same as the department numbers of Chart 19.26, Part A.

Using the input data from Charts 19.26, Part A, and 19.27 and plugging this data into QS, we generate the optimal output from Chart 19.26, Part B. But this solution is not practical for implementation in the way some of the departments were arranged. Suggestions from this solution were used in the development of the final solution. For example, the supervisor (Department 10) is kept close to the front office

(Department 12) and inventory (Department 8). Grinding (Department 9) is kept close to heat treatment (Department 3) and welding (Department 2), and polish (Department 4) is kept close to painting (Department 1). Also note that inventory (Department 8) is kept highly accessible to quality (Department 7), which is the last step in the receiving and production process. The result is the final, practical solution of Chart 19.26, Part C.

Queuing

Queuing is another one of those subjects that people turn into careers. This segment will only give you a taste for it. If you feel it will be beneficial to you, then you need to get more material on the subject.

What happens in queuing is that we study the people or products waiting in line. We want the waiting time to be minimized and the efficiency of the flow to be maximized. So we study the process and calculate how long each step takes. There are several types of queuing:

1. *Single-Channel, Single-Phase:* One line and one server. This is similar to a product waiting to go down an assembly line. Two examples of this type of analysis will be given later in this section.
2. *Single-Channel, Multiple-Phase:* One server and one line, but as soon as the item being processed gets through with the first line and its server, it is immediately routed to another line with a single server. This is the process you go through when you are trying to get your driver's license.
3. *Multiple-Channel, Single-Phase:* Multiple servers and multiple lines. Think of the grocery store or the bank.
4. *Multiple-Channel, Multiple-Phase:* Multiple lines with multiple steps so you travel from one group of lines to the next. This reminds me of the college registration process.

The bottom line in queuing is that we are trying to determine how many servers we need, how long the line will be, and an acceptable wait time. When we consider materials movement through a plant, we encounter lots of examples where queuing would be helpful.

The two examples of single-channel, single-phase queuing are now given. In the first example we have a problem with single-channel and exponential service time. What this means is that we have one line and one server, but we don't know exactly how long it will take to service each customer. We also have a random arrival rate. This relates to customer or vendor arrival. For example, a plant is planning to open a retail outlet (or a new loading dock, or a new shipping dock, etc.) staffed by one employee. It is estimated that requests for service will average 15 per hour, and requests will have a random arrival rate. (Poisson distribution is assumed; if that doesn't mean anything to you, don't worry about it. It's a statistical term that indicates how the random arrivals will occur.) Service time is also assumed to be irregular and random (exponentially distributed, another statistics term). Previous experience with similar operations suggests the mean service time should average about three minutes per request. In our analysis we calculate the following:

1. System utilization. How busy is the system?

   w = arrival rate = 15 per hour
   s = service time = 3 minutes
   u = service rate
   = (60 min. per hr.)/(3 min. per customer)
   = 20 customers per hr.
   r = system utilization = w/u = 15/20 = 0.75

   The system will be utilized 75% of the time.

2. Percent of time the system will be idle.

   i = idle time = 1 − r = 1 − 0.75 = 0.25 or 25%

   The system will be idle 25% of the time.

3. Expected number of customers, vendors, or entrants into the system that are waiting to be served.

   n = average number waiting in line
   = $w^2/[u \times (u - w)] = 15^2/[20 \times (20 - 15)]$
   = $225/(20 \times 5)$ = 2.25 customers

   The expected line length can be 2.25 customers.

4. The average time customers will spend in the system.

   t = average time waiting in the system
   = (n/w) + (1/u)
   = (2.25/15) + (1/20) = 0.15 + 0.05
   = 0.2 hrs. = 12 min.

   Each customer will spend approximately 12 minutes in the system.

Using the information we have calculated above, we now need to decide if 12 minutes is a reasonable amount of time to wait. Do we need more servers (machines, loading docks, etc.)?

Our second example of single-channel queuing is with constant service time. This is a case in which the arrivals are still random, but each entrant into the system will take a very specified amount of time to serve. Preventive maintenance or numerous production operations fall into this category. Some loading dock operations also fall into this category.

In my example we are unloading wood chips for our pulping process. The wood chips come in on trucks that are lifted and dumped by our automatic dumper. The dumping process is automatic and takes five minutes. On a typical working day, trucks arrive at a mean rate of eight per hour, with arrivals tending to follow a Poisson distribution (the same random arrival rates as in the previous problem). Again, we will calculate:

1. The average number of trucks in line

   w = arrival rate = 8 trucks per hour
   u = service rate = 1 every 5 minutes or 12 per hour
   r = system utilization = $w/u = 8/12 = 0.67$

   The system will be utilized 67% of the time.

2. Percent of time the system will be idle.

   $i = \text{idle time} = 1 - r = 1 - 0.67 = 0.33$ or 33%

   The system will be idle 33% of the time.

3. Expected number of entrants.

   $$\begin{aligned} n &= \text{average number of trucks waiting in line} \\ &= w^2/[2 \times u \times (u - w)] \\ &= 8^2/[2 \times 12 \times (12 - 8)] = 64/96 \\ &= 0.667 \text{ trucks} \end{aligned}$$

   The average truck line length is 0.667.

4. The average time trucks spend in line and service

   $$\begin{aligned} t &= (n/w) + (l/u) = (0.667/8) + (1/12) \\ &= 0.0834 + 0.0833 = 0.167 \text{ hours} = 10 \text{ min.} \end{aligned}$$

   Each truck will spend approximately 10 minutes in the system.

Using the information we have calculated, we now need to decide if 10 minutes is a reasonable amount of time for the truckers to wait. It makes a difference, of course, if we have to pay their salary while they wait. We now can answer questions such as "Do we need more unloaders?"

Summary

We have now conquered the chapter on shop floor control. We have discovered that the major function of shop floor control is to make sure that what we have planned is actually happening. The shop floor control system gives us two key elements—control and feedback, both of which are critical if we are to plan what will happen in the future. Shop floor control is a matter of collecting the most appropriate data quickly enough for us to make critical planning decisions.

We have now conquered the information flow diagram from top to bottom. The book now turns to a discussion of some other aspects of running a factory that may be important to your operation. This discussion starts with quality control.

Chapter

20 Quality Control Department

Quality is not the function of a particular department, it is the function of the company. As long as we think about quality as someone else's job, we never get involved in it ourselves. However, today's competitive market requires that we must be totally involved in quality. This means involvement by every department, every employee, and every job function. In this chapter we will discuss some of the ways this can be done. But remember, *you've got to want to be involved in quality* before a quality program will work. Involvement requires time; time spent in training, time spent in meetings discussing quality improvements, and time spent sharing and coordinating the quality effort.

The Quality Control Department is an interesting department because their goal should be to make themselves obsolete. It is the responsibility of this department to train everyone else and to incorporate systems and procedures everywhere that will assure that every product produced gets done right the first time and every time. If this could be achieved, then there wouldn't be a need for a Quality Department.

It is not the function of the Quality Control Department to inspect the products produced by the shop floor and then to fix up the ones that don't pass the quality test. It is much more important to inspect the products, find the defects, and investigate the cause of the defects. However, this inspection process cannot be a finger-pointing process. It needs to be a cooperative improvement process. Often the operators are not even aware that a problem is occurring. That is why the quality process involves everyone. The Quality Department needs to educate employees about quality and then help them implement appropriate improvements.

Definitions

As we begin our discussion of quality, we need to start with a definition of what quality is. If you ask 10 people you'll get 10 different answers. Traditionally, in U.S. industry, quality has been defined as "meeting engineering standards" (whatever that means). If an engineering drawing has a specified set of measurements and tolerances and if the product we produce is within those tolerances, we can claim that we have a "quality" product. The difference between U.S. and European standards has simply been that for Europe the tolerances have been tighter. Therefore, the Europeans have claimed "higher quality" than the United States.

A new definition of quality has evolved that has received a lot of attention. This new definition is customer based and therefore it is an external (to the shop floor) definition. This new definition has received widespread acceptance in Japan, and we in the United States are also trying to adapt it. The new definition of quality is:

> The product we produce is considered to be of the "best" quality if the customer likes our product so well that he/she wouldn't think of buying from anyone else.

Note that in this definition we don't say anything about engineers and tolerances. We also don't say anything about durability or longevity. Features and functions may be more important than durability. It depends entirely on what the customers expect from the product when they purchase it.

Internally, in your factory, there is also a definition of quality that orients itself around the external definition. The internal definition is:

> Every employee has a job function and that job function has a customer. On the factory floor my customer is the next work station that works on the product after I'm done. In the office the next customer is the user of the data or information I generate. For the employee, the definition of quality is that the employee's customer will always be delighted with the employee's output.

Think about this internal definition of quality. This definition states that it's not the company that has a customer. Rather, every employee has a customer. The employee's customer is whoever receives the employee's output. If I am a drill press operator, then my customer is the next person who will receive the materials after I have completed my function.

The internal definition of quality suggests that each employee who receives output from me must be able to evaluate if what I have produced is "quality." To do this, every employee needs to be trained in quality. This means that they need to know what to look for, how to measure it, and how to report it. If each employee understands what is required of the products they receive in order to make them "quality," then they will be able to stop production on items that do not meet the standard. The employees will not be wasting their time working on materials that will eventually be scrapped.

Another advantage of having each employee trained in quality is that we will be able to define the cause of quality problems better. We will know where the quality problems occur, before they are buried under a series of production steps.

You've got to want to improve quality both externally and internally. It's the only competitive edge that you have. Let's take a look at some of the tools that are available to help you improve quality.

Cost of Quality

There is no such thing as "cost of quality." The term "cost of quality" gives quality a negative connotation. It suggests that quality has a "cost" associated with it and we all know that costs are undesirable and painful. Just ask your accountant. Quality is not a cost, it is a must. Without it you are guaranteed only one thing—that you will go out of business, because someone will come along and do it better and drive you out of business. Quality is an "opportunity." It is the opportunity for you to grow, to take over market share, and to become the best at what you do. Throw the "cost of quality" concept out the window and worry about the "cost of not having quality." Now there is a concept that should scare you!

Areas of Quality Control

Quality control occurs in three major areas. The first area is in the raw materials purchasing area (refer to Chart 19.9). When materials arrive at the dock, they are unpacked and the Quality Department assures that the received materials meet the required standards. This involves the traditional inspection process where some specific measures are taken. Then the accepted parts are transferred to inventory.

The second area of quality control is the work-in-process inventory quality inspections. For work-in-process inventory, we do a quality check during each production order. Sometimes the only quality check that occurs is when the product is finished, just before it is transferred to inventory (see Chart 19.9). Other times there are interim quality checks, for example, when the product is half done. The interim checks

assure that we are not wasting time working on garbage.

For work-in-process inventory quality checks, we transfer the entire batch of parts to the Quality Department. Then we inspect the parts and transfer them back into production (if it is an interim quality check) or transfer them to inventory (if the process is completed). There is also the option of in-line quality inspection. This is the process described previously (internal definition of quality) where each employee is trained on quality and will do their own quality inspection. With each employee inspecting quality, we may still want to do the final quality check at the Quality Department, however, the hope is that eventually the employees on the line will become so good at inspecting quality that the work-in-process inspections done by the Quality Department will no longer be needed.

The third type of quality inspection occurs for finished goods that are about to be shipped to the customer (see Chart 19.9). When we receive a customer order we pick the materials, send them to the Quality Department for inspection, package them, and ship them. There should never be quality problems in this area if all the other quality

processes are done correctly. If we have quality problems here it is because the inspection process and feedback mechanism is not working correctly. We are not getting our quality problems corrected early enough in the production process.

Interaction and Integration versus Over-the-Wall Quality

Quality requires interaction and integration throughout the factory. We have heard about the "quality circles" of Japan. These circles are nothing more than meetings that focus on interaction and integration.

What happens is that all the individuals involved in the production of a product get together and discuss the development of that product. This includes engineers, marketers responsible for the product, production planners, shop floor employees, and quality inspectors—everyone. They discuss the "problems" that are occurring with the product. They start with the biggest problems and try to improve those. Then they work on the next biggest, and so on down the line until there are no more problems. Then they start working on opportunities. For example, opportunities to improve productivity, improve efficiency, reduce cost, etc. These meetings occur about once a week and last a couple of hours. But the important thing is that they never stop. We are continually looking for areas of improvement. This process has been given the name *continuous improvement*. The objective of this process is to achieve the external definition of quality using the internal definition of quality—and because this is our goal, it is appropriate to bring customers and vendors into the meetings occasionally. They need to be able to say what they think is important.

There is another interesting aspect that comes out of these quality improvement meetings. It is motivation. If the incentive system of your organization is tied to quality and productivity improvements, both of which should occur as a result of these meetings, then the employees will become more quality conscious. By necessity this incentive system will need to be some form of group incentive (often referred to as *gain-sharing*), rather than an individualized incentive. But the thing that's interesting is that once the incentive system is operational, motivation is no longer a problem. Members of the "circle" will pressure each other to get the improvements installed. Managers no longer need to be pushers. Managers now take on the role of facilitators, which means that they are responsible for implementing the ideas of the "circle" rather than being responsible for driving the employees.

Modifications to the incentive and motivation programs require careful thought. For example, we can't have a team motivation and incentive program and still measure employee efficiency (see the last chapter). This sends a mixed signal to the employees and they are likely to believe that nothing has changed, meaning that the employee efficiency system is considered to be the most important. However, if we throw out the employee efficiency system, we will also be affecting the method of cost accounting that is currently being used because we will no longer have actual labor costs for each job. Job costing will have to be done by an averaging process. Think these changes through before you do them, however; my experience is that the team incentive programs have been demonstrated to be extremely effective.

The "circle" meetings bring integration and interaction. They move away from the traditional "over the wall" form of quality that is characterized by the traditional definition of quality (meeting engineering standards).

Another form of integration and interaction that needs to occur is that employees from our plant need to visit other plants. This is also part of the education process. They need to visit plants similar to ours to get new and fresh ideas for improvements. They need to visit our customers' plants or locations to get a better feel for what their needs are. Our employees need to visit our vendors' plants so that they can look for ways to make the vendors' jobs easier and more cost effective.

Measures of Quality

There are numerous measures of quality. Here we will discuss a few of them, including the ones that should be the most useful to you.

Control Charts

A control chart is a diagram (see Chart 20.1) where we have a desired value ("Avg."), and an upper and lower control limit ("UCL" and "LCL").[1] There are lots of things we may be measuring. For example, we may be measuring a dimension, or a hardness, or a gloss, etc. Whatever we are measuring has a desired value and a tolerance range. Using these values we set up the chart shown in Chart 20.1. Then, as we do our quality measurements, we plot the value on the control chart. If we are outside of the limits, we know that we need to reject the part. If we are within the limits, we look for a tendency or trend (see Chart 20.2). These trends warn us of pending error and encourage us to take corrective action before we actually start having failures.

Looking at Chart 20.2 we see two control chart examples. On the top chart we see a series of measures (the last four points) that are steadily going higher and higher toward the UCL. This is a sign of danger and suggests that soon our measures will go off the top end of the chart. We should take a close look at our production process to see if we can correct this tendency before we start producing bad parts. The bottom chart shows a fairly evenly disbursed set of data with one outlier above the UCL causing that one part to be rejected. Near the end of the bottom control chart we start to see the data edging their way closer and closer toward the control limits. This suggests that we will soon be rejecting lots of parts if we don't find the production problem and correct it soon.

We may be measuring several things each time we take a measurement. In that case, we may have several control charts. Each control chart would be the indicator of a different type of problem.

If we are doing in-line quality control checks where each employee is trained in quality, we will not have each employee recheck all the previous quality checks that had occurred earlier. Each employee would only check the areas of quality that need checking based on the last couple of functions. There may be a little overlap, but that is OK. Just as long as there isn't a lot of overlap. With in-line quality control

---

[1] The upper and lower control limits are developed initially using engineering standard tolerance limits. Eventually these limits can be tightened by setting the limits as three standard deviations off the mean. The tightening occurs because of improvements in the process allowing our quality to improve. The calculation of these tighter limits, and several other concepts that surround these issues, is discussed in the quality books referred to near the end of this chapter.

CHART 20.1 Control Chart

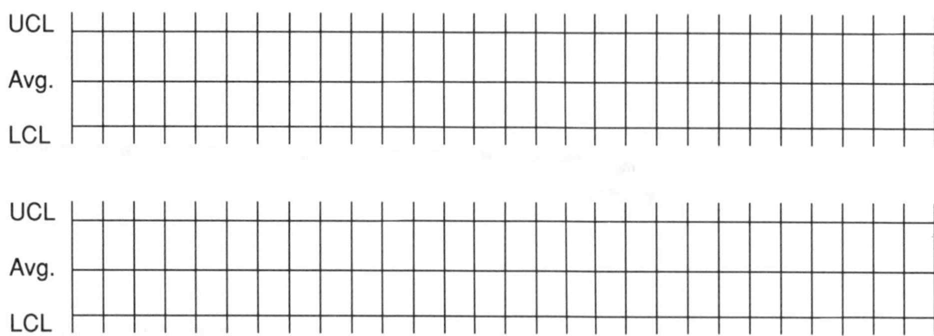

CHART 20.2 Control Chart Example

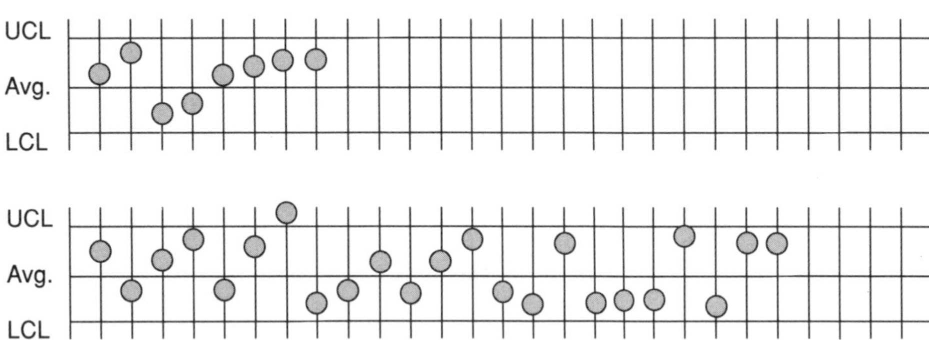

checks, we can add quality checks or delete checks as they are needed to help assure quality and to assist in tracking down quality problems.

Sampling

There are two major ways of validating the quality of a batch of materials. The first is by checking all the parts. This is called 100 percent inspection. However, sometimes, especially in raw materials receipts, we are evaluating small or inexpensive parts and 100 percent inspection seems a waste of time so we use sampling. Sampling is where we randomly inspect a few of the parts. If we find an adequate number of the random sample to be acceptable, we declare the entire batch to be acceptable. Sampling becomes especially important if our testing process is destructive (i.e., the part is destroyed during the testing process).

The control charts of Chart 20.1 work best under the 100 percent inspection environment. But in a sampling environment we need to be able to determine what makes up a random sample and what number of inspections is sufficient to declare the batch acceptable. To accomplish this, we need to determine three things: what the sample size should be, which products should be checked, and at what level we should accept or reject our sample. The best source for this information is the Military Standard Sampling Procedures and Tables for Inspection by Attitude (MIL-STD-105D). We will work through a very brief and summarized version of the information that is available in these tables. However, if you do a lot of sampling, you should get a copy of these tables and work through them in detail.

Sample Size

Chart 20.3 lists a sample size for a specified lot size that is being sampled.

Which Products to Check

To select which products to check we need a random number generator. We use this random number generator to identify which parts should be sampled. Grab a statistics book and look at the back of the book. In it you'll find a random number table. Use this table to identify which parts to select for sampling.

Acceptance and Rejection Level

Chart 20.4 lists the rejection levels at specific levels of defect rates. The quality levels across the top are the levels at which we want to accept the batch. For example, if we want to accept the entire batch of parts if at least 99 percent of the parts are good (1 percent or less bad) we would look at the quality levels and select the column marked 1.0. The quality level of 0.10 is where less than one tenth of one percent (00.10 percent) of the parts is bad.

In Chart 20.4, if we are trying to verify a batch of 15 parts at a 0.40 percent quality level we will see the "zzz" entry on the table. This means that in order to assure that high a level of acceptance you will have to do 100 percent inspection. There are also numbers in the table; for example, if our batch size is 500 and we are working for a one percent quality level, we get a 2 off of the table. This means that if we have two or more failures out of our sample size of 50 parts (see Chart 20.3), we will reject the batch. Fewer than two failures will cause us to accept the batch.

CHART 20.3 Sample Size Table

Lot Size	Sample Size
2–8	2
9–15	3
16–25	5
26–50	8
51–90	13
91–150	20
151–280	32
281–500	50
501–1,200	80
1,201–3,200	125
3,201–10,000	200

CHART 20.4 Acceptance and Rejection Level

Lot Size	Quality Levels							
	0.065	0.10	0.40	0.65	1.0	1.5	4.0	6.5
2–8	zzz	zzz	zzz	zzz	zzz	zzz	zzz	1
9–15	zzz	zzz	zzz	zzz	zzz	zzz	1	1
16–25	zzz	zzz	zzz	zzz	zzz	zzz	1	1
26–50	zzz	zzz	zzz	zzz	zzz	1	1	2
51–90	zzz	zzz	zzz	zzz	1	1	2	3
91–150	zzz	zzz	zzz	1	1	1	3	4
151–280	zzz	zzz	1	1	1	2	4	6
281–500	zzz	zzz	1	1	2	3	6	8
501–1,200	zzz	zzz	1	2	3	4	8	11
1,201–3,200	zzz	1	2	3	4	6	11	15
3,201–10,000	1	1	3	4	6	8	15	22

Here is another example of how sampling works. Assume a batch size of 1,000 parts coming in and we want to make sure that the batch is at least 99 percent good before it is accepted (1 percent or less bad). Chart 20.3 says that my sample size should be at least 80. We randomly select 80 items from the batch using my random number table. Then we will test those 80 parts to see how many failures occurred. If there are three or more failures (see Chart 20.4), we reject the batch. If there are fewer than three failures, we accept the batch as being 99 percent acceptable.

Quality Reports

After we have performed our inspections we need to report them on some type of history report. For example, if we have performed inspections on the same part from the same vendor repeatedly, we want to know how that vendor is performing on that part versus some other vendor's performance on the same part. This process often demonstrates that the cheaper part may not be worth it because of the low quality experienced with this cheaper part. At one plant the part we were producing had such a low level of quality, and we experienced such a high level of waste, that it was actually cheaper to ship the stamped metal part to Japan and let them grind out the gears and ship the finished gears back to us. We need to recognize these problems and ask ourselves, "Why is our level of quality so low?"

A sample quality report is shown on Chart 20.5. Here we see the same part delivered to us by two different vendors. We see that the performance of the two vendors is different and that the first vendor is more reliable in the production of this particular part. The calculations are as follows (using vendor ABCD as the example):

$$\% = \frac{\text{Percentage Good}}{\text{for That Batch}} = \frac{\text{Sample Size} - \text{Rejects}}{\text{Sample Size}} \times 100$$

$$= \frac{10 - 2}{10} \times 100 = 80\%$$

CHART 20.5 Quality Performance Report—Example

Part	Vendor	Date	Quantity	Sample Size	Rejects	%
AXBC	ABCD	1/1/92	100	10	2	80
		1/2/92	200	20	3	85
		1/4/92	100	10	1	90
				Vendor average performance:		85
	AXXX	1/3/92	100	10	2	80
		1/5/92	200	20	3	85
		1/6/92	100	10	2	80
				Vendor average performance:		82.5

$$\text{Vendor Average Performance} = \frac{\Sigma \text{ of Quantities} \times \text{Percentage}}{\Sigma \text{ of Quantities}} \times 100$$

$$= \frac{100 \times 0.80 + 200 \times 0.85 + 100 \times 0.90}{100 + 200 + 100} \times 100$$

$$= \frac{340}{400} \times 100 = 85\%$$

The analysis performed on Chart 20.5 can be used for the analysis of the quality inspection history for any process. This should be done for raw materials, work-in-process, and finished goods items. Analyzing this history will give you some indication of where the majority of your quality problems occur, which is the first step toward solving those problems.

Shelf Life and Quarantine

An interesting twist to the quality control issue is the aspect of shelf life and quarantine. Some products have a limited amount of time during which they are usable (chemical and food products). These products need to get used before their shelf life expires. Similarly, there are other products that need to be aged before they are usable (lumber).

Quality control and inventory management need to work together in order to assure the correct use of shelf life or quarantine restricted items. Inventory management reports the batch number of the materials used on the traveler or pick list. Quality validates that this batch is an appropriate batch available to be used during the time frame when it was used.

Problem Analysis

A lot of organizations have started diagramming their error process. The reason for this is that it allows the user of the diagram to make a quick assessment of where the error may have occurred. For example, if

CHART 20.6 Fish Bone Chart or Ishakawa Diagram

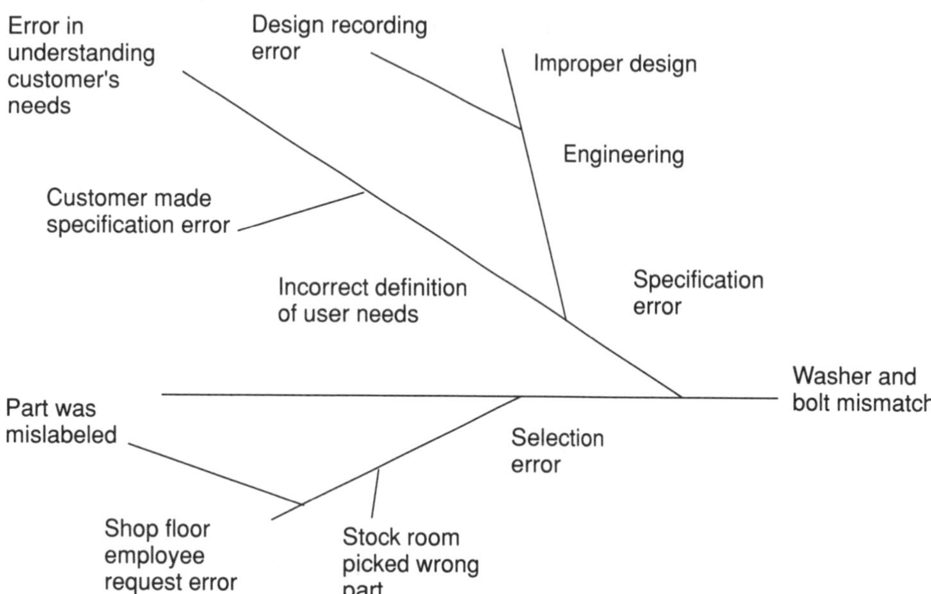

the operator who is filling out the control chart of Chart 20.2 on the top is interested in finding out why a particular measurement is starting to come out of range at the UCL, he or she can look at the error diagram (referred to as a *fish bone chart* or *Ishikawa diagram*) to determine the different causes of the error.

Chart 20.6 is an example of a fish bone chart. Note that each "bone" is a possible cause of an error. Using this diagram we can quickly analyze all the possible reasons for an error and focus on the solution.

Total Quality Management

This book has been trying to avoid buzzwords because they tend to be short lived and faddish. However, there is one buzzword that needs addressing—*total quality management* (TQM). TQM means that the total organization is focused on quality. It is not a program—it is an attitude. It is an organization filled with a positive attitude. The quality focus starts with management and permeates throughout the organization. It incorporates training in quality at all levels of the organization. It includes in-line quality control where the operators are doing quality checks. It involves both internal and external quality concepts. TQM uses quality meetings to coordinate efforts toward productivity and quality improvements, and it utilizes continuous quality improvement concepts. Basically, TQM is the implementation and integration of all the concepts discussed in this chapter on an ongoing basis.

TQM is not a big leap into quality. It is a step-by-step, one-small-step-at-a-time process that will focus on quality. In TQM we look for those items that will give us the most "bang for the buck" as far as quality improvements go, and we make those improvements first. Then we focus on the next area of improvement. Then, one small step at a time, we walk toward quality and productivity improvements that will make us more competitive.

Further Reading

This chapter has been a brief overview of quality and the functions of a Quality Control Department. Entire books have been written on the subject, and this book does not pretend to be comprehensive in its discussion. This is only intended to be a starting point. For further reading, review:

Military Standard Sampling Procedures and Tables for Inspection by Attitude, MIL-STD-105D.

QS (Quant Systems) by Chang and Sullivan, Prentice Hall, 1991, Chapter 28 on quality control.

Quality Control by Dale Besterfield, Prentice Hall, 1990.

The Deming Guide to Quality and Competitive Position by Gitlow and Gitlow, Prentice Hall, 1987.

Quality Is Free by Philip B. Crosby, New American Library, 1979.

Summary

Quality is not a program. It is you. It is your ability to perform as an organization and as an individual. It is your ability to defeat your competition. No production planning and control program is complete without a focus on quality.

PART III OTHER TOPICS

Chapter

21 Support Functions

Tool Room

Tool rooms are like minifactories. Often they have their own production process, which includes the sharpening and even construction of tools, jigs, dies, etc. They also have their own inventory area that needs a perpetual inventory control process. Tool room personnel need to be able to check tools out, and they need to know who took the tool. In this chapter I'm not going to repeat some of the subjects that were already discussed in detail, such as inventory planning and control (Chapters 8, 9, and 11). In these previous chapters we learned how to organize the tool room (ABC analysis), and how to track the quantities of tools and other materials stored in the tool room (EOQ ordering and perpetual inventory tracking).

This chapter discusses a few of the new concepts that relate to the tool room, like a check-out procedure (tool picking) and a replacement scheduling procedure. But before starting the discussion of these new concepts, a recommendation needs to be made about the operation of the tool room. The tool room supervisor should be the most intimidating individual in your plant. The intimidation factor helps to make sure that the tool check-out and check-in procedures are complied with.

A second recommendation for the tool room is that it needs its own incentive system. For example, pay a bonus to the tool room manager during any month when no tools are lost, missing, or otherwise unaccounted for. We can't have tools disappearing, because then, when they are needed, production is delayed.

Check-out and Check-in Procedures

Tools are checked out of the tool room and checked back in. These check-outs and check-ins give us a history of tool usage that will later become important in tool replacement scheduling. Chart 21.1 is an example of a check-out/check-in form that could be used by a tool room. One form would be used for each transaction. This form is filled out when a tool is checked out. Then the form is filed away in tool number order until the tool is returned. When the tool is returned the receiving information is filled in and the form is placed into a history file.

The tool number is the same for all tools of the same type. However, each tool needs to have a unit number attached to it that identifies each specific tool individually. For example, there are six of tool number ABABAB in the tool room. It is important to identify each one of the six with a unit number, for example unit 5, 6, 7, 8, 9, and 10. This way we can keep track of how much life we got out of each individual tool.

Tool Rework or Scrap Report

As tools become old, they break or wear out. Perhaps they can be resharpened or reworked in some way. Or perhaps they need to be scrapped. We need to report this so that we can complete our estimate of the life of the tool. As we rework or scrap a tool, we need to fill out the

CHART 21.1 Tool Check-out and Check-in Form

Tool number ______________________ Unit # __________
Tool description ______________________
Issue information (to):
Employee ______________________
Work station ______________________
Date ____/____/____ Time ____:____
Receiving information (from):
Employee ______________________
Work station ______________________
Date ____/____/____ Time ____:____
Jobs completed ______________________ Quantity __________

CHART 21.2 Tool Rework or Scrap Report

Date: ____/____/____
Tool number: ______________________ Unit # __________
Tool description: ______________________
Part scrapped: __________
Work performed:
Employee: ______________________
Work station: ______________________
Date: ____/____/____ Start time: ____:____
Date: ____/____/____ End time: ____:____
Lapse time: ____:____

report shown on Chart 21.2. If the part is to be scrapped, we fill out the information through the part scrapped line and check this line. If the part is to be reworked, we fill out all the information expect the part scrapped line. Then we file this form with the check-in/check-out history documents.

Replacement Scheduling

The key to replacement scheduling is the development of a history of tool usage. If we know how often a tool is used before it breaks, then we can calculate some kind of average life for the tool. Then, if we know the average life of a tool we can estimate how often the tool will need to be replaced. This process starts with the history that has already been accumulated on check-in/check-out and rework/scrap tickets. We sort these documents into part number/unit number sequence and report them on the report form shown in Chart 21.3.

Some of the tools in the tool room may be considered too inexpensive to be worth documenting, for example, allen wrenches or small screwdrivers. In this case we use an EOQ reorder point system in conjunction with a perpetual inventory system, or we may use a two-bin system (see

CHART 21.3 History Analysis Report

Period From ____/____/____ Through ____/____/____

Tool Number	Unit #	Usage Information: Date	Lapse Time	Quantity	Rework Time	Scrap

CHART 21.4 Tool Check-out and Check-in Form—A Few Examples

Tool number: ABABAB Unit #: 5
Issue information (to):
  Employee: Joe
  Work station: Lathe
  Date: 1/1/1992 Time: 8:00
Receiving information (from):
  Employee: Joe
  Work station: Lathe
  Date: 1/1/1992 Time: 11:00
  Jobs completed: R2D2-1 Quantity: 100

Tool number: ABABAB Unit #: 5
Issue information (to):
  Employee: Judy
  Work station: Lathe
  Date: 1/2/1992 Time: 8:00
Receiving information (from):
  Employee: Judy
  Work station: Lathe
  Date: 1/2/1992 Time: 11:30
  Jobs completed: R2D2-2 Quantity: 200

Tool number: ABABAB Unit #: 6
Issue information (to):
  Employee: Jim
  Work station: Lathe
  Date: 1/2/1992 Time: 8:00
Receiving information (from):
  Employee: Jim
  Work station: Lathe
  Date: 1/2/1992 Time: 11:00
  Jobs completed: C3PO Quantity: 100

Chapters 8, 9, and 11). Either system will track the number of tools we have and trigger the purchase of additional tools when necessary.

Examples of how to fill out the toolroom reports we've discussed are shown in the next three charts. An example of Chart 21.1 is shown in Chart 21.4. Chart 21.2 is demonstrated in Chart 21.5. Chart 21.3 is demonstrated in Chart 21.6.

Using the data from Chart 21.3 (or the example of Chart 21.6), we are now able to update a cumulative history record for each tool. The cumulative history record is kept by tool number and is a summary for each unit number. An entry is reported on the accumulative history when a tool is scrapped. At this point we go back and summarize the life of the tool-unit by reviewing all the history analysis reports back until when the tool was initially used. This information is reported on the cumulative history record (Chart 21.7 or see the example in Chart 21.8).

On Chart 21.7 we report tools that have been scrapped. We report the unit number of the scrapped tool. We report the total life of the tool, from when it was first used until it was finally scrapped. We report the hours of machine usage that the tool received and the number of units produced by the tool. We also report the amount of time spent reworking the tool, for example, sharpening, and we report the reason for finally scrapping the tool. With the cumulative history report we are now able to average the approximate life expectancy of each tool, either in terms of total life, hours of usage, or number of units produced. Then,

CHART 21.5 Tool Rework or Scrap Report—Examples

Date: 1/3/1992
Tool number: ABABAB Unit #: 5
Part scrapped: *

Date: 1/3/1992
Tool number: ABABAB Unit #: 6
Work performed:
Employee: Bobby
Work station: Grind-02
Date: 1/3/1992 Start time: 8:00
Date: 1/3/1992 End time: 10:00
Lapse time: 2:00

CHART 21.6 History Analysis Report—Example (Period from 1/1/1992 through 1/4/1992)

		Usage Information				
Tool Number	Unit #	Date	Lapse Time	Quantity	Rework Time	Scrap
ABABAB	5	1/1/1992	3:00	100		
		1/2/1992	3:30	200		
						1/3/1992
ABABAB	6	1/2/1992	3:00	100		
		1/3/1992			3:00	

CHART 21.7 Cumulative History Report

Tool Number ____________

Unit #	Total Life	Hours of Usage	Number of Units Produced	Rework Time	Reason for Scrap

CHART 21.8 Cumulative History Report—Example

Tool Number ABABAB

Unit #	Total Life	Hours of Usage	Number of Units Produced	Rework Time	Reason for Scrap
1	16 weeks	200	1000	6 hrs.	break
2	17 weeks	220	1000	7 hrs.	break
3	20 weeks	250	1200	7 hrs.	break
4	15 weeks	190	900	5.5 hrs.	break

based on these values, we can estimate how often the tool will need to be replaced.

Reviewing Chart 21.8, we see that tool ABABAB lasts an average of 17 weeks, or 215 production hours, or 1,025 production units. From this we can estimate that every 17 weeks we will need to order a new tool of this type, assuming the demand for the tool remains constant.

Another way to plan the replacement of tools is to have a safety stock of the tool based on the tool's usage. For example, if we keep two extra ABABABs on hand, and then order an ABABAB every time one breaks, then, assuming that the lead time to get a new ABABAB is less than the 17 weeks, we should always recover our inventory satisfactorily. This second method usually generates more tool inventory and the cost of this inventory may encourage you to use the planning method recommended earlier where we order an ABABAB every 17 weeks.

The tool room is a mini-plant that needs its own mini-planning system to assure that we have the appropriate tools when they are needed. By using a replacement tracking and scheduling system and an inventory control system, we should be able to control the flow of tools in and out of the tool room.

Purchasing

The Purchasing Department receives purchase requisitions from two different sources depending on whether we are using an MRP (Chapters 12 and 16) or an EOQ (Chapter 11) production planning system. In the case where we are running an MRP-based system, we get our current purchase requisitions from the order release report. We also get future pending purchase requisitions from the planned order report (both are described in detail in Chapter 16).

If we are running an EOQ-based system, we receive purchase requisitions for current needs only. These current needs are triggered when the perpetual inventory system hits the reorder point. Then the stockroom employee will fill out a purchase requisition for an EOQ quantity of parts (see Chapters 8, 9, and 11 for a detailed explanation of how this should work).

Purchase requisitions may also be triggered by the tool room, by the front office, by maintenance, and by engineering. These are also routed to the Purchasing Department.

Once the Purchasing Department has received the purchase requisitions, it becomes their responsibility to turn these requisitions into purchase orders. The format of the purchase requisition was explained and diagrammed in Chart 9.10 (an example is shown in Chart 9.11). The purchase order is then triggered based on this requisition (see Chart 21.9).

The purchase order form of Chart 21.9 gets filled out by the purchasing agent. The information that is filled out initially is:

Due date

Purchase order number (usually preprinted)

Product number

Product description

Quantity

Estimated price

Shipping information (if there are special requirements)

The purchasing agent gets the necessary approvals signed off on the bottom of the form. The number of approvals needed usually depends on the size (in terms of dollars) of the order.

Next the purchasing agent will talk to various vendors, getting price estimates for the materials needed. Once agreement with a vendor has been reached, the vendor will be given the purchase order number and that number will be referenced in the shipping and billing documents. The purchase order number is usually a preprinted form number so that there are never any duplicate numbers. The vendor name and

CHART 21.9 Purchase Order

Due Date ____/____/____ Purchase Order Number ________

Vendor ________________

Product Number	Product Description	Order Quantity	Price	Quantity Received	Date Received

Approvals ________ ________ ________

Shipping instructions ________________

address information is entered on the form and the cost of the product is adjusted to match the vendor's quote. Shipping information is also filled out at this time if not already specified.

The purchase order then becomes a control document, one copy of which remains in purchasing, and the remaining copies are sent to the receiving dock awaiting the delivery of the materials. At this point, the receiving process takes over. This process has been detailed in Chapter 9, specifically in Chart 9.1, which discusses the flow of raw materials into our shop. Review this information carefully. In step RM3 of Chart 9.1 we see how the purchase order is used to accept or reject goods that have arrived at the receiving dock. In step RM9, we see the return of the purchase and shipping documents for payment purposes.

If we are running an MRP system, the release of the purchase order needs to be reported to the production planning system. It then becomes a pending purchase order (see Chapter 12) and it adjusts the planned purchase orders of the future. Also, when the purchase order is finally returned to the Purchasing Department, the MRP system needs to have the closing of the order reported to it so that the order is no longer pending. The previous pending order has now been replaced by on-hand inventory in the inventory storeroom.

Inventory and Product Costing

The purchasing system is critical in assessing the cost of both our inventory and our manufactured product. We need to track the price paid for our raw materials (purchased) items so that when we do our physical inventory we know what the most appropriate prices of our products will be. In costing our inventory we have several different accounting standards. The selection of which accounting standard you use is a strategic planning decision based on what you think will turn the best after-tax profit. This selection process is strictly a numbers game. Some of the options include:

LIFO: Last in–first out, which assumes that any materials in inventory cost us the price of the first materials we ever purchased. The logic is that we always use the most expensive (most recently purchased) items first.

FIFO: First in–first out, which assumes that we always have the most expensive items in inventory and that we always use the oldest parts up first.

Average: Here we take the average of the costs and use that average value for evaluating our inventory costs.

For operations purposes, the most realistic assessment of inventory is FIFO. This suggests that we always use the most recently paid prices for our evaluation of inventory costs. Review the Chapter 8 discussion of physical inventories.

For product costing, in operations we would also prefer the FIFO value. This will give us the most realistic cost of the product. Product costing is developed from the cost roll that was discussed in detail in Chapter 14.

Product Cost Tracking

Regardless of which accounting method you use for calculating inventory costs, we need to keep a history of the purchases of each inventory item in order to analyze these costs. Chart 21.10 is a sample report form that can be used for tracking product costs. One form should be used for each purchased item and these forms should be kept in some kind of file or binder. Then, as purchasing receives the completed purchasing and shipping information back, they can report the transaction on the form (see step RM9 in Chart 9.1). See Chart 21.11 for a filled-out example of this report.

In the product cost history we report one line item for each completed purchase order. We report:

The vendor number (or some abbreviation that is significant)

The quantity actually received and accepted into inventory (see Chapter 9, Chart 9.1)

The price actually paid for the total quantity including shipping costs

The per unit price, which is the total price divided by the quantity (in the first example this would be \$200.00/10 units = \$20.00 per unit)

Deviations from the actual purchase order. For example, if the wrong quantity was received as in the second example of Chart

21.11 we would report the difference. If the price was not the same as originally quoted, we would report that difference on a per unit basis. If the due date was late, we would report the number of days late (days early can also be reported if that is important, but it is usually not as important as days late).

With this report we have a summarized history of the purchase transactions of a product. This is used for product costing and for vendor analysis, which is discussed next.

Vendor Analysis

Occasionally it is helpful to check on a vendor's performance or to check on the performance of several vendors on a particular part. These vendor analysis reports can be developed and run using the data from the

CHART 21.10 Product Cost History

Product Number ________ Product Description ________

Purchase Order Number	Vendor Number	Quantity	Price	Per Unit Price	Deviations		
					Quantity	Price	Due Date

CHART 21.11 Product Cost History—Example

Product Number ABABAB Product Description ________

Purchase Order Number	Vendor Number	Quantity	Price	Per Unit Price	Deviations		
					Quantity	Price	Due Date
11111	123	10	200.00	20.00			1
11222	123	11	220.00	20.00	10		
11333	122	10	210.00	21.00			

product cost history report. If we want to validate a vendor's performance, we would collect all the data for that vendor and group the data, by part, as shown on Chart 21.12. Note that the only difference between Chart 21.12 and Chart 21.10 is that the vendor information and the part information are switched.

CHART 21.12 Vendor Performance Report

Date ____/____/____

Vendor Number ________ Vendor Name ________________

Part Number	Purchase Order Number	Quantity	Price	Per Unit Price	Deviations		
					Quantity	Price	Due Date

CHART 21.13 Vendor Performance Report—Example

Date 1 / 1 / 1992

Vendor Number 111111 Vendor Name ________________

Part Number	Purchase Order Number	Quantity	Price	Per Unit Price	Deviations		
					Quantity	Price	Due Date
ABABAB	123	10	200.00	20.00			1
ABABAB	133	11	220.00	20.00	10		
ABABAB	134	10	210.00	21.00			
Totals:		31	630.00	20.32	10		1
ACACAC	127	100	210.00	2.10			1
ACACAC	147	120	220.00	1.83	10		
ACACAC	156	100	210.00	2.10		.10	
Totals:		320	640.00	2.00	10	.10	1
Overall Totals:					20	.10	2

Chart 21.13 is an example of Chart 21.12. We calculate totals at the part number level for:

Quantity

Price

Unit price = total price/total quantity

Each of the deviations

Using Chart 21.13 as our example, we can see the vendor's performance on each product, and we can also see overall totals of the deviations so we can see how the vendor performed in all categories. We can also generate a vendor performance report for a particular part to see which vendor performed best on that part (see Chart 21.14). Again, we would start with the data listed on Chart 21.10. These data would be regrouped by vendor. Note that the format of the report is very similar to Chart 21.10 except that the data are grouped by vendor.

The calculations for Chart 21.14 or 21.15 are the same as for Charts 21.12 and 21.13. From Chart 21.15 we see that the quantity and due date performance of vendors 122 and 123 are about the same, but the price performance of vendor 122 is better and, therefore, would be the preferable vendor.

Vendor Contracts

There are two general philosophies about relationships with vendors. The traditional approach is to consider purchase price the most important criteria in vendor selection. The vendor that can give you the products at the lowest price is the one we select. This means that

CHART 21.14 Vendor—Product Performance Report

Date _____/_____/_____

Product Number __________ Product Description ____________________

Purchase Order Number	Vendor Number	Quantity	Price	Per Unit Price	Deviations		
					Quantity	Price	Due Date

CHART 21.15 Vendor—Product Performance Report—Example

Date 1 / 1 / 1992

Product Number ABABAB Product Description ______

Purchase Order Number	Vendor Number	Quantity	Price	Per Unit Price	Deviations		
					Quantity	Price	Due Date
11333	122	10	210.00	21.00			
11367	122	10	200.00	20.00			1
11414	122	11	220.00	20.00	10		
11555	122	10	210.00	21.00			
Totals:		41	840.00	20.49	10		1
12121	123	100	210.00	2.10			
12333	123	120	220.00	1.83	10		
11223	123	100	210.00	2.10		.10	
Totals:		320	640.00	2.00	10	.10	1
Overall Totals:					20	.10	2

purchase agents spend a lot of their time getting price quotes and then making vendor selections.

The second approach for vendor selection is based on quality and reliability. In this approach we look for a long-term relationship with a vendor. We want a vendor that will be involved in the design of their portion of the product and who will accept more responsibility in the quality of the product. This also means that the vendor becomes the sole supplier of that part for us. We establish a contract with the vendor, and we look to the vendor for timely and accurate deliveries. We do not spend time collecting bids, but we spend more time up front establishing our relationship with the vendor.

Purchasing is an extremely important function for any organization. By not establishing a good purchasing policy and by not properly defining our vendor relationships, we can end up spending more time than necessary—and getting poor quality—at higher costs than necessary.

Maintenance

The Maintenance Department is similar to the tool room in that they have a somewhat independent operation with schedules that are dependent on what the rest of the factory floor does. There are two major types of maintenance: urgent and preventive. *Urgent maintenance* is when something breaks down and needs immediate repair. *Preventive maintenance* is regularly scheduled maintenance, such as oiling, greasing, or gear changes, that is performed at regular intervals in order to prevent urgent maintenance. The primary systems needed to run a maintenance shop are: inventory planning and control, preventive maintenance scheduling, setup scheduling, and budgeting.

Inventory planning and control is performed in the same way as discussed in Chapters 8, 9, and 11, with the exception that maintenance has their own inventory area with their own perpetual inventory system. Inventory is carried for spare parts and cleaning and maintenance supplies. This inventory system needs to be controlled tightly just the way it has been described in the previous chapters. If a needed spare part is missing during a machine breakdown, it can shut the entire factory down.

Preventive or urgent maintenance is triggered through a centrally located maintenance office. Preventive maintenance is triggered by the preventive maintenance scheduling system and urgent maintenance is triggered by a phone call from someone having a problem. In either case, a work order is generated that identifies what is to be done and how urgent the work is.

Often, in an urgent care situation, the specific part may not be known and won't be known until the work is completed. We would fill out as much of the information as possible in the Maintenance Department, and the employee doing the repairs will have to fill in the remaining missing information. After the work has been completed the employee doing the work would describe what was done, how long it took, and what parts were used in the process. Then the work order would be returned to the Maintenance Department for posting and costing.

As work orders are generated they are posted on a log. The purpose of this log is to let the office know who is doing what, and what jobs are in process. The flow of work orders would follow Chart 21.16.

CHART 21.16 Work Order Flow

Maintenance Department

A work order is generated by either the preventive maintenance department or by a phone call from someone having a problem. The work order is written up and posted on a log. The work order is assigned to a specific employee to be completed.

Work Area

The work is performed and the employee performing the work fills out the rest of the form.

Maintenance Department

The completed work order is returned to the maintenance area. The log is updated to show the completion date of the job. The master work order file is updated showing the last maintenance performed, thereby scheduling the next preventive maintenance that should occur. The work order information is filed and saved for the costing reports.

Preventive Maintenance Scheduling

For preventive maintenance scheduling we need a master file of every item that is replaced or repaired. This master file would contain the following information (as a minimum).

Building or work area number

Machine number

Component group

Replacement part

Maintenance type

Installed date

Maintenance cycle, the number of days between maintenance

Last maintenance date

Next maintenance date, the last maintenance date (or installed date if no maintenance date exists) added to the maintenance cycle. This is the date that will trigger maintenance work orders.

Location

Drawing, a brief sketch of where the part is and what is to be done is often helpful and can be included on the master record.

This master record is used as a tracking device for what maintenance has occurred on a part and when the next scheduled maintenance should occur. The maintenance master may be copied and attached to the work order if the drawing, location description, or maintenance history information is helpful to the employee doing the work.

Setup Scheduling

Setups are scheduled and performed in a variety of ways in every factory. In some factories, each employee does his or her own setups. In other factories there is a special department whose function is to do the setup process. Sometimes setups are performed by employees housed in the tool room, and sometimes setups are performed by employees housed in the Maintenance Department.

If setups are to be performed by someone other than the shop floor employee who does the work, a scheduling mechanism will be needed to let the "setup" employee know where he or she should be, what tools will be needed, and when the employee should do the setup. The process is similar to the work order process described in this chapter. However, the work order for setups would be triggered by the Production Scheduling Department. When production scheduling initiated a production traveler (production packet) and sent it to the shop floor supervisor (see Chapter 19, Chart 19.1, steps 2 and 3), they also initiated a pick list for inventory. At the same time they would also initiate a work order for the machine setups required. Production scheduling is expected to know which processes will require setups. These work orders for setups are sent to the department responsible for the setups. These work orders hang in limbo, acting as a warning that work will soon need to be performed. The setup is performed when the work station on the shop floor is ready to have the setups done. The shop floor employee would call ahead and warn the setup employees when they will be ready to have the setups performed so that the setup employees can be available when needed.

Costing and Budgeting

When the work orders are returned to the Maintenance Department, they are kept on file by the control number (Building or Work Area Number/Machine Number/Component Group/Replacement Part). This activity file is used when it comes time to perform costing and budgeting analysis. There are several important costing reports:

Machine costing
Work center costing
Employee performance
Maintenance department costing/budgeting

We now analyze how each of these is generated.

Machine Costing. For machine costing we would pull out all the master records for that particular machine and review all the corresponding maintenance work orders that have been filed away. We would summarize this information on a machine costing report. This machine costing report could be run for the total life of the machine or for just a fixed period of time (such as annually).

Work Center Costing. The work center costing report format is almost identical to the machine maintenance costing report. In fact, it is possible to run a costing report for any category, and for any time period, following this same basic format.

Employee Performance. The employee performance or employee efficiency report is a little messier than the ones that were discussed under shop floor control because data for a particular employee may be spread throughout all the work orders. A summary of these data would require searching through a lot of work orders. Another alternative is to go through the log and look at what work orders a specific employee worked on. Again this is going to take time digging up all the work orders. The employee performance report is not something you want to run too often.

Maintenance Department Costing/Budgeting. This report is again exactly like the previous reports in format. However, this report can be run separately for urgent maintenance and for preventive maintenance. An effective preventive maintenance program would have the urgent care maintenance decreasing from one year to the next.

The Maintenance Department costing report helps define what the operating costs of the Maintenance Department are. This report is helpful in budgeting the expenses of this department for the next year.

Computerization

The Maintenance Department master and activity processing can be handled very nicely on a small data base management package. This package will greatly reduce the processing and summarizing tasks that are required of the completed work orders. This summary is crucial for generating the costing reports. The data base can also keep track of due dates in the preventive maintenance system and it can print out a nice listing of pending work orders. To do this by hand, you would need to go through all the master records and see which ones need work orders created. Although it is not necessary, a computer system would be very helpful in this situation.

Summary

The tool room and Maintenance Department are like little factories within a factory. They are critical functions in the factory in making sure that the correct equipment is available and that it is functioning properly. A preventive maintenance program is critical in reducing the number of urgent maintenance calls. With an effective maintenance program, the production planning process has learned to control one of its most critical assets, its equipment. With an effective tool room we should never have a tool shortage. With an effective Purchasing Department we will have all the materials available to us when they are needed.

Chapter

22 Information Functions

Accounting Interfaces
Inventory
Fixed Assets
Costing
Sales, Customer Order Processing, and Accounts Receivable
Purchasing and Accounts Payable
Labor and Payroll
Production Planning, Monitoring, Feedback, and Review
Shop Floor Errors
Integration
Summary

Accounting Interfaces

Believe it or not, accountants do generate useful management information, and not just stab-you-when-you're-down cost reports. But it is our responsibility to let them know what we need.

As discussed in Chapter 4, there is an information flow for production planning and control, and there is also an information flow for accounting. These two flows are integrated at several points in the total flow. Chart 22.1 diagrams the flow of information for production planning and control. Chart 22.2 diagrams the flow of information for accounting, and Chart 22.3 integrates these two flows of information.

In Chart 22.3 we can see the production information flow down the right-hand side of the diagram, and we can see the accounting information flow down the left-hand side of the diagram. In Chart 22.3 we see all the elements of Chart 22.1 and Chart 22.2 plus a few extra elements. In this chapter we will discuss Chart 22.3. Specifically we will discuss several of the integration points that occur in the diagram.

CHART 22.1 The Production and Accounting Integrated Information Flow Diagram

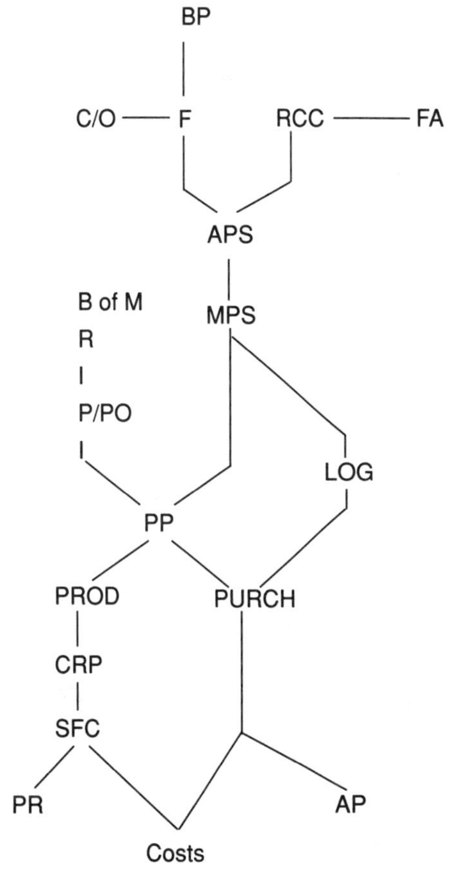

CHART 22.2 Total Flow of Financial Information

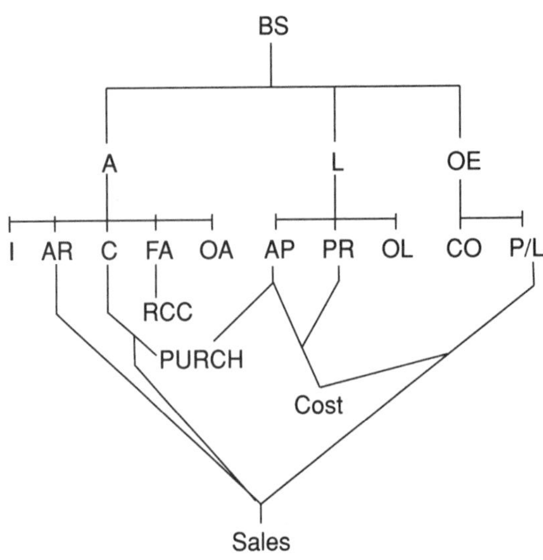

CHART 22.3 The Total Integrated Information Flow Diagram

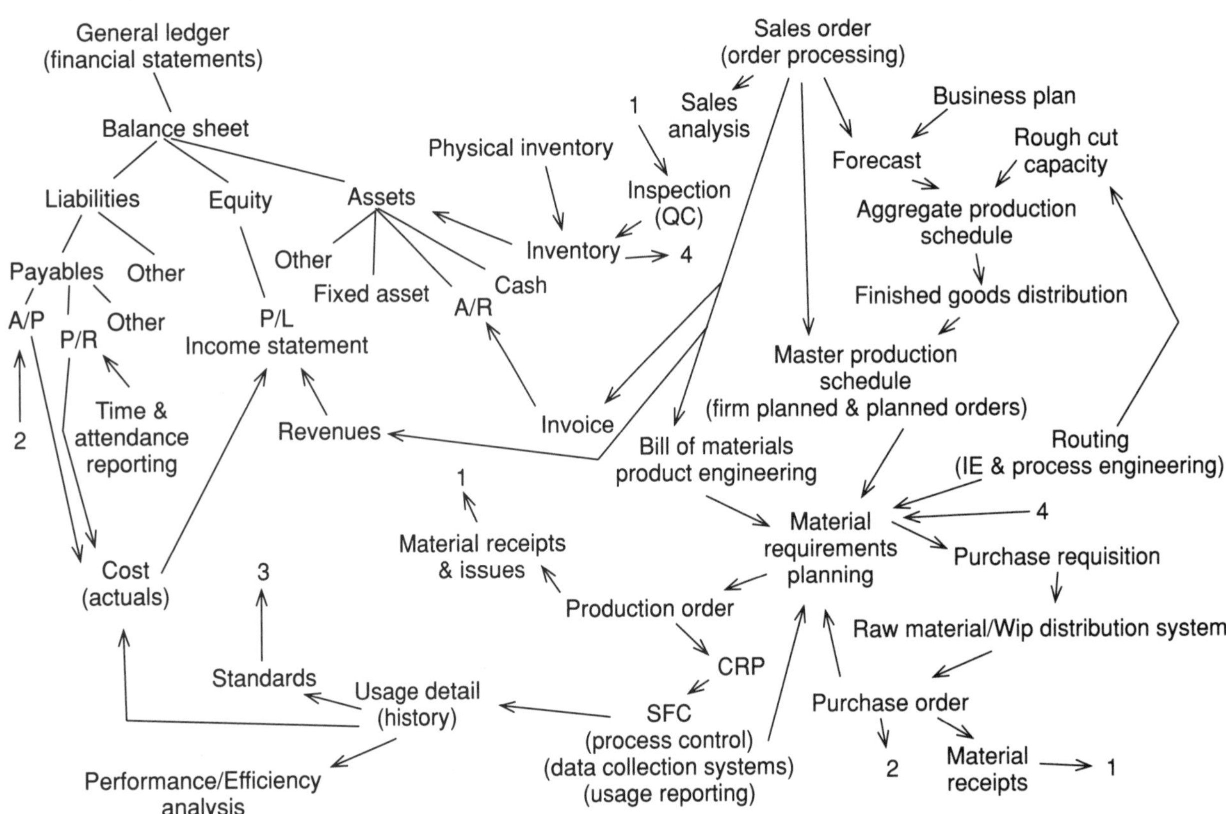

Inventory

Inventory is a major control area in the factory, as we have discussed numerous times throughout this book. Inventory is also a key element in the accounting information flow, since it often makes up the largest portion of current assets. Therefore, the tracking of what inventory is purchased (purchasing), what inventory is being stored (raw materials, work-in-process, and finished goods), what inventory is being worked on (work-in-process), and what inventory is sold (sales) is critical to both the production and the accounting information cycle.

In Chart 22.3 we see inventory feeding the assets of the accounting information flow. We also see inventory (the perpetual inventory system) being updated through quality control (QC) from purchase material receipts and production materials issues and receipts. Both of these are important in planning production (EOQ or MRP), as is the physical inventory.

Fixed Assets

Fixed assets such as machinery are tracked in the accounting system. They are depreciated, eliminated, and replaced. In the production system, machinery tracking is important because it is used for capacity evaluations, especially in the aggregate planning process. For example, machinery evaluations are used to calculate rough-cut capacity (RCC).

Although hard to place in Chart 22.3, the tool room is an important part of the fixed asset evaluation for both accounting information and for production control. Similarly, maintenance plays a key role in the life of the equipment we use.

Costing

Costing flows throughout the production system. Accountants like to collect data on every cost element they can. There's even a new fad called "activity-based costing" which encourages this massive data collection. However, for the employees that are expected to collect all these data, this massive costing process is a major pain.

There are three traditional areas of cost evaluation. Labor costs, material costs, and everything else are thrown into something called *overhead cost*. This traditional model is too simplistic because, as mentioned in numerous previous chapters, labor and materials may not be the critical resource elements that we need to control. We need to identify our critical resource and focus our cost evaluations on that resource.

The costing systems that exist are of two major types: standard costing and actual costing. Most U.S. companies use some form of standard costing where they establish standards for labor and materials usages (routings and bill of materials) and do a cost roll (see Chapters 13 and 14) to figure out product cost. The risk here is in the way overhead is allocated. Overhead can be as much as 50 percent of the value-added cost component, which means that by missallocating overhead, we can make or break the feasibility of a product.

Actual costing is usually performed by some kind of averaging. For example, if we produce a batch of 100 of an item, we accumulate the actual costs that went into the production of that item. The purchase order has the materials prices (Chapter 21), the production traveler has the labor and machine usage costs (Chart 19.10), and, depending on how isolated our work area is, we may be able to identify other actual costs associated with the batch we produced. Again, the way we allocate our remaining costs (overhead) can make a major difference in whether we consider a product profitable or not.

Regardless of the costing method we use (this is primarily an accounting decision anyway; it's part of the numbers game), costing is extremely important to the accounting information flow since it is offset directly against sales to show profit or loss for the organization. For the production information flow, the development of the labor time and machine usage standards used by the costing system is more important than the actual costs. These standards are used in the development of routings, which in turn are used for capacity analysis and production lead time planning. Costing information also comes from the Purchasing Department where materials costs are generated.

Sales, Customer Order Processing, and Accounts Receivable

Sales, or customer order processing, are extremely important to the accounting information flow because they generate the revenues reported on the profit and loss statements. These sales also become entries into the current assets of the balance sheet, either in the form of cash or in the form of accounts receivable.

Sales are, of course, extremely important to production control. If we are a make-to-order factory that only produces to customer orders, then no sales means no work. If we are a make-to-stock plant, then a lack of sales may mean an excessive buildup of inventory. Sales are also used in future production planning projections.

Purchasing and Accounts Payable

The purchasing effects on accounting information occur through several areas. The purchased items add to inventory (current assets), they update the actual materials cost information (expenses), and they either reduce cash (current assets) or they increase accounts payable (current debts). The purchasing effects on the production information flow include the updating of inventory on hand balances and the adjustment of planned purchase orders.

Labor and Payroll

In the shop floor control chapter (Chapter 19) we discussed two types of shop floor labor reporting documents. One was the traveler on which we reported the amount of labor time expended on a particular job. This information is used for job costing and for the updating of actual and standard costs. The second document was the time card, which reported when an employee was "on the job." The time card is used to calculate the payroll, which becomes part of the costs included in the profit and loss statements.

For production information flow, the time cards are not very important. The labor expended information of the production traveler, however, is extremely important in validating our production standards and in costing out the jobs.

This section is not intended to be an all-inclusive lecture on the accounting information flow. This section is included simply to impress you with the fact that the information generated and used by the shop floor is also critical for the financial reporting of the company. The financial side focuses on different bits of information, for example, costing is really big, whereas for the production side of the organization, timing is much more important. But there are still a large number of commonalities, and access to these common areas (common data bases) should be shared and made easily accessible to both sides.

Production Planning, Monitoring, Feedback, and Review

In this section we want to look at the diagram of Chart 22.1 again. Up to now, the entire book has focused on looking down the production information flow diagram, but now we will spend a little time reversing that process in order to show that "What comes up, must come down!" Taking a look at Chart 22.1 (or Chart 22.3), if we look down the diagram we are looking at planning information that is to be passed down to lower levels of the organization. If we look up the diagram we see control data being passed up. The control data that are passed up indicates what has really happened in the plant. These data modify the planning information that is passed down to the next cycle.

The bottom of the production information flow diagram has the labor and materials control systems (refer to Chart 22.1). The production planning (PP) system has generated a labor plan for the production floor (PROD). This labor plan was analyzed against the departmental capacity of the shop floor to produce a capacity plan (CRP, capacity requirements planning). Then these schedules were given to the shop floor and the shop floor performs its tasks (SFC, shop floor control). The feedback mechanism is that as the shop floor performs, they report their performance on the shop floor travelers (see Chapter 19). The completion (or lack of completion) of the shop floor travelers tells the production planning system what the status is of jobs on the shop floor. This feedback updates the purchase and production orders (P/PO), which are fed back into the production planning process on the next cycle.

Similarly, the purchasing schedules (PURCH) generated by the production planning (PP) process help the Purchasing Department order raw materials. As these materials arrive into the plant, the purchase order is filled and closed. The closing of the purchase order is also reported to the production planning system through the purchase and production (P/PO) input into the production plan.

There is also a third feedback mechanism that reports the status of the shop floor back to the production plan. This third feedback is the Inventory Department. As materials are received into inventory, the perpetual inventory system is updated. As materials are issued out of inventory, the perpetual inventory system is updated. The status of the inventory balances for all items—whether they are raw materials, work-in-process, or finished goods—is reported to production planning through the inventory (I) input.

Using the inventory and the purchase and production order inputs (I and P/PO) to the production planning (PP) system, the production planning system always knows what is on hand and what is in process, both for production and for purchasing. With this information, along with the knowledge of what new demands are coming up in the future (MPS, master production schedule), the production planning system can now generate a new set of production (PROD) and purchasing (PURCH) requirements for the next cycle. Chart 22.4 demonstrates the

CHART 22.4 The Production Planning Feedback Process (Taken from Charts 4.9 and 22.1)

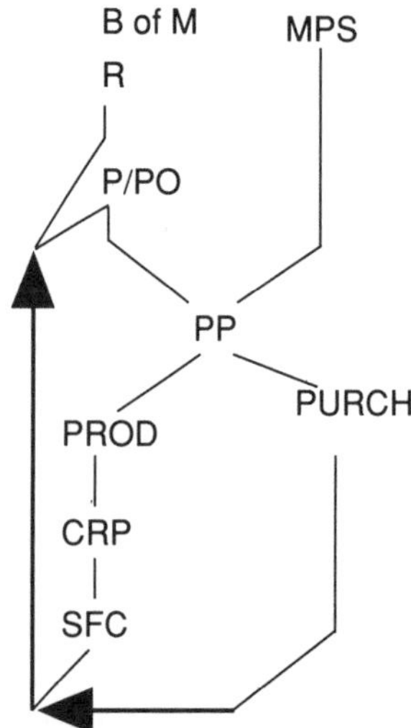

feedback mechanism that is wrapped around the production planning process.

Working our way up the chart we find another feedback mechanism. As the shop floor attempts to produce the output required of it, we monitor its performance to the schedules. As we identify problems in the schedule (where production or purchasing are not able to meet the schedules), we analyze the reasons for these problems. Difficulties in meeting the schedules can be caused by a number of problems. For example:

Inaccurate Routings (R): The timings or capacity requirements are defined incorrectly, causing the expectation that the shop floor can actually produce more than it has the capacity to produce.

Inaccurate Bill of Materials (BofM): The component breakdown of the product is incorrect, causing the wrong parts to be built or purchased.

Invalid Master Production Schedule (MPS): The MPS defines what should be produced. However, I often find plant managers using the MPS as a pushing tool to prod the production floor along. They will require more than is really needed (make the MPS larger than is really needed) in the hope that this will push the production floor to greater productivity. What actually happens is that the shop floor learns not to trust the MPS. An inaccurate MPS gives the production floor inaccurate direction.

Invalid Data Collection System: The data collection system that feeds information back to the production plan has to be accurate and complete or it will misrepresent inventory balances and production and purchase order activity.

Feedback on how effective the schedules actually are working helps the Production Planning Department monitor the ability of the factory to produce on time. (An example of a reporting mechanism that will help in assessing the performance of the factory to produce is shown in Chart 22.7, the production performance report.) As production floor travelers are returned to the Production Planning Department, the transactions from these travelers are logged on a production order performance log (Chart 22.5). This performance appraisal process is similar to the purchasing appraisal process shown in Chapter 21, except now we are evaluating production orders rather than purchase orders.

In Chart 22.5 the control number is the same as on the traveler. The batch size in the control number is the quantity we planned to produce. The date in the control number is the due date by which we want to be finished. The actual quantity produced is the final production quantity that we transferred into inventory. The date completed is the date this final quantity was transferred into inventory. The deviations are the differences. For example, quantity deviations are the difference between the desired quantity and the quantity actually produced. If we overproduced, then the deviation would be positive. If we underproduced, the quantity would be negative. Similarly, the date deviation is a negative number of working days if we are early and a

CHART 22.5 Production Order Performance Log

Control Number			Actual Quantity Produced	Date Completed	Deviations	
Product Number	Batch Size	Date			Quantity	Date

CHART 22.6 Production Order Performance Log—Example

Control Number			Actual Quantity Produced	Date Completed	Deviations	
Product Number	Batch Size	Date			Quantity	Date
CCCC	50	1/1/1992	52	1/2/1992	2	1
AAAA	150	1/3/1992	149	1/3/1992	−1	0
CCAA	500	1/5/1992	510	1/3/1992	10	−2
AACC	50	1/7/1992	50	1/9/1992	0	2

positive number of working days if we are late. Chart 22.6 is an example of how Chart 22.5 would look when filled out.

The data recorded on the production order performance log are collected over a specified period of time (monthly or quarterly). The next step is to summarize these data in the production performance report (Chart 22.7). This report has one page per product and as you go through the log you record the activity under the appropriate product number. Sometimes, if we have a high product variability, we may want to have one page per family of product, rather than one page per individual product. Note that the information transferred is identical in format to Chart 22.5. It is just the sequence that has been changed. Chart 22.8 is an example of how Chart 22.7 should look.

With the production performance report we are able to evaluate the plant's performance on any particular product produced. From Chart

22.8 we see that on the average we are doing pretty well. We average one-quarter day late and one-half unit over.

With this production performance information we can monitor products that are having problems. We would check out which of these products are giving us the most deviations and we would find out why. If we are receiving bad deviations (late products or not enough quantity), then we need to investigate the potential problems discussed earlier in this chapter. If we are experiencing early production, then we should tighten up the lead time, which improves our ability to be responsive to our customer's needs. If we are experiencing overproduction then perhaps we are starting the production process with excessive materials. Regular overproduction builds up inventory that may be more costly than we would like.

CHART 22.7 Production Performance Report

Product Number ____________
Period From ____/____/____ To ____/____/____

Control Number				Deviations	
Batch Size	Date	Actual Quantity Produced	Date Completed	Quantity	Date

CHART 22.8 Production Performance Report—Example
Product Number CCCC

Period From 1/1/1992 To 2/1/1992

Control Number				Deviations	
Batch Size	Date	Actual Quantity Produced	Date Completed	Quantity	Date
50	1/1/1992	52	1/2/1992	2	1
50	1/3/1992	49	1/3/1992	−1	0
50	1/5/1992	51	1/3/1992	1	−2
50	1/7/1992	50	1/9/1992	0	2
			Totals:	2 over	1 day late

We have now established a feedback loop that reports on the production planning and master scheduling abilities of the plant. This feedback mechanism is diagrammed in Chart 22.9. Note that the initial data for this feedback mechanism originated from the shop floor, then were passed to production planning, and now passed to the master production scheduler.

The next step in our look up the feedback loop is up to the aggregate production planning level. This step is an exception step in that when we were analyzing the production performance report, we may have found that some of our production inefficiencies were caused by errors in our evaluations of capacity. For example, if we look at the demand on capacity, it actually takes more capacity to build our product than our summarized routings claim (see Chapter 14). We may have scheduled more production than we are actually capable of producing. This may have occurred because of errors in our routings or because we did a poor job of summarizing our routings for our capacity evaluations.

The other capacity error that may occur is in the evaluation of available capacity. In this case, we have overstated available capacity. This often occurs because we assume a level of capacity that is not realistic. For example, machines are not available for production for the full eight hours of a shift. We may only get four or five hours of capacity out of the machine. Machine breakdowns may also reduce the capacity available even more.

Receiving feedback from the master scheduling analysis has now provided feedback for the aggregate production scheduling process. This step is diagrammed in Chart 22.10.

CHART 22.9 The Master Scheduling Feedback Process (Taken from Charts 4.9, 22.1, and 22.4)

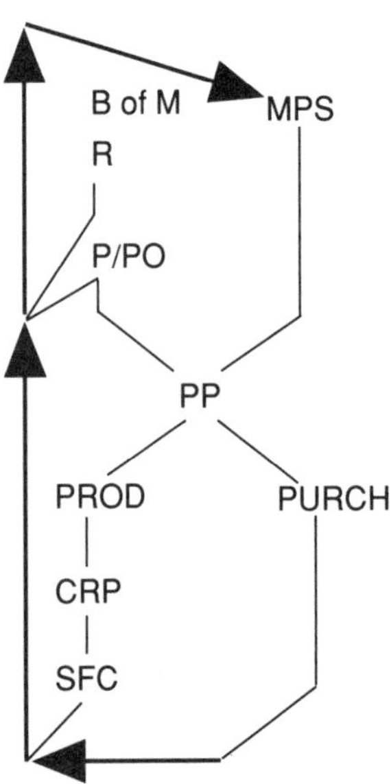

CHART 22.10 The Aggregate Planning Feedback Process (Taken from Charts 4.9, 22.1, 22.4, and 22.9)

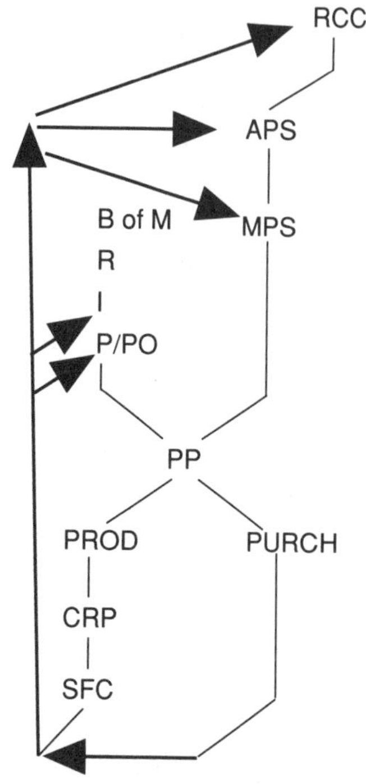

CHART 22.11 Feedback of Financial Information (Taken from Charts 4.8 and 22.2)

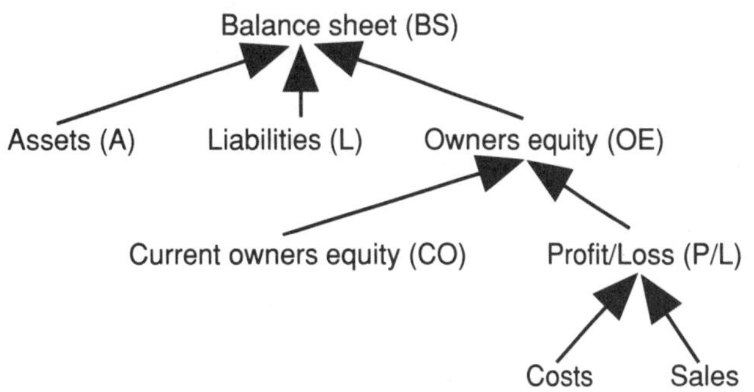

The final step in the feedback mechanism is the feedback to the business plan (BP). This feedback occurs primarily through the accounting process described in the last chapter. Business plan feedback occurs through the profit and loss report, which is made up of the costs and the revenues. This is diagrammed in Chart 22.11. Additionally, feedback to the business plan occurs through an analysis of the operating ratios. These feedback measures are quantifiable improvement measurements that can be monitored to see if things are getting better or worse (see Chapter 7). It also gives focus as to where the problems exist and what corrections or improvements should be made.

Shop Floor Errors

As we look for improvements throughout our factory, I often find that there are three major reasons for most of the shop floor errors. The first is improper engineering (see Chapter 19), which I have already discussed in some detail. The second is improper documentation. The third is inadequate training and education programs.

When we discuss documentation we are not after a detailed, step-by-step procedure on how to do every function. That's insulting. Some of the best documentation I have seen is in comic book format offering pictures that show what is to be done as well as explain the process. I realize that this takes some time, but if you have a production area that is showing repeated errors or failures, it may well be worth the trouble to develop this level of documentation.

Education and training are also important. We can't expect employees to perform properly if they don't understand what it is they are supposed to do. Additionally, if we train them in the areas of quality, maintenance, and setup, they will be able to fix many of the production problems themselves without you ever knowing about it, and thereby improve productivity and efficiency. The next level of training should teach about the job functions that come before and after the employee's work station. With a better understanding of what they should expect from their suppliers and what they should deliver to their customers (see the new internal definition of quality in Chapter 20), they will be able to perform their job function better. Additional training about the other departments and aspects of the company should also be provided. The more employees understand how they fit into the organization, the more pride they will have in their organization and the better able they will be to perform their roles as employees.

Integration

The keyword in information flow, whether it is down the information flow diagram (Chart 22.1) or back up (Chart 22.10), is *integration.* These functions are integrated and depend on each other. A weak link in the information flow can distort the corrective action taken by others in the planning and control process. This integration is also important when we link up with the accounting information flow (Chart 22.2 or 22.11). Integration will allow us to have valid information at all levels and thereby allow us to improve our competitiveness.

The movement of data up the information flow diagram is just as important as the movement of planning and control information down the information flow diagram. Without the upward feedback we wouldn't know what has happened, and without the downward planning we wouldn't know what to do. All of these systems are important, and the integration of them is critical to our success.

Summary

The flow of information was stressed in the first chapters of this book. It is now stressed again in one of the last chapters of the book. All the pieces of this book aid in building this flow of information. By building a successful information flow and feedback mechanism, the entire organization will be information integrated and will flow much smoother.

Chapter

23 Leading Edge Strategies

World-Class Manufacturing Techniques

World class manufacturing is a term that has come to be identified with leading edge philosophies. The current leading edge philosophies include:

Strategic Philosophies:
- Information sharing
- International focus (global management)
- Long-term strategy
- Manager vs. facilitator
- Time-to-market strategies
- Harmony vs. adversarial relationships
- MRP II or MRP III philosophies
- Simplification and focus

Employee Involvement Philosophies:
- Teaming
- Empowerment vs. top-down management
- Shorter organization charts
- Gainsharing
- Job security
- Cross training and job rotation

Improvement Philosophies:
- Planning for change
- Continuous improvement
- Benchmarking
- Risk and uncertainty assessments

Measurement Philosophies:
- Restructured accounting
- Activity-based costing

Quality Philosophies:
- Deming principles (or Juran or Crosby)
- Total quality management
- Total quality control
- Quality circles
- In-line quality control
- Statistical process control

Production Planning Philosophies:
- Just-in-time production philosophies
  - KANBAN
  - Christmas trees
- Theory of constraints
- Bottleneck allocation methodologies
- Bill of energy

Computerization/Automation Philosophies:
- Computer-integrated manufacturing
- Decision support systems
- Expert systems
- Artificial intelligence
- Computer-aided design/computer-aided manufacturing

This chapter discusses some of these philosophies. Many of these have already been incorporated in this book where appropriate. This chapter will not be able to do a good job at discussing any of them in detail because they are very involved and books have been written about each one individually. However, it is useful for you to be familiar with these terms and how they are used because many of these concepts are the next step toward your achievement of manufacturing excellence. Note that some of the fads actually contradict each other, for example, simplification and focus vs. activity-based costing, so they should be implemented very carefully.

Strategic Philosophies

In attempting to reestablish our competitive edge, a number of studies were done to look at why we lost it to begin with. The following items have been identified as major areas of weakness.

Information Sharing. In order for lower levels of managers to manage, and for employees to perform their job functions better, they need to know what is expected. They need to know what the focus and the direction of the corporation is, and they need to understand how their specific function fits into the big picture.

International Focus (Global Management). No company can think of itself as local or regional any longer. Even if the company does not manufacture overseas, they often have customers or vendors that are overseas; and when they do a competitive analysis, they better take a close look at the competition that is being generated overseas.

International manufacturing also introduces an entirely new bag of tricks into the planning process. Customs, shipping, distribution and logistics planning, tariffs, etc., can become very complicated and require close attention if you plan to get into these areas.

Long-Term Strategy. Short-term thinking is triggered by a lack of trust. Stockholders and their board of directors do not trust their CEOs, who do not trust their VPs, who do not trust their line managers, who do not trust their employees. So if anybody slips up at any of these levels they immediately get fired. With this lack of trust we find that the strategy of most organizations is to make themselves look good on the short term, regardless of the long-term consequences. For example, we tend to patch up an old piece of junk rather than replace it with new technology because the cost of the new technology will hurt our financial numbers for the next couple of years.

Manager vs. Facilitator. As employees take on a larger role in decision-making, managers also take on a new role. They no longer direct, rather they become facilitators. They take the ideas of the employees and attempt to find ways to implement these ideas. If the team philosophies are working correctly, the teams will monitor themselves, and the manager becomes their interface with the rest of the world.

Time-to-Market Strategies. This concept focuses on the slowness of the implementation process. The United States is the world's biggest generator of new ideas. Unfortunately, it is also one of the world's slowest implementators of those ideas. Many of our ideas are implemented by our foreign competitors long before we implement them at home. Competitiveness can be greatly increased if we can shorten this implementation time cycle.

Harmony vs. Adversarial Relationships. Many countries attempt to coordinate the goals of the corporation with the goals of the employees. However, in the United States we insist on having an adversarial and untrusting relationship between employee and employer. A harmonious relationship would be much more productive.

MRP II or MRP III Philosophies. MRP II (manufacturing resource planning) is a corporate-wide management philosophy. MRP (material requirements planning) is a production planning tool. Look at Chart 23.1, which diagrams the total information flow of the organization. If you have this integration working properly in your organization, you have MRP II. Whereas, MRP is the material requirements planning system used for production planning. It is diagrammed in the lower right-hand corner of Chart 23.1.

MRP II focuses on the total integration of all information flow functions. If you can get all the pieces discussed in this book to work together, and get them to integrate with the accounting information flow, then you will have achieved an MRP II environment. MRP III uses the same MRP II flow but uses the just-in-time method (discussed later in this chapter) as the shop floor control mechanism.

Simplification and Focus. The strategy here is to get away from overcomputerizing everything. Sometimes we tend to become obsessed with data collection and lose sight of the real problem. The philosophy here is to step back and take a look at the big picture.

Employee Involvement Philosophies

Teaming. This involves putting the employees into teams and making their brains work as well as their hands. Employees are asked to be part of a team, to communicate problems, and to search for solutions. These teams are formed across all disciplines so that we have engineers, shop floor employees, and accountants all working on teams together.

Empowerment vs. Top-down Management. Empowerment involves the giving of decision power to the employees. If the employee team makes a decision, they have the power to implement the decision. Decisions flow upward as opposed to the traditional top-down approach.

Shorter Organization Charts. The communication linkage between top management and the line worker needs to be shortened. With em-

CHART 23.1 The Total Integrated Information Flow Diagram

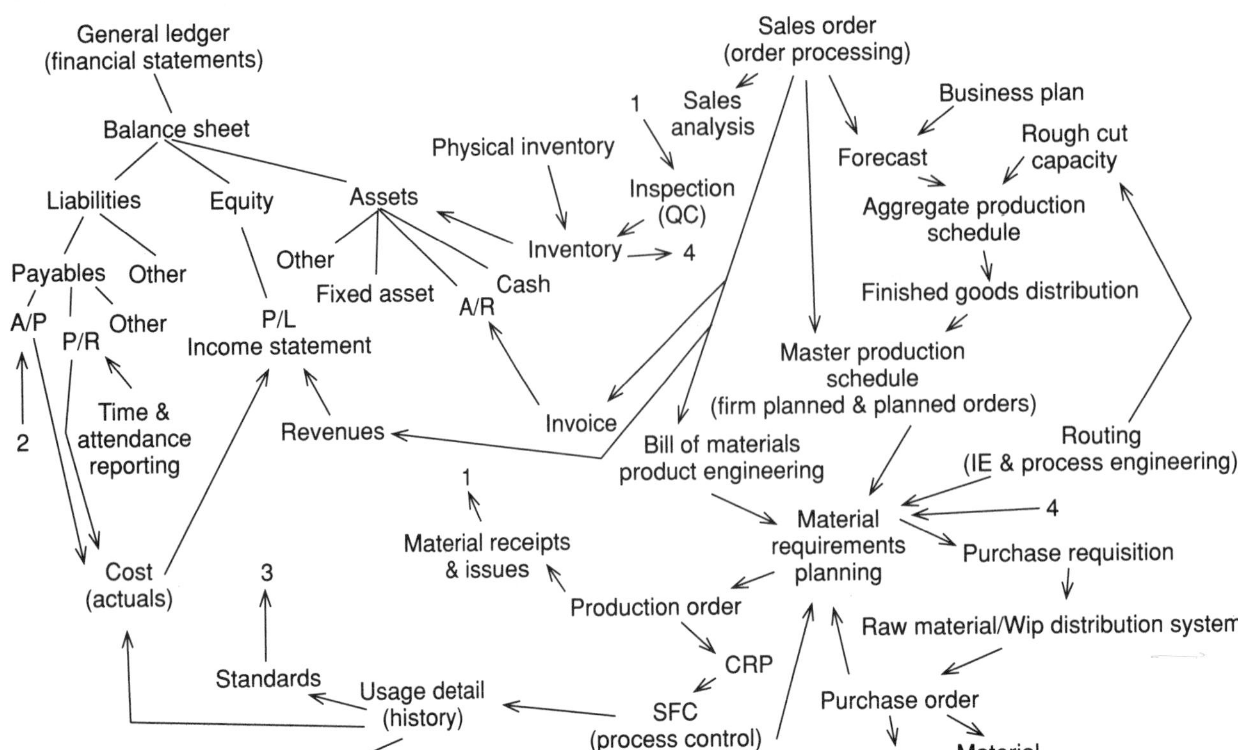

powerment and teaming the span of control for each manager can be much greater, and the current number of middle management levels is no longer necessary.

Gainsharing. The motivator behind the teaming concepts is gainsharing. Employees benefit from the improvements they generate by sharing in the gains of the organization.

Job Security. A fundamental principle behind proper motivation and improvements in quality is that employees need to have their primary concern eliminated, which is that they might lose their jobs. If employees are afraid to make suggestions because they may work themselves out of a job, or if they are afraid to speak up because they may offend someone and get fired, many of the improvements that could be made will never be made. To avoid this problem, employees are guaranteed their job for the life of the corporation.

Cross Training and Job Rotation. Employees are rotated out of their job every two years and trained into a new job. They are not only trained on how to do the job, but they are also trained about the quality and maintenance issues that go along with the job. The principle here is that an employee with a well-rounded background about how the company operates will be more valuable to the company in making improvements.

Improvement Philosophies

Planning for Change. There is an interesting quote from *Breakthrough Thinking* by Nadler and Hibino that defines "insanity" as "continuing to do the same thing while expecting different results." That is basically the theme of this concept. We can't get better if we don't change, and we can't change positively if we don't plan for change.

Continuous Improvement. We should look continuously for areas of improvement. This is different than problem solving. This is looking for new areas of improvement that will strengthen our competitive edge.

Benchmarking. Benchmarking is comparing yourself with the best in your industry. Look for areas where you can improve, and look for vulnerabilities in your competitor on which you can take advantage.

Risk and Uncertainty Assessments. Risk and uncertainty assessments are an attempt to put a number on failure. We financially evaluate the benefits of success and compare them with the costs of failure.

Measurement Philosophies

The measurement system tells the employees where to focus their efforts. An inappropriate measurement system, for any employee no matter what the level, will give them the wrong signals.

Restructured Accounting. New accounting methods are currently being experimented with by the big accounting firms and the federal government. They include things like adding costs for the amount of time you hold on to inventory rather than thinking of inventory as an asset, and they treat employees as an asset rather than a cost.

Activity-Based Costing. Here we attempt to collect cost data on all activities that occur rather than just the three primary resources (materials, labor, and machinery). This is an attempt to define the components of burden. The objective of this system is to look at all areas where cost reductions can be made.

Quality Philosophies

Quality has become the principle buzzword in industry. There is still some confusion on exactly what quality is (review the chapter on quality). Here are some of the latest fads in quality.

Deming Principles (or Juran or Crosby). The three major gurus of quality are Deming, Crosby, and Juran. They each have their own program on how quality improvements can be made. Each individual teaches good principles and has demonstrated numerous success stories. Most companies' quality programs find themselves somewhere in the middle of the three programs.

Total Quality Management. Total quality management is a philosophy of corporate-wide quality improvement on a continuous basis. This concept is discussed in more detail in the chapter on quality.

Total Quality Control. The difference between total quality management and total quality control is epitomized by the phrase *management vs. control.* Most companies "control" quality by a series of inspection processes. But "managing" quality is a continuous quality improvement program. However, a good control system is the first step in the development of a management system.

Quality Circles. Quality circles were the first step in the "teaming" concept discussed earlier. Quality circles are teams that meet to discuss quality improvement issues.

In-line Quality Control. Quality control should not be the function of some department. Quality should be everyone's responsibility, and everyone should be trained in quality so that errors can be caught as they occur, not at the end of the production process. This provides significant cost savings.

Statistical Process Control. Statistical monitoring of production output allows you to watch trends, not just check a specific part. These trends indicate potential problems. The chapter on quality discusses this concept in more detail.

Production Planning Philosophies

There are many production philosophies. I have written a book titled *International Management and Production: Survival Techniques for Corporate America*, published by Tab Professional and Reference Books, Blue Ridge Summit, PA, 1990. In this book I discuss a variety of production philosophies used throughout the world. The book you have been reading discusses two of these philosophies, EOQ and MRP. Here are a few more.

Just-in-Time Production Philosophies. JIT (just-in-time) is the production philosophy the Japanese use. This is a materials flow-oriented production planning philosophy that is extremely effective if you manufacture a highly repetitive product. JIT is an EOQ-based planning strategy that uses KANBANs to track the levels of shop floor inventory. A KANBAN is a card attached to or a box holding inventory, something that tracks the inventory level. These KANBANs are used as the production scheduling tool. A "Christmas tree," which is a board of lights, is used to monitor the flow of work on the production floor.

The basic principle behind JIT is that the factory is laid out with the machines in the sequence in which the product is produced. At this stage JIT is used as a shop floor control mechanism. Most U.S. versions of JIT are of this form. MRP III, discussed earlier, is of this type.

JIT can also be a production planning tool that totally replaces MRP. Very few sites of this type exist in the United States. If you want to go full out in JIT and run it the way the Japanese do, you would replace MRP, MRP II, and MRP III with a JIT-global management philosophy. To do this you need to have employee-based goals and a continuous improvement philosophy.

Theory of Constraints. Another production planning philosophy is TOC (theory of constraints; also known as OPT, optimized production technology), which is a bottleneck-oriented production planning philosophy. This technique is effective when you are trying to optimize throughput through a bottleneck.

Bottleneck Allocation Methodologies. One last production planning philosophy is BAM (bottleneck allocation method), which works on a philosophy similar to OPT, however, it treats the entire plant as a bottleneck.

Bill of Energy. In the production planning process we currently plan our production and purchasing based on materials (bill of materials) and labor (routings) requirements. Additional inputs can be planned like energy using a bill of energy, which would track energy requirements for production. Products that are high energy users can be scheduled during times of the day when energy may be cheaper. Or a high-energy-using product may be scheduled on a routing that uses less energy. Similar resource planning enhancements can be incorporated into your production planning system for maintenance, set ups, tooling, etc.

Computerization/Automation Philosophies

Most of these concepts were discussed in the chapter on the manufacturing data base.

Computer-Integrated Manufacturing. This is the integration of all aspects of the plant operation into one data base. This includes financial, engineering, production control, CAD/CAM, maintenance, tooling, and shop floor data collection.

Decision Support Systems. These are computerized mathematical models that help solve production planning models.

Expert Systems. These are systems that incorporate the experiences of experts and attempt to reproduce them through a computerized decision-making process.

Artificial Intelligence. This is a system that learns from its experiences. It records all its decisions and experiences and makes subsequent decisions based on what it has learned.

Computer-Aided Design/Computer-Aided Manufacturing (CAD/CAM). In this process we take the engineering designs and test them using computer simulations. We then transfer these designs directly to the production floor and the production machinery performs its production functions based on these designs. There is no translation or human intervention.

Summary

As you can see, having gone through this book, we have come a long way. We now have an understanding of how our plant should operate. We have a feel for what measures and feedback systems will help us stay in control of the production process. But, as this chapter has already pointed out, there will always be ways to improve even more. That's what being competitive is all about—continuous improvement. Go out, implement what you have learned, put it to good use, and then look for even more areas of improvement. The search goes on for bigger and better ways to change but remember a quote from Einstein, you need to "apply a little imagination" to all that you do. That little bit of imagination is what will keep you a little better than your competition.

Chapter

24 Conclusion

Don't let any system control you, whether it's the computer system, or the production control system, or the accounting system, or your data collection system. The system is yours to use, not yours to be controlled by. And, believe it or not, if used correctly, it can be an enjoyable experience.

We made it! Hopefully this book was what you needed. It was intended to give you simple, straightforward ideas that will help you run your plant more effectively. If you read this book through one time quick, you should have a feel for how everything ties together. Now you need to go back and review all those areas that affect your job function and see what you can improve. Start implementing some of these ideas. You'll probably need to modify them so that they work well for you. That's expected. Not every factory works exactly the same way. But you do need to get the upward flow of data and the downward flow of information and planning systems working. You need integration.

If there are any subjects that were introduced in this book that you feel you need further information on, there are many books available. It was not the intent of this book to be comprehensive in the tools. Instead, the overall information and planning process was emphasized. It attempted to present enough tools so that you can start improving your operation.

Now I'd like you to do me a favor. If you have any questions, comments, suggestions, frustrations, anxieties, or mood changes caused by this book, contact me. I can use your ideas to make this book better. Your experiences are extremely valuable. Write to me at:

Gerhard Plenert
Brigham Young University
Institute of Business Management
660 TNRB
Provo, Utah 84602

I hope you had fun. I did. I look forward to hearing about your successes, failures, and future.

Gerhard Johannes Plenert

Index

OTHER BUSINESS ONE IRWIN TITLES OF INTEREST TO YOU:

COMPUTER INTEGRATED MANUFACTURING
Guidelines and Applications from Industrial Leaders
Steven A. Melnyk and Ram Narasimhan
The Business One Irwin/APICS Series in Production Management
Computer Integrated Manufacturing (CIM) can greatly improve speed and precision in manufacturing operations. *Computer Integrated Manufacturing* takes a management/strategic perspective and offers case studies that illustrate the implications of the CIM approach to manufacturing. (275 pages)
ISBN: 1-55623-538-0

FRONTLINE MANUFACTURING
Rules, Tools, and Techniques for Line Workers
Robert A. Forcier and Marsha M. Forcier
The Business One Irwin/APICS Series in Frontline Education
Finally, a clear and concise "how-to" manual aimed at the millions of entry level and semi-skilled laborers, assembly line workers, and production supervisors. *Frontline Manufacturing* is a convenient resource that compiles the latest trends and concepts in manufacturing improvement. (253 pages)
ISBN: 1-55623-671-9

FORECASTING SYSTEMS FOR OPERATIONS MANAGEMENT
Stephen A. DeLurgio and Carl D. Bhame
The Business One Irwin/APICS Series in Production Management
Understand and implement practical, theoretically sound, and comprehensive forecasting systems. This book will assist you in moving products, materials, and timely information through your organization effectively. (648 pages)
ISBN: 1-55623-040-0

BENCHMARKING GLOBAL MANUFACTURING
Understanding International Suppliers, Customers, and Competitors
Jeffrey G. Miller, Arnoud De Meyer, and Jinichiro Nakane
The Business One Irwin/APICS Series in Production Management
Reveals valuable data about the track records, operations, and strategies of over 1,000 manufacturing companies worldwide. With these comparisons, and with the book's hands-on benchmarking toolkit, you will be equipped to challenge assumptions and think strategically in every decision. (443 pages)
ISBN: 1-55623-674-3

MRP
Integrating Material Requirements Planning and Modern Business
Terry Lunn with Susan A. Neff
Business One Irwin/APICS Series in Production Management
Demonstrates how material requirements planning (MRP) can effectively manage and maintain material flow, solve scheduling dilemmas, and integrate the various functions of your business. By maximizing MRP, you can better satisfy the demands of your company and most important, your customers (315 pages)
ISBN: 1-55623-656-5

Available in fine bookstores and libraries everywhere.